<u>The Best Way to Use Thi</u>

The Ultimate SAT Math Course

Learn How to Master SAT Math with Perfect Scorer Michael Stroup

To have the best experience with this book, sign up for the Ultimate SAT Math Course. **It's like having your own private math tutor, only cheaper!** The course includes:

- **50-Point Score Improvement Guarantee** (see full details at preppros.io/50-point-guarantee)
- **40+ Hours of On-Demand Lessons and Practice Question Explanations.**
- **Video Lessons Teaching All 36 Chapters in This Book.**
- **1,500 Video Explanations For Every Practice Question in This Book!**
- **Proven Score-Raising Lessons, Strategies, and Test-Taking Tips.**

<u>Ultimate SAT Math Course</u>	<u>Answer Explanations Course</u>
$49.99/month (with discount code below)	$19.99/month
• **50-Point Score Improvement Guarantee!** • Video tutorials teaching all 36 Chapters. • 1,500 video explanation for every practice question in this book. • 4+ practice Digital SAT Math tests & full video explanations.	• 1,500 on-demand video explanation for every practice question in this book. • Only includes answer explanations. • Does not include 50-Point Score Improvement Guarantee.

Free Trial & Secret $25 Off Discount Code!

Chapters 12 is **FREE** in the Free Trial (no credit card needed to sign up). With this book, **you get a lifetime $25 discount on the Ultimate SAT Math Course! Enter coupon code "DS24" at checkout to make the course $49.99/month** (normally $74.99/month).

To sign up, go to www.preppros.io/sat-math-course.

Preparing For The Entire SAT?

Check out the Ultimate SAT Course! Get full access to the Ultimate SAT Math Course and so much more for **only $99/month**!

- **100-Point Improvement Guarantee**
- **70+ Hours of Expert Tutoring**
- **SAT Math Course**
- **SAT Writing Course** (book included)
- **SAT Reading Course** (book included)
- **Study Plans**
- **4+ Practice SATs and Explanations**

We also offer a **FREE trial** that includes 2+ hours of lessons. To sign up for the free trial or the full course, go to **www.preppros.io/sat-course.**

PrepPros Presents

The Complete Guide to

Digital SAT Math

By Matthew Stroup and Michael Stroup

1ST Edition

Copyright © 2024 PrepPros

All Rights reserved. Photocopying any portion of this publication is strictly prohibited unless express written authorization is first obtained from PrepPros, www.preppros.io.

Test names and other trademarks are the property of their respective trademark owners. *SAT is a registered trademark of the College Board, which is not affiliated with PrepPros.

For more information about this book and additional SAT Tutoring services offered by PrepPros, visit www.preppros.io.

Quantity discounts are available for teachers, companies, and other educational purposes. Please contact info@preppros.io for more information or to purchase books.

About the Authors

Matthew Stroup and Michael Stroup are both master tutors, brothers, and the founders of PrepPros. Together, they have over 19,000 hours of private tutoring experience and have both achieved perfect scores on the SAT. Their students have improved their SAT scores up to 400 points. Matthew Stroup graduated from Johns Hopkins University, where he studied biology, economics, and was pre-med, and Georgetown University, where he obtained a master's degree in biotechnology. Michael graduated from Georgetown University with a degree in Marketing and Entrepreneurship.

Matthew and Michael both work as full-time tutors. If you want to learn directly from Matthew and Michael in private tutoring, group classes, or online courses, check out the PrepPros website at www.preppros.io

Table of Contents

Introduction To The Digital SAT Math Test i
- Format of the Digital SAT Math Test
- Difficult of the Questions
- Time Management
- Guessing
- 6 Test Day Tips to Maximize Your Score

Introduction to The Complete Guide to Digital SAT Math iii
- How to Best Use This Book
- Sign Up for On-Demand Video Lessons and Explanations **($25 Off Discount Code)**
- Difficult of Practice Questions
- What Else to Do?

How Our 4 Level System Works v
- How To Find Your Level
- The 4 Levels
- How To Best Use the 4-Level System

SAT Math Study Guides vii
- How to Best Use the Study Guides

Level 1 Study Guide – Core Fundamentals vii

Level 2 Study Guide – Additional Fundamentals xii

Level 3 Study Guide – Advanced Topics xviii

Level 4 Study Guide – Expert Level Topics xxv

Chapter 1: Backsolving 1
- How To Backsolve
- Backsolving With Points

Chapter 2: Substitution 5

Chapter 3: Equivalent Questions 9
- Equivalent Trick
- Desmos Equivalent Hack

Chapter 4: Desmos Hacks 14
- Desmos Hack #1 – Solving Algebra Questions
- Desmos Hack #2 – Solving Systems of Equations
- Desmos Hack #3 – Solving Equivalent Questions
- Desmos Hack #4 – Solving Quadratics Without Factoring

Chapter 5: Algebra Skills 18

PEMDAS
Negative Numbers
Combing Like Terms
Cross Multiply Fractions
Square Both Sides of an Equation Correctly
Algebra with Inequality Signs
Taking Square Roots in Algebraic Equations
Factoring to Isolate a Variable
Factor by Grouping for Cubic Functions
Solving Directly for Answers

Chapter 6: Fractions 30

Combining Fractions
Dividing Fractions
Simplifying Fractions
Getting Rid of Fractions
Turn Fractions into Decimals
Use Desmos to Turn Decimals into Fractions

Chapter 7: "In Terms of" 39

Chapter 8: Inequalities 44

Algebra with Inequalities
Graphing Inequalities
Systems of Inequalities
Inequalities and Word Problems

Chapter 9: Percentages 53

Simple Percentages
Percentage Increase and Decrease
Percentage Change

Chapter 10: Exponents and Roots 63

Exponent Rules
Root Rules
Simplifying Square Roots and Cube Roots
Roots and Variables with Powers

Chapter 11: Quadratics 74

Multiplying Binomials
Factoring Quadratics
Solutions, Roots, x-intercepts, and Zeros for Quadratic Equations
How Solutions Appear on a Graph
The Quadratic Formula
The Discriminant
Finding the Vertex
3 Forms of a Parabola

Chapter 12: Systems of Equations 93

    Solving with Elimination, Substitution, and Setting Equal
    The Shortcut Method
    Word Problems
    More Complex Systems of Equations Questions

Chapter 13: Functions 102

    Function Basics
    Composite Functions
    Functions on Graphs
    Inverse Functions

Chapter 14: Geometry Part 1 – Angles 110

    Intersecting Lines
    Parallel Lines
    Exterior Angle Theorem
    Interior Angles in Polygons
    Types of Triangles (Equilateral, Isosceles, and Scalene)

Chapter 15: Geometry Part 2 – Shapes 117

    Area and Volume
    Similar Shapes and Scale Factors
    Right Triangles
    Special Right Triangles
    Third Side of a Triangle
    Other Geometry Rules You Might Need To Know

Chapter 16: Geometry Part 3 – Similar Shapes and Congruent Triangles . 130

    Similar Triangles
    Other Similar Shapes
    Congruent Triangles & 5 Rules for Proving Congruent Triangles
    3 Rules for Proving Similar Triangles

Chapter 17: Lines 141

    Finding the Slope
    Slopes of Parallel and Perpendicular Lines
    Slope-Intercept Form, Point-Slope Form, and Standard Form
    Solving for Intercepts
    Midpoint Formula
    Distance Formula

Chapter 18: Interpreting Lines 155

    Interpreting the Constants in a Given Equation
    Selecting the Right Equation
    The "Plug In Points" Method

Chapter 19: Exponential Growth and Decay 164
- Exponential Growth and Decay Equations
- Graphing Exponential Growth and Decay
- General Exponential Form
- Advanced Exponential Growth and Decay Questions
- Graphing General Exponential Form

Chapter 20: Trigonometry 177
- Basics of Trigonometry – SOH-CAH-TOA
- Using Trigonometry to Find Side Lengths in Right Triangles
- Basic Trigonometry in Similar Triangles
- 2 Important Trigonometry Identities to Know
- Inverse Trigonometric Functions
- Radians vs. Degrees
- Unit Circle
- Coterminal Angles and The Unit Circle

Chapter 21: Probability 197
- The Basics of Probability
- Probability and Data Tables
- Conditional Probability
- 3 More Probability Rules to Know

Chapter 22: Statistical Analysis 208
- Sampling and Proper Data Collection
- Interpreting and Generalizing Sample Findings
- Standard Deviation
- Dot Plots
- Margin of Error
- Statistical Bias
- Box and Whisker Plot

Chapter 23: Ratios and Proportions 224
- Ratio and a Total
- Ratios as Proportions
- Comparing Across Ratios
- Ratios and Geometry

Chapter 24: Mean, Median, Mode, and Range 230
- Calculating the Mean
- Weighted Average
- Finding the Median in a Data Set, Table, Box Plot, and Bar Graph

Chapter 25: Unit Conversion 241
- Basic Unit Conversion
- Dimensional Analysis
- Advanced Unit Conversions with Squared and Cubed Units

Chapter 26: Scatter Plots and Lines of Best Fit 248
        3 Principles for Scatter Plots and Lines of Best Fit

Chapter 27: Circles 253
        Equation of a Circle
        Graphing a Circle
        General Form and Completing the Square
        Advanced Circle Questions
        Finding Points On, Inside, and Outside the Circle

Chapter 28: Shifting and Transforming Functions 263
        Rules for Shifting Functions
        Shifting and Transforming Lines, Parabolas, and Other Functions

Chapter 29: Absolute Value 271
        Absolute Values with Numbers
        Absolute Value and Unknown Variables
        Advanced Absolute Value Questions
        Absolute Value with 1 Solution, No Solution, and Infinite Solutions

Chapter 30: Word Problems 277
        4 Proven Tips to Solve Word Problems

Chapter 31: Solving for Constants 281
        Solving for Constants in Equivalent Equations
        Solving for Constants in Equivalent Equations with Multiple Unknowns
        Solving for Constants with No Solution
        Solving for Constants with Infinite Solutions
        Solving for Constants with One Solution

Chapter 32: Systems of Equations with Infinite Solutions, No Solution, and One Solution 291
        One Solutions (Intersecting Lines)
        No Solution (Parallel Lines)
        Infinite Solutions (Identical Lines)
        Identifying The Correct System of Equations

Chapter 33: Arcs and Sectors 301
        Arcs, Sectors, and the Inscribed Angle Theorem

Chapter 34: Extraneous Solutions 307

Chapter 35: Interpreting Constants in Linear, Quadratic, and Exponential Functions.. 311

        Interpreting Constants in Linear Functions
        Interpreting Constants in Vertical and Horizontal Parabolas
        Interpreting Constants in Exponential Functions

Chapter 36: Special Quadratics – Perfect Squares and Difference of Squares 321

        Difference of Squares
        Perfect Squares

Answer Key 326

Introduction to the Digital SAT Math

Before we start this book, let's begin by understanding the basic format of the SAT Math Test and general strategies you will need for success.

Format of the Digital SAT Math Test

The Digital SAT Math Test consists of two 35-minute modules, each with 22 questions. On the Digital SAT, **all students complete the same 1st Math module**, which has a mix of easy, medium, hard, and very hard questions. As you work through the 1st Math module, the questions increase in difficulty.

The Digital SAT is adaptive, so your performance on the first module determines which 2nd module you get. **If you do well on the 1st module, the 2nd module will have much more difficult questions.** The harder 2nd module begins with medium questions and then has many hard and very hard questions. **If you do not do well on the 1st module, the 2nd module will have easy, medium, and a few hard questions.** The easier 2nd module begins with easier questions and then progresses to more difficult questions.

The diagram below helps explain how the adaptive test works.

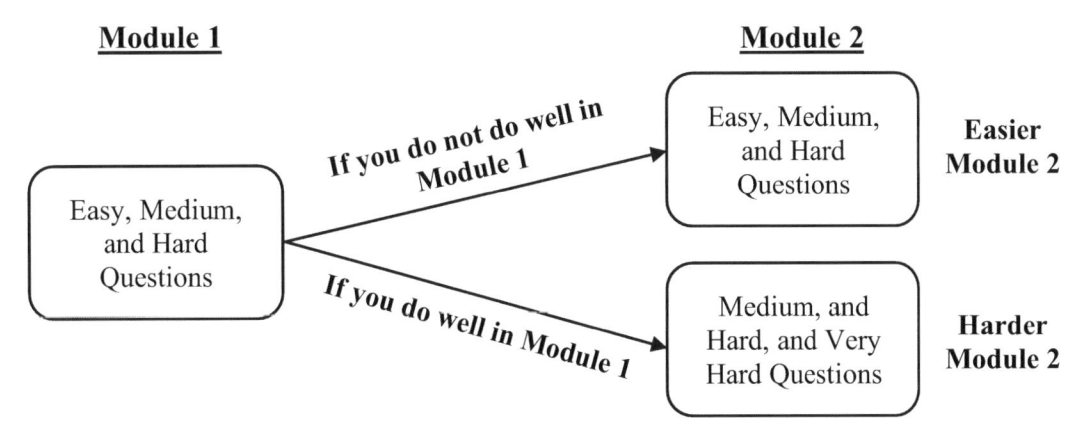

Module 1 → (If you do not do well in Module 1) → Easy, Medium, and Hard Questions — **Easier Module 2**

Easy, Medium, and Hard Questions → (If you do well in Module 1) → Medium, and Hard, and Very Hard Questions — **Harder Module 2**

Difficulty of the Questions

As you progress through each module, the questions increase in difficulty. Module 1 includes easy, medium, and hard questions. For students who do well in module 1, the harder module 2 will include medium, hard, and very hard questions. For students who do not do as well in module 1, the easier module 2 will include easy, medium, and hard questions. The table below breaks down where you will generally see easy, medium, hard, and very hard questions in each module by question number.

Question Difficulty	Module 1	Module 2 (Easier)	Module 2 (Harder)
Easy	1 – 8	1 – 13	None
Medium	9 – 14	14 – 19	1 – 10
Hard	15 – 19	20 – 22	11 – 16
Very Hard	20 – 22	None	17 – 22

Of course, this is a rough breakdown and the SAT most likely will not follow these patterns exactly. However, it is still helpful to know the general pattern of difficulty in each module.

Time Management

On average, you have 95 seconds (1 minute and 35 seconds) to answer each question. Some questions can be solved very quickly while others can take much longer to solve. In general, you should be solving the easier questions in less than 60 seconds, as the later, more difficult questions will require more time.

If you get to a question that you do not know how to solve, mark the question for review, select an answer, and move on. You can always come back to the questions that you marked for review at the end if you have time left. It is important to answer questions as quickly as possible but not to go so fast that you make mistakes. Keep yourself moving through the section and find the questions that you know how to solve.

Guessing

There is no penalty for guessing. Make sure that you select an answer for every single question. On multiple-choice questions, there is no best method for guessing, so look at the answer choices and pick the answer that looks best to you.

For free response questions (where you type in your own answer), still make a guess. Integers, particularly from 1 to 9, are the common answers on grid-in questions. The odds that you will guess correctly are, of course, quite low, but you might get lucky so do not leave any answer blank.

6 Test Day Tips to Maximize Your Score

The 6 test-taking tips below will help you maximize your scores on test day.

1. **Keep Moving.** Do not get stuck on any one question for too long. We often see students make this mistake and run out of time on the last few questions of a section. If you get stuck on a question, mark it for review, select your best guess, and move on. You can come back to the question at the end if you have time left over. Remember, there is no penalty for guessing.

2. **Look for Shortcuts.** Often, solving SAT math questions algebraically is not the easiest or fastest method. In this book, we will refer to solving questions algebraically as the "math teacher way." Look for shortcuts to get to the answer more quickly and easily. We will teach you a variety of different strategies to help you learn to "cheat" the test, spot shortcuts and avoid doing questions the "math teacher way."

3. **Do Your Best To See All The Questions.** As you progress through the module, the questions generally increase in difficulty but that does not mean the hardest questions are always last! If you see a question that stumps you, mark the question for review, select a guess, and move on. Many students make the mistake of getting stuck on difficult questions and running out of time. If you instead skipped questions that stump you and move on, you might find more questions that you know how to answer and achieve a higher score!

4. **Memorize the Equations.** In this book, all of the equations, formulas, and rules that you need to memorize are in bold lettering. Having all of equations, formulas, and rules memorized for test day will help you solve questions more quickly and will help maximize your score.

5. **Use Desmos and Your Calculator!** Use Desmos and your calculator as much as possible. Even for simple calculations, avoid mental math as much as possible, as mental math often leads to avoidable errors.

6. **Practice Like Its Test Day.** The best way to get ready for test day is to treat your practice SATs like it is the real thing. Do not exit the Bluebook app. Do not take breaks. Do not look at your notes.

Introduction to The Complete Guide to Digital SAT Math

The Digital SAT Math is an incredibly repetitive and predictable standardized test. You do not need to be a gifted math student to achieve a top score. If you are willing to put in the time and effort to learn everything in this book, you can improve your SAT Math score by up to 250 points. In this book, we will teach you all of the content, strategies, tips, and techniques that have helped drastically improve the SAT math scores for over 3,000 of our students, many of whom have achieved a perfect 800.

How to Best Use This Book

Great, you purchased *PrepPros The Complete Guide to Digital SAT Math*. Now what? To maximize your improvement, make sure to follow these tips:

1. **Find Your Level.** To make this book as effective as possible for each student, we have split the book into 4 levels. The levels are based on your math ability and scoring goals. The levels are listed below. **Make sure to read the complete description of the 4 Level System on page iii.**

    - **Level 1 – Core Fundamentals**
        - **For Students Scoring Below 550 on SAT Math**
    - **Level 2 – Advanced Fundamentals**
        - **For students Scoring 550-650 on SAT Math**
    - **Level 3 – Advanced Topics**
        - **For Students Scoring from 660-720 on SAT Math**
    - **Level 4 – Expert Level Topics**
        - **For Students Aiming for 730+ on SAT Math**

    In each chapter, the logos above label each concept, example question, and practice question with its corresponding level. **To have the best experience with this book, focus on the concepts in each chapter and practice questions that are AT AND BELOW your level.** If you are a weaker math student, start with level 1. If you master all level 1 topics, move onto level 2. If you are a stronger math student, make sure that you still know all level 1 and 2 topics before moving onto the level 3 topics. Level 4 topics are for advanced math students aiming for perfect and near perfect scores.

2. **Sign Up For The Ultimate Digital SAT Math Course (On-Demand Lessons and Answer Explanations, and Desmos Hacks). The course includes over 40 hours of on-demand videos of expert tutor and perfect scorer Michael Stroup** teaching all the concepts and showing you how to solve all 1,500 questions in this book. Start by watching the lessons for each chapter, where Michael teaches you everything that you need to know and shows you how to apply the concepts on example questions. These lessons are the same ones that he teaches students in private tutoring sessions for $225/hr.

    Next, complete the practice questions at the end of each chapter. Do not watch the video explanations before attempting to solve the question. The struggle is one of the best ways to learn. If you are stuck, look back at the teaching pages in the chapter first. Once you are done with the practice questions, check your answers with the answer key in the back of the book and watch the video explanations for any questions that you answered incorrect or did not confidently know how to solve.

    To sign up, go to www.preppros.io/sat-math-course. Chapter 12 is FREE in the Free Trial (no credit card needed). **The Ultimate SAT Math Course starts at $19.99/month for the answer explanations and $49.99 for the full course with discount code DS24 at checkout** (the course is normally $74.99

but with this book you get a lifetime $25 discount! **For even more information on the course, go to the first page of this book inside the front cover.**

3. **Use The Study Guides.** In the next section, there are 4 study guides: one for each level. **Each study guide lists the topics and equations that you should memorize based on your math level and scoring goals.** You can use the study guide as a checklist of all the concepts you need to learn and equations you need to memorize.

4. **Work Front To Back.** This book is designed to be completed from front to back. The most commonly tested topics are in the front and less commonly tested topics are in the back. To maximize your improvement, we recommend working through all the chapters. That being said, each chapter is written to be independent of the other chapters. If you are already proficient in certain topics, you can skip around and focus on the chapters that you need to learn to improve your score.

5. **Practice Makes Perfect.** We recommend completing all practice questions at your level and below in each chapter. For example, if you are a level 3 student, complete all level 1, 2 and 3 practice questions.

6. **Learn From Your Mistakes.** The students who improve most are the ones who learn the most from their mistakes. We recommend keeping an "Improvement Notebook" where you keep a list of the equations you need to memorize and takes notes when you make mistakes on practice questions.

7. **Mark Questions You Answer Incorrectly and Repeat These Question in The Final 2 Weeks Before Your SAT.** Repeating questions that you answer incorrectly as you lead up to test day helps students review challenging concepts, learn from their mistakes, and maximize their scores.

Difficulty of Practice Questions

In each chapter, the difficulty of the practice questions increases as you work through the problem sets. As you work through each chapter, keep your math level and scoring goals in mind. **If you are aiming for a math score of 700+, make sure you understand how to solve every level 3 question in this book and attempt the level 4 questions as well.**

If you are a weaker math student who is currently scoring below 600, do not be intimidated by the level 3 and 4 questions at the end of each chapter. These questions are written to challenge top math students. That being said, you can still learn by attempting these questions and watching the video explanation in the Ultimate SAT Math Course if you have time to do so, but do not be discouraged if you find them very difficult. You can still see great improvements in your math score without knowing how to solve the most advanced questions on the test.

What Else to Do?

Take practice tests…lots of them! In addition to this book, you should take at least 4 full practice SATs. The College Board has released 4 full practice Digital SATs so far. To take a practice SAT, go to https://bluebook.collegeboard.org/ and download the Bluebook App. Once you download the app and log in, you can take 4 Digital Practice SATs.

To give you more practice, we will also be writing our own practice SATs. PrepPros' practice SATs are included in the Ultimate SAT Course and the Ultimate SAT Math Course. Students who are not enrolled in those courses can be purchased our practice SATs separately on our website www.preppros.io.

How Our 4 Level System Works

To make this book as effective as possible for each student, we created a 4-level system. The levels are based on your math ability and scoring goals. The topics included in each level are based on the difficulty of the math topics and how often the topic appears. You can learn more about each level below to find which level is best for you!

How To Find Your Level

The best way to find your level is to complete a practice SAT and use the table below. Go to page ii and read tip "What Else To Do?" to find where to get a practice SAT. If you have not completed a practice SAT, you can use the general descriptions in the table below to find what level sounds like the best match for you.

Level	SAT Math Score	General Description of Student
1	Below 550	Weak math student
2	550-650	Average math student
3	650-720	Strong math student, often in advanced/honors math courses
4	730+	Very strong math student in advanced/honors math courses

As your scores increase on practice SATs and/or as you master the concepts for your level, you can move up to the next level! **To have the best experience with this book, focus on the concepts in each chapter and practice questions that are AT AND BELOW your level.**

The 4 Levels

Level 1 – Core Fundamentals
- **For Students Scoring Below 550 on SAT Math**

Level 1 is designed for students who find SAT Math difficult and are scoring below 550 on the SAT Math Test. **Level 1 concepts are the topics on the SAT that are easiest to learn and most commonly tested.**

Learning Level 1 concepts helps weaker math students improve their scores quickly and teaches them how to solve many of the easier questions that appear on the SAT Math Test.

Level 2 – Advanced Fundamentals
- **For Students Scoring 550-650 on SAT Math**

Level 2 is designed for average math students who need to review and relearn many concepts they have forgotten from math class. Level 2 also includes some easy-to-learn concepts that students are often never taught in math class. **Level 2 concepts are medium difficulty and are very commonly tested.**

Mastering Level 2 concepts allows average math students to solve more easy and medium difficulty questions that appear in questions on the SAT Math Test quickly and easily, leading to much higher scores.

Level 3 – Advanced Topics
- For Students Scoring 660-720 on SAT Math

Level 3 is designed for strong math students aiming for scores 700+ on the SAT Math Test. Level 3 concepts focus on the advanced topics tested on the SAT Math. **If you do well in the module 1 of math, get the more difficult set of questions in module 2, and then struggle in module 2, you are definitely a level 3 student!**

Overall, Level 3 concepts include all advanced topics that are commonly and somewhat commonly tested on the SAT Math. Additionally, level 3 includes other less commonly tested topics that are easy to master for students at this math level. Mastering level 3 concepts prepares students to achieve scores of 700+ on test day.

Level 4 – Expert Level Topics
- For Students Aiming for 730-800 on SAT Math

Level 4 is designed for very strong math students aiming for scores of 750+ on the SAT Math Test. **You should only complete Level 4 concepts after you have mastered all Level 3 concepts.** Level 4 includes the concepts that are the most advanced and the most difficult to master. However, if you want to achieve near perfect or perfect SAT Math scores, you need to know EVERYTHING tested. Mastering level 4 concepts prepares students to achieve scores of 750+ on test day.

How To Best Use The 4-Level System

To have the best experience with this book, focus on the concepts in each chapter and practice questions that are <u>AT AND BELOW</u> your level. More detailed instructions for each level are written below.

Level 1 Instructions
- **Complete all Level 1 concepts and practice questions.** On chapters you feel confident, try level 2 practice questions as well.
- After mastering Level 1 concepts, start working on Level 2 concepts to keep improving.

Level 2 Instructions
- **Complete all Level 1 & 2 concepts and practice questions.** On chapters you feel confident, try Level 3 practice questions as well.
- After mastering Level 1 & 2 concepts, move onto the commonly tested Level 3 concepts (see Level 3 study guide on pg. xxi for a list of these concepts).

Level 3 Instructions
- **Complete all Level 1-3 concepts and practice questions.** Many Level 3 concepts are topics that challenge many strong math students, so they are important to review to prepare you for scoring 700+ on the SAT.
- Attempt to solve Level 4 practice questions on chapters where you feel confident.

Level 4 Instructions
- **Complete all Level 2-4 concepts and practice questions.** You need to understand EVERYTHING in this book to be ready for a perfect score on test day. You can skip Level 1 questions, as you likely do not need to practice easy questions.

SAT Math Study Guide (Level 1)

SAT Math Study Guides

The Complete Guide to Digital SAT Math Book can be overwhelming. With 36 chapters and 1,500 practice questions, it can be difficult to know where you should focus your studying. Not to worry! We have created this SAT Math Study Guide to help you know what topics to study.

How To Use The Study Guides

There are 4 study guides: one for each of the 4 levels. Each study guide lists the concepts you need to understand and equations you need to memorize based on your math level and scoring goals. If you need to find your level, go back to page v.

We recommend that you use the study guides in 2 ways:

1. **Use the study guide as a checklist of chapters to complete in the book**. As you complete each concept and chapter, you can check them off.
2. **Use the study guide to review before test day**. In the 2 weeks before your SAT, go back through the topics you have learned. Make sure that you have all equations memorized, know the concepts you learned, and review any questions you answered incorrectly.

Level 1 Study Guide – Core Fundamentals

Math Level: Easy

Best For: Students Scoring Below 550 on SAT Math

Overview & Strategy for Level 1 Students:

Level 1 concepts are commonly tested topics on the SAT and the ones that everyone needs to know. If you are a weaker math student, start by learning all the topics listed below. Level 1 concepts are the easiest to learn and do not require advanced math skills. Questions in core fundamentals most commonly appear in the first 10 questions of module 1. If you get the easier module 2, core fundamentals questions will appear in the first half of the module. If you get the harder module 2, core fundamentals questions will rarely be tested.

As a weaker math student, you should focus on trying to answer as many of the first 10-15 questions of module 1 (most commonly easy and medium difficulty questions) correctly. These topics will help you do that! **You may run out of time on the SAT Math Test – that is okay!** You should not worry about the more advanced math questions at the end of module 1, as these are designed to stump advanced math students. If you get the easier module 2, you should be able to answer many questions correctly.

If you do well on module 1 and get the harder module 2, it is going to feel very difficult, and you will likely run out of time. Do the best that you can to find questions that you know how to answer (these will likely be the medium difficulty questions in the first 8 questions of module 2). For questions that you do not know how to answer, select your best guess, mark the question for review, and move on. If you get to the harder module 2, your goal is to answer as many questions as possible on topics that you know correctly and guess on the rest.

PrepPros

Level 1 Topics to Learn

The study guide below lists all the Level 1 topics that you should know for test day. We recommend that you use this study guide as a checklist of chapters for you to complete in this book.

Test-Taking Tricks To Know

Chapter 1: Backsolving (A Powerful Test-Taking Trick)
- Backsolving (p. 1) – learn backsolving, understand examples 1-2.
- Backsolving With Points (p. 2) learn backsolving with points, understand examples 3-4.

Chapter 2: Substitution (Another Test-Taking Trick)
- Substitution (pp. 5-6) – understand examples 1-3.

Chapter 3: Equivalent Questions
- Equivalent Trick (p. 9) – understand equivalent trick, understand examples 1-2.
- Desmos Equivalent Hack (pp. 9-11) – understand how to use Desmos equivalent hack.

Chapter 4: Desmos Hacks
- Desmos Hack #1 – Solving Algebra Questions (pp. 14-15) – understand how to use Desmos to solve examples 1-2.
- Desmos Hack #2 – Solving Systems of Equations (p. 15) – understand how to use Desmos to solve systems of equations, understand example 3.
- Desmos Hack #4 – Solving Quadratics Without Factoring (p. 16) – understand how to use Desmos to find solutions to quadratics without factoring, understand example 4.

Math Concepts To Know

Chapter 5: Algebra Skills
- PEMDAS (p. 18) – understand example 1.
- Negative Numbers (p. 19) – understand example 2, understand negative numbers and exponents.
- Combining Like Terms (p. 20) – understand example 4.
- Cross Multiply Fractions (p. 21) – understand example 5.
- Algebra with Inequality Signs (pp. 22-23) – know when to switch inequality sign.

Chapter 6: Fractions
- Combining Fractions (p. 30) – know how to add and subtract fractions with numbers, do not worry about example 1.
- Dividing Fractions (pp. 30-31) – know the flip and multiply trick, try to understand example 2.
- Simplifying Fractions (pp. 31-32) – understand simplifying with numbers, do not worry if variables examples and example 2 are confusing.
- Getting Rid of Fractions (p. 33) – know how to get rid of fractions if you hate fractions!
- Turn Fractions Into Decimals (p. 34) – great trick to make fractions questions easier.
- Use Desmos to Turn Decimals into Fractions (p. 34) – know how to turn decimals into fractions with Desmos.

Chapter 7: "In Terms of"
- "In Terms of" Questions (p. 39) – understand what "in terms of" questions are asking you to do, understand example 1.

Chapter 8: Inequalities

- Algebra with Inequalities (p. 44) – know when to switch direction of inequality sign, understand example 1.
- Graphing Inequalities (pp. 45-46) – learn how to graph inequalities, understand example 2.

Chapter 9: Percentages

- Simple Percentage (p. 53) – understand examples 1-2.
- Percentage Increase and Decrease (p. 57) – memorize equations, understand example 1.
- Percentage Change (p. 58) – memorize equation, understand example 4.

Chapter 10: Exponents and Roots

- Basic Exponent Rules (pp. 63-64) – memorize rules, understand examples 1-3.
- Simplifying Square Roots (pp. 65-66) – understand examples 5-6.

Chapter 11: Quadratics

- Multiplying Binomials (p. 74) – understand example 1.
- Factoring Quadratics (p. 75-76) – know how the box method works, try to understand example 2.
- "Easy to Factor" Quadratics (p. 75) – memorize equations.
- Solutions, Roots, x-intercepts, and Zeros for Quadratic Equations (pp. 76-77) – know 2 methods to solve quadratics, understand examples 3 and 5.
- Sum of Solutions (p. 77) – memorize rule.

Chapter 12: Systems of Equations

- Elimination (p. 93) – know how to solve using Desmos, try to understand how to solve mathematically but do not worry too much if it seems confusing, understand example 1.
- Substitution (p. 94) – know how to solve using Desmos, try to understand how to solve mathematically but do not worry too much if it seems confusing, understand example 2.
- Set Equal (pp. 94-95) – know how to solve using Desmos, try to understand how to solve mathematically but do not worry too much if it seems confusing, understand example 3.
- More Complex Systems of Equations (p. 96) – know how to solve using Desmos.

Chapter 13: Functions

- Function Basics (p. 102) – understand examples 1-2.
- Composite Functions (pp. 102-103) – try to understand example 3.
- Functions on Graphs (pp. 103-104) – understand how functions are graphed, try to understand example 5.

Chapter 14: Geometry Part 1 - Angles

- Intersecting Lines (p. 110) – memorize rules.
- Parallel Lines (p. 110) – memorize rules, understand example 1.
- Interior Angles of Polygons (pp. 111-112) – memorize equation for total interior angles, understand example 3.
- Drawn to Scale Trick (p. 112)
- Types of Triangles (pp. 112-113) – memorize definitions, understand example 4.

Chapter 15: Geometry Part 2 - Shapes
- Area and Volume (p. 117) – memorize equations, understand example 1.
- Right Triangles (pp. 120-121) – memorize Pythagorean Theorem and Pythagorean Triples, understand example 6.

Chapter 16: Geometry Part 3 – Similar Shapes and Congruent Triangles
- Similar Triangles (p. 130) – memorize similar triangle definition, understand example 1, try to understand example 2.
- Other Similar Shapes (p. 131) – memorize similar shapes definition, try to understand example 3.

Chapter 17: Lines
- Slope (p. 141) – memorize equation, understand examples 1-2.
- Slopes of Parallel and Perpendicular Lines (p. 142) – memorize rules, understand example 3.
- Slope-Intercept Form (p. 143) – memorize equation, understand example 5.
- Standard Form (pp. 145-146) – know how to turn standard form into slope-intercept form, understand example 8.
- Solving for Intercepts (p. 146) – memorize rules, understand example 9.
- Midpoint Formula (p. 147) – memorize equation, understand example 11.
- Distance Formula (p. 148) – memorize equation, try to understand example 12.

Chapter 18: Interpreting Lines
- Interpreting the Constants in a Given Equation (p. 155) – understand example 1.

Chapter 20: Trigonometry
- Basic Trigonometry – SOH-CAH-TOA (pp. 177-178) – understand examples 1-2.
- Using Trigonometry to Find Side Lengths in Right Triangles (pp. 178-179) – try to understand example 4.

Chapter 21: Probability
- The Basics of Probability (p. 197) – understand example 1 (questions 1-2).
- Probability and Data Tables (p. 198) – understand example 2, try to understand example 3.
- 3 More Probability Rules to Know (pp. 200-201) – memorize the 3 rules, understand examples 6-8.

Chapter 22: Statistical Analysis
- Sampling (pp. 208-209) – memorize 3 principles about sampling, understand examples 1-2.
- Standard Deviation (pp. 209-210) – memorize definition, understand example 3.
- Dot Plots (p. 211) – understand how dot plots display data.
- Statistical Bias (pp. 213-214) – understand 3 types of bias, understand example 9.
- Box and Whisker Plot (p. 215) – learn how box and whisker plot displays data, understand example 11.

Chapter 23: Ratios and Proportions
- Ratio and a Total (p. 224) – memorize the "x" trick, understand example 1.
- Ratios as Proportions (p. 225) – understand example 2.

Chapter 24: Mean, Median, Mode, and Range
- Finding the Average (p. 230) – memorize definitions, understand example 1.
- Finding the Median (p. 233) – understand example 6.

Chapter 25: Unit Conversion

- Simple Unit Conversions (p. 241) – understand examples 1-2.

Chapter 26: Scatter Plots and Lines of Best Fit

- Scatter Plots and Lines of Best Fit (pp. 248-249) – memorize 3 principles, understand examples 1-3.
- Is that really the y-intercept? (p. 249) – understand the concept and don't let the SAT trick you!

Chapter 27: Circles

- Equation of a Circle (pp. 253-254) – memorize equation, understand example 1.

Chapter 29: Absolute Value

- Basics of Absolute Value (p. 271) – understand example 1.

Chapter 30: Word Problems

- Understand 4 Tips for Solving Word Problems (p. 250)

Chapter 34: Extraneous Solutions

- Backsolving Method For Extraneous Solutions (pp. 307-309) – learn how to use the answer choices to make extraneous solutions questions easy.

Level 2 Study Guide – Additional Fundamentals

Math Level: Easy, Medium

Best For: Students Scoring 550-650 on SAT Math

Overview & Strategy for Level 2 Students:

Level 2 concepts are commonly tested topics that do not require advanced math skills. These are the concepts, rules, and equations you can learn to quickly boost your score. Some of these concepts are ones that you have learned in school before but may have forgotten because you only covered them briefly in math class or learned them years ago. Others are ones that you may have never learned in school but are easy to learn quickly for the SAT.

This Level 2 study guide includes some Level 1 concepts that students often need to review and additional Level 2 concepts. **The Level 2 additional fundamentals in this study guide expand your math knowledge and allow you to answer more questions correctly.** Level 2 concepts are of medium difficulty and are all easy to learn.

Questions in this Level 2 study guide most commonly appear in the first 10-15 questions of module 1. If you get the easier module 2, questions on topics from this study guide will appear throughout the module. If you get the harder module 2, questions on topics from this Level 2 study guide will most commonly appear in the first 8 questions.

After completing this Level 2 study guide, **you should be able to answer many of the questions in module 1 confidently.** As you get to the end of Module 1, there will likely be some more difficult questions that challenge you. If you see any questions that stump you, mark the question for review, select your best guess, and move on. Do not get stuck for too long! It is important to manage your time well, so you have time to answer all the questions in module 1.

If you do well on module 1 and get the harder module 2, it is going to feel very difficult, and you may run out of time. **Do the best that you can to find questions that you know how to answer** (these will likely be the medium difficulty questions in the first 8 questions of module 2). For questions that you do not know how to answer, select your best guess, mark the question for review, and move on. If you get to the harder module 2, your goal is to answer as many questions as possible on topics that you know correctly and to bubble in guesses for the rest.

If you get the easier module 2, you should be able to answer many questions correctly, as this level 2 study guide covers most of the topics covered in the easier modules. Timing should not be an issue.

Level 2 Topics to Learn

The study guide below lists all the Level 2 topics that you should know for test day. We recommend that you use this study guide as a checklist of chapters for you to complete in this book.

Test-Taking Tricks To Know

Chapter 1: Backsolving (A Powerful Test-Taking Trick)

- Backsolving (p. 1) – learn backsolving, understand examples 1-2.
- Backsolving With Points (p. 2) learn backsolving with points, understand examples 3-4.

Chapter 2: Substitution (Another Test-Taking Trick)

- Substitution (pp. 5-6) – understand examples 1-3.

Chapter 3: Equivalent Questions

- Equivalent Trick (p. 9) – understand equivalent trick, understand example 1-2.
- Desmos Equivalent Hack (pp. 9-11) – understand how to use Desmos equivalent hack.

Chapter 4: Desmos Hacks

- Desmos Hack #1 – Solving Algebra Questions (pp. 14-15) – understand how to use Desmos to solve examples 1-2.
- Desmos Hack #2 – Solving Systems of Equations (p. 15) – understand how to use Desmos to solve systems of equations, understand example 3.
- Desmos Hack #4 – Solving Quadratics Without Factoring (p. 16) – understand how to use Desmos to find solutions to quadratics without factoring, understand example 4.

Math Concepts To Know

Chapter 5: Algebra Skills

- PEMDAS (p. 18) – understand example 1.
- Negative Numbers and Exponents (pp. 19-20) – memorize rule, understand example 3.
- Square Both Sides of an Equation Correctly (pp. 21-22) – understand example 6.
- Algebra with Inequality Signs (pp. 22-23) – know when to switch inequality sign, understand example 7.
- Taking Square Roots in Algebraic Equations (pp. 23-24) – memorize rule, understand example 8.
- Solving Directly for the Answer (p. 25) – understand concept, try to understand example 11.

Chapter 6: Fractions

- Combining Fractions (p. 30) – know how to add and subtract fractions with numbers and variables, try to understand example 1.
- Dividing Fractions (pp. 30-31) – know the flip and multiply trick, understand example 2.
- Simplifying Fractions (pp. 31-32) – know rules for simplifying, understand example 3.
- Getting Rid of Fractions (p. 33) – understand example 2.
- Turn Fractions Into Decimals (p. 34) – great trick to make fractions questions easier.
- Use Desmos to Turn Decimals into Fractions (p. 34) – know how to turn decimals into fractions with Desmos.

Chapter 7: "In Terms of"

- "In Terms of" Questions (p. 39) – understand what "in terms of" questions are asking you to do, understand examples 1-2.

PrepPros

Chapter 8: Inequalities

- Algebra with Inequalities (p. 44) – know when to switch direction of inequality sign, understand example 1.
- Graphing Inequalities (pp. 45-46) – learn how to graph inequalities, understand example 2.
- Systems of Inequalities (pp. 46-47) – understand backsolving and Desmos method for example 3.
- Inequalities and Word Problems (p. 48) – understand example 5.

Chapter 9: Percentages

- Simple Percentage (p. 53) – understand examples 1-2.
- Percentage Increase and Decrease (p. 57) – memorize equations, understand examples 1-2.
- Percentage Change (p. 58) – memorize equation, understand example 4.

Chapter 10: Exponents and Roots

- Basic Exponent Rules (pp. 63-64) – memorize rules, understand examples 1-3.
- Simplifying Square Roots (pp. 65-66) – understand examples 5-6.
- Roots and Variables with Powers (pp. 67-68) – understand example 8.

Chapter 11: Quadratics

- Factoring Quadratics (p. 75-76) – know how the box method works, understand example 2.
- "Easy to Factor" Quadratics (p. 75) – memorize equations.
- Solutions, Roots, x-intercepts, and Zeros for Quadratic Equations (pp. 76-77) – know 2 methods to solve quadratics, understand examples 3 and 5, understand Desmos method for solving example 4.
- Sum of Solutions (p. 77) – memorize rule.
- How Solutions Appear on a Graph (pp. 79-80) – memorize rules, understand example 6.
- The Quadratic Formula (p. 80) – memorize equation, understand example 7.
- The Vertex (p. 83) – memorize vertex form, understand example 11.
- Finding the x-coordinate of the vertex (p. 84) – memorize rule on the top of the page.
- 3 Forms of a Parabola (p. 84) – memorize information in table.

Chapter 12: Systems of Equations

- Elimination (p. 93) – know how to solve using Desmos and the "Math Teacher Way", understand example 1.
- Substitution (p. 94) – know how to solve using Desmos and the "Math Teacher Way", understand example 2.
- Set Equal (pp. 94-95) – know how to solve using Desmos and the "Math Teacher Way", understand example 3
- The Shortcut (p. 95) – understand example 4.
- Word Problems (p. 95) – understand example 5.
- More Complex Systems of Equations (p. 96) – know how to solve using Desmos, understand example 6.

Chapter 13: Functions

- Function Basics (p. 102) – understand examples 1-2.
- Composite Functions (pp. 102-103) – understand example 3.
- Functions on Graphs (pp. 103-104) – understand how functions are graphed, understand example 5.
- Inverse Functions (pp. 104-105) – understand example 6.

Chapter 14: Geometry Part 1 - Angles

- Intersecting Lines (p. 110) – memorize rules.
- Parallel Lines (p. 110) – memorize rules, understand example 1.
- Interior Angles of Polygons (pp. 111-112) – memorize equation for total interior angles, understand example 3.
- Drawn to Scale Trick (p. 112)
- Types of Triangles (pp. 112-113) – memorize definitions, understand example 4.

Chapter 15: Geometry Part 2 - Shapes

- Area and Volume (pp. 117-118) – memorize equations, understand examples 1-2.
- Similar Shapes and Scale Factors (pp. 118-120) – understand example 4, try to understand example 5.
- Similar Shapes and Scale Rules (p. 120) – memorize rules in table.
- Right Triangles (pp. 120-121) – memorize Pythagorean Theorem and Pythagorean Triples, understand example 6.
- Special Right Triangles (pp. 121-122) – memorize triangle proportions, understand example 7.
- Third Side of a Triangle (p. 123) – memorize rule, understand example 9.

Chapter 16: Geometry Part 3 – Similar Shapes and Congruent Triangles

- Similar Triangles (p. 130) – memorize similar triangle definition, understand examples 1-2.
- Other Similar Shapes (p. 131) – memorize similar shapes definition, understand example 3.
- Congruent Triangles (pp. 132-134) – know congruent triangles definition, memorize 5 rules for proving congruent triangles, understand example 4.
- 3 Rules for Proving Similar Triangles (pp. 134-135) – memorize 3 rules, try to understand example 5.

Chapter 17: Lines

- Slope (p. 141) – memorize equation, understand examples 1-2.
- Slopes of Parallel and Perpendicular Lines (p. 142) – memorize rules, understand examples 3-4.
- Slope-Intercept Form (p. 143) – memorize equation, understand example 5.
- Point-Slope Form (pp. 144-145) – memorize equation, understand example 7.
- Standard Form (pp. 145-146) – know how to turn standard form into slope-intercept form, understand example 8.
- Solving for Intercepts (p. 146) – memorize rules, understand example 9, try to understand example 10.
- Midpoint Formula (p. 147) – memorize equation, understand example 11.
- Distance Formula (p. 148) – memorize equation, understand example 12.

Chapter 18: Interpreting Lines

- Interpreting the Constants in a Given Equation (p. 155) – memorize rules, understand examples 1-2.
- Selecting the Right Equation (p. 156) – understand example 3.
- The "Plug In Points" Method (p. 156) – understand the method, try to understand example 4.

Chapter 19: Exponential Growth and Decay

- Exponential Growth and Decay Equations (p. 164) – memorize equations.
- Exponential Growth (pp. 164-165) – know how exponential growth appears on a graph, understand example 1.
- Exponential Decay (pp. 165-166) – know how exponential decay appears on a graph, understand example 2.
- General Exponential Form (p. 166) – memorize equation and what the variables represent, understand the 2 examples given at bottom of the page.

Chapter 20: Trigonometry

- Basic Trigonometry – SOH-CAH-TOA (pp. 177-178) – understand examples 1-3.
- Using Trigonometry to Find Side Lengths in Right Triangles (pp. 178-179) – understand examples 4-5.
- Basic Trigonometry in Similar Triangles (p. 180) – understand concept and example 6.
- Inverse Trigonometric Functions (p. 183) – memorize rules, understand example 10.
- Radians vs. Degrees (p. 184) – know how to convert from radians to degrees and degrees to radians, understand examples 12-13.
- Unit Circle (p. 185) – memorize unit circle, understand example 14.

Chapter 21: Probability

- The Basics of Probability (pp. 197-198) – understand example 1 (questions 1-3).
- Probability and Data Tables (pp. 198-199) – understand examples 2-4.
- Conditional Probability (p. 199) – understand the concept, try to understand example 5.
- 3 More Probability Rules to Know (pp. 200-201) – memorize the 3 rules, understand examples 6-8.

Chapter 22: Statistical Analysis

- Sampling (pp. 208-209) – memorize 3 principles about sampling, understand examples 1-2.
- Standard Deviation (pp. 209-210) – memorize definition, understand examples 3-4.
- Dot Plots (p. 211) – understand how dot plots display data, understand example 5.
- Margin of Error (pp. 211-213) – understand examples 6-8.
- Statistical Bias (pp. 213-214) – understand 3 types of bias, understand examples 9-10.
- Box and Whisker Plot (p. 215) – learn how box and whisker plot displays data, understand example 11.

Chapter 23: Ratios and Proportions

- Ratio and a Total (p. 224) – memorize the "x" trick, understand example 1.
- Ratios as Proportions (p. 225) – understand example 2.
- Comparing Across Ratios (p. 225) – understand example 3.
- Ratios and Geometry (p. 226) – understand example 4.

Chapter 24: Mean, Median, Mode, and Range

- Finding the Average (p. 230) – memorize definitions, understand examples 1-2.
- Weighted Average (p. 232) – memorize equation, try to understand example 4.
- Outliers and the Median (p. 232) – understand example 5.
- Finding the Median (p. 233) – understand example 6.
- Finding the Median in a Table (pp. 233-234) – understand example 7.
- Finding the Median in a Dot Plot (p. 234) – understand example 8.
- Finding the Median in a Bar Graph (p. 235) – understand how to find median in a bar graph.

Chapter 25: Unit Conversion

- Simple Unit Conversions (p. 241) – understand examples 1-2.

Chapter 26: Scatter Plots and Lines of Best Fit

- Scatter Plots and Lines of Best Fit (pp. 248-249) – memorize 3 principles, understand examples 1-3.
- Is that really the *y*-intercept? (p. 249) – understand the concept and don't let the SAT trick you!

Chapter 27: Circles

- Equation of a Circle (pp. 253-255) – memorize equation, understand examples 1-4.

Chapter 28: Shifting and Transforming Functions

- Rules for Shifting and Transforming Functions (p. 263) – memorize rules.
- Lines (pp. 263-264) – understand graphs and shifts, understand example 1.
- Parabolas (p. 265) – understand graphs and shifts, try to understand example 3.
- All Other Functions (p. 266) – understand graphs and shifts.

Chapter 29: Absolute Value

- Basics of Absolute Value (p. 271) – understand example 1.
- Absolute Value and Unknown Variables (pp. 271-272) – memorize steps for how to solve these questions, understand example 2.

Chapter 30: Word Problems

- Understand 4 Tips for Solving Word Problems (p. 250)

Chapter 31: Solving for Constants

- Solving for Constants in Equivalent Equations (p. 281) – understand examples 1-2.
- Solving for Constants in Equivalent Equations with Multiple Unknowns (pp. 282-283) – try to understand examples 5-6.
- Solving for Constants with No Solution (pp. 283-284) – memorize rule, understand example 7.
- Solving for Constants with Infinite Solutions (pp. 284-285) – memorize rule, try to understand examples 9-10.
- Solving for Constants with One Solution (p. 286) – memorize rule.
- Two Solutions for Algebraic Expressions (p. 286)

Chapter 33: Arcs and Sectors

- Arcs (p. 301-302) – memorize equations, understand examples 1-3.
- Inscribed Angle Theorem (p. 302) – memorize rule.
- Sectors (pp. 303-304) – memorize equations, understand examples 4-6.

Chapter 34: Extraneous Solutions

- Backsolving Method For Extraneous Solutions (pp. 307-309) – learn how to use the answer choices to make extraneous solutions questions easy, learn how to use Desmos to solve.

Chapter 35: Interpreting Constants in Linear, Polynomial, and Exponential Functions

- Linear Equations (p. 311) – memorize rules in table, understand example 1.
- Finding the x-intercept and y-intercept (p. 312) – memorize rules, understand example 2.

Level 3 Study Guide – Advanced Topics

Math Level: Medium, Hard

Best For: Students Scoring 660-720 on SAT Math

Overview & Strategy for Level 3 Students:

Level 3 is designed for strong math students aiming for scores 700+ on the SAT Math Test. The Level 3 study guide includes the advanced topics commonly tested on the difficult questions on the SAT. Now, do not let the "advanced" name intimidate you. Yes, some of these topics are difficult, but many are "advanced" simply because most students do not know how to set up and solve these questions effectively. As you work through this study guide, you will learn the most effective methods, strategies, and test-taking tricks to make many difficult questions feel easy.

Questions in this Level 3 study guide most commonly appear on the difficult and very difficult questions at the end of module 1 and throughout the harder module 2. **To get a score of 700+ on the SAT, you cannot miss very many questions, so your goal is to learn all the concepts in this book** so that you will be prepared for any concept that is included on your SAT. **You should complete the level 1-3 practice questions for every chapter in this book.**

As a stronger math student, module 1 should feel easier, and you should have no issue with time management. On the first 10-15 easier and medium difficulty questions, make sure that you read the questions carefully and take your time! You do not want to make any dumb mistakes, as the SAT punishes mistakes on easy questions quite heavily (you can lose up to 50 points for missing an easy question!). As you get to the hard questions at the end of module 1, do you best to answer these correctly as well. If a question stumps you, it is best to mark the question for review, select your best guess, and move on to the next question. You can always come back at the end if you still have time. If you finish the section and have time left, go back and re-do the questions to make sure that you did not make any dumb mistakes.

You should get the harder module 2, which will feel significantly harder than module 1. **Since the harder module 2 has medium, difficult, and very difficult questions, time management is more challenging.** You now need to work more efficiently to complete the section. As your progress through the section, the questions increase in difficulty. You will likely see a few expert level questions that really challenge you. If you get to a question that you do now know how to answer, select your best guess, mark the question for review, and move on. It is important not to get stuck on any 1 question for too long. Keep moving to make sure that you can get to see all the questions on module 2 and get as many points as possible. If you run out of time, at least you know that you were able to answer all of the questions that you knew how to do. If you finish with any extra time, you can go back to any questions you marked for review or can check your work.

Once you complete this level 3 study guide, you will be in a great best position to score 700+ on test day!

Level 3 Topics to Learn

The study guide below lists all the Level 3 topics that you should know for test day. We recommend that you use this study guide as a checklist of chapters for you to complete in this book.

Test-Taking Tricks To Know

Chapter 1: Backsolving (A Powerful Test-Taking Trick)
- o Backsolving (p. 1) – learn backsolving, understand examples 1-2.

- Backsolving With Points (p. 2) learn backsolving with points, understand examples 3-4.

Chapter 2: Substitution (Another Test-Taking Trick)
- Substitution (pp. 5-6) – understand examples 1-3.

Chapter 3: Equivalent Questions
- Equivalent Trick (p. 9) – understand equivalent trick, understand example 1-2.
- Desmos Equivalent Hack (pp. 9-11) – understand how to use Desmos equivalent hack.

Chapter 4: Desmos Hacks
- Desmos Hack #1 – Solving Algebra Questions (pp. 14-15) – understand how to use Desmos to solve examples 1-2.
- Desmos Hack #2 – Solving Systems of Equations (p. 15) – understand how to use Desmos to solve systems of equations, understand example 3.
- Desmos Hack #4 – Solving Quadratics Without Factoring (p. 16) – understand how to use Desmos to find solutions to quadratics without factoring, understand example 4.

Level 1 and Level 2 Topics to Make Sure You Know

Before starting the level 3 topics listed on the following pages, make sure you know the topics listed below from the core fundamentals (Level 1) and advanced fundamentals (Level 2). These topics are ones that we have seen many students, even very strong math students, struggle on. To score 700+ on the SAT Math Test, you NEED to know all these fundamental topics.

Chapter 5: Algebra Skills
- Negative Numbers and Exponents (pp. 19-20) – memorize rule, understand example 3.
- Square Both Sides of an Equation Correctly (pp. 21-22) – understand example 6.
- Taking Square Roots in Algebraic Equations (pp. 23-24) – memorize rule, understand example 8.
- Solving Directly for the Answer (p. 25) – understand concept, try to understand example 11.

Chapter 6: Fractions
- Dividing Fractions (pp. 30-31) – know the flip and multiply trick, understand example 2.
- Simplifying Fractions (pp. 31-32) – know rules for simplifying, understand example 3.
- Turn Fractions Into Decimals (p. 34) – great trick to make fractions questions easier.
- Use Desmos to Turn Decimals into Fractions (p. 34) – know how to turn decimals into fractions with Desmos.

Chapter 7: "In Terms of"
- "In Terms of" Questions (p. 39) – understand what "in terms of" questions are asking you to do, understand examples 1-3.

Chapter 8: Inequalities
- Algebra with Inequalities (p. 44) – know when to switch direction of inequality sign.
- Graphing Inequalities (pp. 45-46) – learn how to graph inequalities, understand example 2.
- Systems of Inequalities (pp. 46-47) – understand backsolving and Desmos method for examples 3-4.
- Inequalities and Word Problems (p. 48) – understand example 5.

PrepPros

Chapter 9: Percentages
- Simple Percentage (pp. 53-54) – understand examples 1-3.
- Percentage Increase and Decrease (pp. 57-58) – memorize equations, understand examples 1-3.
- Percentage Change (p. 58) – memorize equation, understand example 4.

Chapter 10: Exponents and Roots
- Basic Exponent Rules (pp. 63-64) – memorize rules, understand examples 1-4.
- Simplifying Square Roots (pp. 65-66) – understand examples 5-6.

Chapter 11: Quadratics
- "Easy to Factor" Quadratics (p. 75) – memorize equations.
- Solutions, Roots, x-intercepts, and Zeros for Quadratic Equations (pp. 76-77) – know 2 methods to solve quadratics, understand examples 3-5.
- How Solutions Appear on a Graph (pp. 79-80) – memorize rules, understand example 6.

Chapter 13: Functions
- Composite Functions (pp. 102-103) – understand examples 3-4.
- Functions on Graphs (pp. 103-104) – understand how functions are graphed, understand example 5.
- Inverse Functions (pp. 104-105) – understand example 6.

Chapter 14: Geometry Part 1 - Angles
- Intersecting Lines (p. 110) – memorize rules.
- Parallel Lines (p. 110) – memorize rules, understand example 1.
- Interior Angles of Polygons (pp. 111-112) – memorize equation for total interior angles, understand example 3.
- Drawn to Scale Trick (p. 112)

Chapter 15: Geometry Part 2 - Shapes
- Area and Volume (pp. 117-118) – memorize equations, understand examples 1-3.
- Third Side of a Triangle (p. 123) – memorize rule, understand example 9.

Chapter 16: Geometry Part 3 – Similar Shapes and Congruent Triangles
- Similar Triangles (p. 130) – memorize similar triangle definition, understand examples 1-2.
- Other Similar Shapes (p. 131) – memorize similar shapes definition, understand example 3.

Chapter 17: Lines
- Slope (p. 141) – memorize equation, understand examples 1-2.
- Slopes of Parallel and Perpendicular Lines (p. 142) – memorize rules, understand examples 3-4.
- Slope-Intercept Form (pp. 143-144) – memorize equation, understand examples 5-6.
- Point-Slope Form (pp. 144-145) – memorize equation, understand example 7.
- Standard Form (pp. 145-146) – know how to turn standard form into slope-intercept form, understand example 8.
- Solving for Intercepts (pp. 146-147) – memorize rules, understand examples 9-10.
- Midpoint Formula (p. 147) – memorize equation, understand example 11.
- Distance Formula (p. 148) – memorize equation, understand example 12.

Chapter 18: Interpreting Lines
- Interpreting the Constants in a Given Equation (p. 155) – memorize rules, understand examples 1-2.
- Selecting the Right Equation (p. 156) – understand example 3.

Chapter 20: Trigonometry
- Using Trigonometry to Find Side Lengths in Right Triangles (pp. 178-179) – understand examples 4-5.
- Inverse Trigonometric Functions (p. 183) – memorize rules, understand examples 10-11.

Chapter 23: Ratios and Proportions
- Ratio and a Total (p. 224) – memorize the "x" trick, understand example 1.
- Ratios as Proportions (p. 225) – understand example 2.
- Comparing Across Ratios (p. 225) – understand example 3.
- Ratios and Geometry (p. 226) – understand example 4.

Chapter 26: Scatter Plots and Lines of Best Fit
- Scatter Plots and Lines of Best Fit (pp. 248-249) – memorize 3 principles, understand examples 1-3.
- Is that really the y-intercept? (p. 249) – understand the concept and don't let the SAT trick you!

Chapter 30: Word Problems
- Understand 4 Tips for Solving Word Problems (p. 250)

Chapter 33: Arcs and Sectors
- Arcs (p. 301-302) – memorize equations, understand examples 1-3.
- Inscribed Angle Theorem (p. 302) – memorize rule.
- Sectors (pp. 303-304) – memorize equations, understand examples 4-6.

Level 3 Math Concepts To Know

The advanced topics (Level 3) listed below are commonly tested on difficult and very difficult questions on the SAT. Some of the topics listed below are labelled as level 1 and 2 topics in the teaching pages of each chapter, but we have included the topics in this list of Level 3 concepts to know because we have seen many strong math students struggle on these topics. **Mastering the advanced topics and memorizing the rules and equations in the list below will put you in the best position to score 700+ on test day!**

Chapter 5: Algebra Skills
- Factoring to Isolate a Variable (p. 24) – understand example 9.
- Factoring by Grouping for Cubic Functions (p. 25) – understand example 10.
- Solving Directly for the Answer (p. 25) – understand example 11.

Chapter 6: Fractions
- Combining Fractions (p. 30) – understand example 1.

Chapter 10: Exponents and Roots
- Simplifying Cube Roots (p. 67) – understand example 7.
- Roots and Variables with Powers (pp. 67-68) – understand example 8, try to understand example 9.

Chapter 11: Quadratics

- Sum of Solutions (pp. 77-78) – memorize rule, understand example 4.
- Product of Solutions (p. 77) – memorize rule at bottom of page.
- The Quadratic Formula (pp. 80-81) – memorize equation, understand examples 7-8.
- The Discriminant (p. 82) – memorize rules in table, understand example 9, try to understand example 10.
- The Vertex (p. 83) – memorize vertex form, understand examples 11-12.
- Finding the x-coordinate of the vertex (p. 84) – memorize rule on the top of the page, try to understand example 13.
- 3 Forms of a Parabola (pp. 84-85) – memorize information in table, try to understand example 14.

Chapter 12: Systems of Equations

- Elimination (p. 93) – know how to solve using Desmos and the "Math Teacher Way", understand example 1.
- Substitution (p. 94) – know how to solve using Desmos and the "Math Teacher Way", understand example 2.
- Set Equal (pp. 94-95) – know how to solve using Desmos and the "Math Teacher Way", understand example 3
- The Shortcut (p. 95) – understand example 4.
- Word Problems (p. 95) – understand example 5.
- More Complex Systems of Equations (pp. 96-97) – understand examples 6-7.

Chapter 14: Geometry Part 1 - Angles

- Exterior Angle Theorem (p. 111) – memorize rule, understand example 2.

Chapter 15: Geometry Part 2 - Shapes

- Similar Shapes and Scale Factors (pp. 118-120) – understand examples 4-5
- Similar Shapes and Scale Factors Rules (p. 120) – memorize rules in table.
- Special Right Triangles (pp. 121-122) – memorize triangle proportions, understand examples 7-8.
- Other Rules You Might Need to Know (p. 124) – memorize rules and definitions.

Chapter 16: Geometry Part 3 – Similar Shapes and Congruent Triangles

- Congruent Triangles (pp. 132-134) – know congruent triangles definition, memorize 5 rules for proving congruent triangles, understand example 4.
- 3 Rules for Proving Similar Triangles (pp. 134-135) – memorize 3 rules, understand example 5.

Chapter 18: Interpreting Lines

- The "Plug In Points" Method (pp. 156-158) – understand the method, understand example 4, try to understand example 5.

Chapter 19: Exponential Growth and Decay

- Exponential Growth and Decay Equations (p. 164) – memorize equations.
- Exponential Growth (pp. 164-165) – know how exponential growth appears on a graph, understand example 1.
- Exponential Decay (pp. 165-166) – know how exponential decay appears on a graph, understand examples 2-3.
- General Exponential Form (p. 166) – memorize equation and what the variables represent, understand example 4.
- Advanced Exponential Growth and Decay (pp. 167-168) – understand example 5.

- o Graphing General Exponential Form (pp. 168-170) – memorize key points to understand and 3 key takeaways, try to understand example 6.

Chapter 20: Trigonometry

- o Basic Trigonometry in Similar Triangles (pp. 180-181) – understand concept and examples 6-7.
- o 2 Important Trigonometry Identities To Know (pp. 181-182) – memorize equations, understand example 8, try to understand example 9.
- o Radians vs. Degrees (p. 184) – know how to convert from radians to degrees and degrees to radians, understand examples 12-13.
- o Unit Circle (pp. 185-186) – memorize unit circle, understand examples 14-15.
- o Coterminal Angles and The Unit Circle (pp. 186-189) – memorize definition and 6 principles.

Chapter 21: Probability

- o Probability and Data Tables (pp. 198-199) – understand examples 2-4.
- o Conditional Probability (p. 199) – understand example 5.
- o 3 More Probability Rules to Know (pp. 200-201) – memorize the 3 rules, understand examples 6-8.

Chapter 22: Statistical Analysis

- o Sampling (pp. 208-209) – memorize 3 principles about sampling, understand examples 1-2.
- o Standard Deviation (pp. 209-210) – memorize definition, understand examples 3-4.
- o Dot Plots (p. 211) – understand how dot plots display data, understand example 5.
- o Margin of Error (pp. 211-213) – understand examples 6-8.
- o Statistical Bias (pp. 213-214) – understand 3 types of bias, understand examples 9-10.
- o Box and Whisker Plot (p. 215) – learn how box and whisker plot displays data, understand example 11.

Chapter 24: Mean, Median, Mode, and Range

- o Finding the Average (p. 230) – memorize definitions, understand examples 1-3.
- o Weighted Average (p. 232) – memorize equation, try to understand example 4.
- o Outliers and the Median (p. 232) – understand example 5.
- o Finding the Median (p. 233) – understand example 6.
- o Finding the Median in a Table (pp. 233-234) – understand example 7.
- o Finding the Median in a Dot Plot (p. 234) – understand example 8.
- o Finding the Median in a Bar Graph (p. 235) – understand how to find median in a bar graph.

Chapter 25: Unit Conversion

- o Dimensional Analysis (pp. 242-243) – understand examples 3-4.
- o Advanced Unit Conversion with Squared and Cubed Units (pp. 243-244) – understand examples 6-7.

Chapter 27: Circles

- o Equation of a Circle (pp. 253-255) – memorize equation, understand examples 1-4.
- o General Form and Completing the Square (pp. 255-256) – know how to complete the square, understand example 5, try to understand example 6.
- o Advanced Circles Questions (pp. 257-258) – understand examples 7-8.
- o Finding Points On, Inside, and Outside the Circle (pp. 258-259) – memorize rules in table, try to understand example 9.

Chapter 28: Shifting and Transforming Functions

- Rules for Shifting and Transforming Functions (p. 263) – memorize rules.
- Lines (pp. 263-264) – understand graphs and shifts, understand examples 1-2.
- Parabolas (p. 265) – understand graphs and shifts, understand example 3.
- All Other Functions (p. 266) – understand graphs and shifts, try to understand example 4.

Chapter 29: Absolute Value

- Absolute Value and Unknown Variables (pp. 271-272) – memorize steps for how to solve these questions, understand example 2.
- Advanced Absolute Value (p. 273) – understand example 3.
- Absolute Value with 1 Solution, No Solution, and Infinite Solutions (pp. 274-275) – memorize rules in table, understand examples 4-5.

Chapter 31: Solving for Constants

- Solving for Constants in Equivalent Equations (pp. 281-282) – understand examples 1-4.
- Solving for Constants in Equivalent Equations with Multiple Unknowns (pp. 282-283) – understand examples 5-6.
- Solving for Constants with No Solution (pp. 283-284) – memorize rule, understand examples 7-8.
- Solving for Constants with Infinite Solutions (pp. 284-285) – memorize rule, understand examples 9-10.
- Solving for Constants with One Solution (pp. 286-287) – memorize rule, understand example 11.
- Two Solutions for Algebraic Expressions (p. 286)

Chapter 32: Systems of Equations with Infinite Solutions, No Solutions, and One Solution

- One Solution (p. 291) – understand when equations have 1 solution.
- No Solution (pp. 291-292) – memorize ratio shortcut, understand examples 1-2.
- Infinite Solutions (pp. 293-295) – memorize ratio shortcut, understand example 3-5.
- Identifying The Correct System of Equations (pp. 295-296) – understand examples 6-7
- Summary of Rules (p. 296) – memorize rules in table.

Chapter 34: Extraneous Solutions

- Extraneous Solutions (pp. 307-309) – learn "math teacher way" for solving extraneous solutions questions without answer choices, understand examples 1-2.

Chapter 35: Interpreting Constants in Linear, Polynomial, and Exponential Functions

- Linear Equations (p. 311) – memorize rules in table, understand example 1.
- Finding the x-intercept and y-intercept (p. 312) – memorize rules, understand examples 2-3.
- Parabolas (pp. 313-314) – memorize rules in table, understand examples 4-6, try to understand example 7.
- Exponential Functions (pp. 315-317) – memorize 3 rules, understand example 8, try to understand example 9.

Chapter 36: Special Quadratics – Perfect Squares and Difference of Squares

- Special Quadratics (p. 321) – memorize equation in table.
- Difference of Squares (pp. 321-322) – understand examples 1-3, try to understand example 4.
- Perfect Squares (pp. 322-323) – understand example 5, try to understand example 6.

Level 4 Study Guide – Expert Level Topics

Math Level: Hard, Very Hard

Best For: Students Scoring 730+ on SAT Math

Overview & Strategy for Level 4 Students:

If your goal is 750-800 on SAT Math, you need to know EVERYTHING tested on the SAT. That means you should understand EVERYTHING in this book. While knowing everything tested on the SAT is a challenging task, it is an achievable one with this book and study guide. Level 4 concepts cover the most advanced and challenging topics that you can see on test day.

Before you start working on the Level 4 concepts, make sure that you know ALL the topics in the Level 3 study guide and have all the equations memorized. All topics in this study guide are the most advanced and not as commonly tested, so You should NOT start this study guide until you have mastered everything in the level 3 study guide.

Since there are only 44 questions on the entire SAT Math Test, **you need to answer almost every single question correctly to score a 750-800.** If you answer more than 2 or 3 questions incorrectly, you score will almost certainly be below 750. To achieve this level of mastery over the SAT Math, you need to be a bit obsessive about making sure you know everything tested on the SAT and that you learn from all your mistakes. Having a few additional equations and rules memorized can be the difference between a 730 and an 800.

Important Tips to Achieve 750-800

To be ready to score 750-800 on the SAT Math, make sure you know how to solve all level 4 questions at the end of each chapter. These questions are written specifically for students like you and will help you learn how to solve the most advanced questions that appear on the SAT.

On the SAT, difficult and expert level questions can include any topic. Most commonly, it is a mix of advanced topics (exponential graphing, special quadratics, etc.) and regular topics (averages, systems of equations, percentages, etc.) presented in a very difficult way. Therefore, **it is important to make sure you work through the level 2-4 question in all chapters of this book** even if the general topic of the chapter seems easy.

The expert level questions appear at the end of module 1 (usually in questions 18-22) and in the later questions in the harder module 2. **As a stronger math student, module 1 should feel easier, and you should have no issue with time management.** Your goal in module 1 is to answer every question correctly. You will likely finish this section with plenty of time leftover. When you do finish early, use that time to go back and check your work and make sure that you did not make any dumb mistakes!

Module 2 will feel significantly harder than module 1, and time management is more challenging. You now need to work more efficiently to complete the section. If you get to a question that you do now know how to answer, select your best guess, mark the question for review, and move on. It is important not to get stuck on any 1 question for too long. Keep moving to make sure that you can get to see all the questions on module 2 and get as many points as possible.

To achieve a 750-800, you need to (1) have all the equations and rules memorized and (2) be familiar with all topics on the SAT so you can set up and solve questions quickly and efficiently on test day. Time management can be the difference between a 700 and a 780. Putting in the time and working through all chapters of this book will put you in the best position for achieving your goals on test day!

Level 4 Topics to Learn

The study guide below lists all the topics that you should know for test day if you are aiming for 750-800. We recommend that you use this study guide as a checklist of chapters for you to complete in this book.

Test-Taking Tricks To Know

Chapter 1: Backsolving (A Powerful Test-Taking Trick)

- Backsolving (p. 1) – learn backsolving, understand examples 1-2.
- Backsolving With Points (p. 2) learn backsolving with points, understand examples 3-4.

Chapter 2: Substitution (Another Test-Taking Trick)

- Substitution (pp. 5-6) – understand examples 1-3.

Chapter 3: Equivalent Questions

- Equivalent Trick (p. 9) – understand equivalent trick, understand example 1-2.
- Desmos Equivalent Hack (pp. 9-11) – understand how to use Desmos equivalent hack.

Chapter 4: Desmos Hacks

- Desmos Hack #1 – Solving Algebra Questions (pp. 14-15) – understand how to use Desmos to solve examples 1-2.
- Desmos Hack #2 – Solving Systems of Equations (p. 15) – understand how to use Desmos to solve systems of equations, understand example 3.
- Desmos Hack #4 – Solving Quadratics Without Factoring (p. 16) – understand how to use Desmos to find solutions to quadratics without factoring, understand example 4.

Level 4 Topics To Know

The expert level topics (Level 4) listed below are commonly tested on difficult and very difficult questions on the SAT. There are some level 2 and level 3 topics included as well because we have seen many strong math students struggle on these topics or forget the rules/equations. **Mastering the advanced and expert topics and memorizing the rules and equations in the list below will put you in the best position to score 750-800 on test day!**

Chapter 5: Algebra Skills

- Taking Square Roots in Algebraic Equations (p. 23) – remember when to use $\pm$ sign, understand example 8.
- Factoring to Isolate a Variable (p. 24) – understand example 9.
- Factoring by Grouping for Cubic Functions (p. 25) – understand example 10.
- Solving Directly for the Answer (p. 25) – understand example 11.

Chapter 6: Fractions

- Combining Fractions (p. 30) – understand example 1.
- Use Desmos to Turn Decimals into Fractions (p. 34) – know how to turn decimals into fractions with Desmos.

Chapter 9: Percentages

- Simple Percentage (pp. 53-54) – understand example 3.
- Percentage Increase and Decrease (pp. 57-58) – memorize equations, understand example 3.
- Percentage Change (p. 58) – memorize equation, understand example 4.

Chapter 10: Exponents and Roots

- Basic Exponent Rules (pp. 63-64) – memorize rules (especially fraction power rule), understand example 4.
- Simplifying Cube Roots (p. 67) – understand example 7.
- Roots and Variables with Powers (pp. 67-68) – understand example 8-9.

Chapter 11: Quadratics

- Sum of Solutions (pp. 77-78) – memorize rule, understand example 4.
- Product of Solutions (p. 77) – memorize rule at bottom of page.
- The Quadratic Formula (pp. 80-81) – memorize equation, understand examples 7-8.
- The Discriminant (p. 82) – memorize rules in table, understand examples 9-10.
- The Vertex (p. 83) – memorize vertex form, understand examples 11-12.
- Finding the x-coordinate of the vertex (p. 84) – memorize rule on the top of the page, understand example 13.
- 3 Forms of a Parabola (pp. 84-85) – memorize information in table, understand example 14.

Chapter 12: Systems of Equations

- The Shortcut (p. 95) – understand example 4.
- Word Problems (p. 95) – understand example 5.
- More Complex Systems of Equations (pp. 96-97) – understand examples 6-7.

Chapter 13: Functions

- Inverse Functions (pp. 104-105) – understand example 6.

Chapter 14: Geometry Part 1 - Angles

- Exterior Angle Theorem (p. 111) – memorize rule, understand example 2.
- Interior Angles of Polygons (pp. 111-112) – memorize equation for total interior angles, understand example 3.
- Drawn to Scale Trick (p. 112)

Chapter 15: Geometry Part 2 - Shapes

- Area and Volume (pp. 117-118) – memorize equations, understand example 3.
- Similar Shapes and Scale Factors (pp. 118-120) – understand examples 4-5.
- Similar Shapes and Scale Factors Rules (p. 120) – memorize rules in table.
- Special Right Triangles (pp. 121-122) – memorize triangle proportions, understand examples 7-8.
- Third Side of a Triangle (p. 123) – memorize rule, understand example 9.
- Other Rules You Might Need to Know (p. 124) – memorize rules and definitions.

Chapter 16: Geometry Part 3 – Similar Shapes and Congruent Triangles

- Congruent Triangles (pp. 132-134) – know congruent triangles definition, memorize 5 rules for proving congruent triangles, understand example 4.
- 3 Rules for Proving Similar Triangles (pp. 134-135) – memorize 3 rules, understand example 5.

Chapter 18: Interpreting Lines

- The "Plug In Points" Method (pp. 156-158) – understand the method, understand examples 4-5.

Chapter 19: Exponential Growth and Decay

- Exponential Growth and Decay Equations (p. 164) – memorize equations.

PrepPros

- Exponential Growth (pp. 164-165) – know how exponential growth appears on a graph, understand example 1.
- Exponential Decay (pp. 165-166) – know how exponential decay appears on a graph, understand examples 2-3.
- General Exponential Form (p. 166) – memorize equation and what the variables represent, understand example 4.
- Advanced Exponential Growth and Decay (pp. 167-168) – understand example 5.
- Graphing General Exponential Form (pp. 168-170) – memorize key points to understand and 3 key takeaways, understand example 6.

Chapter 20: Trigonometry

- Basic Trigonometry in Similar Triangles (pp. 180-181) – understand concept and examples 6-7.
- 2 Important Trigonometry Identities To Know (pp. 181-182) – memorize equations, understand examples 8-9.
- Radians vs. Degrees (p. 184) – know how to convert from radians to degrees and degrees to radians, understand examples 12-13.
- Unit Circle (pp. 185-186) – memorize unit circle, understand examples 14-15.
- Coterminal Angles and The Unit Circle (pp. 186-189) – memorize definition and 6 principles.

Chapter 21: Probability

- Conditional Probability (p. 199) – understand example 5.
- 3 More Probability Rules to Know (pp. 200-201) – memorize the 3 rules, understand examples 6-8.

Chapter 22: Statistical Analysis

- Sampling (pp. 208-209) – memorize 3 principles about sampling, understand examples 1-2.
- Standard Deviation (pp. 209-210) – memorize definition, understand examples 3-4.
- Dot Plots (p. 211) – understand how dot plots display data, understand example 5.
- Margin of Error (pp. 211-213) – understand examples 6-8.
- Statistical Bias (pp. 213-214) – understand 3 types of bias, understand examples 9-10.
- Box and Whisker Plot (p. 215) – learn how box plot displays data, understand example 11.

Chapter 24: Mean, Median, Mode, and Range

- Weighted Average (p. 232) – memorize equation, try to understand example 4.
- Finding the Median in a Table (pp. 233-234) – understand example 7.
- Finding the Median in a Dot Plot (p. 234) – understand example 8.
- Finding the Median in a Bar Graph (p. 235) – understand how to find median in a bar graph.

Chapter 25: Unit Conversion

- Dimensional Analysis (pp. 242-243) – understand examples 3-5.
- Advanced Unit Conversion with Squared and Cubed Units (pp. 243-244) – understand examples 6-7.

Chapter 27: Circles

- Equation of a Circle (pp. 253-255) – memorize equation, understand examples 1-4.
- General Form and Completing the Square (pp. 255-256) – know how to complete the square, understand examples 5-6.
- Advanced Circles Questions (pp. 257-258) – understand examples 7-8.
- Finding Points On, Inside, and Outside the Circle (pp. 258-259) – memorize rules in table, understand example 9.

Chapter 28: Shifting and Transforming Functions

- Rules for Shifting and Transforming Functions (p. 263) – memorize rules.
- Lines (pp. 263-264) – understand graphs and shifts, understand examples 1-2.
- Parabolas (p. 265) – understand graphs and shifts, understand example 3.
- All Other Functions (p. 266) – understand graphs and shifts, understand example 4.

Chapter 29: Absolute Value

- Advanced Absolute Value (p. 273) – understand example 3.
- Absolute Value with 1 Solution, No Solution, and Infinite Solutions (pp. 274-275) – memorize rules in table, understand examples 4-5.

Chapter 31: Solving for Constants

- Solving for Constants in Equivalent Equations (pp. 281-282) – understand examples 1-4.
- Solving for Constants in Equivalent Equations with Multiple Unknowns (pp. 282-283) – understand examples 5-6.
- Solving for Constants with No Solution (pp. 283-284) – memorize rule, understand examples 7-8.
- Solving for Constants with Infinite Solutions (pp. 284-285) – memorize rule, understand examples 9-10.
- Solving for Constants with One Solution (pp. 286-287) – memorize rule, understand example 11.
- Two Solutions for Algebraic Expressions (p. 286)

Chapter 32: Systems of Equations with Infinite Solutions, No Solutions, and One Solution

- One Solution (p. 291) – understand when equations have 1 solution.
- No Solution (pp. 291-292) – memorize ratio shortcut, understand examples 1-2.
- Infinite Solutions (pp. 293-295) – memorize ratio shortcut, understand example 3-5.
- Identifying The Correct System of Equations (pp. 295-296) – understand examples 6-7.
- Summary of Rules (p. 296) – memorize rules in table.

Chapter 33: Arcs and Sectors

- Arcs (p. 301-302) – memorize equations, understand examples 1-3.
- Inscribed Angle Theorem (p. 302) – memorize rule.
- Sectors (pp. 303-304) – memorize equations, understand examples 4-6.

Chapter 34: Extraneous Solutions

- Extraneous Solutions (pp. 307-309) – learn "math teacher way" for solving extraneous solutions questions without answer choices, understand examples 1-2.

Chapter 35: Interpreting Constants in Linear, Polynomial, and Exponential Functions

- Linear Equations (p. 311) – memorize rules in table, understand example 1.
- Finding the x-intercept and y-intercept (p. 312) – memorize rules, understand examples 2-3.
- Parabolas (pp. 313-314) – memorize rules in tables for vertical and horizontal parabolas, understand examples 4-7.
- Exponential Functions (pp. 315-317) – memorize 3 rules, understand examples 8-9.

Chapter 36: Special Quadratics – Perfect Squares and Difference of Squares

- Special Quadratics (p. 321) – memorize equation in table.
- Difference of Squares (pp. 321-322) – understand examples 1-4.
- Perfect Squares (pp. 322-323) – understand examples 5-6.

Not sure what the circle indicates? Go back to the page iii to learn about the 4 levels and how to best use this book.

Chapter 1: Backsolving

Chapter 1: Backsolving

In these first two chapters, you will learn two important test taking techniques: backsolving and substitution. **As you work through the rest of the book, use these techniques whenever you can to solve questions.**

Backsolving is plugging the answer choices back into the question. On the SAT, you are given 4 answer choices for multiple choice questions, and one of those 4 choices must be correct. Rather than solving the question algebraically and determining whether your answer matches one of the answer choices, you can guess-and-check with the answer choices to find which one is correct. Backsolving is often the fastest and easiest way to solve SAT questions, especially if you get stuck and cannot solve a question algebraically, so use it to your advantage.

Backsolving can be done using five steps:

1. **Start with answer choice B or C.** Plug the value back into the question. The answer choices are always in order of smallest to largest or largest to smallest so starting in the middle saves you time.

2. **Solve the question using this value.** Find any other unknowns if necessary.

3. **If the answer choice you select works correctly, you're done!** Bubble it in and move on.

4. **If the answer choice you select does not work, cross it off.** If you know the correct answer needs to be smaller or larger than the value you just tried, cross off any other incorrect answers.

5. **Pick one of the remaining answer choices and plug it back into the question.** Repeat this until you find the correct answer. Remember, one of the 4 answer choices must work!

Example 1: If $\sqrt{x+10} - 2\sqrt{x-2} = 0$ what is the value of x?

A) 2   B) 6   C) 14   D) 18

Solution: The quickest and easiest way to solve this question is backsolving. Finding the right answer is just a process of guess-and-check. Below, you can see how the correct answer, when $x = 6$, makes the equation true.

$$\sqrt{6+10} - 2\sqrt{6-2} = 0$$
$$\sqrt{16} - 2\sqrt{4} = 0$$
$$4 - 2(2) = 0$$
$$4 - 4 = 0$$
$$0 = 0$$

The answer is B. If we plug in any of the other answer choices, we get an equation that is not equal on both sides and is incorrect.

Example 2: If $\frac{3}{x+1} = \frac{2}{x}$, what is the value of x?

A) -2 B) 0   C) 1   D) 2

Solution: As in the last example, the quickest way to solve this question is backsolving. Plug the answer choices back into the question. Below, you can see how the correct answer $x = 2$ makes the equation true.

$$\frac{3}{2+1} = \frac{2}{2}$$
$$\frac{3}{3} = \frac{2}{2}$$
$$1 = 1$$

The answer is D.

Backsolving With Points

For questions with points in the question or answer choices, it is usually easiest to backsolve with points. Let's start with the first type of question we can backsolve with points, where points are in the answer choices.

> **Example 3:** Which of the following points is a solution to the set of inequalities shown below?
> $$3x + 4 < 2y$$
> $$5y - x > 4$$
> A) $(1, 2)$ B) $(1, 4)$ C) $(-3, -5)$ D) $(2, -5)$

Solution: If we see points in the answer choices, plug the points back into the question to see which point makes the equation(s) true. In Example 3, it is much easier to backsolve and test the 4 points in the answer choices than it is to solve the two inequalities. To test each answer choice, we plug the x and y values into the inequalities and look for the point that makes both inequalities true.

To start, let's plug in $(1, 4)$ from answer choice B. To do so, we plug in $x = 1$ and $y = 4$.

$$3(1) + 4 < 2(4)$$
$$5(4) - (1) > 4$$

Solving the inequalities, we get

$$7 < 8$$
$$19 > 4$$

Both of those statements are true, so the point $(1, 4)$ is a solution. **The answer is B.** If we plug in any other answer choice, one or both of the inequalities will not work.

Next, let's look at the second type of question where we should backsolve with points: we see equations in the answer choice and point(s) in the question.

> **Example 4:** A linear function f passes through the points $(1, 5)$, $(3, 9)$, and $(7, 17)$. Which of the following equations defines f?
> A) $f(x) = 2x + 5$ B) $f(x) = x + 5$ C) $f(x) = 4x + 1$ D) $f(x) = 2x + 3$

Solution: Here, the simplest way to solve is to test the answer choices using the points in the question. Let's start with the point $(1, 5)$. When we plug in $x = 1$, we need to get $f(1) = 5$.

For answer choice A: $f(1) = 2(1) + 5$ → $f(1) = 7$ (A is incorrect.)
For answer choice B: $f(1) = 1 + 5$ → $f(1) = 6$ (B is incorrect.)
For answer choice C: $f(1) = 4(1) + 1$ → $f(1) = 5$ (C works.)
For answer choice D: $f(1) = 2(1) + 3$ → $f(1) = 5$ (D works.)

Answer choices A and B do not work, so we can eliminate those answer choices. Answer choices C and D both work, so we need to use a second point to test answer choices C and D. Let's use the point $(3, 9)$.

For answer choice C: $f(3) = 4(3) + 1$ → $f(1) = 13$ (C is incorrect.)
For answer choice D: $f(3) = 2(3) + 3$ → $f(1) = 9$ (D is correct.)

The answer is D. As you can see, we can solve this question by backsolving with points. This method is much easier than solving this question algebraically.

Backsolving Practice: Answers on page 326.

1. If the area of a rectangle is 16 and one side has a length of 20, what is the width of the rectangle?

   A) $\frac{2}{5}$
   B) $\frac{1}{2}$
   C) $\frac{4}{5}$
   D) 1

2. If $\sqrt{3x} = 9$, what is the value of x?

   A) 3
   B) 9
   C) 27
   D) 81

3. For what value of x is the equation $\frac{13}{4}x + 6 = 5x - 8$ true?

   A) 12
   B) 8
   C) 6
   D) 4

4. The length of a rectangle is 8 inches longer than the width. If the perimeter of the rectangle is 52 inches, what is the width of the rectangle?

   A) 4
   B) 9
   C) 11
   D) 18

5. In the triangle below, the value of y is twice the value x and the value of z is three times the value of x. What is the value of x?

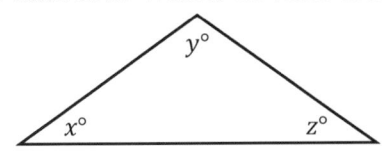

   Note: Figure not drawn to scale.

   A) 30
   B) 45
   C) 60
   D) 90

6. $\frac{12x}{5} + 2 = \frac{4}{10}x$

   What is the value of x in the equation above?

   A) -1
   B) 1
   C) 2
   D) 5

7. A graph shows the linear relationship between the number of yards of red yarn, x, and blue yarn, y, that can be purchased for a certain amount of money. If the points, $(2, 12)$ and $(8, 3)$ are on the graph, which of the following could be the equation of the line of the graph?

   A) $6x + 7y = 80$
   B) $4x + 6y = 68$
   C) $12x + 8y = 120$
   D) $6x + 12y = 80$

8. Which of the following is a solution to the equation of $x^3 + 5x^2 + 6x = 0$

   A) -3
   B) -1
   C) 1
   D) 2

9. The sum of 2 numbers is 85. If the smaller number is 45 less than the larger number, what is the larger number?

   A) 40
   B) 55
   C) 65
   D) 70

10. $\sqrt{x} = x - 2$

    For the equation above, what value(s) of x make the equation true?

    A) 4
    B) -1
    C) 0
    D) $-1, 4$

11. For which of the following tables are all the values of x and their corresponding values of y solutions to the given system of inequalities?

$$y < -4x + 17$$
$$y > -3x - 6$$

A)
x	y
5	5
7	12
8	14

B)
x	y
-2	5
0	3
1	2

C)
x	y
1	9
3	5
8	2

D)
x	y
1	9
5	5
7	2

12. For the quadratic function f, the table shows three values of x and their corresponding values of $f(x)$. Which equation defines f?

x	-1	0	1
$f(x)$	7	13	21

A) $f(x) = 7x^2 + x + 13$
B) $f(x) = 11x^2 - 3x + 13$
C) $f(x) = 5x^2 + 3x + 13$
D) $f(x) = x^2 + 7x + 13$

13. James withdrew one fifth of his savings last week. This week, James withdrew one quarter of the remaining amount. He is left with $150. How much did he originally have?

A) $280
B) $250
C) $220
D) $195

14. The function f is given below. Which table of values represents $y = f(x) + 4$?

$$f(x) = (x + 3)(x + 2)$$

A)
x	y
-6	12
1	12
2	20

B)
x	y
-6	16
1	16
2	24

C)
x	y
-1	6
1	14
2	16

D)
x	y
-10	12
-3	12
-2	20

15. A sheet of origami paper is cut 4 times in a specific manner to create 5 identical smaller pieces of paper. Then, the five smaller pieces of paper are each cut 4 more times to form 25 identical smaller pieces. This process continues until the pieces of paper are too small to cut. Which of the following functions gives the number of pieces of paper, $p(c)$, that result after c cuts, where c is a multiple of 4?

A) $p(c) = 5^{\frac{c}{4}}$
B) $p(c) = 5^{\frac{c}{4}+2}$
C) $p(c) = 5^{4c}$
D) $p(c) = 5^{4c+2}$

16. Skyscrapers have gaps between their floors to allow for expansion and contraction caused by temperature variation. The gap is a part of dynamic riser structure. The size of the gaps between the floor $g(T)$, in inches, is a linear function of temperature T, in degress Fahrenheit (°F). For a certain skyscraper, the gap is 3.625 inches at 35°F and is 2.625 inches at 85°F. Which of the following defines the relationship between temperature and the size of the gap?

A) $g(T) = -\frac{1}{50}(T - 50) + 5.325$
B) $g(T) = -\frac{1}{50}(T + 50) + 5.325$
C) $g(T) = 50(T - 50) + 5.325$
D) $g(T) = 50(T + 50) - 5.325$

17. The first term of a sequence is 7. Each term after the first is 6 times the preceding term. If k represents the nth term of the sequence, which equation gives k in terms of n?

A) $k = 6(7^n)$
B) $k = 6(7^{n-1})$
C) $k = 7(6^n)$
D) $k = 7(6^{n-1})$

Chapter 2: Substitution

Do you prefer working with numbers or variables? We would guess your answer is numbers! On the SAT, some questions have many unknown variables and few or no numbers at all. Most students hate these questions. If you prefer to work with numbers, let's work with numbers. With substitution, **we substitute simple numbers in for variables and solve the question using numbers instead of relying on more complex algebra with variables.**

Substitution can be done with these four steps:

1. **Pick a number for the variable(s) in the question.**
    a. **Pick easy numbers...avoid using 0 but instead pick 1 or 2.** Use 10 for percent problems, 10 or 20 for group size, etc.
    b. **Select different numbers for each variable.** For example, if a question has an x and a y, pick $x = 1$ and $y = 2$.
    c. **Follow any rules in the question.** For example, if a question says x is a number that is negative and even, pick $x = -2$.
2. **Write down the number(s) that you have picked.**
3. **Use your numbers to work your way through the question and find your answer.**
4. **Plug your numbers into the answer choices. The correct answer will be the one that matches your answer.**

Substitution may seem a bit confusing just reading the steps, so let's take a look at some example questions to see how useful this technique can be.

Example 1: Jeremy has n boxes of candy bars. Each box contains m bars of candy. Jeremy has to sell 70% of his candy bars to make enough money for rent. Which of the following expresses the number of candy bars Jeremy must sell in terms of m and n?

A) $0.7(m + n)$ B) $70nm$ C) $nm + m$ D) $0.7nm$

Solution: This question may at first seem intimidating with all the variables. To make this question easier, let's plug in numbers. We can say that Jeremy has 2 boxes of candy, so $n = 2$, and that each box contains 5 bars of candy, so $m = 5$. With our numbers, Jeremy has a total of 10 candy bars. He needs to sell 70% to make enough money for rent, so we can find the total candy bars that he must sell by finding 70% of 10.

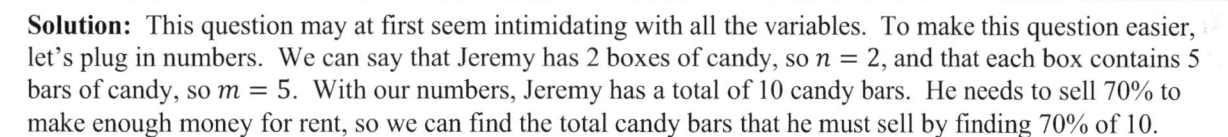

$$0.7(10) = 7$$

With our numbers, Jeremy must sell 7 candy bars, so our answer is 7. Now, we can plug in the values we selected for n and m into the answer choices and see which one is equal to 7. Here, we find that D works.

$$0.7nm = 0.7(2)(5) = 7$$

None of the other answer choices are equal to 7 when we plug in our values for n and m. No matter what numbers you pick for n and m, you will find that **D is the answer**.

Example 2: If $\cos(2x) = a$, which of the following must be true for all values of x?

A) $\sin(2x) = a$ B) $\cos(x) = a$ C) $\sin(90 - 2x) = a$ D) $\cos(90 - 2x) = a$

Solution: The easiest way to solve this question is to pick a value for x and solve for a using your calculator. Let's pick $x = 10$. First, we need to find out what a equals if $x = 10$.

$$\cos(20) = 0.9397$$

PrepPros

Now that we know what a equals, we can plug in $x = 10$ for the x-values in the answer choices to see which is equal to 0.9397. Here, we can see how the correct answer choice of C works.

$$\sin(90 - 20) = \sin(70) = 0.9397$$

This trick will work for any value of x that we pick. **The answer is C.**

Example 3: If the length of a rectangle is tripled and the width is halved, how many times larger is the area of the new rectangle than the area of the original rectangle?

  A) 1.5   B) 2   C) 3   D) 6

Solution: To make this question easier, we can pick values for the length and width of the rectangle. Let's make the length 3 and the width 2. Now, we just follow the steps in the questions.

The length is tripled: $3(3) = 9$ The new length is 9.

The width is halved: $2(\frac{1}{2}) = 1$ The new width is 1.

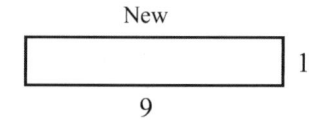

Next, we find the areas of the rectangles and compare. The new rectangle has an area of 9. The original rectangle has an area of 6, so we find that the new rectangle is 1.5 times as large. **The answer is A.**

Substitution Practice: Answers on page 326.

1. If x is an odd integer and y is an even integer, which of the following must be an odd integer?

   A) $2x^2 + y$
   B) $3x + y$
   C) $2x + 6$
   D) $x - \frac{y}{2}$

2. For variables a, b and c, the expression $0 < a < b < c$ is true. Which of the following expressions has the smallest value?

   A) $\frac{b}{c}$
   B) $\frac{c}{b}$
   C) $\frac{a}{c}$
   D) $\frac{c}{a}$

3. When each side length of a square with sides s is increased by 4 inches, which of the following expresses the new area of the square?

   A) $s^2 + 4$
   B) $s^2 + 16$
   C) $(s^2 + 4)^2$
   D) $(s + 4)^2$

4. If x and y are positive integers such that $x + y = 11$, what is the value of $\frac{x-11}{3y}$?

   A) $-\frac{1}{3}$
   B) $\frac{1}{3}$
   C) $\frac{4}{5}$
   D) 1

5. If $\frac{x}{5} = \frac{y}{2}$, which of the following is equal to $\frac{y}{3}$?

   A) $\frac{4x}{15}$
   B) $\frac{2x}{15}$
   C) x
   D) $\frac{2x}{3}$

Chapter 2: Substitution

6. Money raised by m school clubs will be divided equally among the clubs. Based on school records, n people each gave p dollars? Which of the following describes how much money, in dollars, will each club receive?

    A) mpn
    B) $\frac{mp}{n}$
    C) $\frac{np}{m}$
    D) $pn + m$

7. In the xy-plane, line a has slope $\frac{7}{5}$, and line b has slope $\frac{5}{7}$. Both lines contain the point $(0,0)$. For which of these lines is $y > x$ for all positive values of x?

    I. Line a
    II. Line b

    A) I only
    B) II only
    C) I and II
    D) Neither I nor II

8. If the sides of a triangle are all quadrupled, how many times greater is the area of the new triangle than the area of the original triangle?

    A) 4
    B) 8
    C) 10
    D) 16

9. The map of a country is drawn to scale where 2 inches represents 7 miles. The actual distance between two locations is x miles. Which expression represents the distance on the map, in inches, between the two locations?

    A) $\frac{2x}{7}$
    B) $\frac{7x}{2}$
    C) $2x + 7$
    D) $2x - 7$

10. The distance between Albert's front door and the end of his driveway is d miles. If he can run at c miles per hour, how long, in minutes, will it take him to run from his front door to the end of the driveway?

    A) $\frac{d}{c}$
    B) $60c$
    C) $\frac{60d}{c}$
    D) $\frac{60c}{d}$

11. Drew is training for a 50-mile race in the desert by going for a long run every Sunday. He will run 5 miles on the first Sunday that he trains. Every Sunday after the first, he will run 1.5 more miles than he ran on the preceding Sunday. Which of the following equations represents the number of miles m Drew will run on the nth Sunday of his training?

    A) $m = 5 + 1.5n$
    B) $m = 3.5 + 1.5n$
    C) $m = 5(1.5)^n$
    D) $m = 1.5(5)(n)$

12. The sides of a rectangle are in the proportion of $28:10$. The longer side of the rectangle is increased by x inches. By how many inches must the shorter side of the rectangle be increased to maintain the same proportion of the side lengths?

    A) $\frac{7}{4}x$
    B) $\frac{4}{7}x$
    C) $\frac{14}{5}x$
    D) $\frac{5}{14}x$

13. A drawing of an object has a scale where a length of 6 inches on the drawing represents an actual length of 8 feet. The actual length of the object is $5y$ feet. Which expression represents the length, in inches, of the object in the drawing?

A) $\frac{5}{8}y$
B) $\frac{8}{5}y$
C) $\frac{15}{4}y$
D) $\frac{20}{3}y$

14. If $3x = 4y = 6z$, which of the following expresses the average of x and y in terms of z?

A) $\frac{7z}{4}$
B) $\frac{5z}{3}$
C) $\frac{10}{4z}$
D) $\frac{13z}{9}$

15. Two quantities x and y are related such that $y = 7$ when $x = 1$. When the value of x increases by 1, the value of y is multiplied by 2. Which of the following represents this relationship?

A) $y = 7x^2$
B) $y = 7(x-1)^2$
C) $y = 7(2)^x$
D) $y = 7(2)^{x-1}$

16. The table below shows the list price, discount, and installation fee for a window company. The window company's total expenses for selling and installing 5 windows is $250. Which function represents the profit p, in dollars, from selling and installing 5 windows to which the company's discount is applied? (Note: profit = total amount of money received − expenses)

List Price ($)	Discount	Installation fee
x per window	Buy 4 windows at list price and get the 5th free	$150 for 5 windows

A) $p(x) = 5x + 150$
B) $p(x) = 5x - 100$
C) $p(x) = 4x + 150$
D) $p(x) = 4x - 100$

17. The population, in thousands, of Carmel Valley, California can be modeled by the function $p(t) = 247{,}000(1.072)^t$, where t represents the number of years after 2021 and $0 \le t \le 20$. Which of the following equations best models the population, in thousands, of Carmel Valley, California, where y represents the number of years after 2025, and $0 \le y \le 16$?

A) $p(n) = 247{,}000(1.072)^{4y}$
B) $p(n) = 247{,}000(1.072)^{y-4}$
C) $p(n) = 247{,}000(1.072)^4(1.072)^y$
D) $p(n) = (247{,}000)^4(1.072)^4(1.072)^y$

18. If x is an even integer and $3^{2x} + 3^{2x} + 9^x = z$, which of the following expresses z in terms of x?

A) 3^{2x+1}
B) 3^{3x}
C) 9^{2x}
D) $9^x + 27$

Chapter 3: Equivalent Questions

Equivalent questions ask us to identify which of the answer choices is equivalent to a given expression. These questions often look difficult, but they are easy as long as we use our Equivalent Trick or Desmos Equivalent Hack!

Equivalent Trick

1. **Plug in $x = 1$ to the original expression and solve.**
2. **Plug in $x = 1$ to the answer choices and solve.**
3. **Find which answer choice gives you the same value as the original expression. This is the correct answer.** Incorrect answer choices give you a value that is not the same as to the original expression.
4. **If you cannot tell which answer choice is correct after plugging in $x = 1$ because multiple answer choices equal the same value, plug in $x = 2$ or another simple value for x.**

If you do the math correctly, you can identify the correct answer for any equivalent questions without doing any fancy algebra!

Let's see how this works with some examples. To begin, we will start with an easier example.

> **Example 1:** Which of the following expressions is equivalent to $8x^3 - 4x$?
> A) $2x(4x^2 - 2)$ B) $-2x^2(2x - 1)$ C) $8x(x^2 - 1)$ D) $2x(2x - 2)^2$

Solution: Method #1 – Equivalent Trick: First, we plug in $x = 1$ to the expression $8x^3 - 4x$ and solve.

$$8(1)^3 - 4(1) = 8 - 4 = 4$$

We know that if $x = 1$, the expression equals 4. The equivalent answer choice must also equal 4. To find which answer choice is correct, plug in $x = 1$ to the answer choices and find which one equals 4.

For answer choice A: $2(1)(4(1)^2 - 2)$ → $2(4 - 2) = 4$ (A is correct)
For answer choice B: $-2(1)^2(2(1) - 1)$ → $-2(2 - 1) = -2$ (B is incorrect)
For answer choice C: $8(1)((1)^2 - 1)$ → $8(1 - 1) = 0$ (C is incorrect)
For answer choice D: $2(1)(2(1) - 2)^2$ → $2(2 - 2)^2 = 0$ (D is incorrect)

When we plug in $x = 1$ to the answer choices and solve, only answer choice A give us 4. Since both the original expression and the expression in answer choice A give us the same value, they must be equivalent! **The answer is A.**

Desmos Equivalent Hack

Method #2 – Use Desmos: We can solve any equivalent question with Desmos. That's right, we can solve equivalent questions without doing any math at all! To do this, we just need to understand one principle:

If two expressions are equivalent, the graphs of the expressions are identical. So, if we graph 2 expressions in Desmos and only see 1 graph, we know that the expressions are equivalent.

If the 2 expressions are not identical, we will see 2 separate graphs when they expressions are graphed in Desmos.

PrepPros

To solve any equivalent question with Desmos, use the following steps:

Step 1: Graph the original expression. To graph the original expression, type $y =$ and then type in the expression.

Step 2: Graph answer choice A. Use the same $y =$ method we outlined in Step 1 to graph answer choice A. **If the graphs are identical, the answer is A.** If the graphs are identical, you will only see 1 line. **If the graphs are not identical, A is incorrect.**

Step 3: Graph answer choice B and repeat Step 2. Repeat this process with answer choices C and D (if necessary) until you find the correct answer.

Now, we know that may seem confusing, so let's see how this works for Example 1.

To start, we type in the original equation and answer choice A to Desmos. Note how we need to write the expressions with $y =$ before the expression.

Answer Choice A: $y = 8x^3 - 4x$
                    $y = 2x(4x^2 - 2)$

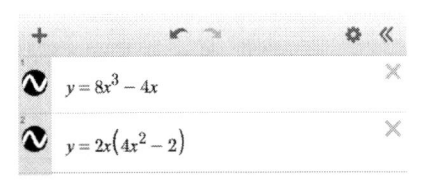

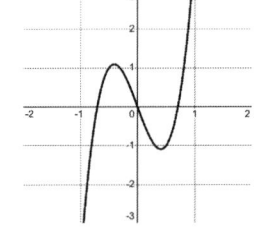

When the original expression and answer choice A are graphed, **we only see 1 line**. This tells us that answer choice A is equivalent to the original expressions, so **the answer is A.**

For the other answer choices, you can see below how each answer choice shows 2 graphs when graphed in Desmos, which tells us the expressions are NOT equivalent.

Answer Choice B: $y = 8x^3 - 4x$
                    $y = -2x^2(2x - 1)$

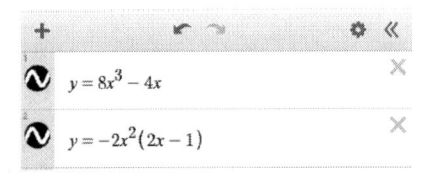

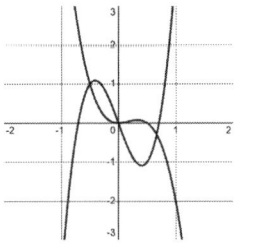

Answer Choice C: $y = 8x^3 - 4x$
                    $y = 8x(x^2 - 1)$

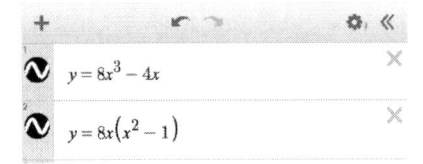

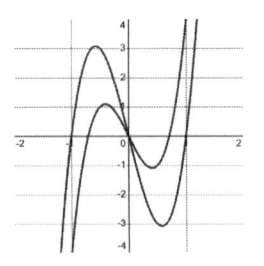

Answer Choice D: $y = 8x^3 - 4x$
                    $y = 2x(2x - 2)^2$

- 10 -

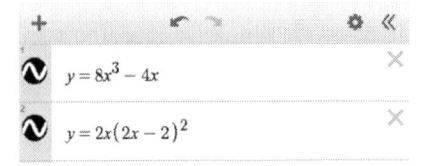

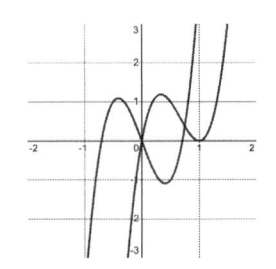

Chapter 3: Equivalent Questions

Method #3 – Factoring: The SAT wants you to solve this question by using your algebra skills and factoring the original expression. If we factor $2x$ out from both terms, we get

$$8x^3 - 4x = 2x(4x^2 - 2)$$

The answer is A. The challenging aspect of this method is that (1) many students are not comfortable with factoring and (2) this answer choice is not the simplest form that you are used to solving for in math class. If you were asked to factor the expression in math class, you would instead factor it like this:

$$8x^3 - 4x = 4x(2x^2 - 1)$$

The SAT loves to play tricks like this in equivalent questions! That's why **we recommend that you always use the Equivalent Trick or Desmos Equivalent Hack** when you see any equivalent questions on test day.

For some of you, the first example might have seemed easy to solve algebraically. However, that is certainly not always the case on the SAT. Equivalent questions can range from very easy to ridiculously hard. Let's take a look at a more difficult example next.

Example 2:
$$\frac{x^2 - 5x + 1}{x - 2}$$

Which of the following expressions is equivalent to the one above for $x \neq 2$?

A) $x - 3 + \frac{13}{x-2}$

B) $x - 3 - \frac{5}{x-2}$

C) $x + 1 + \frac{4}{x-2}$

D) $x + 1 - \frac{17}{x-2}$

(1-4)

Solution: Method #1 – Equivalent Trick: First, we plug in $x = 1$ to the original expression and solve.

$$\frac{(1)^2 - 5(1) + 1}{1 - 2} = \frac{1 - 5 + 1}{-1} = \frac{-3}{-1} = 3$$

We know that if $x = 1$, the expression equals 3. The equivalent answer choice must also equal 3. To find which answer choice is correct, plug in $x = 1$ to the answer choices and find which one equals 3.

A) $1 - 3 + \frac{13}{1-2} = 1 - 3 + \frac{13}{-1} = 1 - 3 - 13 = -15$ (A is incorrect)

B) $1 - 3 - \frac{5}{1-2} = 1 - 3 - \frac{5}{-1} = 1 - 3 - (-5) = 3$ (B is correct)

C) $1 + 1 + \frac{4}{1-2} = 1 + 1 + \frac{4}{-1} = 1 + 1 + (-4) = -2$ (C is incorrect)

D) $1 + 1 - \frac{17}{1-2} = 1 + 1 - \frac{17}{-1} = 1 + 1 - (-17) = 19$ (D is incorrect)

When we plug in $x = 1$ to the answer choices and solve, only answer choice B give us 3. Since both the original expression and the expression in answer choice B give us the same value, they are equivalent! **The answer is B.**

Method #2 – Desmos Equivalent Hack: We can graph the original expression and the answer choices to solve. The correct answer choice will only show 1 graph. You can go to Desmos and test this on your own.

To solve this question algebraically, we need to do polynomial division and then remember how to write the answer with a remainder. We know what you are probably thinking..."no thanks to that!" The Equivalent Trick and Desmos Equivalent Hack are amazing methods because they allow you to solve advanced equivalent questions even if you do not know how to do the algebra.

PrepPros

> **Test Day Tip – Know When to Use The Shortcut Methods**
>
> **If you see an equivalent question and are 100% confident that you can solve the question quickly with algebra, do NOT use the Equivalent Trick or Desmos Equivalent Hack.** Solving the question algebraically will likely be faster, so you can go ahead and use your algebra skills to save time.
>
> **If you are not 100% confident you can solve an equivalent question quickly with algebra or recognize that solving algebraically will take a long time, use the Equivalent Trick or Demos Equivalent Hack.** Plugging in $x = 1$ or graphing all 4 answer choices may feel slow, but you are guaranteed to get the question correct as long as you use one of our shortcut methods correctly.

Equivalent Questions Practice: Answers on page 326.

1. Which of the following is equivalent to $x^2 - 5x - 18$?

   A) $(x + 3)(x - 6) - 2x$
   B) $(x + 3)(x - 6) + 5x$
   C) $(x + 2)(x - 9) - 2x$
   D) $(x + 2)(x - 9) + 5x$

2. Which of the following expressions is equivalent to $18x^2 + 6x$?

   A) $2x(18x + 3)$
   B) $6x(3x + 6)$
   C) $18x(x + 1)$
   D) $3x(6x + 2)$

3. Which of the following is equivalent to the expression below?

   $$2(3x + 1)(2x + 2)$$

   A) $8x + 3$
   B) $12x^2 + 4$
   C) $6x^2 + 8x + 2$
   D) $12x^2 + 16x + 4$

4. Which of the following expressions is an equivalent form of the expression $(2x + 2)^2 + (2x + 2)$?

   A) $2x^2 + 10x + 6$
   B) $4x^2 + 16x + 10$
   C) $(2x + 2)(2x + 3)$
   D) $(4x + 8)(x + 1)$

5. Which of the following expressions is an equivalent form of $x^2 + 10x + 20$?

   A) $(x + 4)(x + 6) - 4$
   B) $(x + 4)(x + 6) + 4x$
   C) $(x + 12)(x - 2) + 4$
   D) $(x + 12)(x - 2) + 24$

6. $$\frac{2}{x+7} + \frac{1}{2}$$

   Which of the following expressions is equivalent to the one above where $x \neq -7$?

   A) $\frac{x+11}{2x+14}$
   B) $\frac{x+7}{2x+14}$
   C) $\frac{5}{x+7}$
   D) $\frac{3}{x+9}$

7. Which of the following is equivalent to the expression below?

   $$x^2 + 8x + 11$$

   A) $(x + 4)^2 - 5$
   B) $(x + 4)^2 + 3$
   C) $(x + 4)^2 + 11$
   D) $(x + 4)^2$

8. Which of the following is equivalent to $(-3x + 4)^2 - 9x^2$?

   A) $-16(x + 1)$
   B) $4(-2x + 4)$
   C) $-8(3x - 2)$
   D) $8(x + 2)$

- 12 -

Chapter 3: Equivalent Questions

9. Which of the following expressions is equivalent to $x + 2 + \frac{3}{x+1}$ where $x \neq -1$?

   A) $\frac{x+5}{x+1}$
   B) $\frac{x^2+3x+5}{x+1}$
   C) $\frac{x^2+5x}{x+1}$
   D) $x + 3$

10. For $a > 0$, which of the following is equivalent to $\frac{6a^2-3a}{2a+1}$?

    A) $3a$
    B) $3a - 3$
    C) $3a - 3 + \frac{3}{2a+1}$
    D) $3a - \frac{a}{2a+1}$

11. Which of the following is equivalent to the expression below?

    $$16x^4 + 8x^3 - 24x^2 - 12x$$

    A) $(2x + 1)(2x^2 - 3)$
    B) $x(4x + 2)(4x^2 - 6)$
    C) $4x(2x - 1)(2x^2 - 3)$
    D) $4x(2x + 3)(2x^2 + 1)$

12. Which expression is equivalent to $5x^6y^3 + 20x^4y^3$?

    A) $5x^4y^3(x^2 + 4)$
    B) $5x^4y^3(x^{\frac{3}{2}} + 4)$
    C) $5x^4y^3(4x^2)$
    D) $5x^4y^3(4x^4)$

13. Which expression is equivalent to $\frac{7x(x-9)-6(x-9)}{3x-27}$, where $x > 9$?

    A) $\frac{x-9}{3}$
    B) $\frac{7x^2-69x-54}{3x-27}$
    C) $\frac{7x^2-69x+54}{x-9}$
    D) $\frac{7x-6}{3}$

14. Which expression is equivalent to $\frac{3+4x}{81-256x^4}$, where $x > 1$?

    A) $\frac{1}{27-64x^3}$
    B) $27 - 64x^3$
    C) $\frac{1}{(9+16x^2)(3-4x)}$
    D) $(9 + 16x^2)(3 - 4x)$

15. For $x \neq 4$, which of the following expressions is equivalent to $\frac{y+7}{x-4} + \frac{y(x-4)}{x^2y-4xy}$?

    A) $\frac{xy+y+3}{x^3-4xy^2+16xy}$
    B) $\frac{xy^2+6xy-4y}{x^2y-4xy}$
    C) $\frac{xy^2+8xy-4y}{x^2y-4xy}$
    D) $\frac{xy^2+8xy-4y}{x^3y-8x^2y+16xy}$

PrepPros

Chapter 4: Desmos Hacks

When you are taking the SAT, you are given Desmos to use as your calculator. Desmos has a scientific calculator and a graphing calculator built in. Desmos is an incredible tool if you know how to use it properly! **In this chapter, we will teach you how to use Desmos to solve many SAT questions without doing any math at all.**

Desmos Hack #1 – Solving Algebra Questions

We can use Desmos to solve any algebra question on the SAT by graphing the two sides of the equation and finding the point(s) of intersection. **When two sides of an equation are graphed, the point(s) of intersection shows the solution(s) to equation.**

Example 1: If $\frac{2}{5}x - 2 = 2x - 4$, what is the value of x?

Solution: To solve, we graph both sides of the equation and find the point of intersection. To do this in Desmos, we write each side of the equation as $y =$ and then type in the equation. Here, we write the left side in Desmos as $y = \frac{2}{5}x - 2$ and the right side as $y = 2x - 4$.

Next, we graph the functions in Desmos and find the point of intersection. Below, you can see the graph.

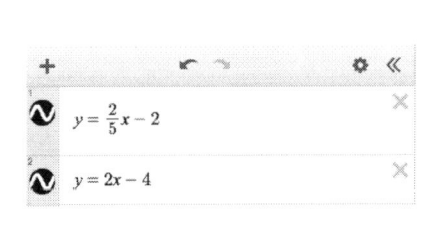

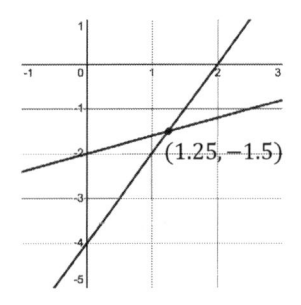

The x-coordinate at the point of intersection shows the solution to the equation. The graph above has a point of intersection at $(1.25, -1.5)$ so **the answer is 1.25.**

You can use this method for ANY algebra question on the SAT. Example 1 is not too difficult to solve algebraically, but we can also use this method for more advanced questions like Example 2.

Example 2: What is the larger of the two solutions to the equation $8x - 4(x - 10)^2 = 80$?

Solution: Even though this question looks hard, we can use the exact same method we did for Example 1. We can graph both sides of the equation and look for the point(s) of intersection. Here, we can write the two sides of the equation as $y = 8x - 4(x - 10)^2$ and $y = 80$.

The graph to the right shows 2 points of intersection.

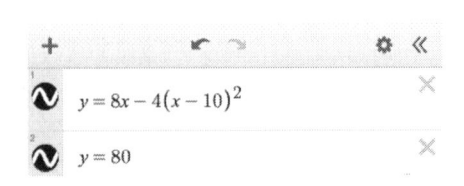

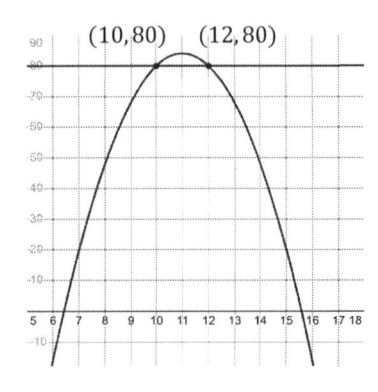

The x-coordinates at the points of intersection show the solutions to the equation. Here, the points of intersection are at $(10, 80)$ and $(12, 80)$, so we have 2 solutions at $x = 10$ and $x = 12$. The question asks us to solve for the larger solution, so **the answer is 12.**

This question can be solved algebraically using quadratics and factoring, skills which we will learn in Chapter 11. However, solving Example 2 algebraically is much more difficult than letting Desmos do the math for you!

Desmos Hack #2 – Solving Systems of Equations

We can also use Desmos to solve a system of equations. For any system of equations, the point(s) of intersection show the solution(s) to the system of equations.

Example 3: For the system of equations below, one solution is point (a, b), where $a > 0$ and $b > 0$. What is the value of $2a - b$?
$$y - 5x = 4x^2 - 7$$
$$y = -3x + 5$$

Solution: To solve, we can graph the equations in the system of equations and find the points of intersection. To graph each equation from the system of equations above, type in the equation as it appears in Desmos. **You do NOT need to write an equation that has both x and y in $y =$ form for Desmos to graph it!**

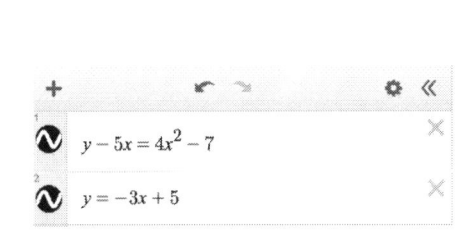

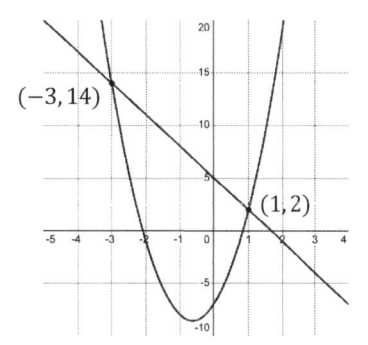

Again, notice that **we can type in the equation in exactly as it appears in the system of equations**. This is an important thing to remember when solving a system of equations with Desmos.

The points of intersection at $(-3, 14)$ and $(1, 2)$ show the solutions to the system of equations. Remember that the x-coordinate shows the solution for x and that the y-coordinate shows the solution for y. In Example 3, the question tells us that the solution at point (a, b) has $a > 0$ and $b > 0$. So, we must use the point at $(1, 2)$ as the solution at point (a, b).

Therefore, $a = 1$ and $b = 2$, so
$$2a - b = 2(1) - 2 = 0$$

The answer is 0. We will learn how to solve questions like Example 3 algebraically in Chapter 12, but the fastest and easiest way to solve Example 3 is using our Desmos Hack for solving systems of equations.

Desmos Hack #3 – Solving Equivalent Questions

You have already learned our 3rd Desmos Hack in Chapter 3. We can use Desmos to solve any Equivalent Questions on the SAT. To review this method, go back to pages 9-10 to see how we used this Desmos Hack to solve Example 1.

Desmos Hack #4 – Solving Quadratics Without Factoring

We can also find the solutions to quadratics by graphing the function in Desmos. If you are given a quadratic that is set equal to 0, such as $4x^2 - 5x - 21 = 0$, you probably think, "oh no, I need to factor that." But do not fear; there is an easier way! **We can solve for the solution(s) to any quadratic that is equal to 0 by graphing the function in Desmos and finding the x-intercept(s).**

Example 4: For $4x^2 - 5x - 21 = 0$, what is the sum of the solutions?

A) $\frac{15}{4}$ B) $\frac{5}{4}$ C) $-\frac{5}{4}$ D) $-\frac{15}{4}$

Solution: To find the solutions (the x-intercepts), we write the function in $y =$ form and look for the x-intercepts. Here, we type the quadratic into Desmos as $y = 4x^2 - 5x - 21$.

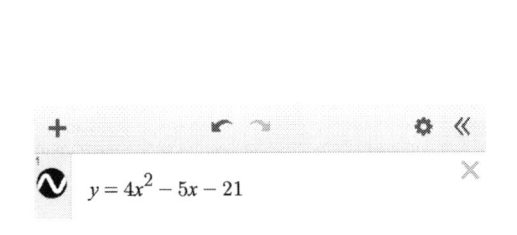

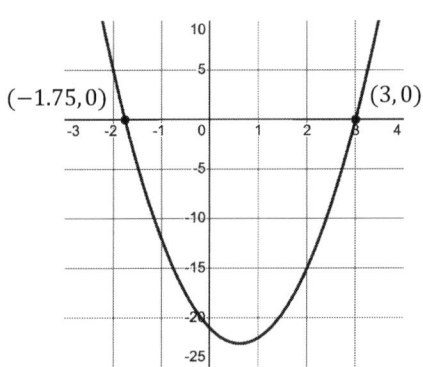

The x-intercepts are at $(-1.75, 0)$ and $(3, 0)$. When a quadratic is equal to zero, as in this example, the solutions are the x-coordinate of the x-intercepts. So here, the solutions are $x = -1.75$ and $x = 3$. The sum of the solutions is $-1.75 + 3 = 1.25$. In fraction form, $1.25 = \frac{5}{4}$, so **the answer is B.**

This question can be solved algebraically by factoring the quadratic and setting each factor equal to zero, a method that we will learn in Chapter 11. However, for most students it is much easier to solve this question using this Desmos Hack!

Desmos Hacks Practice: Answers on page 326.

1. If $42x - 225 = 18x + 309$, what is the value of x?

   A) 3.5
   B) 22.25
   C) 309
   D) 709.5

2. What is the solution to the equation $5x^2 + 20x = -20$?

   A) -2
   B) 0
   C) 4
   D) 10

3. If $22x + 549 = 6x + 717$, what is the value of x?

4. If $20.2x + 15.65 = 19 - 5.6x$, what is the value of x?

   A) -0.25
   B) 0
   C) 0.13
   D) 0.45

Chapter 4: Desmos Hacks

5. For the equation $x^2 + 12x = 15 - 2x$, what is the smallest value of x that is a solution to the equation?

6. Which of the following equations is equivalent to $2(x + 3)^2 - 4x$?

   A) $2x^2 + 2x + 9$
   B) $2x^2 + 8x + 18$
   C) $4x^2 - 4x + 18$
   D) $4x^2 - 4x + 36$

7. For $x^2 + 4x - 396$, what is the sum of the solutions?

   A) -40
   B) -22
   C) -4
   D) 4

8. For the system of equations below, the solution is at the point (a, b). What is the value of b?

   $$80x - 47y = 220$$
   $$16x + 3y = -80$$

9. For the equation below, what is the value of x?

   $$\frac{5x}{6} - \frac{2}{3} = \frac{x}{6} + 2$$

10. If $5x + 8y = 67$ and $2x - y = 31$, what is the value of $x + y$?

    A) 16
    B) 15.5
    C) 15
    D) 14

11. If one of the zeros to the equation $ax^2 - 24x - 64$ is at $x = 8$, what is the value of a?

    A) 2
    B) 4
    C) 7
    D) 10

12. What is the sum of the solutions to the equation $\frac{x^2}{4} - \frac{x}{8} - \frac{15}{8} = 0$?

13. If x is a solution to the equation below, what is the value of $\sqrt{x + 10}$?

    $$\sqrt{x + 3} = x - 3$$

14. For the system of equations below, the solution is at the point (a, b). What is the value of $3a - b$?

    $$4x - y^2 = 12$$
    $$3x = 9$$

15. For the system of equations below, one point is $(m, n - 13)$ where $m > 0$. What is the value of n?

    $$y = 0.25x^2 - 10x - 3$$
    $$0.5x = 17 - y$$

    A) 31
    B) 18
    C) 10
    D) -3

Chapter 5: Algebra Skills

Many SAT questions test your core algebra skills. To answer these questions correctly, you need to be able to isolate the unknown variable, such as x or y, or solve for a more complex term, such as $3a + b$. **For any algebra question, take your time, write out each step of your analysis and calculation, and use the calculator to avoid silly mistakes** like making a mental math error or forgetting to distribute a negative sign.

In this section, we will cover the algebra skills that you need in your toolbox for test day.

1. PEMDAS

In algebra, order of operations is critical to solving math questions correctly. PEMDAS is an acronym to help you remember the order of operations in algebra. The rules of PEMDAS are below:

1. **P – Parentheses:** Complete any calculations inside parentheses first.
2. **E – Exponents:** Next, complete any exponents or square roots.
3. **MD – Multiplication and Division:** Complete any multiplication and division (left-to-right)
4. **AS – Addition and Subtraction:** Complete any addition and subtraction (left-to-right)

Make sure you do the multiplication and division step left-to right! This is where the SAT most often tries to trick students. For example, if we are given

$$16 \div 4 \times 2 - 3$$

We need to work left-to-right when completing multiplication and division. If solved correctly, we will start by dividing 16 by 4 and then multiply by 2. Once we complete the multiplication and division, we will subtract 3.

Correct: $16 \div 4 \times 2 - 3 = 4 \times 2 - 3 = 8 - 3 = 5$

Many students make the mistake of doing the multiplication first and then dividing.

Incorrect: $16 \div 4 \times 2 - 3 = 16 \div 8 - 3 = 2 - 3 = -1$

Example 1: What is the value of the expression $22 + (-4)^2 \div 2 \times (5 + 10)$?
A) 40   B) 72   C) 120   D) 142

Solution: First, complete any calculations in parentheses.

$$22 + (-4)^2 \div 2 \times 15$$

Next, complete the exponents.

$$22 + 16 \div 2 \times 15$$

Complete any multiplication and division from left-to-right.

$$22 + 16 \div 2 \times 15 = 22 + 8 \times 15 = 22 + 120$$

Finally, complete the addition.

$$22 + 120 = 142$$

The answer is D. As long as you follow the PEMDAS steps correctly and work left-to-right correctly, these questions should be easy!

Shortcut Solution – Use Your Calculator: You can also enter these questions directly into your calculator. Your calculator is programed to do PEMDAS correctly, so as long as you enter the equation correctly, the calculator will just tell you the answer. It's that easy!

Chapter 5: Algebra Skills

2. Negative Numbers

The SAT loves questions with negative numbers. These questions are a prime place where students make simple mistakes by not knowing how to properly do algebra with negative numbers. Let's review where students most often make mistakes to make sure that you ace these questions on test day.

Subtracting Negative Numbers

You likely already know that when subtracting a negative number, the negative signs turn into a positive sign, and you add the numbers together. For example

$$2 - (-4) = 2 + 4 = 6$$

That's easy! The mistake students more often make is forgetting to distribute a negative sign to multiple terms. For example, if you are solving

$$5x - (2x - 5)$$

make sure to distribute the negative sign to both the $2x$ and the -5. Many students forget to distribute the negative sign.

Incorrect: $5x - (2x - 5) = 5x - 2x - 5 = 3x - 5$

Correct: $5x - (2x - 5) = 5x - 2x - (-5) = 3x + 5$

Example 2: Which of the following expressions is equivalent to $2(a + b) - 3(a - 4b)$?
A) $-a - 11b$ B) $-a - 3b$ C) $-a + 6b$ D) $-a + 14b$

Solution: Distribute the -3 to both the a and $-4b$ and combine like terms.

$$2(a + b) - 3(a - 4b) = 2a + 2b - 3a - 3(-4b) = 2a + 2b - 3a + 12b = -a + 14b$$

The answer is D.

Negative Numbers and Exponents

The second common mistake occurs when negative numbers are raised to a power. The important thing to understand is

$$-2^2 \text{ is not the same as } (-2)^2$$

For -2^2, you first square the 2 and then multiply by the negative sign. For $(-2)^2$, you just square -2. As a result, we see

$$-2^2 = -4$$
$$(-2)^2 = 4$$

This principle is very important to understand and can be tested on more difficult SAT questions. **Make sure you always put negative numbers in parentheses when you enter them into the calculator!** If you do not use the parentheses, you will get the wrong answer.

Example 3: Given the function $f(x) = 4 - x^3$, for which of the following values of x is $f(x) = 31$ true?
A) -9 B) -3 C) 3   D) 9

Solution: Method #1 – Backsolving: The easiest way to solve this question is to backsolve using the answer choices. We can plug the answer choices in for x in the function to find which one equals 31. Below, we can see how the correct answer of $x = -3$ makes $f(x) = 31$.

$$f(-3) = 4 - (-3)^3$$

- 19 -

PrepPros

Remember our PEMDAS. First, we have to cube -3, so we get
$$f(-3) = 4 - (-27)$$
Since we are subtracting a negative number (-27), we add and get
$$f(-3) = 31$$

The answer is B.

Solution: Method #2 – Desmos Hack #1 for Solving Algebra Equations: After we realize that we plug in 31 for $f(x)$, we get the equation
$$31 = 4 - x^3$$
To solve, we can use our Desmos Hack #1 for solving algebra equations. We write the equations in Desmos as $y = 31$ and $y = 4 - x^3$ and look for the point of intersection. The graphs intersect at $(-3, 31)$. We are looking for the x-value in this question, which is $x = -3$, so **the answer is B.** To review the Desmos Hack #1, go to p. 14.

Solution: Method #3 – "Math Teacher Way": We can also solve this with algebra. Since we are finding the x when $f(x) = 31$, we can plug in the 31 for $f(x)$ and solve.
$$31 = 4 - x^3$$
We need to get the x^3 term by itself. To do so, we add x^3 to both sides and subtract 31 from both sides to get
$$x^3 = -27$$
Now, we have to take the cube root of both sides to solve for x.
$$\sqrt[3]{x^3} = \sqrt[3]{27} \quad \rightarrow \quad x = -3$$

The answer is B. For many of you, this third method is much more difficult. That is why we recommend backsolving or using our Desmos Hack on questions like this! If any of the steps in this explanation are confusing to you, do not worry: we will cover cube roots in Chapter 9 and functions in Chapter 12.

3. Combining Like Terms

Whenever we have the chance, we should combine like terms. Doing so will help us simplify the equation and get to the correct answer more quickly.

Example 4: If $2(3x - 6) + 3y = 6x - y + 8$, what is the value of y?

Solution: First, distribute the 2 on the left side of the equation.
$$6x - 12 + 3y = 6x - y + 8$$
We have x and y terms on both sides of the equation, so we need to combine like terms. Here, the $6x$ terms on both sides cancel, so we get
$$-12 + 3y = -y + 8$$
Now, combine the y-terms and the numbers and solve.
$$4y = 20$$
$$y = 5$$

The answer is 5.

4. Cross Multiply Fractions

Whenever we have two fractions equal to one another, we can cross multiply to get rid of the fractions.

$$\frac{x}{z} = \frac{y}{w}$$

Cross multiplying, we get

$$xw = yz$$

Example 5: If $\frac{3x}{4} = \frac{6}{7}$, what is the value of x?

Solution:
$$\frac{3x}{4} = \frac{6}{7}$$
$$21x = 24$$
$$x = \frac{24}{21} = \frac{8}{7}$$

The answer is $\frac{8}{7}$.

5. Square Both Sides of an Equation Correctly

In algebra questions with square roots, we often need to square both sides to get rid of the square root. It is important to remember that we need to square both sides and not just each individual term. Students will often make a mistake on a question like the example below.

Example 6:
$$\sqrt{x} = x - 2$$

What value(s) of x solve the equation above?

A) 1 B) 4 C) 1, 4 D) 1, 2

Solution: Method #1 – "Math Teacher Way": When we see the square root in this question, we should start by squaring both sides of the equation. Most students will properly get rid of the square root on the left side of the equation, but they make a mistake on the right side by doing this:
$$x = x^2 - 4$$

WRONG! We cannot just square each individual term. We must square the entire equation on each side, so it should look like this:
$$(\sqrt{x})^2 = (x - 2)^2$$

If you prefer, you can also write out the right side of the equation to help make sure you remember to properly expand the term.
$$(\sqrt{x})^2 = (x - 2)(x - 2)$$

If we properly square both sides of the equation, we get
$$x = x^2 - 4x + 4$$

From here, we combine like terms, set the equation equal to zero, and factor. Moving all of the terms to the right side, we get
$$0 = x^2 - 5x + 4$$
$$0 = (x - 4)(x - 1)$$
$$x = 1, 4$$

It looks like there are two answers to this question, but that is not the case! **Anytime you square both sides of an equation, you NEED to plug the answers back into the original equation to look for extraneous solutions** (we will learn more on extraneous solutions in Chapter 32). Sometimes when we square both sides of an equation, we get answers that look correct but do not actually work in the original equation. Let's start by checking $x = 1$.

$$\sqrt{1} = 1 - 2$$
$$1 \neq -1$$

We see that $x = 1$ does not work in the original equation, so it is an extraneous solution. Now, we can check $x = 4$.

$$\sqrt{4} = 4 - 2$$
$$2 = 2$$

We find that $x = 4$ works in the original equation, so **the answer is B**. Now, that was a lot of work! **You should NOT solve a question like this with this method!** Instead, use one of our shortcut methods below.

Solution: Method #2 – Backsolving: We can backsolve using the answer choices. By plugging the answer choices in of 1, 2, and 4 in for x, we can test each answer choice. Only 4 works, so **the answer is B**.

Whenever you see a multiple-choice question like this, you should backsolve by plugging the answer choices back in. If you see a question like this without answer choices, you should use the Desmos Hack.

Solution: Method #3 – Desmos Hack #1 for Solving Algebra Equations: Write the equations in Desmos as $y = \sqrt{x}$ and $y = x - 2$ and look for the point of intersection. The graphs intersect at $(4, 2)$. We are finding the x-value in this question, which is $x = 2$, so **the answer is B**. To review the Desmos Hack #1, go to p. 14.

6. Algebra with Inequality Signs

To solve inequalities on the SAT, treat the inequality signs ($<, >, \leq, \geq$) like an $=$ sign and solve using algebra. Inequalities can be solved as normal algebraic expressions with the exception of one very important rule:

When multiplying or dividing by a negative number, switch the direction of the inequality sign.

This rule is the most important thing to remember from this section and where students most commonly make mistakes on inequalities questions. As a quick example, let's see how to solve the equation below.

$$-5x - 3 > 11$$
$$-5x > 14$$

When dividing by -5, we switch the direction inequality sign, so

$$x < -\frac{14}{5}$$

Let's see a second example:

$$5x + 10 \leq 2x - 44$$

The first step is combining like terms. We subtract $2x$ from both sides to get the x-terms on the left side. We then subtract 10 from both sides to get the numbers on the right side.

$$5x - 2x \leq -44 - 10$$
$$3x \leq -54$$
$$x \leq -\frac{54}{3}$$

$$x \leq -18$$

In this example, we never multiply or divide by a negative number, so the inequality sign stays the same. Just because we are working with a negative number does not mean we need to flip the inequality sign. Some students flip the sign whenever they divide and see a negative sign. Don't make that mistake! Only flip the inequality when you multiply or divide both sides by a negative number.

> **Example 7:** Which of the following inequalities is equivalent to $2x - 6y < 4x - 14$?
> A) $x < 3y - 7$ B) $x > 3y - 7$ C) $x < -3y + 7$ D) $x > -3y + 7$

Solution: Method #1 – Solve Algebraically: To solve, we need to isolate x. We need to do this because all the answer choices have x isolated on the left side of the equation. To isolate x, we need to move the x-terms to the left side and all other terms to the right side. To do this, we need to subtract $4x$ from both sides and add $6y$ to both sides.

$$2x - 6y < 4x - 14$$
$$2x - 4x < 6y - 14$$
$$-2x < 6y - 14$$

To get x by itself, we need to divide both sides by -2. Since we are dividing by a negative, we also need to switch the direction of the inequality sign.

$$x > \frac{6y - 14}{-2}$$

Now, we can simplify the terms on the right side of the equation and solve.

$$x > -3y + 7$$

The answer is D.

Solution: Method #2 – Desmos Hack #3 for Equivalent Questions: We can solve this question with our Desmos #3 Hack for equivalent questions. To review this method, go back to pp. 9-10 in Chapter 3.

7. Taking Square Roots in Algebraic Equations

When solving an algebra question, you may need to find the value of a variable that is squared. For example, if we have the equation

$$x^2 = 9$$

we need to take the square root of both sides to solve. Many students take the square root and get $x = 3$, which is WRONG! To take the square root properly, we need to use the following rule:

When taking the square root of a squared variable (x^2), add a $\pm$ in front of the number.

For the example equation above, we should solve using the following steps to solve properly.

$x^2 = 9$	1. Take square root of both sides.
$\sqrt{x^2} = \pm\sqrt{9}$	2. Add a $\pm$ sign in front of the number.
$x = \pm 3$	3. Simplify
$x = -3, 3$	

Notice that we get 2 answers! This makes sense because both $(-3)^2$ and 3^2 equal 9.

Now, it is important to clarify that this only applies to taking the square root of algebraic equations with squared terms, like x^2. **You do not add a $\pm$ sign when taking the square root of only a number.**

Correct: $\sqrt{9} = 3$ **Incorrect:** $\sqrt{9} = \pm 3$

The square root of 9 is only 3, not ± 3. Square roots are always positive. Understanding this difference is important for solving questions involving square roots and variables correctly.

Example 8: What value(s) of x are solutions to the equation $x^2 + 10 = 46$?

A) $-6, 6$ B) $0, 6$ C) 6 D) -6

Solution: Method #1 – "Math Teacher Way": When solving an equation with an x^2 term and numbers, start by getting the x^2 term on one side by itself. To do that, we need to subtract 10 from both sides.

$$x^2 + 10 = 46$$
$$x^2 = 36$$

Now, we can take the square root of both sides. Since we are taking the square root with an x^2 term, we need to add a $\pm$ sign in front of the number.

$$\sqrt{x^2} = \pm\sqrt{36}$$
$$x = -6, 6$$

The answer is A.

Solution: Method #2 – Desmos Hack #1 for Solving Algebra Equations: Write the equations in Desmos as $y = x^2 + 10$ and $y = 46$ and look for the points of intersection. The graphs intersect at points $(-6, 46)$ and $(6, 46)$. We are finding the x-values in this question, which are $x = -6$ and $x = 6$, so **the answer is A.** To review the Desmos Hack #1, go to p. 14.

8. Factoring to Isolate a Variable

Variables in some equations can be more difficult to isolate. If the variable we are trying to isolate is in multiple terms, we need to be able to factor to isolate the variable.

Example 9: $$z = \frac{x}{x - 3y}$$

Which of the following equations expresses x in terms of y and z?

A) $\frac{y}{z+3}$ B) $\frac{3y}{1-z}$ C) $\frac{3yz}{z-1}$ D) $\frac{1+z}{3yz}$

Solution: To start, multiply both sides by $x - 3y$ to get rid of the fraction.

$$z(x - 3y) = x$$
$$zx - 3yz = x$$

We want to isolate x, so we need to put all terms containing x on the left side and all other terms on the right side.

$$zx - x = 3yz$$

To isolate x, factor x out of the terms on the left side and solve.

$$x(z - 1) = 3yz$$
$$x = \frac{3yz}{z-1}$$

The answer is C.

Chapter 5: Algebra Skills

9. Factoring by Grouping for Cubic Functions

If you ever see an equation with an x^3 term that you need to factor, you should always try to factor by grouping. To see how this works, let's take a look at the example below.

> **Example 10:** For the equation $x^3 - 5x^2 + 4x - 20 = 0$, x is an integer that solves the equation. What is the value of x?

Solution: Method #1 – "Math Teacher Way": To factor by grouping, we want to look at the terms in pairs to see what we can factor out. Here, we can factor out x^2 from the first two terms and 4 from the last two terms.

$$x^2(x - 5) + 4(x - 5) = 0$$

Notice that the terms inside the parentheses are the same. **To factor by grouping, the terms in parentheses must match!** We can rewrite the equation as

$$(x^2 + 4)(x - 5) = 0$$

To solve, set each term equal to 0 and solve for x.

$$x^2 + 4 = 0 \qquad\qquad x - 5 = 0$$
$$x^2 = -4 \qquad\qquad x = 5$$

Since x^2 is always positive, no real solution can come from the $(x^2 + 4)$ term. **The answer is $x = 5$.**

Solution: Method #2 – Desmos Hack #4 for Solving Quadratics: We can graph the equation in Desmos as $y = x^3 - 5x^2 + 4x - 20$ and look for the x-intercept(s). We see only one x-intercept at $(5, 0)$, so **the answer is $x = 5$.** To review Desmos Hack #4, go to p. 16.

10. Solving Directly for the Answer

Some questions ask us to solve for an expression like $2x + y$. Anytime we see a question that asks us to solve for an expression, such as $2x + y$, instead of solving for only a single variable, such as x, we should look to see if we can solve directly for the answer before solving for any specific variable.

> **Example 11:** $\sqrt{x - 3} = \dfrac{5 - \sqrt{2}}{\sqrt{x-3}}$
>
> For the equation above, what is the value of $x - 3$?
>
> A) $8 - \sqrt{2}$ B) 23 C) $5\sqrt{2} - 4$ D) $5 - \sqrt{2}$

Solution: Here, we should first determine if we can solve directly for $x - 3$. There is no need to even bother solving for x if we can solve for $x - 3$. Can we solve directly for $x - 3$?

Yes, we can! If we multiply both sides by $\sqrt{x - 3}$, we get

$$x - 3 = 5 - \sqrt{2}$$

It's that simple. **The answer is D.** For any questions like this, **always try to solve directly for the answer first.** If you cannot solve for the answer directly, solve the unknown(s) and plug them in to find the answer.

Solution: Method #2 – Desmos Hack #1 for Solving Algebra Equations: Write the equations in Desmos as $y = \sqrt{x - 3}$ and $y = \dfrac{5 - \sqrt{2}}{\sqrt{x-3}}$ and look for the point of intersection. The graphs intersect at point $(6.586, 1.894)$. So $x = 6.585$, which means $x - 3 = 3.585$. Plug the answer choices into your calculator to find which one equals approximately 3.585. **The answer is D.** To review the Desmos Hack #1, go to p. 14.

PrepPros

Algebra Skills Practice: Answers on page 326.

1. $(x^4 + x) + (x^3 - x)$

   Which of the following is equivalent to the expression above?

   A) x^7
   B) $x^4 + x^3 - x^2$
   C) $x^4 + x^3$
   D) x^{12}

2. If $3(x + 5) = 16$, what does x equal?

   A) $\frac{1}{3}$
   B) 1
   C) 3
   D) $5\frac{1}{3}$

3. If $4x - 18 = 14$, what is the value of x?

   A) -1
   B) 4
   C) 8
   D) 12

4. If $3x = 36$, what is the value of $4x - 6$?

   A) 6
   B) 12
   C) 30
   D) 42

5. If $x^2 + 4 = 40$, what does $x^2 - 8$ equal?

   A) 24
   B) 28
   C) 30
   D) 36

6. If $x = 3$ in the equation $x - \frac{15}{b} = 0$, what is the value of b?

7. Which expression is equivalent to $(3x^2 - 2x + 5) - (-2x^2 + 3x - 2)$?

   A) $x^2 + x + 3$
   B) $x^2 - 5x + 7$
   C) $5x^2 + x + 3$
   D) $5x^2 - 5x + 7$

8. If $7 + x = 13$, what is the value of $28 + 4x$?

9. Which value of x satisfies the equation below?

   $3(5x - 20) - (5x - 60) = 80$

10. The solution set of $3 - 5x \geq -22$ is the set of all real values of x such that:

    A) $x \geq -5$
    B) $x \leq -5$
    C) $x \geq 5$
    D) $x \leq 5$

11. If $\frac{x}{7} = 8$, what is the value of $\frac{7}{x}$?

12. If $3x + 4 = 4x - 1$, what is the value of $2x + 3$?

    A) 5
    B) 8
    C) 13
    D) 17

13. Which expression is equivalent to $(x^2 + 5) - (-2x^2 - 2)$?

    A) $-x^2 + 3$
    B) $-x^2 + 7$
    C) $3x^2 + 3$
    D) $3x^2 + 7$

14. If $13(x + 7) = 9(x + 7) + 36$, what is the value of $4(x + 7)$?

15. If $x = -1$ and $y = 3$, what is the value of $x^3 + 2x^2y - 5xy^2 + 3y$?

    A) -43
    B) -1
    C) 47
    D) 59

16. What is the value of x in the equation below?

    $$\frac{2x}{3} = \frac{5}{6}$$

    A) $\frac{5}{4}$
    B) $\frac{9}{5}$
    C) $\frac{5}{9}$
    D) $\frac{4}{5}$

17. If $x - y = 14$ and $\frac{y}{3} = 12$, what is the value of x?

    A) 12
    B) 24
    C) 36
    D) 50

18. If $\frac{x+4}{4} = k$ and $k = 2$, what is the value of x?

    A) 2
    B) 4
    C) 6
    D) 8

19. Which of the following inequalities describes the solution set for $6x - 7 > 2x + 4$?

    A) $x > -\frac{3}{4}$
    B) $x > \frac{11}{8}$
    C) $x < \frac{11}{4}$
    D) $x > \frac{11}{4}$

20. If $5(3x - 3) - 2(2x - 4) = 5(2x + 2)$, what is the value of x?

21. Which of the following is equivalent to the expression below?

    $$(x^2y^2 - 4x^3 + 2xy^2) - (2x^2y^2 + 2x^3 - 3xy^2)$$

    A) $3xy^2 + 6x^3 - xy^2$
    B) $-x^2y^2 + 2x^3 - 5xy^2$
    C) $-x^2y^2 - 6x^3 + 5xy^2$
    D) $x^2y^2 + 6x^3 - 3xy^2$

22. If $5x + 4 = 9$, what is the value of $20x + 16$?

    A) 36
    B) 45
    C) 53
    D) 58

23. Given that $\frac{2}{x} = 10$ and $\frac{x}{y} = 8$, what is the value of y?

    A) $\frac{1}{40}$
    B) $\frac{1}{8}$
    C) 8
    D) 40

24. If $\sqrt{4x} = 8$, what is the value of x?

25. Which of the following values of x is the solution to the equation below?

    $$x - 3 = \sqrt{x + 17}$$

    A. -1
    B. 1
    C. 5
    D. 8

PrepPros

26. Which of the following inequalities is equivalent to $-2a - 8b > 30a - 48$?

    A) $b > 4a - 6$
    B) $b < 4a + 6$
    C) $b < -4a + 6$
    D) $b > -4a + 6$

27. If $\sqrt{x-3} = x - 3$, what value(s) of x solve the equation?

    A) 1
    B) 3
    C) 4
    D) 3, 4

28. Which of the following expressions is equivalent to $\frac{2a}{3b} = \frac{5}{a+1}$?

    A) $3a + 1 = 15b$
    B) $2a^2 + 1 = 15b$
    C) $2a^2 + 2a = 15b$
    D) $2a^2 + 2a = 8b$

29. If $ab = 24$ and $\frac{b}{4} = 2$, what is the value of $a - b$?

    A) -5
    B) 3
    C) 5
    D) 8

30. What value(s) of x satisfy the equation below?

    $$2(x-3)^2 + 3 = 21$$

    A) $-3, 3$
    B) 3
    C) 6
    D) 0, 6

31. Based on the equation below, what is the value of $ax - b$?

    $$5ax - 5b - 7 = 28$$

    A) 5
    B) $\frac{28}{5}$
    C) 7
    D) 14

32. In the equation below, what is the value of $x - 2$?

    $$x - 2 = \frac{3^2}{x-2}$$

    A) 1
    B) 3
    C) 5
    D) 9

33. If $\sqrt{3x + 10} = x + 2$, what is the value of x?

34. For the equation $3x^2 + 15 = 18$, b is a solution. If $b < 0$, then $b = $

35. For the equation below, which of the following expresses a in terms of b, and c?

    $$ab = \frac{a + bc + 6c}{3}$$

    A) $\frac{bc + 6c}{3b}$
    B) $\frac{bc + 6c}{3b - 1}$
    C) $\frac{a + bc + 6c}{3b}$
    D) $\frac{3a - bc + 6c}{3b + 1}$

36. For the equation $x^3 - 4x^2 + 3x - 12 = 0$, x is an integer that solves the equation. What is the value of x?

- 28 -

Chapter 5: Algebra Skills

37. Given that the equation $\frac{8k}{4b} = \frac{1}{3}$ is true, what is the value of $\frac{b}{k}$?

38. What value(s) of x satisfy the equation $12x^3 + 4x^2 - 3x - 1 = 0$?

   A) $-\frac{1}{3}$
   B) $\frac{1}{2}$
   C) $-\frac{1}{2}, \frac{1}{2}$
   D) $-\frac{1}{2}, -\frac{1}{3}, \frac{1}{2}$

39. What is the solution to the equation below?
$$\frac{11x-22}{x-2} = x + 5$$

40. For the equation below, which of the following expresses x in terms of y, and z?
$$y = \frac{xz - z^2}{x-1}$$

   A) $\frac{z^2 - y}{z - y}$
   B) $\frac{1+y}{z^2+y}$
   C) $\frac{y-z^2}{z+1}$
   D) $\frac{z^2+y}{1-y}$

41. For the equation below, what is the value of $x + 3$?
$$\frac{8x+24}{x+3} = 5x + 15$$

42. If $\frac{4x+y}{2x+y} = \frac{8}{5}$, what is the value of $\frac{y}{x}$?

   A) $\frac{3}{4}$
   B) $\frac{4}{3}$
   C) $\frac{5}{8}$
   D) $\frac{8}{13}$

43. Which expression is equivalent to $\frac{9x(x-5)-4(x-5)}{2x-10}$, where $x > 5$?

   A) $\frac{x-5}{2}$
   B) $\frac{9x-4}{2}$
   C) $\frac{9x^2-4x+20}{2x-10}$
   D) $\frac{9x^2-4x-25}{2x-10}$

PrepPros

Chapter 6: Fractions

For success on the SAT, you need to be comfortable with fractions. Fractions are a topic that many students struggle with. If you are one of those students, fear not! In this chapter, we cover all of the fundamental techniques that will allow you to answer any question involving fractions quickly and efficiently.

1. Combining Fractions

To add or subtract fractions, we must make the denominators the same by finding the least common multiple of the numbers or expressions in the denominators. For example, consider adding the fractions below:

$$\frac{1}{2} + \frac{2}{5}$$

Here, the least common denominator is 10. An easy trick to find the least common denominator is to multiply the numbers in the denominator together. For the fractions above, $2 \times 5 = 10$. Once we find the least common denominator, we convert all fractions to have the same common denominator and then combine.

$$\frac{1}{2} \times \frac{5}{5} + \frac{2}{5} \times \frac{2}{2} = \frac{5}{10} + \frac{4}{10} = \frac{9}{10}$$

On the SAT, you will often see questions with expressions in the denominators instead of just numbers. These are more difficult, but the concept and approach are the exact same.

Example 1: $\quad \frac{1}{x} + \frac{3}{x-4}$

Which of the following is equivalent to the equation above for $x \neq 0$ and $x \neq 4$?

A) $\frac{4x-4}{x(x-4)}$ B) $\frac{4}{2x-4}$ C) $\frac{4x-12}{x-4}$ D) $\frac{x-1}{x(x-4)}$

Solution: To start, we need to find the common denominator. Here, the common denominator is the product of the two denominators: $x(x-4)$. To make both terms have the same denominator, we need to multiply the top and bottom of each fraction by the term they are missing in the denominator.

$$\frac{1}{x} \times \frac{x-4}{x-4} + \frac{3}{x-4} \times \frac{x}{x} = \frac{x-4}{x(x-4)} + \frac{3x}{x(x-4)} = \frac{x-4+3x}{x(x-4)} = \frac{4x-4}{x(x-4)}$$

The answer is A.

Shortcut Solution: For any "equivalent" questions like this one, we can also use the method we discussed in Chapter 3 and just plug in $x = 1$.

2. Dividing Fractions

Let's say that we are solving an equation and get to

$$\frac{2}{3}x = \frac{1}{5}$$

To solve for x, we divide both sides by $\frac{2}{3}$. How do we divide a fraction by a fraction? **Take the fraction on the bottom, flip it to get the reciprocal, and then multiply the top fraction by the reciprocal of the bottom fraction.** It's as easy as that! For this example, the reciprocal of the bottom fraction is $\frac{3}{2}$, so we multiply the top fraction by $\frac{3}{2}$.

$$x = \frac{\frac{1}{5}}{\frac{2}{3}} = \frac{1}{5} \times \frac{3}{2} = \frac{3}{10}$$

- 30 -

We can use this method anytime you are dividing by a fraction, even if the right side is a whole number. For example,
$$\frac{2}{7}x = 3$$
To solve for x, we need to divide both sides by $\frac{2}{7}$, so we use the same trick of flipping the fraction and multiplying by the reciprocal, which here is $\frac{7}{2}$.
$$x = \frac{3}{\frac{2}{7}} = 3 \times \frac{7}{2} = \frac{21}{2}$$

Example 2: $\quad \frac{2}{7}x + \frac{1}{4} = \frac{2}{5}$

For the equation above, what is the value of x?

Solution: Method #1 – Solve Algebraically: First, we need to combine like terms by subtracting $\frac{1}{4}$ from both sides.
$$\frac{2}{7}x = \frac{2}{5} - \frac{1}{4}$$
Next, we need to combine the fractions on the right side by finding the common denominator. For 5 and 4, the least common denominator is 20.
$$\frac{2}{5} \times \frac{4}{4} - \frac{1}{4} \times \frac{5}{5} = \frac{8}{20} - \frac{5}{20} = \frac{3}{20}$$
Now, substitute this back into the equation.
$$\frac{2}{7}x = \frac{3}{20}$$
To isolate x, we divide both sides by $\frac{2}{7}$, so we flip the fraction and multiply by the reciprocal of $\frac{7}{2}$.
$$x = \frac{3}{20} \times \frac{7}{2} = \frac{21}{40}$$
The answer is $\frac{21}{40}$ or **0.525**.

Solution: Method #2 - Desmos Hack #1 for Solving Algebra Equations: Write the equations in Desmos as $y = \frac{2}{7}x + \frac{1}{4}$ and $y = \frac{2}{5}$ and look for the point of intersection. The graphs intersect at point $(0.525, 0.4)$. We are finding the x-values in this question, which are $x = 0.525$, so **the answer is 0.525**. We can also turn this decimal to a fraction in Desmos (we will learn this on p. 34) to $\frac{21}{40}$.

3. Simplifying Fractions

When simplifying fractions, you must be able to divide all terms in the numerator and denominator by the same number. Simplifying fractions with only numbers is easy.
$$\frac{6}{15} \div \frac{3}{3} = \frac{2}{5}$$
Many students struggle when there are multiple terms in the numerator or denominator. Let's start with a variable in the numerator.
$$\frac{2x + 10}{4}$$

Can we simplify this fraction? Yes, but only if we can divide all terms by the same number. Here, we can divide every term by 2, so we can simplify the fraction.

$$\frac{2x+10}{4} \div \frac{2}{2} = \frac{x+5}{2}$$

Many students will make the mistake and will only divide the first term and not the 10 like this:

$$\frac{2x+10}{4} \neq \frac{x+10}{2}$$

WRONG! You must divide all terms by the same number to simplify. If you cannot divide all terms by the same number, you cannot simplify the fraction. For example, if we instead had

$$\frac{8x+3}{4}$$

We can no longer simplify this fraction, but we can split this fraction into two:

$$\frac{8x+3}{4} = \frac{8x}{4} + \frac{3}{4} = 2x + \frac{3}{4}$$

If you cannot simplify a fraction by dividing all terms by the same number, you should look to split and simplify the fraction this way.

The same concept applies for simplifying fractions when we have a variable in the denominator.

$$\frac{3}{6x+30}$$

Can we simplify this fraction? Yes, all terms can be divided by 3, so we can simplify the fraction.

$$\frac{3}{6x+30} \div \frac{3}{3} = \frac{1}{2x+10}$$

Again, make sure that you divide all terms by the same number. If you cannot divide all terms by the same number, the fraction cannot be simplified. For example, if we had

$$\frac{3}{6x+10}$$

we cannot simplify the fraction. While we just saw that you can split up the numerators of a fraction, you cannot split up the denominators.

$$\frac{3}{6x+10} \neq \frac{3}{6x} + \frac{3}{10}$$

We cannot simplify a fraction like this one at all.

Example 3: $\frac{12x+2}{6} + \frac{1}{3}$

Which of the following is equivalent to the equation above?

A) $2x + \frac{1}{2}$ B) $2x + \frac{2}{3}$ C) $\frac{7}{3}x + \frac{1}{3}$ D) $4x + \frac{7}{3}$

Solution: Method #1 – "Math Teacher Way": First, we need to make the denominators the same, so we can combine the fractions. The least common denominator of 3 and 6 is 6.

$$\frac{12x+2}{6} + \frac{1}{3} \times \frac{2}{2} = \frac{12x+2}{6} + \frac{2}{6} = \frac{12x+4}{6}$$

Next, we simplify the fraction. All of the terms can be divided by 2.
$$\frac{12x+4}{6} \div \frac{2}{2} = \frac{6x+2}{3}$$
Finally, we can split the numerator and simplify to solve.
$$\frac{6x+2}{3} = \frac{6x}{3} + \frac{2}{3} = 2x + \frac{2}{3}$$

The answer is B.

Solution: Method #2 – Use Equivalent Question Shortcut: Since this is an "equivalent" question, we can also use the Equivalent Trick (plug in $x = 1$) or Desmos Equivalent Hack we learned earlier in Chapter 3.

4. Getting Rid of Fractions

For questions with only numbers in the denominator, it is usually easiest to get rid of the fractions. We can get rid of the fractions by multiplying both sides by the least common denominator.
$$\frac{1}{4}x + \frac{1}{2} = \frac{3}{8}x$$
The least common denominator of 4, 2, and 8 is 8, so we can multiply all terms by 8 to eliminate all of the fractions.
$$\frac{1}{4}x \times 8 + \frac{1}{2} \times 8 = \frac{3}{8}x \times 8$$
The equation becomes
$$2x + 4 = 3x$$
Now, solving is easy!
$$x = 4$$

If you struggle with fractions, always use this method to convert fractions to whole numbers whenever there are only numbers in the denominator.

Example 4: If $\frac{3x}{5} - \frac{2x}{6} - \frac{1}{2} = \frac{x}{10}$, what is the value of x?

Solution: Since all the terms in denominator are numbers, we can get rid of the fractions. The least common denominator of 5, 6, 2, and 10 is 30, so we can multiply all the terms by 30.
$$\frac{3x}{5} \times 30 - \frac{2x}{6} \times 30 - \frac{1}{2} \times 30 = \frac{x}{10} \times 30$$
$$18x - 10x - 15 = 3x$$
$$8x - 15 = 3x$$
$$8x = 3x + 15$$
$$5x = 15$$
$$x = 3$$

The answer is 3. It is important to understand how the math works here, but if you a question like this with just number, there is an easier way to solve!

PrepPros

Solution: Method #2 - Desmos Hack #1 for Solving Algebra Equations: Write the equations in Desmos as $y = \frac{3x}{5} - \frac{2x}{6} - \frac{1}{2}$ and $y = \frac{x}{10}$ look for the point of intersection. The graphs intersect at point $(3, 0.3)$. We are finding the x-value in this question, which is $x = 3$, so **the answer is 3.** To review the Desmos Hack #1, go to p. 14.

5. Turn Fractions into Decimals

If you really dislike fractions, another trick is to turn fractions into decimals using your calculator.

Example 5: $\frac{3}{4}x - \frac{4}{10} = \frac{1}{2}x$

For the equation above, what is the value of x?

Solution: We can change the fractions to decimals with the calculator. If we do this, the equation becomes

$$0.75x - 0.4 = 0.5x$$

Now, we solve for x algebraically.

$$0.75x = 0.5x + 0.4$$
$$0.25x = 0.4$$
$$x = \frac{0.4}{0.25} = \frac{8}{5} = 1.6$$

The answer is $\frac{8}{5}$ or 1.6. Both answers are counted as correct on the SAT. We can also use our Desmos Hack #1 to solve Example 5 by graphing both sides of the equation and finding the point of intersection.

6. Use Desmos to Turn Decimals into Fractions

Desmos has a button that turns a decimal into a fraction and vice versa. This can make fractions questions on the SAT far easier and faster to solve.

Decimal ↔ Fraction button

How To Turn a Decimal into a Fraction

1. Enter the number in the Desmos calculator in decimal form. In the picture below, we entered 5.25.

2. Press the Decimal ↔ Fraction button. This button appears on the left side after you enter a number.

3. The fraction form will appear on the right side, as you can see with the $\frac{21}{4}$ below.

How To Turn a Fraction into a Decimal

1. Enter the fraction into the Desmos calculator. To enter a fraction, use the / button on your keyboard or click the ÷ in the calculator. For the fraction shown, we typed in 5/4.

2. Desmos automatically displays the decimal form of the fraction. We can see here that 5/4 is equal to 1.25.

Chapter 6: Fractions

Fractions Practice: Answers on pages 326-327.

1. $\frac{4}{3} + \frac{3}{2} =$

2. $\frac{3}{5} - \frac{1}{4} =$

3. $\frac{7}{8} + \frac{1}{2} =$

4. $\frac{2a}{3} - \frac{5}{2} =$

5. $\frac{6y}{7} - \frac{x}{3} =$

6. $\frac{21}{5} + \frac{z}{y} =$

7. $\frac{16}{3x} - \frac{7}{6x} =$

8. $\frac{\frac{3}{5}}{\frac{4}{3}} =$

9. $\frac{\frac{x}{2}}{\frac{y}{3}} =$

10. $\frac{\frac{2}{z}}{\frac{3}{2}} =$

11. $\frac{\frac{4}{m}}{\frac{1}{m}} =$

12. If $\frac{2}{7}x + 8 = 15$, then $x = ?$

13. If $\frac{2a}{3} = \frac{4}{3}$, what is the value of a?

14. The expression $\frac{1}{3} + \frac{1}{2} + \frac{3}{5}$ is equal to:

15. If $x = 3$ in the equation below, what is the value of b?
$$x - \frac{2}{3}b = 0$$

16. Monique, Cassandra, and Maria decorated a cake together. Cassandra decorated $\frac{2}{7}$ of the cake and Monique decorated $\frac{1}{3}$ of the cake. How much of the cake did Maria decorate?

    A) $\frac{1}{3}$
    B) $\frac{8}{21}$
    C) $\frac{13}{21}$
    D) $\frac{7}{10}$

17. What value of x is the solution to the equation below?
$$\frac{8}{3}x = \frac{2}{3}$$

18. If $x = \frac{2}{5}y$ and $y = 10$, what is the value of $3x + 3$?

    A) 4
    B) 9
    C) 12
    D) 15

19. What value of x is the solution to the equation below?
$$\frac{2x+8}{3} = \frac{10}{3}$$

20. If $\frac{11a}{6} = \frac{18}{5}$, what is the value of a?

    A) $\frac{108}{55}$
    B) $\frac{55}{108}$
    C) $\frac{108}{5}$
    D) $\frac{90}{66}$

- 35 -

PrepPros

21. What is the solution to $\frac{1}{3}x + \frac{2}{7} = \frac{4}{7}x$?

22. If $\frac{x}{y} = 3$, what is the value of $\frac{3y}{x}$?

    A) 0
    B) 1
    C) 3
    D) 9

23. What is the solution to $\frac{4}{3}x - \frac{1}{2} = \frac{3}{6}x$?

24. Which of the following is equivalent to $\frac{3+9x}{15}$?

    A) $\frac{3+3x}{5}$
    B) $\frac{1+9x}{5}$
    C) $\frac{1+3x}{5}$
    D) $\frac{1}{5} + 3x$

25. A gas tank has a capacity of 270 gallons and is $\frac{7}{9}$ full of gas. Anissa then removes $\frac{1}{5}$ of the gas in the tank. How many gallons of gas are left in the tank?

    A) 84
    B) 168
    C) 210
    D) 252

26. If $\frac{7}{5}x = \frac{9}{8}$, what is the value of x?

    A) $\frac{8}{9}$
    B) $\frac{9}{7}$
    C) $\frac{45}{56}$
    D) $\frac{56}{45}$

27. Which of the following is equivalent to $\frac{x^2+5x}{x}$ where $x \neq 0$?

    A) $\frac{x+5}{x}$
    B) $\frac{x^2+5}{x}$
    C) $x + 5$
    D) 6

28. What is the solution to $x - \frac{4}{5} = 2 + \frac{1}{3}x$?

29. Which of the following is equivalent to the equation below where $x \neq 2$?

    $$\frac{4}{x-2} + \frac{6}{3(x-2)}$$

    A) $\frac{6}{x-2}$
    B) $\frac{22}{3x-2}$
    C) $\frac{16}{3x-6}$
    D) $\frac{28}{3x-6}$

30. Which of the following is equivalent to $\frac{2}{x-1} + \frac{3}{x}$ where $x \neq 0$ and $x \neq 1$?

    A) $\frac{5x-3}{x^2-x}$
    B) $\frac{3x-3}{x^2-x}$
    C) $\frac{5x+3}{x^2-x}$
    D) $\frac{-1}{x-1}$

Chapter 6: Fractions

31. If $x > 0$, which of the following is equivalent to $\dfrac{2}{x} + \dfrac{1}{3}$?

    A) $\dfrac{6x+3}{3x}$
    B) $\dfrac{3}{x+3}$
    C) $\dfrac{6+x}{3x}$
    D) $\dfrac{6+x}{x}$

32. If $x > 1$, which of the following is equivalent to $\dfrac{x}{x+1} - \dfrac{3}{x-1}$?

    A) $\dfrac{x^2-4x-3}{x^2-1}$
    B) $\dfrac{x^2+2x-3}{x^2-1}$
    C) $\dfrac{x^2+4x+3}{x^2-1}$
    D) $\dfrac{x-3}{x^2-1}$

33. Given consecutive positive integers $a, b, c,$ and d, such that $a > b > c > d$, which of the following has the largest value?

    A) $\dfrac{d}{c}$
    B) $\dfrac{a+b}{d}$
    C) $\dfrac{a+c}{b+d}$
    D) $\dfrac{a+b}{c+d}$

34. If $\dfrac{m+3}{m+5} = 8$, what is the value of m?

    A) $-\dfrac{3}{5}$
    B) $-\dfrac{5}{3}$
    C) $-\dfrac{37}{7}$
    D) $-\dfrac{40}{7}$

35. If $\dfrac{8k}{4b} = \dfrac{1}{3}$, what is the value of $\dfrac{b}{k}$?

    A) $\dfrac{1}{6}$
    B) $\dfrac{1}{2}$
    C) 2
    D) 6

36. For the equation below, which of the following gives y in terms of x?

    $$y\left(\dfrac{2}{x+3}\right) = \left(\dfrac{x+1}{x}\right)$$

    A) $y = \dfrac{x^2+4x+3}{2x}$
    B) $y = \dfrac{x^2+3x+3}{2x}$
    C) $y = \dfrac{2x+2}{x^2+3x}$
    D) $y = \dfrac{2x+4}{2x}$

37. In the equation below, what is the value of a?

    $$\dfrac{x}{x-3} + \dfrac{2}{3} = \dfrac{ax-6}{3x-9}$$

38. In the equation below, what is the value of $a+b$?

    $$\dfrac{x}{x-3} + \dfrac{4}{x+2} = \dfrac{ax^2+bx-12}{x^2-x-6}$$

39. Which of the following expressions is equivalent to $\dfrac{\frac{2x+12}{x/2}}{x+20}$?

    A) $\dfrac{2x}{2x^2+52x+240}$
    B) $\dfrac{2x^2+52x+240}{2x}$
    C) $\dfrac{2x^2+240}{2x}$
    D) $\dfrac{4x+24}{2x^2+20x}$

40. In the equation below, what is the value of $a + b$?

$$\frac{x+2}{x-3} + \frac{5}{x+3} = \frac{ax^2 + bx - 9}{x^2 - 9}$$

41. For the equation below, which of the following gives y in terms of x?

$$\left(\frac{xy - 2y}{x+3}\right) = \left(\frac{x+2}{x+1}\right)$$

A) $y = \frac{x^2 - 4}{x^2 + 4x + 3}$

B) $y = \frac{x^2 - x - 2}{x^2 + 5x + 6}$

C) $y = \frac{x^2 + x - 6}{x^2 + 3x + 2}$

D) $y = \frac{x^2 + 5x + 6}{x^2 - x - 2}$

42. What value of x satisfies the equation below?

$$\frac{5x^2 + 2x}{x^2 - 4} - \frac{3x}{x-2} = \frac{3}{x+2}$$

A) -2

B) $-\frac{3}{2}$

C) $\frac{3}{2}$

D) 2

43. The equation below is true for all values of x where $x > 1$, where a and b are positive constants. What is the value of ab?

$$\frac{4}{x-1} + \frac{3}{x+2} = \frac{ax+b}{x^2 + x - 2}$$

44. The expression below is equivalent to $ax^3 + bx^2 + cx + d$ for all values of x, where $x \neq 4$ or $x \neq 3$, and $a, b, c,$ and d are constants. What is the value of bc?

$$\frac{x^2}{x-4} - \frac{x+12}{2x-3} = \frac{ax^3 + bx^2 + cx + d}{2x^2 - 11x + 12}$$

45. The equation below is true for all values of x where $x > 2$, where a and b are positive constants. What is the value of $a + b + c + d$?

$$\frac{2}{x^2 + 4} + \frac{5}{x-2} = \frac{ax^3 + bx^2 + cx + d}{x^4 - 16}$$

- 38 -

Chapter 7: "In Terms of"

"In Terms of" questions ask you to express a certain variable "in terms of" the other variables. If a question says, "solve for x in terms of y and z," you need to isolate x and determine what it is equal to. If you have done this correctly, the x will be isolated on one side the equation and the y and z values, along with any numbers, will be on the other side of the equation.

The expressions in these questions can range from very simple to extremely complex and intimidating, but as long as you use the algebra skills that we learned in Chapter 4, you should be able to solve these questions without any issue. The answer choices usually make it obvious which variable you are being asked to isolate.

Example 1: A painter uses the formula $z = 20hw$ to estimate that z liters of paint are needed to paint a wall that is h feet high and w feet wide. Which of the following expresses w in terms of h and z?

A) $w = 20z - h$ B) $w = \frac{z}{h-20}$ C) $w = \frac{z}{20h}$ D) $w = \frac{h}{20z}$

Solution: The question asks for w in terms of h and z, so to solve we isolate w. To get w by itself, we divide both sides by $20h$.

$$z = 20wh$$

$$\frac{z}{20h} = w$$

The equation above can also be written as $w = \frac{z}{20h}$, so **the answer is C**.

Example 1 is an easy example of an "in terms of" questions. Now, let's look at another example that is a bit more challenging but still not too difficult.

Example 2: The equation below describes how a water pump displaces w gallons of water from a well every h minutes when the water is at a depth of x feet. Which of the following equations expresses x in terms of h and w?

$$2000 + xh^2 = 4wh$$

A) $x = \sqrt{4wh - 2000}$

B) $x = 4wh - 2000 + h^2$

C) $x = \frac{4wh - 2000}{h^2}$

D) $x = \frac{4w}{h} - 2000$

Solution: We need to isolate x. To start, we want to get all terms with x on the left side and all other terms on the right side. To do so, we subtract 2000 from both sides.

$$2000 + xh^2 = 4wh$$

$$xh^2 = 4wh - 2000$$

Now, we can divide both sides by h^2 to solve for x.

$$x = \frac{4wh - 2000}{h^2}$$

The answer is C.

Next, let's see an example that is more challenging. The SAT can make "in terms of" questions more difficult by asking you to do more advanced algebra to isolate a variable.

> **Example 3:** For the equation below, which of the following expresses m in terms of p and q?
> $$15p - 2m = 2mq + 300$$
>
> A) $m = 15p + 2q + 300$
>
> B) $m = \frac{15p + 300 + 2q}{2}$
>
> C) $m = \frac{300 - 15p}{2q}$
>
> D) $m = \frac{15p - 300}{2q + 2}$

Solution: We need to isolate m. To do this, we need to move all terms with m to the left side and move all other terms to the right side. We do this by subtracting $15p$ and $2mq$ from both sides to get
$$-2mq - 2m = -15p + 300$$
Now, we need to factor out m from the terms on the left side.
$$m(-2q - 2) = -15p + 300$$
To isolate m, we divide both sides by $-2q - 2$.
$$m = \frac{-15p + 300}{-2q - 2}$$
This does not match any of the answer choices yet, but we are close. If we multiply the right side by $\frac{-1}{-1}$, the equation instead will look like
$$m = \frac{15p - 300}{2q + 2}$$
The answer is D.

If the variable that you are trying to isolate appears in multiple terms, as with m in Example 3 above, we always need to move all terms including that variable to one side and then factor to isolate the variable. Once the term is factored out, you can then use division to isolate the term and find the correct answer. If you need to review how to factor to isolate a variable, go to page 24.

"In Terms of" Practice: Answers on page 327.

1. The velocity v of an object is found by taking the change in position m of an object and dividing it by the time s. Which of the following gives time s in terms of m and v?

   A) $s = mv$

   B) $s = \frac{v}{m}$

   C) $s = \frac{m}{v}$

   D) $s = m - v$

2. Due to a new tax, steel prices have recently increased. The original pre-tax price of a steel bar is p dollars. The new price of steel bar after the increase is represented by n dollars. The equation below shows this relationship. What is p in terms of n?

   $$1.18p + 40 = n$$

   A) $p = 40n - 1.18$

   B) $p = 1.18n - 40$

   C) $p = \frac{n - 40}{1.18}$

   D) $p = \frac{1.18}{n - 40}$

Chapter 7: "In Terms of"

3. The given equation below relates the positive numbers b, x, and z. Which equation correctly expresses x in terms of b and z?

$$\frac{1}{9b} = \frac{13x}{z}$$

A) $x = \frac{9bz}{13}$
B) $x = z - 117b$
C) $x = \frac{z}{117b}$
D) $x = 113bz$

4. The given equation relates the positive numbers $a, b,$ and c. Which equation correctly expresses c in terms of a and b?

$$\frac{4}{9a} = \frac{16b}{3c}$$

A) $c = 144ab$
B) $c = 12ab$
C) $c = \frac{1}{144ab}$
D) $c = \frac{1}{12ab}$

5. For the expression below, which of the following expresses p in terms of g, m, and q?

$$g = \frac{m + 3p + 5}{q}$$

A) $p = \frac{gq+5}{m}$
B) $p = \frac{gq-m-5}{3}$
C) $p = \frac{gq-5}{3+m}$
D) $p = \frac{gq+m+5}{3}$

6. The equation below relates the positive real a, b and c. Which equation correctly expresses c in terms of a and b?

$$a = b(17 - c)$$

A) $c = \frac{a}{b} - 17$
B) $c = \frac{b}{a} - 17$
C) $c = -\frac{a}{b} - 17$
D) $c = -\frac{a}{b} + 17$

7. If $5x = \sqrt{a}$, what is a in terms of x?

A) $\sqrt{5x}$
B) $5x^2$
C) $25x$
D) $25x^2$

8. The given equation below relates the numbers $l, m,$ and k. Which equation correctly expresses l in terms of m and k?

$$18k + \frac{3l}{2} = 3m$$

A) $l = -18k + 3m$
B) $l = -24k + 4m$
C) $l = -12k - 3m$
D) $l = -12k + 2m$

9. Approximately 25% of the height of Mauna Kea is visible above the surface of the ocean. If v represents the height in meters of Mauna Kea visible above the surface of the ocean and h represents the total height in meters of Mauna Kea, including the portion below the ocean's surface, which of the following equations best approximates h in terms of v?

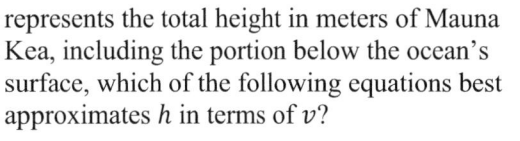

A) $h = 0.25v$
B) $h = \frac{v}{0.25}$
C) $h = 1.25v$
D) $h = \frac{v}{1.25}$

10. If x is 30% of y, which expression represents y in terms of x?

A) $0.03x$
B) $0.70x$
C) $\frac{10}{3}x$
D) $\frac{3}{10}x$

11. If $3\sqrt{5x} = b$, what is $5x$ in terms of b?

A) $\frac{b}{3}$
B) $\frac{b^2}{3}$
C) $\frac{b^2}{9}$
D) $15b^2$

12. The line $y = kx - 3$, where k is a constant, is graphed in the xy-plane. If the point (a, b) is on the line, where a and b do not equal to zero, what is the slope of the line in terms of a and b?

A) $\frac{a+3}{b}$
B) $\frac{a-3}{b}$
C) $\frac{b+3}{a}$
D) $\frac{b-3}{a}$

13. The map of a country is drawn to scale where 3 inches represents 5 miles. The actual distance between two locations is x miles. Which expression represents the distance on the map, in inches, between the two locations?

A) $\frac{5x}{3}$
B) $\frac{3x}{5}$
C) $3x + 5$
D) $3x - 5$

14. Which of the following gives e in terms of $a, b, c,$ and d?

$$abd - bcd = ed - cd$$

A) $abd - bcd - cd$
B) $abd - bcd + cd$
C) $ab - bc + c$
D) $ab - bc - c$

15. The equation below relates the positive real numbers $a, b, c,$ and d. Which equation correctly expresses b in terms of $a, c,$ and d?

$$a = b + bcd$$

A) $b = \frac{a}{1+cd}$
B) $b = \frac{1+cd}{a}$
C) $b = a - 2cd$
D) $b = \frac{a}{2cd}$

16. A helium machine blows up balloons such that after starting with an empty balloon, the machine will fill the balloon at a rate of c cubic inches of air every t seconds, where $c = 6t\sqrt{t}$. Which of the following gives the average rate at which the balloon is filled in terms of t?

A) $\sqrt{t}$
B) $6\sqrt{t}$
C) $\frac{6}{\sqrt{t}}$
D) $6t$

17. If $2\sqrt[3]{5x} = b$, what is x in terms of b?

A) $\frac{b^3}{\frac{2}{5}}$
B) $\frac{b^3}{10}$
C) $\frac{b^3}{20}$
D) $\frac{b^3}{40}$

18. If $a^2 = 16b^4$, what is b in terms of a?

A) $\frac{a}{4}$
B) $\frac{\sqrt{a}}{4}$
C) $\frac{\sqrt{a}}{2}$
D) $\frac{\sqrt{a}}{16}$

19. The formula below is used to show E, the expected time to complete a marathon, where f is the fastest time to finish the race, A is the average time to finish, and s is the slowest time to finish. Which of the following correctly gives s in terms of $E, f,$ and A?

$$E = \sqrt{\frac{s^2 + 2f}{A}}$$

A) $s = \sqrt{E^2 A - 2f}$
B) $s = E\sqrt{A - 2f}$
C) $s = \sqrt{\frac{E^2 A}{2f}}$
D) $s = EA - 2$

Chapter 7: "In Terms of"

20. The equation below relates the positive real numbers $a, b, c,$ and d. Which equation correctly expresses d in terms of $a, b,$ and c?

$$a = \frac{bc}{\sqrt{1+d}}$$

A) $d = \left(\frac{bc}{a}\right)^2 + 1$

B) $d = \frac{(bc)^2}{a^2 - 1}$

C) $d = \frac{bc}{a^2} - 1$

D) $d = \left(\frac{bc}{a}\right)^2 - 1$

21. The given equation relates the distinct positive real numbers $j, k,$ and l. Which equation correctly expresses l in terms of j and k?

$$\frac{8j}{48k} = \frac{1}{6}\sqrt{l - 17}$$

A) $l = \sqrt{\frac{j}{k}} + 17$

B) $l = \sqrt{\frac{64j}{2304k}} + 17$

C) $l = \left(\frac{j}{k}\right)^2 + 17$

D) $l = \left(\frac{64j}{2304k}\right)^2 + 17$

22. The given equation relates the distinct positive real number $a, b,$ and c. Which equation correctly expresses a in terms of b and c?

$$\frac{35c}{5b} = 7\sqrt{a + 12}$$

A) $a = \sqrt{\frac{c}{b}} - 12$

B) $a = \sqrt{\frac{245c}{35b}} - 12$

C) $a = \left(\frac{c}{b}\right)^2 - 12$

D) $a = \left(\frac{245c}{5b}\right)^2 - 12$

23. The formula below expresses s in terms of $d, e,$ and t. Which of the following gives e in terms of the other variables?

$$s = d^2\sqrt{1 - \frac{e^2}{t^2}}$$

A) $e = t\sqrt{1 - \frac{s^2}{d^4}}$

B) $e = t\sqrt{1 + \frac{s^2}{d^4}}$

C) $e = t(1 - \frac{s}{d^2})$

D) $e = t(1 + \frac{s}{d^2})$

24. The equations below relate the distinct positive real numbers $a, b, c,$ and d. Which equation correctly expresses b in terms of d?

$$c = 2a^2$$
$$a^{3b} = \left(\frac{c}{2}\right)^{d-1}$$

A) $b = \frac{d}{3} + \frac{1}{3}$

B) $b = \frac{4d}{3} - \frac{4}{3}$

C) $b = \frac{2d}{3} - \frac{2}{3}$

D) $b = \frac{2d}{3} - \frac{1}{3}$

25. The number of hours h for Saturn's moon Dione to complete an orbit around Saturn can be modeled by the equation below, where d is the average distance from Saturn, in thousands of miles. Which of the following expresses the distance in terms of the number of hours?

$$h = 18 \cdot \sqrt[3]{\left(\frac{d}{67}\right)^4}$$

A) $d = \frac{67}{18}(h)^{\frac{3}{4}}$

B) $d = \frac{67}{18}(h)^{\frac{4}{3}}$

C) $d = 67\left(\frac{h}{18}\right)^{\frac{4}{3}}$

D) $d = 67\left(\frac{h}{18}\right)^{\frac{3}{4}}$

- 43 -

PrepPros

Chapter 8: Inequalities

In math, two values are not always equal. Sometimes, we just know that one value is bigger or smaller when compared to another value. In these situations, we use inequalities.

① Algebra with Inequalities

To solve inequalities on the SAT, treat the inequality signs ($<, >, \leq, \geq$) like an = sign and solve using algebra. Inequalities can be solved as normal algebraic expressions with the exception of one very important rule:

When multiplying or dividing by a negative number, switch the direction of the inequality sign.

This rule is the most important thing to remember from this section. Students most commonly make mistakes on inequalities questions involving multiplication and division with negative numbers. As a quick example, let's see how to solve the equation below.

$$-2x + 5 \leq 11$$

Subtract 5 from both sides to get

$$-2x \leq 6$$

When dividing by -2 to isolate x, we switch the direction of the inequality sign, so we get

$$x \geq -3$$

Let's see a second example:

$$3x + 6 > x - 4$$

The first step is combining like terms. We subtract x from both sides to get the x-terms on the left side. We then subtract 6 from both sides to get the numbers on the right side.

$$3x - x > -4 - 6$$
$$2x > -10$$
$$x > -5$$

In this example, **we never multiply or divide by a negative number, so the inequality sign stays the same**. Just because we are working with a negative number does not mean we need to flip the inequality sign. Some students flip the sign whenever they divide and see a negative sign. Don't make that mistake! **Only flip the inequality when you multiply or divide both sides by a negative number.**

---

① Example 1: Which of the following shows the solution for $6x + 12 \leq 9x + 17$?

A) $x \geq \frac{29}{3}$ B) $x \geq \frac{29}{3}$ C) $x \leq -\frac{5}{3}$ D) $x \geq -\frac{5}{3}$

Solution: To solve, we need to isolate x. Here, let's move all the x-terms to the left side and all the numbers to the right side. To do this, we subtract $9x$ from both sides and 12 from both sides to get

$$-3x \leq 5$$

Now we divide both sides by -3. Since we are dividing by a negative number, we switch the direction of the inequality sign.

$$x \geq -\frac{5}{3}$$

The answer is D.

Chapter 8: Inequalities

Graphing Inequalities

Desmos can graph inequalities for you! If you are given an equation like $2x + 3y \geq 6$, you can write that directly into Desmos and it will graph it for you! However, the SAT can make graphing inequalities questions more difficult by including variables, so you need to know how to solve these algebraically as well.

When graphing inequalities in the coordinate plane, you need to remember three simple steps:

1) **Rearrange the equation into $y = mx + b$ form.**

2) **Plot the line. For greater than and less than ($>$ *and* $<$), draw a dashed line. For greater than or equal to and less than or equal to ($\geq$ *and* $\leq$), draw a solid line.**

3) **For greater than and greater than or equal to ($>$ *and* $\geq$), shade above the line. For less than and less than or equal to ($<$ *and* $\leq$), shade below the line.**

Let's start by graphing the inequality $2x + 3y \geq 6$. We can type this directly into Desmos, but for practice let's learn how to solve this algebraically.

First, we need to rearrange this into slope-intercept form to isolate y. If we do this correctly, we will get

$$y \geq -\frac{2}{3}x + 2$$

Since this is greater than or equal to, we draw a solid line and shade above the line, so the graph looks like

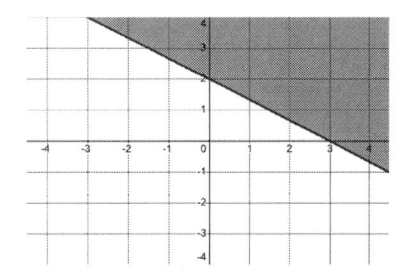

The solution set is the shaded area of the graph. Any points in the shaded area are solutions to the inequality.

For a system of inequalities in the coordinate plane, the solution is where the shaded regions overlap. For example, let's consider the inequalities $4x - 2y > 8$ and $x + 3y > -2$

To graph these inequalities, we need to rearrange them into slope-intercept form to isolate y. If we do this correctly, we get

$$y < 2x - 4 \quad \text{and} \quad y > -\frac{1}{3}x - \frac{2}{3}$$

For the $y < 2x - 4$ line, we draw a dashed line and shade below the line. For the $y > -\frac{1}{3}x - \frac{2}{3}$ line, we draw a dashed line and shade above the line.

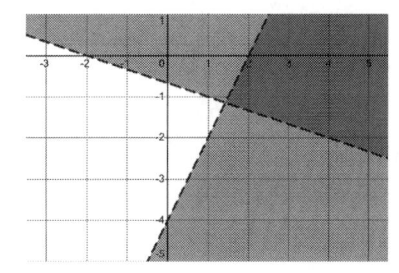

The solution set to this system of inequalities is the area in the top right where the shaded regions overlap. Any points in that shaded region are a solution to the system of inequalities.

- 45 -

PrepPros

Example 2: The dark shaded region in the graph below represents the solution set to which of the following systems of inequalities?

A) $y > 2x - 1$
$y > \frac{1}{2}x + 2$

B) $y < 2x - 1$
$y > \frac{1}{2}x + 2$

C) $y > 2x - 1$
$y < \frac{1}{2}x + 2$

D) $y < 2x + 2$
$y > \frac{1}{2}x - 1$

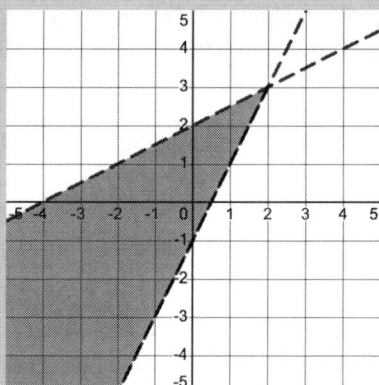

Solution: Method #1 – Solving Algebraically: First, we need to find the equations of the lines. The steeper line has a slope of 2 and a y-intercept at -1. The shaded region is above the line and the line is dashed, so the first equation is $y > 2x - 1$. The flatter line has a slope of $\frac{1}{2}$ and a y-intercept at 2. The shaded region is below the line and the line is dashed, so the second equation is $y < \frac{1}{2}x + 2$. **The answer is C.**

Solution: Method #2 – Graphing in Desmos: We can graph the answer choices in Desmos to see which one matches the graph shown in the question. If you are not confident on how to solve a question like Example 2 algebraically, use Desmos instead.

Systems of Inequalities

A system of inequalities is a set of multiple inequalities with multiple variables. On the SAT, systems of inequalities questions usually include two inequalities with two variables.

Example 3:
$y > 3x + 1$
$2y + x < 13$

In the xy-plane, point A is contained in the graph of the solution set of the system of inequalities above. Which of the following could be the coordinates of point A?

A) $(-2, -8)$ B) $(1, 5)$ C) $(1, 7)$ D) $(3, 3)$

Solution: Method #1 – Backsolving: If you see a question with two inequalities with both x-terms and y-terms, one easy way to solve is to plug the answer choices back into the inequalities. Whichever answer choice has true statements for both inequalities is the correct answer.

To test each answer choice, we plug in the values from the point for x and y in the inequalities and see if the statement is true or false.

A) $-8 > 3(-2) + 1$ → $-8 > -5$ (false)   (A is incorrect)
$2(-8) + (-2) < 13$ → $-18 < 13$ (true)

B) $5 > 3(1) + 1$ → $5 > 4$ (true)   (B is correct)
$2(5) + 1 < 13$ → $11 < 13$ (true)

C) $7 > 3(1) + 1$ → $7 > 4$ (true)   (C is incorrect)
$2(7) + 1 < 13$ → $15 < 13$ (false)

Chapter 8: Inequalities

D) $3 > 3(3) + 1$ → $3 > 10$ (false)   (D is incorrect)
     $2(3) + 3 < 13$ → $9 < 13$ (true)

Since both inequalities are true with the point $(1, 5)$, **the answer is B.**

Solution: Method #2 – Graph On Desmos: For any question with inequalities and points, we can graph the inequalities and the points in Desmos to solve. To do this, type the inequalities into Desmos as they appear in the question. Next, graph all 4 points from the answer choices.

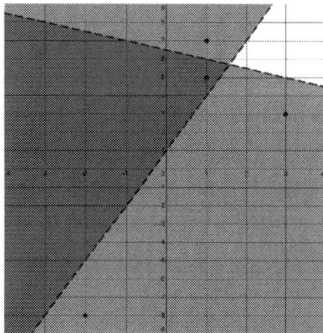

- $y > 3x + 1$
- $2y + x < 13$
- $(-2, -8)$
- $(1, 5)$
- $(1, 7)$
- $(3, 3)$

The solution set to the system of inequalities is the dark shaded region on the left. Any point in that shaded region will be part of the solution set, so we are looking for a point that is in that shaded region. The only point that is in the shaded region is $(1, 5)$, so **the answer is B.**

Example 4:
$$2x > 15$$
$$3y - 2x > 21$$

Which of the following consists of the y-coordinates of all the points that satisfy the system of inequalities above?

    A) $y > 36$ B) $y > 12$ C) $y > 7$ D) $y > 3$

Solution: To solve a system of inequalities, we need to solve each inequality. We can solve using normal algebra. In addition, we use the substitution method that we will learn in Chapter 12 to combine the inequalities.

To start, we solve the first inequality by dividing both sides by 2 to get

$$x > \frac{15}{2}$$

Now for the tricky part: solving the second inequality for y. To solve for y, we want to get rid of the x using substitution, so that equation is expressed wholly in terms of y. From solving the first equation, we know that $x > \frac{15}{2}$. The trick here is to think of the first inequality as $x = \frac{15}{2}$ and substitute the $\frac{15}{2}$ for the x. Now, we have

$$3y - 2(\tfrac{15}{2}) > 21$$
$$3y - 15 > 21$$

This looks like an equation we can solve.

$$3y > 36$$
$$y > 12$$

The solution to this system of inequalities is $x > \frac{15}{2}$ and $y > 12$. **The answer is B.**

Shortcut Method – Use Desmos: Graph the inequalities in Desmos and then look at the solution set, the area where the shaded regions overlap. The inequalities cross at the point $(7.5, 12)$, and the rest of the solution set is above that point and to the right. Since the minimum y-value is at $y = 12$, the solution set is $y > 12$. **The answer is B.** This more advanced example requires a higher level of understanding to use Desmos to solve.

2-4 Inequalities and Word Problems

The SAT also includes word problems with inequalities and asks you to select the answer choice that properly models the situation described. As always with word problems, read the question very carefully and try to convert the words into equations. If you have trouble writing the equations yourself, use the answer choices to help.

Example 5: Trevor is ordering lunch for the office. He has to spend less than $500 and buy lunch for 35 people. The options for lunch today are a salmon salad for $18 and a roast beef sandwich for $11. If s represents salmon salads and r represents roast beef sandwiches, which of the following inequalities correctly represents this situation?

A) $r + s > 35$
   $11r + 18s > 500$
B) $r + s = 35$
   $18r + 11 = 500$
C) $r + s = 35$
   $18s + 11r < 500$
D) $18r + 11s < 500$
   $r - s < 35$

Solution: We are told that Trevor has to buy lunch for 35 people, so the total number of meals needs to be 35. The first equation needs to be $r + s = 35$. Trevor also needs to spend less than $500. To find the total dollars spent on salmon salad, we need to multiply the number of salads, s, by the price, $18. To find the total dollars spent on roast beef sandwiches, we need to multiply the number of sandwiches, r, by the price, $11. Putting all of this together, the second equation needs to be $18s + 11r < 500$. **The answer is C.**

Inequalities Practice: Answers on page 327.

1. Which of the following inequalities describes the solution set for $4x - 2 \geq 10x - 14$?

    A) $x \leq 2$
    B) $x \geq 2$
    C) $x \leq -1$
    D) $x \geq -2$

2. The solution set to $3x + 4 > -11$ is all real values of x such that:

    A) $x > -15$
    B) $x < -15$
    C) $x > -5$
    D) $x < -5$

3. The point $(x, 56)$ is a solution to the system of inequalities below in the xy-plane. Which of the following could be the value of x?

    $$y > 7$$
    $$5x + 2y < 18$$

    A) -19
    B) -17
    C) 17
    D) 19

4. Which of the following is the solution set for $\frac{2}{5}x + 6 \leq x + 10$?

    A) $x \leq -\frac{20}{3}$
    B) $x \geq -\frac{20}{3}$
    C) $x \geq \frac{4}{7}$
    D) $x \leq \frac{20}{3}$

Chapter 8: Inequalities

5. The solution set to $\frac{1}{3}x < \frac{3}{2}x + \frac{11}{6}$ is all real values of x such that:

   A) $x > -\frac{11}{7}$
   B) $x < -\frac{11}{7}$
   C) $x > 2$
   D) $x < 2$

6. Which of the following inequalities is equivalent to $5x + 9y \leq 2x - 6$?

   A) $x \geq -3y - 2$
   B) $x \leq -3y - 2$
   C) $x \geq 3y - 2$
   D) $x \leq 3y - 2$

7. The point $(x, -12)$ is a solution to the system of inequalities in the xy-plane. Which of the following could be the value of x?

   $$y < 3$$
   $$4x - 8y < 18$$

   A) -20
   B) -17
   C) -14
   D) -8

8. Which of the following inequalities is equivalent to the inequality below?

   $$18x - 12y > 24$$

   A) $6x - 4y > 8$
   B) $6x - 9y > 12$
   C) $9x - 4y > 12$
   D) $6x - 4y < 8$

9. John plants trees at a constant rate of 40 trees per hour. John planted 200 trees so far today and plans to spend h hours planting trees for the rest of the day. If John wants to plant at least 440 trees by the end of the day, which of the following inequalities best represents this situation?

   A) $40h \geq 440$
   B) $40h - 200 \geq 440$
   C) $40h + 200 \geq 440$
   D) $200h + 40 \geq 440$

10. Which ordered pair (x, y) is a solution to the given system of inequalities in the xy-plane?

    $$y > 2x + 6$$
    $$3x + 4y < 12$$

    A) $(-2, 4)$
    B) $(-4, -3)$
    C) $(2, 1)$
    D) $(4, -2)$

11. The minimum value of x is 7 less than 4 times another number n. Which inequality shows the possible values of x?

    A) $x \geq 4n - 7$
    B) $x \leq 4n - 7$
    C) $x \geq 7 - 4n$
    D) $x \leq 7 - 4n$

12. At the beginning of the day, John had 15 pieces of candy. John gave away x pieces of candy to his friend Tom, and Dave gave John y pieces of candy. At the end of the day John had at least 23 pieces of candy. Which of the following inequalities can be used to correctly represent this situation?

    A) $15 - x + y \geq 23$
    B) $15 + x - y \geq 23$
    C) $-x + 15 + y \leq 23$
    D) $23 - x + y \geq 15$

13. Shawn has two jobs. He works as a server, which pays \$13 per hour, and as a surf instructor, which pays \$15 per hour. He can work no more than 25 hours per week, and he wants to earn at least \$340 per week. Which of the following systems of inequalities represents this situation in terms of x and y, where x is the number of hours he works as a server and y is the number of hours he works as a surf instructor?

    A) $13x + 15y \geq 340$
       $x + y \geq 25$
    B) $13x + 15y \geq 340$
       $x + y \leq 25$
    C) $13x + 15y \leq 340$
       $x + y \geq 25$
    D) $13x + 15y \leq 340$
       $x + y \leq 25$

14. The maximum value of a is 13 more than 6 times another number b. Which inequality shows the possible values of a?

   A. $a \geq 13 + 6b$
   B. $a \geq 13b + 6$
   C. $a \leq 13 + 6b$
   D. $a \leq 13b + 6$

15. In the xy-plane, which of the following does NOT contain any points (x, y) that are solutions to the $6y - 4x > 16$?

   A) The region where $x > 0$ and $y > 0$
   B) The region where $x < 0$ and $y > 0$
   C) The region where $x > 0$ and $y < 0$
   D) The x-axis.

16. James has 3,000 square feet of wood. He wants to make at least 10 dressers and 5 bed frames. Each dresser requires 150 square feet of wood, and each bed frame requires 120 square feet of wood. If d represents dressers and b represents bed frames, which of the following systems of inequalities correctly represents this situation?

   A) $d + b \leq 3,000$
      $d \geq 10$
      $b \geq 5$
   B) $120d + 150b \leq 3,000$
      $d \geq 10$
      $b \geq 5$
   C) $10d + 5b \leq 3,000$
      $d \geq 150$
      $b \geq 120$
   D) $150d + 120b \leq 3,000$
      $d \geq 10$
      $b \geq 5$

17. A model estimates that the African Hyena can travel 9 to 13 km per day. Based on this model, which inequality represents the estimated total number of miles, m, an African Hyena could travel in 12 days?

   A) $9 + 12 \leq m \leq 13 + 12$
   B) $9 \leq 12m \leq 13$
   C) $9 \leq m + 12 \leq 13$
   D) $9 \leq \frac{m}{12} \leq 13$

18. Which of the following inequalities includes the y-coordinates of all points that satisfy the system of inequalities below?

$$y > 3x - 3$$
$$3x > 12$$

   A) $y > 1$
   B) $y > 4$
   C) $y > 9$
   D) $y > 15$

19. A workshop class is split into groups that are building large and small coffee tables. A large coffee table requires 6 legs and 4 segments of plywood. A small coffee table requires 3 legs and 2 segments of plywood. There are 85 legs and 79 segments of plywood. Each group must construct at least 2 small coffee tables and 1 large coffee table. What is the maximum number of groups that the workshop class can be split into?

20. Dimitri works a barista for $15 per hour and babysits for $25 per hour. Last week, he made at least $160 working x hours as a barista and y hours as a babysitter. Which of the following inequalities models this situation?

   A) $25x + 15y \geq 160$
   B) $3x + 5y \geq 32$
   C) $15x + 25y \geq 32$
   D) $5x + 3y \geq 32$

21. In the equation $ax \leq 2b - by$, a and b are constants and $0 < b < a$. Which of the following could represent the graph of the equation in the xy-plane?

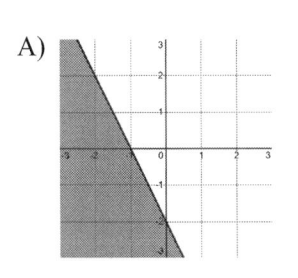

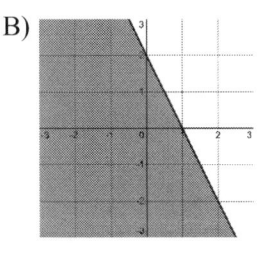

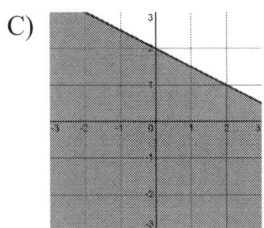

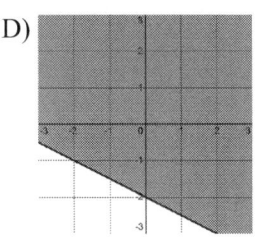

A)

B)

C)

D)

22. A group of counselors and students take a trip to an aquarium. A maximum of 46 counselors and students are on the trip. Each counselor can lead a group of no more than 5 students. If c represents the number of counselors and k represents the number of students, which of the following system of inequalities best describes the possible number of counselors and students who can go on the trip?

A) $c + k \leq 46$
   $c \leq 5k$
B) $c + k \leq 46$
   $c \geq 5k$
C) $c + k \leq 46$
   $c \leq \frac{k}{5}$
D) $c + k \leq 46$
   $c \geq \frac{k}{5}$

23. If a and b are positive integers that satisfy the inequalities below, how many different values of $a - b$ are possible?
$$a^2 < 8$$
$$b^2 < 21$$

24. A geologist conducted a study on soil erosion in 2014 for farmers in the United States. Flooding was responsible for 0.63 billion tons of soil loss in 2014. Wind erosion and overgrazing were also responsible for soil loss on farms. Flooding, wind erosion, and overgrazing together were responsible for 1.37 billion tons of soil loss in 2014. Which inequality represents the possible amounts of soil loss, s, in billions of tons, on farms from overgrazing in 2014 in the United States?

A) $0 < s < 0.74$
B) $0.63 < s < 1.37$
C) $0.74 < s < 1.37$
D) $1.37 < s < 2.00$

25. A taco stand is buying pork for carnitas and flank steak for carne asada from its distributer. The distributer will deliver no more than 400 pounds of meat in a shipment. Pork comes in 9-pound packages, and flank steak comes in 6-pound packages. The taco stand wants to order at least three times as many packages of pork as packages of flank steak. Let p represent the number of packages of pork and let f represent the number of packages of flank steak. Which of the following systems of inequalities best represents this situation?

A) $9p + 6f \leq 400$
   $3p \geq f$
B) $9p + 6f \leq 400$
   $p \geq 3f$
C) $27p + 6f \leq 400$
   $3p \geq f$
D) $27p + 6f \leq 400$
   $p \geq 3f$

PrepPros

26. A heat wave is defined as 5 or more days where the daily temperature is at least 9 °F higher than the average temperature during that month. If the month of June in San Diego has an average temperature of A °F and the daily temperature each of the last five 5 days is defined by x °F, which of the following would give the inequality for a heat wave occurring in the last 5 days in San Diego in June?

A) $A = x + 9$
B) $A \leq x - 9$
C) $A \geq x + 9$
D) $A \geq x - 9$

27. For the system of inequalities below, $c = 2b$ and $b < 0 < a$. Which of the graphs below shows a possible solution set to the system of inequalities?

$$ax + 2by \geq c$$
$$3ay - 2bx \geq 3a$$

A)
B)
C)
D)

28. A car manufacturer is shipping two types of cars across the Atlantic Ocean on a car ferry. Car A is 3 tons and Car B is 6 tons. The car manufacturer wants to transfer at least 50% more of Car A than Car B. The ferry can transport up to 230 tons of cars and hold no more than 50 cars. What is the maximum number of Car B cars that can be transported on the ferry?

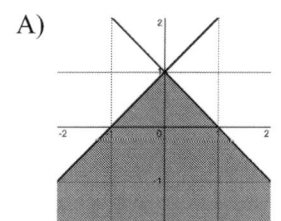

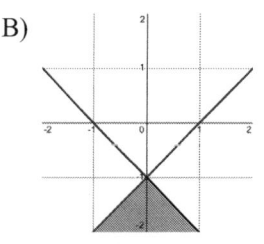

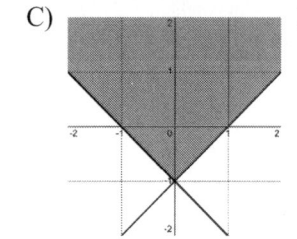

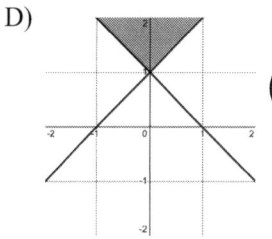

29. Sadie plans to make at least 20 pounds of baked goods that will consist of brownies and cookies. If Sadie wants at least 75% of the baked goods to be made up of cookies, which of the following systems of inequalities represents b, pounds of brownies, and c, pounds of cookies?

A) $b + c \leq 20$
   $0.75c \leq b$
B) $b + c \geq 20$
   $0.75b \leq c$
C) $b + c \geq 20$
   $3c \leq b$
D) $b + c \geq 20$
   $3b \leq c$

30. For the equations below, $a > 2$, $d \leq -1$, and $-1 < b < 0 < c < 1$. When graphed in the xy-plane, which of the following inequalities has a solution that does not include any values in the 1st quadrant?

A) $ax + (a + b)y < cx - c$
B) $2ax + by < cx - d$
C) $a - cx < ady + b$
D) $dx + (c - a)y > 4b$

- 52 -

Chapter 9: Percentages

On the SAT, you need to know how to solve questions with simple percentages and with percentage increase and decrease. While percentages may seem simple, they can often stump students who do not know how to set them up correctly. This chapter provides you all of the skills that you need to know in order to handle percentage questions quickly and easily on test day.

Simple Percentages

Simple percentage questions can be solved by properly setting up a proportion:

$$\frac{\text{new}}{\text{original}} = \frac{\%}{100}$$

You can think of the "original" as the starting value (the 100%) and the "new" as the percentage of the starting value. If you are given a percentage value, always put it where the % is.

Example 1: Isaiah purchased a new watch for 72% of the original price. Isaiah paid no sales tax. If the original price was $160, how much did Isaiah pay for the watch?

Solution: Method #1 – Proportion: To solve, we set up a proportion:

$$\frac{x}{160} = \frac{72}{100}$$

$$100x = 11{,}520$$

$$x = \frac{11{,}520}{100} = 115.20$$

Isaiah paid $115.20 for the watch. **The answer is 115.2.**

Solution: Method #2 – Decimal Shortcut: Here, we can turn the 72% into 0.72. Let the price Isaiah paid for the watch be p. We know that Isaiah paid 72% of the original price of $160 so

$$p = 0.72(160)$$

$$p = 115.2$$

Isaiah paid $115.20 for the watch.

Example 2: Joey buys a new set of golf clubs for $720 when the clubs are on sale for 80% of the original price. What was the original price, in dollars, of the set of golf clubs?

Solution: Method #1 – Proportion: To solve, we can set up a proportion:

$$\frac{720}{x} = \frac{80}{100}$$

$$80x = 72{,}000$$

$$x = \frac{72{,}000}{80} = 900$$

The answer is 900.

Method #2 – Decimal Shortcut: We can also turn percentages into decimals by dividing the percentage value by 100. 120% is the same as 1.2. 85% is the same as 0.85. For this question, we can turn 80% in 0.8 and solve:

$$0.8x = 720$$

$$x = \frac{720}{0.8} = 900$$

The answer is 900. We recommend the decimal shortcut, as it is faster for solving percentage questions.

PrepPros

The SAT also asks questions with multiple percentage changes in the same question. To solve these questions the fastest, you should do all the percentage changes together in one step.

> **Example 3:** Fred got a great deal on a new road bicycle at a garage sale. To make some money, Fred decides to sell the bicycle for 195% of the original price to Dave. Dave sells the bicycle 6 months later for 80% of the price that he purchased the bicycle for from Fred. The price that Dave sells the bicycle for is what percent of the original price of the bicycle?

Solution: Method 1 – "Math Teacher Way": Let the original price of the bicycle be p. When Fred sells the bicycle to Dave for 195% of the original price, you multiply by 1.95. When Dave later sells the bicycle for 80% of the purchase price, you multiply by 0.8. The final price that Dave sold the bicycle for is then:

$$p(1.95)(0.8) = 1.56p$$

The final price is 156% of the original price. **The answer is 156.**

Method 2 – Plug in Numbers: The most confusing part of this question is that we are never given any actual price for the bicycle. To make this question easier, pick an original price for the bicycle and use that price to solve. Let's say the original price of Fred's bicycle $100. 100 is always a good number to pick for percentage problems because it is easy to calculate percent changes from 100. Since Dave buys the bicycle for 195% of the original price, Dave pays $195 for the bicycle. Dave then sells the bicycle for 80% of the $195, so you can solve for the final price:

$$\text{Final Price} = 0.8(195) = 156$$

The final price is $156. Since the original price was $100, the final price is 156% of the original price. **The answer is 156.**

Simple Percentages Practice: Answers on page 327.

1. What is 80% of 50?

   A) 20
   B) 40
   C) 42
   D) 45

2. On his English test, Justin missed 8 of the 50 questions. What percentage of the questions did Justin answer correctly?

   A) 40%
   B) 60%
   C) 75%
   D) 84%

3. Jim is a farmer. Last year, Jim planted 280 acres of corn and 420 acres of soybeans. What percentage of the acres that Jim planted was corn?

   A) 28%
   B) 40%
   C) 66%
   D) 75%

4. 48 is 150% of what number?

   A) 30
   B) 32
   C) 40
   D) 72

5. If $y = 200$ and x is 40% of y, what is 125% of x?

   A) 80
   B) 100
   C) 120
   D) 150

6. When a black bear hibernates, its heart rate drops by 15 beats per minute. This drop is 25% of its normal heart rate. What is the black bear's normal heart rate?

   A) 30
   B) 45
   C) 60
   D) 75

7. Cardiff Market is selling their famous tri-tip steak sandwiches at a local music and arts festival. As a special promotion, they promise to donate 27% of the sandwich sales to charity. If they sold $870 dollars in sandwiches, how much will they be donating to charity?

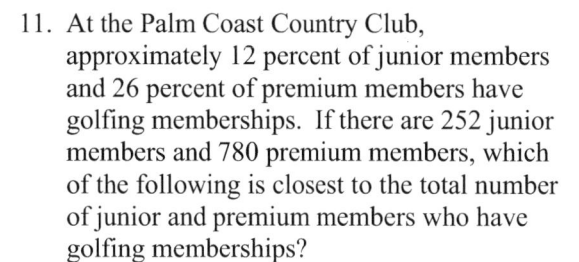

   A) $234.90
   B) $247.00
   C) $469.80
   D) $722.10

8. Last month, Amanda spent a total of $800. She spent $240 on food, $90 on gas, $400 on rent, and $70 on clothing. The category in which that Amanda spent the second largest sum of money on is closest to what percentage of her total spending?

   A) 20%
   B) 30%
   C) 50%
   D) 60%

9. How Did Attendees First Hear About Coachella?

Source	Percent
Social Media	35%
Friend Attended	12%
TV	5%
Internet	38%
Other	10%

   The table above shows a summary of 1,500 responses from attendees at Coachella when asked how they first learned about the festival. Based on the table, how many people learned from a friend who attended or from social media?

   A) 525
   B) 675
   C) 705
   D) 720

10. Christina has 10 hours of free time each week. If she spends 18% of her free time reading, how many <u>minutes</u> per week does she read?

    A) 1.8
    B) 18
    C) 64
    D) 108

11. At the Palm Coast Country Club, approximately 12 percent of junior members and 26 percent of premium members have golfing memberships. If there are 252 junior members and 780 premium members, which of the following is closest to the total number of junior and premium members who have golfing memberships?

    A) 467
    B) 233
    C) 203
    D) 30

12. If 8% of x is the same as 10% of 120, what is the value of x?

13. A popsicle stand buys popsicles at a wholesale price of $0.70 per popsicle and sells them each at a retail price that is 250% of the wholesale price. During the last 30 minutes of the day, any leftover popsicles are sold for 40% of the retail price. What is the price of a popsicle, in dollars, that is sold during the last 30 minutes of the day?

14. Rebecca sells her pickup truck to Jeremy for 76% of the original price. Jeremy does some work on the car and then sells it for 110% of the price at which he purchased the car. Which of the following is closest to percent of the original price that Jeremy sold the pickup truck for?

    A) 84
    B) 86
    C) 93
    D) 110

15. $p\%$ of x is 7. Which expression represents x in terms of p?

A) $\dfrac{7}{p}$

B) $\dfrac{7p}{100}$

C) $\dfrac{(100)(7)}{p}$

D) $\dfrac{7}{(100)(p)}$

16. The groups of students who are graduating with honors from a university have a variety of different majors. 30% are science majors, 15% are history majors, 25% are humanities majors, and the remaining 24 students are all business majors. Of the students graduating with honors, how many more science majors are there than history majors?

A) 6
B) 12
C) 15
D) 25

17. x is 320% of y. x is also 60% of z. What percentage of z is equal to y? (Round your answer to the nearest hundredth)

18. 48% of the gifts in a donation basket are balls. Of those 48%, 26% are blue. Of the blue balls, 36% are basketballs. Which of the following is closest to the percentage of items in the basket that are not blue basketballs?

A) 0.044%
B) 4.49%
C) 87.52%
D) 95.51%

19. If $y\%$ of x is $13x$, and x is a positive number, what is the value of y?

20. How many liters of a 40% saline solution must be added to 8 liters of a 10% saline solution to obtain a 30% saline solution?

21. Big Storage is offering a new storage shed. The original storage shed was 6 feet wide, 10 feet long, and 8 feet tall. The new storage shed's dimensions will be 80% of the original width, 75% of the original length, and 90% of the original height. To the nearest 1%, what percent will the volume of the new storage shed be when compared to the volume of the original storage shed?

A) 54
B) 66
C) 78
D) 81

22. A scientist is creating a sugar water solution for his lab. If there are currently 10 liters of a 32% sugar solution in a bucket, how many liters of a 12% sugar solution need to be added to the bucket to create a 20% sugar solution??

23. $h\%$ of 12 is equal to 220% of z. Which of the following correctly expresses z in terms of h?

A) $z = \dfrac{3}{55}h$

B) $z = \dfrac{11}{60}h$

C) $z = \dfrac{55}{3}h$

D) $z = \dfrac{60}{11}h$

24. 7.5 gallons of a $p\%$ chlorine solution are added to 10 gallons of a 5% chlorine solution to make a 20% chlorine solution. What is the value of p?

Chapter 9: Percentages

Percentage Increase and Decrease

Percentage questions are more difficult when there is an increase or a decrease to the percentage, but you can still set them up as a proportion.

Percentage increase: $\frac{\text{New}}{\text{Original}} = \frac{100 + \%}{100}$ **Percentage decrease:** $\frac{\text{New}}{\text{Original}} = \frac{100 - \%}{100}$

The "original" is the starting value (the 100%), and the "new" is the percentage increase or decrease from the starting value. **If you are given a percentage value, always insert it into the equation where the % sign is.**

Example 1: Jarvis construction company is building a new exit ramp for the local highway. The company initially said that the project would take 250 days, but a forecast for bad winter weather led the company to estimate that the project would take 12% longer to finish. How many days does Jarvis now estimate that the new exit ramp will take to complete?

Solution:
$$\frac{x}{250} = \frac{100+12}{100}$$

$$100x = (250)(112)$$

$$x = \frac{(250)(112)}{100} = 280$$

The answer is 280.

It is also important to know the shortcut for solving percentage increase and decrease questions. Let's say you want to increase x by 30%. Normally if we want to increase x by 30%, you will find 30% of the value and then add it to x:

$$x + 0.3x$$

This is the same as

$$x + 0.3x = x(1 + 0.3) = 1.3x$$

Instead of finding 30% of x and adding it to the original value, you can simply multiply x by 1.3. This shortcut will work for any percent value. To increase a value by 4%, multiply by 1.04. To decrease a value by 10%, multiply by 0.9. This technique will help you solve percentage increase and decrease questions more quickly and effectively on the SAT.

Both this shortcut technique and the proportion technique work, so use the one that you are more comfortable with.

Example 2: Tim grew 15% more tons of tomatoes in 2019 than in 2018. If Tim grew 23 tons of tomatoes in 2019, how many tons of tomatoes did Tim grow in 2018?

Solution:
$$(1.15)(\text{tons in 2018}) = \text{tons 2019}$$
$$(1.15)(\text{tons in 2018}) = 23$$
$$\text{tons in 2018} = \frac{23}{1.15}$$
$$\text{tons in 2018} = 20$$

The answer is 20.

PrepPros

Example 3: The price of a painting decreased by 8% in 2017, increased by 25% in 2018, and increased by 40% in 2019. What percentage greater is the price of the painting in 2019 than the original price at the beginning of 2017?

Solution: Let the original price of the painting be p. When the price is decreased by 8% in 2017, we multiply by $(1 - 0.08)$ because it is the original price minus 8%. When the price is increased by 25% in 2018, we multiply by $(1 + 0.25)$ because we are adding 25% onto the price from 2017. When the price is increased by 40% in 2019, we multiply by $(1 + 0.40)$ because you are adding 40% onto the price from 2018. The final price is then:

$$p(1 - 0.08)(1 + 0.25)(1 + 0.40) = p(0.92)(1.25)(1.40) = 1.61p$$

The $1.61p$ shows that the price in 2019 is 61% higher than the price in 2017. **The answer is 61.**

For other percentage questions, you will need to know how to calculate the percent by which a value increases or decreases. To solve these questions, you just need to use the equation below:

$$\text{Percentage Change} = \frac{\text{Final Value} - \text{Initial Value}}{\text{Initial Value}} \times 100$$

If the percent change is a positive number, it is a percent increase. If the percent change is a negative number, it is a percentage decrease.

Example 4: In 2017, the average price of an avocado in California was $1.43. In 2018, the average price of an avocado in California was $1.54. Which of the following is closest to the percentage increase of the price of an avocado from 2017 to 2018?

A) 7.1% B) 7.7% C) 8.2% D) 8.4%

Solution:

$$\text{Percentage Change} = \frac{1.54 - 1.43}{1.43} \times 100 = 7.7\%$$

The answer is B.

<u>Percentage Increase and Decrease Practice</u>: Answers on page 327.

1. Bob bought a house at a 20% discount. If the house was initially priced at 600,000 dollars, what was the price, in dollars, Bob paid?

    A) 120,000
    B) 480,000
    C) 720,000
    D) 750,000

2. The value of b is equal to the value of a increased by 47%. If $a > 0$, which of the following expresses b in terms of a?

    A) $b = 0.47a$
    B) $b = 0.53a$
    C) $b = 1.47a$
    D) $b = 1.53a$

3. The price of the new PowerBros external phone charger is 30% more than the price of the old version. If the old version costs $85.00, which of the following best approximates the cost, in dollars, of the new external phone charger?

    A) $25.50
    B) $59.50
    C) $110.50
    D) $283.35

4. The price of two sandwiches was $20 before sales tax. If a sales tax of 8% is added, how much do the two sandwiches cost including the sales tax?

A) $18.40
B) $20.08
C) $20.80
D) $21.60

5. In 2017, Jimmy's Surfboard Shapers made 1,231 surfboards. In 2018, Jimmy's Surfboard Shapers made 1,391 surfboards. Which of the following is closest to the percentage increase in surfboards made from 2017 to 2018?

A) 11%
B) 13%
C) 16%
D) 18%

6. The total number of bicycles manufactured at a facility increased by 17% from 2018 to 2019. If the total number of bicycles manufactured in 2019 is k times the number manufactured in 2018, what is the value of k?

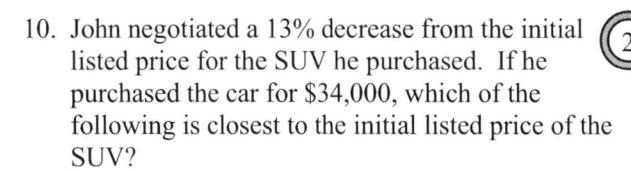

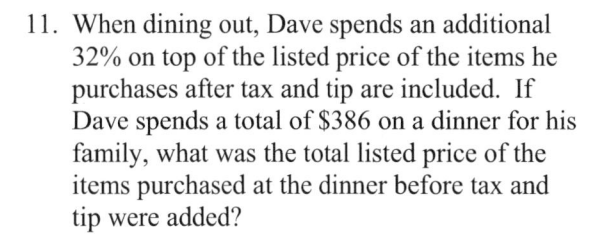

7. The expression $0.65x$ represents decreasing the positive quantity x by what percentage?

8. Max bought a new pair of hiking shoes for $118.00 dollars after an 8% sales tax. What was the price of the hiking shoes before the sales tax was added?

A) $108.56
B) $109.26
C) $110.92
D) $112.00

9. Last year, 700 students graduated from Eastlake High. This year, 8% fewer students graduated than last year. How many students graduated this year?

A) 620
B) 644
C) 648
D) 756

10. John negotiated a 13% decrease from the initial listed price for the SUV he purchased. If he purchased the car for $34,000, which of the following is closest to the initial listed price of the SUV?

A) $4,420
B) $29,580
C) $38,500
D) $39,000

11. When dining out, Dave spends an additional 32% on top of the listed price of the items he purchases after tax and tip are included. If Dave spends a total of $386 on a dinner for his family, what was the total listed price of the items purchased at the dinner before tax and tip were added?

A) $292.43
B) $262.48
C) $509.52
D) $567.65

12. This month, Stella decided to try to be more energy efficient by turning off the lights in her house when she was not in the rooms and by using her air conditioning less. If her energy bill last month was $85.95 and her energy bill this month is $76.24, to the nearest tenth of a percent, what percent did her energy bill decrease?

A) 12.7%
B) 12.4%
C) 11.8%
D) 11.3%

13. James bought three shirts for $168 during a 30% off sale. How much would the three shirts have cost without the sale?

    A) $118
    B) $200
    C) $218
    D) $240

14. John's average weekly grocery bill for 2016 was $176.45. His average weekly grocery bill for 2017 was $190.56. Which of the following is the closest to the percent increase in John's average grocery bill from 2016 to 2017?

    A) 7.1%
    B) 7.4%
    C) 8.0%
    D) 8.6%

15. Julie drives an average of 50 miles per hour during her 30-mile commute to work. Today, Julie is in a rush, so she drives 20% faster. How many minutes does it take her to drive to work today?

16. Andrew and Cole both work on a farm picking apples. Andrew picks apples 30% faster than Cole. If Andrew picked 325 apples yesterday, how many apples did Cole pick?

    A) 200
    B) 250
    C) 290
    D) 425

17. Julie spent 2 hours and 20 minutes per day studying for her SAT over the first three weeks of April. During the last week in April, she studied an extra 30% each day. How much time did Julie spend studying during the last week?

    A) 3 hours and 2 minutes
    B) 2 hours and 51 minutes
    C) 20 hours and 2 minutes
    D) 21 hours and 14 minutes

18. Dave is currently making 250 pies per week. His boss wants him to increase the number of pies he is making by 12% each week. In two weeks, approximately how many pies will Dave be making?

    A) 274
    B) 280
    C) 308
    D) 314

19. The quantity b is reduced by 67% of its value which equals c. Which of the following is equivalent to b in terms of c?

    A) $0.67c$
    B) $0.33c$
    C) $\dfrac{c}{0.33}$
    D) $\dfrac{c}{0.67}$

20. At the beginning of the month, there were 5,000 items in stock at a warehouse. The number of items remaining in stock at the warehouse at the end of the month was $p\%$ less than the number at the beginning of the month. Which expression represents the number of items for sale at the end of the month?

    A) $\left(\dfrac{100-p}{100}\right)5{,}000$
    B) $\left(\dfrac{100+p}{100}\right)5{,}000$
    C) $\left(\dfrac{p}{100}\right)5{,}000$
    D) $(100-p)5{,}000$

21. Bob's Woodshop buys 2 tons of wood from The Wood Depot. Each ton of wood costs $2,500. Bob gets a 15% discount for being a frequent customer. After the discount is applied, Bob has to pay a 10% sales tax. How much did Bob pay for the 2 tons of wood?

    A) $2,125
    B) $2,750
    C) $4,250
    D) $4,675

Chapter 9: Percentages

22. In 2021, 275 biology majors make up 2.5% of the undergraduate students at Washington University. In 2022, 450 biology majors make up 3.6% of the undergraduate students at Washington University. Which of the following statements about the undergraduate students at Washington University is correct?

    A) There are 13.6% more students in 2022 than in 2021.
    B) There are 12.0% more students in 2022 than in 2021.
    C) There are 1.1% fewer students in 2022 than in 2021.
    D) There are 12.0% fewer students in 2022 than in 2021.

23. Julie's bakery sold 1,200 cookies in September and 1,403 cookies in October. If the percent increase from September to October was the same as the percent increase from August to September, which of the following is closest to the number of cookies Julie's bakery sold in August?

    A) 997
    B) 1026
    C) 1061
    D) 1613

24. The number c is 140% greater than the number d. The number d is 80% less than 30. What is the value of c?

25. A bakery sold n muffins on Monday. The bakery sold 8% more muffins on Tuesday than on Monday and sold 25% more on Wednesday than on Tuesday, how many muffins were sold on Wednesday in terms of n?

    A) $0.35n$
    B) $1.33n$
    C) $1.35n$
    D) $2.33n$

26. Thomas recently purchased a new computer for college. Thomas had a coupon for a 20% discount from the original price. All items sold from the computer store also include an 8% sales tax added at the register. If Thomas paid a final price of $850.76, which included the discount and sales tax, what was the original price of the computer?

    A) $1,148.52
    B) $1,063.45
    C) $984.68
    D) $898.45

27. The manager of an online newsletter received the report below on the number of subscribers that were signed up for the newsletter. The manager estimated that the percentage decrease from 2019 to 2020 would be double the percentage decrease from 2020 to 2021. How many subscribers did the manager estimate would be signed up for the newsletter in 2021?

Year	Subscribers
2019	560,000
2020	520,800

    A) 447,888
    B) 484,344
    C) 502,572
    D) 505,176

28. John's business made $18,000 in profit in 2015. In 2016, he made 30% more in profit than in 2015. In 2017, he made 6% less in profit than in 2016. Which of the following correctly expresses the profit John's business made in 2017?

    A) $(1.30)(1.06)(18,000)$
    B) $(1.30)(0.94)(18,000)$
    C) $(0.70)(1.06)(18,000)$
    D) $(0.70)(0.94)(18,000)$

- 61 -

29. The product of three numbers is 2160. One of the numbers, z, is 25% greater than the other two numbers, which are the same. What is the value of z?

30. a is 280% greater than b. a is also 24% less than c. What percent of b is equal to c?

31. James has an online newsletter he sends out once a month. In December, James had 3.4 times as many subscribers as he had in June. What was the percent increase in his number of subscribers from June to December?

A) 3.4%
B) 34%
C) 240%
D) 340%

32. A pair of sneakers were originally purchased for p dollars. The first owner sold the sneakers and made a 130% profit. The second owner resold the sneakers and made a 65% profit. Which of the following correctly solves for the final price the sneakers were sold for?

A) $(1.3)(0.65)p$
B) $(1.3)(1.65)p$
C) $(2.3)(0.65)p$
D) $(2.3)(1.65)p$

33. When 50 is increased to 60, the percent increase is the same as when the number n is increased to 12. What is the value of n?

34. 81 is x% greater than 9. What is the value of x?

35. The number y is 60% greater than the number x. The number z is 0.5% less than y. The number z is what percentage of x? (Round your answer to the nearest tenth)

36. A rectangle is changed by decreasing its length by 20% and increasing its width by q percent. If these changes increased the area of the rectangle by 8%, what is the value of q?

37. TicketHub has a service fee for all concert tickets purchased online. The service fee is equal to k% of the final price at checkout. The final price at checkout is the original price of the tickets plus a 1.4% processing fee. If Pam purchased 5 tickets to a concert that all have an original price of m dollars, TicketHub charges Pam a service fee that is equal to $0.01521m$ dollars. What is the value of k?

Chapter 10: Exponents and Roots

Exponents

Let's start by reviewing the common exponent rules that you need to know for the SAT.

Rule Name	Rule	Example
Product Rule	$a^x \times a^y = a^{x+y}$	$3^3 \times 3^4 = 3^7$
Quotient Rule	$\dfrac{a^x}{a^y} = a^{x-y}$	$\dfrac{5^9}{5^4} = 5^5$
Power Rule	$(a^x)^y = a^{xy}$	$(2^4)^3 = 2^{12}$
Fraction Power Rule	$a^{\frac{x}{y}} = \sqrt[y]{a^x}$	$6^{\frac{2}{3}} = \sqrt[3]{6^2}$
Negative Exponent Rule	$a^{-x} = \dfrac{1}{a^x}$	$11^{-4} = \dfrac{1}{11^4}$
One Power Rule	$a^1 = a$	$(-4)^1 = -4$
Zero Power Rule	$a^0 = 1$	$13^0 = 1$

Make sure that you memorize all of these rules for test day. The product, quotient, and power rules are tested most often, but you will also need to know the fraction power rule and negative exponent rule for more difficult questions. To successfully solve exponent questions, you will need to use several of these rules together.

Example 1:
$$\frac{2x^6 y^7}{16x^2 y^{14}}$$

Which of the following equations is equivalent to the one above?

A) $\dfrac{x^3 y^7}{8}$ B) $\dfrac{x^4}{8y^7}$ C) $\dfrac{x^3 y^2}{8}$ D) $\dfrac{y^7}{14x^4}$

Solution: To solve, we use the quotient rule for the exponents. For the numbers, we just follow our normal algebra rules to simplify, so $\dfrac{2}{16}$ simplifies to $\dfrac{1}{8}$.

$$\frac{x^{6-2} y^{7-14}}{8}$$

$$\frac{x^4 y^{-7}}{8}$$

Using the negative exponent rule, we get

$$\frac{x^4}{8y^7}$$

The answer is B. A good trick with negative exponents is that if we switch the term from a numerator to the denominator or vice versa, the negative power turns into a positive power. In the last step of the solution to Example 1, the y^{-7} term in the denominator switches to y^7 when we move the term from the numerator to the denominator.

Example 2:
$$\frac{(-2xy^3)^2}{x}$$

Which of the following equations is equivalent to the equation above?

A) $-2xy^6$ B) $-2x^2y^5$ C) $4xy^6$ D) $4x^2y^5$

Solution: Here, it is easiest to start with the power rule and simplify the numerator. Make sure that you remember to distribute the power to all the terms including the -2 at the front.

$$\frac{4x^2y^6}{x}$$

Now, we use the quotient rule to simplify the x-terms.

$$4xy^6$$

The answer is C.

Example 3: If $4^{3x+1} = 4^{-x+7}$, what is the value of x?

Solution: In this question, the bases are the same, so the exponents must be equal.

$$3x + 1 = -x + 7$$
$$4x = 6$$
$$x = \frac{3}{2}$$

The answer is $\frac{3}{2}$.

Example 4: For what value of x is $9^{2x} = 27^{x+4}$ true?

Solution: To use any of our exponent rules, we need the bases of our exponents to be equal. The trick to this question is to recognize that 9 is the same as 3^2 and 27 is the same as 3^3, so we can make the bases of both terms 3. Plugging in 3^2 for 9 and 3^3 for 27, we get

$$(3^2)^{2x} = (3^3)^{x+4}$$
$$3^{4x} = 3^{3x+12}$$

Since the terms are equal, we can set the exponents equal and solve.

$$4x = 3x + 12$$
$$x = 12$$

The answer is 12.

Example 4 is a more difficult than the first three because the bases of the exponents are different. Anytime you see different bases, look to find a way to substitute as we did in this question to make the bases the same. Once the bases are the same, we can use the exponent rules to solve.

Chapter 10: Exponents and Roots

Exponents Exercise: For questions 1-12, simplify the expressions until you only have positive exponents. For questions 13-20, solve for x. Answers on page 328.

1. $(x^4y)(x^2y^2) =$
2. $(3x^3)(2x^4)\left(\frac{1}{2}x^{-2}\right) =$
3. $(8x^{-3}y^4)(3x^6y^3) =$
4. $(2xy^3)^2 =$
5. $3x^{-2}y^5 =$
6. $\frac{18x^8}{2x^4} =$
7. $9x^{-3}yz^{-2} =$
8. $(x^{-2}y^2)(xy^{-2}) =$
9. $\frac{x^{-3}yz^2}{xyz} =$
10. $(3x^5y^{-2}z)^2 =$
11. $\frac{(4xy^2)^2}{xy} =$
12. $\frac{(5x^4y^{-2})^2}{(2x^{-3}y)^3} =$
13. $12^{-3} \times 12^5 = 144^x$
14. $\frac{7^2 \times 7^x}{49} = 7^8$
15. $\frac{x^7}{x^5} = 25$
16. $7^{-2x+3} = 7^{2-x}$
17. $(2^x)^3 = 2^4 \times 2^{\frac{3}{2}}$
18. $9^{\frac{3}{2}} = 3^{\frac{x}{2}}$
19. $16^{\frac{3}{2}} = 2^x$
20. $\frac{8}{8^{-3}} = 2^{2x-4}$

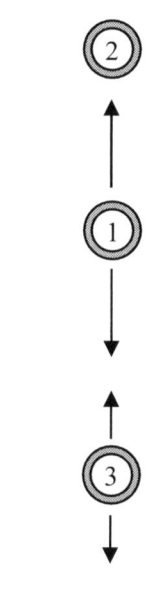

Roots

On the SAT, you need to know how to simplify and solve equations with roots. Let's begin by reviewing the common root rules:

$$\sqrt{xy} = \sqrt{x} \times \sqrt{y} \qquad\qquad \sqrt{18} = \sqrt{9} \times \sqrt{2} = 3\sqrt{2}$$

$$\sqrt{\frac{x}{y}} = \frac{\sqrt{x}}{\sqrt{y}} \qquad\qquad \frac{\sqrt{24}}{\sqrt{6}} = \sqrt{\frac{24}{6}} = \sqrt{4} = 2$$

To simplify a square root, factor the number underneath the radical and take out any pairs of the same number.

$$\sqrt{50} = \sqrt{5 \times 5 \times 2} = 5\sqrt{2}$$

In the example above, there were a pair of 5's underneath the radical, so we can take the 5 out. The 2 is not part of a pair, so it stays underneath the radical. Here's one more example:

$$\sqrt{108} = \sqrt{2 \times 2 \times 3 \times 3 \times 3} = (2 \times 3)\sqrt{3} = 6\sqrt{3}$$

Here, we have a pair of 2's and a pair of 3's, so we take both out and move them to the front. The third 3 is not part of a pair, so it stays underneath the radical.

For some questions, you might need to go backwards and put a number outside back underneath the radical. To do this, take the number outside and put it back under the radical as a pair.

$$6\sqrt{3} = \sqrt{6 \times 6 \times 3} = \sqrt{108}$$

Example 5: If $\sqrt{45} + \sqrt{20} = x\sqrt{5}$, what is the value of x?

Solution: Method #1 – Solve Algebraically: We need to simplify the radicals on the left side of the equation.

$$\sqrt{45} = \sqrt{3 \times 3 \times 5} = 3\sqrt{5}$$

$$\sqrt{20} = \sqrt{2 \times 2 \times 5} = 2\sqrt{5}$$

Plugging these values into the left side of the equation, we get

$$3\sqrt{5} + 2\sqrt{5} = x\sqrt{5}$$
$$5\sqrt{5} = x\sqrt{5}$$
$$x = 5$$

The answer is 5.

Solution: Method #2 - Desmos Hack #1 for Solving Algebra Equations: Write the equations in Desmos as $y = \sqrt{45} + \sqrt{20}$ and $y = x\sqrt{5}$, and look for the point of intersection. The graphs intersect at point $(5, 11.18)$. We are finding the x-value in this question, which is $x = 5$, so **the answer is 5.** To review the Desmos Hack #1, go to p. 14.

Example 6: If $\sqrt{2x} = 5\sqrt{6}$, what is the value of x?

Solution: Method #1 – Solve Algebraically: To solve for x, move the 5 back underneath the radical.

$$\sqrt{2x} = \sqrt{6 \times 5 \times 5}$$
$$\sqrt{2x} = \sqrt{150}$$

For these to be equal, the terms under the radical must be equal, so

$$2x = 150$$
$$x = 75$$

The answer is 75.

Solution: Method #2 – Square Both Sides: We can also solve this question by squaring both sides.

$$(\sqrt{2x})^2 = (5\sqrt{6})^2$$
$$2x = 25 \times 6$$
$$2x = 150$$
$$x = 75$$

The answer is 75.

Solution: Method #3 - Desmos Hack #1 for Solving Algebra Equations: Write the equations in Desmos as $y = \sqrt{2x}$ and $y = 5\sqrt{6}$, and look for the point of intersection. The graphs intersect at point $(75, 12.247)$. We are finding the x-value in this question, which is $x = 75$, so **the answer is 75.** To review the Desmos Hack #1, go to p. 14.

It is important to understand how to solve Examples 5 and 6 algebraically, as the SAT can test you on these concepts with questions that cannot be solved in Desmos. However, if you see questions like Examples 5 and 6 that can be solved in Desmos, you should absolutely use our Desmos Hack!

Chapter 10: Exponents and Roots

Remember, these same rules still apply to roots other than just square roots.

$$\sqrt[3]{xy} = \sqrt[3]{x} \times \sqrt[3]{y}$$

$$\sqrt[5]{\frac{x}{y}} = \frac{\sqrt[5]{x}}{\sqrt[5]{y}}$$

$$\sqrt[3]{16} = \sqrt[3]{8} \times \sqrt[3]{2} = 2\sqrt[3]{2}$$

$$\sqrt[5]{\frac{5}{32}} = \frac{\sqrt[5]{5}}{\sqrt[5]{32}} = \frac{\sqrt[5]{5}}{2}$$

To simplify a cube root, factor underneath the radical and take out triples of the same number.

$$\sqrt[3]{24} = \sqrt[3]{2 \times 2 \times 2 \times 3} = 2\sqrt[3]{3}$$

To simplify a 4th root, factor underneath the radical and take out four of the same number.

$$\sqrt[4]{80} = \sqrt[4]{2 \times 2 \times 2 \times 2 \times 5} = 2\sqrt[4]{5}$$

You are unlikely to see any higher roots on the SAT, but if you do just follow this same pattern to simplify any root.

Example 7: If $a = \sqrt[3]{162}$ and $b = \sqrt[3]{40}$, which of the following is equal to $a + b$?

A) $3\sqrt[3]{18} + 2\sqrt[3]{10}$ B) $2\sqrt[3]{20} + 2\sqrt[3]{5}$ C) $6\sqrt[3]{2} + 5\sqrt[3]{2}$ D) $3\sqrt[3]{6} + 2\sqrt[3]{5}$

Solution: To start, let's simplify to find the value of a.

$$a = \sqrt[3]{162} = \sqrt[3]{3 \times 3 \times 3 \times 6} = 3\sqrt[3]{6}$$

Now, simplify b.

$$b = \sqrt[3]{40} = \sqrt[3]{2 \times 2 \times 2 \times 5} = 2\sqrt[3]{5}$$

We can solve

$$a + b = 3\sqrt[3]{6} + 2\sqrt[3]{5}$$

The answer is D.

Roots and Variables with Powers

When you have exponent questions with roots and variables with powers underneath the root, **it is easiest to convert the root to a power and then use the exponent rules to solve.** For example,

$$\sqrt[3]{x^5 y} = (x^5 y)^{\frac{1}{3}} = (x^5)^{\frac{1}{3}} y^{\frac{1}{3}} = x^{\frac{5}{3}} y^{\frac{1}{3}}$$

This could also be solved using our fraction power rule, but the trick we just used makes complicated roots questions much easier.

Example 8: Which of the following is equivalent to $\sqrt[3]{5x^6 y^{18}}$?

A) $\sqrt[3]{5}\, x^2 y^6$ B) $\sqrt[3]{5} x^3 y^{15}$ C) $\sqrt[3]{5x^3 y^{15}}$ D) $5x^2 y^6$

Solution: The first step is to convert the root to an exponent.

$$(5x^6 y^{18})^{\frac{1}{3}}$$

Next, distribute the exponent to all terms.

$$(5x^6 y^{18})^{\frac{1}{3}} = 5^{\frac{1}{3}} (x^6)^{\frac{1}{3}} (y^{18})^{\frac{1}{3}}$$

Use the exponent rules to solve.

PrepPros

$$5^{\frac{1}{3}}(x^6)^{\frac{1}{3}}(y^{18})^{\frac{1}{3}} = \sqrt[3]{5}\, x^2 y^6$$

The answer is A.

> **Example 9:** If b is a positive integer in the equation below what is the value of b?
>
> $$4^{\frac{3b}{5}} = \sqrt[4]{32^{b-3}}$$

Solution: First, we use the fractional exponent rule to rewrite the right side of the equation. Anytime we see an expression like the one on the right side of the equation above with a root and a power underneath the root, we need to use the fractional exponent rule.

$$4^{\frac{3b}{5}} = 32^{\frac{b-3}{4}}$$

Next, we need to make the bases of the exponent equal. We need to recognize that 4 is the same as 2^2 and 32 is the same as 2^5, so we can make the bases of both terms 2. Plugging in 2^2 for 4 and 2^5 for 32, we get

$$(2^2)^{\frac{3b}{5}} = (2^5)^{\frac{b-3}{4}}$$

Now, we apply our power rules and multiply the exponents.

$$2^{\frac{6b}{5}} = 2^{\frac{5b-15}{4}}$$

Since the bases are equal, we can set the exponents equal and solve.

$$\frac{6b}{5} = \frac{5b-15}{4}$$

Now, we can cross multiply and then solve for b.

$$24b = 5(5b - 15)$$
$$24b = 25b - 75$$
$$-b = -75$$
$$b = 75$$

The answer is 75. Example 9 is a very hard example and one that is meant to challenge the best math students. Many advanced roots and exponents questions on the SAT test similar skills as to the ones in Example 9. If you are aiming for an 800 on the SAT Math, make sure you are very comfortable with the fractional power rule.

Chapter 10: Exponents and Roots

Roots Exercise: For questions 1-12, simplify the radical. For questions 13-20, solve for x. Answers on page 328.

1. $\sqrt{60} =$
2. $\sqrt{150} + \sqrt{24} =$
3. $6\sqrt{5} - \sqrt{80} =$
4. $\sqrt{32} - \sqrt{18} + \sqrt{72} =$
5. $\sqrt[3]{48} + \sqrt[3]{162} =$
6. $\frac{\sqrt{45}}{\sqrt{15}} =$
7. $\frac{5\sqrt{12}}{10\sqrt{3}} =$
8. $\sqrt{8ab^4} =$
9. $\sqrt{16x^2y} =$
10. $\sqrt[4]{a^{12}b^2} =$
11. $\sqrt[3]{24x^6y^4} =$
12. $\sqrt{16x^{10}} =$
13. $\sqrt{3x-2} = \sqrt{18}$
14. $\sqrt{15} = \frac{\sqrt{x}}{\sqrt{3}}$
15. $\sqrt{18} \times \sqrt{3} = x\sqrt{6}$
16. $\sqrt{x} - \sqrt{40} = \sqrt{10}$
17. $\sqrt{3x} + \sqrt{8} = \sqrt{50}$
18. $(3\sqrt{5})^2 = 2x$
19. $\sqrt{6x} = 2\sqrt{6}$
20. $\sqrt[3]{54} + \sqrt[3]{16} = x\sqrt[3]{2}$

Exponents and Roots Practice: Answers on page 328.

1. Which of the following is equivalent to $(2x^4)(9x^9)$?

   A) $11x^{14}$
   B) $11x^{36}$
   C) $18x^{13}$
   D) $18x^{36}$

2. Which of the following expressions is equivalent to $(a^3b^4c^2)(a^5b^3c^6)$ for all real values of $a, b,$ and c?

   A) $a^{15}b^{12}c^8$
   B) $a^9b^7c^{10}$
   C) $a^8b^{12}c^{12}$
   D) $a^8b^7c^8$

3. Which of the following is equal to $x^{\frac{3}{4}}$, for all values of x?

   A) $\sqrt{x^{\frac{1}{4}}}$
   B) $\sqrt[3]{x^4}$
   C) $\sqrt[4]{x^3}$
   D) $\sqrt{x^3}$

4. For all nonzero values of x and y, which of the following expressions is equivalent to $-\frac{24x^3y^6}{6x^2y}$?

   A) $-18xy^5$
   B) $-4x^5y^7$
   C) $-4x^3y^6$
   D) $-4xy^5$

5. If $x > 0$, which of the following is equivalent to the given expression below?

   $$\sqrt{16x^2}$$

   A) $4x$
   B) $4x^2$
   C) $36x$
   D) $36x^4$

6. For all nonzero numbers $a, b,$ and c, the expression $\frac{3a^7b^2c^5}{6a^2b^5c}$ is equivalent to:

   A) $\frac{a^5c^5}{2b^3}$
   B) $\frac{a^5c^4}{2b^3}$
   C) $\frac{a^5bc^5}{2b^3c^2}$
   D) $\frac{(3abc)^{14}}{(6abc)^6}$

PrepPros

7. In the equation below, what is the value of z?

$$(x^{\frac{1}{3}})^6 (x^{\frac{4}{3}})^5 = x^z$$

8. Which of the following expressions is equivalent to $\sqrt[y]{x^z}$?

A) $x^{\frac{z}{y}}$
B) $x^{\frac{y}{z}}$
C) x^{y+z}
D) x^{z-y}

9. What value of x makes the equation below true?

$$\frac{16^x}{4^3} = 4^7$$

A) 3
B) 5
C) 10
D) 16

10. Given m and n such that $x^{2m-10} = x^6$ and $(x^n)^3 = x^{15}$, what is the value of $x^m x^n$?

A) x^{11}
B) x^{13}
C) x^{21}
D) x^{40}

11. For what value is $4^{x+4} = 2^{3x}$ true?

A) 4
B) 8
C) 12
D) 16

12. For all positive real numbers x, which of the following expressions is equivalent to $\dfrac{\left(\frac{x^{17}}{x^6}\right)}{\left(\frac{1}{x^4}\right)}$?

A) x^7
B) x^{11}
C) x^{15}
D) x^{19}

13. For $x \neq 0$, what is the value of $\dfrac{(4x^4)^2}{(2x^2)^4}$?

14. Which of the following is an equivalent form of $\sqrt[4]{g^8 m^2}$?

A) $\sqrt{g}\, m^{-2}$
B) $g^2 \sqrt{m}$
C) $g^{\frac{1}{2}} m^{\frac{1}{2}}$
D) $g^{-\frac{1}{2}} m^{-2}$

15. The expression $\dfrac{x^{-3} y^{\frac{1}{3}}}{x^2 y^{-2}}$, where $x > 1$ and $y > 1$, is equivalent to which of the following?

A) $\dfrac{y^{\frac{2}{3}}}{x^5}$

B) $\dfrac{y^{\frac{7}{3}}}{x^5}$

C) $\dfrac{y^{\frac{7}{3}}}{x^{-5}}$

D) $\dfrac{\sqrt[3]{y}}{x^5}$

16. Which expression is equivalent to $\sqrt[7]{x^5} \cdot \sqrt[7]{x}$, where $x > 0$?

A) $x^{\frac{6}{7}}$
B) $x^{\frac{7}{6}}$
C) $x^{\frac{5}{35}}$
D) x^7

17. Which of the following is equivalent to $\sqrt[3]{8a^{27}}$?

A) $\frac{8}{3} a^3$
B) $\frac{8}{3} a^9$
C) $2a^3$
D) $2a^9$

- 70 -

Chapter 10: Exponents and Roots

18. If $x > 0$ and $\sqrt{x\sqrt{x}} = x^b$, what is the value of b?

19. Which of the following is an equivalent form of $\sqrt[2]{16a^2b^6c}$?

   A) $16ab^4\sqrt{c}$
   B) $16ab^3\sqrt{c}$
   C) $4ab^4\sqrt{c}$
   D) $4ab^3\sqrt{c}$

20. If a and b are positive real numbers, which of the following is equivalent to $\dfrac{(4a^{-3}b^2)^3}{16ab^{-4}}$?

   A) $\dfrac{b}{4a^{10}}$
   B) $\dfrac{b^9}{4a^{10}}$
   C) $\dfrac{4b^9}{a}$
   D) $\dfrac{4b^{10}}{a^{10}}$

21. For a positive real number x, where $x^4 = 4$, what is the value of x^8?

   A) 2
   B) 8
   C) 16
   D) 64

22. If x and y are positive rational numbers such that $x^{5y} = 10$, what does x^{10y} equal?

   A) 20
   B) 50
   C) 80
   D) 100

23. Which expression is equivalent to $\sqrt[3]{x^4} \cdot \sqrt[4]{x^5}$, where $x > 0$?

   A) $x^{\frac{31}{12}}$
   B) $x^{\frac{12}{31}}$
   C) $x^{\frac{20}{12}}$
   D) $x^{\frac{31}{20}}$

24. For a positive real number y, where $y^{20} = 16$, what is the value of y^5?

   A) 2
   B) $2\sqrt{4}$
   C) 4
   D) $4\sqrt{2}$

25. For all positive values of x, $(\sqrt[3]{x^5})(\sqrt[4]{x^{-3}})$ is equal to:

   A) $x^{\frac{1}{2}}$
   B) $x^{\frac{11}{12}}$
   C) x^2
   D) $x^{\frac{8}{3}}$

26. Which of the following expressions is equivalent to $(27x^3)^{\frac{1}{3}}$?

   A) $3x$
   B) $9x$
   C) $27x$
   D) $\sqrt[3]{27x}$

27. An exponential function g is defined by $g(x) = c^x$, where c is a constant greater than one. If $g(5) = 9g(4)$, what is the value of c?

28. If $27^{a-1} = 3$ and $4^{a+b} = 64$, then $b = $?

   A) $\dfrac{1}{2}$
   B) $\dfrac{5}{3}$
   C) $\dfrac{8}{3}$
   D) 3

29. If a and b are positive numbers in the equation below, what is the value of $\dfrac{a}{b}$?

$$\left(\sqrt{27}\right)^a = 9^{\frac{b}{3}}$$

PrepPros

30. The equation below has the solution $x = a$, where a is positive integer. What is the value of a?

$$\sqrt[3]{\frac{10x}{5}} = \frac{1}{2}x$$

31. Which of the following is equivalent to $\sqrt[3]{x^2 + 6x + 9}$?

A) $(x+3)^3$
B) $(x+3)^2$
C) $(x+3)^{\frac{2}{3}}$
D) $(x+3)$

32. An exponential function is defined by $f(x) = a^x$, where a is a constant greater than 1. If $f(9) = 25f(7)$, what is the value of a?

33. Which of the following is an equivalent form of $\sqrt[3]{24x^4y^2z^3}$?

A) $2xz\sqrt{3xy^2}$
B) $8xz\sqrt[3]{3xy^2}$
C) $2xz\sqrt[3]{3xy^2}$
D) $8xz\sqrt{xy^2}$

34. If $3x + 4y = 16$, what is the value of $(8^x)(16^y)$?

A) $\frac{1}{2}$
B) $(\frac{1}{2})^2$
C) 2^8
D) 2^{16}

35. If p and q are positive integers such that $(\sqrt[3]{4})^p = 16^{3q}$, what is the value of $\frac{q}{p}$?

36. If $\frac{x^2\sqrt{x^3}}{\sqrt[5]{x^2}} = x^{\frac{a}{b}}$ for all positive values of x, what is the value of $\frac{a}{b}$?

37. If $2x - 3y = 7$, what is the value of $\frac{9^x}{27^y}$?

A) $\frac{1}{3}$
B) 3^7
C) 9^7
D) Cannot be determined.

38. Which of the following is expressions is equivalent to $(-4x^6)^{\frac{2}{3}}$?

A) $-2x^6 \cdot \sqrt[3]{2}$
B) $-x^6 \cdot \sqrt[3]{16}$
C) $2x^4 \cdot \sqrt[3]{2}$
D) $2x^4 \cdot \sqrt[3]{16}$

39. Two numbers a and b, are each greater than zero, and the square root of a is equal to the cube root of b. For what value of x is a^{3x-4} equal to b?

40. The expression $5\sqrt[4]{4^4 x^{16}} \cdot \sqrt[6]{3^6 x^2}$ is equivalent to ax^b, where a and b are positive constants and $x > 1$. What is the value of $a + b$?

- 72 -

Chapter 10: Exponents and Roots

41. In the equations below, a and b are constants, $a > 1$, and $b > 1$. What is the value of x?

$$\sqrt[3]{a^5} = \sqrt[2]{b^3}$$
$$a^{4x} = b^2$$

42. If a is a positive integer, which of the following is the equivalent to the expression below?

$$2^{\frac{3}{a}} \cdot \sqrt[a]{3}$$

A) $3^{\frac{1}{a}}$
B) $6^{\frac{1}{a}}$
C) $\sqrt[a]{6}$
D) $\sqrt[a]{24}$

43. For all positive values of a and b, $a^{\frac{1}{5}}b^{\frac{3}{2}}$ can be written in which of the following radical forms?

A) $\sqrt[10]{ab^3}$
B) $\sqrt[10]{a^2b^3}$
C) $\sqrt[10]{a^3b^6}$
D) $b\sqrt[10]{a^2b^5}$

44. Two numbers r and s are each greater than zero, and the cube root of r is equal to the fourth root of s. For what value of x is r^{2x-4} equal to s?

45. If $3x + 2y - 1 = 4$, what is the value of the expression below?

$$\frac{27^x \cdot 9^y}{3}$$

46. For all positive values of x and y, $\sqrt{\frac{4x}{y}} - \sqrt{\frac{y}{x}}$ is equivalent to which of the following?

A) $\frac{2\sqrt{xy}}{x-y}$
B) $\frac{4\sqrt{xy}}{y-x}$
C) $\frac{4x-y}{y-x}$
D) $\frac{2x-y}{\sqrt{xy}}$

47. Which of the following expressions is equivalent to $\left(3\sqrt{x} - 2\sqrt{y}\right)^{\frac{2}{5}}$, where $x > y$ and $y > 0$?

A) $(9x - 4y)^5$
B) $(9x - 4y)^{\frac{1}{5}}$
C) $(9x - 12xy + 4y)^{\frac{1}{5}}$
D) $(9x - 12\sqrt{xy} + 4y)^{\frac{1}{5}}$

48. If a and b are positive numbers in the equation below, what is the value of $\frac{a}{b}$?

$$(\sqrt[3]{8})^{2a} = 2^{\frac{2b}{5}}$$

49. Two numbers a and b are each greater than 0 and 9 times the cube root of a is equal to 25 times the square root of b. If $a = \frac{3}{5}$, for what value of x is $a^x = b$.

PrepPros

Chapter 11: Quadratics

Quadratics are mathematical expressions containing a term to the second degree with a standard form of

$$y = ax^2 + bx + c$$

For quadratics on the SAT, you need to be able to multiply binomials (FOIL), factor, interpret quadratics on a graph, use the quadratic equation, find the vertex, and solve complex word problems.

① Multiplying Binomials

In order to multiply binomials, you will need to FOIL, which stands for First, Outer, Inner, Last. You are likely familiar with how to multiply binomials by now, but for a quick review, here is an example of how to FOIL:

To multiply $(2x + 3)(x + 6)$ ...

First terms: $(2x)(x) = 2x^2$

Outer terms: $(2x)(6) = 12x$

Inner terms: $(3)(x) = 3x$

Last terms: $(3)(6) = 18$

so we get: $(2x + 3)(x + 6) = 2x^2 + 12x + 3x + 18 = \mathbf{2x^2 + 15x + 18}$

Multiplying Perfect Squares – Don't Forget to FOIL

When multiplying perfect squares, make sure to avoid the common mistake of forgetting to FOIL.

$$(x + 5)^2 \neq x^2 + 25$$

To help avoid this mistake, you can write the perfect square as two terms and then FOIL.

$$(x + 5)^2 = (x + 5)(x + 5) = x^2 + 5x + 5x + 25$$

Combine like terms to get

$$(x + 5)^2 = x^2 + 10x + 25$$

Example 1: Which of the following is equivalent to $(2x + 3)^2 + 4x$?

A) $4x^2 + 16x + 9$ B) $4x^2 + 4x + 9$ C) $2x^2 + 4x + 3$ D) $6x^2 + 9$

Solution: To solve, multiply out the squared term and then combine like terms.

$$(2x + 3)^2 + 4x$$
$$(2x + 3)(2x + 3) + 4x$$
$$4x^2 + 12x + 9 + 4x$$
$$4x^2 + 16x + 9$$

The answer is A.

Shortcut Method – Use Equivalent Question Shortcut: Since this is an "equivalent" question, we can also use the Equivalent Trick (plug in $x = 1$) or Desmos Equivalent Hack we learned earlier in Chapter 3. To review this method, go to pp. 9-10.

Factoring Quadratics

You also need to know how to factor quadratics. Factoring can help you simplify expressions or identify the solution(s) to a quadratic equation.

The "Box" Method

We can use the "box" method to find the factors for a quadratic equation. The factors appear on the outside of the box and the quadratic appears in the box.

To see how this works, let's factor the quadratic below:
$$x^2 - x - 12 = 0$$

1. Place the x^2 term in the top left of the box. Place the number in the bottom right.

2. Write down the two terms that must multiply to the top left term outside the box. In this example, x and x multiply to x^2.

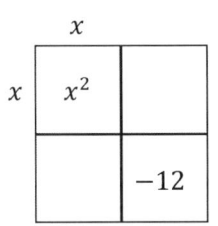

3. Identify which number(s) can multiply to the number in the bottom right of the box. In this example, we need a pair of numbers that multiply to -12.

4. Place a pair of numbers that multiply to the bottom right value (-12 in this example) outside the box. You have the correct setup when the two other boxes (the x-terms) add up to the middle term in the quadratic. In this example, $3x + (-4x) = -x$, so we know the numbers are set up correctly. The factors appear on the outside of the box.

5. Write down the quadratic in factored form. $x^2 - x - 12 = (x+3)(x-4)$

There are other ways to factor quadratics algebraically. If you know a different method that works for you, use that method. We will not review factoring beyond this example in this book. If you need to review factoring, look up some lessons and practice problems online and in your textbooks.

"Easy to Factor" Quadratics

Keep an eye out for perfect squares and difference of squares on the SAT. These are very common in quadratics questions, and they can be factored quickly and easily as long as you spot the pattern. The table below shows the three common "easy to factor" quadratics you should know.

Equation	Formula	Example
Perfect Square (Addition)	$(x+y)^2 = x^2 + 2xy + y^2$	$(x+2)^2 = x^2 + 4x + 4$
Perfect Square (Subtraction)	$(x-y)^2 = x^2 - 2xy + y^2$	$(x-3)^2 = x^2 - 6x + 9$
Difference of Squares	$(x+y)(x-y) = x^2 - y^2$	$(x+6)(x-6) = x^2 - 36$

Example 2: If $x \neq 3$, which of the following expressions is equal to $\frac{x^2-7x+12}{x-3} + 3x + 1$?

A) $\frac{x^2-4x-11}{x-3}$ B) $x^2 + 3x + 9$ C) $x - 4$ D) $4x - 3$

Solution: To simplify, we need to factor the numerator of the fraction and see if any expressions cancel.

$$\frac{x^2-7x+12}{x-3} + 3x + 1 = \frac{(x-3)(x-4)}{x-3} + 3x + 1$$

Since there is an $x - 3$ in the numerator and the denominator, we can cancel these and then combine like terms.

$$\frac{\cancel{(x-3)}(x-4)}{\cancel{x-3}} + 3x + 1 = x - 4 + 3x + 1 = 4x - 3$$

The answer is D.

Shortcut Method – Use Equivalent Question Shortcut: Since this is an "equivalent" question, we can also use the Equivalent Trick (plug in $x = 1$) or Desmos Equivalent Hack we learned earlier in Chapter 3. To review this method, go to pp. 9-10.

Solutions, Roots, x-intercepts, and Zeros for Quadratic Equations

The SAT may ask you to find the "solutions," "roots," "x-intercepts," or "zeros" of a quadratic equation. All of these terms refer to the values of x that make $f(x) = 0$. Remember, all these terms mean the same thing. We will refer to these terms collectively as the "solutions" in the rest of this chapter.

Method #1 – Factor and Solve

Our first method is what you have likely learned at school. If we are asked to find the solution(s) to a quadratic equation, we follow these steps:

1. **Set the quadratic equal to zero.** For example, if you are given $x^2 - x - 8 = 4$, we must subtract 4 from both sides to get $x^2 - x - 12 = 0$.

2. **Factor the quadratic.** You can use the box method we just learned or any other method you are comfortable with. For the quadratic $x^2 - x - 12 = 0$, we just showed how we can factor to get $(x + 3)(x - 4) = 0$.

3. **Set each factor equal to 0 and solve for x.** The factors are $(x + 3)$ and $(x - 4)$. To find the solutions, we set each factor to 0 and solve for x.

$$x + 3 = 0 \qquad \qquad x - 4 = 0$$
$$x = -3 \quad \text{and} \quad x = 4$$

4. **Write down the solutions.** For our example, the solutions are $x = -3$ and $x = 4$. The solutions are also the x-intercepts if the quadratic is graphed (more on this below).

Method #2 – Desmos Hack for Solving Quadratics Without Factoring

We can also find the solutions to quadratics by graphing the function in Desmos. If you are given a quadratic that is set equal to 0, such as $x^2 - x - 12 = 0$, you probably think, "oh no, I need to factor that." But do not fear; there is an easier way! **We can solve for the solution(s) to any quadratic by graphing the function in Desmos and finding the x-intercept(s).** We learned this method in Chapter 4 on p. 16.

Chapter 11: Quadratics

To graph a quadratic in Desmos, we type it in as $y =$ and then type in the quadratic equation. So for our example, we type in $y = x^2 - x - 12 = 0$.

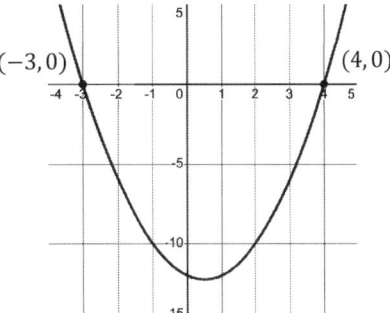

The x-intercepts are at $(-3, 0)$ and $(4, 0)$. When a quadratic is equal to zero, as in this example, the solutions are the x-coordinate of the x-intercepts. So here, the solutions are $x = -3$ and $x = 4$.

If you use the Desmos Hack, it is important to understand the relationship between solutions and factors. To go from a solution to a factor, we just switch the sign. For the solution $x = -3$, the factor is $(x + 3)$. For the solution $x = 4$, the factor is $(x - 4)$. Understanding this principle is not necessary for this example, but it is a commonly tested concept and one your need to know.

Solving quadratics with Desmos is much easier than factoring, so **we recommend that you ALWAYS use this Desmos Hack when you can.** That being said, **you still need to know how to factor quadratics**, as the SAT can test that skill in a variety of other ways.

Example 3: What is the sum of the solutions of the polynomial $f(x) = x^2 - 11x + 18$?

Solution: Method #1 – Factor and Solve: To solve, we need to find the values of x that make $f(x) = 0$.

$$x^2 - 11x + 18 = 0$$
$$(x - 2)(x - 9) = 0$$
$$x = 2, 9$$

The solutions are 2 and 9. The sum of the solutions is $2 + 9 = 11$. **The answer is 11.**

Solution: Method #2 – Desmos Hack for Solving Quadratics Without Factoring: We can graph the function in Desmos by typing in $y = x^2 - 11x + 18$. The x-intercepts are at $(2, 0)$ and $(9, 0)$, so the solutions are $x = 2$ and $x = 9$. The sum of the solutions is $2 + 9 = 11$. **The answer is 11.**

Solution: Method #3 – Sum of Solutions Shortcut: To find the sum of solutions, we can use the rule below:

For any quadratic equation in the form of $ax^2 + bx + c = 0$, the sum of the solutions to the quadratic is always equal to $-\frac{b}{a}$.

For the equation in Example 3, $a = 1$ and $b = -11$, so

$$-\frac{b}{a} = -\frac{-11}{1} = 11$$

The answer is 11. Make sure to memorize this rule, as it is very useful for any questions that asks for the sum of solutions to a quadratic equation.

*****Additional Rule to Memorize:** For any quadratic equation in the form of $ax^2 + bx + c = 0$, the product of the solutions to the quadratic is always equal to $\frac{c}{a}$. This rule is rarely tested but one you should memorize if you are aiming for top scores.

PrepPros

> **Example 4:** If (x, y) is a solution to the system of equations below, what is a possible value of y given that $x > 0$?
>
> $$y = 2x - 3$$
> $$y = x^2 + 12x - 27$$
>
> A) 1   B) 2   C) 8   D) 12

Solution: Method #1 – "Math Teacher Way": This system of equations question involves quadratics. We will more thoroughly cover how to solve systems of equations in Chapter 12. When solving a system of equations, the solution(s) are the intersection point(s) of the two functions. Here, we are given the equations

$$y = 2x - 3$$
$$y = x^2 + 12x - 27$$

To solve this system of equations algebraically, we set the equations equal to each other and solve for x.

$$x^2 + 12x - 27 = 2x - 3$$

$$x^2 + 10x - 24 = 0$$

$$(x - 2)(x + 12) = 0$$

$$x = 2, -12$$

Since the question specifies that $x > 0$, we must use $x = 2$. To find the y, plug in $x = 2$ to either of the original equations. Here, we will use the easier first equation.

$$y = 2(2) - 3$$

$$y = 1$$

Therefore, a point of intersection is at $(2, 1)$. **The answer is A**.

Solution: Method #2 – Desmos Hack for Solving Systems of Equations: If the first method seemed challenging, we have good news for you – there is a much easier way to solve Example 4! In Chapter 4, we learned how to use Desmos to solve a system of equations. For any system of equations, the point(s) of intersection show the solution(s) to the system of equations. To review this method, go to p. 15.

If we graph the system of equations, we find the points of intersection at $(-12, -27)$ and $(2, 1)$. The question specifies that $x > 0$, so we must use the point $(2, 1)$. We are asked to solve for y, so we want the y-coordiante at this point of intersection, which is $y = 1$. **The answer is A**.

For any questions like Example 4 that you can graph, you should ALWAYS solve using this Desmos Hack. This method is both easier and faster than solving algebraically.

> **Example 5:** Tom's math teacher is offering to buy Tom's sandwich. The teacher writes the equation $x^2 - 11x + 14 = 26$ on the board and says he will pay Tom t dollars for the sandwich, where t is equal to the positive solution to the equation on the board. What is the value of t?

Solution: Method #1: Factor and Solve

$$x^2 - 11x + 14 = 26$$

$$x^2 - 11x - 12 = 0$$

$$(x - 12)(x + 1) = 0$$

$$x = 12, -1$$

The question tells us that t is positive, so **the answer is 12.** Notice how we had to subtract the 26 before factoring. **You cannot factor a quadratic until the equation is set equal to 0.** This is a very common mistake that students make, so make sure you remember this critical step.

Solution: Method #2 – Desmos Hack for Solving Quadratics Without Factoring: We can graph the function in Desmos by typing in $y = x^2 - 11x - 12$. The x-intercepts are at $(-1, 0)$ and $(12, 0)$, so the solutions are $x = -1$ and $x = 12$. t is positive, so **the answer is 12.**

How Solutions Appear on a Graph

Solutions appear as the x-intercepts when graphed in the xy-plane. When we have a quadratic or other polynomial in factored form, we can see where the x-intercepts are. We will review the rules for multiplicity (the power to which a factor is raised) and zeros for polynomial functions below:

$y = (x + 2)(x - 4)$	$y = (x - 1)^2$	$y = (x + 3)^3$
$(-2, 0)$ $(4, 0)$	$(1, 0)$	$(-3, 0)$
Multiplicity = 1	Multiplicity = 2	Multiplicity = 3
Zeros: The function has 2 solutions at $x = -2$ and $x = 4$.	Zeros: The function has 1 solution at $x = 1$.	Zeros: The function has 1 solution at $x = -3$.
Behavior: The function passes straight through the x-axis at the solution.	Behavior: The function bounces at the solution and does not cross the x-axis.	Behavior: The function flattens and passes through the x-axis at the solution.

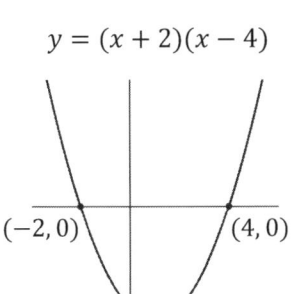

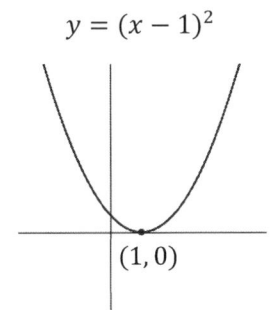

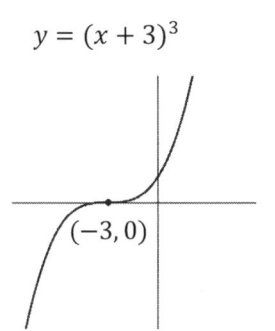

TIP – Functions with No Real Solution

If a function never crosses the x-axis, the function has no real solution. In other words, the function has no x-intercept.

As an example, the function $f(x)$ to the right has no real solution. This function cannot be factored to solve for x. If you use the quadratic formula to solve, the solutions are imaginary numbers.

$f(x) = x^2 - 2x + 2$

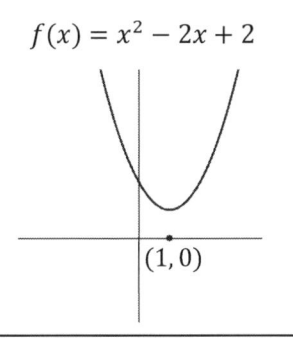

$(1, 0)$

Example 6: Which of the following equations correctly describes the function in the graph below?

A) $y = (x+2)^2(x-1)^2(x-3)$
B) $y = (x+2)(x-1)(x-3)$
C) $y = (x-2)^2(x+1)(x+3)$
D) $y = (x+2)(x-1)^2(x-3)^2$

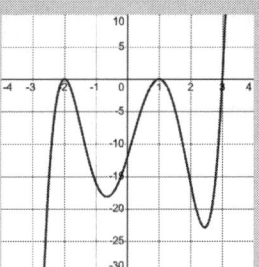

Solution: To solve this question, we need to look at the behavior of the function at each of the x-intercepts. There are x-intercepts at $x = -2$, $x = 1$, and $x = 3$, so we need to see the factors $(x+2)$, $(x-1)$, and $(x-3)$ in the correct answer. Now, we need to find out what power each term should be raised to. At $x = -2$ and $x = 1$, the function bounces, so the $(x+2)$ and $(x-1)$ terms are squared. At $x = 3$, the function goes straight through, so the $(x-3)$ should be to the first power. **The answer is A.**

Shortcut Solution – Graph in Desmos: We can graph the answer choices and see which one matches the graph! Sure, it may take some time, but you will be able to guarantee that you get the correct answer.

The Quadratic Formula

If a quadratic is not easily factorable, you will need to use the quadratic formula to solve for the roots of a quadratic function. You will need to have the quadratic formula memorized.

For $ax^2 + bx + c = 0$, the solution(s) are given by: $x = \dfrac{-b \pm \sqrt{b^2 - 4ac}}{2a}$

Example 7: One solution to the equation $x^2 - 8x + 4 = 0$ can be written as $4 - 2\sqrt{k}$. What is the value of k?

A) 3   B) 8   C) 12   D) 24

Solution: Since this quadratic cannot be factored, we must use the quadratic formula.

$x = \dfrac{-(-8) \pm \sqrt{(-8)^2 - 4(1)(4)}}{2(1)}$ 1. Plug in the values for a, b, and c.

$x = \dfrac{8 \pm \sqrt{64 - 16}}{2}$ 2. Begin to simplify terms.

$x = \dfrac{8 \pm \sqrt{48}}{2}$ 3. Combine terms under the radical.

$x = \dfrac{8 \pm 4\sqrt{3}}{2}$ 4. Simplify radical (if possible).

$x = 4 \pm 2\sqrt{3}$ 5. Simplify terms further (if possible).

$x = 4 + 2\sqrt{3}$ and $x = 4 - 2\sqrt{3}$ 6. Identify the value(s) of x.

The solutions are $x = 4 + 2\sqrt{3}$ and $x = 4 - 2\sqrt{3}$. The question says one of the solutions can be written as $4 - 2\sqrt{k}$. Since one of our solutions is $4 - 2\sqrt{3}$, we can see that $k = 3$. **The answer is A.**

Chapter 11: Quadratics

> **Example 8:** The equations below intersect at the point (x, y). Which of the following is a value of x?
>
> $$y = x^2 + 3x + 15$$
> $$y = -3x + 11$$
>
> A) 2   B) $6 + \sqrt{5}$ C) $-3 + \sqrt{13}$ D) $-3 - \sqrt{5}$

Solution: Method #1 – "Math Teacher Way": This is another system of equations question like the one we solved in Example 4. The solutions to the system of equations are where the functions intersect. To solve this system of equations, we set the equations equal to each other and solve for x.

$$x^2 + 3x + 15 = -3x + 11$$
$$x^2 + 6x + 4 = 0$$

At this point, we cannot easily factor, so we need to use the quadratic formula.

$$x = \frac{-6 \pm \sqrt{6^2 - 4(1)(4)}}{2(1)}$$

$$x = \frac{-6 \pm \sqrt{20}}{2}$$

$$x = \frac{-6 \pm 2\sqrt{5}}{2}$$

$$x = -3 \pm \sqrt{5}$$

The x-values at the points of intersection for the system are at $x = -3 + \sqrt{5}$ and $x = -3 - \sqrt{5}$. **The answer is D.**

Solution: Method #2 – Desmos Hack for Solving Systems of Equations: If we graph the system of equations, we find the points of intersection at $(-5.236, 26.708)$ and $(-0.764, 13.292)$. We are solving for x, so the solutions are at $x = -5.236$ and $x = -0.764$. The answer choices are not in decimal form, so we have a bit more work to do.

To see which answer choices matches one of the solutions we found, we need to type in the answer to our calculator to turn them into decimal form. A and B are clearly incorrect since both of those are positive values. So, we can type in answer choices C and D into the calculator.

$$\text{C) } -3 + \sqrt{13} = 0.6055 \qquad \text{(C is incorrect)}$$
$$\text{D) } -3 - \sqrt{5} = -5.236 \qquad \text{(D is correct)}$$

We see that $-3 - \sqrt{5}$ matches the intersection point at $(-5.236, 26.708)$ we found on the graph, so **the answer is D.** This method does involve a bit more work when the answer choices are not pretty, but you are guaranteed to get the questions correct. So, we recommend that you use this method whenever you can.

- 81 -

The Discriminant

In the quadratic formula, the discriminant is the $b^2 - 4ac$ term under the radical. This term is very important because it can quickly tell us how many real or complex solutions there will be for any quadratic equation. **The exact value of the discriminant is not important, but whether it is positive, negative, or zero is.**

Discriminant Value	Types of Solutions
$b^2 - 4ac > 0$	2 real solutions
$b^2 - 4ac = 0$	1 real solution
$b^2 - 4ac < 0$	0 real solutions, 2 complex solutions

Memorize these rules. **If you ever see a question about the number of solutions to a system of equations, use the discriminant to solve.**

Example 9: How many real solutions are there to the function $h(x) = 2x^2 - 7x + 9$?

A) 0   B) 1   C) 2   D) 3

Solution:
$$\text{Discriminant} = b^2 - 4ac = (-7)^2 - 4(2)(9)$$
$$\text{Discriminant} = -23$$

The discriminant is negative, so there are no real solutions. **The answer is A.**

Example 10: In the system of equations below, m is a constant. For which of the following values of m does the system of equations have exactly 1 real solution?

$$y = x^2 - 8x + 10$$
$$y = m - 2x$$

A) -1 B) 0   C) 1   D) 2

Solution: To start, we set the equations equal.
$$x^2 - 8x + 10 = m - 2x$$
$$x^2 - 6x + (10 - m) = 0$$

If the system of equations has one real solution, the equation above must have one real solution and the discriminant must be equal to 0.

$$\text{Discriminant} = b^2 - 4ac = (-6)^2 - 4(1)(10 - m) = 0$$

At this point, you can either test each of the answer choices to see which one makes the discriminant equal 0 or solve algebraically for m. The steps below show how to solve algebraically.

$$36 - 4(10 - m) = 0$$
$$36 - 40 + 4m = 0$$
$$-4 + 4m = 0$$
$$4m = 4$$
$$m = 1$$

The answer is C.

The Vertex

The vertex is the highest or lowest point of a parabola. For the parabola shown below, the vertex is at $(1, -4)$. You should memorize the vertex form equation shown below.

$$y = (x - 1)^2 - 4$$

Vertex Form: $y = a(x - h)^2 + k$

- vertex at (h, k)
- when $a > 0$, parabola opens up
- when $a < 0$, parabola opens down

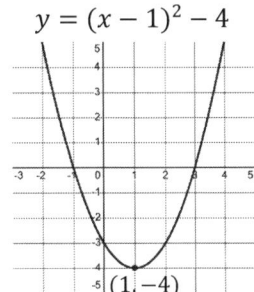

When a quadratic is written in vertex form, we can tell what the vertex is without graphing. As you can see in the example above, we can tell the vertex is at $(1, -4)$. We can think of the vertex as the midpoint of a parabola because the x-coordinate of the vertex is always the midpoint of the two solutions, or x-intercepts. The x-coordinate of the vertex is equal to the average of the solutions. Using the parabola above as an example, we can see how this works. Since the solutions to the parabola are located at $x = -1$ and $x = 3$, the x-coordinate of the vertex is at $x = \frac{-1+3}{2} = 1$, which matches the graph.

Remember, the vertex is always the maximum or minimum value of a quadratic. For the example above, the minimum is at $y = -4$.

Example 11: The graph of the equation $y = 2(x + p)^2 + 3q$ in the xy-plane is a parabola, where p and q are constants. What is the vertex of this parabola?

A) (p, q) B) $(-p, q)$ C) $(-p, 3q)$ D) $(-2p, -3q)$

Solution: Let's start with the x-coordinate of the vertex. In the vertex form shown above, the x-coordinate is the h-value in the $(x - h)^2$ term. In the equation in Example 11, we have $(x + p)^2$, which tells us that the x-coordiante of the vertex is at $-p$. If the x-coordinate was at $+p$, vertex form would be $(x - p)^2$. The x-coordinate of the vertex is always the opposite sign of the h-value we see in vertex form.

The y-coordinate of the vertex is shown by the k-value. In the equation in Example 11, we have $+3k$, which tells us that the y-coordinate is at $3k$. For the y-coordinate, the value in the equation directly shows the value, so we do not need to do the same sign switch that we did for the x-coordinate.

The vertex is at $(-p, 3q)$, so **the answer is C.**

Example 12: $f(x) = (x - a)(x - b)$ has a minimum value at point (c, d). Which of the following correctly expresses c in terms of a and b?

A) $\frac{ab}{2}$ B) $\frac{a+b}{2}$ C) $\frac{a-b}{2}$ D) $\frac{ab}{a+b}$

Solution: The minimum value of a parabola is at the vertex, so point (c, d) is at the vertex. Since the function is already in factored form, we see the solutions are at $x = a$ and $x = b$. We are asked to find c, which is the x-coordinate of the vertex. The x-coordinate of the vertex is the average of the roots, so

$$c = \frac{a + b}{2}$$

The answer is B.

The average method works perfectly if you are given a quadratic that is already factored. But what if you are not given a quadratic in factored form? Good news! There is a second way to quickly find the vertex.

For any quadratic in the form of $y = ax^2 + bx + c$, you can find the x-coordinate of the vertex using

$$x = -\frac{b}{2a}$$

Make sure you memorize this equation! It can really help you quickly and easily solve any questions where you need to find the vertex of a parabola.

Example 13: The graph of the equation $y - 4n^2 = 4mx^2 - 12mnx + 9n^2$ in the xy-plane, where m and n are constants, has what value of x at its vertex?

A) $\frac{3}{2}n$ B) $-\frac{3}{2}n$ C) $-3mn$ D) $3mn$

Solution: To find the x-coordinate of the vertex, we can use the equation we just introduced above. But before we use this rule, we need to isolate y so the the equation is in the form $y = ax^2 + bx + c$. To do so, we add $4n^2$ to both sides to get

$$y = 4mx^2 - 12mnx + 13n^2$$

Looking at the equation, we can see the $a = 4m$, $b = -12mn$, and $c = 13n^2$. We can now use our rule above to find the x-coordinate at the vertex.

$$x = -\frac{b}{2a} = -\frac{-12mn}{2(4m)} = \frac{12mn}{8m} = \frac{3n}{2} = \frac{3}{2}n$$

The answer is A. It is important to memorize this rule! You will need to use it if you are asked to find the vertex of a parabola that is written in standard form.

3 Forms of a Parabola

Finally, we need to understand the 3 forms of a parabola: standard form, factored form, and vertex form. All 3 forms are shown in the table below. We need to know what the constants represent in these various forms.

Form	Equation	What the Constants Represent
Standard	$y = ax^2 + bx + c$	c is the y-intercept
Factored	$y = a(x - d)(x - f)$	d and f are the x-intercepts
Vertex	$y = a(x - h)^2 + k$	vertex is at (h, k)

For standard form, note that the c-values shows the y-intercept. As we covered earlier in this chapter, factored form shows the x-intercepts. And we just reviewed how vertex form shows the vertex at point (h, k).

For many advanced quadratics questions on the SAT, you need to understand these 3 forms of a parabola.

Example 14: The height h, in meters of a rocket can be modeled by a quadratic function that is defined in terms of t, where t is the time after launch in seconds. At a time of 10.0 seconds after launch, the rocket is at a height of 200.0 meters, and at a time of 20.0 seconds after launch, the rocket is at a height of 800.0 meters. If the rocket was at a height of 0 meters when $t = 0$, then what is the height of the rocket, in meters, 8.0 seconds after launch?

Solution: The question tells us height of the rocket can be modeled by a quadratic function, which is another word for a parabola. For this question, we are not given any information about the vertex or x-intercepts, so

we need to use the standard form of a parabola. We can write the equation in terms of h and t by plugging in h for y and t for x:
$$h = at^2 + bt + c$$
The question tells us that the rocket has a height of 0 meters when $t = 0$, so the y-intercept is at $(0, 0)$. In standard form, the c-value is the y-intercept, so we know that $c = 0$. So, we can remove the c and simplify the equation to
$$h = at^2 + bt$$
Now is the fun (hard) part. We need to solve for a and b. To do this, we plug in the values that we are given in the question. We are told that at a time of 10.0 seconds ($t = 10$), the rocket is at a height of 200.0 meters ($h = 200$). Plugging these values into the equation, we get
$$200 = a(10)^2 + b(10)$$
We can simplify this equation to
$$200 = 100a + 10b$$
We cannot solve an equation with 2 unknowns. However, we still have more information from the question. We are told that at a time of 20.0 seconds ($t = 20$), the rocket is at a height of 800.0 meter ($h = 800$). Plugging these values into the equation, we get
$$800 = a(20)^2 + b(20)$$
We can simplify this equation to
$$800 = 400a + 20b$$

Now, we have a system of equations that we can solve.
$$200 = 100a + 10b$$
$$800 = 400a + 20b$$
We will learn how to solve systems of equations in Chapter 12. For a system of equations like this, our favorite method is elimination. To get rid of the b-values, we can multiply the top equation by -2 to get
$$-400 = -200a - 20b$$
$$800 = 400a + 20b$$
When we add these equations together, the b-terms cancel out, so we get
$$400 = 200a$$
$$a = 2$$
Now that we know $a = 2$, we can solve for b using either equation in the system of equations. Let's use the equation $200 = 100a + 10b$.
$$200 = 100(2) + 10b$$
$$200 = 200 + 10b$$
$$0 = 10b$$
$$b = 0$$
We find that $b = 0$. Plugging in our values of a and b to the standard form equation, we get
$$h = 2t^2$$
To find the height at 8.0 seconds after launch, we plug in $t = 8$.
$$h = 2(8)^2 = 128$$

The answer is 128. This is an advanced question that is designed to challenge top math students.

PrepPros

Quadratics Practice: Answers on pages 328-329.

1. What is the sum of the solutions of the polynomial $f(x) = x^2 - 7x + 12$?

   A) -7
   B) 3
   C) 4
   D) 7

2. What is the sum of the solutions to $(x - 1.2)(x + 5) = 0$?

   A) -6.2
   B) -3.8
   C) 3.8
   D) 6.2

3. Which of the following is equivalent to $(3x - 5)(-x + 7)$?

   A. $(3x + 5)(x + 7)$
   B. $(3x - 5)(x + 7)$
   C. $(-3x + 5)(x - 7)$
   D. $(-3x + 5)(x + 7)$

4. What is the sum of the solutions of the equation $x^2 - 4x - 21 = 0$?

   A) -10
   B) -4
   C) 3
   D) 4

5. What is one of the solutions to the given equation?

   $$0 = a^2 + 6a - 27$$

6. What is the positive solution to the function $f(x) = x^2 - 8x - 65$?

7. What is the sum of the solutions to the given equation?

   $$x^2 - 12x + 26 = 2x + 2$$

8. The function $f(x) = \frac{1}{3}(x - 9)^2 + 14$ models the height of a pendulum, x, seconds after it is released. What is the minimum value of $f(x)$?

9. In the equation below, a and b are constants. Which of the following could be the value of a?

   $$9x^2 - 16 = (ax - b)(ax + b)$$

   A) 3
   B) 4
   C) 9
   D) 16

10. In the equation below, $j, l, k,$ and m are constants. If the equation has roots of $-4, 3,$ and -5. Which of the following could be a factor of the equation below?

    $$jx^3 + lx^2 - kx - m = 0$$

    A) $x - 4$
    B) $x - 5$
    C) $x - 3$
    D) $x + 3$

11. What is the sum of the solutions to the given equation?

    $$x^2 - 13x + 40 = 6x - 8$$

    A) -13
    B) -19
    C) 13
    D) 19

12. What is the positive solution to the given equation?

    $$\frac{78}{x + 7} = x$$

13. $(80x - 42)(15x + 12) = ax^2 + bx + c$

    For the equation above, what is the value of $a + b + c$?

- 86 -

Chapter 11: Quadratics

14. If (x, y) is a solution to the system of equations below, what is a possible value of x?

    $$y = x^2 + 6x + 6$$
    $$y = 2x + 2$$

    A) -2
    B) 0
    C) 2
    D) 4

15. The function $f(x) = \frac{1}{7}(x - 6)^2 + 13$ gives a marble's height above the ground $f(x)$, in feet, x seconds after it began moving down a track, where $0 \leq x \leq 10$. Which of the following is the best interpretation of the vertex of the graph of $y = f(x)$ in the xy-plane?

    A) The marble's minimum height was 6 feet above the ground.
    B) The marble's minimum height was 13 feet above the ground.
    C) The marble's height was 6 feet above the ground when it started moving.
    D) The marble's height was 13 feet above the ground when it started moving.

16. Which of the following is a solution to the equation below?

    $$x^2 + 6x + 3 = 0$$

    A) $-3 + \sqrt{6}$
    B) $-3 + \sqrt{13}$
    C) $3 - \sqrt{6}$
    D) $3 - \sqrt{13}$

17. In the xy-plane, the parabola with equation $y = (x + 3)(x + 4)$ intersects the equation $y = 20$ at two points. Which of the following is an x-value of a point of intersection?

    A) -8
    B) -1
    C) 3
    D) 4

18. What is the larger of the two solutions to the equation below?

    $$4(x - 10)^2 = 8x - 80$$

19.
    $$x^3 + 8x^2 - 27x - 28 = 0$$

    The polynomial above can be written as $(x + 1)(x + 7)(x^2 - 4) = 0$. What are all of the roots of the equation?

    A) $-1, -7$
    B) $-1, -7, \sqrt{2}$
    C) $-2, -1, 2, 7$
    D) $-7, -2, -1, 2$

20. Ben is throwing a ball from the top of his building. The ball's height is modeled by the function $H(x) = -x^2 + 10x + 56$, where x is the number of seconds after he throws the ball. How many seconds after throwing the ball does it hit the ground?

    A) 4
    B) 5
    C) 14
    D) 56

21. The given equation below defines function f. For what value of x does $f(x)$ reach its maximum?

    $$f(x) = -6x^2 - 96x - 86$$

22. The graph of the equation $y = 3(x + a)^2 - b$ in the xy-plane is a parabola, where a and b are constants. What is the vertex of this parabola?

    A) $(-3a, -b)$
    B) $(-a, -b)$
    C) $(a, -b)$
    D) $(3a, -b)$

23. Which of the following is a solution to the equation below?

    $$x^2 - 4x + 1 = 0$$

    A) $2 - \sqrt{6}$
    B) $-2 + \sqrt{6}$
    C) $2 + \sqrt{3}$
    D) $-2 - \sqrt{3}$

24. The system of equations below is graphed in the xy-plane. If x is negative, what is a possible value of x?

$$y = x^2 + 5x + 8$$
$$y = 8 - 2x$$

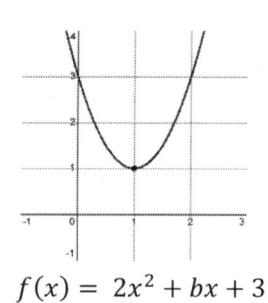

25. $h(x) = x^4 + 2x^3 - 8x^2 - 18x - 9$

The polynomial above can be written as $(x^2 - 9)(x + 1)^2$. What are all the real roots of the equation?

A) 9, 1
B) 9, 1, and -1
C) 3, -3, and -1
D) 3, -3, 1, and -1

26. What is the solution set for $5x^2 + 6x = 8$?

A) $\{\frac{1}{5}, \frac{1}{2}\}$
B) $\{-\frac{1}{5}, -\frac{1}{2}\}$
C) $\{\frac{4}{5}, 2\}$
D) $\{\frac{4}{5}, -2\}$

27. The number of containers of canned tuna, in thousands, processed by a seafood company each year from 2002 to 2015 can be modeled by the given function f, where x is the number of years after 2002. Based on the model, which year from 2002 to 2015 had the greatest number of containers of canned tuna processed?

$$f(x) = -127(x - 7)^2 + 73{,}000$$

A) 2003
B) 2009
C) 2010
D) 2015

28. One of the factors of $4x^3 + 28x^2 + 48x$ is $x + a$, where a is a positive constant. What is one possible value of a?

29.

$$f(x) = 2x^2 + bx + 3$$

The graph and equation of the function $f(x)$ are shown above. Which of the following is the value of b?

A) -1
B) -2
C) -4
D) -8

30. The function $g(x)$ is defined as $g(x) = x^3 + ax^2 + bx + c$. If the zeros of the function are $-9, 5$, and 4, what is the value of c?

31. Given that $(2x + 3)$ and $(x - 4)$ are the factors of the quadratic below, what is the value of z?

$$2x^2 + (z - 1)x + 2z = 4$$

32. The equation below is graphed in the xy-plane. If a and b are positive constants and $a \neq b$, how many distinct x-intercepts does the graph have?

$$y = (x + a)(x - a)(x + b)^2$$

A) 1
B) 2
C) 3
D) 4

Chapter 11: Quadratics

33. If $k < 0$ and $(4k)^2 - 5(4k) - 24 = 0$, what is the value of k?

34. The expressions $x^2 + bx + 13$ and $(x + 4)^2 + c$, where b and c are constants, are equivalent. What is the value of $b + c$?

   A) 11
   B) 8
   C) 5
   D) -3

35. A positive value x that satisfies the equation below can be written in the form $x = j + j\sqrt{k}$, where j and k are integers. What is the value of k?

$$x^2 - 2x - 10 = 0$$

36. In the quadratic equation below, z is a constant. For what value of z, will the equation have one real solution?

$$zx^2 + 6x = 3$$

   A) -3
   B) 1
   C) 3
   D) 6

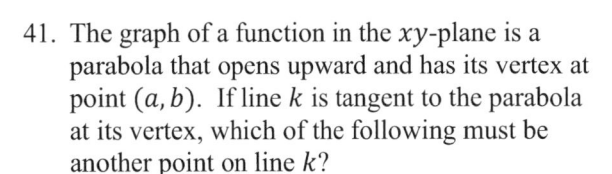

37. Which of the following quadratic equations has no real solution?

   A) $x^2 + 6x - 9 = 0$
   B) $x^2 - 6x + 9 = 0$
   C) $3x^2 - 6x - 6 = 0$
   D) $3x^2 - 6x + 6 = 0$

38. One of the factors of $3x^3 + 60x^2 + 288x$ is $x + k$, where k is a positive constant. What is the largest possible value of k?

39. The system of equations below is graphed in the xy-plane. Which of the following is the x-coordinate of an intersection point (x, y) of the system of equations?

$$y = x^2 + 8x + 9$$
$$y = 2x + 3$$

   A) $-3 + \sqrt{3}$
   B) $3 + 2\sqrt{3}$
   C) $-5 - \sqrt{13}$
   D) $3 - \sqrt{3}$

40. In the given equation below, c is a constant. The equation has no real solutions if $c > k$. What is the least possible value of the integer k?

$$x^2 - 56x + c = 0$$

41. The graph of a function in the xy-plane is a parabola that opens upward and has its vertex at point (a, b). If line k is tangent to the parabola at its vertex, which of the following must be another point on line k?

   A) $(-13, b)$
   B) $(-13, -b)$
   C) $(0, 0)$
   D) $(a, -13)$

42. The expression $\frac{1}{4}x^2 - 6$ can be rewritten as $\frac{1}{4}(x - a)(x + a)$, where a is a positive constant. What is the value of a?

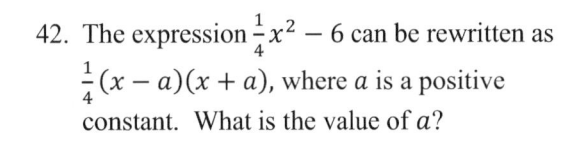

   A) 6
   B) 24
   C) $\sqrt{6}$
   D) $\sqrt{24}$

- 89 -

43. The equation below has solutions $x = a + b\sqrt{c}$ and $x = a - b\sqrt{c}$, where a, b and c are positive integers. What is the value of $ab - c$?

$$x^2 - 4x - 4 = 0$$

44. What is the sum of solutions to the given equation?

$$x(2x + 3) + 723 = 5x(2x - 6)$$

45. In the given equation below, c is a positive integer. The equation has two real solutions. What is the greatest possible value of c?

$$4x^2 - 28x + c = 0$$

46. $(kx + 3)(4x^2 - mx - 3) = 20x^3 - 3x^2 - 24x - 9$

For the equation above, what is the value of km?

A) -15
B) -5
C) 3
D) 15

47. In the xy-plane, a parabola has a vertex $(5,1)$ and intersects the x-axis at two points. If the equation of the parabola is written in the form $y = -ax^2 + bx + c$, where a, b, and c are constants and $a > 0$, which of the following could be a value of c?

A) -5
B) 2
C) 3
D) 9

48. In the given equation below, k is a positive integer. The equation has no real solution. What is the greatest possible value of k?

$$-x^2 + kx - 5{,}329 = 0$$

49. Which of the following is a solution to the equation below?

$$5x^2 + 4x - 4 = 6x - 2$$

A) $\frac{4}{5}$
B) $\frac{1-\sqrt{11}}{5}$
C) $\frac{1}{5} - \sqrt{11}$
D) $\frac{\sqrt{11}}{5}$

50. In the given system of equations, a is a constant. The graphs of the equations intersect at exactly one point, (x, y) in the xy-plane. What is the value of x?

$$y = 2x^2 - 12x + 24$$
$$y = 2x - a$$

51. The equation includes point $(3, p)$. If $a > 0$, which of the following could be the value of p?

$$y = a(x - 2)(x + 1)(x - 4)$$

A) -47
B) 0
C) 23
D) 401

52. A quadratic function can be used to model the height, in meters, of an object above the ground in terms of time, in seconds, after the object was launched into the air from a height of 0 feet. The object reached a maximum height of 375 meters 5 seconds after it was launched. Based on the model, what was the height, in meters, of the object 3.5 seconds after it was launched? (Round your answer to the nearest tenth.)

Chapter 11: Quadratics

53. Which of the following equations has $x + 3a$ as a factor where a is a positive integer?

   A) $3x^2 - 24x + 18a = 0$
   B) $3x^2 + 8x + 18a = 0$
   C) $3x^2 + 16x + 18a = 0$
   D) $3x^2 + 24x + 18a = 0$

54. The given equation $ax^2 + 180x + c$, where a and c are constants has at least 1 real root and a factor of $kx + m$. What is the greatest possible product of ac?

55. The equation below is graphed in the xy-plane. If a and b are positive constants and $a \neq b$, how many distinct x-intercepts does the graph have?

$$x^2 + ax + bx + ab = 0$$

   A) 0
   B) 1
   C) 2
   D) 3

56. If x is the solution to the equation below, what is the value of $\sqrt{x-5}$?

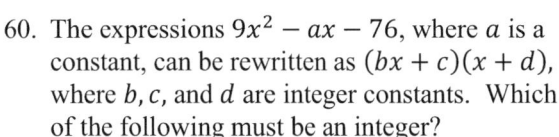

$$\sqrt{x-5} = 5 - \sqrt{x}$$

57. In the given equation $18x^2 + (18j + k)x + jk$, the product of the solutions is equal to jky. What is the value of y?

58. The total distance d, in feet, traveled by an object moving in a straight line can be modeled by a quadratic function that is defined in terms of t, where t is the time in seconds. At a time of 30.0 seconds, the total distance traveled by the object is 1,920 feet, and at a time of 50.0 seconds, the total distance traveled by the object is 5,200 feet. If the object was at a distance of 0 feet when $t = 0$, then what is the total distance traveled, in feet, by the object after 10.0 seconds?

59. In the expression below, a and b are positive integers. If the expression is equivalent to $x + b$ and $x \neq b$, which of the following could be the value of a?

$$\frac{x^2 - a}{x - b}$$

   A) 5
   B) 6
   C) 9
   D) 12

60. The expressions $9x^2 - ax - 76$, where a is a constant, can be rewritten as $(bx + c)(x + d)$, where $b, c,$ and d are integer constants. Which of the following must be an integer?

   A) $\frac{a}{b}$
   B) $\frac{a}{c}$
   C) $\frac{76}{b}$
   D) $\frac{76}{d}$

- 91 -

61. The flight path of a ball launched into the air is modeled by a quadratic function. Its initial height is 12 feet. After 4 seconds, it reaches its maximum height of 252. What is the height after 5 seconds?

64. If the vertex of a parabola is at the point $(1, 24)$ and the quadratic can be written in the form $-a(x^2) + bx + c$ and $a, b,$ and c are all positive integers, what is the maximum value of b?

62. The given equation $ax^2 + 78x + c = 0$, where a and c are constants has no real solutions and a factor of $gx + p$. The product of $ac > k$. What is the least possible value of k?

65. For the system of equations below, $b = 2a$. For the system of equations below to have one solution, the value of a must be equal to what?

$$y = 2ax^2 - bx - b$$
$$y = 4x^2 + 8x - 2a$$

63. In the system of equations below, a and b are constants. For which of the following values of a and b does the system of equations have exactly one real solution?

$$y = 6x + 2$$
$$y = ax^2 + b$$

A) $a = 3, b = 1$
B) $a = 3, b = 3$
C) $a = 9, b = 3$
D) $a = -3, b = 1$

66. In the xy-plane, a parabola has a vertex $(7, 12)$ and intersects the x-axis at two points. If the equation of the parabola is written in the form $y = ax^2 + bx + c$, where $a, b,$ and c are constants, which of the following could be the value of $a + b + c$?

A) 10
B) 14
C) 18
D) 36

Chapter 12: Systems of Equations

A system of equations is a set of two equations with the same set of variables. The SAT most commonly gives you two equations and asks you to solve for x, for y, or for some combination of the two. **The easiest method for solving most systems of equations on the SAT is using Desmos!** To review our Desmos Hack for solving systems of equations, go back to page 15.

In case you see any system of equations questions that cannot be solved with Desmos, you also need to know 3 methods for solving a system of equations: elimination, substitution, and setting equal. We will start with these methods in this chapter and also learn how to spot word problems that must be solved by writing and solving a system of equations.

Elimination

We cannot solve an equation with two variables, so elimination is all about one variable to get to an equation with only one variable that can be solved. To do this, we make the coefficients of one variable have the same number and the opposite signs. With addition, one of the variables cancels out, leaving an equation with just one variable that can be solved.

Example 1: If $10x - 4y = 16$ and $2x + 4y = 8$, what is the value of y?

Solution: Method #1 – "Math Teacher Way": Whenever we have a system of equations question where none of the variables are already isolated, "elimination" is the fastest way to get to the answer. Since we are asked to solve for y, we want to cancel the x-terms. To do so, we multiply the second equation by -5.

$$10x - 4y = 16$$
$$-5(2x + 4y = 8)$$

$$10x - 4y = 16$$
$$-10x - 20y = -40$$

Next, add the equations together. Notice that the x-terms cancel out, so we get

$$-24y = -24$$
$$y = 1$$

The answer is 1.

Solution: Method #2 – Desmos Hack for Solving Systems of Equations: If the first method seemed challenging, we have good news for you – there is a much easier way to solve Example 1! In Chapter 4, we learned how to use Desmos to solve a system of equations. For any system of equations, the point(s) of intersection show the solution(s) to the system of equations. To review this method, go to p. 15.

If we graph the system of equations, we find the point of intersection at $(2, 1)$. We are asked to solve for y, so we want the y-coordiante at this point of intersection, which is $y = 1$. **The answer is 1.**

Notice how **we can type the equations into Desmos exactly as they are given in the question.** This trick is a helpful one when solving system of equations in Desmos.

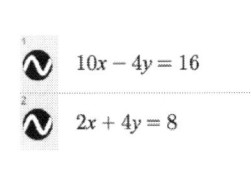

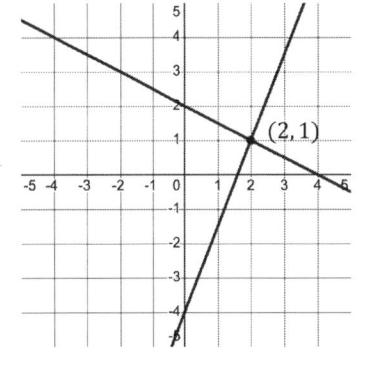

Substitution
1-4

In substitution, we want to isolate one variable in the fastest and easiest way possible. Once we have an isolated variable in one equation, we can substitute that value into the second equation to get an equation with one variable that we can solve. This is not the same substitution (plug in numbers) we learned in Chapter 2.

Example 2: If $12a + 8b = 8$ and $b = 6a - 14$, what does a equal?

Solution: Method #1 – "Math Teacher Way": If we are given a system of equations where one variable is isolated in an equation, use the "substitution" method. In this question, b is isolated in the second equation. Since $b = 6a - 14$, we can substitute $6a - 14$ for the b in the first equation.

$$12a + 8(6a - 14) = 8$$
$$12a + 48a - 112 = 8$$
$$60a - 112 = 8$$
$$60a = 120$$
$$a = 2$$

The answer is 2.

Solution: Method #2 – Desmos Hack for Solving Systems of Equations: If we type in the equations in Example 2 as they are written (with a and b), Desmos gives an error and does not show any graphs. So how do we use our Desmos Hack to solve? **Change a and b to x and y.** Once we change a to x and b to y, we can graph the equations in Desmos and solve!

If we graph the system of equations, we find the point of intersection at $(2, -2)$. We are asked to solve for a, which we changed to x. We want the x-coordiante at this point of intersection, which is $x = 2$. This tells us that $a = 2$, so **the answer is 2.**

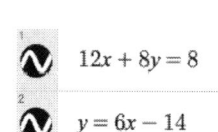

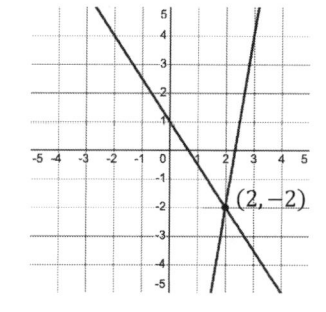

Set Equal
1-4

When we are given two equations that both isolate the same variable, the fastest and easiest way to solve algebraically is to set the equations equal and solve.

Example 3: If $y = 10x - 60$ and $y = -3x - 8$, what is the value of x at the point (x, y) where the lines intersect?

Solution: Method #1 – "Math Teacher Way": The point where the lines intersect is another way to ask for the solution to a system of equations. At the point where two lines intersect, the y-value must be the same for both equations, so we can set the equations equal and solve for x.

$$10x - 60 = -3x - 8$$
$$13x - 60 = -8$$
$$13x = 52$$
$$x = 4$$

The answer is 4.

Chapter 12: Systems of Equations

Solution: **Method #2 – Desmos Hack for Solving Systems of Equations:** If we graph the system of equations, we find the point of intersection at $(4, -20)$. We are asked to solve for x, so we want the x-coordiante at this point of intersection, which is $x = 4$. **The answer is A.**

The Shortcut

If a question asks you for a value that is a combination of x and y-terms, such as $2x + 3y$, always look to see if you can add or subtract directly to the answer to save time. If you cannot get directly to the answer, use the Desmos Hack, elimination, or substation to solve.

Example 4: If $8a + 17b = 90$ and $5a + 14b = 50$, what is the value of $3a + 3b$?

Solution: The fastest way to solve this question is to subtract the second equation from the first. In 1 step, we can get directly to the answer.

$$\begin{array}{r} 8a + 17b = 90 \\ -\underline{5a + 14b = 50} \\ 3a + 3b = 40 \end{array}$$

The answer is 40.

Word Problems

Many word problems are systems of equations questions in disguise. For these questions, the greatest challenge is turning the words into equations. If you can do that successfully, then you only need to solve the system of equations. Let's see how this works with Example 5.

Example 5: For her garden, Mary buys 42 plants for a total of $108.00. Mary is only going to plant tomatoes and peppers. If a tomato plant costs $3.00 and pepper plant costs $2.00, how many pepper plants did Mary buy?

Solution: Let x be the number of tomato plants and y be the number of pepper plants. We can write two equations. The first equation comes from the fact that we know Mary bought a total of 42 plants.

$$x + y = 42$$

The second equation uses the prices of each plant to add to the $108.00 Mary spent buying plants.

$$3x + 2y = 108$$

Once we have these two equations, **we can graph the equations in Desmos or use elimination to solve.** If we graph the equations in Desmos, we find the point of intersection is at $(24, 18)$. We are solving for the number of pepper plants, y, so we want the y-coordinate, which is at $y = 18$. **The answer is 18.** The x-coordinate at this point tells us that Mary bought 24 tomato plants.

If we solve with elimination, we can eliminate the tomato plants, x, by multiplying the first equation by -3.

$$-3(x + y = 42)$$
$$3x + 2y = 108$$

$$-3x - 3y = -126$$
$$3x + 2y = 108$$

Next, add the equations together and solve for y.

$$-y = -18$$
$$y = 18$$

The answer is 18.

1-4 More Complex Systems of Equations

The SAT often includes more complex systems of equations with terms that are squared. For these questions, **we always recommend using the Desmos hack to solve**. For questions that cannot be solved with Desmos, setting the equations equal is the quickest and easiest way to solve.

> **Example 6:** The equations $y = x^2 - 11$ and $y = 10x + 13$ intersect at a point (x, y) where $x < 0$. What is the y-coordinate of this point of intersection?
>
> A) 12   B) 5   C) -2 D) -7

Solution: Method #1 – Desmos Hack for Solving Systems of Equations:

If we graph the system of equations, we find two points of intersection at $(-2, -7)$ and $(12, 133)$.

The question asks us for the point of intersection where $x < 0$, so we must use $(-2, -7)$. The y-coordinate at this point is $y = -7$, so **the answer is D.**

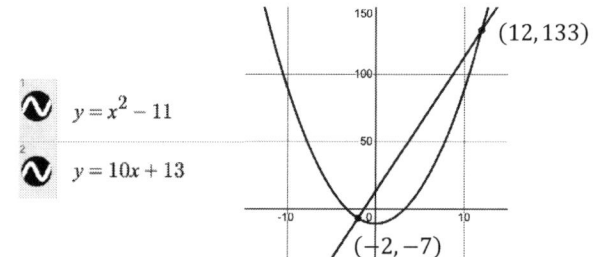

Solution: Method #2 – "Math Teacher Way": In this question, y is already isolated in both equations, so we can set the equations equal and solve for x.

$$x^2 - 11 = 10x + 13$$

Since we have a quadratic, we need to move all the terms to the left-hand side to make the equation equal to zero and factor.

$$x^2 - 10x - 24 = 0$$
$$(x - 12)(x + 2) = 0$$
$$x = -2, 12$$

The question tells us that $x < 0$, so we must use $x = -2$. To solve for the y-coordinate, plug $x = -2$ into either of one of our initial equations. We will use the first equation.

$$y = (-2)^2 - 11 = -7$$

The answer is D. Of course, you can see this method is a lot more work than using Desmos. However, you should still understand the math we did here if you are aiming for high math scores, as the SAT can present questions with variables that cannot be solved in Desmos.

> **Example 7:** The equations $y = x^2 + p$ and $x^2 + (y - 4)^2 = 25$ intersect at the point $(x, 8)$. What is the value of p?

Solution: This question is more difficult because we cannot solve it in Desmos since we do not know the value of p. We are told that the equations intersect at the point $(x, 8)$, so we can plug in $y = 8$ to the equations.

$$8 = x^2 + p$$
$$x^2 + (8 - 4)^2 = 25$$

Simplifying the bottom equation, we get

$$8 = x^2 + p$$
$$x^2 + 16 = 25$$

Since both equations have x^2, we can isolate the x^2 term in the top equation and use substitution to plug in for the x^2 term in the bottom equation. By subtracting p from both sides in the top equation, we get

$$8 - p = x^2$$

We can now substitute $8 - p$ in for the x^2 term in the bottom equation.

$$8 - p + 16 = 25$$

Now, we have an equation that we can solve for p.

$$24 - p = 25$$
$$-p = 1$$
$$p = -1$$

The answer is −1. This is a much more challenging question, but it is one that you need to understand how to solve if you are aiming for top scores. We expect the SAT to include more questions like this that you cannot solve with the Desmos Hack.

System of Equations Practice: Answers on page 329.

1.
$$x - 3y = 3$$
$$x + y = 7$$

   The solution to the system of equations above is (x, y). What is the value of x?

   A) 2
   B) 4
   C) 5
   D) 6

2. The solution to the given system of equations is (x, y). What is the value of $x - y$?

$$6x = 30$$
$$3x + 2y = 8$$

   A) −3.5
   B) 1.5
   C) 5
   D) 8.5

3.
$$x - y = 3$$
$$y = 3 - 2x$$

   For the system of equations above, what is the value of x?

   A) 6
   B) 2
   C) 0
   D) −3

4.
$$3m + 5n = 26$$
$$m + n = 34$$

   In the system of equations above, what is the value of m?

   A) 18
   B) 36
   C) 72
   D) 144

5.
$$2x - 3z = -6$$
$$3x + 2z = 4$$

   For the system of equations above, what is the value of $x + z$?

   A) −2
   B) 0
   C) 1
   D) 2

6.
$$0.25a - 2b = -4$$
$$a + b = 2$$

   The solution to the system of equations above is the point (a, b). What is the value of b?

7. If (x, y) satisfies the system of equations below, what is the value of x?

$$3x - 2y = -1$$
$$10x + 4y = 50$$

8. Max has $150 to spend on a picnic. He is going to buy cookies and brownies for the picnic. The table below gives the number of brownies and cookies in each box and the price per box.

Food Item	Number in each box	Price per box
Cookies	18	6
Brownies	12	8

Max will order a total of 20 boxes of cookies and brownies. Which system of equations gives a true relationship between the boxes of brownies, B, and boxes of cookies, C, that Max will order?

A) $C + B = 20$
    $6C + 8B = 150$
B) $C + B = 20$
    $18C + 12B = 150$
C) $C + B = 300$
    $6C + 8B = 150$
D) $6C + 8B = 20$
    $18C + 12B = 150$

9. If (x, y) is the solution to the system of equations below, what is the value of $y - x$?

$$2x - 3y = -9$$
$$3x + 2y = 19$$

A) -2
B) 2
C) 3
D) 8

10.
$$6x = y + 8$$
$$y = 96 - 7x$$

In the system of equations above, what is the value of $x - y$?

A) -32
B) 32
C) 104
D) 736

11. The solution to the given system of equations is (p, q). What is the value of q?

$$8x + y = 48$$
$$3x + y = 12$$

12. Monique, a manager at a local bakery, is taking all of the $10 and $20 bills in the cash register to the bank at the end of her shift. On her way back to work, she lost the deposit slip, but she remembers that there were 19 bills totaling $260. How many $10 bills were in the cash register at the end of her shift?

A) 6
B) 9
C) 11
D) 12

13. The system of equations below has a solution (x, y). What is the value of y?

$$\tfrac{1}{4}x = 4y - 4$$
$$-\tfrac{3}{4}x + 5y = -\tfrac{55}{10}$$

14. The drama club is selling two types of tickets for the play: student tickets for $7 each and regular tickets for $12 each. If the drama club sold a total of 200 tickets and the ticket sales were $2,025, how many student tickets were sold?

15.
$$4a + 3b = 22$$
$$3a + 2b = 16$$

In the system of equations above, what is the value of $a + b$?

Chapter 12: Systems of Equations

16. At Franky's Surf Shop, the price of a t-shirt is $20, and the price of a hat is $17. Javaun spent $282 on 15 items and only bought t-shirts and hats. How many hats did he buy?

17. Kiki's teacher wrote the following riddle on the board: "There are two integers I am thinking of. The difference between the two integers is 21, and the sum of the larger integer and twice the smaller integer is -15. What is the value of the larger integer?" The answer is:

    A) -12
    B) -9
    C) 9
    D) 12

18. $$-4x - 15y = 78$$
    $$3y + x = -30$$

    The system of equations above is graphed in the xy-plane. At which point do the graphs intersect?

    A) $(14, -14)$
    B) $(-72, 14)$
    C) $(7, -52)$
    D) $(228, 66)$

19. $$y = x^2 - 11x + 14$$
    $$2y = 4 - 6x$$

    The system of equations above is graphed in the xy-plane. Which of the following is the x-coordinate of an intersection point of the two equations?

    A) 1
    B) 4
    C) 6
    D) 10

20. At the Pacific Beach boardwalk, there is a taco stand that sells carnitas tacos and fish tacos. Carnitas tacos have 50 more calories than fish tacos. If 3 carnitas tacos and 2 fish tacos have a total of 650 calories, how many calories does each fish taco have?

21. $$x = y^2 + 8y$$
    $$x + 2y = 24$$

    The system of equations above is graphed in the xy-plane. Which of the following is the y-coordinate of an intersection point of the graphs of the two equations?

    A) 8
    B) 4
    C) -2
    D) -12

22. A group of 150 people went whitewater rafting. The group took 20 total rafts. The rafts could carry either 6 or 8 people. How many 8-person rafts did the group take?

    A) 4
    B) 6
    C) 10
    D) 15

23. The graphs of the equations in the given system of equations intersect at the point (x, y) in the xy-plane. What is a possible value of x?

    $$14x + \frac{1}{2}y = -28$$
    $$2x^2 = y - 40$$

24. Jimmy's Deli sells Reuben sandwiches for $7.35 and brisket sandwiches for $8.10. Yesterday, the deli made $759.90 from selling a total of 99 Reuben and brisket sandwiches. How many Reuben sandwiches were sold yesterday?

- 99 -

25. The solution to the given system of equations is (a, b). What is the value of a?

$$a + b = 17$$
$$3(a - b) = 33$$

26. The product of 2 integers is 96. The greater integer is 2 less than triple the lesser integer. What is the greater integer?

27.
$$(x - 1)^2 + (y - 2)^2 = 35$$
$$x = 2y + 2$$

Which of the following could be the x-coordinate of the solution to the system of equations above?

A) $\sqrt{6}$
B) $\dfrac{\sqrt{30}}{2}$
C) $2\sqrt{6} + 2$
D) $\sqrt{30} + 2$

28. The solution to the given system of equations is $(2, 3)$. What is the value of $a + b$?

$$4ax = by + 12$$
$$2ax - 5by = 15$$

29. The equations $c = x^2 - y$ and $(x - 3)^2 + (y + 1)^2 = 49$ intersect at the point $(3, y)$. What is the value of c?

A) -1
B) 1
C) 3
D) 4

30.
$$4x - 5qy = 36$$
$$px + 10qy = 54$$

In the given system of equations, p and q are constants. The lines of the two equations intersect at $(4, y)$. What is the value of p?

31. The linear function f is defined by $f(x) = ax + b$, where a and b are constants. If $f(15) = 850$ and $f(28) = 1{,}305$, what is the value of $a + b$?

32.
$$8kx + 8my = -8$$
$$3xk + 6my = -24$$

In the system of equations above, k and m are constants. The system has a solution of $(6, y)$. What is the value of k?

33. The system of equations below intersects at the point $(-3, y)$. What is the value of h?

$$20 + 2y = 8x$$
$$y = x^2 - 16hx - 43$$

34. In the system of linear equations below, c is a nonzero constant. The graphs of the equations are two lines in the xy-plane that intersect at $(-7, a)$. What is the value of a?

$$5y + 7x = 3c$$
$$4y + 9x = c$$

35.
$$(a - b) + 12(c + d) = 589$$
$$(a - b) + 18(c + d) = 1251$$

For the system of equations above, what is the value of $2a - 2b$?

Chapter 12: Systems of Equations

36. James took a trip from Maryland to Boston by car and train. When travelling by car, he averaged 40 miles per hour. When traveling by train, he averaged 60 miles per hour. The trip took him 7 hours and was 400 miles. How far did he travel by train?

   A) 120
   B) 200
   C) 240
   D) 360

37. $$y = x - 18$$
    $$y^2 + (x - 14)^2 - 12 = 0$$

   For the system of equations above, what is a possible value of y?

   A) $-2 + \sqrt{2}$
   B) $\sqrt{2}$
   C) $2 + \sqrt{3}$
   D) $-2 - \sqrt{6}$

38. The quadratic function f is defined by $f(x) = ax^2 + bx + c$, where a, b, and c are constants. If $f(9) = 251$, $f(3) = 71$, and $c = 35$, what is the value of $f(7)$?

39. In the system of equations below, a is a constant. What is the y-value of the solution to the system in terms of a?

    $$3x + 4y = 6$$
    $$-5x + y = a$$

   A) $\frac{30 + 3a}{23}$
   B) $-\frac{30 + 3a}{23}$
   C) $\frac{6 + 4a}{23}$
   D) $-\frac{6 + 4a}{23}$

40. In a chemistry classroom, when experiments are performed, students are seated at lab tables. If the teacher assigns 4 students to each lab table, 2 additional lab tables will be needed to seat all of the students. If the teacher assigns 8 students to each lab table, there will be 2 extra tables. How many students are in the science class?

41. The difference of 2 positive integers is 5. The square of the greater number is 95 more than the square of the lesser number. What is the value of the sum of the two integers?

42. In a group of 750 college students, some are premed students, and the rest are business students. There are 150 more women than men and there are 300 fewer business students than premed students. If there are 90 female business students and a man is to be selected at random, what is the probability that the man is a premed student?

43. For the system of equations below, the lines intersect at the point $(2, 4)$. If $b > 0$, what is the value of b?

    $$\frac{1}{2}ay - \frac{1}{2}bx = 7x$$
    $$\frac{1}{2}ay = \frac{1}{2}b^2y - 3bx + 5x$$

PrepPros

Chapter 13: Functions

A function is defined as a mathematical relationship between a variable x and the function $f(x)$. For every value of x, there is exactly one value of $f(x)$. For any function, there will be an input x, which appears as the term in the parentheses of a function, and an output, which will be the value that $f(x)$ equals.

① Function Basics

In order to solve functions questions on the SAT, we first need to know where to properly plug in the input to a function. For the function

$$f(x) = 5x - 2$$

you plug in the input for x. You are likely used to the input being a number, but the input can include variables as well. No matter what the input, just plug it in for the x in the equation:

$$f(3) = 5(3) - 2 = 13$$
$$f(-2x) = 5(-2x) - 2 = -10x - 2$$
$$f(a - 11) = 5(a - 11) - 2 = 5a - 57$$

① Example 1: If $f(x) = 3\sqrt{x} + 11$, what is the value for $f(25)$?

Solution: To solve, plug in the input to the function.

$$f(25) = 3\sqrt{25} + 11 = 3(5) + 11 = 15 + 11 = 26$$

The answer is 26.

① Example 2: If $f(x) = \frac{10x}{x+4}$, for what value of x does $f(x) = 5$?

Solution: If you are given the output, which is 5 in this question, and need to find the input, plug in the output for $f(x)$ and solve for the input x.

$$5 = \frac{10x}{x+4}$$
$$5(x + 4) = 10x$$
$$5x + 20 = 10x$$
$$20 = 5x$$
$$4 = x$$

The answer is 4.

②/③ Composite Functions

Quite often, the SAT will ask you to solve composite functions. A composite function is a function that is written inside of another function. We will use the examples below to learn how to solve composite functions questions correctly.

② Example 3: If $f(x) = 3x + 10$ and $g(x) = x - 5$, what is the value of $f(g(8))$?

Solution: If you are asked to solve a composite function, there are two methods to solve: (1) solve for the composite function or (2) work inside out. Let's learn how to solve with both methods:

- 102 -

Method #1 - Solve for the composite function: We want to solve for the function $f(g(x))$. To do so, we plug the entire $g(x)$ function in for the x in the $f(x)$ function. So, we plug $x - 5$ in for x in the $f(x)$ function.

$$f(g(x)) = 3(x-5) + 10 = 3x - 15 + 10 = 3x - 5$$

Now that we know the composite function, we can plug in 8 for x and solve.

$$f(g(8)) = 3(8) - 5 = 24 - 5 = 19$$

The answer is 19.

Method #2 - Work inside out: Rather than solve for the composite function, we can also work from the inside out to solve for $f(g(8))$. To start, we can solve for $g(8)$.

$$g(8) = 8 - 5 = 3$$

We now know that $g(8) = 3$, so we can simplify the function we are solving for.

$$f(g(8)) = f(3)$$

Now, we solve for $f(3)$.

$$f(3) = 3(3) + 10 = 19$$

The answer is 19.

Both of these methods work for any composite function questions on the SAT, so you should use the one that you are more comfortable with.

Example 4: If $f(x) = 2x^2 - 7$ and $g(x) = x + 3$, what is $f(g(x - 1))$?

A) $2x^2 + 2$ B) $2x^2 + 8x + 1$ C) $2x^2 + 12x + 11$ D) $2x^2 - 3$

Solution: This question looks more difficult since we now have $x - 1$ as the input, but you should still treat this as a composite function. Both of the methods outlined in Example 3 work to solve. Below, we will use the inside out method. First, we solve for $g(x - 1)$:

$$g(x - 1) = (x - 1) + 3 = x + 2$$

We now know that $g(x - 1) = x + 2$, so we can simplify the function that we are solving for.

$$f(g(x-1)) = f(x+2)$$

Now, solve for $f(x + 2)$

$$f(x+2) = 2(x+2)^2 - 7 = 2(x^2 + 4x + 4) - 7 = 2x^2 + 8x + 8 - 7 = 2x^2 + 8x + 1$$
$$f(g(x-1)) = 2x^2 + 8x + 1$$

The answer is B.

**Common Mistake to Avoid: Remember that $(x + 2)^2 \neq x^2 + 4$. You need to multiply out the terms because $(x + 2)^2$ is the same as $(x + 2)(x + 2)$.

Functions on Graphs

When a function is graphed, the input, x, is on the x-axis and the output, $f(x)$, is on the y-axis. To see how any function appears on a graph, remember that for any function **we can type and function directly in Desmos** and Desmos will graph the function.

$$f(x) = mx + b \quad \text{is the same as} \quad y = mx + b$$
$$f(x) = ax^2 + bx + c \quad \text{is the same as} \quad y = ax^2 + bx + c$$

PrepPros

For any specific point on the graph of a function, we can think of the $f(x)$ as the y-coordinate and x as the x-coordinate. For example, if we are told $f(2) = 7$, the point $(2, 7)$ is on the graph.

Example 5: The graph of the function f is shown below. If $f(a) = 3$ and $f(2) = b$, what is the value of $a + b$?

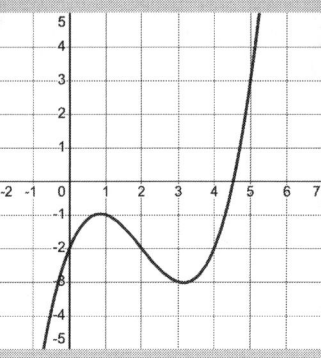

Solution: To solve this question, we need to understand how to interpret the input, x, and output, $f(x)$, of a function when the function is graphed. Remember, the input of the function is the x-value and the output as the y-value.

Let's start with $f(a) = 3$. We are asked to find the input, a, that has an output of 3. On the graph, the output is the y-value, so we need to find the x-value (the input) where $y = 3$. On the graph, the only point where $y = 3$ is at the point $(5, 3)$. So, we see that $a = 5$.

Now, let's find b. We are told that $f(2) = b$. We are given the input, so we know the x-value is 2. To find b, we need to find the y-value when $x = 2$. On the graph, the point where $x = 2$ is at $(2, -2)$, so $b = -2$.

Now, that we know a and b, we can solve. $a + b = 5 + (-2) = 3$. **The answer is 3.**

2-4 Inverse Functions

Inverse functions, written as $f^{-1}(x)$, are less commonly tested on the SAT, but they are pretty easy to solve. The problem is that many students forget how to solve for inverse function! So be sure to memorize this one simple method: **To find the inverse of any function, switch the input x and the output $f(x)$ and solve for $f(x)$.** Let's see how this works in the example below.

Example 6: Given the function $f(x) = \frac{10x-7}{2}$, what is the value for $f^{-1}(6.5)$?

Solution: To find the inverse of a function, switch the input x and the output $f(x)$. Most students find it easiest to start by replacing $f(x)$ with y, so our function becomes

$$y = \frac{10x - 7}{2}$$

To find the inverse function, switch the x and y and then solve for y.

$$x = \frac{10y - 7}{2}$$

$$2x = 10y - 7$$

$$2x + 7 = 10y$$

$$\frac{2x + 7}{10} = y$$

Once we have solved for y, we have found the inverse function. Now, plug in $f^{-1}(x)$ for y.

$$f^{-1}(x) = \frac{2x + 7}{10}$$

Now that we know the inverse, we can find $f^{-1}(6.5)$ by plugging in 6.5

$$f^{-1}(6.5) = \frac{2(6.5) + 7}{10} = \frac{20}{10} = 2$$

$$f^{-1}(6.5) = 2$$

The answer is 2.

Functions Practice: Answers on page 329.

For questions 1-15, use the functions below.

$$f(x) = 2x^2 - 7$$
$$g(x) = -3x + 10$$
$$h(x) = x - 3$$

1. What is the value of $f(4)$?

2. What is the value of $g(-31)$?

3. What is the value of $f(-10)$?

4. What is the value of $h(-19)$?

5. What is the value of $f(3x)$?

6. What is the value of $g(x - 3)$?

7. For what value of x does $h(x) = -5$?

8. For what value of x does $g(x) = 31$?

9. For what value of x does $f(x) = 43$?

10. For what value of x does $g(x) = -11$?

11. What is the value of $g(h(-11))$?

12. What is the value of $f(h(2x))$?

13. What is the value of $f(h(-4))$?

14. For what value of x does $g(h(x)) = 18$?

15. What is the value of $g(f(3x))$?

16. The function f is defined as $f(x) = x^2 - 4x$. What is the value of $f(2)$?

    A) -12
    B) -4
    C) 0
    D) 12

17. What is the value of $f(-3)$ given $f(x) = 3x^2 + 3x + 10$?

    A) -46
    B) -26
    C) 28
    D) 36

18. The function $f(x) = 6x - 1$ gives the total number of students on a field trip with x teachers. What is the total number of students on a field trip with 5 teachers?

19. For the function $m(x) = 8 - 6x$, for what value of x does $m(x)$ equal -1?

20. The function f is defined as $f(x) = -6x^3 + 2x^2$. What is $f(-4)$?

PrepPros

21. The function f is defined by $f(x) = 95(0.8)^x$. What is the value of $f(0)$?

22.

The graph of the function f is shown above. The function f has a minimum value when $x = k$. If $g(x) = 2x - 7$, what is the value of $g(k)$?

A) -3
B) -1
C) 3
D) 7

23. The function $h(t) = -2(t-4)^2 + 32$ models the height h, in meters, of a rocket t seconds after it was launched. What is the height of the rocket 5 seconds after it was launched?

24. If $h(x) = 4x - 7$, what is the value of $h(-2x)$ equal to?

A) $-8x - 7$
B) $8x - 14$
C) $8x - 7$
D) $-8x + 7$

25. The graph of the function f is shown below, where the function f is defined by $f(x) = ax^3 + bx^2 + cx + d$ and a, b, c, and d are constants. For how many values of x does $f(x) = 0$?

A) One
B) Two
C) Three
D) Four

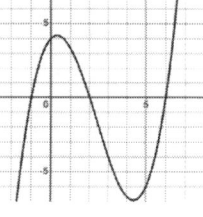

26. For functions f and g defined by $f(x) = 2x^2 + x$ and $g(x) = 2x - 1$, what is the value of $g(f(2))$?

A) 10
B) 15
C) 19
D) 22

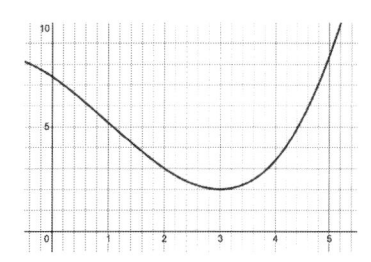

27. The function $p(x) = 10.5x + 20.25$ gives the height of a lemon tree in inches x years after it is planted. If the height of a tree is now 67.5 inches, how many years ago was it planted?

28. The function $f(x) = 3x + 7$ and the function $g(x) = 2x - 3$. What is the value of $f(g(5))$?

A) 11
B) 22
C) 28
D) 41

29.
$$f(x) = -5x + 2$$
$$g(x) = 10 - f(x)$$

The functions f and g are defined above. What is the value of $g(3)$?

A) -13
B) -3
C) 7
D) 23

30. If $f(x) = x + \frac{1}{2x}$ and $g(x) = \frac{1}{x}$ what is the value of $f(g(\frac{1}{4}))$?

31. The function p is defined by $p(n) = 3n^3 + 8$. What is the value of n when $p(n)$ is equal to 89?

- 106 -

32.

x	t(x)	p(x)
1	-3	4
2	0	3
3	2	-1
4	9	-7

The table above shows some values for the functions t and p. For what value of x does $t(x) + p(x) = 2$?

A) 1
B) 2
C) 3
D) 4

33.

x	g(x)
2	11
4	23
6	35

Some values of a linear function g are shown above. Which of the following defines $g(x)$?

A) $g(x) = 4x + 3$
B) $g(x) = 6x - 1$
C) $g(x) = 4x + 7$
D) $g(x) = 5x + 5$

34.

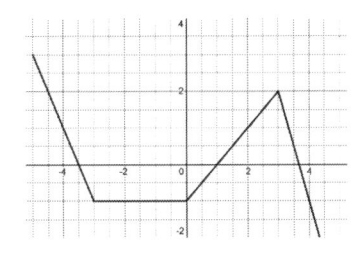

The complete graph of the function f is shown in the xy-plane above. Which of the following statements are true?

I. $f(-4) = -1$
II. $f\left(-\frac{5}{2}\right) = -1$
III. $f(4) = 0$

A) III only
B) II only
C) I and III only
D) II and III only

35. The table below shows values of a quadratic function $f(x)$ for specific values of x. Which of the following could define $f(x)$?

x	f(x)
1	3
3	-1
5	3

A) $f(x) = (x - 3)^2 - 1$
B) $f(x) = (x - 3)^2 + 1$
C) $f(x) = (x + 3)^2- 1$
D) $f(x) = (x + 3)^2 + 1$

36. The graph below shows the entire function f in the xy-plane. If $f(c) = -2$, what is the sum of all possible values of c?

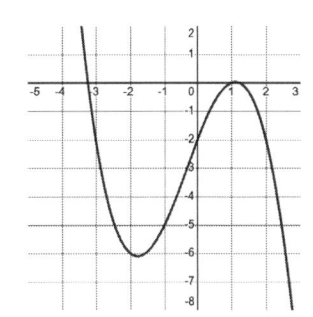

37. In the xy-plane, the point $(3, 18)$ lies on the graph of the function f. If $f(x) = k - 2x^2$, where k is a constant, what is the value of k?

38. The function f is defined by $f(a) = \frac{-3a}{5} + 10$. For what value of a does $f(a) = -32$?

39. A function g satisfies $g(5) = 11$ and $g(6) = 8$. A function h satisfies $h(8) = -3$ and $h(6) = 5$. What is the value of $g(h(6))$?

A) -3
B) 5
C) 8
D) 11

40. $$p(x) = x^2 + 2x - b$$

For the function p defined above, b is a constant and $p(2) = 5$. What is the value of $p(-3)$?

A) -18
B) 0
C) 5
D) 12

41. For the function $f(x) = \frac{x+1}{3}$, what is the value of $f^{-1}(x)$?

A) $\frac{3x-1}{3}$
B) $3x - 1$
C) $\frac{x+1}{3}$
D) $\frac{-x-1}{-3}$

42. In the xy-plane, the point $(2, 8)$ lies on the graph of the function $f(x) = 2x^3 - tx - 6$. What is the value of t?

43.

x	$k(x)$
-2	10
1	19
7	37

Some values of the linear function k are shown in the table above. What is the value of $k(4)$?

A) 22
B) 25
C) 27
D) 28

44. $$f(x) = 2ax^2 - 5x - 4$$

In the xy-plane, the point $(3, 17)$ lies on the graph of the function $f(x)$. What is the value of a?

A) 2
B) 4
C) 9
D) 36

45. Two functions are defined as $f(x) = x^2 - 2$ and $g(x) = 2x - 3$. Which of the following expressions represents $f(g(x))$?

A) $2x^2 - 5$
B) $2x^2 - 11$
C) $4x^2 - 12x + 7$
D) $4x^2 - 12x - 11$

46. The function f is defined by the given equation below. What is the product of $f(a - 4)$ and $f(a)$, where $a > 4$?

$$f(x) = \frac{x}{x+4}$$

A) $\frac{a+4}{a-4}$
B) $\frac{4}{a+4}$
C) $\frac{a-4}{a}$
D) $\frac{a-4}{a+4}$

47. The function f is defined by $f(x) = 3x^2 - 5x + 10$. If the function $f(x - 2)$ is written in the form $ax^2 + bx + c$, what is the value of $a + b + c$?

Chapter 13: Functions

48. The function f is defined by the $f(x) = (x - c)^2$, where c is a constant. If $f(4) = f(12)$, what is the value of $f(2)$?

49. Consider the functions $f(x) = \sqrt{x}$ and $g(x) = 4x + b$. In the standard coordinate plane, the function $y = f(g(x))$ passes through $(5, 4)$. What is the value of b?

50. For the function g, if $g(4x) = x - 8$ for all values of x, what is the value of $g(12)$?

    A) -5
    B) 2
    C) 4
    D) 5

51. Given functions $f(x) = x^2 + 6x - 7$ and $g(x) = 3^x$, for what values of x does $g(f(x)) = 1$?

    A) 1 only
    B) -1 and 7 only
    C) 0 and -1 only
    D) -7 and 1 only

52. For the function f, if $f(10x) = 2x - 8$ for all values of x, what is the value of $f(5)$?

    A) -8
    B) -7
    C) -6
    D) 0

53. For all values of x, there is a function g such that $3g(x) = g(5x)$. If $g(20) = 18$, what is the value of $g(4)$?

54. The function g is defined by $g(t) = (t - 7)(t + 3)^2$. If $g(a - 3) = 0$, what is one possible value of a?

55. The 2 functions f and g are defined as $f(x) = 6x - a$ and $g(x) = 4x + 4$, where a is a real number. If $f(g(x)) = g(f(x))$, then what is the value of a?

- 109 -

PrepPros

Chapter 14: Geometry Part 1 - Angles

In this chapter, we will cover all of the rules that you need to know for angles on the SAT. For angles questions, **we recommend finding and labeling any unknown angles**. The more angles you label, the easier it will be to find the angle that you need to answer the question.

① Intersecting Lines

If two lines intersect, what do we know about the relationships between the angles?

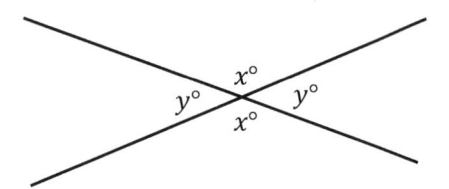

1. **Vertical angles are equal.**

2. **Adjacent angles are supplementary (x and y add to 180°).**

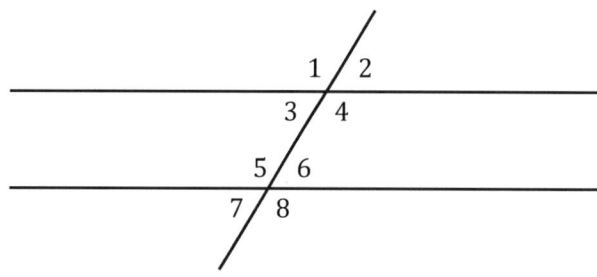

① Parallel Lines

Given two parallel lines, we know the following are true:

1. **Vertical angles are equal** (ex: $\angle 1 = \angle 4$).
2. **Alternate interior angles are equal** (ex: $\angle 3 = \angle 6$).
3. **Opposite interior angles are supplementary** (ex: $\angle 3 + \angle 5 = 180°$ and $\angle 4 + \angle 6 = 180°$).
4. **Corresponding angles are equal** (ex: $\angle 2 = \angle 6$).

All of those rules and fancy terms are nice, but all you really need to know is that one line intersecting two parallel lines creates two sets of identical angles.

$$\angle 1 = \angle 4 = \angle 5 = \angle 8$$
$$\angle 2 = \angle 3 = \angle 6 = \angle 7$$

Any of the angles from the first list will be supplementary with any of the angles from the second list. For example, $\angle 1 + \angle 6 = 180°$ and $\angle 4 + \angle 7 = 180°$. As long as you memorize which angles are identical, you will be able to handle parallel lines questions.

Example 1:

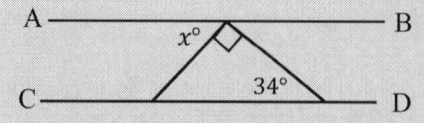

Note: Figure not drawn to scale.

In the figure above, $\overline{AB}$ is parallel with $\overline{CD}$. What is the value of x?

Solution: We know that all angles in a triangle add up to 180°, so we can find the unknown third angle in the triangle above.

$$\text{Third angle} = 180° - 34° - 90° = 56°$$

The third angle we just found and $x°$ are alternate interior angles, so they must be equal. **The answer is 56.**

Chapter 14: Geometry Part 1 - Angles

> **TIP – Extend Parallel Lines**
>
> Often on the SAT, questions with parallel lines will not always look like the parallel lines in the figure on the previous page (the one with angles 1-8 labelled). If the lines just hit and stop (ex: the corner of a parallelogram), take your pencil and extend the lines yourself. Then, it will be much easier to tell which angles are identical.

Exterior Angle Theorem

The exterior angle of a triangle is the angle outside of the triangle when any side is extended. In the triangle below, $a°$ is an exterior angle. The exterior angle theorem states:

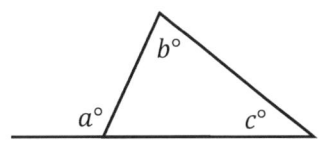

The exterior angle is equal to the sum of the two opposite interior angles. For the triangle above, $a° = b° + c°$.

Example 2:

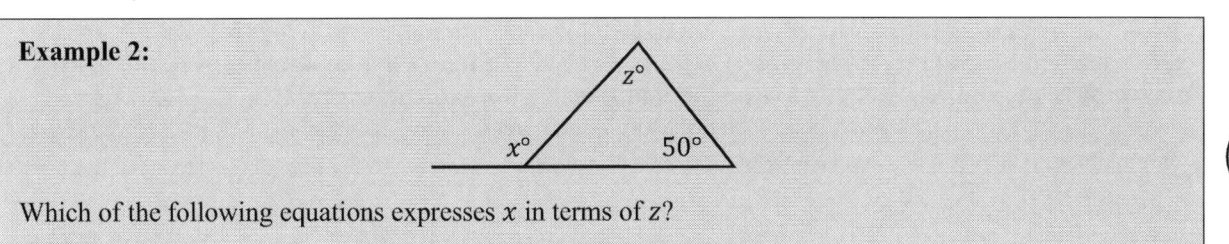

Which of the following equations expresses x in terms of z?

A) $180 - z$ B) $130 - z$ C) $50 + z$ D) $z - 50$

Solution: By definition, $x°$ is an exterior angle, so it must be equal to the sum of the two opposite interior angles 50° and $z°$. **The answer is C.**

Interior Angles in Polygons

You need to know the sum of the interior angles of a...

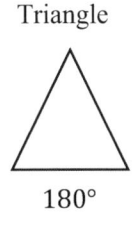

Triangle	Quadrilateral	Pentagon	Hexagon
180°	360°	540°	720°

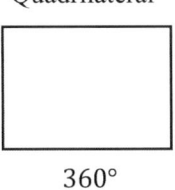

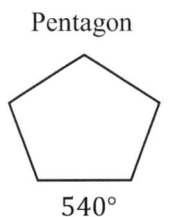

For any polygon,

Sum of Interior Angles $= 180°(n - 2)$ where n is the number of sides.

It does not matter what the shape looks like. All that matters for the sum of the interior angles is the number of sides. You can see how this works with the examples below:

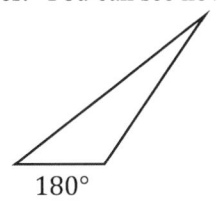

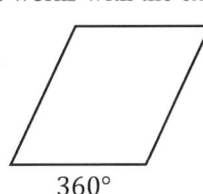

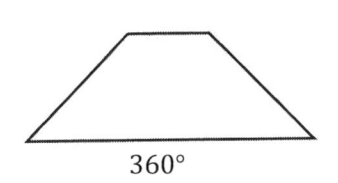

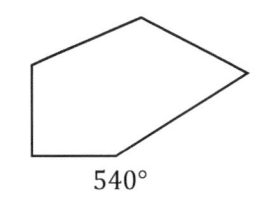

180°   360°   360°   540°

PrepPros

Example 3: For the figure below, what is the value of x?

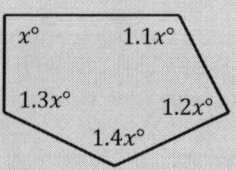

$x°$ $1.1x°$
$1.3x°$ $1.2x°$
$1.4x°$

Note: Figure not drawn to scale.

Solution: The figure above has 5 sides, so the total interior angles are equal to $180°(5-2) = 540°$.

$$x° + 1.3x° + 1.4x° + 1.2x° + 1.1x° = 540°$$
$$6x° = 540°$$
$$x = 90$$

The answer is 90.

TIP – Note: Figure Not Drawn to Scale.

If you see a question with "Note: Figure not drawn to scale," do not trust the figure! The SAT often draws the figure incorrectly to trick you. On the other hand, **if a figure has no note below it, the figure is drawn to scale, and you can trust the angles and side lengths in the figure.** If a figure is drawn to scale and you do not know how to solve the question algebraically, look at the answer choices to see if you can make an educated guess on which answer looks correct.

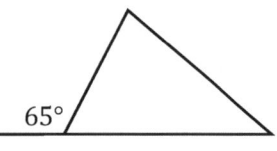

65°   115°

Note: Figure not drawn to scale.

In the figures above, we see that the angle labelled as 65° in the figure on the left is clearly incorrect. On the other hand, the figure on the right has no note, so we know the 115° is correct and know that the figure is drawn to scale.

Types of Triangles

An **equilateral triangle** is a triangle in which all three sides are equal, and all angles are equal to $60°$.

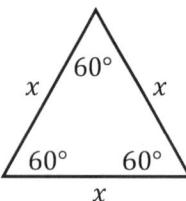

x /60°\ x
/60° 60°\
x

An **isosceles triangle** is a triangle in which two sides are equal and two angles are equal.

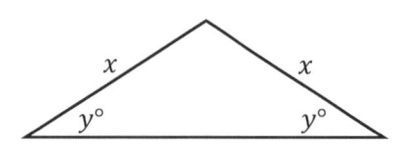

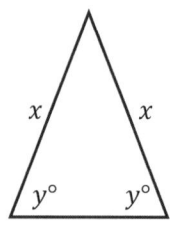

x x x x
$y°$ $y°$ $y°$ $y°$

- 112 -

A scalene triangle is a triangle with three sides and three angles that are all different.

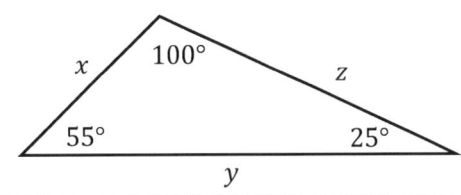

Example 4:

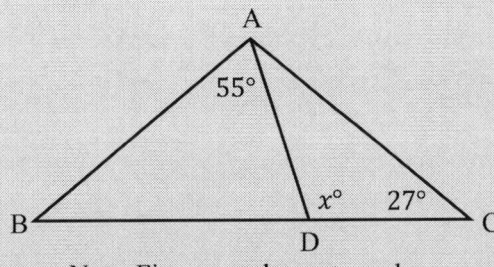

Note: Figure not drawn to scale.

Triangle ABC is an isosceles triangle in which BC is the longest side. What is the value of x?

A) 82   B) 98   C) 125   D) 151

Solution: Since ABC is an isosceles triangle and BC is the longest side, we know $AB = AC$. That means we can find $\angle B$:

$$\angle B = \angle C = 27°$$

Once we know $\angle B = 27°$, we can find $\angle ADB$ because we know the other two angles in triangle ADB.

$$\angle ADB = 180° - 27° - 55° = 98°$$

The angle $x°$ that we are looking for is adjacent to $\angle ADB$, so we can solve:

$$x° = 180° - 98° = 82°$$

The answer is A.

Remember that we cannot trust the figure when we see "Note: Figure not drawn to scale." The correct answer is an acute angle, but the figure makes it look like $x°$ should be obtuse. The question tried to trick you! The SAT Math Test may include curveball questions like this, so make sure you always read questions and figures carefully.

Angles Practice: Answers on page 329.

1. In the triangle below, what is the value of x?

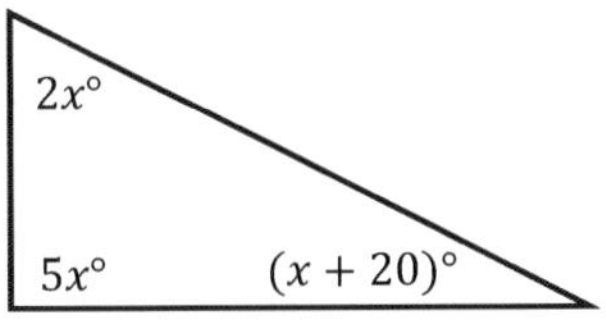

   Note: Figure not drawn to scale.

2. What is the value of x in the figure below?

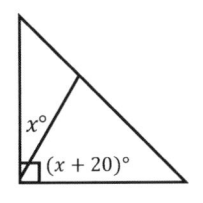

   A) 25
   B) 30
   C) 35
   D) 40

3. In the figure below, what is the measure of $\angle JKL$?

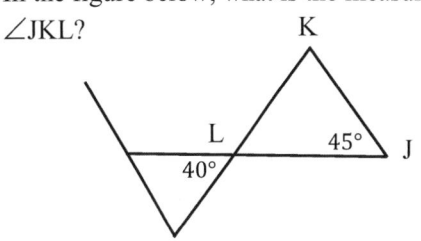

   Note: Figure not drawn to scale.

   A) 40
   B) 45
   C) 85
   D) 95

- 113 -

PrepPros

4. In the figure below, if $y = 54$, what is the value of x?

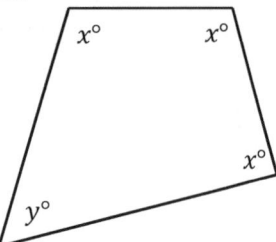

Note: Figure not drawn to scale.

A) 102
B) 108
C) 112
D) 126

5. In the figure below, $AE = DE$, $BE = CE$, and $\overline{BC}$ is parallel to $\overline{AD}$. If $x = 32$, what is the measure of $\angle BCE$?

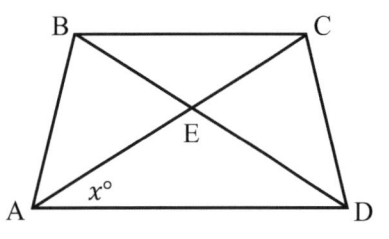

A) 28
B) 32
C) 48
D) 64

6. In the figure below, $\overline{LN}$ intersects $\overline{KM}$ at point P. What is the measure of $\angle LPM$?

A) 12
B) 61
C) 129
D) 143

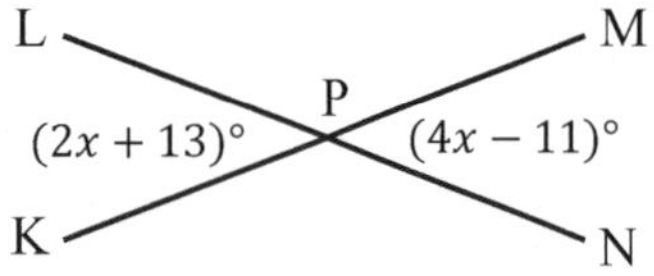

Note: Figure not drawn to scale.

7.

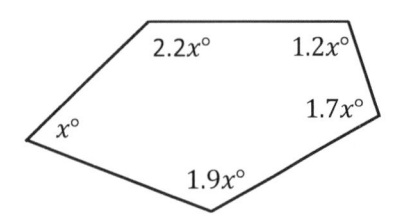

Note: Figure not drawn to scale.

In the figure above, what is the value of x?

8. In the figure below, two parallel lines are intersected by $\overline{AB}$. What is the value of x?

A) 30
B) 40
C) 50
D) 80

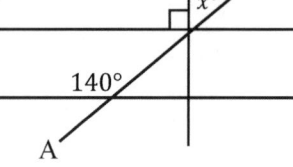

9.

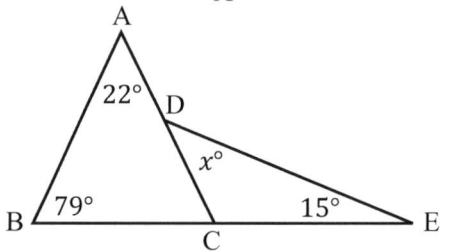

Note: Figure not drawn to scale.

In the figure above, what is the value of x?

A) 101
B) 86
C) 79
D) 64

10. The measures of four of the interior angles of a hexagon are $65°, 70°, 95°$ and $110°$. What is the sum of the last two interior angles?

A) 180
B) 340
C) 380
D) 440

11.

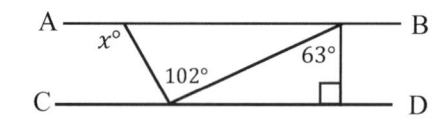

Note: Figure not drawn to scale.

In the figure above, $\overline{AB}$ and $\overline{CD}$ are parallel. What is the value of x?

- 114 -

12. Triangle LMN and the collinear points L, N, and P are shown below. What is the measure of ∠M?

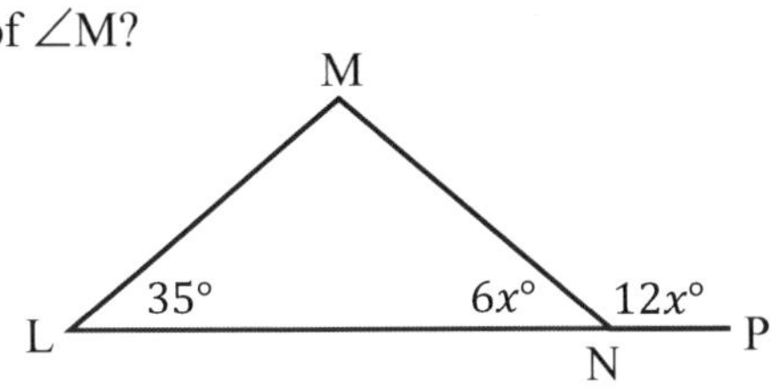

Note: Figure not drawn to scale.

A) 55
B) 65
C) 85
D) 95

13.

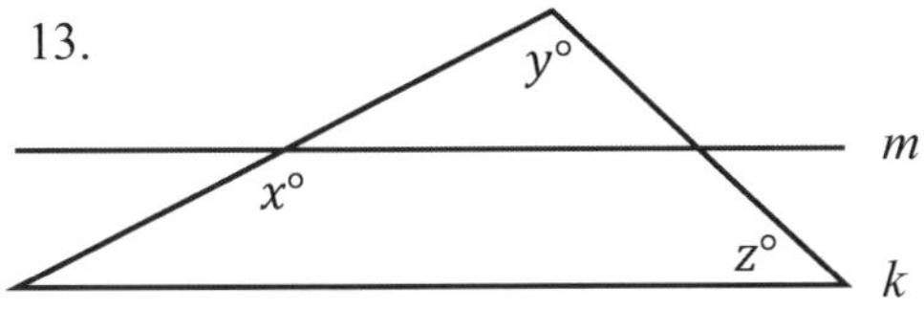

Note: Figure not drawn to scale.

In the figure above, lines k and m are parallel. If $x = 148$ and $y = 70$, what is the value of z?

A) 102
B) 78
C) 44
D) 32

14.

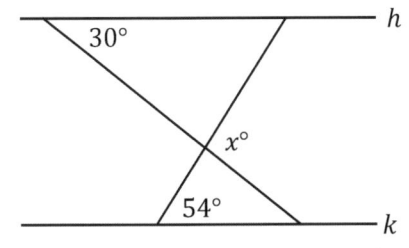

Note: Figure not drawn to scale.

In the figure above, lines h and k are parallel. What is the value of x in the figure above?

15.

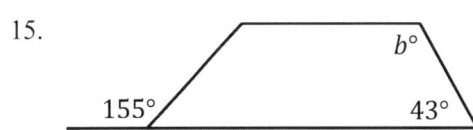

Note: Figure not drawn to scale.

In the figure above, the shape is a trapezoid. What is the value of b?

A) 43
B) 112
C) 137
D) 155

16.

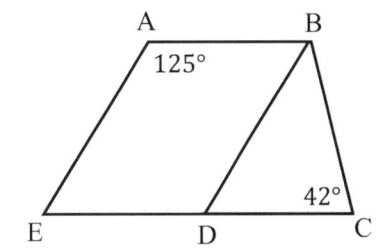

Note: Figure not drawn to scale.

In the figure above, $\overline{AB}$ and $\overline{EC}$ are parallel, $\overline{AE}$ and $\overline{BD}$ are parallel. What is the measure of ∠ABC in degrees?

A) 138
B) 125
C) 97
D) 83

17.

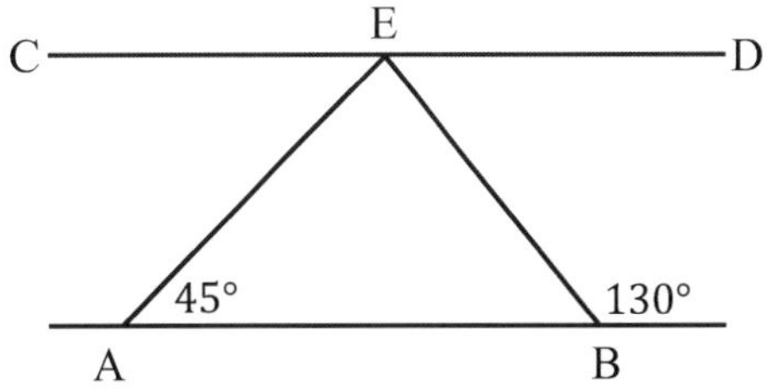

Note: Figure not drawn to scale.

In the figure above, what is the measure of ∠AED in degrees?

- 115 -

18. In the figure shown below, line c intersects lines a and b. Which additional pieces of information is sufficient to prove that lines a and b are parallel? (Note: Figure not drawn to scale.)

 A) $y = z$
 B) $x = y$
 C) $x = 180 - z$
 D) $y = 180 - x$

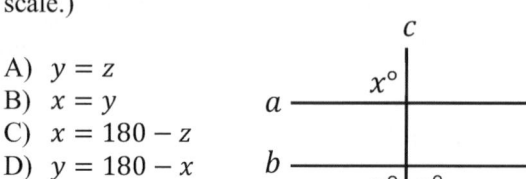

19. In the figure above, $\overline{AB}$ is parallel to $\overline{DE}$. What is the measure of $\angle ACB$?

 A) 51
 B) 55
 C) 68
 D) 74

20. Which statement must be true in the figure below for lines a and b to be parallel?

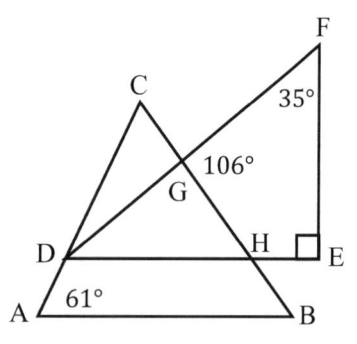

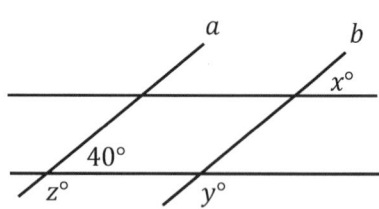

 A) $z = 180 - 40$
 B) $x = 180 - y$
 C) $z - 40 = y$
 D) $z = 180 - x$

21. In the figure below, two sides of the triangle have been extended. If $y = 66°$ and $c = 2b$, what is the value of x?

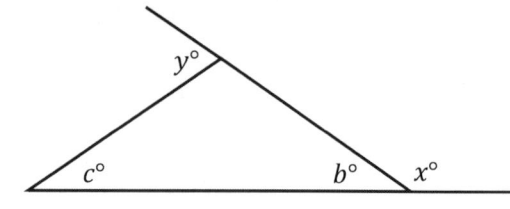

Note: figure not drawn to scale

22. Which of the following expressions is correct for the figure above?

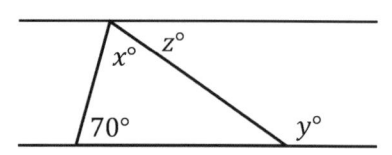

 A) $x + y = 180$
 B) $x + 70 - y$
 C) $x + 70 + z = 180 - y$
 D) $z - 70 = x$

23. In the figure above, $AG = CG$. What is the measure of $\angle AKB$?

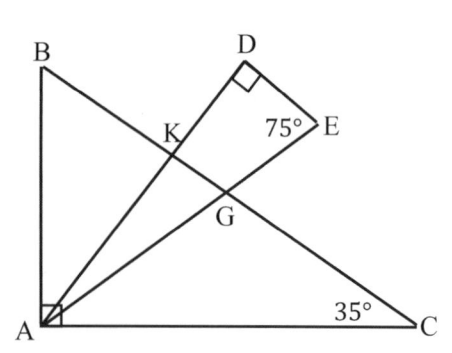

 A) 70
 B) 75
 C) 80
 D) 85

Chapter 15: Geometry Part 2 - Shapes

For each SAT Math section, you are given a reference sheet with equations for certain shapes. There are additional equations in this chapter that you need to have memorized for test day as well. Whether the SAT gives you the equations or not, you should have all the equations in this chapter memorized, as it will help you solve questions more quickly on test day.

Area and Volume

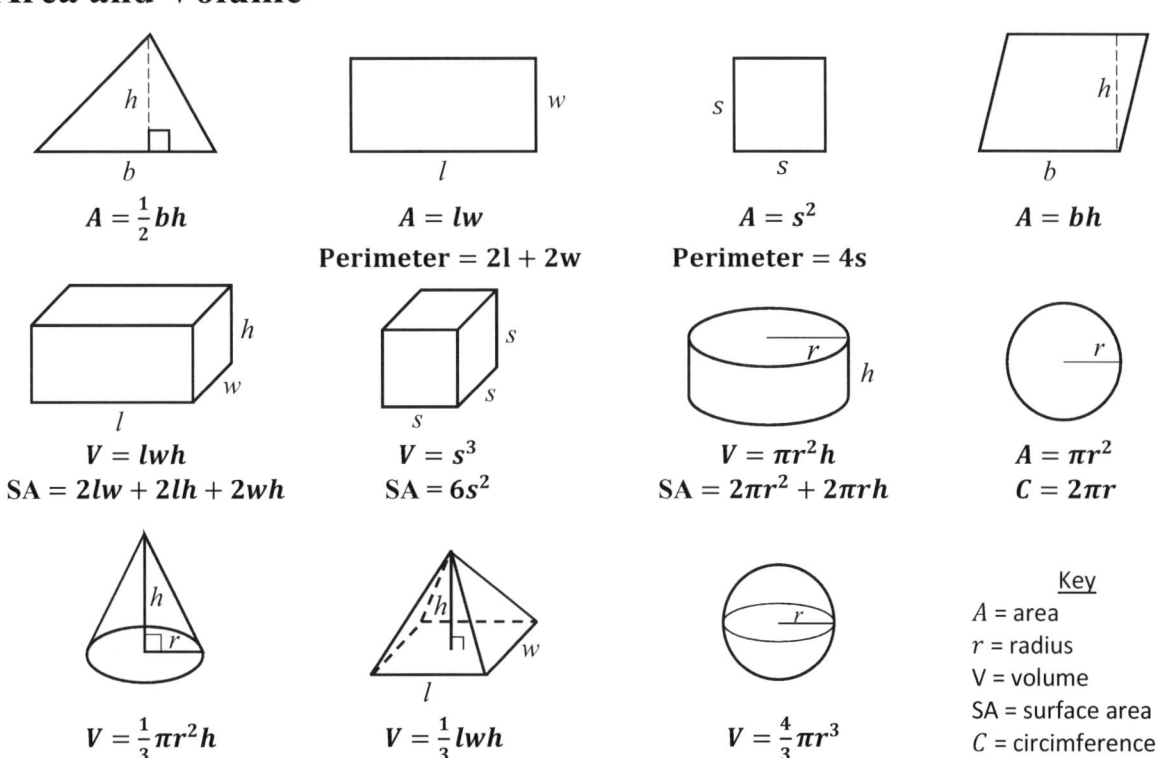

$A = \frac{1}{2}bh$

$A = lw$
Perimeter $= 2l + 2w$

$A = s^2$
Perimeter $= 4s$

$A = bh$

$V = lwh$
$SA = 2lw + 2lh + 2wh$

$V = s^3$
$SA = 6s^2$

$V = \pi r^2 h$
$SA = 2\pi r^2 + 2\pi r h$

$A = \pi r^2$
$C = 2\pi r$

$V = \frac{1}{3}\pi r^2 h$

$V = \frac{1}{3}lwh$

$V = \frac{4}{3}\pi r^3$

Key
A = area
r = radius
V = volume
SA = surface area
C = circumference

Example 1: A rectangular solid has a square base. If one side of the base is 6 inches and the rectangular solid has a height of 16, what is the volume, in cubic inches, of the rectangular solid?

Solution: To solve, we use the rectangular solid equation $V = lwh$. We are told that the base is a square with a side length of 6 inches, so we know that 2 sides, the base and length, are equal 6. We know that the height is 16 inches. So, we can find the volume by plugging those values into the volume equation:

$$V = lwh \quad \rightarrow \quad V = (6)(6)(16) = 576$$

The answer is 576.

Example 2:

Amanda is freezing ice cream in the cake tin above to make an ice cream cake. The cake tin has a diameter of 25 cm. If Amanda uses 2,000 cm³ of ice cream to make the ice cream cake, which of the following is closest to the height, in centimeters, of the ice cream cake?
  A) 12   B) 8   C) 4   D) 2

Solution: To solve, we will use the equation for the volume of a right circular cylinder. We know the volume is equal to 2,000 cm³. The radius of a circle is equal to half of the diameter, so the radius is equal to 12.5 cm. Now, we can solve for the height.

$$V = \pi r^2 h$$
$$2000 = \pi(12.5)^2 h$$
$$\frac{2000}{\pi(12.5)^2} = h$$
$$4.07 = h$$

The height is equal to 4.07 cm, which is closest to 4. **The answer is C.**

> **Example 3:** Morgan is making a poster for her room. The original poster did not fit on her wall, so she is changing the dimensions by tripling the width and halving the length. If the original area of the poster was 4A, what is the area of the new poster in terms of A?
>
> A) $\frac{3}{2}A$ B) $4A$ C) $6A$ D) $9A$

Solution: Method #1 – The Math Teacher Way: We know the area of the original poster is 4A, so

$$4A = lw$$

Now, we need to see how the area changes with the new length and width:

$$\text{New Area} = (3l)(0.5w) = 1.5lw$$

The new area is 1.5 times as large as the old area. From the first equation, we know that $4A = lw$, so plugging in the 4A for lw, we can find the new area in terms of A.

$$\text{New Area} = 1.5(4A) = 6A$$

The answer is C.

Method #2 – Substitution: If solving this question algebraically seems confusing, that's because it is! To make this question easier, use the substitution method we learned in Chapter 2 and pick values for the length and width of the original poster. Let's say the length is 2 and the width is 3, so the original poster has an area of 6. Now, use the numbers we picked to solve the rest of the question.

$$\text{New Width} = 3(3) = 9$$
$$\text{New Length} = 2(0.5) = 1$$
$$\text{New Area} = lw = (9)(1) = 9$$

The original area was 6 and the new area is 9. The new area is 1.5 times larger than the original area, so we can apply that same change to the poster's original area of 4A.

$$\text{New Area} = 1.5(\text{Original Area}) = 1.5(4A) = 6A$$

The answer is C.

Similar Shapes and Scale Factors

Similar shapes have the same shape but different sizes. **All corresponding angles in similar shapes are equal and the corresponding sides are all in the same ratio.** For example, the two rectangles below are similar shapes.

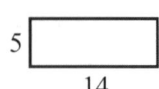

In similar shapes, the side lengths are multiplied by the same scale factor. In the example above, the scale factor is 2. Notice how all side lengths in the first rectangle are multiplied by 2 to get to the side lengths in the second rectangle.

Example 4: If the base and height of a triangle are quadrupled, how many times larger is the new area than the original area?

A) 4   B) 8   C) 12   D) 16

Solution: Method #1 – Scale Factors Rules: This question is challenging because we are not given values for the base and height, so we need to conceptually understand how the changes affect the area of the triangle. The good news is that there is a rule that we can memorize:

For any 2-dimensional shape, the area is equal to (scale factor)² times the original area.

This rule applies for all 2-dimensional shapes (triangles, squares, rectangles, circles, trapezoids, etc.). In Example 4, all sides are quadrupled, so the scale factor is 4. Applying our rule, we find that the area of the triangle is equal to $(4)^2$ the original area. Solving, we find that the area is 16 times the original area, so **the answer is D.**

Now, let's examine why that rule always works. The equation for the area of a triangle is $A = \frac{1}{2}bh$. If we quadruple both the base and height, the equation becomes

$$A = \frac{1}{2}(4b)(4h)$$

When we simplify, we end up with

$$A = \frac{1}{2}(16bh)$$

Since we multiply the base and height, the scale factor, 4, is always squared. Therefore, the area of a 2-dimensional similar shape is always equal to (scale factor)² times the original area.

There is one other rule you should memorize as well in case a similar shapes question asks about perimeter.

For any 2-dimensional shape, the perimeter or circumference is equal to (scale factor) times the original perimeter or circumference.

For the triangle in Example 4, the new perimeter would be 4 times as long as the original perimeter.

Method #2 – Substitution: We can also "cheat" this question by selecting values for the base and height of the original triangle. Let's say the base is 2 and the height is 3, so the original triangle has an area of 3. Now, let's quadruple the numbers we picked to find the base and height of the new triangle.

$$\text{New Base} = 4(2) = 8$$
$$\text{New Height} = 4(3) = 12$$
$$\text{New Area} = \frac{1}{2}bh = \frac{1}{2}(8)(12) = 48$$

The original area was 3 and the new area is 48. The new area is 16 times larger than the original area, so **the answer is D.** While substitution is great for Example 4, you should still make sure that you understand the scale factors rules, as the SAT may include questions where we cannot use substitution.

Example 5: Rectangular prism $ABCD$ has side lengths of x, y, and z, and rectangular prism $EFGH$ has side lengths ax, ay, and az. If rectangular prism $ABCD$ has a volume of 16 cubic feet and rectangular prism $EFGH$ has a volume of 2,000 cubic feet, what is the value of a?

Solution – Scale Factor Rules: All sides of the rectangular prism are multiplied by a, so we know that the two rectangular prisms are similar. We now have a 3-dimensional shape, so let's learn the rule that we can apply for 3 dimensional shapes when solving for volume:

For any 3-dimensional shape, the volume is equal to (scale factor)³ times the original volume.

In Example 5, the scale factor is a. We know that the original volume is 16 and the new volume is 2000, so we can use our rule to set up the equation below.

$$2{,}000 = a^3(16)$$

The volume, 2,000 cubic feet, is equal to the scale factor, a, cubed times the original volume, 16 cubic feet. To solve for a, we divide both sides by 16 and then take the cube root.

$$\frac{2{,}000}{16} = a^3$$

$$125 = a^3$$

$$\sqrt[3]{125} = a$$

$$5 = a$$

The answer is 5.

There is one other rule you should memorize as well in case a similar shapes question asks about surface area.

For any 3-dimensional shape, the surface area is equal to (scale factor)^2 times the original surface area.

In Example 5, we found the scale factor was 5, so rectangular prism $EFHG$ would have a surface area that is 25 times as large as the surface area of $ABCD$.

Similar Shapes and Scale Factors Rules

The table below summarizes all the scale factor rules that we learned in this chapter. **Make sure you memorize the rules in the first row!** We have also included some common scale factors that can appear on the SAT to help you better understand the rules.

Scale Factor	2-Dimensional Shapes		3-Dimensional Shape	
	Perimeter	Area	Surface Area	Volume
(scale factor)	(scale factor)	(scale factor)^2	(scale factor)^2	(scale factor)^3
$\frac{1}{2}$	$\frac{1}{2}$	$\frac{1}{4}$	$\frac{1}{4}$	$\frac{1}{8}$
2	2	4	4	8
3	3	9	9	27
4	4	16	16	64

Right Triangles

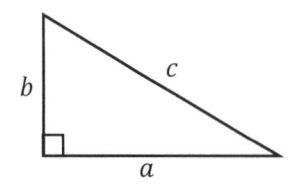

All right triangles follow the Pythagorean theorem:

$$a^2 + b^2 = c^2$$

where a and b are the lengths of the legs and c is the hypotenuse. Remember that **you can only use the Pythagorean theorem for right triangles.**

Chapter 15: Geometry Part 2 - Shapes

Example 6:

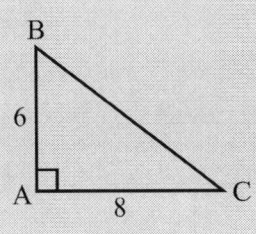

In the triangle above, point D (not shown) is the midpoint of BC. What is the length of CD?

Solution: We first need to use the Pythagorean theorem to find the length of BC.

$$6^2 + 8^2 = c^2$$
$$100 = c^2$$
$$10 = c$$

We now know $BC = 10$. Since D is the midpoint of BC, the length of CD is half of BC, so CD is 5. **The answer is 5.**

TIP – Pythagorean Triples

Pythagorean triples are sets of whole numbers that work in the Pythagorean theorem. On the SAT, you should look out for the two common Pythagorean triples.

3, 4, 5 Right Triangle

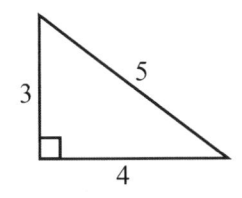

5, 12, 13 Right Triangle

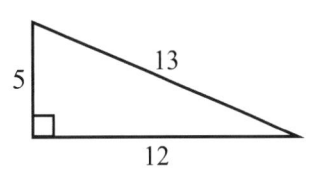

These triangles can also be scaled up by multiplying all of the side lengths by the same number to create more Pythagorean triples. For example, a 3, 4, 5 right triangle can be doubled to become a 6, 8, 10 right triangle, tripled to become 9, 12, 15, and so on.

Special Right Triangles

You need to be familiar with two special right triangles: $45° - 45° - 90°$ and $30° - 60° - 90°$. The side lengths of these triangles are always in a particular ratio.

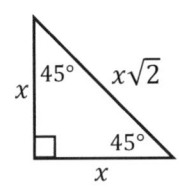

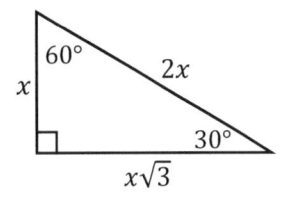

$45° - 45° - 90°$

$30° - 60° - 90°$

You are given the two pictures in the reference table for each math section. It is still critical to memorize the ratio of the side lengths, so you can spot special right triangles questions.

PrepPros

Example 7:

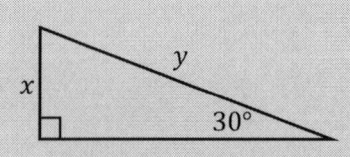

Note: Figure not drawn to scale.

In the triangle above, $y = 10$. What is the value of x?

A) 3   B) 5   C) 6   D) 8

Solution: This is a $30° - 60° - 90°$ right triangle, so we need to use the ratio of side lengths to solve. The shortest side, x, is always half the length of the hypotenuse, y. We know that $y = 10$, so $x = \frac{1}{2}(10) = 5$.
The answer is B.

Example 8:

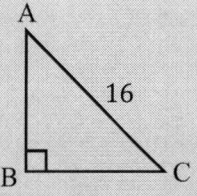

Triangle ABC above is a right isosceles triangle. What is the area of triangle ABC?

A) 128   B) $128\sqrt{2}$ C) 64   D) $64\sqrt{2}$

Solution: A right isosceles triangle is the same as a $45° - 45° - 90°$ right triangle. To find the area of triangle ABC, we need to know the side lengths AB and BC. To find these sides lengths, we can use the ratio from the $45° - 45° - 90°$ right triangle. We are looking for the legs of the triangle, which are the x's, and we are given that the hypotenuse, which is the $x\sqrt{2}$. Since we know the hypotenuse is equal to 16, we can solve for x.

$$x\sqrt{2} = 16$$

$$x = \frac{16}{\sqrt{2}} = \frac{16}{\sqrt{2}} \times \frac{\sqrt{2}}{\sqrt{2}} = \frac{16\sqrt{2}}{2} = 8\sqrt{2}$$

We know that $AB = BC = 8\sqrt{2}$. Now that we know the lengths of the base and height of the triangle, we can solve for the area of triangle ABC.

$$\text{Area of ABC} = \frac{1}{2}(8\sqrt{2})(8\sqrt{2}) = \frac{1}{2}(128) = 64$$

The answer is C.

Third Side of a Triangle

Can you make a triangle with side lengths of 4, 5, and 10? What about one with side lengths of 4, 5, and 9? Or one with side lengths of 4, 5, and 8? While this may at first seem confusing, there is a simple rule:

The sum of the two shorter sides of a triangle, a and b, must be greater than the longest side of a triangle, c.

$$a + b > c$$

Let's use this rule to review the three potential triangles introduced above. We will start with a triangle with side lengths of 4, 5, and 9.

$$4 + 5 \not> 9$$

Since the sum of the shorter side lengths are equal to the longest side, we cannot make a triangle.

Let's try side lengths of 4, 5, and 10.

$$4 + 5 \not> 10$$

Now, the two shorter sides cannot even reach the end of the longest side, so again we cannot make a triangle.

What about side lengths of 4, 5, and 8?

$$4 + 5 > 8$$

Since the smaller sides are greater than the longest side, we can finally make a triangle!

Example 9: Triangle ABC has two sides of length 10 and 15. Which of the following could NOT be the third side of triangle ABC?

    A) 5   B) 13   C) 19   D) 23

Solution: To solve, we just need to test each answer choice to find which one does not work with our third side of the triangle rule. For answer choices A and B, the longest side would be 15. For answer choices C and D, the number in the answer choice would be the longest side.

Let's start with answer choice A.

$$5 + 10 \not> 15$$

The sides of 5 and 10 are equal to 15, so no triangle can be formed.

If we test the rest of the answer choices, we see that each of them works.

$$\text{For B: } 13 + 10 > 15$$
$$\text{For C: } 10 + 15 > 19$$
$$\text{For D: } 10 + 15 > 23$$

The answer is A.

PrepPros

Other Rules You Might Need to Know

Below are some additional geometry rules that you may need to know for test day. Any students aiming for very high math scores should memorize all the rules below.

1. Area of an Equilateral Triangle

To find the area of an equilateral triangle with side lengths s, use the equation. $A = \frac{s^2\sqrt{3}}{4}$

Memorize this equation! It can be extremely helpful for advanced triangles questions.

2. Half of an Equilateral Triangle is a 30° − 60° − 90° right triangle.

Cutting an equilateral triangle in half vertically creates two 30° − 60° − 90° right triangles.

3. Side Lengths and Angles in a Triangle

The smallest side in a triangle is opposite from the smallest angle. The largest side in a triangle is opposite from the largest angle.

4. Other Triangle Definitions

- **An acute triangle** has angles that are all less than 90°.
- **An obtuse triangle** has 1 angle that is greater than 90°.
- **A right triangle** has 1 angle that is equal to 90°.

5. Tangent Lines and Circles

A tangent line to a circle is a straight line that just touches the circle at one point. The angle between the radius of the circle to the point of tangency and the tangent line is always 90°. In the diagram below, lines BC and CD are both tangent lines. The points of tangency are at point B and point D.

The radius from the center of the circle to the point of tangency is perpendicular to the tangent line. In the diagram below, the slope of line AB is perpendicular to BC, and the slope of line AD is perpendicular to DC.

Two tangent lines to a circle from a single point are congruent. In the diagram below, BC = DC.

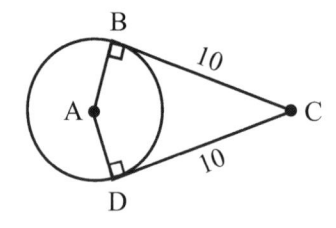

Shapes Practice: Answers on page 330.

1. If the area of rectangle ABCD below is 80, what is area of the shaded region?

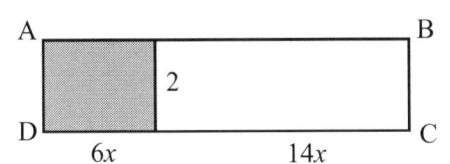

   A ▬▬▬▬▬▬▬▬▬▬▬▬▬▬▬▬ B
   ░░░░░│ 2
   D ──6x── ──14x── C

   Note: Figure not drawn to scale.

   A) 12
   B) 18
   C) 24
   D) 36

2. What is the area of a circle with a circumference of 12π?

   A) 12π
   B) 24π
   C) 30π
   D) 36π

3. The diameter of a circle is $\frac{22}{\pi}$ centimeters. What is the circumference of the circle?

4. For the triangle below, which of the following correctly solves for side BC?

   A) $\sqrt{6^2} + \sqrt{17^2}$
   B) $\sqrt{6^2 + 17^2}$
   C) $\sqrt{6 + 17}$
   D) $\sqrt{17^2 - 6^2}$

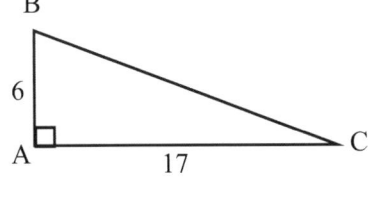

5. Triangle ABC has two sides of length 7 and 12. Which of the following could NOT be the length of the third side of the triangle?

   A) 5
   B) 7
   C) 12
   D) 15

6. The circumference of a circle is 16π. What is the area of half of the circle?

   A) 16π
   B) 32π
   C) 64π
   D) 128π

7. A swimming pool has a volume of 2,880 cubic feet. If the pool is 15 feet deep and 16 feet long, how wide, in feet, is the pool?

8. In the shape below, all angles are right angles. Which of the following is closest to the area of the shape?

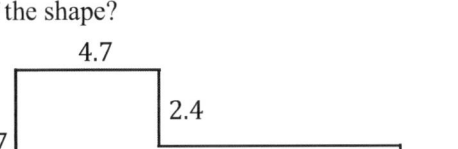

   A) 40.5
   B) 42.5
   C) 53.5
   D) 59.7

9. Each side of a square ABCD has a length of 40 meters. A certain rectangle whose area is equal to the area of square ABCD has a width of 25 meters. What is the length, in meters, of the rectangle?

10. The length of a rectangle's diagonal is $13\sqrt{2}$, and the length of the rectangle's shorter side is 7. What is the length of the rectangle's longer side?

- 125 -

PrepPros

11. In the figure below, the larger shaded circle has a radius of 10, and the smaller circles each have a radius of 2. What is the area of the shaded region?

A) 64π
B) 81π
C) 92π
D) 100π

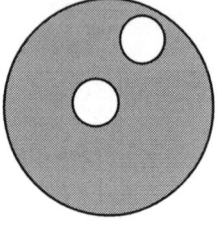

12. Equilateral triangle ABC is shown below. What is the value of k?

A) -2
B) 0
C) 4
D) 6

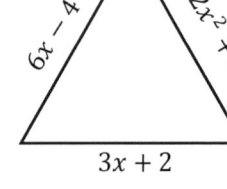

(sides labeled: $6x - 4$, $2x^2 + k$, $3x + 2$)

13. If a triangle has two sides with lengths 6 and 8, what is the length of the third side?

A) 2
B) 6
C) 8
D) Cannot be determined

14. Simone is building a box to store her textbooks. She has a spot in the corner of her room to put the box that is 20 inches wide and 24 inches long. If the box must have a total volume of 7,200 cubic inches, what is the height, in inches, of the box?

15. Michelle is filling up a ball with water as part of a science fair project. If the ball can hold a total of 950 cubic inches of water when it is completely filled, approximately what is the radius of the ball?

A) 6.1
B) 8.9
C) 20.1
D) 26.7

16. What is the area of the triangle below?

A) $36\sqrt{3}$
B) 36
C) $18\sqrt{3}$
D) 18

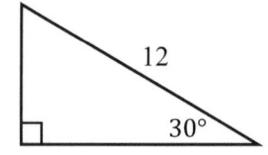

(triangle with hypotenuse 12, angle 30°)

17. The area of a rectangle is 500 square inches, and its width is 5 times its length. What is the perimeter of the rectangle?

A) 20
B) 50
C) 120
D) 250

18. A right triangle has sides of lengths $7\sqrt{2}$, $9\sqrt{2}$ and $\sqrt{260}$. What is the area of the triangle, in square units?

A) $16\sqrt{2} + \sqrt{260}$
B) 63
C) $126\sqrt{260}$
D) 126

19.

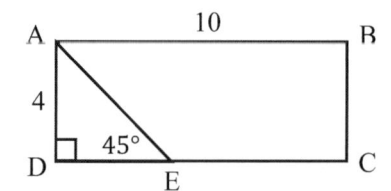

(Figure: rectangle ABCD with AB = 10, AD = 4, point E on DC with angle at E = 45°)

For the figure above, what is the perimeter of quadrilateral AECB?

A) $20 + 4\sqrt{2}$
B) $28 + 4\sqrt{3}$
C) $24 + 4\sqrt{2}$
D) 24

20. Circle A has a radius of $7n$ and circle B has a radius of $119n$, where n is a positive constant. The area of circle B is how many times the area of circle A?

A) 17
B) 34
C) 119
D) 289

- 126 -

Chapter 15: Geometry Part 2 - Shapes

21. There are two similar rectangles. The area of the larger rectangle is 9 times larger than the area of the smaller rectangle. The perimeter of the smaller rectangle is 44. What is the perimeter of the larger rectangle?

   A) $\frac{44\sqrt{3}}{3}$
   B) $44\sqrt{3}$
   C) 132
   D) 396

22. The length of the rectangular prism is 3 times the width. The height and the width are the same. The volume of the prism is 81 cubic inches. What is the length, in inches, of the prism?

23. Ayesha is making a flowerpot for her Mom for Mother's Day. Her Mom's current favorite flowerpot, which is in the shape of a right circular cylinder, holds Q liters of water. Ayesha is going to make a new flowerpot with twice the width and twice the height. How many liters of water will the new flowerpot hold?

   A) $2Q$
   B) $4Q$
   C) $6Q$
   D) $8Q$

24. The length of a diagonal of a square is $\frac{9\sqrt{2}}{2}$. What is the length of a side of the square?

25. An isosceles right triangle has a hypotenuse of length $34\sqrt{2}$ centimeters. What is the perimeter, in centimeters, of this triangle?

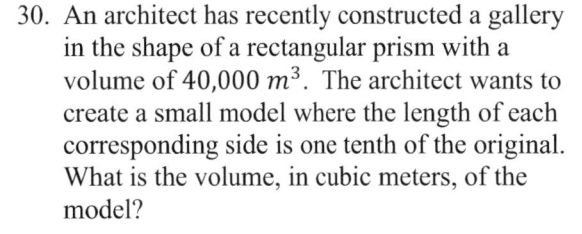

   A) $34\sqrt{2}$
   B) $68\sqrt{2}$
   C) $68 + 34\sqrt{2}$
   D) $68 + 68\sqrt{2}$

26. Two pool floats are each in the shape of a sphere. The larger pool float has a diameter of $4x$ and the smaller pool float has a diameter of x. What is the ratio of the volume of the larger pool float to the volume of the smaller pool float?

   A) 4 to 1
   B) 8 to 1
   C) 16 to 1
   D) 64 to 1

27. The dimensions of a right rectangular prism are 6 inches by 5 inches by 3 inches. What is the surface area, in square inches, of the prism?

   A) 63
   B) 66
   C) 90
   D) 126

28. In the figure below, the diameter of the circle is 10 inches. What is the area of the square inside of the circle?

29. The area of a triangle is 14 square units. A second triangle has side lengths 8 times those of the first triangle. What is the area, in square units, of the second triangle?

30. An architect has recently constructed a gallery in the shape of a rectangular prism with a volume of $40,000 \ m^3$. The architect wants to create a small model where the length of each corresponding side is one tenth of the original. What is the volume, in cubic meters, of the model?

- 127 -

31. A manufacturer determined that right cylindrical containers with a height that is 3 inches longer than the radius offer the optimal number of containers to be displayed on a store shelf. Which of the following expresses the volume, V, in cubic inches, of such containers, where r is the radius, in inches?

   A) $V = 3\pi r^2$
   B) $V = 3\pi r^3$
   C) $V = \pi r^2 + 3\pi r$
   D) $V = \pi r^3 + 3\pi r^2$

32. The volume of cube A is k cubic units. The edge length of cube B is four times the edge length of cube A. Which expression represents the volume of cube B in terms of k?

   A) $4k$
   B) $8k$
   C) $16k$
   D) $64k$

33. The volume of rectangular solid X is 100 cubic units. The length, the width, and the height of rectangular solid Y are 3 times the corresponding dimension of rectangular solid X. What is the volume, in cubic units, of rectangular solid Y?

34. In the figure below, $\triangle ABC$ is equilateral and each side of $\triangle ABC$ is the diameter of a semicircle. If the total length of the three semicircles is 12π, what is the perimeter of $\triangle ABC$?

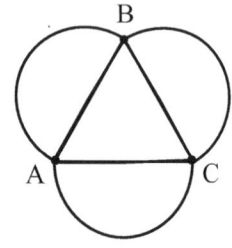

35. A paint can in the shape of a right circular cylinder has a paper label covering all of the can except the circular top and bottom. If the radius of the top of the can is 1.5 inches and the height of the can is 7 inches, which of the following best approximates the area, in square inches, of the part of the can covered by the label?

   A. 33
   B. 49
   C. 66
   D. 198

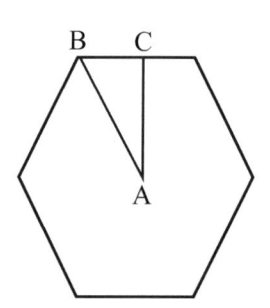

36. In the regular hexagon above, $AB = 20$. What is the area of $\triangle ABC$?

   A) 20
   B) $20\sqrt{2}$
   C) $50\sqrt{3}$
   D) 50

37. Jake is going to cut a regular hexagon, where all the sides are the same length, out of a rectangle, leaving only the shaded region behind. What is the sum of the area of the shaded region?

   A) $25\sqrt{3}$
   B) $25\sqrt{2}$
   C) $50\sqrt{3}$
   D) 50

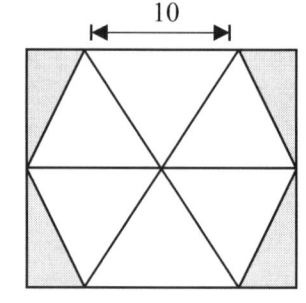

38. Square A has a side length of x inches. Square B has a perimeter that is 148 inches less than the perimeter of square A. The function f gives the area of square B, in square inches. Which of the following defines f?

A) $f(x) = (x + 37)^2$
B) $f(x) = (x - 37)^2$
C) $f(x) = (148x - 37)^2$
D) $f(x) = (148x + 37)^2$

39. A triangle has interior angles with measures in the ratio of 4:8:12. If the shortest side of the triangle is 6, what is the length of the second longest side?

A) $6\sqrt{3}$
B) 9
C) 12
D) 18

40. The perimeter of an equilateral triangle can be expressed as $x\sqrt{3}$. If the height of the triangle is 24, what is the value of x?

41. An isosceles right triangle has a perimeter of $38 + 38\sqrt{2}$ centimeters. What is the length, in centimeters, of one leg of this triangle?

A) 19
B) $19\sqrt{2}$
C) 38
D) $38\sqrt{2}$

42. The volume of a rectangular prism with a square base is 12,000 cubic inches. If the area of each of the four lateral faces is 600 square inches, what is the area, in square inches, of the square base?

43. Rectangular prism A is similar to rectangular prism B, where the shortest side of rectangular prism A corresponds to the shortest side of rectangular prism B. The volume of rectangular prism A, in cubic meters, is 3,402, and the volume of rectangular prism B, in cubic meters, is 126. The shortest side of rectangular prism A is 9. What is the shortest side of rectangular prism B?

44. In the figure below, the circle below has an area of 16π. What is the area of the equilateral triangle?

A) 64
B) $64\sqrt{3}$
C) $\frac{64\sqrt{3}}{3}$
D) $\frac{128\sqrt{3}}{3}$

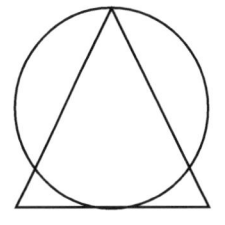

45. What is the perimeter of an equilateral triangle with an area of $49\sqrt{3}$

Chapter 16: Geometry Part 3 – Similar Shapes and Congruent Triangles

Similar triangles have the same shape but different size, and congruent triangles are identical in both shape and size. In addition to knowing the definitions of similar and congruent triangles, we must also know how other similar shapes work and how to prove when two triangles are similar and when two triangles are congruent.

Similar Triangles

Similar triangles have the same shape but different size. In similar triangles, **all corresponding angles are identical, and all corresponding side lengths are proportional.** To understand this better, let's consider the two triangles below:

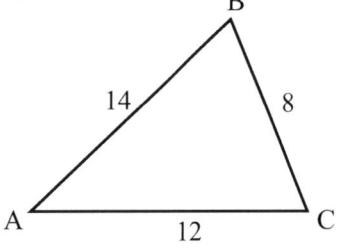

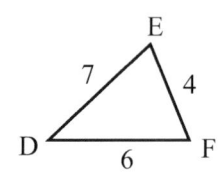

Triangle ABC is similar to triangle DEF. In similar triangles, the corresponding angles are identical. Corresponding angles share the same relative position in each triangle. The pairs of corresponding angles are

$$\angle A = \angle D \qquad \angle B = \angle E \qquad \angle C = \angle F$$

Corresponding side lengths share the same relative position in each triangle. AB corresponds with DE, BC corresponds with EF, and AC corresponds with DF. In any similar triangles, **the ratio of corresponding side lengths is always constant**, so

$$\frac{AB}{DE} = \frac{BC}{EF} = \frac{AC}{DF}$$

We will need to understand these 2 rules to solve similar triangles questions on the SAT.

Example 1: Triangle *JKL* is similar to triangle *XYZ* such that *J*, *K*, and *L* correspond to *X*, *Y*, and *Z* respectively. The measure of ∠Y is 87°. What is the measure of ∠K ?

Solution: Since triangles *JKL* and *XYZ* are similar, the corresponding angles are identical. So, we need to find which angle in triangle *JKL* corresponds with ∠Y. ∠K corresponds with ∠Y, so we know that ∠K = ∠Y. The question tells us that ∠Y is 87°, so ∠K is also 87°. **The answer is 87.**

Example 2:

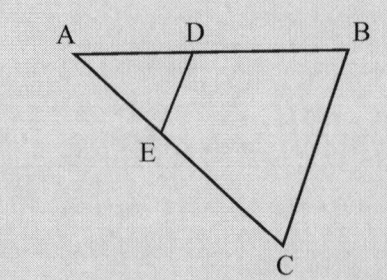

Note: Figure not drawn to scale.

In the triangle above, $\overline{DE}$ is parallel to $\overline{BC}$, AE = 8, AC = 40, and AB = 28. What is the length of AD?

Solution: Triangles ADE and ABC are similar triangles. Anytime a line that is parallel to one of the bases creates a smaller triangle, the smaller triangle will be similar to the larger triangle. Here, DE creates the smaller similar triangle. Since the triangles are similar, we know the sides must be proportional.

$$\frac{AD}{AB} = \frac{AE}{AC}$$

$$\frac{AD}{28} = \frac{8}{40}$$

$$40\,AD = 224$$

$$AD = \frac{224}{40} = \frac{28}{5} = 5.6$$

The answer is $\frac{28}{5}$ or 5.6.

Other Similar Shapes

The SAT also includes other similar shapes beyond triangles. All similar shapes follow the same 2 rules that we learned for similar triangles: (1) all corresponding angles must be identical, and (2) all corresponding side lengths are proportional. To solve any similar shapes questions, we use the same approach that we learned for similar triangles.

Example 3: In the figure below, ACEF and BCDG are similar rectangles, the ratio of AB: BC is 3: 2, and AF = 75. What is the length of BG ?

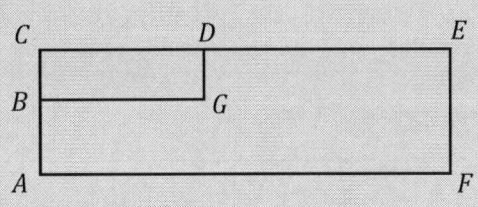

Solution: Since ACEF and BCDG are similar rectangles, we know that all side lengths must be proportional. The hardest part about this question is the ratio. Before we can find BG, we first need to find the proportion for corresponding side lengths for the similar rectangles. BC on the small rectangle corresponds with AC on the large rectangle. We have to find the ratio of BC: AC. Since $AC = AB + BC$ and AB: BC is 3: 2, we can think of AC as having a length of 5. Using this, we find that the ratio of BC: AC is 2: 5.

Since the rectangles are similar, the ratio of all corresponding side lengths in BCDG to ACEF is 2: 5. Side length BG corresponds with side length AF. We can set up a ratio as

$$\frac{BG}{AF} = \frac{2}{5}$$

Since we know that AF = 75, we can plug in 75 for AF and cross multiply to solve for BG.

$$\frac{BG}{75} = \frac{2}{5}$$

$$BG = 30$$

The answer is 30.

Congruent Triangles

Congruent triangles have the same shape and same size. In other words, congruent triangles are identical. **All corresponding angles are identical, and all corresponding side lengths are identical.** Triangles *ABC* and *DEF* below are congruent.

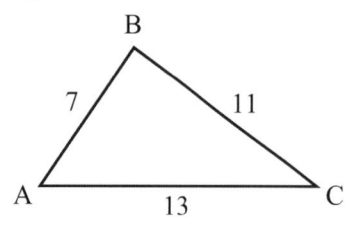

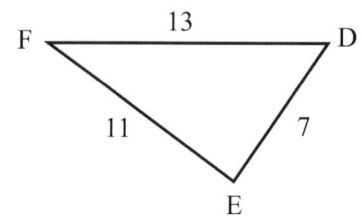

In congruent triangles, the corresponding angles are identical. Corresponding angles share the same relative position in each triangle. The pairs of corresponding angles are

$$\angle A = \angle D \qquad \angle B = \angle E \qquad \angle C = \angle F$$

Corresponding side lengths are identical and share the same relative position in each triangle. The corresponding side lengths are

$$AB = DE \qquad BC = EF \qquad AC = DF$$

The naming for congruent triangles is important. When naming triangles, the ordering of the letters describes the corresponding side lengths and angles. For example, triangles *ABC* and *DEF* are congruent: *AB* and *DE* both have side lengths of 7, *BC* and *EF* both have side lengths of 11, and *AC* and *DF* both have side lengths of 13. The angles all also correspond. However, *ABC* and *EFD* are not: *AB* and *EF* have different side lengths. Understanding the naming rules is important for congruent triangles questions.

5 Rules for Congruent Triangles

For most congruent triangles question on the SAT, we need to know how to prove that two triangles are congruent. For proving two triangles are congruent, there are 5 rules we need to know:

Rule #1: SSS (Side-Side-Side): If all 3 side lengths on one triangle are equivalent to all 3 corresponding side lengths on another triangle, the triangles are congruent.

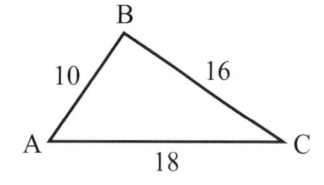

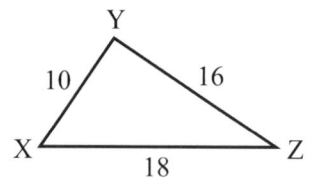

Triangle ABC and XYZ are congruent by SSS.

Rule #2: SAS (Side-Angle-Side): If 2 side lengths and the angle included between those sides in one triangle are equivalent to the corresponding 2 sides and angle in another triangle, the triangles are congruent.

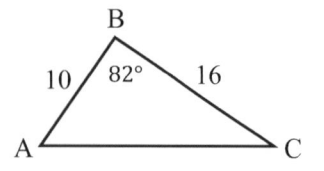

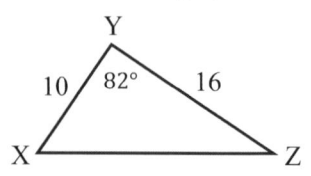

Triangle ABC and XYZ are congruent by SAS.

Rule #3: ASA (Angle-Side-Angle): If any 2 angles and the side included between those two angles in one triangle are equivalent to the corresponding 2 angles and side length between the angles in another triangle, the triangles are congruent.

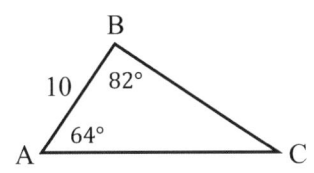

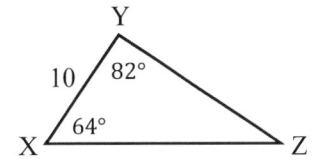

Triangle ABC and XYZ are congruent by ASA.

Rule #4: AAS (Angle-Angle-Side): If any 2 angles and the side not included between those two angles in one triangle is equivalent to the corresponding 2 angles and side not included between those angles in another triangle, the triangles are congruent.

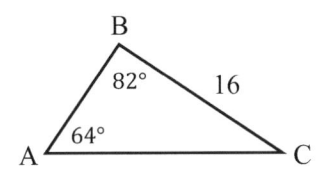

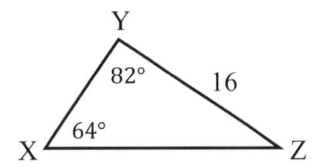

Triangle ABC and XYZ are congruent by AAS.

Rules #5: RHS (Right Angle-Hypotenuse-Side): If the hypotenuse and side length of a right triangle is equivalent to the hypotenuse and side length of another right triangle, the triangles are congruent.

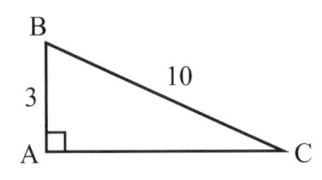

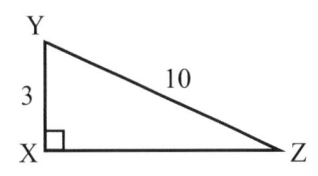

Triangle ABC and XYZ are congruent by RHS.

To solve congruent triangles questions on the SAT, you should memorize and know how to apply these 5 rules. Now, let's see how the SAT tests you on congruent triangles.

Example 4: Triangles ABC and XYZ are shown below. Which of the following pieces of information is NOT sufficient to prove that triangle ABC is congruent to triangle XYZ ?

A) $\angle A = \angle X$
B) $\angle C = \angle Z$
C) $AB = XY$
D) $AC = XZ$

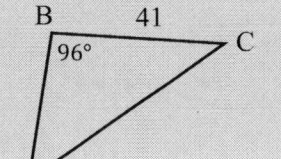

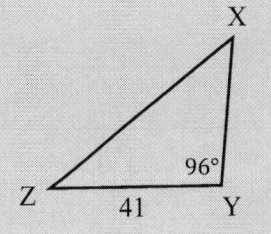

Solution: In the diagram of the triangle, we see that one set of corresponding angles ($\angle B = \angle Y$) and one corresponding side length ($BC = YZ$) are equivalent. To solve, we need to consider each additional piece of information in the answer choices to see if we can use one of our 5 rules to prove the triangles are congruent.

Let's start with answer choice A, which tells us that $\angle A = \angle X$. With this second set of corresponding angles, we have 2 corresponding angles that are equivalent and 1 set of corresponding side lengths that is not included between the angles that is equivalent. Therefore, we can use AAS to prove that triangles ABC and XYZ are congruent. A is incorrect.

Next, let's consider answer choice B, which tell us that ∠C = ∠Z. With this second set of corresponding angles, we have 2 corresponding angles that are equivalent and 1 set of corresponding side lengths that is included between the angles that is equivalent. Therefore, we can use ASA to prove that triangles ABC and XYZ are congruent. B is incorrect.

Next, let's consider answer choice C, which tell us that $AB = XY$. With this second set of corresponding side length, we have 2 sets of corresponding side lengths that are equivalent and 1 set of corresponding angles that is equivalent. The set of corresponding angles is between the two corresponding side lengths, so we can use SAS to prove that triangles ABC and XYZ are congruent. C is incorrect.

Finally, let's consider answer choice D, which tells us that $AC = XZ$. With this second set of corresponding side lengths, we have 2 sets of corresponding side lengths that are equivalent and 1 set of corresponding angles that is equivalent. However, the set of corresponding angles is NOT between the two corresponding side lengths. If we start at point A and work counterclockwise, we have two consecutive side lengths (AC and BC) and then an angle (∠B). SSA (side-side-angle) is not one of our 5 rules, so we cannot prove that triangles ABC and XYZ are congruent. **D is correct.**

3 Rules for Proving Similar Triangles

(2-4)

For advanced similar triangles questions, we need to know how to prove when triangles are similar. To prove two triangles are similar, there are 3 rules we need to know:

Rule #1: AA (Angle-Angle): If 2 angles on one triangle are equivalent to 2 corresponding angles on another triangle, the triangles are similar. Note that AA (Angle-Angle) is the same as AAA (Angle-Angle-Angle) since the sum of angles in a triangle must equal 180°.

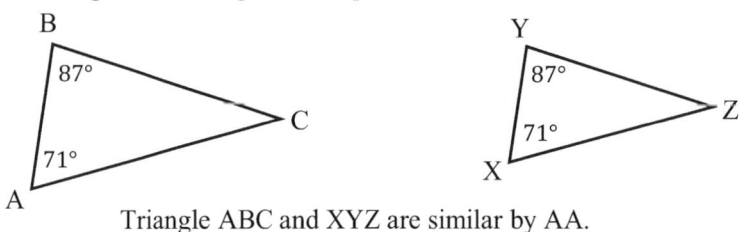

Triangle ABC and XYZ are similar by AA.

Rule #2: SSS (Side-Side-Side): If all 3 side lengths in a triangle are proportional to all 3 corresponding side lengths in another triangle, the triangles are similar.

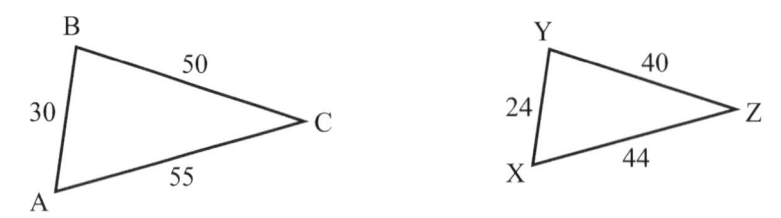

Triangle ABC and XYZ are similar by SSS.

As we learned earlier in this chapter, **the ratio of corresponding side lengths must be constant in similar triangles**. For the triangle above, the ratio of corresponding side lengths for triangle ABC to triangle XYZ is $5:4$.

$$\frac{AB}{XY} = \frac{BC}{YZ} = \frac{AC}{XZ} = \frac{5}{4}$$

$$\frac{30}{24} = \frac{50}{40} = \frac{55}{44} = \frac{5}{4}$$

Rule #3: SAS (Side-Angle-Side): If 2 side lengths in a triangle are proportional to 2 corresponding side lengths in another triangle and the angle between the 2 side lengths are equivalent, the triangle are similar.

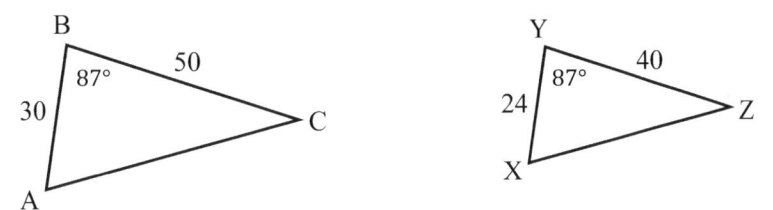

Triangle ABC and XYZ are similar by SAS.

To solve similar triangles questions on the SAT, you should memorize and know how to apply these 3 rules. Now, let's see an example of how the SAT can test proving similar triangles.

Example 5: In triangle ABC and DEF, angle A and angle D have measures of 60°, $AB = 24$ and $BC = 40$. Which additional piece of information is sufficient to prove that triangle ABC is similar to triangle DEF?

A) $DE = 48$ and $EF = 80$.
B) $AC = 60$ and $DF = 30$.
C) The measures of angles B and F are 85° and 35° respectively.
D) The measures of angles C and E are 65° and 70° respectively.

Solution: We recommend drawing a sketch of the triangles. The visual for a question like this makes the question much easier. To prove that two triangles are similar, we need to use one of the 3 rules that we just learned. Any one of the rules is sufficient to prove that two triangles are similar. With these rules in mind, let's assess each answer choice.

First, let's consider answer choice A. In answer choice A, we are given the side lengths of DE, which corresponds with AB, and EF, which corresponds with BC. The length of DE is twice AB, and the length of EF is twice BC, which looks good for the triangles being similar. However, we do not know if the final pair of corresponding sides AC and DF have the same proportion. To prove that two triangles are similar using SSS, all corresponding side lengths must have the same proportion, so we cannot prove that triangles ABC and DEF are similar. We also cannot prove the triangles are similar using SAS, as the angles we know are identical are not between the corresponding sides. A is incorrect.

Next, let's consider answer choice B. In answer choice B, we are given AC, the third side of triangle ABC, and DF. We only have one pair of corresponding side lengths, AC and DF, and one pair of corresponding angles, $\angle A = \angle D$, so we cannot use any of our 3 rules. B is incorrect.

Now, let's consider answer choice C. We are told $\angle B = 85°$ and that $\angle F = 35°$. Let's start with triangle ABC. The question tells us that $\angle A = 60°$. If we know that $\angle B = 85°$, we can find that $\angle C = 35°$ because all angles in a triangle add up to 180° (and $180° - 60° - 85° = 35°$). What about triangle DEF? The question told us that $\angle D = 60°$. If we know that $\angle F = 35°$, we can find that $\angle E = 85°$. So, we can prove that all corresponding angles are equal. $\angle A = \angle D = 60°$, $\angle B = \angle E = 85°$, and $\angle C = \angle F = 35°$. Since all corresponding angles are equal, triangles ABC and DEF are similar using AA (or AAA in this case). **The answer is C.**

For answer choice D, we are told that $\angle C = 65°$ and that $\angle E = 35°$. For triangle ABC, if we know that $\angle A = 60°$ and $\angle C = 65°$, we can find that $\angle B = 55°$. For triangle DEF, if we know that $\angle D = 60°$ and $\angle E = 70°$, we can find that $\angle F = 50°$. Since the angles in triangles ABC and DEF are not equivalent, we know that the triangles are not similar. D is incorrect.

PrepPros

Similar Triangles Practice: Answers on page 330.

1. Triangle XYZ is similar to triangle ABC such that $X, Y,$ and Z correspond to $A, B,$ and C, respectively. The measure of $\angle B$ is $45°$. What is the measure of $\angle Y$?

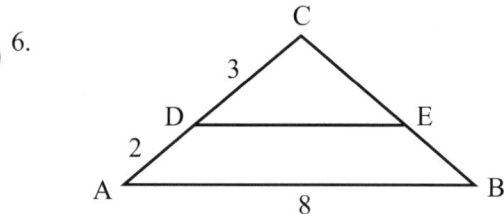

   A) $15°$
   B) $45°$
   C) $90°$
   D) $135°$

2. Triangle JKL is similar to triangle XYZ such that $X, Y,$ and Z correspond to $J, K,$ and L, respectively. The measure of $\angle K$ is $39°$ and $3JL = XZ$. What is the measure of $\angle Y$?

   A) $13°$
   B) $39°$
   C) $78°$
   D) $117°$

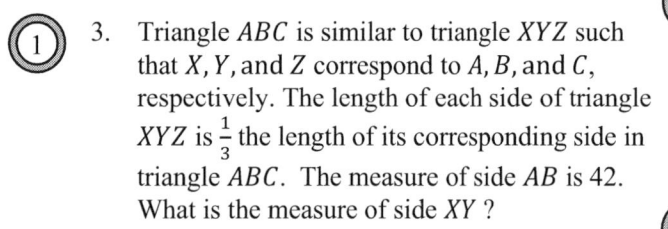

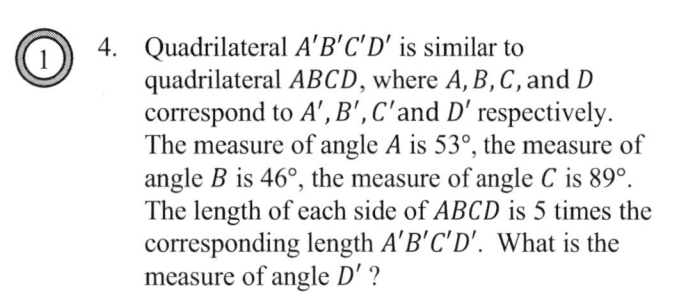

3. Triangle ABC is similar to triangle XYZ such that $X, Y,$ and Z correspond to $A, B,$ and C, respectively. The length of each side of triangle XYZ is $\frac{1}{3}$ the length of its corresponding side in triangle ABC. The measure of side AB is 42. What is the measure of side XY ?

4. Quadrilateral $A'B'C'D'$ is similar to quadrilateral $ABCD$, where $A, B, C,$ and D correspond to A', B', C' and D' respectively. The measure of angle A is $53°$, the measure of angle B is $46°$, the measure of angle C is $89°$. The length of each side of $ABCD$ is 5 times the corresponding length $A'B'C'D'$. What is the measure of angle D' ?

5. Right triangles ABC and DEF are similar, where A and B, correspond to D and E, respectively and angles C and F are right angles. Angle B has a measure of $63°$. What is the measure of angle D ?

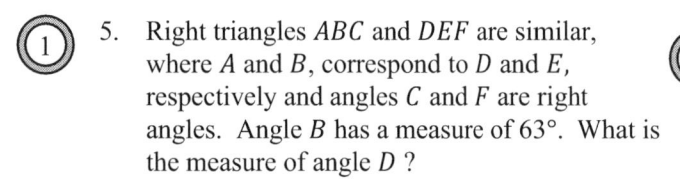

   A) $27°$
   B) $63°$
   C) $117°$
   D) $153°$

6. In the figure above, $\overline{AB}$ is parallel to $\overline{DE}$. Which of the following is equal to the length of DE ?

   A) $\frac{16}{3}$
   B) $\frac{13}{2}$
   C) $\frac{24}{5}$
   D) $\frac{40}{3}$

7. Triangles ABC and DEF are congruent, where A corresponds to D and B and E are right angles. The measure of angle A is $17°$. What is the measure of angle F ?

8. Triangles ABC and DEF are shown below. Which of the following pieces of information is sufficient to prove that triangle ABC is congruent to triangle DEF?

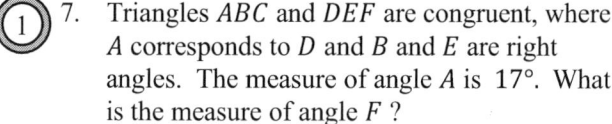

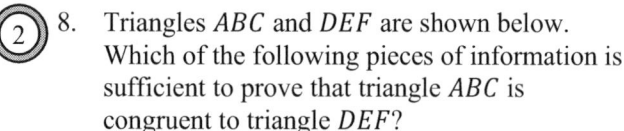

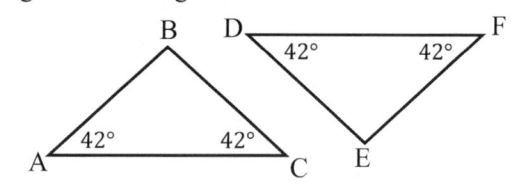

   A) $\angle ABC = \angle DEF$
   B) $\overline{BC} = \overline{ED}$
   C) $\overline{AC} = \overline{EF}$
   D) No additional information is necessary.

9. In the figure below, $\overline{BE}$ is parallel with $\overline{CD}$. Which of the following statements is true?

   A) $\frac{AB}{BC} = \frac{BE}{CD}$
   B) $\frac{AB}{AC} = \frac{AE}{AD}$
   C) $\frac{BE}{AE} = \frac{AE}{CD}$
   D) $\frac{BC}{ED} = \frac{BE}{AB}$

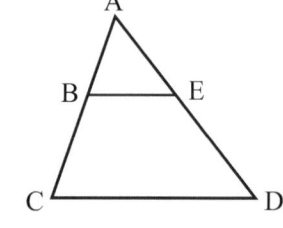

- 136 -

10. Triangles *ABC* and *DEF* are shown below. Which of the following is equal to the ratio of $\frac{AB}{BC}$?

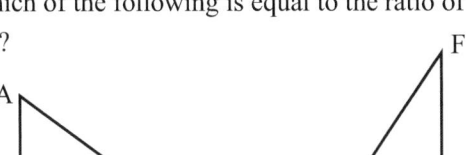

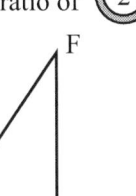

   A) $\frac{DF}{DE}$
   B) $\frac{DE}{DF}$
   C) $\frac{DE}{EF}$
   D) $\frac{EF}{DF}$

11. In the figure shown below, line segments *AC* and *DE* are parallel. The measure of angle *CAB* is 51°, and $CB = \frac{5}{3}EB$. What is the measure, in degrees, of angle EDB?

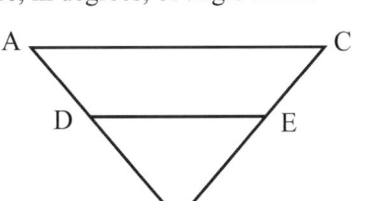

12. Triangles *ABC* and *DEF* each have a corresponding angle measuring 78°. Which additional piece of information is sufficient to determine whether these two triangles are similar?

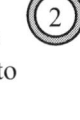

   A) The length of line segment *BC*
   B) The length of line segment *EF*
   C) The measure of another pair of corresponding angles in the triangles.
   D) The lengths of one pair of corresponding sides in the two triangles.

13. Triangles *JLK* and *MNO* correspond such that *J, L,* and *K* correspond to *M, N,* and *O*, respectively. If $\overline{JL} = \overline{MN}$ and $\overline{LK} = \overline{NO}$, which of the following facts would be sufficient to prove the two triangles are congruent?

   A) ∠*L* = ∠*N*
   B) ∠*J* = ∠*O*
   C) ∠*K* = ∠*M*
   D) ∠*K* = ∠*N*

14. In the figure below, $\overline{AD}, \overline{EF},$ and $\overline{BC}$ are parallel. If $AB = 25$ and $EA = 6$, and $FD = 7$, what is the length of *CD* to the nearest tenth?

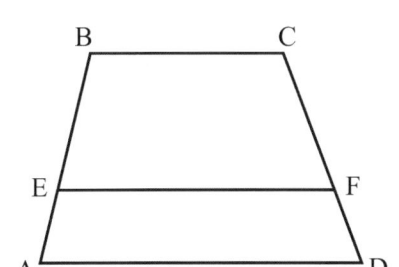

15. In triangles *XYZ* and *DEF*, angles *X* and *D* each have measures of 37° and angles *Z* and *F* each have measures of 52°. Which additional piece of information is sufficient to determine whether triangle *XYZ* is congruent to triangle *DEF*?

   A) The measure of angle *Y*
   B) The length of side *EF*
   C) The lengths of sides *XY* and *DE*
   D) No additional information is necessary.

16. In the figure below, $\overline{AB}$ and $\overline{DE}$ intersect at point C. Which of the following additional statements is (are) sufficient to prove that triangle ABC is similar to triangle DCE?

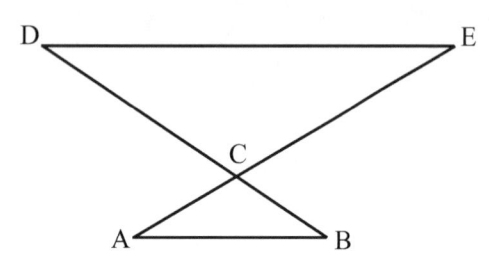

   I. The length of $\overline{DE}$ is 3 times the length of $\overline{AB}$.
   II. AB is parallel to DE.

   A) I is sufficient, but II is not.
   B) II is sufficient, but I is not.
   C) I is sufficient, and II is sufficient.
   D) Neither I nor II is sufficient.

17. In triangle XYZ, the measure of angle X is 14 degrees, and the measure of angle Z is 68 degrees. Point K lies on $\overline{XY}$, point J lies on $\overline{YZ}$, and $\overline{KJ}$ is parallel to $\overline{XZ}$. What is the measure, in degrees, of angle YJK?

18. In triangle XYZ, the measure of angle Z is 45°. In triangle ABC, the measure of angle A is 45°. Which of the following additional pieces of information is(are) sufficient to prove that triangle XYZ is similar to triangle ABC?

   I. Angle Y is 90°.
   II. Angle B is 90°.
   III. Side lengths $\overline{XY}$ and $\overline{AB}$ are equivalent.

   A) I only.
   B) III only.
   C) I and II only.
   D) I and III.

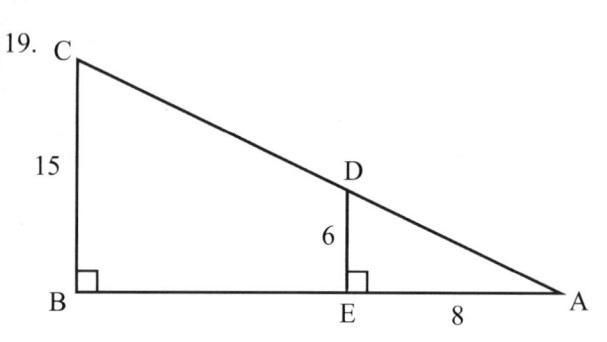

19.

   Note: Figure not drawn to scale.

   In the figure above, $\overline{BC}$ is parallel to $\overline{DE}$. What is the length of AC?

20. In the figure below, $\overline{AB}$ is parallel to $\overline{ED}$, and the length of $\overline{AC}$ is $\frac{9}{11}$ units, the length of $\overline{CD}$ is $\frac{12}{11}$ units, and the length of ED is $\frac{44}{9}$ units. What is the length of AB in units?

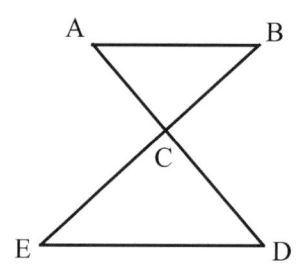

   Note: Figure not drawn to scale.

21. In the figure shown, $\overline{JM}$ and $\overline{KN}$ intersect at point L. Which of the following additional pieces of information is NOT sufficient to prove that $\triangle KLM$ is similar to $\triangle JLN$? (Note: Figure not drawn to scale.)

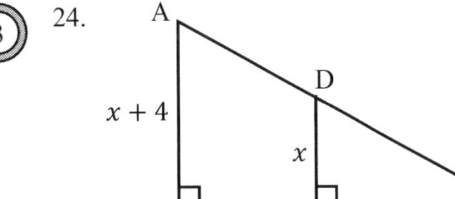

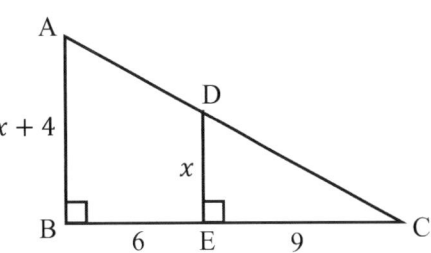

A) The measure of $\angle M$ is equal to the measure of $\angle K$, and $\angle N$ is equal to the measure of $\angle J$.
B) $\overline{KM}$ is parallel to $\overline{JN}$.
C) The measure of $\angle M$ is equal to the measure of $\angle J$
D) The length of $\overline{LM}$ is $\frac{5}{4}$ the length of $\overline{JL}$.

22. In triangles ABC and LMN, angles B and M both have measure of $65°$, angles A and L correspond, angles C and N correspond, and $AB = \frac{9}{2}$ and $AC = \frac{27}{4}$. Which additional piece of information is sufficient to prove that triangle ABC and LMN are congruent?

A) $LM = \frac{9}{2}$
B) $LM = \frac{9}{2}$ and $MN = \frac{27}{4}$
C) $LM = \frac{9}{2}$ and angles A and L are congruent.
D) The measures of angles A and L are congruent, and the measure of angles C and N are congruent.

23. In triangles ABC and DEF, AB and DE each are 7 inches. Angle A and Angle D are both $37°$. Which of the following is sufficient to determine that triangles ABC and DEF are congruent?

   I. The measures of angles B and C are equal.
   II. $AC = DF$
   III. $BC = EF$

A) I only
B) II only
C) III only
D) II or III only

24.

Note: Figure not drawn to scale.

In the figure above, $\overline{AB}$ is parallel to $\overline{DE}$. If $AC = \sqrt{a}$, what is the value of a?

25. In the figure below, $AB = 9$, and the length of line segment EC is one third of the length of line segment BC. Lines AB and DC are parallel. What is the length of line segment CD ?

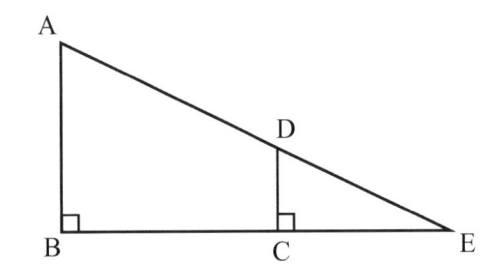

Note: Figure not drawn to scale.

A) $\frac{4}{9}$
B) $\frac{3}{4}$
C) $\frac{9}{4}$
D) 3

26. In triangles ABC and JKL, angles C and L each have measures of $57°$, $BC = 7$, and $KL = 28$. Which additional piece of information is sufficient to prove that triangles ABC and JKL are similar?

A) $AB = 11$ and $JK = 44$
B) $AC = 12$ and $JL = 12$
C) The measures of angles A and K are $58°$ and $65°$, respectively.
D) The measure of A and J are $58°$ and $65°$, respectively.

PrepPros

27. In triangle ABC, angle C is a right angle, point Point D lies on $\overline{AB}$, point E lies on $\overline{AC}$, and $\overline{DE}$ is parallel to $\overline{CB}$. If the length of $\overline{BC}$ is 68 units, the length of $\overline{DE}$ is 17 units, and the area of triangle ABC is 646 square units, what is the length of $\overline{AE}$ in units?

28. In the figure below, Point D lies on the hypotenuse of right triangle ABC. What is the length of line segment DB ?

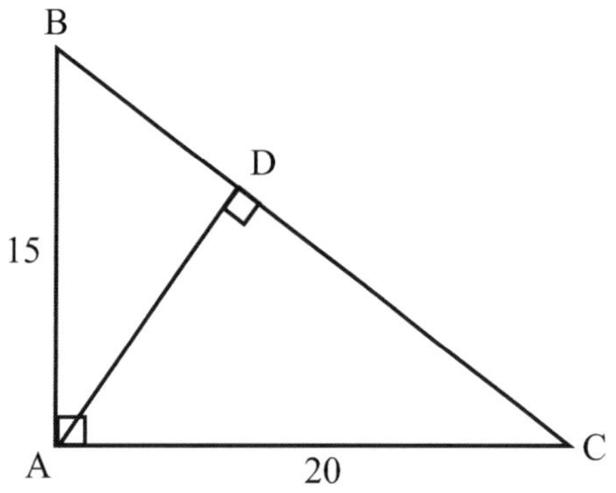

29. In the figure shown below, $\overline{ED}$ is parallel to $\overline{AC}$. Which of the following is enough to prove that $\triangle FBE$ is similar to $\triangle EDB$?

A) $z + k = x + y$
B) $z + x = m + y$
C) $z + k = y$
D) $z + k = x$

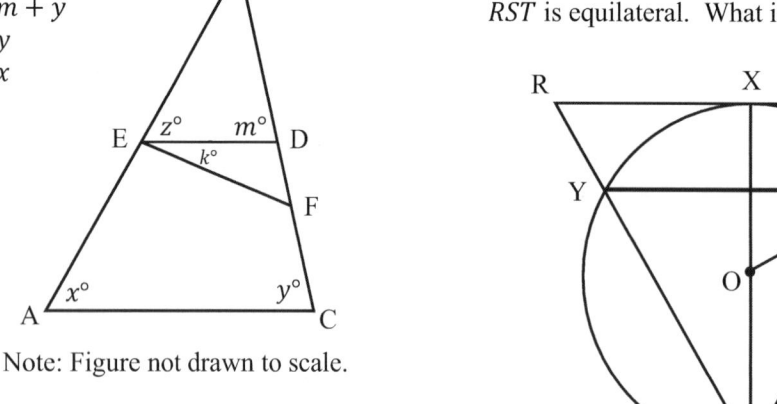

Note: Figure not drawn to scale.

30. In the figure below, $\triangle ABC$ and $\triangle BDC$ are right triangles, $AD = 4$, and $BD = 3$. What is the length of $\overline{DC}$?

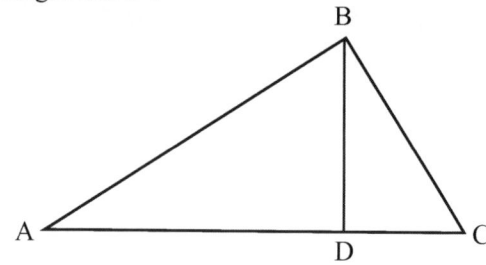

31. In the figure below, $\overline{BD}$ is a diameter of the circle and $\triangle ABC$ is a right triangle. The circle is tangent to $\overline{AC}$ at point D. If $\overline{AD} = 27$ and $\overline{CD} = 12$, what is the length of $\overline{BD}$?

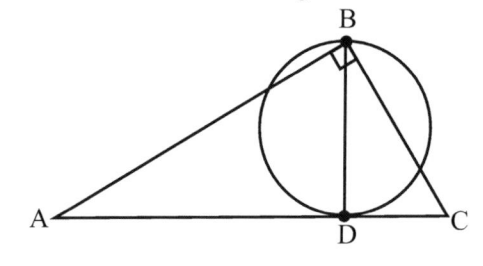

32. In the figure below, O is the center of the circle and $\overline{RT}$ is tangent to the circle at X. If triangle RST is equilateral. What is the ratio of $\frac{RT}{YZ}$?

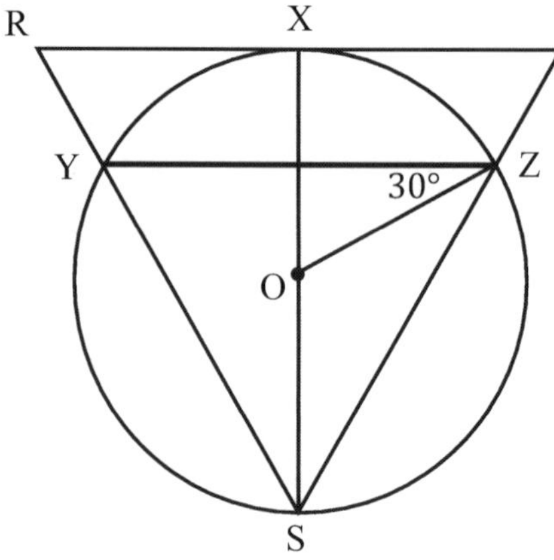

- 140 -

Chapter 17: Lines

Many SAT questions will ask you how to use and solve linear functions, which is just a fancy term for lines. Linear functions appear in the form $y = mx + b$. In this chapter, we will cover all the equations that you need to know and common types of lines questions on test day.

Slope

Given any two points on a line (x_1, y_1) and (x_2, y_2),

$$\text{Slope} = \frac{\text{rise}}{\text{run}} = \frac{y_1 - y_2}{x_1 - x_2}$$

The slope measures how steep a line is. A line with a higher slope is steeper while a line with a lower slope is flatter. The rise is the change in the y-coordinates, and the run is the change in the x-coordinates. For example, if a line has a slope of $\frac{1}{2}$, the line will go up 1 unit for every 2 units we move to the right, or it will go down 1 unit for every 2 units we move to the left. Lines with a positive slope go up and to the right, and lines with a negative slope go down and to the right.

Example 1: Line l passes through points $(9, y)$ and $(-1, 3)$ and has a slope of 3. What is the value of y?

Solution: To solve, plug the given values into the slope equation

$$\text{Slope} = \frac{y-3}{9-(-1)} = 3$$

$$\frac{y-3}{10} = 3$$

$$y - 3 = 30$$

$$y = 33$$

The answer is 33.

Example 2: Line m is graphed below, what is the slope of line m?

A) $\frac{1}{5}$

B) 1

C) -1

D) $-\frac{1}{5}$

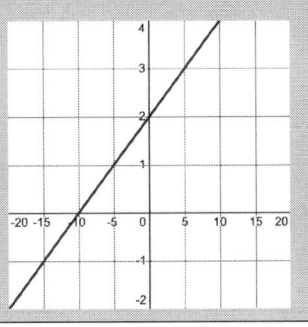

Solution: To find the slope, we need to pick two points on the line. We can pick any 2 points on the graph, so here let's use $(-10, 0)$ and $(0, 2)$.

$$\text{Slope} = \frac{0-2}{-10-0} = \frac{-2}{-10} = \frac{1}{5}$$

The answer is A.

*Test-Taking Tip – Never count squares to find the slope! The graphs on the SAT often have different scales on the x-axis and y-axis. In the graph above, each box on the x-axis represents 5 units, and each box in the y-axis represents 1 unit. If you counted boxes to find the slope from $(-10, 0)$ to $(0, 2)$, you would count 2 boxes up and 2 boxes to the right. So, you would think the slope is 1 and would get this question wrong!

PrepPros

1-2 Slopes of Parallel and Perpendicular Lines

If two lines are parallel, the lines have the same slope. For example, if lines A and B are parallel and line A has a slope of 3, line B also has a slope of 3.

If two lines are perpendicular, the slopes of the lines are the negative reciprocals of one another. To find the negative reciprocal, take the slope of the initial line, flip the fraction, and make it negative. For example, if lines A and B are perpendicular and line A has a slope of $\frac{3}{2}$, the slope of line B is $-\frac{2}{3}$.

> **Example 3:** Points $(4, 10)$ and $(1, 31)$ are located on line q. If line p is perpendicular to line q, which of the following equations could be the equation of line p?
>
> A) $y = 7x + 28$ B) $y = \frac{1}{7}x - \frac{5}{2}$ C) $y = -7x + 10$ D) $y = -\frac{1}{7}x + 2$

Solution: To start, we need to find the slope of line q.

$$\text{Slope} = \frac{10-31}{4-1} = \frac{-21}{3}$$

$$\text{Slope} = -7$$

Line q has a slope of -7. Line p is perpendicular to line q, so line p must have a slope of $\frac{1}{7}$. **The answer is B.**

> **Example 4:** In the xy-plane, line d is parallel to line f. Line d has an equation of $y = \frac{3}{5}x + \frac{9}{2}$. Which of the following could be the equation of line f?
>
> A) $3x + 5y = 20$ B) $10x - 6y = 3$ C) $9x - 15y = 40$ D) $-5x + 3y = 18$

Solution: Line d has a slope of $\frac{3}{5}$. Since lines d and f are parallel, they must have the same slopes, so line f must have a slope of $\frac{3}{5}$. To find which answer choice has a slope of $\frac{3}{5}$, we must convert the answer choices from standard form to slope-intercept form by isolating y. If you have not learned how to do this, we will learn this later in this chapter on page 135.

Let's start with answer choice A. To convert to slope-intercept form, we must isolate y. To do so, we must subtract $3x$ and then divide by 5.

$$3x + 5y = 20$$
$$5y = -3x + 20$$
$$y = -\frac{3}{5}x + 4$$

Answer choice A has as slope of $-\frac{3}{5}$, so A is incorrect. We can repeat this process with the remaining answer choices. In the last step of each answer choice below, we simplify the fractions.

For answer choice B:

$$10x - 6y = 3$$
$$-6y = -10x + 3$$
$$y = \frac{10}{6}x - \frac{3}{6}$$
$$y = \frac{5}{3}x - \frac{1}{2}$$

For answer choice C:

$$9x - 15y = 40$$
$$-15y = -9x + 40$$
$$y = \frac{9}{15}x - \frac{40}{15}$$
$$y = \frac{3}{5}x - \frac{8}{3}$$

For answer choice D:

$$-5x + 3y = 18$$
$$3y = 5x + 18$$
$$y = \frac{5}{3}x + \frac{18}{3}$$
$$y = \frac{5}{3}x + 6$$

Answer choice C has a slope of $\frac{3}{5}$, so **the answer is C.**

Chapter 17: Lines

Slope-Intercept Form

Slope-intercept form is the simplest form of a line and the one that you are likely most comfortable with.

$$y = mx + b$$

where **m is the slope** and **b is the y-intercept**.

As an example, consider the graph of $y = 2x - 2$ below:

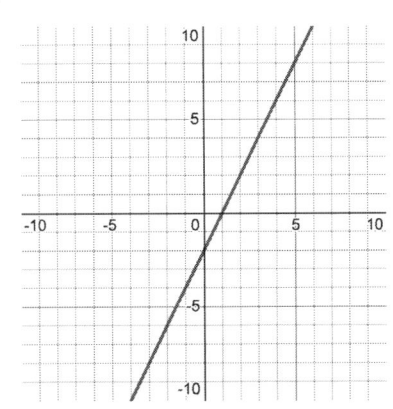

We can see both the slope and the y-intercept on the graph. The y-intercept is where the line crosses the y-axis, which we can clearly see at the point $(0, -2)$. We can also see the slope is 2 by tracing how the line moves: for every 2 units we move up (the rise), the graph moves one unit to the right (the run). **You need to be comfortable identifying the y-intercept and slope of a line from a graph.**

Example 5: Which of the following is the correct equation for the graph pictured in the xy-plane below?

A) $y = x + 5$
B) $y = x - 5$
C) $y = -x + 5$
D) $y = -x - 5$

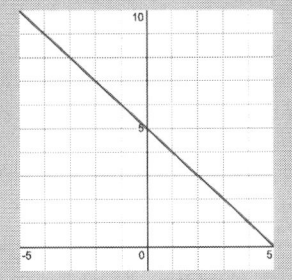

Solution: To solve, we need to find the y-intercept and the slope. The y-intercept is at $y = 5$. To find the slope, we can pick two points on the line. Here, we will use $(0, 5)$ and $(1, 4)$.

$$\text{Slope} = \frac{5-4}{0-1} = \frac{1}{-1} = -1$$

The answer is C.

Example 6: There is a linear relationship between x and $f(x)$. The table shows three values of x and their corresponding values of $f(x)$ in terms of a constant p. Which of the following equations could represent $f(x)$?

A) $f(x) = px$ B) $f(x) = \frac{5}{2}x + p$ C) $f(x) = \frac{2}{5}x + p$ D) $f(x) = 10x + \frac{p}{4}$

x	$f(x)$
0	p
4	$p + 10$
8	$p + 20$

Solution: Method #1 – "Math Teacher Way": First, it is important to understand that $f(x)$ is the same as y, so we can use the values in the $f(x)$ column as the y-values. The values in the table tell us that three points on the linear function $f(x)$ are $(0, p)$, $(4, p + 10)$, and $(8, p + 20)$.

- 143 -

To find the equation of $f(x)$, we need to find the slope and the y-intercept. We see that when $x = 0$, $f(x) = p$, so we can tell that the y-intercept of the graph is at $(0, p)$. We know that A and D are incorrect. A has a y-intercept at $(0, 0)$, and D has a y-intercept at $(0, \frac{p}{4})$. B and C have y-intercepts at $(0, p)$, so we next must find the slope.

To find the slope, we can select two points and use the slope equation. Let's use points $(0, p)$ and $(4, p + 10)$.

$$\text{Slope} = \frac{p-(p+10)}{0-4} = \frac{p-p-10}{-4} = \frac{-10}{-4} = \frac{10}{4} = \frac{5}{2}$$

The slope of $f(x)$ is $\frac{5}{2}$, so **the answer is B.**

Method #2 – Plugging In Test Points: Anytime we have a point or points that are on a graph, or in this case on a function, the points must make the equation of the graph true. **If we plug the point(s) back into the equation of the graph, the equation must be true!** Plugging test point(s) into an equation of a line, or any other type of graph or function, is a great method for solving questions that seem difficult to solve mathematically.

For Example 6, we use $(0, p)$, $(4, p + 10)$, and $(8, p + 20)$ as test points. To solve, we can plug these points into the answer choices to test which answer choices work. It is best to start with 1 point, plug it into all the answer choices, eliminate any answer choices that do not make the equation true, and then repeat with a second test point (if necessary).

Let's start with $(0, p)$ as a test point. We plug in 0 for x and the equation must equal p.

For answer choice A: $f(x) = px$ → $f(x) = p(0) = 0$ (A is incorrect)

For answer choice B: $f(x) = \frac{5}{2}x + p$ → $f(x) = \frac{5}{2}(0) + p = p$ (B works)

For answer choice C: $f(x) = \frac{2}{5}x + p$ → $f(x) = \frac{2}{5}(0) + p = p$ (C works)

For answer choice D: $f(x) = 10x + \frac{p}{4}$ → $f(x) = 10(0) + \frac{p}{4} = \frac{p}{4}$ (D is incorrect)

Both B and C work for $(0, p)$, so we need to use a second test point. Let's use point $(4, p + 10)$. We plug in 4 for x and the equation must equal $p + 10$.

For answer choice B: $f(x) = \frac{5}{2}x + p$ → $f(x) = \frac{5}{2}(4) + p = 10 + p$ (B works)

For answer choice C: $f(x) = \frac{2}{5}x + p$ → $f(x) = \frac{2}{5}(4) + p = \frac{8}{5} + p$ (C is incorrect)

Using the plugging in test points method, only answer choice B works for both points we tested, so **B is correct.** Anytime you have the opportunity to plug in test points, you should do it! Plugging in points can allow you to find the correct answer on very difficult questions that you may not be able to solve the "Math Teacher Way."

2-4 Point-Slope Form

If we only know the slope of a line and a point on the line, we will need to use point-slope form:

$$y - y_1 = m(x - x_1)$$

where (x_1, y_1) **is a point on the line and m is the slope**. Once we plug in the slope and point to point-slope form, we can then turn the equation back into slope-intercept form by solving for y.

Chapter 17: Lines

> **Example 7:** Line w passes through points $(2, 10)$ and $(5, -2)$. What is the y-intercept of line w?

Solution: To start, we need to find the slope of line w.

$$\text{Slope} = \frac{10-(-2)}{2-5} = \frac{12}{-3} = -4$$

Now that we know the slope, we can use point-slope form. We can use either point. For this example, we will use the point $(2, 10)$.

$$y - 10 = -4(x - 2)$$
$$y - 10 = -4x + 8$$
$$y = -4x + 18$$

Once we have the equation in slope-intercept form, we see that the y-intercept is 18. **The answer is 18.**

Alternate Method – Plug a point into $y = mx + b$ form.

When dealing with lines in $y = mx + b$ form, you can also plug the (x, y) coordinates of a point on the line into the equation and then solve for the y-intercept. To see how this works, let's go back to example 5. Once we found the slope was -4, we could have set the equation up like this:

$$y = -4x + b$$

To solve for the b-value, we can plug in one of the points from the line for x and y and solve for b. Here, we will use $(2, 10)$.

$$10 = -4(2) + b$$
$$b = 18$$

Now that we know the b-value, we can write the equation in slope-intercept form:

$$y = -4x + 18$$

Note that this "Plug a point into $y = mx + b$ form" approach and the point-slope form method we used in the solution to Example 5 both find slope-intercept form. You can use whichever one you feel more comfortable with on test day.

Standard Form

Lines can also appear in standard form:

$$Ax + By = C$$

The coefficients in this form do not show the slope or the y-intercept. They actually show nothing, so standard form is not particularly useful. **To turn standard form into slope-intercept form, solve for y.** Once you have the equation in slope-intercept form, you can find the slope and the y-intercept for the line.

> **Example 8:** Line n has an equation of $-4x + 3y - 15 = 0$. When written in $y = ax + b$ form, what is the value of $a + b$?

Solution: To Convert line n from standard form to slope-intercept form, we solve for y. First, we should get the y-term, $3y$, on one side and the x-term and constants, $-4x$ and -15, on the other side.

$$-4x + 3y - 15 = 0$$
$$3y = 4x + 15$$

Now, we divide by 3 to isolate y.

$$y = \frac{4}{3}x + 5$$

- 145 -

PrepPros

After putting line n in slope-intercept form, we see the slope is $\frac{4}{3}$, so $a = \frac{4}{3}$, and the value of the y-intercept is 5, so $b = 5$. So, we can solve.

$$a + b = \frac{4}{3} + 5$$

$$a + b = \frac{19}{3} = 6.33$$

The answer is $\frac{19}{3}$ or **6.33**.

1-4 Solving for Intercepts

The x-intercept is the point where a line crosses the x-axis. **To solve for the x-intercept, set $y = 0$ and solve for x.**

The y-intercept is the point where the line crosses the y-axis. **To solve for the y-intercept, set $x = 0$ and solve for y.**

Example 9: For the line $10 - 2y = 5x$, what is the sum of the x-intercept and the y-intercept?

Solution: To find the x-intercept, set $y = 0$ and solve for x.

$$10 - 2(0) = 5x$$
$$10 = 5x$$
$$x = 2$$

The x-intercept is 2.

To find the y-intercept, set $x = 0$ and solve for y.

$$10 - 2y = 5(0)$$
$$10 - 2y = 0$$
$$2y = 10$$
$$y = 5$$

The y-intercept is 5.

The sum of the x-intercept and y-intercept is $2 + 5$, so the **answer is 7**.

Example 10: The graph of $3x + 6y - 30 = 0$ is translated up 4 units in the xy-plane. What is the x-coordinate of the x-intercept of the resulting graph?

Solution: To start, we need to turn the graph into slope-intercept form. We are asked to find the x-intercept of the graph after it is translated up 4 units, so finding the x-intercept of the current graph is not helpful. To turn the graph into slope-intercept form, we isolate y.

$$3x + 6y - 30 = 0$$
$$6y = -3x + 30$$
$$y = -\frac{3}{6}x + \frac{30}{6}$$
$$y = -\frac{1}{2}x + 5$$

- 146 -

Now that we know have the graph in slope-intercept form, we can translate the graph up 4 units by increasing the y-intercept, the b-value in $y = mx + b$ form, by 4. So, after translating the graph up 4 units, the graph has an equation of $y = -\frac{1}{2}x + 9$.

To find the x-intercept, set $y = 0$ and solve for x.

$$0 = -\frac{1}{2}x + 9$$

$$\frac{1}{2}x = 9$$

$$x = 18$$

The answer is 18.

Midpoint Formula

Given any two points on a line (x_1, y_1) and (x_2, y_2),

$$\text{midpoint} = \left(\frac{x_1 + x_2}{2}, \frac{y_1 + y_2}{2}\right)$$

> **Example 11:** C is the midpoint of AB. If point A is at $(3, 6)$ and point C is at $(5, 2)$, which of the following is point B?
>
> A) $(4, 4)$ B) $(6, 0)$ C) $(7, -2)$ D) $(8, -1)$

Solution: We are given the midpoint, point C, and one of the endpoints, point A. We can plug the values into the midpoint formula to solve for the coordinates of point B.

To solve for the x-coordinate of point B, plug in the x-coordinates that we are given for the midpoint ($x = 5$) and the endpoint at point A ($x = 3$) to the midpoint formula.

$$5 = \frac{3+x}{2}$$

$$10 = 3 + x$$

$$x = 7$$

The x-coordinate of point B is 7. If we look at the answer choices, **we can already tell that the answer is C**. Make sure that you always check the answer choices on questions like this. If we could not tell which answer is correct at this point, we would still need to solve for y, which we do below.

To solve for the y-coordinate of point B, plug in the y-coordinates that we are given for the midpoint ($y = 2$) and the endpoint at point A ($y = 6$) to the midpoint formula.

$$2 = \frac{6+y}{2}$$

$$4 = 6 + y$$

$$y = -2$$

The y-coordinate is -2. **The answer is C.**

Distance Formula
1-4

Given any two points (x_1, y_1) and (x_2, y_2),

$$\text{Distance} = \sqrt{(x_1 - x_2)^2 + (y_1 - y_2)^2}$$

The distance formula is used to solve for the distance between any two points.

If you do not like the distance formula, **you can also use the Pythagorean Theorem to find the distance between two points.** To do so, sketch a coordinate plane and draw a triangle, and solve for the hypotenuse. You can see how this works in the example below.

Example 12: The endpoints of line X are at $(-2, 1)$ and $(5, 4)$. The length, in coordinate units, of line X can be expressed as $\sqrt{a}$. What is the value of a?

Solution: Method #1 – Distance Formula: We can use the distance formula with $(-2, 1)$ as (x_1, y_1) and $(5, 4)$ as (x_2, y_2).

$$\text{Distance} = \sqrt{(-2 - 5)^2 + (1 - 4)^2}$$

$$\text{Distance} = \sqrt{(-7)^2 + (-3)^2}$$

$$\text{Distance} = \sqrt{58}$$

Since the distance can be expressed as $\sqrt{a}$, we see that $a = 58$. **The answer is 58.**

Method #2 – Draw a coordinate plane and make a triangle.

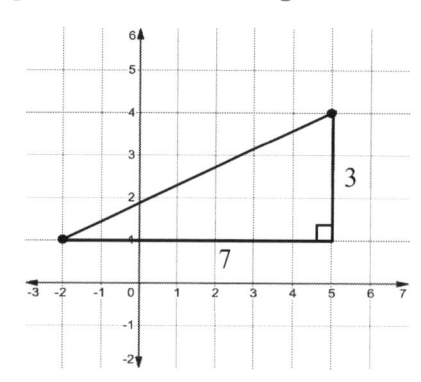

Using the triangle, we see that the base has a length of 7 and the height has a length of 3. To find the length of line X, use the Pythagorean Theorem:

$$7^2 + 3^2 = c^2$$

$$58 = c^2$$

$$c = \sqrt{58}$$

Since the distance can be expressed as $\sqrt{a}$, we see that $a = 58$. **The answer is 58.**

> ***Test-Day Tip – Don't Plan To Rely On Desmos!**
>
> As you can see with this question and the rest of the example questions in this chapter, **the SAT is going to intentionally write lines questions that you cannot solve using Desmos**. You need to understand how to apply all the skills we learned in this chapter to consistently answer lines questions correctly on test day.

Chapter 17: Lines

Lines Practice: Answers on page 330.

1. A line in the standard (x, y) coordinate plane passes through the points $(-7, 5)$ and $(1, -4)$. The slope of the line is:

   A) Negative
   B) Positive
   C) Zero
   D) Undefined

2. In the xy-plane, what is the midpoint of the line segment with endpoints $(2, 6)$ and $(6, 10)$?

   A) $(3, 6)$
   B) $(4, -4)$
   C) $(4, 8)$
   D) $(8, 16)$

3. Which of the following statements is true about the graph of the equation $3y - 4x = -6$ in the xy-plane?

   A) The line has a negative slope and a negative y-intercept.
   B) The line has a negative slope and a positive y-intercept.
   C) The line has a positive slope and a negative y-intercept.
   D) The line has a positive slope and a positive y-intercept.

4. In the standard xy-plane, what is the slope of the line with the equation $7x - 3y = 4$?

5. In the standard xy-plane, what is the slope of a line perpendicular to $6x = 4y + 10$?

   A) -1
   B) $\frac{2}{3}$
   C) $\frac{3}{2}$
   D) $-\frac{2}{3}$

6. Line m is shown in the xy-plane below.

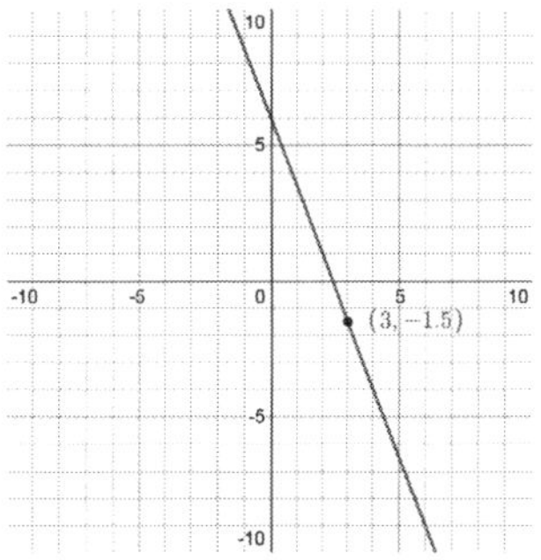

   What is the slope of line m?

7. When the point Y $(2, 4)$ is graphed in the standard xy-plane, the midpoint of XY is at $(-2, 3)$. What are the coordinates of point X?

   A) $(0, 3.5)$
   B) $(4, 0)$
   C) $(6, 5)$
   D) $(-6, 2)$

8. What is the length, in coordinate units, of a line with endpoints at $(-9, -2)$ and $(3, 7)$?

   A) $\sqrt{81}$
   B) $\sqrt{144}$
   C) $\sqrt{169}$
   D) $\sqrt{225}$

9. Which of the following is the correct equation for the graph below?

   A) $y = 4x + 2$
   B) $y = -\frac{x}{2} + 4$
   C) $y = -2x + 4$
   D) $y = 2x + 4$

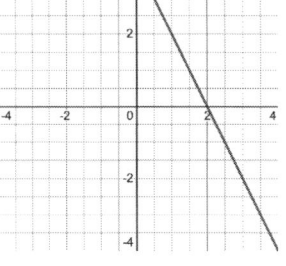

PrepPros

10. In the xy-plane below, line a is parallel to line b (not shown). Which of the following could be the equation of line b?

   A) $y = x - 3$
   B) $y = \frac{1}{2}x - 2$
   C) $y = 2x + 4$
   D) $y = -2x - 5$

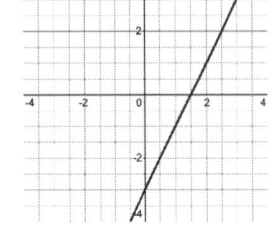

11. Line k is defined by $3x + 5y = 24$. Line a is perpendicular to line k in the xy-plane. What is the slope of line a?

12. The graph below shows the function $f(x)$. $f(x)$ and $g(x)$ (not shown) are perpendicular lines. Which of the following could define $g(x)$?

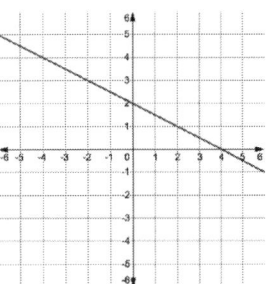

   A) $g(x) = -2x - 2$
   B) $g(x) = -\frac{1}{2}x + 4$
   C) $g(x) = \frac{1}{2}x + 2$
   D) $g(x) = 2x - 3$

13. In the linear function f, $f(0) = 15$ and $f(1) = 20$. Which equation defines f?

   A) $f(x) = 20x + 15$
   B) $f(x) = 5x$
   C) $f(x) = 5x + 15$
   D) $f(x) = 5x + 20$

14. The line the with equation $\frac{5}{4}x + \frac{1}{2}y = 3$ is graphed in the xy-plane. What is the x-intercept of the line?

15. Line m is defined by $y = -\frac{3}{5}x + 7$. Line k is perpendicular to line m in the xy-plane and passes through the point (6, 13). Which equation defines line k?

   A) $y = \frac{5}{3}x + \frac{1}{7}$
   B) $y = \frac{5}{3}x + 3$
   C) $y = \frac{5}{3}x + 7$
   D) $y = \frac{5}{3}x + \frac{47}{3}$

16. Line k passes through the points $(-2, 10)$ and $(4, 28)$. Which of the following is the equation for line k?

   A) $y = 3x + 16$
   B) $y = 3x + 4$
   C) $y = \frac{1}{3}x + 12$
   D) $y = \frac{1}{3}x + 15$

17. In the linear function k, $k(1) = 34$ and $k(2) = 31$. Which equation defines k?

   A) $k(x) = -3x + 37$
   B) $k(x) = 3x + 31$
   C) $k(x) = -37x$
   D) $k(x) = 34x$

18. When a roadmap is drawn in the xy-plane, one rest stop is drawn at $(-2, 6)$ and a second rest stop is drawn at $(8, 14)$. If 1 coordinate unit represents 10 miles, which of the following is the closest to the straight-line distance in miles between the two rest stops?

   A) 80
   B) 100
   C) 130
   D) 164

19. The table shows three values of x and their corresponding values of $f(x)$. There is a linear relationship between x and $f(x)$ that is defined by the equation $f(x) = mx - b$. What is the value of $m + b$?

x	7	13	17
f(x)	54	132	184

- 150 -

20. The point with the coordinates $(a, 6)$ lies on the line that contains the points $(0,8)$ and $(7,0)$. What is the value of a?

   A) $-\frac{7}{4}$
   B) $-\frac{4}{7}$
   C) $\frac{7}{4}$
   D) $\frac{4}{7}$

21. The graph of $9x = 4y + 27$ in the xy-plane has an x-intercept at $(J, 0)$ and a y-intercept at $(0, K)$, where J and K are constants. What is the value of $\frac{J}{K}$?

22. The graph of the line $y = kx - 2$ is graphed in the xy-plane and k is a constant. If the line contains the point (a, b) and $a \neq 0$ and $b \neq 0$, what is the slope of the line in terms of a and b?

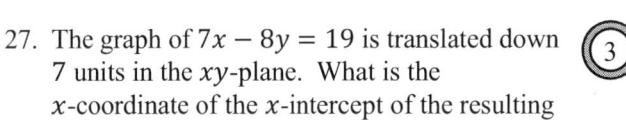

   A) $\frac{a+2}{b}$
   B) $\frac{b+2}{a}$
   C) $\frac{2-a}{b}$
   D) $\frac{b-2}{a}$

23. The graph of $4x - 5y = 20$ is translated down 8 units in the xy-plane. What is the y-coordinate of the y-intercept of the resulting graph?

24. Lines t and v are perpendicular in the xy-plane. The equation of line t is $4x + 3y = 10$, and line v passes through the point $(-3, 3)$. What is the y-intercept of line v?

25. The function f is linear, and $f(3) = 21$. When the value of x increases by 2, the value of $f(x)$ increases by 8. Which of the following equations defines f?

   A) $f(x) = 3x + 12$
   B) $f(x) = 3x + 8$
   C) $f(x) = 4x + 9$
   D) $f(x) = 4x + 21$

26. The graph of a line in the xy-plane passes through the point $(4, 6)$ and crosses the y-axis at the point $(0, 10)$. The line crosses the x-axis at the point $(a, 0)$. What is the value of a?

27. The graph of $7x - 8y = 19$ is translated down 7 units in the xy-plane. What is the x-coordinate of the x-intercept of the resulting graph?

28. Lines l and k are parallel in the xy-plane. The equation for line l is $x + 4y = -5$, and line k passes through the point $(2, 8)$. What is the x-intercept for line k?

29. Which of the following equations represents the line in the xy-plane that passes through the point $(-6, -7)$ and has a slope of $\frac{1}{3}$?

   A) $x - 3y = 15$
   B) $3x + y = 15$
   C) $2x + 5y = -15$
   D) $x + y = 5$

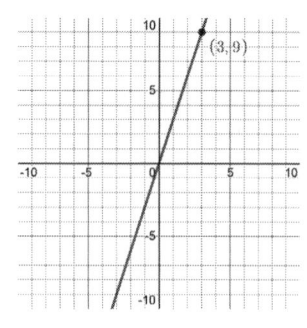

30. In the graph above, point A (not shown) with coordinates (h, k) is on the line $y = f(x)$ shown above. If h and k are negative integers, what is the ratio of k to h?

A) $-3:1$
B) $1:3$
C) $2:3$
D) $3:1$

31. $$y = 6x - 4$$

The equation of line m in the xy-plane is shown above. A second line, w, has half the slope of line m and twice the y-intercept. Where do lines m and w intersect?

A) $\left(\frac{4}{3}, 4\right)$
B) $\left(-\frac{3}{4}, -\frac{9}{2}\right)$
C) $\left(\frac{3}{4}, \frac{1}{2}\right)$
D) $\left(-\frac{4}{3}, -12\right)$

32. Line k in the xy-plane has a slope of $-\frac{1}{5}$ and passes through the point $(13, \frac{8}{5})$. Which equation defines line k?

A) $x + 5y = 21$
B) $x + 5y = 4$
C) $5y - x = 21$
D) $13y + 8x = 21$

33. $$4x - 3y = 10$$

In the xy-plane, the graph of which of the following equations is perpendicular to the graph of the equation above?

A) $-4y + 3x = 3$
B) $6x + 8y = -7$
C) $2x - 3y = 10$
D) $-4x + 3y = 10$

34. The graph shows the relationship between the number of croissants, x, and the number of madeleines, y, that Claire can buy from a bakery for $20.00. The relationship can be modeled by the equation $ax + by = 20$, where a and b are constants. What is the value of $\frac{a}{b}$?

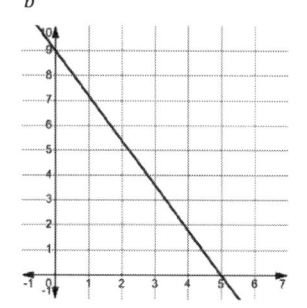

35. The points $(2, 133)$ and $(3, 138)$ lie on line k. Line k is the result of translating line a up 21 units in the xy-plane. What is the x-intercept of line a?

36. The graph of the line l in the xy-plane passes through the point $(2, 6)$ and is perpendicular to the line m with the equation $2x + 3y = 6$. The line l crosses the y-axis at the point $(0, b)$. What is the value of b?

37. In the xy-plane, line m is perpendicular to line l. Line l has an equation of $y = \frac{4}{3}x + 4$. Which of the following is the equation of line m?

A) $4x + 3y + 3 = 0$
B) $4x - 3y + 3 = 0$
C) $3x - 4y + 12 = 0$
D) $3x + 4y + 12 = 0$

38. The variables x and y are related such that each time x decreases by 7, y increases by 3. If $y < 0$ when $x = 0$, which of the following equations could express the relationship between x and y?

   A) $3x + 7y = -21$
   B) $7x + 3y = -30$
   C) $3x + 7y = 14$
   D) $7x + 3y = 9$

39. Line k has a slope of $-\frac{5}{6}$ and an x-intercept of $\left(\frac{p}{2}, 0\right)$, where p is a constant. What is the y-coordinate of the y-intercept of line k in terms of p?

   A) $-\frac{5p}{12}$
   B) $\frac{5p}{12}$
   C) $-\frac{4p}{5}$
   D) $\frac{4p}{5}$

40. In the xy-plane below, lines a and b are perpendicular. Line a passes through the origin. Lines a and b intersect at point $(6, 8)$. What is the x-coordinate of point c?

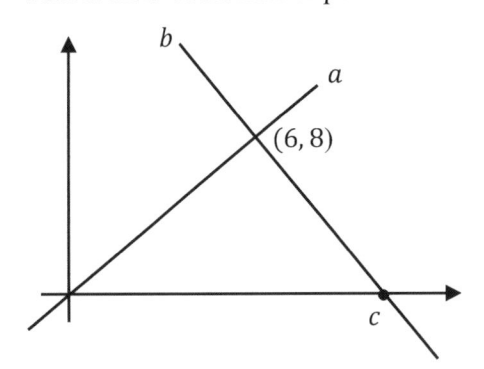

   Note: Figure not drawn to scale.

41. The variables a and b are related such that each time a increases by 5, b decreases by 7. Which of the following equations expresses the relationship between a and b?

   A) $5a - 7b = 9$
   B) $5a - 7b = -56$
   C) $5a + 7b = 56$
   D) $7a + 5b = 45$

42. In the given pair of equations below, a and b are constants. The graph of this pair of equations in the xy-plane is a pair of perpendicular lines. Which of the following pairs of equations also represents a pair of perpendicular lines?

   $$3x + 8y = 10$$
   $$ax + by = 10$$

   A) $3x - 8y = 10$
       $ax + by = 10$
   B) $6x - 16y = 10$
       $2ax + 2by = 5$
   C) $3x + 16y = 10$
       $2ax + by = 10$
   D) $3x + 16y = 10$
       $ax + 2by = 10$

43. For each real number r, which of the following points lies on the graph of the equation $2x + 5y = 9$ in the xy-plane?

   A) $\left(\frac{r}{2} + 9, \frac{r}{5}\right)$
   B) $\left(\frac{5r}{2} + \frac{9}{2}, r\right)$
   C) $\left(r, -\frac{2r}{5} + \frac{9}{5}\right)$
   D) $\left(r, -\frac{5r}{2} + \frac{9}{2}\right)$

44. Line m in the xy-plane has slope $-\frac{4p}{7}$ and y-intercept $(0, p)$, where p is a positive constant. What is the x-coordinate of the x-intercept of line m?

45. In the xy-plane, lines l and k are parallel. Line l passes through the points $(-1, -7)$ and $(1, 3)$. If the point (a, b) lies on line k, which of the following is another point on line k?

A) $(a - 1, b - 5)$
B) $(a - 1, b + 5)$
C) $(a + 5, b + 1)$
D) $(a + 5, b - 1)$

46. In the xy-plane, the point (a, c) lies on the line with equation $y = 4x + b$, where b is a constant. The point $(3a, 4c)$ lies on the line with equation $y = 2x + b$. If $a \neq 0$, what is the value of $\frac{c}{a}$?

47. For each real number r, which of the following points lies on the graph of the equation $5x + 7y = 12$?

A) $\left(-\frac{7r}{5} + \frac{12}{5}, r\right)$
B) $\left(-\frac{5r}{7} - \frac{12}{5}, r\right)$
C) $\left(r, \frac{7r}{5} + \frac{12}{5}\right)$
D) $\left(r, -\frac{5r}{7} - \frac{12}{7}\right)$

48. The table below shows several values of x and their corresponding values of y, where k is a nonzero constant. If the relationship between x and y is linear, which of the following defines this relationship?

x	-1	1	2
y	$-3k - 6$	$3k + 6$	$6k + 12$

A) $y = 3(kx - 2)$
B) $y = 3(kx + 2x)$
C) $y = 3kx + 6$
D) $y = -3k - x - 2$

49. In the given pair of equations below, a and b are constants. The graph of this pair of equations in the xy-plane is a pair of perpendicular lines. Which of the following pairs of equations represents a pair of parallel lines?

$$7x + 11y = 100$$
$$ax + by = 10b$$

A) $7x - 11y = 10$
   $ax + by = 10b$
B) $7x + 33y = 100$
   $2ax - 3by = 50b$
C) $33x - 7y = 100$
   $3ax + by = b$
D) $11x + 7y = 100$
   $ax + by = 10b$

Chapter 18: Interpreting Lines

The SAT includes questions that ask you to interpret the meanings of the terms in a linear equation. Interpreting lines questions ask you to either (1) interpret the meaning of a term in a given equation or (2) select the equation that properly models a described situation. To answer these questions correctly, you need to understand what the constants in slope-intercept form represent.

$$y = mx + b$$

- m **is the slope. The slope represents the change in the y-value per unit of x.** In other words, when the x-value increases by 1, the slope tells you how much the y-value increases or decreases.

- b **is the y-intercept. The y-intercept is the value of y when $x = 0$.** We can think of this as **the initial value**.

These definitions can be very helpful when it comes to solving interpreting lines questions.

1) Interpreting the Constants in a Given Equation

The first type of interpreting lines question on the SAT asks us to interpret the meaning of a constant in a given equation.

> **Example 1:** The price, P, of a kayak purchased in 2010 is estimated by the equation $P = 2,200 - 150t$, where t represents the number of years since the kayak was purchased. Which of the following is the best interpretation of the 2,200 in this context?
>
> A) The initial price of a kayak in 2010.
> B) The decrease in price of a kayak each year.
> C) The price of a kayak in 2019.
> D) The decrease in the price of a kayak from 2010 to 2019.

Solution: The 2,200 is the y-intercept of the given equation, so it represents the initial price when $t = 0$. The 2,200 is equal to the price of the kayak when $t = 0$ years after 2010, which is 2010. **The answer is A.**

It is important to also understand what each of the numbers in a linear equation represents. The -150 in the equation above is the slope. The slope of -150 tells us that the price of a kayak will decrease by $150 each year. If the question above instead asked us, "what is the best interpretation of -150 in this context?" the answer would have been B.

> **Example 2:** The number of bacteria in a colony is modeled by the equation $b(x) = 12.5 + 0.5x$, where x represents the number of weeks and b represents the thousands of bacteria present in the colony. What is the best interpretation of the number 0.5 in this context?
>
> A) The number of bacteria in the colony will increase by 50% each week.
> B) The number of bacteria in the colony will increase by 0.5 bacteria each week.
> C) The number of bacteria in the colony will increase by 500 bacteria each week.
> D) The initial number of bacteria in the colony is 500 bacteria.

Solution: The 0.5 is the slope in this equation. Since the unit of x is in weeks, we know that every 1 week, the value of b increases by 0.5. Since the unit of b is thousands of bacteria, the slope 0.5 shows an increase of 0.5 thousand each week. $0.5 \times 1000 = 500$, so the number of bacteria in the colony will increase by 500 each week. **The answer is C.**

For these types of questions, you need to read carefully and keep an eye out for tricks like this one. The SAT loves to change the units on more difficult questions, just like we saw here, so it is important to make close reading a habit in the math sections.

2) Selecting the Right Equation

The second type of interpreting lines question asks you to select which equation properly models the situation described in the question.

> **Example 3:** The price, P, of printing one copy of a hardcover book at Printing Express starts at a base price of $2.45. The base price only includes the hardcover and does not include the pages. Printing Express charges $0.02 per page, and the book they are currently printing costs $8.98 to print each copy. If x represents the number of pages in the book currently being printed, which of the equations correctly describes this situation?
>
> A) $8.98 = 0.02 + 2.45x$
> B) $8.98 = 0.02x + 2.45$
> C) $8.98 = 0.2x + 2.45$
> D) $8.98 = 0.2 + 2.45x$

Solution: The rate at which the thickness price increases is $0.02 per 1 page, so 0.02 is the slope. The initial price to print the book when $x = 0$ (no pages) is $2.45 mm, so the y-intercept must be 2.45. We are told that the total price must equal $8.98, so **the answer is B.**

Okay, so that was a pretty simple example to start. However, these questions can (and will) get much more challenging on the SAT, so we want to have a method to "cheat" these questions so that we don't have to rely on solving the "Math Teacher Way."

The "Plug In Points" Method

For more challenging questions where it is difficult to write the equation on your own, we can use the "Plug In Points" method. The idea behind this method is that we can select a point or points that we know must work in the equation and can use these points to help identify which answer choice is correct. To use the "Plug In Points" method, follow the steps below:

1. **Select a test point that must work in the equation. We recommend starting with an initial value, when $x = 0$ if possible, that you are given.** For Example 3 above, the first point we select would be $(0, 2.45)$ because we know the price of one copy of a hardcover book is $2.45 when there are 0 pages.

2. **Plug the point we selected into the answer choices. Eliminate any answer choices that are incorrect.** In Example 3, we know that the price is on the left side of the equation where the 8.98 is in the answer choices. If we plug in $x = 0$, the right side of the equation should be equal to a price of $2.45. Answer choices B and C give the correct value of $2.45. Answer choices A and D give us $0.02 and $0.20 respectively, so we know those answer choices are incorrect.

3. **Select a second test point (if necessary) that works in the equation.** Make this point as simple as possible from the information that you are given. For Example 3, let's add 1 page to the book. If we add 1 page to the book, the price increases by $0.02. So, for a 1-page book, the price is $2.47. We can use the point $(1, 2.47)$ as our second test point.

4. **Plug in the second point (if necessary) to the answer choices to find the correct answer.** If we plug in $x = 1$, the equation must be equal to the price of $2.47. We can see that B gives the correct price of $2.47 while C gives an incorrect price of $2.65, so we find that B has the correct equation for how to calculate the price and is the correct answer.

This is an extremely powerful method that we can use to make challenging interpreting lines questions on the SAT feel easy. To see how this works in practice on more advanced questions, let's take a look at the next two examples.

Chapter 18: Interpreting Lines

> **Example 4:** An experiment collected data about the relationship between the pressure within a balloon and the balloon's altitude. The scientists found a linear relationship between pressure and altitude. On the ground, the pressure within the balloon was measured at 14.3 psi. For every 250-meter increase in elevation, the pressure within the balloon dropped by 1.8 psi. Which of the following equations best models the pressure within the balloon, p, at h meters above the ground?
>
> A) $p = 14.3 - 1.8h$
> B) $p = 14.3 - 0.0072h$
> C) $p = 250 - 0.0572h$
> D) $p = 138.8h - 14.3$

Solution: This question is clearly more difficult to solve. We cannot easily tell what the slope is without doing some calculations, so the fastest and easiest way to solve this is using our "Plug In Points" method.

Method 1 – "Plug In Points": Let's start with the point $(0, 14.3)$. We know that this point is on the graph because when the balloon is on the ground ($h = 0$), the pressure is 14.3 psi ($p = 14.3$). We can plug the point $(0, 14.3)$ into the answer choices to see which answer choices work and which answer choices are incorrect.

A) $p = 14.3 - 1.8(0)$	→	$p = 14.3$	(A works)
B) $p = 14.3 - 0.0072(0)$	→	$p = 14.3$	(B works)
C) $p = 250 - 0.0572(0)$	→	$p = 250$	(C is incorrect)
D) $p = 138.8(0) - 14.3.3$	→	$p = -14.3$	(D is incorrect)

Since answer choices A and B both work with our first point, we need to select another point to determine if the answer is A or B.

For a second test point, we can select $(250, 12.5)$. At a height of 250 meters, we know that the pressure will have decreased by 1.8 psi from the original value of 14.3 psi, so the pressure at 250 m will be 12.5 psi.

A) $p = 14.3 - 1.8(250)$	→	$p = -435.7$	(A is incorrect)
B) $p = 14.3 - 0.0072(250)$	→	$p = 12.5$	(B is correct)

The answer is B. By plugging in points, we can solve this difficult question without doing any difficult math.

Method 2 – "Math Teacher Way": This question can also be solved using the more traditional approach of finding the slope and the y-intercept. Here, the y-intercept is easiest to find. When $h = 0$, the pressure is 14.3, so the y-intercept is 14.3.

The slope is a bit more difficult to find. In this equation, the slope represents the change in pressure per meter of elevation. We are told that the pressure decreases by 1.8 psi per 250 m of elevation, so the slope would be

$$\frac{\text{change in pressure}}{\text{change in elevation}} = \frac{-1.8}{250} = -0.0072.$$

The answer is B. As you can see, this method requires more advanced math thinking and understanding of how slopes work. You are welcome to use this method if you are a more advanced math student, but we still recommend our "Plug-in Points" method, as it is easier to make sure you find the correct answer on test day.

> **Example 5:** At a parking garage in downtown Baltimore, the first hour of parking is $2. After the first hour, the rate is $8.25 per hour. Which of the following equations gives the price, $P(h)$, for parking a car for h hours?
>
> A) $P(h) = 8.25h + 2$
> B) $P(h) = 8.25(h - 1)$
> C) $P(h) = 8.25h - 6.25$
> D) $P(h) = 2(h - 1) + 8.25$

- 157 -

PrepPros

Solution: At first glance, most students think, "Oh this question is easy! The answer is A." WRONG!! We like to call questions like this "fake y-intercept" questions. It is important to understand that the y-intercept is not at 2. Remember, the y-intercept is when $x = 0$, or in this case when $h = 0$. We are told the first hour of parking is $2, so when $h = 1$, $P(h) = 2$. Again, this is NOT the y-intercept.

So, how do we solve this? **We recommend using the "Plug In Points" method.** We know that when $h = 1$, $P(h) = 2$, so we can plug in $h = 1$ and test the answer choices and see which one gives us the correct price of $2.

    A) $P(1) = 8.25(1) + 2$ → $p = 10.25$ (A is incorrect)

    B) $P(1) = 8.25(1 - 1)$ → $p = 0$ (B is incorrect)

    C) $P(1) = 8.25(1) - 6.25$ → $p = 2$ (C is correct)

    D) $P(1) = 2(1 - 1) + 8.25$ → $p = 8.25$ (D is incorrect)

The answer is C. All the other answer choices gave us incorrect values. This method is the easiest and most effective to solve questions like this, so it should be your go-to method on test day.

If you are wondering how we would solve this question algebraically, we would need to set up the equation like this:

$$P(h) = 8.25(h - 1) + 2$$

Since the price is $8.25 per hour, the slope is 8.25. However, since that rate does not start until after the 1st hour, we subtract 1 from the number of hours and write the term as $(h - 1)$. The first hour is $2, so we have to add 2 to get the correct price.

If we distribute the 8.25 and combine like terms, we get the same equation as the correct one in answer choice C.

$$P(h) = 8.25(h - 1) + 2 \quad \rightarrow \quad P(h) = 8.25h - 8.25 + 2 \quad \rightarrow \quad P(h) = 8.25h - 6.25$$

If that seems confusing, do not worry about it! It's supposed to. That's why the SAT includes these as difficult questions on test day. However, they are easy as long as you remember to use the "Plug In Points" method to solve these "fake y-intercepts" questions on test day.

Interpreting Lines Practice: Answers on pages 330-331.

1. $$x + y = 200$$
The equation above represents the number of hours, x, Andrew spends fishing each year and the number of hours, y, Andrew spends surfing each year. In the equation, what does the number 200 represent?

    A) The number of hours spent fishing each year.
    B) The number of hours spent surfing each year.
    C) The total number of hours spent fishing and surfing each year.
    D) The number of hours spent fishing for each hour spent surfing.

2. The maximum speed of an F1 racecar in miles per hour is a linear function of the temperature, t, in degrees Fahrenheit of the engine, given by $S(t) = 0.128t + 212.5$. Which of the following statements is the best interpretation of the number 212.5?

    A) The increase in the speed of the car for each 1°C increase in the temperature.
    B) The increase in the speed of the car for each 0.128°C increase in the temperature.
    C) The speed of the car at 0°C.
    D) The speed of the car at 0.128°C.

3. John makes his surfboard by starting with a 28 mm thick piece of foam. He then adds n layers of 2 mm fiberglass. Which of the following gives the total thickness, S, in millimeters for a surfboard with n layers of fiberglass?

A) $S = 2n + 28$
B) $S = n + 14$
C) $S = 28n + 2$
D) $S = 2n + 14$

4. $$w = 9a + 19.5$$

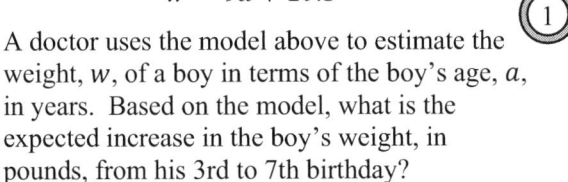

A doctor uses the model above to estimate the weight, w, of a boy in terms of the boy's age, a, in years. Based on the model, what is the expected increase in the boy's weight, in pounds, from his 3rd to 7th birthday?

A) 9
B) 19.5
C) 27
D) 36

5. Nikhil walks at a speed of 4 miles per hour and runs at a speed of 7 miles per hour. He walks for w hours and runs for r hours for a combined total of 17 miles. Which equation represents this situation?

A) $4w + 7r = 17$
B) $\frac{1}{4}w + \frac{1}{7}r = 17$
C) $4w + 7r = 187$
D) $\frac{1}{4}w + \frac{1}{7}r = 187$

6. To draw a mural, a painter charges a onetime fee and $23 per hour of work. The equation $23h + 75 = 236$ represents this situation, where h is the number of hours worked. Which of the following is the best interpretation of the 75 in this context?

A) The onetime fee, in dollars.
B) The number of hours worked.
C) The charge per hour, in dollars.
D) The total charge, in dollars.

7. Julian rents a boat at a cost of $230 per day plus a nonrefundable deposit of $85. Which equation represents the total cost c, in dollars, to rent the boat after putting down the deposit for d days?

A) $c = 85(230 + d)$
B) $c = 230(d + 85)$
C) $c = 230d + 85$
D) $c = 85d + 230$

8. A moving truck rental company charges a flat fee of $124.99 for renting a truck and $1.79 for every ten miles driven. A customer paid a total of $262.82 for a moving truck rental. If x is the number of miles that the customer drove the truck, which of the following equations represents this situation?

A) $262.82 = 1.79x + 124.99$
B) $262.82 = 0.179x + 124.99$
C) $262.82 = 1.79 + 124.99x$
D) $262.82 = 1.79x + 12.499$

9. Total Cost of Renting a Kayak by the Hour

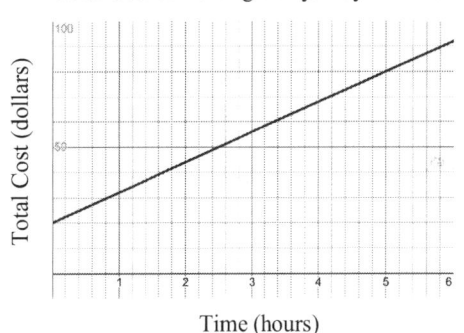

The graph above shows the total cost c, in dollars, of renting a kayak for x hours. What does the y-intercept on the graph represent?

A) The initial cost of renting a kayak.
B) The total number of hours the kayak was rented.
C) The total number of kayaks rented.
D) The increase in cost to rent the kayak for each additional hour.

10. A moving company estimates the price of a job, in dollars, using the equation $P = 150 + 25mh$, where m represents the number of movers and h is the total number of hours the job will take using m movers. Which of the following is the best interpretation of the number 25 in the equation?

A) The company charges 25 dollar per hour for each mover.
B) The price of every job increases by 25 dollars each hour.
C) Each mover works for an average of 25 hours per week.
D) A maximum of 25 movers can be used for the same job.

11. Lucia earns k dollars for every a hours of work. Which expression represents the amount of money, in dollars, Lucia earns for $27a$ hours of work?

A) $\frac{k}{27}$
B) $27k$
C) $k + 27$
D) $k - 27$

12. The Lakewood Country Club plans to increase its membership by a total of m families per year. At the beginning of this year, there were p families with memberships. Which function best models the total number of families, f, the Lakewood Country Club plans to have as members x years from now?

A) $f = px + m$
B) $f = mx + p$
C) $f = m(p)^x$
D) $f = mxp$

13. A 4,864-piece jigsaw puzzle has 276 edge pieces, and the rest are pieces inside of the puzzle. The equation $74x + 276 = 4,864$ describes this situation, where x represents the number of rows that contain inside pieces. Which of the following is the best interpretation of $74x$ in this context?

A) There are $74x$ total pieces.
B) There are $74x$ pieces in each row.
C) There are $74x$ edge pieces.
D) There are $74x$ inside pieces.

14. The number of turtles that went to a certain beach in Costa Rica to lay their eggs from 2005 to 2015 can be modeled by the equation $y = 5.21x + 150$, where x represents the number of years since 2005 and y represents the total number of turtles each year. Which of the following best describes the meaning of the number 5.21 in the equation above?

A) The estimated increase in the number of turtles that came to the beach each additional year after 2005.
B) The total number of turtles who came to the beach in 2005.
C) The estimated difference between the number of turtles in 2005 and in 2015.
D) The average number of turtles who arrived each year.

15. Kyle measured the internal temperature of his brisket while it was being smoked. The temperature of the brisket before being placed in the smoker was 48°F. Kyle discovered that the temperature of the brisket rose at a constant rate. Two and a half hours after being placed in the smoker, the brisket's temperature was 93°F. Four hours after being placed in the smoker, the brisket's temperature was 120°F. Which of the following equations models the temperature $T(h)$ in degrees Fahrenheit h hours after being placed in the smoker?

A) $T(h) = 45h + 48$
B) $T(h) = 30h + 48$
C) $T(h) = 48h + 45$
D) $T(h) = 18h + 48$

16. The amount of juice that the average orange from Mitch's farm produces when juiced can be modeled by the equation $x = -19h + 290$, where x is the milliliters of juice produced and h is the weeks since harvest. Which of the following statements is true based on the equation?

A) On average, an orange produces 19 milliliters less juice at harvest than one week after harvest.
B) Two weeks after harvest, each orange on average produces 252 milliliters of juice.
C) Each orange loses exactly 19 milliliters of juice per week after harvest.
D) One week before harvest, each orange would have produced 308 milliliters of juice.

17. A company that manufactures x dog beds calculates its monthly profit by subtracting its monthly cost from its monthly revenue. The equation $18{,}000 = 12.00x - 1.50x$ models this situation. What is the meaning of $1.50x$ in this context?

   A) The monthly revenue from each dog bed sold.
   B) The monthly revenue from x dog beds sold.
   C) The cost of manufacturing each dog bed.
   D) The cost of manufacturing x dog beds.

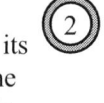

18. An electronic waste disposal service paid $35,000 to dispose of l pounds of lithium batteries and h pounds of hard drives. The equation $35l + 15h = 35{,}000$ represents this situation. What is the interpretation of 35 in this context?

   A) The weight, in pounds, of each lithium battery.
   B) The amount, in dollars, it costs the service to dispose of each lithium battery.
   C) The amount, in dollars per pound, it costs the service to dispose of lithium batteries.
   D) The total amount, in dollars, the disposal service paid to dispose of lithium batteries.

19. Max begins working at a bakery on January 1st. His job is to make chocolate croissants. The number of chocolate croissants that Max can make each day is estimated by the equation $y = 2.2x + 60$, where x is the number of weeks since January 1st and y is the number of croissants he makes per day. Which of the following is the best explanation of 2.2 in this context?

   A) The increase in the estimated number of croissants that Max makes each week with each additional week of experience.
   B) The increase in the estimated number of croissants Max makes each day with each additional week of experience.
   C) The total number of croissants that Max makes during his first week.
   D) The total number of croissants that Max makes during his first day.

20. $$27{,}000 - 180m = v$$

The current value, v, of Jill's car m months after she purchased the car is modeled by the equation above. Which of the following statements is correct?

   A) The value of Jill's car at purchase was $26,820.
   B) Every year, the current value of Jill's car decreases by $180.
   C) Every 6 months, the current value of Jill's car decreases by $1,080.
   D) In ten years, the value of Jill's car will be $25,200.

21. $$W(b) = 0.62b + 5$$

Paleontologists can estimate the wingspan, W, of a Pterosaurs in feet based on beak length, b, in inches using the formula above. What is the correct interpretation of 0.62 in the equation?

   A) The estimated beak length, in inches, of a Pterosaurs at birth.
   B) The estimated increase of a Pterosaurs' wingspan, in feet, for each increase of 5 inches of beak length.
   C) The estimated increase of a Pterosaurs' beak length, in inches, for each one-foot increase in wingspan.
   D) The estimated increase of a Pterosaurs' wingspan, in feet, for each one-inch increase in its beak length.

22. A research team tracked the diameter of the trunk of a redwood tree, w, in inches over seventy-two years. When the study began in 1940, the redwood tree's trunk had a diameter of 46 inches. When the study was completed in 2012, the redwood tree's trunk had a diameter of 104 inches. Which of the following best models the diameter of the redwood tree, w, for y years since 1940?

   A) $w = 46 + 0.806y$
   B) $w = 1.625y + 46$
   C) $w = 46 + 0.64y$
   D) $w = 58y + 46$

23. Annie paid $65 to sign up for a food delivery service that sends her ingredients for 5 meals each week. After the sign-up fee, Annie pays $200 every 4 weeks for the food. Which of the following models how much Annie pays, m, for k meals?

A) $m = 65 + 10k$
B) $m = 200 + 65k$
C) $m = 5k + 65$
D) $m = 65 + 50k$

24. The cost of renting a kayak is $20 for the first hour, plus an additional $12 for each additional hour. If h represents the number of hours the kayak is rented, which of the following functions gives the cost $K(h)$, in dollars, of renting the kayak for h hours?

A) $K(h) = 12h + 20$
B) $K(h) = 12h + 8$
C) $K(h) = 12h$
D) $K(h) = 20h + 12$

25. The given linear function f models the annual percentage increase in the population over the prior year for Tijuana t years since 2010, where $0 \le t < 15$. What is the best interpretation of $f(10) = 2.5$ in this context?

$$f(t) = -0.075t + 3.25$$

A) 2.5 years after 2010, the percentage increase in the population of Tijuana was 10% over the previous year.
B) 2.5 years after 2010, Tijuana's population was approximately 10 times the amount in 2010.
C) 10 years after 2010, the percentage increase in the population of Tijuana was 2.5% over the previous year.
D) 10 years after 2010, Tijuana's population was approximately 2.5 times its population in 2010.

26. Megan is training for her first marathon by going on a long run every Monday. She will run 4 miles on the first Monday that she is training. Every Monday after the first, she will run 2.5 more miles than she ran the preceding Monday. Which of the following equations represent the number of miles m Megan will run on the nth Monday of her training?

A) $m = 4 + 2.5n$
B) $m = 1.5 + 2.5n$
C) $m = 2.5n - 4$
D) $m = 2.5^n + 4$

27. The given function g models the number of gallons of gasoline that remains from a full gas tank in a motorcycle after driving m miles. According to the model about how miles per gallon can the motorcycle travel?

$$g(m) = -0.08m + 8.75$$

A) 0.08
B) 8.75
C) 12.5
D) 109

28. Linh ran from her home to her friend's house in 1 hour and 15 minutes at an average rate of 7 miles per hour. If the equation below represents this situation, what does z represent?

$$\frac{1}{1.25} = \frac{7}{z}$$

A) The distance, in miles, that Linh ran.
B) The time, in hours, that Linh ran.
C) Linh's average speed, in miles per hour.
D) Linh's average speed, in miles per minute.

29. A boxing club membership costs $85 per month. After 1 year, members receive a discount of $30 off the cost of their monthly membership. Which function c gives the total cost $c(t)$, in dollars, that a new member pays after t months of membership, where $t \ge 12$?

A) $c(t) = 1{,}020 + 55t$
B) $c(t) = 55t + 85$
C) $c(t) = 360 + 55t$
D) $c(t) = 1{,}020 + 85(t - 12)$

30. Julia and Drew both work at their own constant rate, either alone or together. When Julia works alone, she can finish her job 18 minutes faster than Drew can. The equation below can be used to find the time x, in minutes, it takes Drew to finish the job alone. Which of the following is the best interpretation of the number 54 in the equation?

$$\frac{1}{54} = \frac{1}{x-18} + \frac{1}{x}$$

A) The number of minutes it takes Julia and Drew to finish the job working together.
B) The number of minutes it takes Julia to complete the Job.
C) The number of minutes it takes Drew to complete the Job.
D) How many fewer minutes it takes Julia to complete the job than Drew.

31. For groups of 50 or more people, an aquarium charges $17 per person for the first 50 people and $12 for each additional person after the 50th person. Which function c gives the total charge, in dollars, for a group of x people, where $x \geq 50$?

A) $c(x) = 12x + 17$
B) $c(x) = 12x + 50$
C) $c(x) = 12x + 250$
D) $c(x) = 12x + 850$

32. A company that manufactures crutches calculates its monthly profit by subtracting its fixed monthly costs from its monthly revenue from sales. The equation $36{,}000 = 20x - 12{,}000$ represents this situation in June when x crutches are manufactured and sold. What is the meaning of $\frac{36{,}000}{x}$ in this context?

A) The average cost of manufacturing x crutches in June.
B) The profit per crutch sold in June.
C) The revenue for each crutch sold in June.
D) The total revenue from selling x crutches in June.

Chapter 19: Exponential Growth and Decay

Any quantity that grows or decays at a fixed rate over time experiences exponential growth or decay. Some examples that you may be familiar with include money in a bank account earning 8% interest each year or the number of bacteria on a plate doubling every week.

For most questions on the SAT, we use the simpler form of the exponential growth and decay equations shown below:

Growth: $A = P(1 + r)^t$

Decay: $A = P(1 - r)^t$

P = initial value
A = current value
r = rate of the growth or decay
t = time interval

We use the simple form of the equation above when the time interval is in years, which is most common on the SAT.

Exponential Growth

To see how these equations work and appear on a graph, let's examine the equation for a bank account that has an initial balance of $100 and an 8% annual interest rate.

$$A = 100(1 + 0.08)^t$$
$$A = 100(1.08)^t$$

The $100 is the initial value, and the 8% is the growth rate. 8% is expressed as 0.08 in decimal form, so we get a value of 1.08 inside the parentheses. A represents the current value after t time intervals. Since the amount of money in the bank account is increasing at a non-linear rate over time, we have **exponential growth**.

Now, let's see how this exponential growth equation appears on a graph.

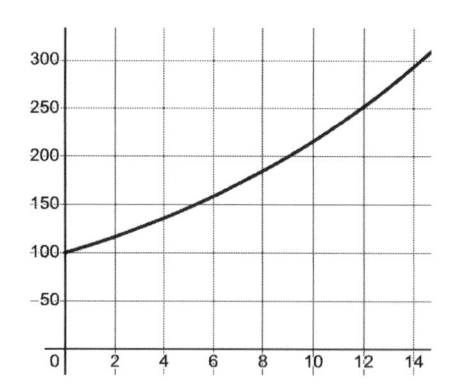

For any exponential growth equation, the graph will have an upward curve like this one. **The y-intercept of the graph shows the initial value**, which in this example is $100.

Note that **the graph is NOT linear**. Even though the growth rate remains constant at 8%, the annual increase in the amount of money in the account will not be the same. In the first year, the $100 grows by 8%, which is $8, so the final amount in the account at the end of year 1 is $108. For the second year, the money is growing at 8% but the starting value is now $108, so the amount of money will increase by 8% of $108, which is $8.64. This explains why a constant rate of change does NOT lead to a constant amount of change and why exponential graphs are not linear.

Example 1: Julia estimates that the numbers of bees in a hive increases by 30% every month. If Julia buys a hive with 50 bees, which of the following properly models Julia's estimate for how many bees, B, will live in the hive in m months?

A) $B = 50 + 30m$ B) $B = 50(0.3)^m$ C) $B = 50m^2 + 30$ D) $B = 50(1.3)^m$

Solution: The initial number of bees in the colony is 50, and the growth rate is 30%. Since the growth is 30% each month and not a fixed numerical value, we have exponential growth and not linear growth. A, which is linear, and C, which is quadratic, are incorrect. The value in the parentheses must be 1.3 and not 0.3 since the growth rate is 30%. The 1.3 comes from the $(1 + 0.3)$ in the growth equation. **The answer is D.**

Exponential Decay

Now let's consider an example of **exponential decay**. A new car purchased for $20,000 loses 10% of its value each year after the purchase date.

$$A = 20,000(1 - 0.1)^t$$
$$A = 20,000(0.9)^t$$

The $20,000 is the initial value, and the 10% is the rate of decay. 10% can be expressed as 0.1 in decimal form, so we get a value of 0.9 inside the parentheses. A represents the current value after t time intervals.

Now, let's see how this exponential decay equation appears on a graph.

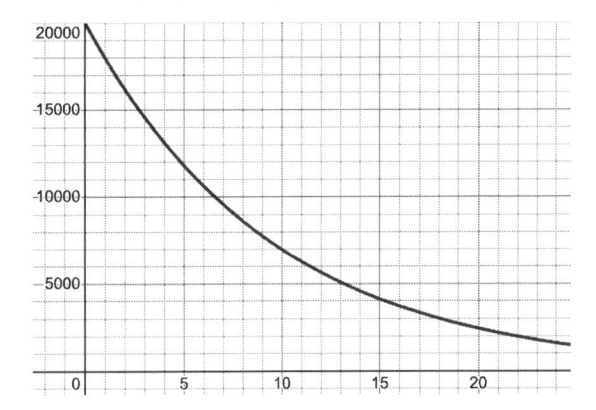

Again, note that the graph is NOT linear. The car continues to lose 10% of its value each year, but the numerical decrease in the car's value is not the same every year. Anytime we have an exponential decay equation, the graph will have a downward curve like this one. **The y-intercept of the graph shows the initial value**, which in this example is the purchase price of $20,000.

In Example 1, we were asked to select the correct equation to describe a given situation. The SAT also commonly asks you to interpret constants in a given exponential equation.

Example 2: A paper published in 1980 estimated that the number of ranchers in the United States can be modeled by the equation $r = 10,500(0.92)^t$, where r is the number of ranchers and t is the number of years since 1980. Which of the following is the best interpretation of 0.92 in this context?

A) The estimated number of ranchers in the United States in 1980 is 920.
B) The estimated number of ranchers in the United States decreased by 920 ranchers each year after 1980.
C) The estimated number of ranchers in the United States decreased at a rate of 92% each year after 1980.
D) The estimated number of ranchers in the United States decreased at a rate of 8% each year after 1980.

Solution: The 0.92 represents the rate of change. Remember, our exponential decay equation is $A = P(1 - r)^t$, so the 0.92 is equal to $1 - r$. Once we recognize this, we can see that $r = 8\%$ (since $1 - 0.08 = 0.92$) so the estimated number of ranchers in the United States decreased by 8% per year after 1980. **The answer is D.**

The 0.92 in the equation means that after each year, there are 92% of the ranchers remaining, so the estimated number of ranchers has decreased by 8%. The 10,500 in the equation shows us the initial value for the estimated initial number of ranchers in the United States in 1980 (when $t = 0$). So, in 1980, there were an estimated 10,500 ranchers in the United States.

The SAT also can ask you to interpret the meaning of a point in an exponential function.

> **Example 3:** The function $p(t) = 23,500(0.93)^t$ models the population, p, of giant river otters in South America since the populations of giant river otters began being tracked in 1970. Given that t represent the number of years since 1970, which of the following statements is the correct interpretation of $p(8) = 13,150$ in this context?
>
> A) The population of giant river otters in South America was 13,150 in 1978.
> B) The population of giant river otters in South America decreased by 13,150 from 1970 to 1978.
> C) The population of giant river otters in South America in 1978 is 7% less than the population of giant river otters in 1970.
> D) The population of giant river otters in South America is decreasing at a rate of 13,150 giant river otters per year in 1978.

Solution: The $p(8) = 13,150$ tells us that if we plug in $t = 8$ to the original equation, we get $p(t) = 13,150$. In words, when $t = 8$, which is 8 years after 1970 (so in 1978), the population of giant river otters in South America is 13,150. **The correct answer is A.**

The other answer choices are all incorrect interpretations of the function. The 23,500 in the equation tells us that the population is originally 23,500 when $t = 0$, which is in 1970. The $(0.93)^t$, which can be rewritten as $(1 - 0.07)^t$, tells us that the population decreases by 7% each year.

General Exponential Form

Exponential equations can also appear in the general form show below.

$$y = ab^x$$

where $a \neq 0$ and b is a positive number and $b \neq 1$. The a and b values are constants. The main points we need to understand about this general exponential form are listed below:

- **a is the y-intercept and shows the initial value of graph when $x = 0$.**
- **b is the rate of change and shows how much the initial value changes per time interval.**
- **x is the time interval.**
- **If $b > 1$, the equation shows exponential growth.**
- **If $0 < b < 1$, the equation shows exponential decay.**

To better understand general form, let's consider two examples with some numbers:

Example 1: A population of 150 endangered Rhinos is doubling every year. Write an equation that models the size of the population, $P(x)$, in x years.

$$P(x) = 150(2)^x$$

The initial Rhino population is 150, so $a = 150$. The population is doubling every year, so the rate of change, b, is 2. x represents the number of years.

Example 2: After a lake is polluted, the population of fish in the lake follow exponential decay. A survey finds that one third of the fish in the lake survived after 1 month. If the estimated initial population of fish in the lake was 12,000, write an equation that models the number of fish, $F(x)$, in m months, assuming the same rate of decay as the first month.

Chapter 19: Exponential Growth and Decay

$$F(x) = 12{,}000 \left(\frac{1}{3}\right)^m$$

The initial population of fish in the lake is 12,000, so $a = 12{,}000$. The population is one third of its starting value after 1 month so $b = \frac{1}{3}$. m represents the number of months.

Now, let's see how the SAT can test you on this concept.

Example 4: The equation $A(x) = 315(2)^x$ shows the number of apricots that an apricot tree produces x years after it begins producing fruit. By looking at the equation above, it can be determined that the apricot tree increases the number of apricots it produces by p percent each year. What is the value of p?

Solution: When written in general exponential form, the b-value, the 2 in the equation above, shows the rate of change. The 2 in the equation above means that the number of apricots that the tree produces doubles every year. Many students mistakenly think that the answer here is 200 since doubling is the same as multiply by 200%.

But here the question asks us to find the percent increase each year. Thinking back to our exponential growth equation $A = P(1 + r)^t$, the $(1 + r)$ shows the growth rate r. This value is 2 is in the equation above, so, to get a 2 inside the parentheses, $r = 1$. We could rewrite the equation above as $A(x) = 315(1 + 1)^x$ to see the r-value. Since $r = 1$, the growth rate if 100%, so $p = 100$. **The answer is 100.**

The 315 shows the initial number of apricots when $x = 0$, so the tree produces 315 apricots the first year that it produces fruit.

Advanced Exponential Growth and Decay

Advanced exponential growth and decay questions take the concepts we have learned in this chapter and present them in a more challenging way.

Example 5: A chemist is growing fungi as part of an experiment. At the beginning of the experiment, there are 105 fungi on the plate. The chemist discovers that the fungi population doubles every 20 minutes. Which of the following equations best models the number of fungi, f, on the plate h **hours** after the start of the experiment?

A) $f = 105(2)^{3h}$

B) $f = 105(2)^{\frac{h}{3}}$

C) $f = 105(2)^{20h}$

D) $f = 105(2)^{\frac{h}{20}}$

Solution: Solving this algebraically can be challenging and confusing, so **the best way to solve questions like this is to use our "Plug In Points" method**. We just learned this method in Chapter 18 (go to p. 146 to review how to use this method).

For this question, we first know that the initial population, when $h = 0$, is 105. So, let's use $(0, 105)$ as our first test point. We can plug in $h = 0$ and see which answer choices give us the correct value of 105 fungi.

A) $f = 105(2)^{3(0)}$ → $f = 105(2)^0$ → $f = 105$ (A works)

B) $f = 105(2)^{\frac{0}{3}}$ → $f = 105(2)^0$ → $f = 105$ (B works)

C) $f = 105(2)^{20(0)}$ → $f = 105(2)^0$ → $f = 105$ (C works)

D) $f = 105(2)^{\frac{0}{20}}$ → $f = 105(2)^0$ → $f = 105$ (D works)

- 167 -

With this test point, all the answer choices work, so we need a second test point. We know that the population doubles every 20 minutes, so after 20 minutes, the population will be 210 fungi. The units of h is hours, so we need to convert 20 minutes to hours. 20 minutes is $\frac{1}{3}$ hours, so we know that when $h = \frac{1}{3}$, the population must be 210 fungi. Therefore, we can use $\left(\frac{1}{3}, 210\right)$ as our second test point. We can plug in $h = \frac{1}{3}$ and see which answer choice gives us the correct value of 210 fungi.

A) $f = 105(2)^{3\left(\frac{1}{3}\right)}$ → $f = 105(2)^1$ → $f = 210$ (A is correct)

B) $f = 105(2)^{\frac{\frac{1}{3}}{3}}$ → $f = 105(2)^{\frac{1}{9}}$ → $f = 113.4$ (B is incorrect)

C) $f = 105(2)^{20\left(\frac{1}{3}\right)}$ → $f = 105(2)^{\frac{20}{3}}$ → $f = 10{,}667.3$ (C is incorrect)

D) $f = 105(2)^{\frac{\frac{1}{3}}{20}}$ → $f = 105(2)^{\frac{1}{60}}$ → $f = 106.22$ (D is incorrect)

The answer is A. All the other answer choices gave us incorrect values. This method is the easiest and most effective to solve questions like this, so it should be your go-to method on test day.

Graphing General Exponential Form
(3/4)

The SAT can include questions where you need to know how to graph exponential equations. If you understand the general shape of the graph and know the key points to understand for 2 examples below, you should be able to solve any exponential graphing questions that appear on test day.

Exponential Growth ($b > 1$)

$y = ab^x$

$y = 2^x$

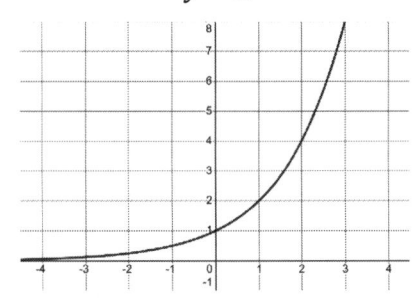

Exponential Decay ($0 < b < 1$)

$y = ab^x$

$y = 2\left(\frac{1}{2}\right)^x$

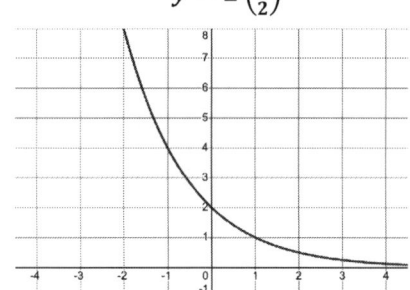

Key Points To Understand

- **y-interecept at $(0, a)$.** In this example, $a = 1$, so the y-intercept is at $(0, 1)$. Notice when $a = 1$, the a-value is not shown in the equation.
- **Graph increasing from left to right when $b > 1$.**
- **Horizontal asymptote at $y = 0$.**

Key Points To Understand

- **y-interecept at $(0, a)$.** In this example, $a = 2$, so the y-intercept is at $(0, 2)$.
- **Graph decreasing from left to right when $0 < b < 1$.**
- **Horizontal asymptote at $y = 0$.**

Chapter 19: Exponential Growth and Decay

Exponential graphs follow the same shifting rules that all other graphs follow. Below are all the shifting rules that you need to understand.

Base Function

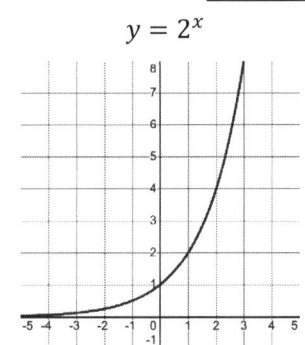

$y = 2^x$

- The y-intercept is at $(0, 1)$.
- The horizontal asymptote is at $y = 0$.
- As we shift this graph, pay attention to how the y-intercept and horizontal asymptote shift.

Horizontal Shift

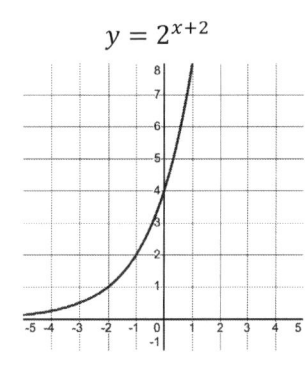

$y = 2^{x+2}$

- Numbers added in the exponent shift the function left.
- Numbers subtracted in the exponent shift the function right.
- The $+2$ shifts the function 2 units left. The initial y-intercept at point $(0, 1)$ is now at $(-2, 1)$.
- The horizontal asymptote is still at $y = 0$.

Vertical Shift

$y = 2^x + 3$

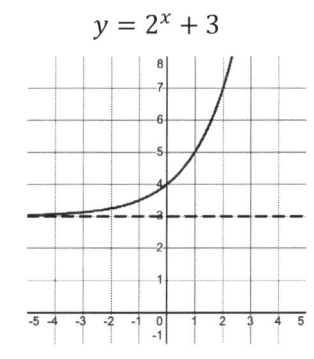

- Numbers added shift the function up.
- Numbers subtracted shift the function down.
- The $+3$ shifts the y-intercept and the horizontal asymptote 3 units up.

Vertical Flip

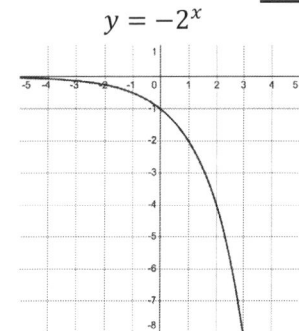

$y = -2^x$

- A negative sign in front causes the function to reflect over the x-axis.
- The y-intercept reflects over the x-axis and is now at $(0, -1)$.
- The horizontal asymptote is still at $y = 0$.

3 Key Takeaways from Graphing and Shifting Exponential Functions

1. **The horizontal asymptote starts at $y = 0$ and only shifts with a vertical shift.**

2. **For an exponential graph in $y = ab^x$ form, the y-intercept starts at $(0, a)$ and then can shift up, down, left, right, and flip vertically.** With all these shifts, the y-intercept can be more difficult to keep track of.

3. **We can always solve for the y-intercept by plugging in $x = 0$ to the function.** It is often good to find the y-intercept and use it as a test point when dealing with exponential growth and decay that involves graphing.

Since you are given Desmos on test day, the SAT will most likely make any exponential graphing questions a bit more challenging by writing questions with variables instead of numbers.

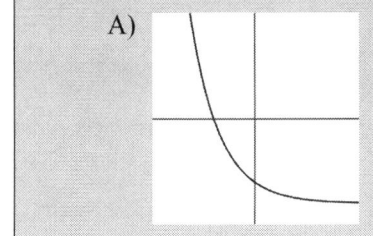

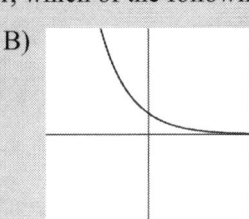

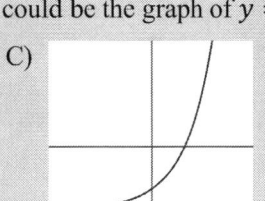

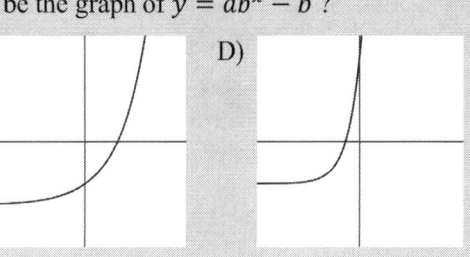

Example 6: If $a > b$ and $b > 4$, which of the following could be the graph of $y = ab^x - b$?

A)   B)   C)   D)

- 169 -

Solution: Method #1 – "Math Teacher Way": Since we are told that $b < 4$ and $a > b$, we know that a and b must both be positive values greater than 4. Since b is positive and greater than 1, we know that the graph should show exponential growth. Answer choices A and B, which show exponential decay, are incorrect.

Now, let's look at answer choices C and D. Both answer choices have a horizontal asymptote that is below the y-axis, which makes sense since the graph is shifted b units down. The notable difference between answer choices C and D is the y-intercepts. Answer choice C has a negative y-intercept while answer choice D has a positive y-intercept. To find the y-intercept, let's plug in $x = 0$ to the original equation.

$$y = ab^0 - b$$

$b^0 = 1$, so the equation becomes

$$y = a - b$$

The y-intercept of the graph is equation to $a - b$. We are told that $a > b$, so $a - b$ must be positive. Therefore, the y-intercept of the graph must be positive, so **the answer is D**.

Method #2 – Substitution: Remember, you have Desmos, so let's use it! We can pick values for a and b and graph the equation. For example, if we select $a = 6$ and $b = 5$, the graph looks like this:

$$y = 6(5^x) - 5$$

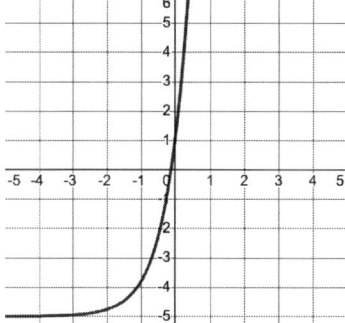

Looking at the answer choices, we can see that the answer choice that most closely resembles our graph is D. **The answer is D.** If you get stumped on any question that involves graphing, you should always try substituting in numbers to see if you can use Desmos to help you solve.

Exponential Growth and Decay Practice: Answers on page 331.

1. Trayvon is buying 5,436 fish to start his fish farm. The number of fish in his pond are estimated to increase at a rate of 3% per year. Which equation models the total number of fish, P, in the pond t years from now?

   A) $P(t) = 5,436(1.03)^t$
   B) $P(t) = 5,436(0.03)^t$
   C) $P(t) = 0.03(5,436)^t$
   D) $P(t) = 1.03(5,436)^t$

2. The function f is defined by $f(x) = 300(0.2)^x$. What is the value of $f(0)$?

   A) 0
   B) 1
   C) 60
   D) 300

3. The equation $H = 29(1.14)^t$ models the number of horses, H, in a population from 1882 to 1896, where t is the number of years since 1882. Based on the model, by what percentage did the number of horses increase each year?

   A) 0.14%
   B) 0.29%
   C) 14%
   D) 29%

4. The function $f(x) = 75,000b^x$ models the annual value for a stock, in dollars, x years after being placed on the stock market, where b is a constant. If the stock's value increases 6% per year, what is the value of b?

5. The value of a motorcycle depreciates at an annual rate of 14 percent. If the initial value is $20,000, which of the following models the value of the motorcycle, in dollars, in t years?

   A) $f(t) = 1.14t + 20{,}000$
   B) $f(t) = 0.86t + 20{,}000$
   C) $f(t) = 20{,}000(1.14)^t$
   D) $f(t) = 20{,}000(0.86)^t$

6. A model predicts that the population of Encinitas was 54,000 in 2007. The model also predicts that each year for the next 10 years, the population p increased by 7% of the previous year's population. Which equation best represents the model, where x is the number of years after 2007, where $0 \leq x \leq 10$?

   A) $p = 0.93(54{,}000)^x$
   B) $p = 1.07(54{,}000)^x$
   C) $p = 54{,}000(0.93)^x$
   D) $p = 54{,}000(1.07)^x$

7. A surfboard depreciates at an annual rate of 15%. If the initial value of the surfboard is $995, which of the following functions P correctly models the price of the surfboard t years from purchase?

   A) $P(t) = 0.15(995)^t$
   B) $P(t) = 0.85(995)^t$
   C) $P(t) = 995(1.15)^t$
   D) $P(t) = 995(0.85)^t$

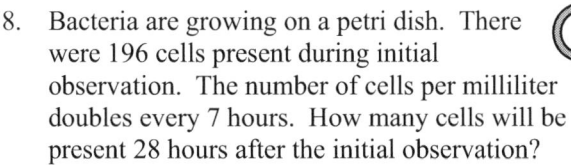

8. Bacteria are growing on a petri dish. There were 196 cells present during initial observation. The number of cells per milliliter doubles every 7 hours. How many cells will be present 28 hours after the initial observation?

9. What is the y-intercept of the graph of $f(x) = 7^x - 7$ in the xy-plane?

   A) $(0, -7)$
   B) $(0, -6)$
   C) $(0, 1)$
   D) $(0, 7)$

10. The function below can be used to estimate the millions of people living within 15 miles of San Diego, where n is the number of years since 2017. Which of the following is the best explanation for 7.86?

    $$F(n) = 7.86(1.02)^n$$

    A) The number of people, in millions, living in San Diego in 2017.
    B) The number of people, in millions, living within 15 miles of San Diego in 2017.
    C) The estimated annual increase in the number of people, in millions, living within 15 miles of San Diego after 2017.
    D) The estimated annual increase in the number of people, in millions, living in San Diego after 2017.

11. For the function b, the value of $b(x)$ decreases by 65% for every increase in the value of x by 1. If $b(0) = 375$, which equation defines b?

    A) $b(x) = 0.65(375)^x$
    B) $b(x) = 0.35(375)^x$
    C) $b(x) = 375(0.35)^x$
    D) $b(x) = 375(0.65)^x$

12. The US population has grown at an average rate of 0.8% per year since 1975. There were 236 million people in the US in 1980. Which of the following functions represents the US population N, in millions of people, y years since 1980?

    A) $N(y) = 236(1.008)^y$
    B) $N(y) = 236(1.08)^y$
    C) $N(y) = 236 + 1.008y$
    D) $N(y) = 236 + 1.08y$

13. Each year after a car is purchased, the price is estimated to be 15% less than the value the previous year. If the initial purchase price of a car was $29,500, which of the following is closest to the price of the car 3 years after it was purchased?

    A) $13,000
    B) $16,000
    C) $16,225
    D) $18,100

14. The given function f models the number of emails a company sent to their customers at the end of each year, where t represents the number of years since the end of 1998, and $0 \leq t \leq 5$. If $y = f(t)$ is graphed in the ty-plane, which of the following is the best interpretation of the y-intercept of the graph in this context?

$$f(t) = 14{,}000(1.45)^t$$

A) The maximum estimated number of emails the company sent to their customers during the 5 years was 29,435.
B) The maximum estimated number of emails the company sent to their customers during the 5 years was 14,000.
C) The estimated number of emails the company sent to their customers at the end of 1998 was 14,000.
D) The estimated number of emails the company sent to their customers at the end of 1998 was 20,300.

15. For the function k, the value of $k(x)$ increases by 55% for every increase in the value of x by 1. If $k(0) = 32$, which equation defines k?

A) $k(x) = 1.55(32)^x$
B) $k(x) = 0.55(32)^x$
C) $k(x) = 32(1.55)^x$
D) $k(x) = 32(0.55)^x$

16. The number of electronic bikes sold by a particular retailer in a city can be modeled with the function $f(t) = 760(1.65)^t$, where t is the number of years since 2019. Which of the following is true?

A) The number of electronic bikes sold by this particular retailer is increasing by 760 per year.
B) The number of bikes sold by this particular retailer in 2020 is 494 more than the number sold in 2019.
C) The number of electronic bikes sold by this particular retailer is increasing by 165% per year.
D) The number of bikes sold by this particular retailer is decreasing by 65% each year.

17. From the 2nd month to the 6th month of its life, a golden retriever experiences exponential growth. The table below shows the weight of a golden retriever every 2 months.

Age (months)	Weight (pounds)
2	8
4	18
6	40.5

Which of the following equations most closely models the weight of the golden retriever, $W(m)$, m months after 2 months from the ages of 2 months to 6 months?

A) $W(m) = 8(2.25)^{\frac{m}{2}}$
B) $W(m) = 8(2.25)^{2m}$
C) $W(m) = 8(1.25)^{\frac{m}{2}}$
D) $W(m) = 8(1.25)^{2m}$

18. The function $f(x) = 450(1.055)^x$ models the value, in dollars, of a certain investment account at the end of each year from 1984 to 2013, where x is the numbers of years after 1984. Which of the following is the best interpretation of $f(4) = 557.47$ in this context?

A) The value of the investment account is $107.47 greater in 1988 than in 1984.
B) The value, in dollars, of the investment account is estimated $557.47 in 1984.
C) The value of the investment account increases by approximately $107.47 every 4 years between 1984 and 2013.
D) The value of the investment account increases by $557.47 from 1984 to 1988.

19. Starting in 1950, the number of people living in Alaska doubled every 20 years. The population of Alaska was 150,000 in 1950. Which of the following expressions gives the population of Alaska in 2010?

A) $150{,}000(2)^3$
B) $150{,}000(2)^{20}$
C) $150{,}000(2)^{60}$
D) $150{,}000(2)(60)$

Chapter 19: Exponential Growth and Decay

20. As a beam of ultraviolet photons passes through a special cloth, the special cloth absorbs some of the photons. The function F, defined by the equation below, models the relationship between the predicted number of photons, $F(n)$, remaining in a beam and the number of special clothes, n, the beam has passed through. Based on this model, the percentage of photons remaining after passing through 2 special cloths is $p\%$. What is the value of p?

$$F(n) = 10,000(1 - 0.1)^n$$

21. Two variables x and y, are related such that for each increase of 1 in the value of x, the value of y increases by a factor of 3. When $x = 0$, $y = 450$. Which equation represents this relationship?

   A) $y = 3(x)^{450}$
   B) $y = 3(450)^x$
   C) $y = 450(3)^x$
   D) $y = 450(x)^3$

22. San Diego estimates that the city's population will increase 8% every 16 years. If the current population is 3 million people, which of the following represents the city's estimate of the number of people, P, in millions that will live in San Diego y years from now?

   A) $P = 3(1.08)^y$
   B) $P = 3 + 1.08y$
   C) $P = (3y)^{1.08}$
   D) $P = 3(1.08)^{\frac{y}{16}}$

23. What is the y-intercept of $y = a(7.2)^x - b$ in the xy-plane, where a and b are positive constants?

   A) $(0, a)$
   B) $(0, -b)$
   C) $(0, a - b)$
   D) $(0, b - a)$

24. The equation below models the number of students, N, who have joined the choir y years after the choir was started. Which of the following equations models the number of students who have joined the choir m months after it started?

$$N = 25(1.15)^y$$

   A) $N = 25(1.15) + 12m$
   B) $N = 25(1.15)^{12m}$
   C) $N = 25(1.15 + \frac{m}{12})$
   D) $N = 25(1.15)^{\frac{m}{12}}$

25. A hedge fund is offering a guaranteed investment return of 7% every three months. If you were to invest $50,000 today, which of the following equations gives the value of the investment, $V(t)$, y years from today?

   A) $V(y) = 50,000(1.07)^y$
   B) $V(y) = 50,000(1.07)^{4y}$
   C) $V(y) = 50,000(1.07 + \frac{y}{4})$
   D) $V(y) = 50,000(1.07)^{3y}$

26. The graph of an exponential function is shown below in the xy-plane. Which of the following is an equation of the graph shown, where a is a positive constant?

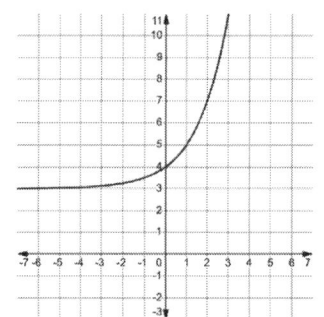

   A) $f(x) = 2^{x+a}$
   B) $f(x) = 2^x + a$
   C) $f(x) = 2^{x-a}$
   D) $f(x) = 2^x - a$

27. If $f(x) = 3(1.75)^x - 2$ and $g(x) = f(x) - 3$, what is the y-intercept of $g(x)$?

- 173 -

28. A researcher conducted a memory experiment on students in an AP Psychology class by giving students a list of 4 number sequences. Immediately after the experiment, the participants remembered 100% of the sequences. The researcher found that the percentage of the sequences that the students remembered decreased by 27% for every 4 second interval that passed. Which function best models this situation where P is the percentage of sequences that students remembered and t is the time, in seconds, that have passed?

A) $P(s) = 100(0.73)^{\frac{t}{4}}$
B) $P(s) = 100(0.73)^{4t}$
C) $P(s) = 100(0.27)^{4}$
D) $P(s) = 100(0.27)^{4t}$

29. The function f below gives the value, in dollars, of a certain piece of equipment after x weeks of use. If the value of the equipment decreases each year by $p\%$ of its value the preceding year, what is the value of p?

$$f(x) = 23{,}000(0.74)^{\frac{x}{52}}$$

A) 13
B) 26
C) 52
D) 74

30. A model estimates that at the end of each year from 2017 to 2023, the number of mice in a population was 125% more than the number of mice at the end of the previous year. The model estimates that there were 450 mice in the population at the end of 2017. Which of the following equations represents this model, where m is the estimated number of mice in the population t years after the end of 2017 and $t \leq 6$?

A) $m = 450(1.25)^t$
B) $m = 450(2.25)^t$
C) $m = 200(1.25)^t$
D) $m = 200(2.25)^t$

31. The number of phosphorescent algae at Moonlight Beach on April 1, 2020, is P_0. For every 5-day period after April 1st, 2020, the number of phosphorescent algae will decrease by 7%. Which of the following equations represents the number of phosphorescent algae at Moonlight Beach, P_t, after t days?

A) $P_t = P_0(0.07)^{5t}$
B) $P_t = P_0(0.07)^{\frac{t}{5}}$
C) $P_t = P_0(0.93)^{\frac{1}{5}t}$
D) $P_t = P_0(0.93)^{5t}$

32. If $h < -1$ and $0 < k < 1$, which of the following could be the graph of $y = -k^x - h$?

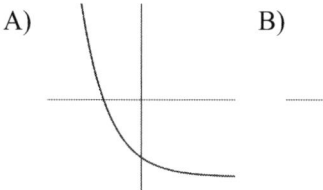

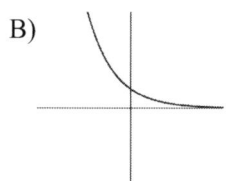

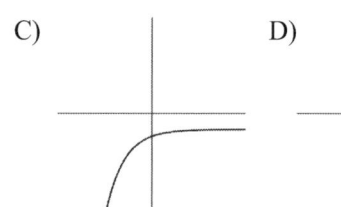

A)
B)
C)
D)

33. A model of how a popular social media message is spread estimates that every 15 minutes the number of people who have seen the message increases by 200%. Which equation represents this model when 300 people initially see the message, where y is the approximate number of people who have seen the message x hours after the message is initially heard?

A) $y = 300(2)^{4x}$
B) $y = 300(2)^{\frac{x}{4}}$
C) $y = 300(3)^{\frac{x}{4}}$
D) $y = 300(3)^{4x}$

34. The function $f(x) = 28{,}000(3)^{\frac{x}{360}}$ gives the number of bacteria in a population x minutes after an initial observation. How much time, in hours, does it take for the number of bacteria in the population to triple?

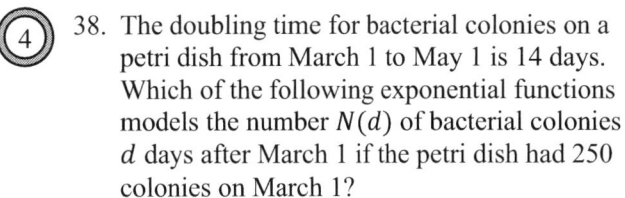

35. A newsletter currently has 2,000 subscribers. If the number of subscribers triples every 15 months, which of the following functions N gives the number of subscribers the newsletter will have y years from now?

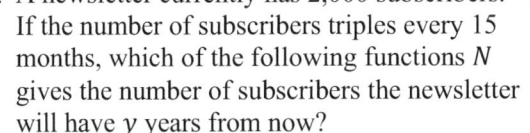

   A) $N(y) = 2{,}000(3)^{\frac{5y}{4}}$
   B) $N(y) = 2{,}000(3)^{\frac{4y}{5}}$
   C) $N(y) = 2{,}000(3)^{\frac{3y}{4}}$
   D) $N(y) = 2{,}000(3)^{\frac{4y}{3}}$

36. Blue light wave intensity below the surface of the ocean, $f(x)$, expressed as a percentage of the intensity at the surface, can be modeled with an exponential function, where x is the depth, in meters, below the surface. For every 9 meters the depth increases, the light intensity decreases by 45%. Which function best models this situation?

   A) $f(x) = 100(0.55)^{\frac{x}{9}}$
   B) $f(x) = 100(0.55)^{\frac{9}{x}}$
   C) $f(x) = 100(0.45)^{\frac{x}{9}}$
   D) $f(x) = 100(0.45)^{\frac{9}{x}}$

37. A group of students participated in a study about the speed of completing a manual task. It was determined that for each prior hour of experience doing the task, the time necessary to complete the task decreased by 10%. Jamil spent approximately 28 minutes to complete the task with 11 hours of prior experience. Which function models the amount of time T, in minutes, it will take Jamil to complete the task after x hours of experience?

   A) $T = 29(0.1)^x$
   B) $T = 29(0.9)^x$
   C) $T = 90(0.1)^x$
   D) $T = 90(0.9)^x$

38. The doubling time for bacterial colonies on a petri dish from March 1 to May 1 is 14 days. Which of the following exponential functions models the number $N(d)$ of bacterial colonies d days after March 1 if the petri dish had 250 colonies on March 1?

   A) $N(d) = 14(2)^{\frac{d}{250}}$
   B) $N(d) = 14(2)^{250d}$
   C) $N(d) = 250(2)^{\frac{d}{14}}$
   D) $N(d) = 250(2)^{14d}$

39. A virus has been shown to increase its viral load by 180% every 24 hours. If a sick individual has a viral load of x when they first get infected and the equation $N = x(b)^d$ models viral load, N, present after d days, what value should be used for b?

40. A scientist initially estimates that there are 90,000 termites in a colony. 12 days later, the scientist estimates 180,000 termites are in the same colony. Assuming exponential growth, the formula $T = A(2)^{rd}$ give the number of termites in the colony, where A and r are constants and T is the number of termites in the colony d days after the initial measurement. What is the value of r?

   A) $\frac{1}{90{,}000}$
   B) $\frac{1}{12}$
   C) 12
   D) 90,000

41. The equation below models the number of bacteria, in thousands, on a petri dish h hours after the dish has been inoculated. According to the model, the number of bacteria is predicted to increase by 2% every n minutes. What is the value of n?

   $$F(h) = 62(1.02)^{\frac{h}{5}}$$

   A) 12
   B) 60
   C) 120
   D) 300

42. The given function f models the balance of an investment account, in dollars, t years after it is opened. Which statement is the best interpretation of $(1.04)^{3t}$?

$$f(t) = 6{,}000(1.04)^{3t}$$

A) Every 4 months, the balance increases by $240.
B) Every 4 months, the balance increases by 4% of the previous 4 months balance.
C) Every 3 years, the balance increases by $240.
D) Every 3 years, the balance increases by 4% of the previous 3 years balance.

43. The graph of $m(x)$ is shown above. Given that $1 < a < 2$ and $a + b < 0$, which of the following could be the equation of $m(x)$?

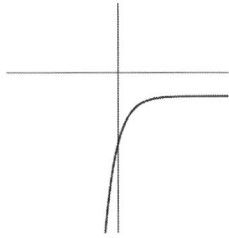

A) $m(x) = a(0.98)^x + b$
B) $m(x) = a(2.21)^x - b$
C) $m(x) = -a(0.81)^x + b$
D) $m(x) = -a(0.49)^x - b$

44. The population, in thousands, of Taos, New Mexico, can be modeled by the function $p(t) = 5{,}789(1.042)^t$, where t represents the number of years after 2022, and $0 \le t \le 20$. Which of the following equations best models the population, in thousands, of Taos, New Mexico, where y represents the number of years after 2029, and $0 \le y \le 20$?

A) $p(n) = 5{,}789(1.042)^{7y}$
B) $p(n) = 5{,}789(1.042)^{y-7}$
C) $p(n) = 5{,}789(1.042)^7(1.042)^y$
D) $p(n) = (5{,}789)^7(1.042)^7(1.042)^y$

45. NASA has just finished building a new ion thruster that will power a spaceship on a mission to Pluto. By using continuous small thrusts, the engine is able to accelerate at an exponential rate of 0.096% per day. When the ion thruster is turned on, the spaceship is moving at 35,000 meters per second. The spaceship will double its speed every 73 days. Which of the following exponential functions models the speed $S(y)$ of the spaceship, in meters per second, y years after the ion thruster is turned on? (1 year = 365 days)

A) $S(y) = 35{,}000(1.0096)^y$
B) $S(y) = 35{,}000(1.0096)^{2y}$
C) $S(y) = 35{,}000(2)^{\frac{1}{5}y}$
D) $S(y) = 35{,}000(2)^{5y}$

46. The function $f(x)$ and $g(x)$ are given below. Given that $a, b, c,$ and d are positive constants, which of the following statement must be true so that $f(x)$ and $g(x)$ never intersect?

$$f(x) = ab^{x-5} + c$$
$$g(x) = -ab^{x+2} + d$$

A) $b > 1$ and $c \ge d$.
B) $c \ge d$ only.
C) $b > 1$ and $c < d$.
D) $0 < b < 1$ and $c \ne d$.

47. Function f is defined by $f(x) = -a^x + b$, where a and b are constants. In the xy-plane, the graph of $y = f(x) + 20$ has a y-intercept at $\left(0, -\frac{86}{6}\right)$. The product of a and b is $\frac{100}{6}$. What is the value of a?

Chapter 20: Trigonometry

Basic Trigonometry

For the easier trigonometry questions on the SAT, just remember **SOH-CAH-TOA**! If you have not heard of **SOH-CAH-TOA**, it is an acronym to memorize the sine, cosine, and tangent functions. **SOH** stands for **S**ine equals **O**pposite over **H**ypotenuse, **CAH** stands for **C**osine equals **A**djacent over **H**ypotenuse, and **TOA** stands for **T**angent equals **O**pposite over **A**djacent.

$$\sin(x) = \frac{\text{opposite}}{\text{hypotenuse}} = \frac{9}{15}$$

$$\cos(x) = \frac{\text{adjacent}}{\text{hypotenuse}} = \frac{12}{15}$$

$$\tan(x) = \frac{\text{opposite}}{\text{adjacent}} = \frac{9}{12}$$

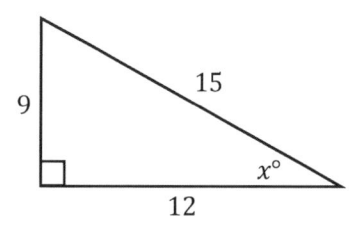

For easy trigonometry questions, you need to set up the basic trigonometry functions correctly.

Example 1: What is the value of $\cos B$ in the triangle below?

A) $\frac{11}{5}$ B) $\frac{5}{11}$ C) $\frac{4\sqrt{6}}{11}$ D) $\frac{11}{4\sqrt{6}}$

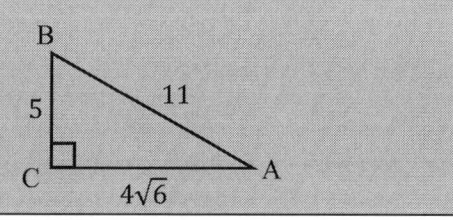

Solution: To find $\cos B$, we need to find the side length adjacent to angle B and the hypotenuse. The side length adjacent to angle B is 5 and the hypotenuse is 11, so we set up the cosine equation as

$$\cos B = \frac{5}{11}$$

The answer is B.

For other similar questions, we may need to use the Pythagorean theorem to find the third side of a triangle and then find the sine, cosine, or tangent.

Example 2: What is the value of $\tan A$ in the triangle below?

A) $\frac{4}{3}$ B) $\frac{4}{\sqrt{33}}$ C) $\frac{\sqrt{33}}{4}$ D) $\frac{3}{4}$

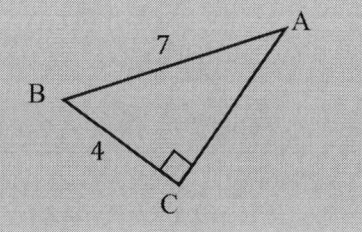

Solution: To find $\tan A$, we need to know the side lengths opposite angle A and adjacent to angle A. The side length opposite angle A is 4. The side length adjacent to angle A, side AC, is currently unknown. To solve for AC, we use the Pythagorean theorem.

$$4^2 + AC^2 = 7^2$$
$$16 + AC^2 = 49$$
$$AC^2 = 33$$
$$AC = \sqrt{33}$$

Now, we can label all sides of triangle ABC and find $\tan A$. The opposite side length is 4, and the adjacent side length is $\sqrt{33}$ so

- 177 -

PrepPros

$$\tan A = \frac{\text{opposite}}{\text{adjacent}} = \frac{4}{\sqrt{33}}$$

The answer is B.

Both examples we have done so far gave us a triangle. **What if we see a basic trigonometry question and a no triangle given? We can draw our own right triangle!** Remember that SOH-CAH-TOA only applies to right triangles.

Questions like these first two examples should be pretty easy to solve. If you found either of those questions difficult, make sure you take some time to review the basics SOH-CAH-TOA.

Example 3: For an angle with a measure of q in a right triangle, $\sin q = \frac{9}{15}$ and $\tan q = \frac{9}{12}$, what is the value of $\cos q$?

A) $\frac{15}{12}$ B) $\frac{12}{15}$ C) $\frac{12}{9}$ D) $\frac{15}{9}$

Solution: We can draw a right triangle, label one of the acute angles as q, and then use the trigonometry functions to label the sides. **If you are ever given a trigonometry question without a drawing, always start by sketching and labelling a triangle.**

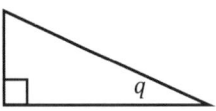

Since $\sin q = \frac{9}{15}$, we can first label the opposite side as 9 and the hypotenuse as 15. Since $\tan q = \frac{9}{12}$ and the opposite side is already labelled as 9, we now also label the adjacent sides as 12. As a result, the triangle now looks like this:

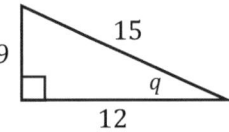

Now, we can see that $\cos q = \frac{12}{15}$. **The answer is B.**

1-4 Using Trigonometry to Find Side Lengths in Right Triangles

The second very common type of easier trigonometry question asks us to use trigonometry to solve for an unknown side of a right triangle. To solve these questions correctly, we need to use SOH-CAH-TOA and then solve for the unknown side.

Example 4: In the triangle below, which of the following expressions is equal to x?

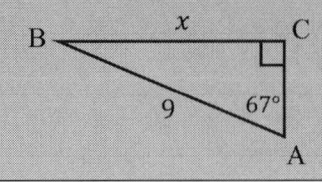

A) $9 \sin 67°$
B) $9 \cos 67°$
C) $\frac{9}{9 \sin 67°}$
D) $\frac{9}{9 \cos 67°}$

Solution: The first step is to identify which trigonometric function involves the values we are given and x. We know angle A, the hypotenuse, and are solving for the opposite, so we use the sine function. We can set up the sine function and plug in the values we are given.

$$\sin A = \frac{\text{opposite}}{\text{hypotenuse}} \quad \rightarrow \quad \sin 67° = \frac{x}{9}$$

Next, we solve for x by multiplying both sides by 9 and get

$$x = 9 \sin 67°$$

The answer is A. If the question was a grid-in questions without answer choices, we can plug 9 sin 67° into the calculator to find the actual length, which here is 8.285.

Another version of a question testing this concept gives us no angle but tells us the value of the sine, cosine, or tangent function. With no angle, using trigonometry seems confusing at first, but, if we know how to set up trigonometric functions, we solve with the same SOH-CAH-TOA knowledge we used in Example 4.

> **Example 5:** In triangle ABC, $\cos B = \frac{2}{3}$, the length of AB is 6, and $\angle BAC = 90°$. What is the length of AC?
> A) 2   B) 4   C) $3\sqrt{5}$ D) 9

Solution: To start, sketch triangle ABC and label the sides and angles we know.

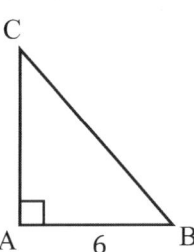

We are not given any angles B or C, but we are told what the $\cos B = \frac{2}{3}$. We also know that $\cos B = \frac{6}{BC}$, so we can set these equal and solve for BC:

$$\frac{6}{BC} = \frac{2}{3}$$

$$2BC = 18$$

$$BC = 9$$

Now that we know $BC = 9$, we can use the Pythagorean theorem to solve for AC.

$$AC^2 + 6^2 = 9^2$$

$$AC^2 = 45$$

$$AC = \sqrt{45} = 3\sqrt{5}$$

The answer is C.

Example 5 introduces one important concept about trigonometric functions that you need to understand: **trigonometric functions only tell us the ratio of the side lengths and not the actual side lengths.** For example, triangle ABC with $\cos B = \frac{2}{3}$ could look like any of these:

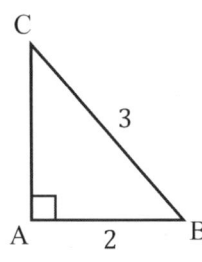

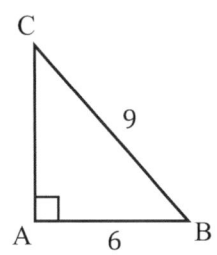

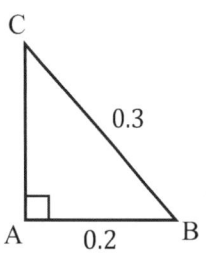

For a triangle where $\cos B = \frac{2}{3}$, we only know that the ratio of the adjacent to hypotenuse is 2 to 3; we do not know the actual side length. Many students make the mistake of labeling the side lengths of triangles from trigonometric functions and assume triangle ABC looks like the one on the left. We do not know what the triangle actually looks like until we are given the length of one of the sides.

Basic Trigonometry in Similar Triangles

2-4

The SAT also loves to ask basic trigonometry questions involving similar triangles. Remember, **all the angles in similar triangles are identical, so all the sine, cosine, and tangent values in similar triangles are identical for corresponding angles.** That wording may seem confusing, so let's use the triangles below to show you how this works.

Below, triangle ABC is similar to triangle DEF, where A corresponds to D and C corresponds to F. The "A corresponds with D" statement tells us that angles A and D are identical and are at the same location in the triangles (top left in the triangles below). Similarly, angles C and F are identical.

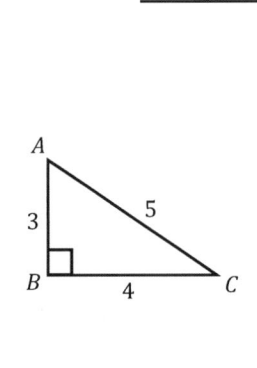

For Triangle ABC

$$\cos A = \frac{3}{5}$$
$$\sin A = \frac{4}{5}$$
$$\tan A = \frac{4}{3}$$

$$\cos C = \frac{4}{5}$$
$$\sin C = \frac{3}{5}$$
$$\tan C = \frac{3}{4}$$

For Triangle DEF

$$\cos D = \frac{6}{10} = \frac{3}{5}$$
$$\sin D = \frac{8}{10} = \frac{4}{5}$$
$$\tan D = \frac{8}{6} = \frac{4}{3}$$

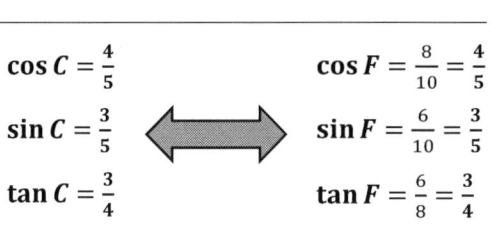

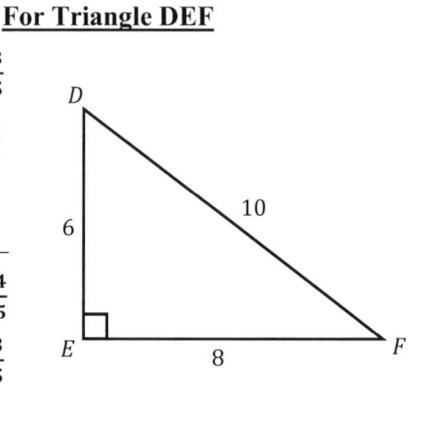

$$\cos F = \frac{8}{10} = \frac{4}{5}$$
$$\sin F = \frac{6}{10} = \frac{3}{5}$$
$$\tan F = \frac{6}{8} = \frac{3}{4}$$

Since the angles are the same, **all of the trigonometric functions (sine, cosine, and tangent) are identical for corresponding angles.** Notice how all the values of sine, cosine, and tangent are identical for corresponding angles A and D and for corresponding angles C and F.

Example 6: Triangle ABC is similar to triangle DEF, where A corresponds to D and angles B and E are right angles. If $\tan(A) = \frac{31}{9}$, what is the value of $\tan(D)$?

Solution: Since angles A and D are corresponding angles in similar triangles, the trigonometric functions are identical. Therefore, we know that
$$\tan(A) = \tan(D)$$
We are told that $\tan(A) = \frac{31}{9}$, so $\tan(D) = \frac{31}{9}$. **The answer is $\frac{31}{9}$.**

Example 7: The side lengths of right triangle XYZ are given below. Triangle XYZ is similar to triangle LMN, where X corresponds to L and Z corresponds to N. What is the value of $\sin N$?

$$XY = 30$$
$$YZ = 72$$
$$XZ = 78$$

A) $\frac{5}{13}$ B) $\frac{12}{13}$ C) $\frac{5}{12}$ D) $\frac{13}{12}$

Solution: Since Z and N are corresponding angle in similar triangle, we know that the trigonometric functions are identical. So,
$$\sin N = \sin Z$$

We are given the side lengths in triangle XYZ, so we can sketch the triangle and find the sin Z.

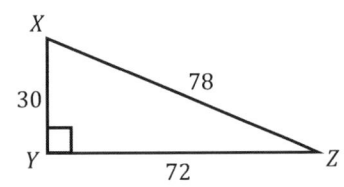

In a right triangle, we know that the longest side, which in this triangle is XZ, is the hypotenuse. So, we know that the right angle is at Y. Once we correctly sketch the triangle, we can find that

$$\sin Z = \frac{30}{78}$$

And since we know that $\sin N = \sin Z$, we can find sin N:

$$\sin N = \frac{30}{78} = \frac{5}{13}$$

The answer is A.

2 Important Trigonometry Identities To Know

Beyond the basic trigonometric functions, you should also memorize these two important identities:

$$\sin x = \cos(90° - x)$$
$$\cos x = \sin(90° - x)$$

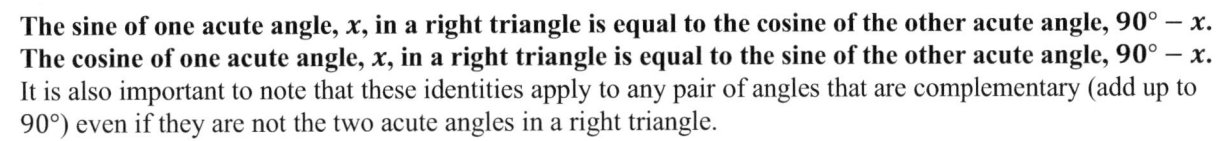

The sine of one acute angle, x, in a right triangle is equal to the cosine of the other acute angle, $90° - x$. The cosine of one acute angle, x, in a right triangle is equal to the sine of the other acute angle, $90° - x$. It is also important to note that these identities apply to any pair of angles that are complementary (add up to 90°) even if they are not the two acute angles in a right triangle.

To help you better understand this identity, let's consider triangle below.

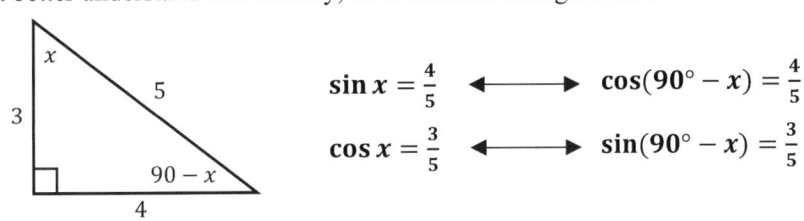

$$\sin x = \frac{4}{5} \longleftrightarrow \cos(90° - x) = \frac{4}{5}$$
$$\cos x = \frac{3}{5} \longleftrightarrow \sin(90° - x) = \frac{3}{5}$$

Let's consider the first identity: $\sin x = \cos(90° - x)$. For $\sin x$, the opposite side length is 4 and the hypotenuse is 5. For $\cos(90° - x)$, the adjacent side length is 4 and the hypotenuse is 5. So, both $\sin x$ and $\cos(90° - x)$ are equal to $\frac{4}{5}$.

We can repeat this thinking for the second identity: $\cos x = \sin(90° - x)$. For $\cos x$, the adjacent side length is 3 and the hypotenuse is 5. For $\sin(90° - x)$, the opposite side length is 3 and the hypotenuse is 5. So, both $\cos x$ and $\sin(90° - x)$ are $\frac{3}{5}$.

Example 8: In right triangle XYZ, the right angle is at Z. If $\cos X = \frac{7}{9}$, what is the value of $\sin Y$?

A) $\frac{2}{9}$ B) $\frac{7}{9}$ C) $\frac{4\sqrt{2}}{9}$ D) $\frac{9}{7}$

Solution: Method #1 – Draw a Triangle: First, sketch and label triangle XYZ. Since we are told that $\cos X = \frac{7}{9}$, we can label the side length adjacent to angle X as 7 and the hypotenuse as 9.

PrepPros

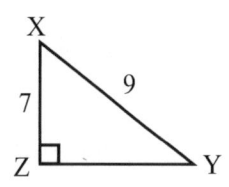

We are asked to solve for the sin Y, which is $\frac{\text{opposite}}{\text{hypotenuse}}$. We already know the opposite side length from angle Y is 7 and the hypotenuse is 9, so we get

$$\sin Y = \frac{7}{9}$$

The answer is B.

Method #2 – Shortcut Solution: In triangle XYZ, angles X and Y are the two acute angles. By definition, the two acute angles in a right triangle add up to 90°, so we know that $\angle X + \angle Y = 90°$. We can rewrite this equation as $\angle Y = 90° - \angle X$. From the identity above, we know that

$$\cos X = \sin(90° - X)$$

In our triangle, angle $Y = 90° - X$, so

$$\cos X = \sin Y$$

The question tells us that $\cos X = \frac{7}{9}$, so $\sin Y = \frac{7}{9}$. **The answer is B.**

Example 9: In a right triangle DEF, the right angle is at point E. A point G lies on $\overline{DF}$ and a line connecting points E and G is drawn. What is the value of $\sin \angle FEG - \cos \angle DEG$?

Solution: To start, let's draw triangle DEF, point G, and the line connecting points E and G.

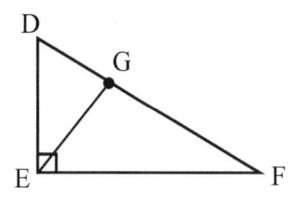

We do not know where point G is exactly, so we can select a point. As you will see shortly, the exact location of point G is not important for solving this question. What's important to notice is that $\angle FEG$ and $\angle DEG$ must add to 90°. No matter where we draw point G on $\overline{DF}$, $\angle FEG$ and $\angle DEG$ together are the same as $\angle E$, which we know is a right angle equal to 90°.

We know that $\angle FEG + \angle DEG = 90°$. We can rewrite this equation as

$$\angle DEG = 90° - \angle FEG$$

To find $\sin \angle FEG - \cos \angle DEG$, we are going to use the identity $\sin x = \cos(90° - x)$. First, let's plug in $\angle FEG$ for x.

$$\sin \angle FEG = \cos(90° - \angle FEG)$$

We know that $\angle DEG = 90° - \angle FEG$, so we can plug in $\angle DEG$ or $90° - \angle FEG$ to get

$$\sin \angle FEG = \cos \angle DEG$$

Since $\sin \angle FEG = \cos \angle DEG$, $\sin \angle FEG - \cos \angle DEG = 0$. **The answer is 0.**

Remember, the trigonometric identities $\sin x = \cos(90° - x)$ and $\cos x = \sin(90° - x)$ apply to any 2 angles that sum to 90°! The angles do not need to be two acute angles in the same right triangle. For more difficult questions like example 9, you have to recognize that you can apply this rule.

Inverse Trigonometric Functions

Inverse trigonometric functions are used to find an unknown angle in a right triangle when the side lengths are known. Inverse trigonometric functions are just like SOH-CAH-TOA except that the angle is switched with the side lengths.

$$\sin^{-1}\left(\frac{\text{opposite}}{\text{hypotenuse}}\right) = x° \quad \rightarrow \quad \sin^{-1}\left(\frac{9}{15}\right) = x°$$

$$\cos^{-1}\left(\frac{\text{adjacent}}{\text{hypotenuse}}\right) = x° \quad \rightarrow \quad \cos^{-1}\left(\frac{12}{15}\right) = x°$$

$$\tan^{-1}\left(\frac{\text{opposite}}{\text{adjacent}}\right) = x° \quad \rightarrow \quad \tan^{-1}\left(\frac{9}{12}\right) = x°$$

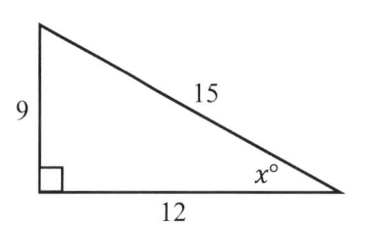

In the example triangle, we can use inverse trigonometry to solve for the unknown angle $x°$. Using a calculator and any of the inverse trigonometric functions, we can find that angle $x = 36.9°$. If you are ever given the side lengths of a right triangle and asked to find an unknown angle, you will need to use the inverse trigonometry functions to find the angle.

Example 10: Find the value of x in the triangle below.

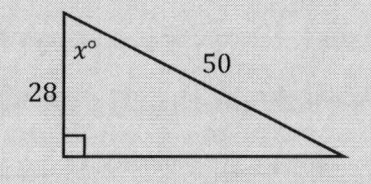

Solution: To find the missing angle, we need to use an inverse trigonometric function. We know the adjacent and opposite lengths in this triangle, so we can solve for x using the inverse cosine function.

$$\cos^{-1}\left(\frac{28}{50}\right) = x$$

$$x = 55.944$$

The answer is 55.94. Remember that for free response questions, you can enter up to 4 digits. If the answer is not exact, you need to round your answer.

Example 11: Anthony is building a ramp from a spot in his backyard to the entrance to his tree house. The tree house is 18 feet off the ground, and the spot that Anthony is going to put the base of the ramp is 45 feet from the base of the tree, which is directly below the entrance to the tree house. What angle of elevation should Anthony use for his ramp?

Solution: Start by sketching and labelling the triangle described in the question. The most difficult part of this word problem is getting the sketch correct.

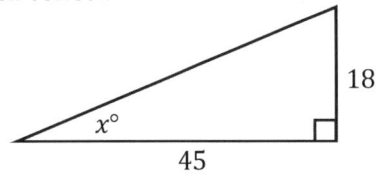

The angle of elevation is the angle of the ramp, labeled above as x. We know the opposite and adjacent lengths in the triangle, so we can solve for the angle of elevation using the inverse tangent function.

$$\tan^{-1}\left(\frac{18}{45}\right) = x$$

$$x = 21.801$$

The answer is 21.80. Again, we can only enter 4 digits, so we must round the answer.

2-4 Radians vs. Degrees

Radians are another unit to measure angles. Just like we can measure temperature in Fahrenheit or Celsius, we can measure an angle in degrees or radians. For the SAT, you need to know how to convert between radians and degrees. In the reference table, the SAT tells you

The number of degrees in a circle is 360.

The number of radians of arc in a circle is 2π.

That is a very complicated way of saying that

$$2\pi \text{ radians} = 360°$$

If we simplify this, we get

$$\pi \text{ radians} = 180°$$

Both of these are correct, so we can use either one of these when working on radians questions. For the rest of this section, we will use π radians = 180°.

To convert between radians and degrees, we need to memorize the following 2 rules:

1. To convert from radians to degrees, we multiply by $\frac{180°}{\pi \text{ radians}}$.
2. To convert from degrees to radians, we multiply by $\frac{\pi \text{ radians}}{180°}$.

Let's learn how to apply these rules in examples 12 and 13.

Example 12: Angle D has a measure of 200°. If angle D can be written in its most simplified form as $\frac{a}{b}\pi$ radians, where a and b are both integers, what is the value of $a + b$?

Solution: We need to convert angle D from degrees to radians, so we multiply by $\frac{\pi \text{ radians}}{180°}$. As in any unit conversion question, start with the given, which is 200°, and then use the conversion factor to change the units.

$$200° \times \frac{\pi \text{ radians}}{180°} = \frac{10}{9}\pi \text{ radians}$$

When we multiply by $\frac{\pi \text{ radians}}{180°}$, the degree signs cancel, so we are left with radians. The question says angle D can be written as $\frac{a}{b}\pi$ radians, so we can see that $a = 10$ and $b = 9$. $a + b = 19$. **The answer is 19.**

Example 13: Angle M has a measure of $\frac{33}{5}$ radians. What is the measure of angle M in degrees?

Solution: We need to convert angle M from radians to degrees, so we multiply by $\frac{180°}{\pi \text{ radians}}$.

$$\frac{33}{5} \text{ radians} \times \frac{180°}{\pi \text{ radians}} = \frac{5,940}{5\pi} = 378.15°$$

We must round to 4 digits, so **the answer is 378.2.** Make sure that you notice the measure of angle M is $\frac{33}{5}$ radians and not $\frac{33}{5}\pi$ radians. Many students make that mistake on a question like this!

Unit Circle

Remember the unit circle? The one your math teacher made you memorize all of those points for? Well, it's back. The unit circle is occasionally tested on the SAT, so **we recommend that all students memorize the unit circle**.

A complete unit circle is shown below.

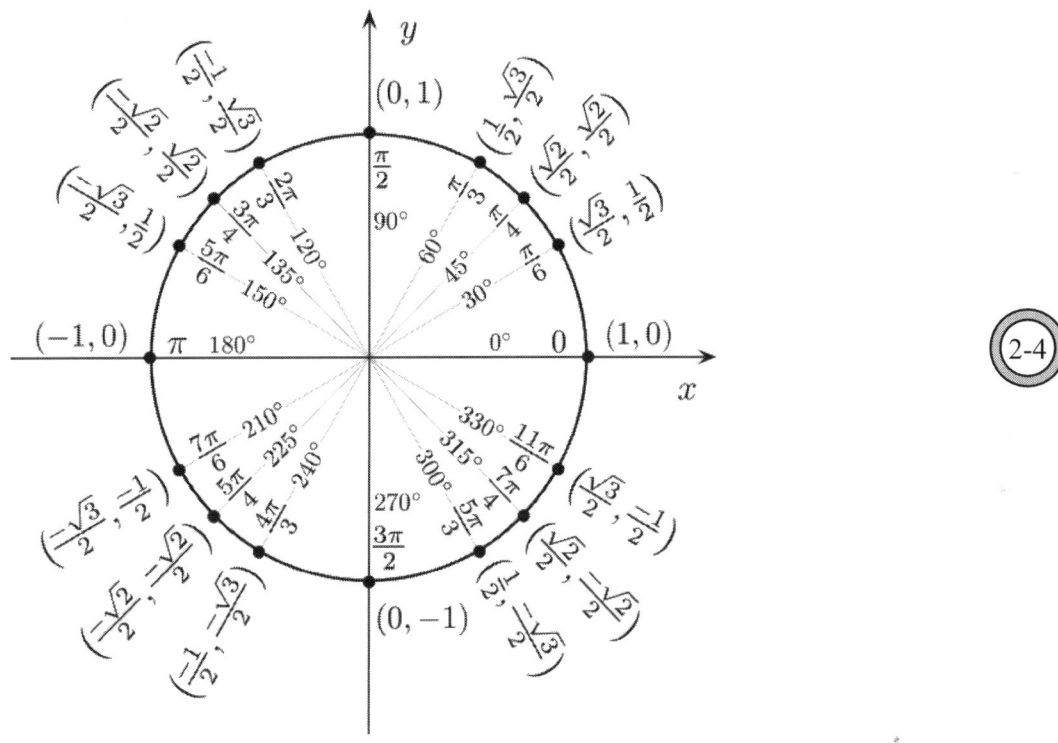

Angles on the unit circle can be expressed in degrees or radians. There are 3 few important principles to know with the unit circle.

1. **The cosine of any angle on the unit circle is equal to the *x*-coordinate of the corresponding point.** For example, $\cos(60°) = \frac{1}{2}$.

2. **The sine of any angle on the unit circle is equal to the *y*-coordinate of the corresponding point.** For example, $\sin(60°) = \frac{\sqrt{3}}{2}$.

3. **The tangent of any angle on the unit circle is equal to $\frac{y-\text{coordinate}}{x-\text{coordinate}}$.** For example, $\tan(60°) = \frac{\frac{\sqrt{3}}{2}}{\frac{1}{2}}$, which simplifies to $\tan(60°) = \sqrt{3}$.

Understanding these three principles and memorizing the unit circle can make many unit circle questions easy.

Example 14: What is the value of $\cos(240°)$?

A) $-\frac{\sqrt{3}}{2}$ B) $-\frac{1}{2}$ C) $\frac{1}{2}$ D) $\frac{\sqrt{3}}{2}$

Solution: To find $\cos(240°)$, we need to find the *x*-coordinate of the corresponding point on the unit circle. The point that corresponds with 240° is $\left(-\frac{1}{2}, -\frac{\sqrt{3}}{2}\right)$, so $\cos(240°) = -\frac{1}{2}$. **The answer is B.**

PrepPros

> **Example 15:** On the interval $0 \leq \theta < 2\pi$, $\sin \theta = \frac{\sqrt{2}}{2}$ is true for what value(s) of θ ?
>
> A) $\frac{\pi}{4}, \frac{5\pi}{4}$ B) $\frac{\pi}{4}, \frac{3\pi}{4}$ C) $\frac{\pi}{4}, \frac{7\pi}{4}$ D) $\frac{\pi}{4}$

Solution: For this question, we need to find the values of θ, in radians, on the unit circle for which $\sin \theta = \frac{\sqrt{2}}{2}$. The interval from $0 \leq \theta < 2\pi$ includes the entire unit circle, but sometimes the SAT limits which portion of the unit circle we should look at with a smaller interval.

Remember, the sine of any angle is equal to the y-coordinate of the point. So, we need to look at the unit circle and find the point(s) that have $\frac{\sqrt{2}}{2}$ as the y-coordinate. If we look at the unit circle (or have it memorized), we see that $\frac{\pi}{4}$ and $\frac{3\pi}{4}$ have $\frac{\sqrt{2}}{2}$ as the y-coordinate, so we know

$$\sin \frac{\pi}{4} = \frac{\sqrt{2}}{2} \quad \text{and} \quad \sin \frac{3\pi}{4} = \frac{\sqrt{2}}{2}$$

The answer is B.

Coterminal Angles and The Unit Circle

Coterminal angles are angles that share the share the same initial side (starting position) and terminal side (ending position). If you have not learned this concept before in math class, let's start with a simple example.

Coterminal Angles - Example 1: 30° and 390° are coterminal angles.

Notice how in the diagram to the right that 30° and 390° have the same terminal side. In simpler terms, they end at the same place on the unit circle.

When drawing angles on the unit circle, we always start from 0°, which is labelled as the "Initial Side" in the diagram to the right, and then move in the counterclockwise direction.

Angles that are greater than 360° complete full rotation(s) around the unit circle and then continue. For 390°, we draw a full rotation, which is equal to 360°, and then continue 30° more to get to the terminal side.

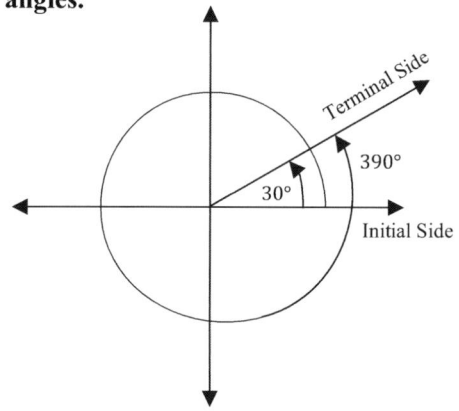

For any angle that is greater than 360°, we can find the terminal side by subtracting 360° repeatedly until the resulting angle is between 0° and 360°. Let's apply this rule to the 390° from Example 1.

$$390° - 360° = 30°$$

So, we find that the terminal side of 390° is at 30°. We can use this trick for much larger angles as well. Let's consider the angle 1,110°. To find the terminal side, we start by subtracting 360°.

$$1,110° - 360° = 750°$$

750° is still greater than 360°, so we subtract 360° again.

$$750° - 360° = 390°$$

390° is still greater than 360°, so we have to subtract 360° one more time to find the terminal side.

$$390° - 360° = 30°$$

The terminal side of 1,110° is at 30°, so we now know that 1,110°, 390°, and 30° are all coterminal angles. To draw 1,110° on the diagram above, we would complete 3 full rotations and draw the final 30°.

In this first example, we have introduced our first 3 principles for coterminal angles:

Coterminal Angles Principle #1: The initial side is always at 0°, for angles measured degrees, or 0π, for angles measured in radians. In simple terms, we always start drawing angles from the right side.

Coterminal Angles Principle #2: Positive angles always are drawn in the counterclockwise direction. As we saw in Example 1, both angles started at the initial side and then are drawn in the counterclockwise direction.

Coterminal Angles Principle #3: For any angle that is greater than 360°, we can find the terminal side by subtracting 360° repeatedly until the resulting angle is between 0° and 360°.

Coterminal Angles - Example 2: 135° and −225° are coterminal angles.

Notice how in the diagram to the right that 135° and −225° have the same terminal side. Coterminal angles always end at the same place on the unit circle.

When drawing angles on the unit circle, we always start from 0°, which is labelled as the "Initial Side" in the diagram to the right. Since 135° is positive, we move in the counterclockwise direction.

When drawing angles with a negative degree measure, we move in the clockwise direction. As we see in the diagram, −225° moves the clockwise direction.

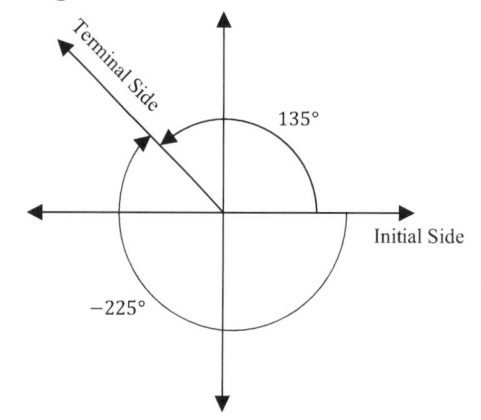

For any angle that has a negative measure (less than 0°), we can find the terminal side by adding 360° repeatedly until the resulting angle is between 0° and 360°. Let's apply this rule to the −225° from Example 2.

$$-225° + 360° = 135°$$

So, we find that the terminal side of −225° is at 135°. We can use this trick for smaller angles as well. Let's consider the angle −585°. To find the terminal side, we start by adding 360°.

$$-585° + 360° = -225°$$

−225° is still less than 0°, so we add 360° again.

$$-225° + 360° = 135°$$

The terminal side of −585° is at 135°, so we now know that −585°, −225°, and 135° are all coterminal angles. To draw −585° on the diagram above, we would complete 1 full rotation in the clockwise direction and draw the final −225°.

In this example, we have learned 2 more principles for coterminal angles:

Coterminal Angles Principle #4: Negative angles always are drawn in the clockwise direction. As we saw in Example 2, −225° started at the initial side and then is drawn in the clockwise direction.

Coterminal Angles Principle #5: For any negative angle (less than 0°), we can find the terminal side by adding 360° repeatedly until the resulting angle is between 0° and 360°.

Coterminal Angles Practice – Part 1: Find a coterminal angle between 0° and 360° for each given angle.

1. 495°
2. 540°
3. 675°
4. −120°
5. 1,350°
6. 405°
7. −45°
8. −330°
9. 3,390°
10. −930°
11. −540°
12. 1,170°
13. −1,215°
14. 5,490°
15. −3,105°
16. 4,860°

So far, we have only worked with angles with degree measurements. Now, let's go over some examples with radians. Coterminal Angles Principles 1, 2, and 4 all apply for radians. We will make some minor modifications to Coterminal Angles Principles 3 and 5 to convert from degrees to radians.

Coterminal Angles - Example 3: $\frac{2\pi}{3}$ and $\frac{8\pi}{3}$ are coterminal angles.

When drawn on the unit circle, $\frac{2\pi}{3}$ and $\frac{8\pi}{3}$ have the same terminal side and are coterminal angles.

When drawing angles on the unit circle, we always start from 0π radians, which is labelled as the "Initial Side" in the diagram to the right. We move in the counterclockwise direction since the angles in this example are positive.

Angles that are greater than 2π complete full rotation(s) around the unit circle and then continue. Since $\frac{8\pi}{3}$ is greater than 2π, we draw a full rotation, which is equal to 2π, and then continue $\frac{2\pi}{3}$ more to get to the terminal side.

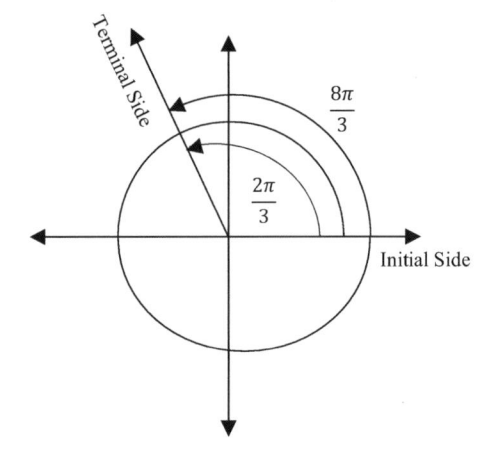

For any angle that is greater than 2π, we can find the terminal side by subtracting 2π repeatedly until the resulting angle is between 0π and 2π. Let's apply this rule to the $\frac{8\pi}{3}$ from Example 3.

$$\frac{8\pi}{3} - 2\pi = \frac{8\pi}{3} - \frac{6\pi}{3} = \frac{2\pi}{3}$$

So, we find that the terminal side of $\frac{8\pi}{3}$ is at $\frac{2\pi}{3}$. We can use this trick for much larger angles as well. Let's consider the angle $\frac{14\pi}{3}$. To find the terminal side, we start by subtracting 2π.

$$\frac{14\pi}{3} - 2\pi = \frac{14\pi}{3} - \frac{6\pi}{3} = \frac{8\pi}{3}$$

$\frac{8\pi}{3}$ is still greater than 2π, so we have to subtract 2π one more time to find the terminal side.

$$\frac{8\pi}{3} - 2\pi = \frac{8\pi}{3} - \frac{6\pi}{3} = \frac{2\pi}{3}$$

The terminal side of $\frac{14\pi}{3}$ is at $\frac{2\pi}{3}$. so we now know that $\frac{14\pi}{3}$, $\frac{8\pi}{3}$, and $\frac{2\pi}{3}$ are all coterminal angles. To draw $\frac{14\pi}{3}$ on the diagram above, we would complete 2 full rotations and draw the final $\frac{2\pi}{3}$.

Chapter 20: Trigonometry

We have learned one new coterminal angle principle.

Coterminal Angles Principle #6: For any angle that is greater than 2π, we can find the terminal side by subtracting 2π repeatedly until the resulting angle is between 0π and 2π.

Coterminal Angles - Example 4: $\frac{3\pi}{2}$ and $-\frac{\pi}{2}$ are coterminal angles.

When drawn on the unit circle, $\frac{3\pi}{2}$ and $-\frac{\pi}{2}$ have the same terminal side and are coterminal angles.

When drawing angles on the unit circle, we always start from 0π, which is labelled as the "Initial Side" in the diagram to the right. Since $\frac{3\pi}{2}$ is positive, we move in the counterclockwise direction.

When drawing angles with a negative radian measure, we move in the clockwise direction. As we see in the diagram, $-\frac{\pi}{2}$ moves the clockwise direction.

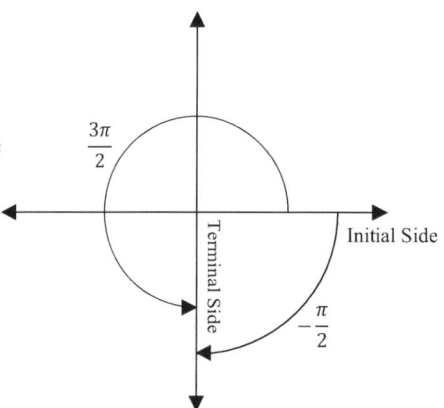

For any angle that has a negative measure (less than 0π), we can find the terminal side by adding 2π repeatedly until the resulting angle is between 0π and 2π. Let's apply this rule to the $-\frac{\pi}{2}$.

$$-\frac{\pi}{2} + 2\pi = -\frac{\pi}{2} + \frac{4\pi}{2} = \frac{3\pi}{2}$$

So, we find that the terminal side of $-\frac{\pi}{2}$ is at $\frac{3\pi}{2}$. We can use this trick for smaller angles as well. Let's consider the angle $-\frac{5\pi}{2}$. To find the terminal side, we start by adding 2π.

$$-\frac{5\pi}{2} + 2\pi = -\frac{5\pi}{2} + \frac{4\pi}{2} = -\frac{\pi}{2}$$

$-\frac{\pi}{2}$ is still less than 0π, so we add 2π again.

$$-\frac{\pi}{2} + 2\pi = -\frac{\pi}{2} + \frac{4\pi}{2} = \frac{3\pi}{2}$$

The terminal side of $-\frac{5\pi}{2}$ is at $\frac{3\pi}{2}$, so we now know that $-\frac{5\pi}{2}$, $-\frac{\pi}{2}$, and $\frac{3\pi}{2}$ are all coterminal angles. To draw $-\frac{5\pi}{2}$ on the diagram above, we would complete 1 full rotation in the clockwise direction and draw the final $-\frac{\pi}{2}$.

Coterminal Angles Practice – Part 2: Find a coterminal angle between 0π and 2π for each given angle.

1. $\frac{11\pi}{3}$
2. $\frac{9\pi}{2}$
3. $\frac{17\pi}{6}$
4. $-\frac{4\pi}{3}$
5. $\frac{-11\pi}{6}$
6. $\frac{25\pi}{4}$
7. $\frac{11\pi}{3}$
8. -9π
9. $-\frac{15\pi}{2}$
10. $\frac{20\pi}{3}$
11. $-\frac{33\pi}{4}$
12. $\frac{19\pi}{6}$
13. $\frac{-104\pi}{12}$
14. $\frac{4{,}360\pi}{30}$

Trigonometry Practice: Answers on pages 331-332.

1. The side lengths of a triangle are given in the figure below. What does sin C equal?

   A) 2
   B) $\frac{2}{3}$
   C) $\frac{1}{2}$
   D) $\frac{3}{4}$

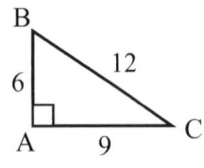

2. Two of the side lengths of a right triangle are given in the figure below. What is cos C?

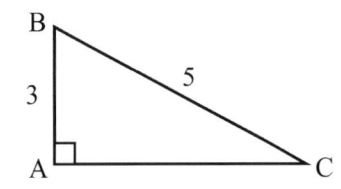

   Note: Figure not drawn to scale.

   A) $\frac{3}{5}$
   B) $\frac{5}{3}$
   C) $\frac{5}{4}$
   D) $\frac{4}{5}$

3. In triangle ABC, which expression represents the length of line segment BC?

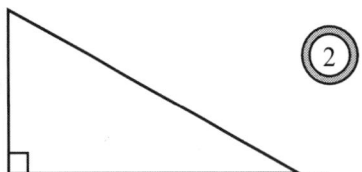

   A) 37 cos B
   B) 37 sin B
   C) $\frac{\cos B}{37}$
   D) $\frac{37}{\cos B}$

4. The side lengths of a triangle are given below. Which of the following expressions gives the measure of the angle θ?

   A) $\tan^{-1}\left(\frac{b}{a}\right)$
   B) $\sin^{-1}\left(\frac{b}{c}\right)$
   C) $\sin^{-1}\left(\frac{c}{b}\right)$
   D) $\cos^{-1}\left(\frac{b}{c}\right)$

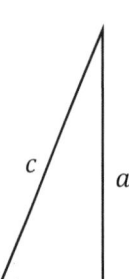

5. The figure below shows a 7-foot stick leaning against a vertical wall. The stick makes a 47° angle. Which of the following expressions gives the height where the top of the ladder hits the wall?

   A) 7 tan 47°
   B) 7 sin 47°
   C) $\frac{7}{\cos 47°}$
   D) $\frac{7}{\sin 47°}$

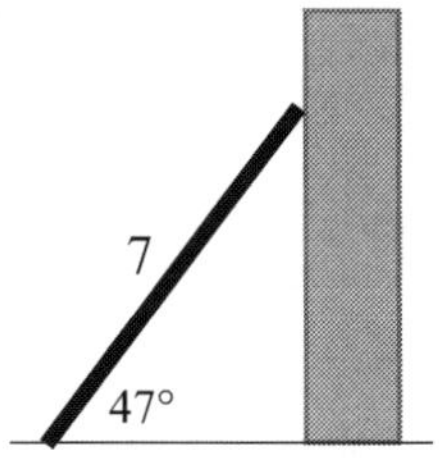

6. What expression is equal to the value of x in the triangle shown below?

   A) 30 tan 37°
   B) 30 sin 37°
   C) $\frac{30}{\tan 37°}$
   D) $\frac{30}{\sin 37°}$

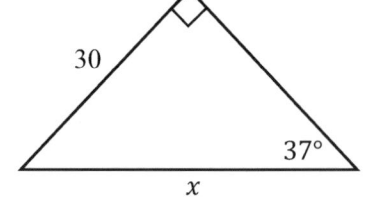

7. If $\sin \theta = 0.8$ in the triangle, below what is the value of x?

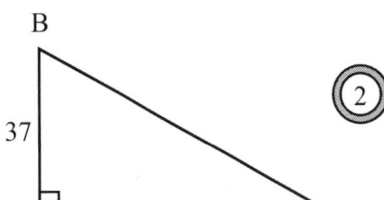

   A) 3.6
   B) 14.4
   C) 21.6
   D) 24.4

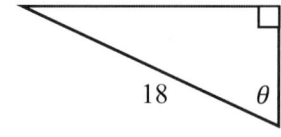

8. Which expression is equivalent to the length of BC?

   A) $\frac{\tan 63°}{60}$
   B) $\frac{60}{\tan 63°}$
   C) $\tan\left(\frac{63°}{60}\right)$
   D) 60 tan 63°

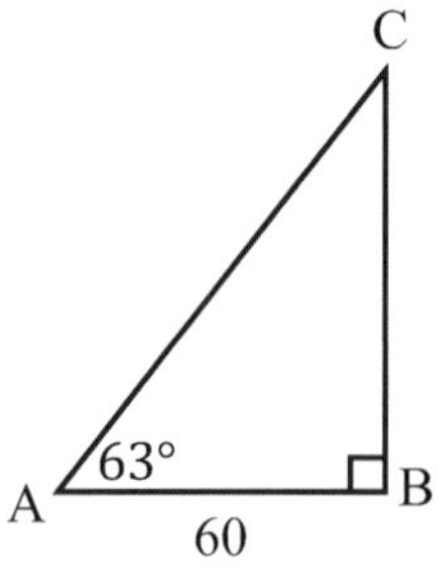

9. If $\angle A = \frac{9\pi}{4}$ radians, what is the measure of $\angle A$ in degreees?

Chapter 20: Trigonometry

10. Triangle ABC has a right angle at point B. If $\sin A = \frac{2}{7}$, what is the value of $\tan C$?

    A) $\frac{7}{2}$
    B) $\frac{\sqrt{45}}{2}$
    C) $\frac{2}{5}$
    D) $\frac{2\sqrt{45}}{45}$

11. Triangle ABC is similar to triangle DEF, where angle A corresponds to angle D and angles C and F are right angles. If $\cos A = \frac{4}{7}$, what is the value of $\cos D$?

12. Point a lies on the unit circle. If the angle of a has a measure of $\frac{7\pi}{4}$ radians, what is the $\cos a$?

    A) $-\frac{\sqrt{2}}{2}$
    B) $\frac{1}{2}$
    C) $\frac{\sqrt{2}}{2}$
    D) $\frac{\sqrt{3}}{2}$

13. Triangle CAB has right angle A. If $\tan C = \frac{6}{8}$, what is the value of $\cos B$?

14. For an angle with measure θ, $\sin \theta = \frac{7}{25}$ and $\cos \theta = \frac{24}{25}$. What is the value of $\tan \theta$?

    A) $\frac{7}{24}$
    B) $\frac{25}{24}$
    C) $\frac{24}{7}$
    D) $\frac{7}{25}$

15. Angle B has a measure of 320°. When written in radians, angle B has a measure of $a\pi$ radians. What is the value of a?

16. In the right triangle ABC, the length of side AB is 35, the measure of angle A is 90°, and the measure of angle C is 43°. Which of the following represents the length of side BC?

    A) $\frac{35}{\sin 43°}$
    B) $\frac{35}{\sin 47°}$
    C) $35\sin 43°$
    D) $35\sin 47°$

17. What is the value of $\sin\left(\frac{3\pi}{4}\right)$?

    A) $-\frac{\sqrt{2}}{2}$
    B) $-\frac{\sqrt{3}}{2}$
    C) $\frac{\sqrt{2}}{2}$
    D) $\frac{\sqrt{3}}{2}$

18. In triangle ABC, $\cos(C) = \frac{10}{26}$ and angle B is a right angle. What is the value of $\cos A$?

19. In the triangle below, the $\sin A = \frac{3}{5}$, what is $\tan B$?

    A) $\frac{4}{3}$
    B) $\frac{3}{4}$
    C) $\frac{4}{5}$
    D) $\frac{3}{5}$

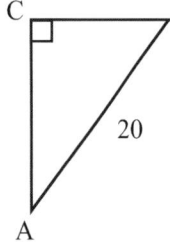

- 191 -

PrepPros

20.

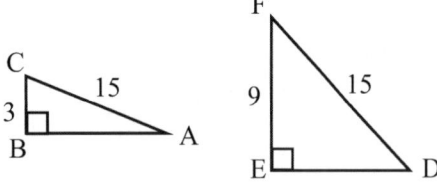

For the triangles above, which of the following expressions is true?

A) $\sin A = 3 \sin D$
B) $\sin A = \frac{1}{3} \sin D$
C) $\cos A = 3 \cos D$
D) $\cos A = \frac{1}{3} \cos D$

21. Points A and B lie on the circle with radius 1 centered at the origin, O. If the measure of $\angle AOB$ is $100°$, what is the measure, in radians, or $\angle AOB$?

A) $\frac{\pi}{2}$
B) $\frac{5\pi}{9}$
C) $\frac{2\pi}{3}$
D) π

22. If $\frac{\pi}{2} < x < \pi$ and $\sin x = \frac{1}{2}$, what is the value of $\cos x$?

A) $-\frac{\sqrt{3}}{2}$
B) $-\frac{\sqrt{2}}{2}$
C) $\frac{\sqrt{2}}{2}$
D) $\frac{\sqrt{3}}{2}$

23. In the triangle below, $\cos x = \frac{5}{17}$. What is $\sin y$?

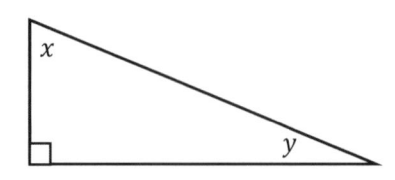

24. In triangle ABC, $\cos(C) = \frac{56}{119}$ and angle A is a right angle. What is the value of $\cos(B)$?

25. The two acute angles of a right triangle have degree measures of a and b. If $\sin a = 0.3$, what does $\cos b$ equal?

26. Triangle DEF is similar to triangle JKL, where D corresponds to J and angles E and K are right angles. If $\sin(D) = \frac{240}{260}$, what is the value of $\sin(J)$?

A) $\frac{100}{240}$
B) $\frac{100}{260}$
C) $\frac{240}{260}$
D) $\frac{260}{240}$

27. In the figure below, ABC is a right triangle. If $BC = 30$ and the tangent of $\angle BCA$ is equal to 0.75, what is the length of AC?

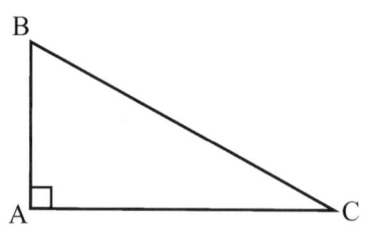

Note: Figure not drawn to scale.

28. The measure of angle A is $\frac{4\pi}{3}$ radians. The measure of angle B is $\frac{7\pi}{12}$ radians less than the measure of angle A. What is the measure of angle B is <u>degrees</u>?

A) 120
B) 135
C) 240
D) 345

- 192 -

29. In the figure, the length of line segment BC can be represented as $x \tan A$. What is the value of x?

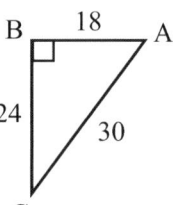

30. Two acute angles in a right triangle have degree measures of x and y. If $\sin x = \frac{21}{29}$, what is the value of $\cos y$?

31. Triangles ABC and DEF are similar right triangles. Angles C and F are both equal to 90° and side BC is corresponding to side EF. The length of side BC is 3.7 times the side EF. If $\tan B = \frac{20}{21}$, what is the value of $\tan E$?

32. For acute angles A and B, $\sin(A) = \cos(B)$. The measure of angle A is 48°. What is the measure of angle B?

A) 42°
B) 48°
C) 58°
D) 78°

33. Points A and B lie on the circle with radius 1 centered at the origin, O. If the cosine of $\cos \angle AOB = -\frac{1}{2}$ and $\sin \angle AOB = -\frac{\sqrt{3}}{2}$, what is the measure, in radians, or $\angle AOB$?

A) $\frac{5\pi}{6}$
B) $\frac{7\pi}{3}$
C) $\frac{2\pi}{3}$
D) $\frac{4\pi}{3}$

34. Triangle ABC is similar to triangle LMN, where B is corresponds to M, what is the $\cos \angle M$?

A) $\frac{\sqrt{2}}{2}$
B) 1
C) $\sqrt{2}$
D) $5\sqrt{2}$

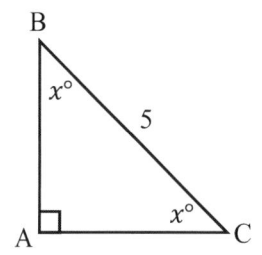

35. The side lengths of right triangle FGH are given below. Triangle FGH is similar to triangle XYZ, where F corresponds to X and G corresponds to Y. What is the value $\sin X$?

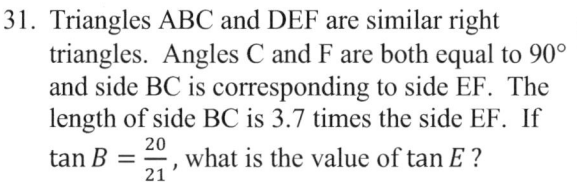

$$FG = 15$$
$$GH = 20$$
$$HF = 25$$

A) $\frac{3}{5}$
B) $\frac{3}{4}$
C) $\frac{4}{5}$
D) $\frac{5}{4}$

36. In the figure below, $\cos(90° - x) = \frac{3}{11}$. What is the value of $\cos x$?

A) $\frac{4\sqrt{7}}{11}$
B) $\frac{11\sqrt{7}}{28}$
C) $\frac{8}{11}$
D) $\frac{11}{3}$

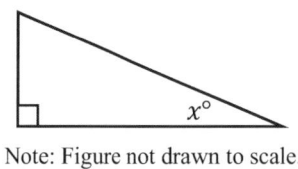

Note: Figure not drawn to scale.

37. Triangle ABC is similar to triangle DEF, where angle A corresponds to angle D and angles C and F are right angles. The length of AB is 0.7 times the length of DE. If $\tan A = \frac{21}{28}$, what is the value of $\cos D$?

PrepPros

38. A circle with center $B\ (0,0)$ is on the xy-plane. Point $A\ (3,0)$ and point $C\ (x,-3)$ lie on the circle. The measurement of $\angle ABC$ in radians if point C is revolved 13 times around the center is represented by $x\pi$. If $\angle ABC$ is measured in the counterclockwise direction, what is the value of x?

39. In the right triangle below, $\tan B = \frac{8}{6}$. What is $\cos C + \cos B$ equal to?

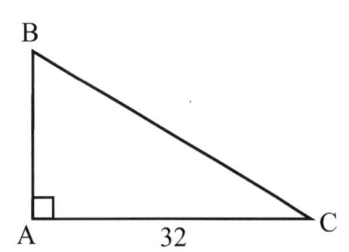

[Triangle with right angle at A, AC = 32, B at top]

Note: Figure not drawn to scale.

40. In the figure below, $AC = 5$. The measure of $\angle C$ is half the measure of $\angle A$, and AB is parallel to ED. In triangle CDE, what is the measure of $\sin C$?

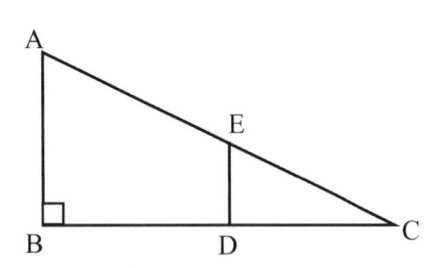

[Triangle figure with A, B, E, D, C]

A) $\frac{1}{2}$
B) $\frac{3}{5}$
C) $\frac{4}{5}$
D) 2

41. In the figure below, $\angle B$ is congruent to $\angle E$. What is the value of $\cos D$?

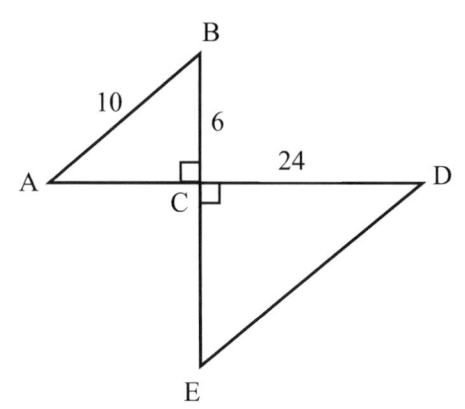

[Figure with triangles, AB side 10, BC = 6, CD = 24]

42. The side lengths of right triangle ABC are given below. Triangle ABC is similar to triangle LMN, where A corresponds to L and B corresponds to M. What is the value of $\tan N$?

$AB = 25$
$BC = 60$
$CA = 65$

A) $\frac{5}{13}$
B) $\frac{5}{12}$
C) $\frac{12}{13}$
D) $\frac{12}{5}$

43. The measure of angle x is $28°$ and $\cos(x) - \sin(C) = 0$, where $0° < C < 90°$. What is the measure, in degrees, of angle C?

A) 17
B) 28
C) 62
D) 152

44. In the xy-plane, points $A\left(-\frac{\sqrt{2}}{2}, \frac{\sqrt{2}}{2}\right)$ and $B\left(\frac{\sqrt{3}}{2}, -\frac{1}{2}\right)$ lie on a circle with radius 1, where O is the center of the circle. The measure, in radians, of angle AOB is θ. If $\theta = \frac{k\pi}{12}$, what is the value of k?

Chapter 20: Trigonometry

45. In a right triangle, the two acute angles are a and b. If the $\sin \angle a = \cos \angle b$, and $a = 2x + 44$ and $b = 3x + 6$, what is the value of x?

46. What is the area of triangle ABC below?

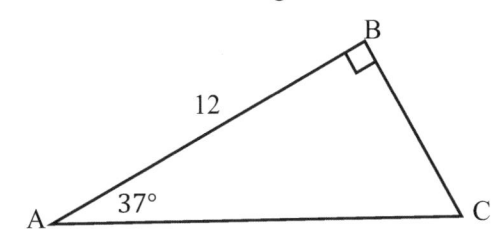

A) $\frac{\tan 37°}{2}$
B) $\frac{72}{\tan 37°}$
C) $72 \tan 37°$
D) $144 \tan 37°$

47. In the xy-plane, there are 3 points $a, b,$ and c. Point a has coordinates of $(1, 0)$, point b has coordinates of $(0, 0)$, and point c has coordinates of $(0, -1)$. Which of the following gives a possible angle measure, in radians, of $\angle abc$?

A) $\frac{33\pi}{2}$
B) 32π
C) 33π
D) $\frac{35\pi}{2}$

48. In the figure below, $\cos C = \frac{4}{5}$. If $CB = 16$ and $ED = 6$, what is the length of AE?

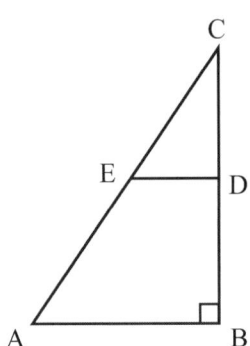

Note: Figure not drawn to scale.

49. If $\cos x = y$, which of the following must be true for all values of x?

A) $\sin x = y$
B) $\sin(90° - x) + \cos x = 2y$
C) $\cos(90° - x) + \sin x = 2y$
D) $\sin(180° + x) = y$

50. In the figure below, $ABCD$ is a rectangle. Which of following must be true?

A) $\sin(\angle BDA) = \cos(\angle DBC)$
B) $\sin(\angle BDA) = \cos(\angle BDC)$
C) $\sin(\angle DAB) = \cos(\angle DBC)$
D) $\sin(\angle DAB) = \cos(\angle BCD)$

51. A circle with center B, $(0, 0)$ is a unit circle on the xy-plane. Point A $(1,0)$ and C lie on the circle. If the measurement of $\angle ABC$ is $\frac{885\pi}{60}$ in radians, what is the x-coordinate of point C?

A) $\frac{\sqrt{2}}{2}$
B) $-\frac{\sqrt{2}}{2}$
C) 0
D) $-\frac{\sqrt{3}}{2}$

52. For a certain angle A, $\sin A = -\frac{\sqrt{2}}{2}$ and $\tan A < 0$. Which of the following angles has a cosine value that is equivalent to $\cos A$?

A) $-1,935°$
B) $-1,305°$
C) $1,755°$
D) $1,350°$

- 195 -

PrepPros

53. In the figure BD and AC intersect at point D, $BD = 16$, and $CD = 12$. What is the value of $\tan A$?

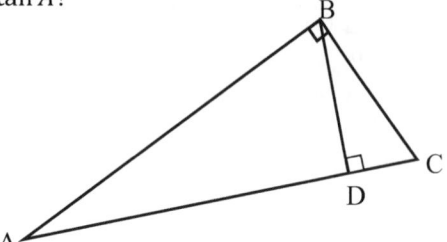

Note: Figure not drawn to scale.

54. A point K $(1, 0)$ lies on the circle. The point O $(0, 0)$ is the center of the circle while point J with coordinates $(a, -1)$ also lies on the circle. What of the following could be the measure $\angle JOK$?

A) $-\frac{53}{2}\pi$
B) -21π
C) -18π
D) $-\frac{39}{2}\pi$

55. A circle with center E, $(0, 0)$ is a unit circle on the xy-plane. Point D $(1,0)$ and F lie on the circle. If the measurement of $\angle DEF$ is $-\frac{276\pi}{18}$ in radians, what is the y-coordinate of point F?

A) $\frac{\sqrt{3}}{2}$
B) $-\frac{\sqrt{3}}{2}$
C) $\frac{1}{2}$
D) $-\frac{1}{2}$

56. In triangle ABC, point D (not shown) lies on $\overline{AC}$. If the measure of $\angle CBD$ is $x°$ and the measure of $\angle ABD$ is $y°$, what is the value of $\sin x° - \cos y°$?

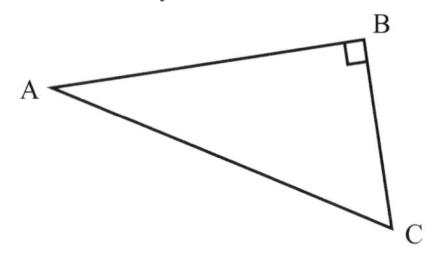

57. Triangle ABC is similar to triangle DEF, where A corresponds to D and C corresponds to F. Angles C and F are right angles. If $\tan(A) = \sqrt{3}$ and $FE = 100$, what is the perimeter of triangle DEF? (Round your answer to the nearest tenth).

58. In the figure, AC and BD intersect at point D, $AD = 12$ and $DC = 5$. What is the value of $\tan A$?

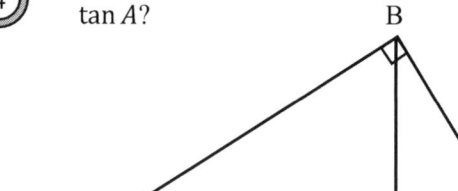

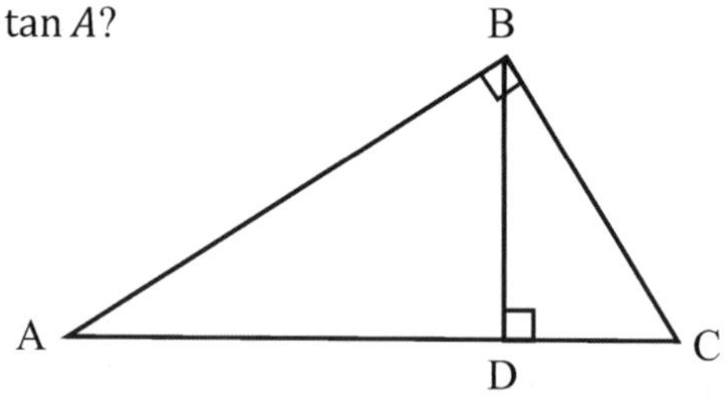

A) $\frac{5}{12}$
B) $\frac{5\sqrt{3}}{4}$
C) $\frac{\sqrt{15}}{6}$
D) $\frac{\sqrt{119}}{12}$

- 196 -

Chapter 21: Probability

The Basics of Probability

Probability is the likelihood of a desired outcome occurring compared to the total number of possible outcomes. On the SAT, probability can be a fraction, a decimal, or, less commonly, a percentage:

$$\text{Probability} = \frac{\text{Desired Outcome}}{\text{All Possible Outcomes}}$$

The SAT often phrases probability questions by asking you the probability of an event occurring. To answer these questions, consider the event that you are counting and compare it to the total number of possible outcomes.

To learn how probability works, let's work through a few questions with the following example:

Example 1: A bag has a total of 38 chocolate candies. 18 of the candies are blue, 10 are red, 5 are yellow, 3 are green, and 2 are pink.

Question 1: Andy will reach into the bag and pick one candy. What is the probability that he will grab a yellow candy?

Solution: Of the 38 candies in the bag, 5 are yellow. Therefore, the probability of selecting a yellow candy is $\frac{5}{38}$. The answer is $\frac{5}{38}$.

Question 2: Evelyn is going to pick one piece of chocolate candy from the bag. What is the probability that she will NOT pick a blue candy?

Solution: There is a total of 18 blue candies in the bag, which means there are 20 candies that are not blue. The probability of selecting a chocolate candy that is not blue is $\frac{20}{38}$. This could also be simplified to $\frac{10}{19}$. The answer is $\frac{10}{19}$.

Pretty easy, right? Now, probability questions get a bit more difficult when you have probabilities that involve multiple events. **To calculate a probability involving multiple events, multiply the probabilities of each individual event.** Make sure that you remember to multiply the probabilities and not add them. Adding instead of multiplying the probabilities for multiple events is the most common mistake students make.

Question 3: Min will select 2 chocolate candies from the bag without replacement. What is the probability that Min will select a red candy and then a green candy?

A) $\frac{13}{75}$ B) $\frac{15}{722}$ C) $\frac{15}{703}$ D) $\frac{13}{76}$

Solution: We have two probabilities: (1) the probability of selecting a red candy and (2) the probability of then selecting a green candy. For the red candy, there are a total of 38 candies in the bag and 10 red candies, so the probability of selecting a red candy is $\frac{10}{38}$. After selecting a red candy, there are 37 candies left in the bag since Min does not replace the first candy. There are still 3 green candies in the bag, so the probability of the second candy being green is $\frac{3}{37}$. Since we have multiple events occurring in a row, we multiply the probabilities together.

$$\frac{10}{38} \times \frac{3}{37} = \frac{30}{1,406}$$

Simplifying the fraction, we get an answer of $\frac{15}{703}$. **The answer is C.**

For questions like #3, **make sure to read carefully to see if the selection is with replacement or without replacement, as it changes the answer**. If Min instead replaced the chocolate candy he selected the first time, there would still be a total of 38 candies in the bag for the 2nd piece of candy he draws from the bag, so the total probability instead would be

$$\frac{10}{38} \times \frac{3}{38} = \frac{30}{1,444}$$

Make sure you understand the difference between replacement and no replacement and how it affects the probability in case you see a question like this on test day!

1-4 Probability and Data Tables

For most probability questions on the SAT, you are given a data table and asked to identify the probability of a certain event occurring. It is critical to read the question carefully and consider (1) what are the events that you are asked to identify (the numerator) and (2) what are the total outcomes you are choosing from (the denominator). For these questions, probability can be defined as

$$\text{Probability} = \frac{\text{Number In Target Group}}{\text{Total Number To Select From}}$$

Let's use the table and examples below to see how this works:

The table below shows the results of a survey asking high school students in two different classrooms about their favorite school lunch.

	Tacos	Chicken Tenders	Vegetable Pasta	Total
Period 1	24	3	6	33
Period 2	9	5	15	29
Total	33	8	21	62

Example 2: What is the fraction of students whose favorite school lunch is tacos?

Solution: We are not given any restrictions on which students to consider, so we include all 62 students in the total. The total number of students who selected tacos is 33.

$$\frac{\text{Student who Selected Tacos}}{\text{Total Students}} = \frac{33}{62}$$

The answer is $\frac{33}{62}$.

When the question includes no restrictions, as in Example 2, we look at the entire table. This is the easiest type of probability and data tables question.

More commonly, SAT probability questions give us a condition that directs us to only consider a certain portion of the table. In math, this is called a **conditional probability**. Let's learn how this works with Examples 3 and 4.

Example 3: Given that a student is in period 2, what is the probability that he or she picked chicken tenders on the survey?

Solution: The statement "given that a student is in period 2" directs us to only consider students from period 2. So, we only look at the 29 students in period 2 not all 62 students at the school. The fact that a student must be in period 2 is the condition, making this conditional probability.

Now, let's find the answer. Of the 29 students in period 2, 5 selected chicken tenders.

$$\frac{\text{Students in Period 2 who Selected Chicken Tenders}}{\text{Total Students in Period 2}} = \frac{5}{29}$$

The answer is $\frac{5}{29}$.

> **Example 4:** What is the probability a student is in period 2, given that the student selects vegetable pasta as his or her favorite food?

Solution: The statement "given that the student selects vegetable pasta as his or her favorite food" directs us to only consider students who selected vegetable pasta. Therefore, we only look at the 21 students who selected vegetable pasta to find the answer. Of those 21 students, 15 are in period 2.

$$\frac{\text{Student who Selected Vegeable Pasta and are in Period 2}}{\text{Total Students who Selected Vegetable Pasta}} = \frac{15}{21}$$

Simplifying the fraction, **the answer is $\frac{5}{7}$.**

Conditional Probability

Conditional probability is the probability that an event occurs given that another condition has already been met. We were introduced to this concept in Examples 3-4, but we want to dive into it a little bit more since the SAT loves to test you on conditional probability.

Let's start with how to spot a conditional probability question. **If a probability question ever includes a conditional statement (most commonly a "given that..." statement), it is a conditional probability question.** Notice how we saw "given that..." statements in both Examples 3 and 4.

To further understand conditional probability, let's consider the following example:

> **Example 5:** A bag has 4 red balls, 2 green balls, and 7 black balls. What is the probability of selecting a red ball, given that a green ball is <u>not</u> selected? (Express your answer as a fraction.)

Solution: To answer any conditional probability question correctly, follow these 4 steps:

1. **Identify The Condition.** The condition is given by the "given that..." statement. In Example 5, the condition is "given that a green ball is <u>not</u> selected."

   Less commonly, the condition can be given by an "if..." statement. Example 5 could also be written as, "If a green ball is <u>not</u> selected, what is the probability of selecting a red ball?" Even though this is worded differently, we are asked to find the same probability.

2. **Find the Total Outcomes Remaining Given the Condition.** This is the most important step to master conditional probability. The given condition limits the total number of outcomes that we consider when finding the probability, so **we have to find which outcome(s) meet the given condition to find the total outcomes that we are selecting from,** which is the number in the denominator of the probability fraction.

   In Example 5, the condition "given that a green ball is not selected" means that we do not count the green balls as a potential outcome. This condition is the same as removing the green balls from the bag. Therefore, we are only selecting from the red and black balls. Therefore, the total outcomes remaining given the condition is 11 since we are selecting from the 4 red balls and 7 black balls.

3. **Find The Number in the Target Group.** The target group is the group that we are being asked to select. In Example 5, we are asked the probability of selecting a red ball, so red ball is the target group. There are 4 red balls in the bag, so the number in the target group is 4.

4. Write Your Answer. Use the value we found in step 2 as the denominator and the value we found in step 3 as the numerator to find the conditional probability.

$$\text{Conditional Probability} = \frac{\text{Number in the Target Group}}{\text{Total Outcomes Remaining Given the Condition}}$$

For Example 5, the number in the target group is 4 (the number of red balls), so we put 4 in the numerator. The total outcomes remaining given the condition is 11 (the total number of balls given that we do not select a green ball), so the conditional probability of selecting a red ball given that a green ball is not selected is

$$\text{Conditional Probability} = \frac{\text{Number in Red Balls}}{\text{Total Number of Balls That Are Not Green}} = \frac{4}{11}$$

The answer is $\frac{4}{11}$.

If you understand these 4 steps and Example 5, you are ready to solve any conditional probability questions that can appear on the SAT.

1-4 3 More Probability Rules to Know

The vast majority of probability questions on the SAT are probability and data tables questions. However, there are three probability rules that you should know just in case. While less commonly tested on the SAT, these 3 rules are easy to learn for students of all levels.

Rule #1 – The sum of the probabilities of all possible outcomes is equal to 1.

For example, let's think of a flipping a coin. The probability of flipping heads is $\frac{1}{2}$, and the probability of flipping tails is $\frac{1}{2}$. Of course, $\frac{1}{2} + \frac{1}{2} = 1$. All coin flips must end in heads or tails, so the sum of the probabilities of those events must equal 1.

Example 6: In a class of fifth graders, students were asked to pick their favorite lunch, and no student was allowed to select more than one lunch as their favorite: $\frac{1}{2}$ picked pizza, $\frac{1}{5}$ picked chicken nuggets, $\frac{1}{10}$ picked pasta, and $\frac{3}{20}$ picked tacos. What is the probability that a randomly selected student did not select any of these lunches?

A) 0   B) $\frac{3}{1600}$ C) $\frac{1}{20}$ D) $\frac{1}{60}$

Solution: All fifth graders selected a favorite lunch, so the sum of the fractions must add up to 1. We can use the given fractions to find the fraction of students, x, who did not select any of the lunches.

$$\frac{1}{2} + \frac{1}{5} + \frac{1}{10} + \frac{3}{20} + x = 1$$

To solve, we need to make the fractions all have a common denominator. Here, the least common denominator is 20. If you need to review adding fractions, go back to Chapter 6.

$$\frac{10}{20} + \frac{4}{20} + \frac{2}{20} + \frac{3}{20} + x = 1 \rightarrow \frac{19}{20} + x = 1$$

$$x = \frac{1}{20}$$

The fraction of students who selected none of the lunches is $\frac{1}{20}$, so the probability that a randomly selected student picked none of the lunches is also $\frac{1}{20}$. **The answer is C.**

Rule #2 – The probability of Event A OR Event B occurring is the sum of the probabilities of the individual events.

$$P(A \text{ or } B) = P(A) + P(B)$$

Example 7: Kristina is on a game show where she plays three games for three different prizes. The first game is for a toaster, the second game is for a couch, and the third game is for a new car. The probability that she wins a toaster is 0.5, the probability that she wins a couch is 0.2, and the probability that she wins a new car is 0.05. What is the probability that she wins a new car or a toaster?

A) 0.025   B) 0.1   C) 0.25   D) 0.55

Solution: Since we are finding the probability of winning a new car OR a toaster, we add the probabilities of both events. The probability of winning a car or a toaster is the sum of the probability of winning a car, 0.05, and the probability of winning a toaster, 0.5.

$$P(\text{car or toaster}) = P(\text{car}) + P(\text{toaster}) = 0.05 + 0.5 = 0.55$$

The answer is D.

Rule #3 – The probability of Event A AND Event B occurring is the product of the probabilities of the individual events.

$$P(A \text{ and } B) = P(A) \times P(B)$$

Example 8: The probability that Event A will occur is 0.3. The probability that Event B will occur is 0.7. Given that Events A and B are mutually exclusive, what is the probability that Event A *and* Event B will occur?

A) 0.21   B) 0.3   C) 0.5   D) 1.0

Solution: We are finding the probability that Events A AND B occur, so we multiply the probabilities of the individual events.

$$P(A \text{ and } B) = P(A) \times P(B) = 0.3 \times 0.7 = 0.21$$

The answer is A.

Make sure that you memorize all 3 of these rules. While these rules are not as commonly tested on the SAT, as long as you know the rules, any probability questions with these 3 rules will be easy!

PrepPros

Probability Practice: Answers on page 332.

1. Andy has a bag of marbles. If the bag has 30 blue marbles, 25 red marbles, and 15 green marbles, what is the probability that he will randomly select a red marble?

   A) $\frac{5}{14}$
   B) $\frac{6}{15}$
   C) $\frac{3}{7}$
   D) $\frac{5}{7}$

2. Each face of a fair 12-sided die is labeled with a number 1 through 12, with a different number appearing on each face. If the die is rolled one time, what is the probability of rolling a 7?

3. Jerry is in a rush and needs to grab one of the premade sandwiches at the market. Jerry's favorite is the Italian sub, but the sandwiches have no labels on them. If there are 27 total sandwiches and 10 are Italian subs, what is the probability that he does NOT get an Italian sub?

   A) $\frac{1}{10}$
   B) $\frac{10}{27}$
   C) $\frac{17}{27}$
   D) $\frac{17}{37}$

4. A box contains 1 red bead, 6 white beads, and 3 blue beads. Jorge will randomly remove one bead from the box, record its color, and place it back in the box. If Jorge repeats this experiment 150 times, what is the expected number of times that Jorge will record a bead that is blue?

   A) 30
   B) 45
   C) 75
   D) 120

5. A bag contains 13 pieces of candy: 5 lemon, 2 strawberry, 3 orange, and 3 grape. What is the probability that one piece of candy randomly selected is not lemon?

   A) $\frac{3}{13}$
   B) $\frac{5}{13}$
   C) $\frac{8}{13}$
   D) $\frac{10}{13}$

6. A group of backpackers were asked to pick their favorite country in Europe. No backpacker was allowed to pick more than one country. $\frac{1}{4}$ picked Italy, $\frac{1}{5}$ picked Spain, $\frac{1}{6}$ picked France, and $\frac{1}{20}$ pick Portugal. If a random backpacker from the group is selected, what is the probability that he or she did not pick any of these 4 countries?

   A) $\frac{3}{20}$
   B) $\frac{1}{3}$
   C) $\frac{4}{10}$
   D) $\frac{1}{2}$

7. A pencil will be randomly selected from a bag. The probability of selecting a white pencil is $\frac{3}{13}$. The probability of selecting a blue pencil is $\frac{2}{13}$. What is the probability of selecting a white or blue pencil?

   A) $\frac{1}{13}$
   B) $\frac{5}{13}$
   C) $\frac{5}{26}$
   D) $\frac{6}{26}$

Use the information below for questions 8 and 9.

The table below shows the impact of two diets on the weights of dogs.

Diet	Type of Weight Change		Total
	Gained	Lost	
A	50	100	150
B	75	75	150

8. If one of the dogs in the table is selected at random, what is the probability of selecting a dog who lost weight and received diet B?

   A) $\frac{75}{300}$
   B) $\frac{75}{150}$
   C) $\frac{100}{175}$
   D) $\frac{100}{300}$

9. Based on the results in the table, what fraction of the dogs in the study received diet A and gained weight?

   A) $\frac{1}{2}$
   B) $\frac{1}{3}$
   C) $\frac{1}{6}$
   D) $\frac{5}{12}$

10. Three squares with the same center have side lengths of 1, 2, and 3 respectively. What is the probability that a point randomly chosen in the interior of the largest square is also in the interior of the smallest square?

    A) $\frac{1}{9}$
    B) $\frac{1}{3}$
    C) $\frac{4}{9}$
    D) $\frac{6}{9}$

Use the information below for questions 11 and 12.

In a survey, biology and chemistry professors from local science departments were asked if their primary focus was teaching or research. The results are shown below.

Type of Professor	Primary Focus		Total
	Teaching	Research	
Biology	86	132	218
Chemistry	142	85	227
Total	228	217	445

11. A speaker for an upcoming event will be selected at random from the professors who participated in the survey. Which of the following is the closest to the probability that the selected professor is a chemistry professor, given the professor's primary focus is research?

    A) 0.191
    B) 0.392
    C) 0.488
    D) 0.510

12. Which of the following is the closest to the probability that a randomly selected chemistry professor has a primary focus on teaching?

    A) 0.319
    B) 0.512
    C) 0.623
    D) 0.626

13. Julia runs out of time on her test and needs to guess on the last 4 questions. Each question has 5 answers. If Julia answers each one randomly, what is the probability she answers all 4 questions correctly?

    A) $\frac{1}{625}$
    B) $\frac{4}{625}$
    C) $\frac{1}{125}$
    D) $\frac{1}{5}$

Use the information below for questions 14-16.

		Crust Style		
		Thin	Deep Dish	Gluten Free
Topping	Cheese	12	19	7
	Pepperoni	8	25	9

The table above shows the pizza orders at Pete's Pizzeria for an hour on a Saturday afternoon.

14. If one of the pizzas is selected at random, what is the probability the pizza was a thin crust pizza?

   A) $\frac{1}{4}$
   B) $\frac{2}{5}$
   C) $\frac{19}{40}$
   D) $\frac{3}{5}$

15. If one of the pizzas is selected at random, what is the probability that the pizza was thin crust or gluten free?

   A) $\frac{19}{28}$
   B) $\frac{1}{2}$
   C) $\frac{19}{40}$
   D) $\frac{9}{20}$

16. If one of the pizzas is selected at random, what is the probability that the pizza selected is a cheese pizza, given the pizza is gluten free?

   A) $\frac{7}{80}$
   B) $\frac{19}{40}$
   C) $\frac{7}{38}$
   D) $\frac{7}{16}$

Use the information below for questions 17 and 18.

	Resting Heart Rate		
	Decrease	Increase	Total
Weight Training	140	60	200
Cardio	160	20	180
Total	300	80	380

The table above shows adults who exercise with weight training or cardio and whether their resting heart rate increased or decreased.

17. What proportion of adults had an increase in resting heart rate?

   A) $\frac{1}{9}$
   B) $\frac{3}{10}$
   C) $\frac{4}{19}$
   D) $\frac{3}{4}$

18. One adult is selected at random. What is the probability of selecting an adult who had a decrease in resting heart rate, given the participant exercised with weight training?

   A) $\frac{7}{19}$
   B) $\frac{3}{5}$
   C) $\frac{7}{15}$
   D) $\frac{7}{10}$

Use the information below for questions 19 and 20.

Beverage	Food	
	Purchased	No Purchase
Purchased	100	85
No Purchase	45	20

The table above shows the purchases made by a random sample of 250 people at a baseball game.

19. What is the probability that someone surveyed purchased both food and a beverage?

    A) $\frac{100}{250}$
    B) $\frac{45}{250}$
    C) $\frac{85}{185}$
    D) $\frac{100}{145}$

20. What is the probability that someone surveyed who purchased food did not purchase a beverage?

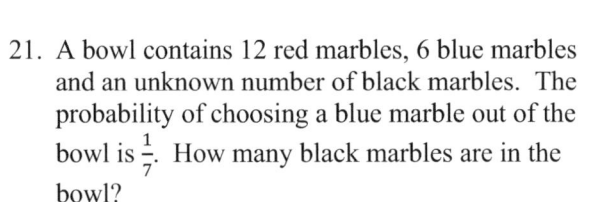

    A) $\frac{45}{250}$
    B) $\frac{45}{65}$
    C) $\frac{45}{145}$
    D) $\frac{85}{250}$

21. A bowl contains 12 red marbles, 6 blue marbles and an unknown number of black marbles. The probability of choosing a blue marble out of the bowl is $\frac{1}{7}$. How many black marbles are in the bowl?

    A) 8
    B) 12
    C) 18
    D) 24

Use the information below for questions 22-24.

The table below shows the distribution of 886 ribbons with different color packages and different color ribbons.

Ribbon Color	Package Color		Total
	Blue	Red	
Pink	246	178	424
White	304	158	462
Total	550	336	886

22. If one of the ribbons is selected at random, which of the following is closest to the probability that it has a red package?

    A) 0.38
    B) 0.48
    C) 0.52
    D) 0.62

23. If a pink ribbon is selected at random, which of the following is closest probability that it has a blue package?

    A) 0.20
    B) 0.27
    C) 0.41
    D) 0.58

24. If a white ribbon is to be selected at random, the probability that the ribbon has a blue package is $\frac{152}{0.5k}$. Which of the following best describes k in this context?

    A) The total number of ribbons in the table.
    B) The number of white ribbons in the table.
    C) The total number of ribbons in the table that have a blue package.
    D) The number of ribbons in the table that have red packages.

Use the information below for questions 25-27.

A bowl contains red and blue balls, each labeled with a letter: A, B, or C. The table below shows the distribution of colors and letters for the balls in the bowl.

	Color		Total
Letter	Blue	Red	
A	7	6	13
B	6	8	14
C	8	5	13
Total	21	19	40

25. If a blue ball is selected at random from the bowl, what is the probability that the selected ball is labeled C?

   A) $\frac{6}{21}$
   B) $\frac{7}{21}$
   C) $\frac{8}{21}$
   D) $\frac{8}{13}$

26. If a ball with the letter C is selected at random from the bag, what is the probability that the selected ball is red?

   A) $\frac{5}{19}$
   B) $\frac{5}{13}$
   C) $\frac{8}{21}$
   D) $\frac{8}{13}$

27. If a ball is selected at random from the bag, what is the probability that the selected ball is red and has the letter A on it?

   A) $\frac{7}{40}$
   B) $\frac{3}{20}$
   C) $\frac{6}{19}$
   D) $\frac{6}{13}$

Use the information below for questions 28-30.

	State A	State B
Liberal	120	30
Conservative	60	90
Moderate	20	80

The table above summarizes the distribution of political views for 400 voters from State A and State B.

28. If one of the 400 voters in the table above is selected at random, what is the probability of selecting a voter from State B, given the voter is not a liberal? (Express your answer as a decimal or fraction, not as a percent)

29. If one of the 400 voters in the table above is selected at random, what is the probability of selecting a conservative voter, given the voter is not from State A? (Express your answer as a decimal or fraction, not as a percent)

30. If one of the 400 voters in the table above is selected at random, what is the probability of selecting a voter from State B, given the voter is not conservative? (Express your answer as a decimal or fraction, not as a percent)

Use the following information to answer questions 31-32.

Data from a random sample of 245 customers of a certain clothing company are listed below. The table indicates the number of customers in 3 age brackets (16-25, 26-35, 36-45) and the number of items of clothing from the company each customer owns.

Age (in years)	Items of Clothing			
	1–3	4–6	7+	Total
16-25	71	17	2	90
26-35	43	32	60	135
36-45	11	6	3	20
Total	125	55	65	245

31. If two customers are chosen at random, what is the probability that they are both above the age of 25 and own less than 4 items of clothing?

A) $\frac{155}{245}$
B) $\frac{54(53)}{245(244)}$
C) $\frac{43(42)}{245(244)}$
D) $\frac{54(53)}{125(124)}$

32. Three customers that are below the age of 36 are chosen at random. Given that the first customer is 17 years old and owns 6 items of clothing, what is the probability that the next 2 customers are in the 16-25 age bracket and own 4-6 items of clothing?

A) $\frac{17(16)}{245(244)}$
B) $\frac{16(15)}{245(244)}$
C) $\frac{17(16)}{90(89)}$
D) $\frac{16(15)}{224(223)}$

33. There are building blocks in a child's construction set. Each block is categorized into only 1 shape. There are 24 squares, 8 triangles, and 32 are circles and trapezoids. The probability that a building block that is randomly picked is a trapezoid, given that the shape is NOT a square is $\frac{1}{8}$. What is the number of circles in the construction set?

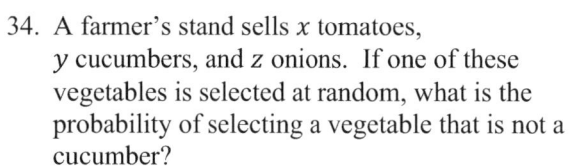

34. A farmer's stand sells x tomatoes, y cucumbers, and z onions. If one of these vegetables is selected at random, what is the probability of selecting a vegetable that is not a cucumber?

A) $\frac{z+x}{y}$
B) $\frac{z+x-y}{z+x+y}$
C) $1 - \frac{y}{x+z+y}$
D) $1 - \frac{y}{x+z}$

35. In the figure below, point B and the center of each circle lie on $\overline{AC}$. The ratio of AB to BC is 5 to 3. If a point is randomly selected in the figure, what is the probability the point is in the shaded region?

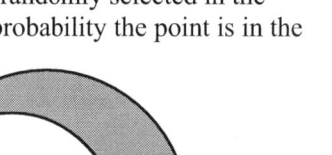

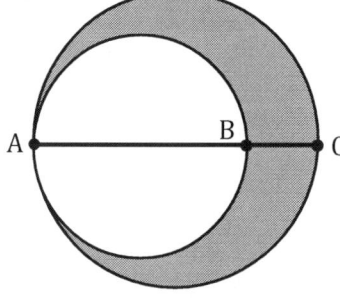

Note: Figure not drawn to scale.

36. There are red, green, blue, and black marbles in a bowl. The probability of randomly selecting a red or green marble is $\frac{3}{5}$. The probability of selecting a red or blue marble is $\frac{2}{3}$. The probability that a randomly selected marble is NOT green is $\frac{11}{12}$. Given that a randomly selected marble is not green, what is the probability of selecting a black marble?

PrepPros

Chapter 22: Statistical Analysis

The SAT loves to ask questions about various statistics terms, proper sampling methods, and the assumptions that can be made from a given data set. Statistical analysis is a topic that many students have not learned before taking the SAT, so it is common to struggle with statistics questions. The good news is we have everything you need to know about statistics in this chapter, so you will be ready for any statistical analysis questions on test day.

Sampling
(1-4)

Data collection in statistical analysis is most commonly gathered through surveying (or sampling) a population. There are 3 important things to remember about sampling:

1. **In order to have reliable data, a survey must be conducted on randomly selected members of a population.**

2. **A larger sample size is better than a smaller sample size as long as both samples are randomly selecting members from a population.**

3. **The findings of a survey can be generalized to the entire population that is being randomly sampled.**

The most important thing to look for in any sampling question is that the sample is random. Any sample that is not randomly selected is not reliable (more on this shortly).

So, what is the point of all of this sampling? The findings of a survey conducted with random sampling can be generalized to the entire population that is being sampled. In other words, sampling is a powerful tool to help estimate the true value for a larger population without having to sample the entire population.

I know this wording seems confusing, so let's use an example to make this clearer:

Blue Top Middle School has 2,500 total students and 700 6th grade students. 40 6th grade students are randomly selected and asked how many pairs of shoes they own. The survey found the 40 randomly selected 6th grade students on average own 5 pairs of shoes.

The survey randomly selects students, so we have a reliable data set. **From this survey, we can estimate that the average number of pairs of shoes owned by each student for the 700 6th grade students at Blue Top Middle School is close to 5.** Even though we did not survey all 700 6th grade students, we can make an educated guess that the average number of pairs of shoes owned by 6th graders at Blue Top Middle School is close to the average from the survey. This is the entire point of conducting a survey! Since we were sampling from the 700 6th grade students at Blue Top Middle School, we can generalize the findings to all 700 students.

Now, **we can NOT assume that the average number of pairs of shoes owned by each student for all 2,500 students at Blue Top Middle School is close to 5.** We can only generalize the survey data to the group that we are randomly sampling from. Since we did not randomly sample from all students at Blue Top Middle School, we cannot make any predictions about the average number of pairs of shoes owned for all 2,500 students at Blue Top Middle School.

In addition, we cannot apply the findings to any other groups of 6th grade students. If there was another Middle School, let's call it Red Top Middle School, down the street from Blue Top Middle School, we cannot apply the findings and say that Red Top Middle School's 6th graders on average own close to 5 pairs of shoes. There may be something different about the students at Red Top Middle School that make them own more or fewer pairs of shoes. Again, we can only apply the findings of a survey to the population that is being randomly sampled.

If you understand the three principles and how they apply to this example, you know everything you need to correctly answer sampling questions on test day.

> **Example 1:** The teachers at Iron Ridge High School want to find out how students use their phones. Which of the following will produce the most reliable data about all of the students at the high school?
>
> A) Listing students' last names alphabetically and then conducting a survey of the last 80 students on the list.
> B) Randomly selecting 30 students to complete an online questionnaire.
> C) Assigning each student a number and then using a random number generator to select 200 students to complete a survey.
> D) Setting up a table with free pizza and getting 75 students to fill out a survey.

Solution: For this survey to have reliable data, we need a random sample. A is not a random sample because we organized the students alphabetically. D is not random because students volunteered for the survey. B and C are both random samples. A larger sample size produces better data than a smaller sample size, so **the answer is C**.

It is important to recognize that A is not a random sample. Even though it may seem random at first, **any type of organization in selecting a sample makes it non-random.**

> **Example 2:** A study about the quality of the health care system is conducted by polling 110 nurses who work at different hospitals in Austin, Texas. The survey found the average rating for the overall quality of the current health care system is 6.5 out of 10. Which of the following is the biggest group that the findings of this study can be applied to?
>
> A) The 110 nurses polled in the study.
> B) All of the nurses that work in hospitals in Austin, Texas.
> C) All of the nurses in Austin, Texas.
> D) All of the nurses who work in hospitals in Texas.

Solution: The results of a study can be generalized to the population that is being randomly survey. In this question, the study surveys nurses who work in hospitals in Austin, Texas, so we can generalize the findings to that group. The study did not survey nurses who did not work in hospitals, so we cannot include all nurses in Austin, Texas. The study also did not include nurses from other parts of Texas, so we cannot assume nurses from the rest of Texas would respond similarly to those in Austin, Texas. **The answer is B.**

Standard Deviation

Standard deviation is a measure of the spread of values in a data set. A low standard deviation indicates the values in the data set tend to be closer to the average of a data set while a high standard deviation indicates that values in the data set tend to be farther from the average of a data set. You do not need to know how to compute standard deviation, but you do need to understand the concept. All that you need to know is

> **A set of values that are closer together has a lower standard deviation, and a set of values that are farther apart has a higher standard deviation.**

If you have this rule memorized, you can answer standard deviation questions correctly on test day. Let's take a look at some examples to see how this commonly is tested on the SAT.

PrepPros

Example 3: Company A: 18, 25, 26, 26, 27, 35, 36, 38
Company B: 64, 66, 66, 66, 68, 68, 68, 70
Company C: 22, 40, 78, 78, 88, 90, 90, 96

Three water filtration companies (A, B, and C) each provided 8 samples of water to be tested for purity. The purity scores are listed above. Which of the following statements about the standard deviation of the purity scores is correct?

A) Company A has the lowest standard deviation.
B) Company B has the lowest standard deviation.
C) Company C has the lowest standard deviation.
D) It cannot be determined which company has the lowest standard deviation.

Solution: To find out which company has the lowest standard deviation, look for which set of values is the closest together. The purity scores for company B are the closest together, so company B has the lowest standard deviation. **The answer is B.**

The purity scores for company C are the farthest apart, so company C has the higher standard deviation. Company A's standard deviation is between the standard deviations of companies A and C. Notice that the actual values of the numbers do not affect standard deviation. **When finding standard deviation, it does not matter how big or small the values are; all that matters is how close the values are to each other.**

Standard deviation questions also commonly include a table or graph. If we are given a table or graph, we are still looking for how spread apart the data points are. Data points that are more closely clustered have a lower standard deviation while data points that are more spread apart have a higher standard deviation.

Example 4: The tables below give the distribution of weekly rainfall for City A and City B over 17 weeks during the summer of 2012.

Weekly Rainfall	City A	City B
0.00-0.99 inches	6	3
1.00-1.99 inches	2	11
2.00-2.99 inches	3	2
3.00-3.99 inches	1	1
>4 inches	5	0

Which of the following is true about the data shown for these 17 weeks?

A) The standard deviation of weekly rainfall is greater in city A than in city B.
B) The standard deviation of weekly rainfall is greater in city B than in city A.
C) The standard deviation of weekly rainfall in city A is the same as in city B.
D) The standard deviation of weekly rainfall cannot be calculated with the data provided.

Solution: To determine standard deviation, we need to see how spread out the data points are. The values for the weekly rainfall for city A are very spread out, with 6 weeks having less than 1 inch of rainfall and 5 weeks having greater than 4 inches of rainfall. City B has very consistent rainfall, with 11 of the 17 weeks falling between 1 and 1.99 inches, so the weekly rainfall is not very spread out. City A is much more spread out than city B, so the standard deviation of weekly rainfall in city A is greater. **The answer is A.**

Chapter 22: Statistical Analysis

Dot Plots

A Dot plot is a way to visually display a data set. **In a dot plot, each dot represents a data point in the set.**

The dot plot below shows the results of a survey that asked 18 students how many hours they spend on homework each weekend. Each dot represents a student who was included in the survey, so we have a total of 18 dots for the 18 students.

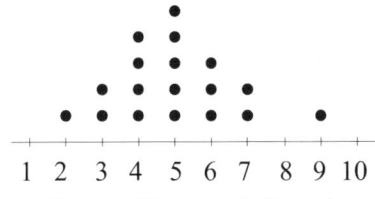

Time on Homework (hours)

In this dot plot, we can see that 1 student in the survey said he or she spent 2 hours on homework each weekend, 2 students said that they spend 3 hours on homework each weekend, 4 students said they spend 4 hours on homework each weekend, 5 students said they spend 5 hours on homework each weekend, and so on. Rather than just listing all these values, the dot plot gives a visual display that allow us to more quickly see the spread of the data points. Looking at the dot plot above, we can see that most students spend 4-6 hours on homework each weekend, with a few students spending fewer or more hours on homework each weekend.

The SAT commonly includes dot plots in standard deviation questions.

Example 5: Dots plots for sets A and B are shown to the right. Which of the following statements about the standard deviations for data sets A and B is correct?

A) The standard deviation for data set A is less than the standard deviation for data set B.
B) The standard deviation for data set A is greater than the standard deviation for data set B.
C) The standard deviation for data set A is equal to the standard deviation for data set B.
D) The standard deviations of the data sets cannot be computed.

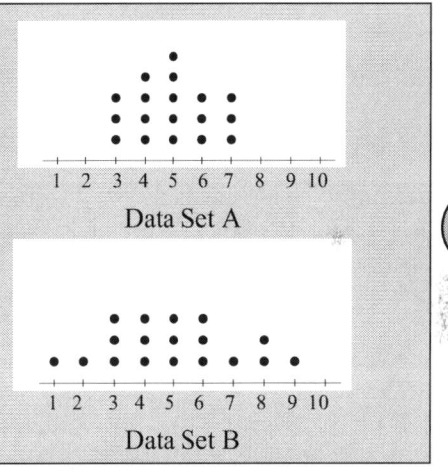

Solution: Standard deviation is a measure of the spread of data points in a set. When given dot plots and asked to compare the standard deviations, we look at how spread apart or close together the data points are. In data set A, the data points are closer together, so data set A has a lower standard deviation. For data set B, the data points are more spread out, so data set B has a greater standard deviation. **The answer is A.**

Margin of Error

Margin of error is a statistic expressing the amount of random sampling error in a survey. The margin of error is the amount by which the findings of a survey may vary from the true value. I know that wording seems confusing, so let's take a look at an example to clarify how margin of error is actually used.

At Smithfield High School, 50 students are randomly selected to complete a survey about their homework habits. The survey found that the estimated mean number of hours spent on homework per week was 9.5 with a margin of error of 2.

PrepPros

From this survey, **an appropriate interpretation of the data would be that it is plausible that the mean number of hours spent on homework per week for all high school students at Smithfield High School is between 7.5 and 11.5 hours.**

The margin of error identifies the range in which we expect the true value of the mean to fall. **The true value of the mean would be the value if you surveyed every student at Smithfield High School and calculated the mean**. However, we do not have time to survey every student, so the margin of error helps us more quickly find out what the mean number of hours students spend on homework each week likely is.

Be sure to notice that we are talking about the mean here. **The margin of error does NOT tell us that all students spend between 7.5 and 11.5 hours of homework per week.** Some students may be lazy and only do 3 hours of homework per week, and others may study much more and spend 15 hours on homework each week. The margin of error just says the mean number of hours spent on homework each week for all students at Smithfield High School is between 7.5 and 11.5 hours.

Example 6: A quality control manager at Clark's Candies is testing to see how many chocolates are in each jar. The quality control manager randomly selects 200 jars that day and counts the number of chocolates in each jar. He finds that the mean number of chocolates in each jar is 58 with an associated margin of error of 4. Which of the following is the most appropriate conclusion based on the data?

A) All of the jars of chocolate ever produced at Clark's Candies have between 54 and 62 chocolates.
B) All of the jars of chocolate produced that day at Clark's Candies have between 54 and 62 chocolates.
C) It is plausible that the mean number of chocolates in each jar produced that day at Clark's Candies is between 54 and 62 chocolates.
D) It is plausible that the mean number of chocolates in each jar ever produced at Clark's Candies is between 54 and 62 chocolates.

Solution: Given the mean and margin of error, it is plausible that the mean number of chocolates in each jar for all of the jars produced that day is between 54 and 62 chocolates. The margin of error does not mean that all of the jars fall within that range; there could have been an error and a jar with only 40 candies could have been produced, so B is incorrect. Also, the sample can only give data about the day when it was conducted, so answer choices A and D, which talk about all of the jars ever produced, are incorrect. **The answer is C.**

Example 7: Researchers want to find the output of orange trees at George's farm in Vero Beach, Florida by randomly selecting 80 orange trees in his grove and counting the number of oranges each tree produces. After gathering the data, the researchers discovered that the trees on average produced 310 oranges per tree with a margin of error of 22 oranges. Which of the following statements is the most appropriate conclusion from these findings?

A) The mean number of oranges produced per tree for all farms in Vero Beach, Florida is between 288 and 332 oranges.
B) The number of oranges per tree on all trees on George's farm is between 288 and 332 oranges.
C) It is plausible that the mean number of oranges produced by each tree on George's farm is between 288 and 332 oranges.
D) All trees in Vero Beach, Florida produce between 288 and 332 oranges.

Solution: Given the mean and margin of error, it is plausible that the mean number of oranges produced by each tree at George's farm is between 288 and 332. We can only apply the data to George's farm since all of the trees selected were on his farm, so A, which talks about all farms in Vero Beach, is incorrect. The margin of error tells us about the mean value for all trees, not the exact value on each individual tree, so answer choices B and D are incorrect. **The answer is C.**

There is one other important principle to understand for margin of error:

> **A larger data set will most likely have a smaller margin of error, and a smaller data set will most likely have a larger margin of error.**

If you think about sampling, this makes perfect sense. The more data points you gather, the more likely you are to be closer to the true mean. For example, let's say that Joe and Tommy are trying to find out how many watches are owned by each student in the 11th grade. If Joe only asks 5 students and Tommy asks 60, the mean value of Tommy's data set will likely be much closer to the true mean value for all students than the mean from Joe's data set. In other words, Tommy's data set will have a much smaller margin of error than Joe's.

Here is an example of how this type of question may appear on the SAT.

> **Example 8:** Rebecca and Simone survey people in their town and ask people to rank, on a scale of 1 to 10, how much they care about saving tigers in the wild. Rebecca surveys 125 people, and Simone surveys 52. Both Rebecca and Simone find that the mean survey response was 5.5. Which of the following statements is most likely to be true?
>
> A) The range for Rebecca's survey responses is larger than the range for Simone's survey responses.
> B) The range for Rebecca's survey responses is smaller than the range for Simone's survey responses.
> C) The margin of error for Rebecca's survey responses is larger than the margin of error for Simone's survey responses.
> D) The margin of error for Rebecca's survey responses is smaller than the margin of error for Simone's survey responses.

Solution: Rebecca surveyed a larger number of people, so the margin of error for her survey responses is most likely smaller. The mean survey response and size of the survey does not tell us anything about the range, as we have no way to know the largest and smallest values in the survey, so answer choices A and B are both wrong. **The answer is D.**

Statistical Bias

Statistical bias is when a model or statistic does not accurately represent the population that was surveyed. Below, we will cover the common surveying mistakes that can lead to a sample having bias and not accurately reflecting the general population. **If statistical bias occurs, the results of the survey will somehow be skewed because participants were not selected at random, and the findings cannot be applied to the general population.**

1. **Sampling bias occurs whenever the population is not randomly sampled.** Anytime the participants are not selected randomly, the results from the sample will not be representative of the population.

   For example, let's say you wanted to find the average number of kids per household in a neighborhood. If you go to the community pool and ask people how many kids they have, this creates sampling bias because individuals at the community pool are more likely to have kids. To do this survey correctly, you would need to randomly select houses in your neighborhood and then ask the people at these houses how many kids they have.

2. **Self-Selection bias occurs when individuals are selecting themselves to be part of a sample.** If a survey is voluntary, only certain people will take the effort to respond to the survey, but this choosing to respond may correlate with other behaviors. The results from any sample with self-selection bias will not be representative of the population.

For example, let's say you want to find out why lawyers in San Francisco think they were successful. To do so, you send out an email to 500 lawyers in San Francisco and ask them to come in and answer a few questions about how they achieved success. This will generate self-selection bias. The most successful lawyers will likely be too busy to take time to come in for an interview for your survey. In addition, the lawyers who did come in may be likely to overexaggerate their success and not give honest feedback. To do this survey correctly, you would need to find a method that generates a completely random sample of lawyers to come in for the interview and gets honest responses to the survey questions.

3. **Cause-Effect bias occurs when a correlation between two variables leads us to incorrectly believe that there is a cause-and-effect relationship.**

For example, after selecting a group of 2,000 people and examining their breakfast diets and health, researchers found that those who ate fruit at breakfast had a lower rate of heart attacks. This does not mean that eating fruit for breakfast lowers the risk of a heart attack. Most likely, people who eat fruit with breakfast have a healthier lifestyle compared to those who eat less healthy options. This healthier lifestyle, not just the fruit at breakfast, more likely causes the lower rate of heart attacks.

Any survey with any of these three biases produces a data set that is not reliable. As a result, the findings cannot be generalized to a larger population.

Example 9: Three separate studies examined the number of countries a junior at Fenwick High could name in 30 seconds. The participants for the studies were selected as follows:

    I.   For Study 1, 200 juniors from Fenwick High volunteered to participate.
    II.   For Study 2, 150 juniors from Fenwick High were randomly selected to participate.
    III.   For Study 3, 125 of the 250 juniors at Fenwick High who are currently enrolled in world history were selected at random to participate.

The results of which studies can appropriately be generalized to the entire population of juniors at Fenwick High?

    A) Study I   B) Study II   C) Studies II and III   D) Studies I, II, and III

Solution: Study I is not random since students volunteer, so Study 1 has self-selection bias. Study III has sampling bias because students who are enrolled in world history may have better knowledge of countries than a randomly selected student. Study II uses a randomly selected population, so we can generalize the results to the entire population of juniors at Fenwick High. **The answer is B.**

Example 10: Penelope wants to find out how much people spend on organic produce each week in her town. To do so, she goes to Mark's Organic Market, a market that specializes in selling organic items, and surveys people at the market. Penelope surveys 218 people and finds that the mean amount spent on organic produce each week is $43 with a margin of error of $4. Which of the following is the best interpretation of Penelope's finding?

    A) The mean number of dollars spent on organic produce each week for all of the people in Penelope's town is $43.
    B) It is plausible that the mean number of dollars spent on organic produce each week for all people in Penelope's town is between $39 and $47.
    C) If Penelope surveys another 218 people at Mark's Organic Market, the mean number of dollars spent on organic produce will be $43.
    D) Penelope's method for collecting data is flawed, so we cannot make any conclusions about the amount of money the rest of the town spends on organic produce.

Solution: Since Penelope conducts the survey at Mark's Organic Market, she is not sampling a random population and her findings cannot be generalized to the rest of the town. People shopping at Mark's Organic Market likely will spend more on organic produce than shoppers at other grocery stores. **The answer is D.**

Box and Whisker Plot

A box and whisker plot is another way that a data set can be visually displayed. The box and whisker plot gives a five-number summary of the data: the minimum, the maximum, the first quartile, the median, and the third quartile.

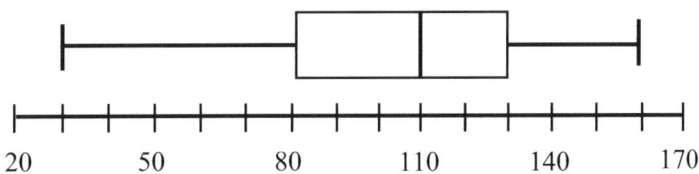

- **The whiskers display the minimum and maximum of the data.** For the example plot, the minimum is at 30 and the maximum is at 160.

- **The box ranges from the first quartile (25th percentile) to the third quartile (75th percentile) of the data.** In other words, the middle 50% of the data points, those from the 25th to 75th percentiles, all fall within the box. The first quartile, the lowest 25% of data points, is from the minimum to the left edge of the box. The fourth quartile, the largest 25% of data points, is from the right side of the box to the maximum.

- **The middle line in the box displays the median for the data.** For the example plot, the median is 110.

Example 11: Ms. Pearson's first and second period classes each sold brownies to raise money for charity after a forest fire destroyed many local businesses. There are 24 students in the first period class and 29 in the second period class. Each student in the class sold brownies and then reported the number of brownies they sold to Ms. Pearson. The data for the number of brownies sold by each student are displayed in the box and whisker plot below. If a represents the median for the first period class and b represents the median for the second period class, what is the value of $a - b$?

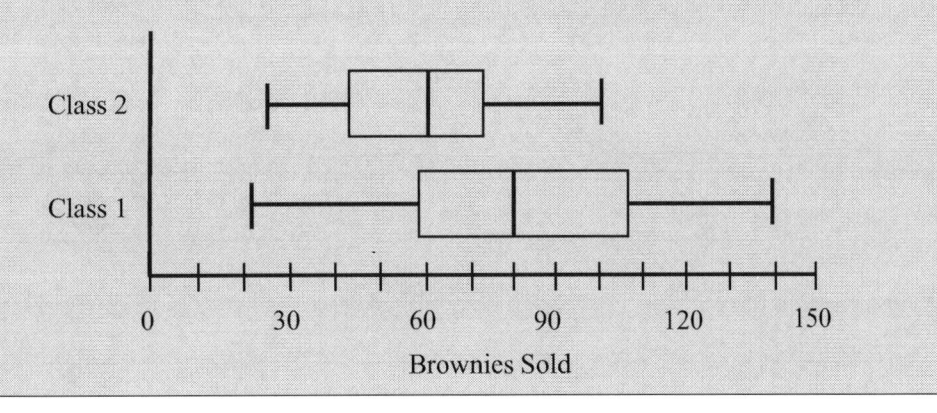

Solution: The median value is the line in the middle of the box. For class 1, the median is 80, so $a = 80$. For class 2, the median is 60, so $b = 60$. So, we know that $a - b = 80 - 60 = 20$. **The answer is 20.**

For a question like this where you are asked approximate values, the SAT will count multiple answers as correct. For the figure above, we cannot tell that the medians are at exactly 60 and 80. If you estimated the median for class 1 as 79 and the median for class 2 was 61 and you wrote your answer as 18, it would still be counted as correct. For Example 10, we would count any answer from 18 to 22 as correct.

Statistical Analysis Practice: Answers on page 332.

1. Which of the following is true about the standard deviations of the two data sets in the table below?

   | Set A | 30 | 45 | 55 | 75 | 80 | 90 |
   | Set B | 8 | 40 | 79 | 90 | 110 | 140 |

   A) The standard deviation of data set A is larger than the standard deviation of data set B.
   B) The standard deviation of data set B is larger than the standard deviation of data set A.
   C) The standard deviation in both data sets is identical.
   D) There is not enough information available to compare the standard deviations of the two data sets.

2. A school librarian wants to predict how often students at Walker High School will want to use a new 3D printer. Which of the following study designs will most likely provide reliable results for the librarian?

   A) Polling 120 random students who are in the library.
   B) Using an online survey that gets responses from 30,000 high school students.
   C) Randomly selecting 500 students at Walker High School to complete a questionnaire.
   D) Asking 1,000 Walker High School students and parents to volunteer to complete a survey.

3. Which of the given data sets has a greater standard deviation?

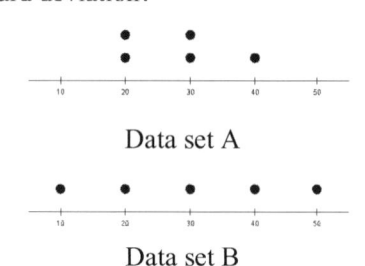

   Data set A

   Data set B

   A) Data set A
   B) Data set B
   C) The standard deviations of data set A and data set B are equal.
   D) There is not enough information to determine which data set has a greater standard deviation.

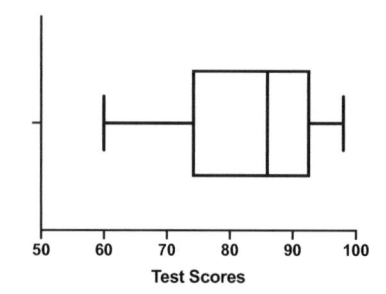

4.

   The box and whisker plot above displays information about the test scores for students on the final exam. Which of the following is the median test score on the final exam?

   A) 60
   B) 75
   C) 87
   D) 94

5. Everyone must pass a driver education test in order to get a driver's license. This year, California offered a new program where students could attend an additional review session for free before taking the test. The students who went to the additional review session scored higher on the test on average than those who did not. Which of the following is a valid conclusion based on this information?

   A) The extra review session caused the enrolled students to do better on the driving test.
   B) The extra review session will cause anyone to do better on the driving test.
   C) An extra review session will help anyone do better in any type of class.
   D) You cannot make a conclusion about the cause and effect of going to an extra review session before taking the driving test.

6. A researcher asked a randomly selected group of 5,000 oncologists if they believed that cancer will be cured in the next 50 years. Using the survey data, the researcher found that 18% of the oncologists believe that cancer will be cured in the next 50 years with a margin of error of 3%. Which of the following is the most appropriate conclusion about all oncologists based on the given findings and margin of error?

   A) It is plausible that the percentage of all oncologists who believe cancer will be cured in the next 50 years is between 15% and 21%.
   B) The researcher is between 15% and 21% sure that most oncologists believe cancer will be cured in the next 50 years.
   C) It is unlikely that less than 18% of oncologists believe cancer will be cured in the next 50 years.
   D) At least 18% but no more than 21% of oncologists believe cancer will be cured in the next 50 years.

7. Two hundred members at Axburry Golf Club will be selected to participate in a survey about the menu for the annual club championship dinner. Which of the following methods would result in a random sample of members of the Axburry Golf Club?

   A) Obtain an alphabetical list of all Axburry Golf Club members. Select the first two hundred people.
   B) Obtain a numbered list of all Axburry Golf Club members. Use a random number generator to select 200 members from the list. Give the survey to those members.
   C) Obtain a list of Axburry Golf Club members attending the club championship dinner. Give the survey to the first 200 members who arrive.
   D) Tell all Axburry Golf Club members that volunteers are needed to take a survey. Give the survey to the first 200 volunteers.

8. To determine if residents of Cardiff would support a measure to spend $50,000 to build a new skate park, Jonathan surveyed 100 people at a popular skate spot. 70% of the people surveyed said they would support the measure. Which of the following statements must be true?

   A) When the measure is voted on, 70% of Cardiff residents will vote yes.
   B) The sample size is too small to have any useful data.
   C) The margin of error is not provided, so we cannot make a valid conclusion.
   D) The sampling method is flawed and will likely produce a biased result.

9. A sample of 75 employees from the legal department at Company A was selected at random. The 75 employees completed a survey about an application's effectiveness at helping them meditate during the workday, and 82% found the application effective. Which of the following is the largest population to which the results of this survey can be generalized?

   A) All employees in the legal department at company A.
   B) All employees in a legal department in the United States.
   C) All employees in the sample.
   D) All employees at Company A.

10. A news website invited readers to respond to a poll at the end of the article that asked, "Do you think the new federal budget will help our economy?" The survey found that 65% of respondents said "Yes" and 31% said "No". Which of the following best explains why these results are unlikely to represent the beliefs of the entire US population?

    A) Those who responded to the poll do not represent a random sample of US residents.
    B) The news website did not share how many people responded to the poll.
    C) The percentages do not add up to 100%, so any possible conclusions from the data are invalid.
    D) The poll was not posted on the website for a long enough time, so there is not enough data to make any valid conclusions.

11.
| Set A | 2,420 | 3,480 | 5,600 | 7,843 | 9,867 |
| Set B | 10,452 | 25,460 | 38,499 | 50,480 | 80,260 |

Which of the following is true about the standard deviations of the two data sets above?

A) The standard deviation for set B is larger than for set A.
B) The standard deviation for set A is larger than for set B.
C) The standard deviations for set A and for set B are equal.
D) There is not enough information to compare the standard deviations of the sets.

12.

The box and whisker plot above displays information about the height of plants in a garden. Which of the following values is closest to the range for the heights of the plants in the garden?

A) 13
B) 18
C) 20
D) 24

13. A market researcher asked 150 randomly selected people who like a local market's tri tip sandwiches if they like the local market's new Reuben sandwich. 78% of the people said that they like the new Reuben sandwich. Which of the following inferences can be appropriately drawn from this survey?

A) Exactly 78% of people will like the new Reuben sandwich.
B) Exactly 78% of people who like the local market's tri tip sandwich will like the new Reuben sandwich.
C) Around 78% of people will like the new Reuben sandwich.
D) Around 78% of people who like the local market's tri tip sandwich will like the new Reuben sandwich.

14. Donovan asked 47 of his classmates about their grades on the last US history test. Christina measured 124 tomato plants one month after sprouting and recorded their heights. Box and whisker plots of their results are below.

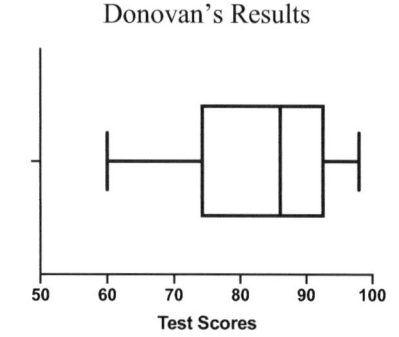

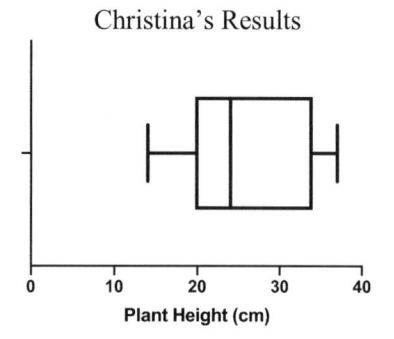

Donovan's Results

Christina's Results

If d is the median test score from Donovan's survey and c is the median plant height from Christina's data and both d and c are integers, what is a possible value of $d - c$? (Note: median values must be estimated for this question, but there are multiple correct answers).

15. Erica wants to predict if over 50% of seniors will vote to change the school mascot. A majority vote is needed to change the mascot. Erica randomly selects 140 of her classmates to ask about the vote, and 51% of her classmates say they will vote to change the mascot. The associated margin of error with Erica's survey is 2.5%. Based on the survey's results, which of the following is accurate?

    A) Erica's survey does not provide sufficient information to conclude if the seniors will vote to change the mascot.
    B) 51% of the seniors will vote to change the mascot.
    C) The seniors will vote to change the mascot, but the exact percentage of votes in favor cannot be predicted.
    D) The seniors will vote to change the mascot with at least 53.5% of the vote.

16. To determine if eating chocolate has an effect on men's standardized test scores, researchers surveyed a random population of 8,000 men. Study participants were identified as regular chocolate eaters or non-chocolate eaters and were given a standardized test. They found that the regular chocolate eaters had higher scores than the non-chocolate eaters. What is the most appropriate conclusion for this study?

    A) Eating chocolate regularly causes higher standardized test scores for men and women.
    B) Eating chocolate regularly causes higher standardized test scores for men but not necessarily for women.
    C) There is an association between eating chocolate and higher standardized test scores for men and women, but it is not necessarily a cause-and-effect relationship.
    D) There is an association between eating chocolate and higher standardized test score for men, but it is not necessarily a cause-and-effect relationship and it does not necessarily exist for women.

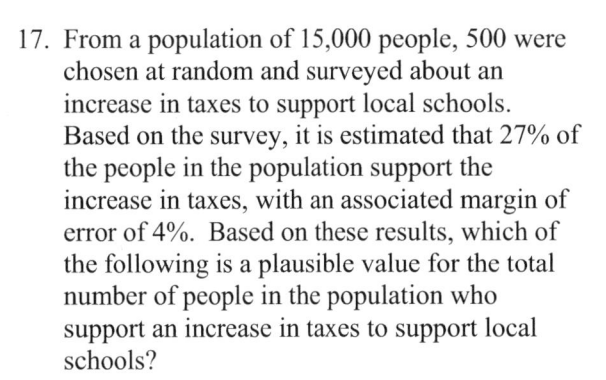

17. From a population of 15,000 people, 500 were chosen at random and surveyed about an increase in taxes to support local schools. Based on the survey, it is estimated that 27% of the people in the population support the increase in taxes, with an associated margin of error of 4%. Based on these results, which of the following is a plausible value for the total number of people in the population who support an increase in taxes to support local schools?

    A) 135
    B) 150
    C) 3,750
    D) 5,250

18. The principal of a local high school is conducting a survey on whether students felt online learning was still effective during the COVID-19 pandemic. Of the 200 students who were randomly sampled, 43% felt that online learning is still effective. Based on the margin of error, the principal expects that somewhere between 35% and 51% of all students feel that online learning is still effective during the COVID-19 pandemic. What is the margin of error?

    A) 43%
    B) 16%
    C) 8%
    D) 2%

19. There are 50 unique numbers in a data set. If the value of each number increases by 25%, which of the following will be true?

    A) The new mean will remain the same, but the new standard deviation will be 25% more than the previous standard deviation.
    B) The new mean will be 25% more than the previous mean, but the standard deviation will remain the same.
    C) The new mean will be 25% more than the previous mean, but the standard deviation will increase.
    D) Neither the mean nor the standard deviation of the values will change.

Questions 20 and 21 refer to the following information.

At a business with 3,000 employees, Chloe and Amy conduct a survey to find out how much money people spent on groceries each week. Both Chloe and Amy mailed out surveys to randomly selected employees. 180 people responded to Chloe's survey and 100 people responded to Amy's survey. The results from Chloe's and Amy's surveys are summarized below:

Chloe's Survey Results

Grocery Spending (USD)	Number of Employees
Less than 100	12
100-199	26
200-299	39
300-400	68
Greater than 400	35

Amy's Survey Results

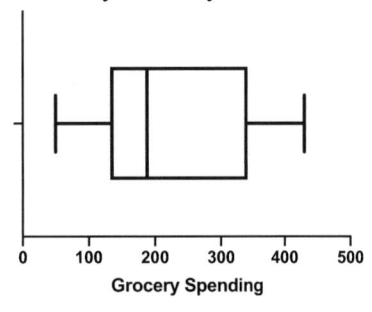

20. Which of the following statements about the median values in Chloe's and Amy's survey results is accurate?

   A) The median value in Chloe's results is higher than the median value in Amy's results.
   B) The median value in Amy's results is higher than the median value in Chloe's results.
   C) The median values in Amy's and Chloe's results are the same.
   D) There is not enough information to determine whether the median value in Amy's or Chloe's results is higher.

21. Which of the following box and whisker plots correctly displays Chloe's survey results?

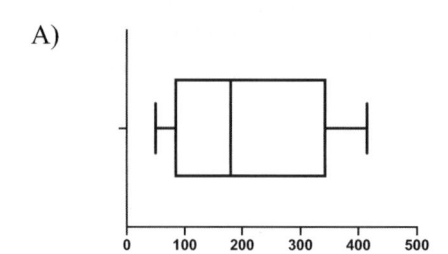

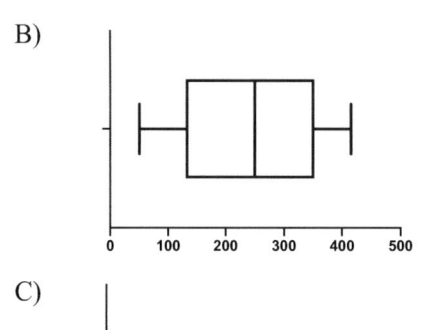

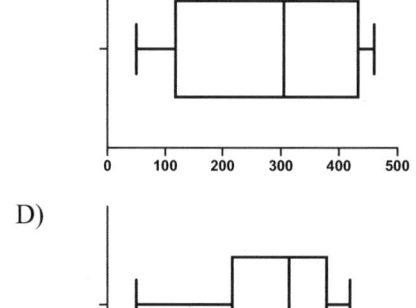

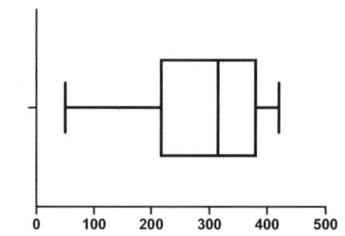

   A)
   B)
   C)
   D)

22. Two companies used the same sampling method to conduct polls to determine the proportion of residents in favor of the construction of a new basketball facility in the town. Both companies surveyed participants selected at random from the same population. Company A used a sample of 730 residents, and Company B used a sample of 430 residents. Which of the following statements is most likely true?

A) The proportion of residents in favor of the construction will be smaller in Company A's survey than in Company B's survey.
B) The proportion of residents in favor of the construction will be smaller in Company B's survey than in Company A's survey.
C) The margin of error associated with the proportion in Company A's survey will be smaller than the margin of error associated with the proportion in Company B's survey.
D) The margin of error associated with the proportion in Company B's survey will be smaller than the margin of error associated with the proportion in Company A's survey.

23. A San Diego marine biologist went to La Jolla and selected a random sample of 15 sea lions for a study about sea lion mass. The marine biologist found that the mean mass of the sea lions in the sample was 480 pounds, with an associated margin of error of 38 pounds. Which of the following is the best interpretation of the marine biologist's findings?

A) All sea lions in the sample have a mass between 442 pounds and 518 pounds.
B) Most sea lions have a mass between 442 pounds and 518 pounds.
C) Any mass between 442 pounds and 518 pounds is a plausible value for the mean mass of the sea lions in La Jolla.
D) Any sea lion at La Jolla shores has a mass between 442 pounds and 518 pounds.

24. A biologist wanted to study the effectiveness of a fertilizer on the growth of corn seeds. To make the conditions as similar as possible for all plants, a greenhouse was used. The greenhouse was split down the middle and half A of the greenhouse was treated with the fertilizer being studied throughout the experiment and half B was not. The biologist obtained two 750-seed packages. The seeds from one package were planted in the soil treated by the fertilizer, and the seeds from one package were planted in the soil not treated by the fertilizer. How should the experiment be changed to allow the researched to conclude whether the fertilizer has an effect on the growth of corn seeds?

A) No changes to the experiment are required.
B) All 1,500 corn seeds should receive the fertilizer.
C) One of the packages of corn seeds should be planted in a field rather than the greenhouse.
D) Half of the seeds from each package should be randomly assigned to each half of the greenhouse.

25. The standard deviation of data set A is x, and the standard deviation of data set B is y. Which of the following statements about the standard deviation of the data sets is true?

Data Set A	19	19	21	21	23	24	24
Data Set B	1	1	3	3	5	6	6

A) $x > y$
B) $x = y$
C) $x < y$
D) The relationship between x and y cannot be determined.

26. A study conducted by a physician found that the average number of hours 11th graders in high school spent sleeping during weeknights was 7.2, with an associated margin of error of 0.7 hours. The study was then repeated with a much smaller sample size, with the mean and margin of error of the new sample being calculated in the same way as the original study. Which of the following is most likely true?

A) The margin of error of the new study is larger than the margin of error of the original study.
B) The margin of error of the new study is smaller than the margin of error of the original study.
C) The mean from the new study is larger than the mean from the original study.
D) The mean from the new study is smaller than the mean from the original study.

27. A data set of 77 different numbers has a mean of 1,073. A new data set is created by adding 93 to each number in the original data set that is greater than the median and subtracting 93 from each number in the original data set that is less than the median. Which of the following measures does NOT have the same value in both the original and the new data sets?

A) Sum of the numbers
B) Mean
C) Standard deviation
D) Median

28. Data set *A* consists of 18 different values that have a minimum of 12, a maximum of 80, a mean of 46 and a standard deviation of 17. The values 12 and 80 are removed from the set to create data set *B*, which consists of 16 different values. Which of the following statements is true?

A) The mean of data set *B* is greater than 46.
B) The mean of data set *B* is less than 46.
C) The standard deviation of data set *B* is greater than 17.
D) The standard deviation of data set *B* is less than 17.

29. The dot plot represents 13 values in data set A. Data set B is created by adding 39 to each of the values is data set A. Which of the following correctly compares the median and standard deviations of data sets A and B?

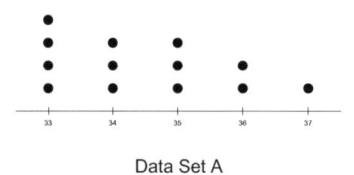

Data Set A

A) The median of data set B is equal to the median of data set A, and the standard deviation of data set B is equal to the standard deviation of data set A.
B) The median of data set B is greater to the median of data set A, and the standard deviation of data set B is equal to the standard deviation of data set A.
C) The median of data set B is greater to the median of data set A, and the standard deviation of data set B is greater than the standard deviation of data set A.
D) The median of data set B is less than the median of data set A, and the standard deviation of data set B is equal to the standard deviation of data set A.

Chapter 22: Statistical Analysis

30. The dot plots shown each represent a data set. Which of the following statements best compares the means and standard deviations of the two data sets?

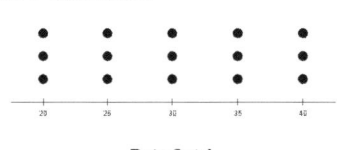

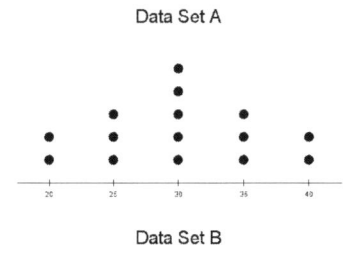

    Data Set A

    Data Set B

    A) The standard deviations are equal: the mean of data set A is less than the mean of data set B.
    B) The standard deviations are equal: the mean of data set B is less than the mean of data set A.
    C) The means are equal: the standard deviation of data set A is less than the standard deviation of data set B.
    D) The means are equal: the standard deviation of data set B is less than the standard deviation of data set A.

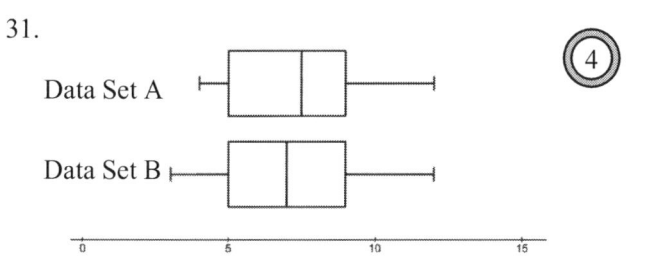

31.

    Data Set A

    Data Set B

    The box plots above summarize data set A and data set B. Each of the data sets consists of a total of 200 integers. Which of the following statements must be true?

    I. The mean of data set A must be greater than the mean of data set B.
    II. The median of data set A must be greater than the median of data set B.

    A) I only
    B) II only
    C) I and II
    D) Neither I nor II

32. The dot plots shown summarize the daily sales of brownies from a bakery for the 23 days the store was open in October and November, respectively. Which of the following was(were) the same for daily sales in October and November?

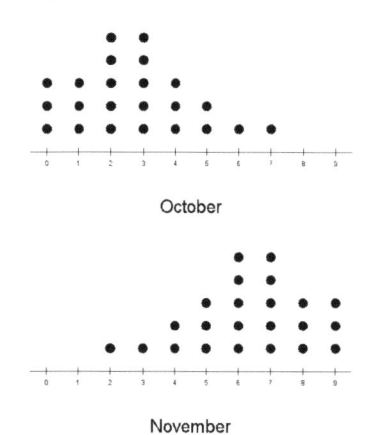

    October

    November

    I. Median
    II. Standard Deviation

    A) I only
    B) II only
    C) Both I and II
    D) Neither I nor II

Chapter 23: Ratios and Proportions

We use ratios to make comparisons between two things. Ratios do not give the exact number of items but instead allow you to concisely compare the relationship between two things at the same time.

As an example, if we have oranges and apples in a basket in the ratio of 2: 3, it does not necessarily mean that we have 2 oranges and 3 apples. Instead, the ratio tells us that for every 2 oranges, there are 3 apples. As a result, **you can think of this ratio as $2x$: $3x$** because we must multiply 2 and 3 by the same value to keep the 2:3 ratio. Using this "x" trick can help you on many ratio questions where you are given a ratio but not any exact numbers.

On the SAT, you will need to solve ratio questions in four different ways. We will review the four types below along with the method(s) to solve them:

#1 - Ratio and a Total

Example 1: The ratio of red marbles to green marbles in a bag is 4: 6. If there are a total of 80 marbles in the bag and all of the marbles in the bag are red or green, how many of the marbles are red?

Solution: Method #1: The "x" trick. We can think of the ratio 4: 6 as $4x$: $6x$, where the $4x$ represents the red marbles and the $6x$ represents the green marbles.

$$\text{Red Marbles} + \text{Green Marbles} = 80$$
$$4x + 6x = 80$$
$$10x = 80$$
$$x = 8$$

To solve for the red marbles, we need to plug the x value back in to the $4x$.

$$\text{Red Marbles} = 4x = 4(8) = 32$$

The answer is 32.

Method #2: Set up a Proportion. We can set up a proportion from the ratio. Since the ratio of red marbles to green marbles is 4: 6, we know that there are 4 red marbles for every 10 total marbles.

$$\frac{\text{red marbles}}{\text{total marbles}} = \frac{4}{10}$$

Since there are 80 total marbles, we can set up an equation to solve for the unknown number of red marbles.

$$\frac{x}{80} = \frac{4}{10}$$
$$10x = 320$$
$$x = 32$$

The answer is 32.

#2 – Ratios as Proportions

Example 2: Beth is baking her famous chocolate cupcakes for her mother's birthday party. For every 3 cupcakes, Beth uses 10 pieces of chocolate. If Beth needs to make 42 cupcakes for the party, how many pieces of chocolate will she need to buy?

Solution: Set up the values from the ratio as a proportion. Here, we set up the proportion as

$$\frac{\text{cupcakes}}{\text{pieces of choclate}} = \frac{\text{cupcakes}}{\text{pieces of choclate}}$$

Now, we can plug in the values from the question and solve.

$$\frac{3 \text{ cupcakes}}{10 \text{ pieces of chocolate}} = \frac{42 \text{ cupcakes}}{x \text{ pieces of chocolate}}$$

$$3x = 420$$

$$x = \frac{420}{3} = 140$$

The answer is 140.

#3 – Comparing Across Ratios

Example 3: The ratio of x to y is 3:4. The ratio of y to z is 2:10. What is the ratio of $x:z$?
A) 3:10   B) 3:20   C) 15:4   D) 4:15

Solution: We need to make the variable that appears in both ratios, y, have the same numerical value. To do that, we multiply the second ratio by 2, so

$$\begin{matrix} x:y & y:z \\ 3:4 & 2:10 \end{matrix}$$

becomes

$$\begin{matrix} x:y & y:z \\ 3:4 & 4:20 \end{matrix}$$

Now that the y-values are the same (both are equal to 4), we can compare across the ratios to find $x:z$.

$$x:z = 3:20$$

The answer is B.

#4 – Ratios and Geometry

Example 4: In rectangle ABCD, the ratio of the lengths of side AB to side BC is 8:5. If the total perimeter of the rectangle is 156 feet, what is the length of the longer side of the rectangle?

Solution: To start, sketch out rectangle ABCD. We can think of the ratio as $8x:5x$ instead of just $8:5$. We can label the sides of our rectangle using $8x$ and $5x$ as the side lengths.

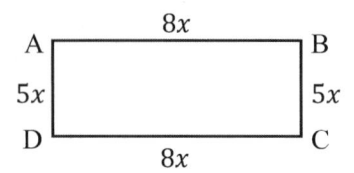

The perimeter of the rectangle is

$$8x + 8x + 5x + 5x = 156$$

$$26x = 156$$

$$x = \frac{156}{26} = 6$$

Now that we have solved for x, we can solve for the longer sides of the rectangle.

$$\text{Longer Sides} = 8x = 8(6) = 48$$

The answer is 48.

Ratios and Proportions Practice: Answers on page 332.

1. If a dodgeball team has 6 girls and 11 total team members, what is the ratio of boys to girls?

    A) 5:6
    B) 6:5
    C) 12:10
    D) 15:6

2. There are 35 goldfish and 42 tetras in a fish tank. What is the ratio of goldfish to tetras?

    A) 1:5
    B) 5:6
    C) 5:11
    D) 6:5

3. On a map, $\frac{1}{5}$ inch represents 10 miles. How many inches represent 350 miles?

4. The ratio of blue blocks to red blocks in a child's building set is 7 to 3. If there are 42 blue blocks, how many red blocks are there?

5. A factory that produces fidget spinners can make 2,000 fidget spinners each hour. Of those 2,000 fidget spinners, 17 are randomly selected and inspected. If the factory produces 30,000 fidget spinners this week, how many will be selected for inspection?

    A) 170
    B) 205
    C) 225
    D) 255

Chapter 23: Ratios and Proportions

6. The combined length of 3 pieces of fabric is 105 inches. The lengths of the pieces are in a 4:5:6 ratio. What is the length, in inches, of the longest piece of fabric?

   A) 7
   B) 28
   C) 35
   D) 42

7. A state lottery has 2 out of every 9 tickets as a winner. Yesterday, 120 people bought a winning ticket. How many total tickets were purchased yesterday?

   A) 240
   B) 540
   C) 780
   D) 1080

8. Bailey is baking bread, and the recipe calls for $\frac{3}{4}$ of a teaspoon of yeast and $3\frac{1}{2}$ cups of flour. She decides to use an entire 3 teaspoon pack of yeast and will keep the same yeast to flour ratio. How many cups of flour will she need?

   A) $3\frac{1}{2}$
   B) 7
   C) $10\frac{1}{2}$
   D) 14

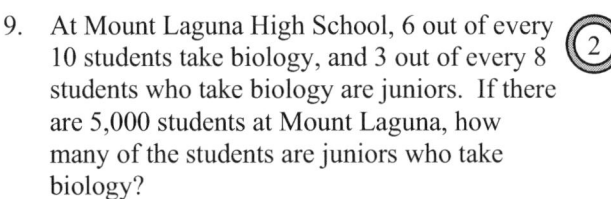

9. At Mount Laguna High School, 6 out of every 10 students take biology, and 3 out of every 8 students who take biology are juniors. If there are 5,000 students at Mount Laguna, how many of the students are juniors who take biology?

   A) 1,125
   B) 1,214
   C) 1,270
   D) 1,596

10. If $x:y = 7:2$ and $y:z = 3:2$, what is the ratio of $x:z$?

    A) 3:1
    B) 7:2
    C) 14:4
    D) 21:4

11. In a triangle, the lengths of the three sides are in the ratio of 3:6:7. If the longest side is 28, what is the length of the perimeter?

12. Abby's age is three times Beth's age, and Beth's age is 5 times Cathy's age. What is the ratio of Abby's age to Cathy's age?

    A) 15:1
    B) 3:5
    C) 5:3
    D) 1:15

13. Atrazine, a weed killer commonly used by farmers, is such a concentrated substance that only 1L can be used to spray up to 4 hectares of farm fields. If one hectare is equal to approximately $2\frac{1}{2}$ acres, how many acres of farm fields could 25 L of atrazine be used to spray?

    A) 100
    B) 150
    C) 250
    D) 1,750

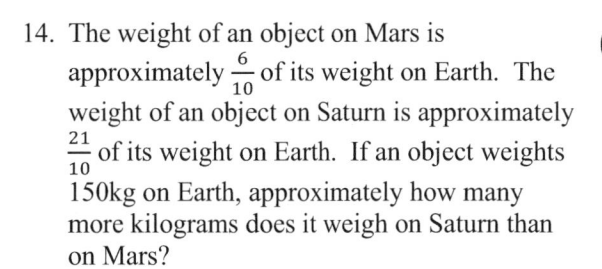

14. The weight of an object on Mars is approximately $\frac{6}{10}$ of its weight on Earth. The weight of an object on Saturn is approximately $\frac{21}{10}$ of its weight on Earth. If an object weights 150kg on Earth, approximately how many more kilograms does it weigh on Saturn than on Mars?

    A) 60
    B) 150
    C) 210
    D) 225

15. A model of the library that will be built next year is currently on display in the principal's office. The model is 36 inches tall and 65 inches wide. The model is $\frac{1}{25}$ the size of the actual building. What will be the height, in feet, of the library?

PrepPros

16. A biologist determined that the healthy ratio of males to females in a healthy zebra herd is 4 to 13. If a zebra herd has a population of 731, how many female zebras are in the herd for it to be healthy?

17. In a certain rectangle, the ratio of the length to the width is 7:4. If the area of the rectangle is 252 square inches, how many inches long is the width?

A) 12
B) 14
C) 18
D) 24

18. A bakery has a daily sales ratio of croissants to cookies of 4:5. The bakery normally sells 104 croissants on Saturday. This Saturday, the bakery sold 24 more croissants than normal. If the daily sales ratio of croissants to cookies remains the same, how many cookies were sold this Saturday?

19. For a certain rectangular region, the ratio of its length to width is 25 to 7. If the width of the rectangular region increases by 14 units, how must the length change to maintain this ratio?

A) It must decrease by 50 units.
B) It must decrease by 3.92 units.
C) It must increase by 3.92 units.
D) It must increase by 50 units.

20. A rectangular painting has a width of 360 inches and a length of 450 inches. A scale drawing of this painting has a length of l inches. Which of the following equations gives the area $A(l)$, in square inches, of the scale drawing of the painting?

A) $1.25l^2$
B) $0.8l^2$
C) $\dfrac{l^2}{0.8}$
D) $\dfrac{l^2}{1.2}$

21. Demi is designing a rectangular planter bed so that the ratio of the length of the garden to its width is 5 to 3. If the area of the garden is 135 square feet, what is the perimeter, in feet, of the garden?

22. A proposal for a new robotics laboratory was voted on by students at a university. The head of the committee assigned to the project stated that 4 times as many people voted against the proposal as people who voted for it did. Additionally, the head of the committee stated that 600 more people voted against the proposal than those who voted for the proposal. Based on this data, how many people voted for the proposal?

23. The high school football team is raising money to upgrade the turf on the field. The team has only sophomore, junior, and senior members. The ratio of sophomores to juniors to seniors on the football team is 2:4:5. Sophomores on average raised $40 per person, juniors on average raised $55 per person, and seniors on average raised $72 per person. What is the average amount raised per team member?

A) 57
B) 59
C) 60
D) 62

- 228 -

24. In the figure below, E is the point of intersection of the line segments AC and BD. Line segments AB and DC are parallel. The length of line segment BD is 286. What is the length of line segment BE?

B
91
　　　　　　　　　C
　　　　E　　　52
A
　　　　　　D

Note: Figure not drawn to scale

25. Javon is constructing a box. The ratio of the length to the width to the height of the box must be 5 to 4 to 2. If the volume of the box is 2,560 in^3, what is the height, in inches, of the box?

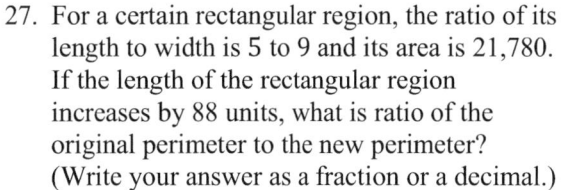

A) 4
B) 8
C) 20
D) 32

26. There are two alpaca farms. Farm A and farm B. The ratio of male alpacas to female alpacas is $1:17$ for the total number of alpacas on farms A and B. The ratio of male alpacas on Farm A to Farm B is $1:10$. Farm A has 360 total alpacas and farm B has 234 total alpacas. How many more female alpacas are there in farm A than farm B?

27. For a certain rectangular region, the ratio of its length to width is 5 to 9 and its area is 21,780. If the length of the rectangular region increases by 88 units, what is ratio of the original perimeter to the new perimeter? (Write your answer as a fraction or a decimal.)

Chapter 24: Mean, Median, Mode, and Range

To start, let's review the basic definitions of mean, median, mode, and range:

Mean (average): The sum divided by the number of items.

Median: The middle number in a list of numbers when ordered from smallest to largest.

Mode: The number that appears most often.

Range: The difference between the smallest and the largest numbers.

On the SAT, you are commonly asked to solve average questions. For these questions, remember that:

$$\text{Average} = \frac{\text{Sum}}{\text{Number of Items}}$$

Example 1: The five students who sit in the front row of Ms. Rashard's class averaged 24 points on last Friday's quiz. If the first four students received scores of 22, 28, 17, and 25, what was the score of the fifth student?

Solution: Let's call the unknown student's score x and set up the question using the average equation.

$$24 = \frac{22+28+17+25+x}{5}$$

$$24 = \frac{92+x}{5}$$

$$120 = 92 + x$$

$$x = 28$$

The answer is 28.

Example 2: The highest possible score on the biology final is 100 points. The first period class of 6 students has an average score of 85. The second period class of 9 students has an average score of 90. What is the average score for all of the students combined?

Solution: To solve this question, we need to find out the total number of points scored by all students from both classes and then divide by the total number of students (15).

In the equations below, x represents the sum of the test scores for students in the 1st period class and y represents the sum of the test scores for students in the second period class. To start, we can find the total number of points that all students in the first period class received.

$$85 = \frac{x}{6}$$

$$x = 510$$

The first period students received a total of 510 points. Even though we do not know each student's test score, we know the total. We can repeat this same calculation for the second period class.

$$90 = \frac{y}{9}$$

$$y = 810$$

The second period class received a total of 810 points. Now, we can solve for the average score for all students combined.

$$\text{Average Score} = \frac{\text{Total Points}}{\text{Total Students}} = \frac{510+810}{15} = \frac{1320}{15} = 88$$

The answer is 88.

> **Example 3:** Erica's golden retriever gave birth twice in the last two years. Her first litter had 7 puppies with an average weight of p lbs. Her second litter had 5 puppies with an average weight of m pounds. Which of the following expressions correctly calculates the average weight w, in pounds, of all of the puppies that Erica's golden retriever gave birth to over the last two years?
>
> A) $w = \frac{p+m}{12}$ B) $w = \frac{p}{7} + \frac{m}{5}$ C) $w = \frac{7p+5m}{12}$ D) $w = \frac{7m+5p}{12}$

Solution: Method #1 – "Math Teacher Way": To find the average puppy weight, we need to find the total weight of all the puppies and divide it by the total number of puppies. First, we can find the total weight of her first litter:

$$p = \frac{\text{sum}}{7}$$

$$7p = \text{total weight of puppies in 1st litter}$$

We can repeat this to find the total weight of the second litter:

$$m = \frac{\text{sum}}{5}$$

$$5m = \text{total weight of puppies in 2nd litter}$$

We know that there are 12 puppies total, so now we can calculate the average weight.

$$w = \frac{7p+5m}{12}$$

The answer is C.

Method #2 – Pick Numbers. For many students, this question is difficult because we are not given any values for the average weights of the litters. To make this question easier, we can use substitution and pick numbers. Let's say the first litter has an average weight of 1 pound ($p = 1$) and the second litter has an average weight of 3 pounds ($m = 3$). We can use our numbers to solve for the average weight of the puppies in both litters.

$$\text{Total Weight of 1st Litter} = 7 \times 1 = 7$$

The first litter had 7 puppies with an average weight of 1 pound, so the total weight of the litter is 7 pounds.

$$\text{Total Weight of 2nd Litter} = 5 \times 3 = 15$$

The second litter had 5 puppies with an average weight of 3 pounds, so the total weight is 15 pounds. Now, we can find the average weight of each puppy from these two litters.

$$w = \frac{7+15}{12} = \frac{22}{12} = \frac{11}{6}$$

With the values $p = 1$ and $m = 3$, we found that $w = \frac{11}{6}$. To find the correct answer choice, plug in $p = 1$ and $m = 3$ to the answer choices and see which one gives us $w = \frac{11}{6}$. Below, you can see how the correct answer choice C gives us the correct value for w.

$$w = \frac{7(1)+5(3)}{12} = \frac{22}{12} = \frac{11}{6}$$

The answer is C.

PrepPros

> **Example 4:** During the first 30 minutes of work at Birkee's Bakery, Vaivani decorated 23 cookies per minute for the first 10 minutes and then at 14 cookies per minute for the next 20 minutes. Which of the following gives the average number of cookies that Vaivani decorated per minute for her first 30 minutes at work?
>
> A. 15   B. 16   C. 16.5   D. 17   E. 18.5

Solution: In this question, we are given two averages that do not equally affect the final result. Since the first average of 23 cookies per minute is for 10 minutes and the second average of 14 cookies per minute is for 20 minutes, these averages cannot be treated equally. In math, this is called a **weighted average**. To solve weighted average questions with two items, we can use the equation below:

$$\text{Weighted Average} = \frac{(\text{average \#1})(\text{weight \#1}) + (\text{average \#2})(\text{weight \#2})}{\text{weight \#1} + \text{weight \#2}}$$

In this equation, the two averages are the given averages, so we plug in 23 for average #1 and 14 for average #2. The weight refers to the significance of the data point. Exactly what the weight is will depend on the question. For Example 4, the weight is the number of minutes, with 10 being weight #1 and 20 being weight #2. If there was a question where we were trying to calculate your final grade and 70% of your grade was from homework and 30% was from tests, the percentages of 70 and 30 would be the weights. The weights are used to reflect that certain averages have more "weight," or more significance, than others.

Now, let's get back to Example 4 and use the weighted average formula to solve:

$$\text{Average Number of Cookies} = \frac{(23)(10)+(14)(20)}{10+20} = 17$$

The answer is D.

The weighted average formula is a very important one and can be used to solve advanced SAT average questions. Looking back to Example 2, we can use a weighted average to solve. In that question, the averages are given as 85 for the first class and 90 for the second class. The weight is the number of students in each class, which is 6 and 9.

$$\text{Average Score} = \frac{(85)(6)+(90)(9)}{6+9} = 88$$

We even could use the weighted average formula for Example 3. The averages are given to be p and m. The weight is the number of puppies in each litter, which is 7 and 5.

$$\text{Average Puppy Weight} = \frac{(p)(7)+(m)(5)}{7+5} = \frac{7p+5m}{12}$$

Make sure that you understand how the weighted average formula works. As you can see, knowing how to properly find a weighted average can allow you to solve many difficult-looking average questions in one quick step.

> **Example 5:** The mean household income in a neighborhood with 80 residents is $90,250 per year. If a new family moves in with a household income of $1,859,000, which of the following values for the neighborhood will change the least?
>
> A) Mean   B) Median   C) Range   D) Standard Deviation

Solution: The new family has a much higher household income than the mean household income for the rest of the neighborhood. In statistics, we call values that are far higher or lower than any other numbers in the data set outliers. **Any outlier will greatly increase the range**. The new family's income is also so large that it will increase the mean household income for the neighborhood. The standard deviation, which is a measure of how close or far apart numbers in a data set are from the average, will also increase from an outlier. The median will change the least. Since the median is the middle value in a data set, **any outlier always has a minimal effect on the median.** **The answer is B.**

- 232 -

Chapter 24: Mean, Median, Mode, and Range

Example 6: For her science fair experiment, Monica wanted to find out whether her tree frog or bullfrog jumps farther. She placed each frog on a starting spot and then measured how far the frogs jumped, in inches. The results for each frog, in inches, are below:

Tree Frog: 41, 18, 30, 8, 14, 33
Bullfrog: 38, 19, 66, 48, 45, 33, 10

If f is the median jump length for the tree frog and h is the median jump length for the bullfrog, what is the value of $h - f$?

Solution: To start, we need to reorder the numbers in each data from smallest to largest.

Tree Frog: 8, 14, 18, 30, 33, 41
Bullfrog: 10, 19, 33, 38, 45, 48, 66

Next, we cross out numbers from both sides to find the median. **For data sets with an odd number of numbers, such as the bullfrog data in this question, the median is just the middle value. For data sets with an even number of numbers, such as the tree frog data in this question, we take the average of the two middle numbers to find the median.** Using this rule, we can find the values of f and h:

Tree Frog: 8̶, 1̶4̶, 18, 30, 3̶3̶, 4̶1̶

Tree Frog median $= f = \frac{18+30}{2} = 24$

Bullfrog: 1̶0̶, 1̶9̶, 3̶3̶, 38, 4̶5̶, 4̶8̶, 6̶6̶

Bullfrog median $= h = 38$

$$h - f = 38 - 24 = 14$$

The answer is 14.

Finding the Median in a Table

The SAT also asks you to find the median value in a frequency table. For these questions, we need to use a more efficient method than listing all of the values and crossing off to find the median value.

Example 7: The school newspaper recently surveyed 51 students about their monthly consumption of cheeseburgers. The results of the survey are summarized in the table below. What was the median number of cheeseburgers eaten each month by the students in the survey?

Number of Burgers Eaten	Number of Students
0	7
1	19
2 - 3	8
4 - 5	13
6 +	4

A) 0   B) 1   C) 2 - 3   D) 4 - 5

Solution: The trick to solving this question is to identify what term represents the median in the data set. To find the median term in a table, there are three quick steps:

1. **Add 1 to the total number of items in the data set.**
2. **Divide that number by 2.**
   - If you have a data set with an odd number of items, the number you get will be the term that it is the median. For example, if we have a group of 31, we will get 16 in step 2. This tell us that the 16th term is the median.

- 233 -

PrepPros

- If you have a data set with an even number of items, you will get an answer that ends in 0.5. In this case, the median will be the average of the two middle terms. The two middle terms will be the integers right above and below the value that we get from our first two steps. For example, if we have a group of 20, we will get 10.5 in step 2. This tell us that two middle terms will be the 10th and 11th terms. We find the median by finding the average of the 10th and 11th terms.

3. **Find where the term is in the table.**

In this question, we have 51 students who were surveyed, so following Step 1 above

$$\frac{51+1}{2} = 26$$

we find the 26th student will be the median data point in the set. To find where the 26th student is in the table, start at the top of the table and add up the students until you find the 26th student. Here, there are 7 students who ate 0 burgers and 19 who ate 1 burger. If we add 7 and 19 together, we get 26, so we can tell that the 26th student ate 1 burger. The median is 1, and **the answer is B**.

2-4 Finding the Median in a Dot Plot

You are commonly asked to find the median in a dot plot on the SAT. We have already introduced dot plots in chapter 22. If you are not familiar with dot plots, go back to chapter 22 to learn what dot plots are and how they work.

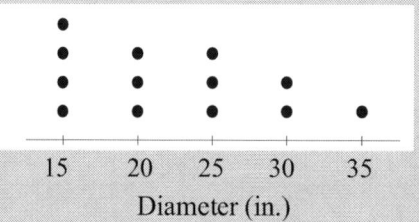

> **Example 8:** The dot plot below shows the diameters of 13 tires in Mitch's garage. What is the median diameter, in inches, for the 13 tires?
>
> [Dot plot with x-axis labeled Diameter (in.) showing values 15, 20, 25, 30, 35 with dots: 15 has 4 dots, 20 has 3 dots, 25 has 3 dots, 30 has 2 dots, 35 has 1 dot]

Solution: Cross Out Dots To Find The Median: To find the median, we can use the same method that we used in Example 6 and cross out the highest and lowest values one by one to find the middle. We recommend drawing an "X" over each dot as you count to keep track.

Remember, the dot plot is just a way to visually display values in a data set, so, compared to a list, the dot plot above is a more organized way of displaying the diameters of the 13 tires. To make the crossing out method super clear, we can also write out the tire diameters as a list:

15, 15, 15, 15, 20, 20, 20, 25, 25, 25, 30, 30, 35

The crossing out dots method is the exact same as the one we used in Example 6 except now we are going to cross out dots instead of the numbers. To start, we cross off the largest value of 35 (put an "X" over the dot at 35) and one of the smallest values at 15 (put an "X" over one of the dots at 15). We can continue this process by crossing off the dots for the next 2 largest values at 30 and 2 more dots of the smallest values at 15. Next, we can cross out one of the dots at 25 and the final dot at 15. Finally, we can cross out the 2 remaining dots at 25 and 2 of the dots at 20. The final dot left is a 20, so **the median is 20. The final dot always shows the median value.** If there are 2 dots remaining, we average the values from the final 2 dots to find the median.

You can also list the values from the dot plot and then cross your way to the middle to find the median.

~~15, 15, 15, 15, 20, 20,~~ 20, ~~25, 25, 25, 30, 30, 35~~

The answer is 20.

Bonus Topic: Finding The Median in A Bar Graph

Less commonly, the SAT asks you to find the median of data in a bar graph. To find the median in a bar graph, we can use the same method we did in Example 8 – by crossing out the larger and smaller values to find the median.

The bar graph below shows the same data set for the 13 tires in Mitch's garage:

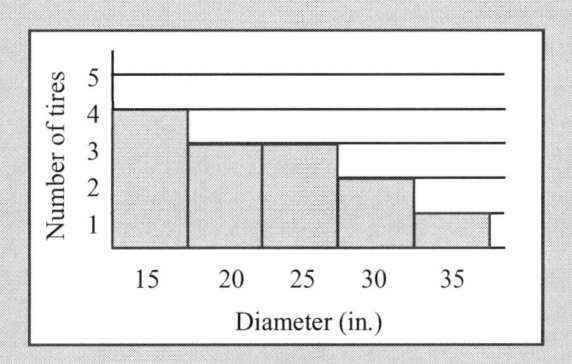

To find the median, we follow the same process that we did with the dot plot in Example 8. Instead of crossing out dots, we are now crossing out the portions of the bar graph. Many students find it easier to split each box into smaller boxes, where each box represents 1 data point. You can see what this looks like with the bar graph below:

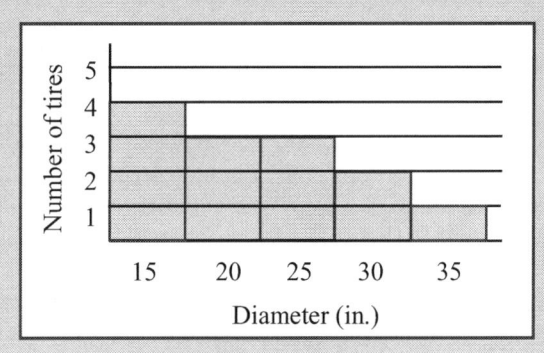

Notice how the number of boxes now match the dots in the dot plot in Example 8. To find the median, we follow the same process we did in Example 8 and cross out the largest and smallest values until we find the median. Now, instead of crossing out dots, we cross out the boxes. If we do this correctly, the final box left will be one at 20, so we can tell that the median is 20.

Make sure that you memorize how to find the median in a bar graph as well in case you see one of these on test day!

*Note: For finding the median in a dot plot or a bar graph, we can also use the same method we just learned for how to find a median in a table. For any questions that include a larger number of data points in a dot plot or a bar graph, the "Add 1 and divide by 2" trick we learned will be easier and faster than the crossing-out method we outlined in Example 8 and the bonus topic box above.

Mean, Median, Mode and Range Practice: Answers on pages 332-333.

1. The tips that a barista earned for 1 week were $25 on Monday, $45 on Tuesday, and $30 on Wednesday, Thursday, and Friday. What was the barista's average daily tips for these 5 days?

   A) $31
   B) $32
   C) $33
   D) $35

2. What is the difference between the mean and the median of the data set {4, 7, 8, 9, 12}?

   A) 0
   B) 1
   C) 2
   D) 3

3. If 4 apartments are rented for $280, $360, $240, and $320, what is the mean rent?

   A) $260
   B) $280
   C) $300
   D) $320

4. John and Aaron tracked their 400-meter race times, which are listed below in seconds. The median for John's race times is x and the median for Aaron's race times is y. What is the value of $x - y$?

   John: 76, 68, 62, 68, 79, 70
   Aaron: 63, 58, 68, 61, 67, 66

5. The average of 6 numbers is 93. What is the 6th number if the first 5 are 99, 86, 93, 89, 92?

   A) 88
   B) 93
   C) 95
   D) 99

6. If $a < b < c < d < e$, which of the following cannot affect the median of the set of numbers?

   A) Increasing the value of a
   B) Decreasing the value of e
   C) Increasing the value of b
   D) Decreasing the value of a

7. The given list below shows a lacrosse team's score for each of its first 8 games. In the ninth game, the team had a score of 13. Which of the following best describes the mean and median of the team's scores for the first 9 games compared to the first 8 games?

   0, 1, 3, 5, 5, 7, 8, 10

   A) The mean increased and the median remained the same.
   B) The median increased and the mean remained unchanged.
   C) Both the mean and the median increased.
   D) Both the mean and the median remained unchanged.

8. A survey was conducted on the value of the cars driven by Orange County residents and found that the mean car value was $65,000 and the median car value was $48,000. Which of the following could explain the difference between the mean and the median car values in Orange County?

   A) Some cars are valued much higher than the rest.
   B) Some cars are valued much lower than the rest.
   C) Many cars have values between $48,000 and $65,000.
   D) The majority of cars have values that are close to each other.

9. The scores for the 43 students in AP Biology were reported, and the mean, median, range, and standard deviation were found. The teacher made an error in grading, and the student with the highest score actually scored 8 points higher. Which of the following will not change after the student's score is corrected?

A) Range
B) Mean
C) Standard Deviation
D) Median

10. If x is equal to $k + 8$ and y is equal to $3k + 12$, which of the following expresses the average of x and y in terms of k?

A) $k + 10$
B) $2k + 10$
C) $4k$
D) $4k + 20$

11. Number of iPhones per Household

iPhones	Frequency
0	6
1	3
2	1
3	5
4	4
5	2

A recent survey asked 21 households how many iPhones they owned. Based on the table above, what was the median number of iPhones?

A) 1
B) 2
C) 3
D) 4

12. As part of a social studies project, Tommy surveyed 50 of his friends about their daily use of Snapchat. The results are shown in the table below.

Number of Snapchats Viewed	Number of Students
0 – 3	4
4 – 6	11
7 – 10	8
11 – 15	9
> 15	18

Which category contains the median number of Snapchats viewed for the survey?

A) 4 – 6
B) 7 – 10
C) 11 – 15
D) > 15

Questions 13-14 refer to the table below.

Points	Frequency
0	3
10	0
20	1
30	2
50	3
100	1

The table above shows the points that a player received on each of his 10 throws while playing Skee-Ball.

13. What was his total score?

A) 200
B) 280
C) 330
D) 350

14. What was the median value of the points scored from the 10 throws?

A) 20
B) 25
C) 30
D) 50

15. The table below shows the distribution of class size for the 217 classes of a high school. What is the median class size at the high school?

Class Size	Frequency
17	44
18	23
20	26
23	40
24	49
27	34

16. There is a list of 29 numbers, all of which are unique. Which of the following never affects the median?

A) Increasing the largest number in the data set.
B) Increasing all numbers in the data set by 10.
C) Making the smallest value in the data set the largest value in the data set.
D) Increasing the smallest value in the data set by 20.

17.

	Mass (g)				
Mike	8.3	7.8	9.2	7.6	8.1
Aaron	5.2	3.5	4.4	3.9	x

Mike and Aaron both conducted a chemistry experiment where they tried to isolate a mystery compound Z. They each ran the experiment 5 times and recorded the mass, in grams, of compound Z that they obtained. The mean of the masses of compound Z that Mike obtained is twice the mean of the masses of compound Z that Aaron obtained. What is the value of x?

18. 80 people each bowled one game at Brick Alley Bowling last Friday. 60 people scored between 50 and 100, 18 people scored score between 101 and 185, and the remaining two players bowled a score between 280 and 300. Which of the following statements about the mean and median of the 80 scores is true?

A) The mean is less than the median.
B) The median is less than the mean.
C) The median and mean are equal.
D) There is not enough information to determine whether the mean or median is greater.

19. A data set of 27 different numbers has a mean of 18 and a median of 18. A new data set is created by adding 20 to all of the values greater than the median while leaving all other numbers in the data set unchanged. Which of the following values will not change?

A) Mean
B) Range
C) Median
D) Sum of the numbers

20. The dot plot represents 13 values in data set A. Data set B is created by adding 39 to each of the values is data set A. Which of the following correctly compares the median and range of data sets A and B?

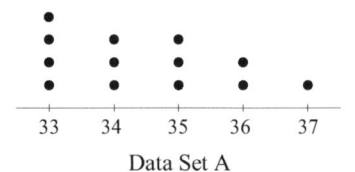

Data Set A

A) The median of data set B is equal to the median of data set A, and the range of data set B is equal to the range of data set A.
B) The median of data set B is greater to the median of data set A, and the range of data set B is equal to the range of data set A.
C) The median of data set B is greater to the median of data set A, and the range of data set B is greater than the range of data set A.
D) The median of data set B is less than the median of data set A, and the range of data set B is equal to the range of data set A.

21. The mean score of 10 students on a 36-point test is 23.8 points. If the student with the highest score is removed, the mean score for the other 9 students is 23 points. How many points did the student with the highest score have?

A) 28
B) 31
C) 33
D) 36

22. John and Karen work at the bakery. John works 7 hours per day, and Karen works 6 hours per day. John produces x brownies per hour and Karen produced y brownies per hour. Which of the following expressions gives the average number of brownies John and Karen produce per hour?

A) $\frac{x+y}{13}$
B) $\frac{7x+6y}{13}$
C) $\frac{xy}{13}$
D) $\frac{6x+7y}{13}$

23. John drove 40 miles per hour for 15 minutes and then drove 20 miles per hour for 10 minutes. Which of the following gives the average rate, in miles per hour, that he drove during the 25 minutes?

24. Each of the three data sets represented by the three dot plots has 18 values. The median of data sets A, B, and C are a, b, and c respectively. What is the relationship between a, b, and c?

A) $a < b < c$
B) $c < b < a$
C) $b < c < a$
D) $a = b = c$

25. Production Run A of axles results in 35 axles with an average weight of a pounds. Production run B of axles results in 15 axles with an average weight of b pounds. Which of the following expressions gives the average weight w of all axles that are produced during two runs of Production run A and one run of Production Run B?

A) $w = \frac{35b+15a}{50}$
B) $w = \frac{2a+b}{3}$
C) $w = \frac{70a+15b}{85}$
D) $w = \frac{35a+15b}{85}$

26. Ashley wanted to save an average of $20 per week over the past 15 weeks. For the first 5 weeks, she saved an average of $15 per week. For the next 5 weeks, she saved an average of $19 per week. For the last 5 weeks, she saved an average of $23 per week. How much more should she have saved each week to hit her goal?

A) $0.75
B) $0.80
C) $1.00
D) $1.50

27. Harold is writing a book. To finish by his deadline, he needs to write an average of 3,000 words per week for 4 weeks. He wrote 4,500 words in the first week, 2,800 words in the second week, and 2,400 words in the third week. Which inequality represents the number of words, x, Harold needs to write in the 4th week to meet or exceed his goal?

A) $4{,}500 + 2{,}800 + 2{,}400 + x \geq 4(3{,}000)$
B) $\frac{4{,}500+2{,}800+2{,}400}{3} + x \geq 3{,}000$
C) $4{,}500 + 2{,}800 + 2{,}400 \geq x(3{,}000)$
D) $\frac{4{,}500}{4} + \frac{2{,}800}{4} + \frac{2{,}400}{4} + x \geq 3{,}000$

28. In the dot plot shown below, each dot represents one of the ten values of data set A. The mean of data set A is 3. A new data set B is created consisting of the ten data values from data set A and the two additional values: 1 and 2. How much less is the mean of data set B than the mean of data set A?

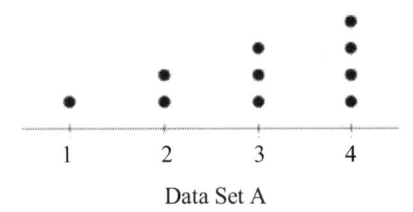

Data Set A

29. On October 2, 2021, a lioness has her 7th, 8th, 9th, 10th, and 11th cubs. The average age of the other 6 cubs was 22 months old. What will be the average age, in months, of the lioness's 11 cubs on October 2, 2022?

30. The average weight of 2 groups of seals at the zoo is 136 pounds. The first group of 18 seals has an average weight of 126 pounds. The second group has 10 seals. What is the average weight of the second group of seals?

A) 136
B) 144
C) 150
D) 154

31. The table below shows the profit of Company X each month for a 4-month period. What is the total profit, in dollars, that Company X must have for the next 3 months in order to have an average monthly profit of $12,000 for the entire 7-month period?

Month	Profit (dollars)
June	-23,000
July	17,000
August	-7,800
September	4,900

32. Sven collects baseball cards. The average price of Sven's 12 most expensive baseball cards is x. After Sven sells the two most expensive baseball cards, the average price of the remaining cards is y. Which of the following expressions represents the total price of Sven's two most expensive baseball cards?

A) $12x - 10y$
B) $12(x - y)$
C) $12y - 10x$
D) $\frac{12x - 10y}{2}$

33. For a set of 71 integers, the mean is greater than the median. Which of the following CANNOT be true about the integers?

A) They are consecutive.
B) They are all even.
C) They are all odd.
D) They are all different.

34. Data set A contains 23 positive integers and has mean score of 83. The highest and two lowest values in data set A are removed to create data set B. The average of data set B is 87. What is the greatest possible range of the 3 values that were removed to create data set B?

35. In order for Mr. Walsh's class to get a pizza party, the class average on the final must be at least 85%. The first fifteen students received an average of 82%. What is the lowest possible score that the 16th student can receive to still allow the class of 20 students to get a pizza party?

Chapter 25: Unit Conversion

You need to know how to properly convert units on the SAT. Two commonly tested conversion factors you should know are listed below.

$$1 \text{ hour} = 60 \text{ minutes} \qquad 1 \text{ minute} = 60 \text{ seconds}$$

For other conversions, such as pounds to kilograms or miles to feet, the SAT provides the conversion factor as part of the question.

Example 1: What weight, in pounds, is equivalent to 15 kilograms? (1 kilogram = 2.2 pounds)

Solution: To solve, we need to convert 15 kilograms to pounds. To do so, we use the conversion factor provided. When setting up a unit conversion, we start with the given, which here is 15 kilograms. We then set up the conversion factor to change the units from kilograms to pounds,

$$15 \text{ kilograms} \times \frac{2.2 \text{ pounds}}{1 \text{ kilogram}} = 37.5 \text{ pounds}$$

The answer is 37.5. Notice how the units for kilograms cancel. **When setting up the conversion factor, the units must cancel.** If the units cancel, the conversion factor is set up correctly. For Example 1, we need the kilograms to cancel and to end with pounds in the numerator since the question is asking for the answer to be in pounds.

$$15 \text{ \sout{kilograms}} \times \frac{2.2 \text{ pounds}}{1 \text{ \sout{kilogram}}} = 37.5 \text{ pounds}$$

If the units do not cancel, the conversion factor is set up incorrectly. You can see the incorrect set up below:

$$15 \text{ kilograms} \times \frac{1 \text{ kilogram}}{2.2 \text{ pounds}} \quad (\text{INCORRECT!})$$

Notice how the units do not cancel when the conversion factor is set up incorrectly.

Example 2: A marathon is 26.2 miles. What is the distance of a marathon in meters? (0.62 miles = 1 kilometers) (1,000 meters = 1 kilometer)

Solution: This question is more advanced than Example 1 because we have 2 unit conversions: (1) miles to kilometers and (2) kilometers to meters.

First, we need to convert miles to kilometers. To do so, we use the conversion factor of 0.62 miles = 1 kilometer to convert 26.2 miles into kilometers.

$$26.2 \text{ miles} \times \frac{1 \text{ kilometer}}{0.62 \text{ miles}} = 42.258 \text{ kilometers}$$

When setting up our conversion factor, we want to make the units cancel. To make the miles cancel, we set up the conversion factor as $\frac{1 \text{ kilometer}}{0.62 \text{ miles}}$. Now that we know the distance in kilometers, we convert 42.258 kilometers to meters:

$$42.258 \text{ kilometers} \times \frac{1{,}000 \text{ meters}}{1 \text{ kilometer}} = 42{,}258 \text{ meters}$$

We set up the conversion factor as $\frac{1{,}000 \text{ meters}}{1 \text{ kilometer}}$ to make the kilometer units cancel. **The answer is 42,258.**

Dimensional Analysis

For more advanced unit conversion questions, you need to know dimensional analysis, which uses conversion factors to convert from one unit to another. In the previous examples, we did some dimensions analysis to convert kilograms to pounds, miles to kilometers, and kilometers to meters.

For unit conversion questions, you need to know dimensional analysis, which uses conversion factors to convert from one unit to another. To do dimensional analysis, complete the following steps:

1. **Start with the value given in the question.**
2. **Use the conversion factor(s) to switch the units.**
3. **Multiply and divide the numbers to find the answer.**

If the conversion factor(s) are setup correctly, the answer will have the correct unit and all other units will cancel! An example of how to do this is shown below:

Example 3: The top speed of Andrew's toy car is 30 meters per second. What is the speed of the toy car in kilometers per hour? (Round your answer the to the nearest whole number) (1 kilometer = 1,000 meters)

Solution: To solve this question, we need to convert meters to kilometers and seconds to hours. **Whenever you are given a rate that includes two units, set it up as a fraction.** In this question, we are given the speed in meters per second, so we can set up 30 meters per second as:

$$\frac{30 \text{ meters}}{1 \text{ second}}$$

From here, we just need to convert the units.

$\frac{30 \text{ meters}}{1 \text{ second}} \times \frac{1 \text{ kilometer}}{1{,}000 \text{ meters}} = \frac{30 \text{ kilometers}}{1{,}000 \text{ seconds}}$ 1. Convert meters to kilometers.

$\frac{30 \text{ kilometers}}{1{,}000 \text{ seconds}} \times \frac{60 \text{ seconds}}{1 \text{ minute}} = \frac{1{,}800 \text{ kilometers}}{1{,}000 \text{ minutes}}$ 2. Convert seconds to minutes.

$\frac{1{,}800 \text{ kilometers}}{1{,}000 \text{ minutes}} \times \frac{60 \text{ minutes}}{1 \text{ hour}} = \frac{108{,}000 \text{ kilometers}}{1000 \text{ hours}}$ 3. Convert minutes to hours.

$\frac{108{,}000 \text{ kilometers}}{1{,}000 \text{ hours}} = \frac{108 \text{ kilometers}}{1 \text{ hour}} = 108 \text{ kilometers/hour}$ 4. Simplify the answer.

You can also solve this question in one big step as shown below:

$$\frac{30 \text{ meters}}{1 \text{ second}} \times \frac{1 \text{ kilometers}}{1{,}000 \text{ meters}} \times \frac{60 \text{ seconds}}{1 \text{ minute}} \times \frac{60 \text{ minutes}}{1 \text{ hour}} = \frac{108{,}000 \text{ kilometers}}{1{,}000 \text{ hours}} = 108 \text{ kilometers}/hr$$

The answer is 108.

The most difficult part of unit conversion questions is setting up the conversion factors correctly, so pay close attention to the units. If the units cancel and you finish with the units the question is asking for, the equation is up properly, and you will have the correct answer.

Example 4: Erica bikes at an average speed of 24 miles per hour for 40 minutes. If Rosie bikes at an average speed of 18 miles per hour, how many minutes does it take Rosie to bike the same distance that Erica biked in 40 minutes?

Solution: We first need to find out how far Erica bikes in 40 minutes:

$$40 \text{ minutes} \times \frac{1 \text{ hour}}{60 \text{ minutes}} \times \frac{24 \text{ miles}}{1 \text{ hour}} = 16 \text{ miles}$$

To bike 16 miles, Rosie will take:

$$16 \text{ miles} \times \frac{1 \text{ hour}}{18 \text{ miles}} \times \frac{60 \text{ minutes}}{1 \text{ hour}} = 53.33 \text{ minutes}$$

The answer is 53.33.

Example 5: A metal pipe that is p feet long will be cut into n pieces that are each x inches long. Which of the following expressions correctly describes length, in inches, of each of the n pieces of pipe?

A) $x = \frac{12p}{n}$ B) $x = \frac{p}{nx}$ C) $x = \frac{px}{12n}$ D) $x = \frac{12n}{px}$

Solution #1 - "Math Teacher Way": We first need to convert the length of the metal pipe from feet to inches:

$$p \text{ feet} \times \frac{12 \text{ inches}}{1 \text{ foot}} = 12p \text{ inches}$$

Then, we need to cut it into n pieces, so we will divide the metal pipe by n:

$$\frac{12p \text{ inches}}{n \text{ pieces of pipe}} = x \text{ inches per piece of pipe}$$

The answer is A.

Method #2 – Substitution: If solving algebraically seems tricky, we can just pick numbers to make this question easier. Let's say that the metal pipe is 2 feet long ($p = 2$) and that we will cut it into 3 pieces ($n = 3$). From here, we can easily solve for x, the length of each piece in inches:

$$2 \text{ feet} \times \frac{12 \text{ inches}}{1 \text{ foot}} = 24 \text{ inches}$$

$$\frac{24 \text{ inches}}{3} = 8 \text{ inches per piece}$$

With the numbers we picked, we found that $x = 8$. From here, we plug our values of p, n, and x into the answer choices to find out which equation is correct. Let's confirm this works by plugging in our values to answer choice A.

$$8 = \frac{12(2)}{3}$$

$$8 = 8$$

The equation works with our numbers, so we know that **the answer is A.**

Advanced Unit Conversions with Squared and Cubed Units

For advanced unit conversion questions, we need to know how to correctly use dimensional analysis for squared and cubed units. For these questions, the challenge is knowing how to correctly convert a basic conversion factor to a squared unit conversion or a cubed unit conversion.

Example 6: A tennis court has an area of 2,808 square feet. What is the area, in *square yards*, of a tennis court? (1 yard = 3 feet)

A. 312   B. 936   C. 2,808   D. 8,424   E. 25,272

Solution: When we are asked to convert the squared units and are given a basic conversion factor, we **square the conversion factor.** In Example 6, our conversion factor is 1 yard = 3 feet. The units of area in this question are square feet and square yards, so squaring the conversion factor we get

$$1 \text{ yard}^2 = 9 \text{ feet}^2$$

PrepPros

The yard² is the same as square yards, and the feet² is the same as square feet, so the conversion factor becomes

$$1 \text{ square yard} = 9 \text{ square feet}$$

Now that we have the conversion factor for square feet to square yards, we can use dimensional analysis to convert 2,808 square feet into square yards and solve:

$$2{,}808 \text{ square feet} \times \frac{1 \text{ square yard}}{9 \text{ square feet}} = 312 \text{ square yards}$$

The answer is A.

③ **Example 7:** A solution that has a volume of 578 cubic inches has what volume in cubic centimeters? (1 inch = 2.54 centimeters)

Solution: When we are asked to convert cubed units and given a basic conversion factor, we cube the conversion factor. In Example 7, our conversion factor is 1 inch = 2.54 centimeters. The units of volume in this question are cubic centimeters and cubic inches, so squaring the conversion factor we get

$$1 \text{ inch}^3 = 16.387064 \text{ centimeters}^3$$

In case it is not clear, $(2.54)^3 = 16.387064$. The inch³ is the same as cubic inches, and the centimeters³ is the same as cubic centimeters, so the conversion factor becomes

$$1 \text{ cubic inch} = 16.387064 \text{ cubic centimeters}$$

Now that we have the conversion factor for cubic inches to cubic centimeters, we can use dimensional analysis to convert 578 cubic inches to cubic centimeters and solve:

$$578 \text{ cubic inches} \times \frac{16.387064 \text{ cubic centimeters}}{1 \text{ cubic inch}} = 9{,}471.73 \text{ cubic centimeters}$$

The answer is 9,472.

Chapter 25: Unit Conversion

Unit Conversion Practice: Answers on page 333.

1. What length, in <u>centimeters</u>, is equivalent to a length of 37 meters?
   (1 meter = 100 centimeters)

   A) 0.037
   B) 0.37
   C) 3,700
   D) 37,000

2. The weight limit of a certain elevator is 1,800 pounds. What is the approximate weight limit of the elevator in <u>kilograms</u>?
   (1 kilogram = 2.2046 pounds)

   A) 816
   B) 1494
   C) 2168
   D) 3968

3. A whale swam a distance of 232,320 yards. How far did the whale swim in <u>miles</u>?
   (1 mile = 1,760 yards)

4. A set of 4 tires weighs 120 pounds. What is the approximate weight of the set of 4 tires in <u>kilograms</u>? (1 kilogram = 2.2046 pounds)

   A) 22
   B) 54
   C) 122
   D) 265

5. If a 6-foot giant sub is cut in half and each half is cut into quarters, how many <u>inches</u> long are the resulting pieces of the sub?
   (1 foot = 12 inches)

   A) 9
   B) 18
   C) 36
   D) 72

6. How many cups, each with a capacity of 6 fluid ounces, can be filled with lemonade from a cooler that holds 9 gallons of lemonade?
   (1 gallon = 128 ounces)

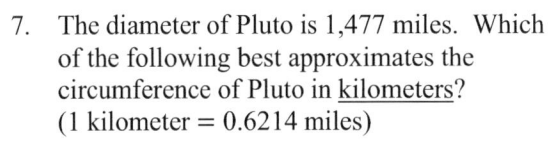

7. The diameter of Pluto is 1,477 miles. Which of the following best approximates the circumference of Pluto in <u>kilometers</u>?
   (1 kilometer = 0.6214 miles)

   A) 2,380
   B) 5,766
   C) 7,467
   D) 14,935

8. James is walking at a speed of 5 miles per hour through downtown Manhattan. If James walks for two hours, how many <u>city blocks</u> does he walk? (1 city block = $\frac{1}{20}$ of a mile)

   A) 10
   B) 50
   C) 100
   D) 200

9. A category 3 hurricane rains 3 inches per hour for 36 hours. Which of the following is closest to the total <u>feet</u> of rain over the 36 hours?
   (1 foot = 12 inches)

   A) 9
   B) 12
   C) 108
   D) 1296

10. A bakery purchases flour in 50-gallon bags. The flour is mixed with water to make loaves of bread. Each loaf of bread is made by mixing 3 quarts of flour with 2 quarts of water. What is the maximum number of loaves of bread that can be made from two 50-gallon bags of flour? (1 gallon = 4 quarts)

    A) 66
    B) 133
    C) 150
    D) 200

11. A 25-foot plank of wood and a 12-foot plank of wood will be cut into 10-inch pieces. How many 10-inch pieces can be cut from the two planks? (1 foot = 12 inches)

    A) 10
    B) 30
    C) 40
    D) 44

- 245 -

12. During the first 24 hours of a snowstorm, snow fell at a constant rate of 3 inches per hour. Which of the following is closest to the total amount of snow that fell during the first 7 hours of the storm in millimeters?
(5 inches = 127 millimeters)

A) 0.12
B) 21
C) 76
D) 533

13. A laboratory receives a compound in 4-decagram vials. How many 1-centigram doses are contained in one 4-decagram vial?
(1 decagram = 10 grams)
(100 centigrams = 1 gram)

A) 0.04
B) 4
C) 400
D) 4,000

14. An Olympic bicyclist broke a record during a race in the French hills. He biked 13 miles in 17 minutes. What was his average speed, to the nearest integer, in miles per hour?

15. A racehorse runs at an average speed of 80 kilometers per hour. Which of the following is closest to this speed in meters per second?
(1 kilometer = 1,000 meters)

A) 22
B) 44
C) 133
D) 1,320

16. On a 14-mile road there are 8 rest stops placed at equal intervals, including one at each end of the road. What is the distance, in feet, between two consecutive stops?
(1 mile = 5,280 feet)

17. A pickup truck bed holds 8 cubic meters of soil. How many cubic centimeters of soil does the pickup truck bed hold?
(100 centimeters = 1 meter)

A) 8,000
B) 80,000
C) 800,000
D) 8,000,000

18. A restoration company sells sand at a rate of $50 per cubic yard. Which of the following is closest to the price the company charges for 108 cubic feet of sand? (1 yard = 3 feet)

A) $108
B) $200
C) $600
D) $1,800

19. A certain state park has an area of 32.8 square miles. What is the area, in square yards, of this state park? (1 mile = 1,760 yards)

A) 0.018
B) 295.2
C) 57,728
D) 101,601,280

20. One gallon of paint will cover 180 square feet of a surface. A room has a total wall area of x square feet. Which equation represents the total amount of paint, P, in gallons, needed to paint the walls of the room three times?

A) $P = \frac{x}{60}$
B) $P = 540x$
C) $P = \frac{x}{180}$
D) $P = 180x$

21. The abyssopelagic zone is the zone from the depth of 4,000 yards to 6,000 yards in the ocean. If an object is sinking at a rate of 2 miles per hour, to the nearest minute how many minutes would it take the object to pass from the beginning to the end of the abyssopelagic zone? (1 yard = 3 feet)
(1 mile = 5,280 feet)

22. The speed of light in a vacuum is 3.00×10^8 meters per second. Given that 1 kilometer is equal to approximately 0.62 miles and 1,000 meters equal 1 kilometer, which of the following is closest to the speed of light in a vacuum, in miles per minute?

   A) 1.12×10^7
   B) 1.12×10^{10}
   C) 2.90×10^7
   D) 2.90×10^{10}

23. A gardener is preparing a potting bed in the shape of a rectangular prism. The dimensions of a rectangular prism are 6 feet by 12 feet by 44 inches. If it costs $108 per cubic yard to prepare the potting bed, how much does the gardener need to spend? (1 yard = 3 feet) (1 foot = 12 inches)

24. A rocket's speed is increasing at a rate of 17.8 meters per second squared. What is the rate in miles per minute squared? (1 mile = 1,609 meters)

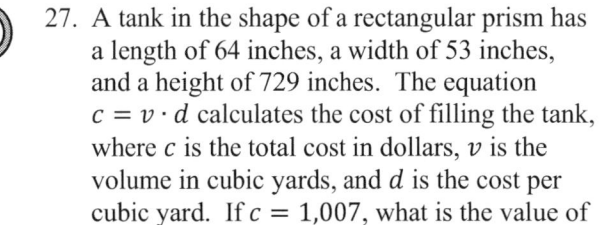

25. A racecar has tires with a radius of 1 foot. The racecar completes one lap of a race in 53 seconds, and the tires rotate at an average rate of 2,876 times per minute. To the closest hundredth of a mile, what is the length of the racetrack? (1 mile = 5280 feet)

26. There are 640 acres in 1 square mile. The area of a nature preserve is increasing at a rate of 4 acres per year. Which of the following is closest to the rate at which the area of the forest is increasing, in square kilometers per year? (Use 1 kilometer = 0.62 mile.)

   A) 0.0024
   B) 0.0040
   C) 0.0100
   D) 0.0163

27. A tank in the shape of a rectangular prism has a length of 64 inches, a width of 53 inches, and a height of 729 inches. The equation $c = v \cdot d$ calculates the cost of filling the tank, where c is the total cost in dollars, v is the volume in cubic yards, and d is the cost per cubic yard. If $c = 1,007$, what is the value of d in dollars? (1 yard = 36 inches)

Chapter 26: Scatter Plots and Lines of Best Fit

Scatter plots show the relationship between two variables in a data set. **Each data point appears as a dot on the scatter plot. A line of best fit is a line (or curve) that best represents the data on a scatter plot.** This line may pass through some of the points, none of the points, or all of the points. Let's see how this works with an example scatter plot:

The scatterplot below shows the root depth and plant height for the tomato plants in Bill's garden one month after the seeds were planted.

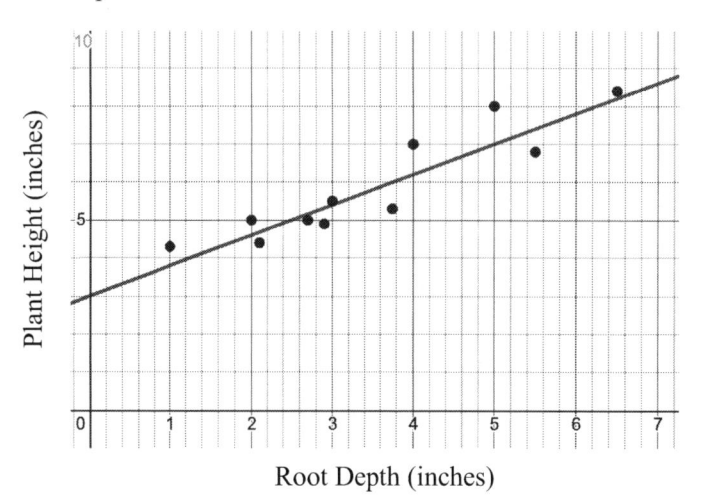

Each of the points in the scatter plot represents a single tomato plant in Bill's garden. The location of the dot corresponds with the root depth and plant height of the tomato plant. Since there are 11 dots, we know there are 11 tomato plants in Bill's garden. This brings us to the first two principles you need to know about scatter plots.

Principle #1 – Each point on a scatter plot represents one data point in the set.

Principle #2 – The total number of points on a scatter plot is equal to the total number of data points in the set.

The line of best fit is used to make an estimate for data points that are not part of the original data set. For example, on the scatter plot above when the root depth is 5 inches, the line of best fit predicts the plant height will be 7 inches. The actual value of the height of the plant with a root depth of 5 inches is 8 inches, which is shown by the dot at (5, 8). This brings us to our second important principle to understand about scatter plots and the line of best fit.

Principle #3 – The predicted value is on the line of best fit while the actual value is at the point in the scatter plot.

We will use the scatter plot above to go over the various ways that the SAT will test you on scatter plots and lines of best fit.

Example 1: Based on the line of best fit, if the value of root depth is 6 inches, what is the predicted plant height in inches?

A) 3.8   B) 5.2   C) 6.7   D) 7.8

Solution: To find the predicted plant height, we want to find the point on the line of best fit where root depths is 6 inches. On the line of best fit, this is at the point (6, 7.8). **The answer is D.**

Example 2: For the tomato plant with a root depth of 4 inches, which of the following is closest to the positive difference between the actual plant height and the plant height predicted by the line of best fit?

A) 1.5   B) 1.2   C) 0.8   D) 0.4

Solution: We first need to find which point the question is directing us to look at, which is where the root depth is 4 inches. The plant height is on the x-axis, so if we look at where $x = 4$, we find a point at $(4, 7)$. This point shows one of the tomato plants had a root depth of 4 inches and a height depth of 7 inches. The 7 inches is the actual height. To find the predicted height, we find the point on the line of best fit where the root depth is 4 inches. We can estimate this point to be at $(4, 6.2)$. The 6.2 inches is the plant height predicted by the line of best fit. The positive difference between the actual height and predicted height is $7 - 6.2 = 0.8$. **The answer is C.**

Notice that even though we had to estimate the value for the predicted value, the answer choices made clear which one is correct. Even if we estimated the point to be at $(4, 6.1)$, we would get an answer of 0.9, which is closest to 0.8.

Example 3: The scatter plot above shows the depth of the tomato plant roots, x, and the height of the tomato plants, y, for 11 tomato plants in Bill's garden. A line of best fit is also shown. Which of the following could be the equation of the line of best fit?

A) $1.4x + 3$ B) $0.8x + 3$ C) $1.4x + 1.2$ D) $0.8x + 1.2$

Solution: For a question like this, start by solving for the slope. To find the slope, find for two points on the line of best fit. Here, we will use $(5, 7)$ and $(0, 3)$.

$$\text{slope} = \frac{7-3}{5-0} = \frac{4}{5} = 0.8$$

Next, find the y-intercept. For the line of best fit, we see the y-intercept is at $y = 3$. **The answer is B.**

TIP – Is that really the y-intercept?

When asked to find the equation of a line of best fit on a scatter plot, make sure that the point that looks like the y-intercept is actually the y-intercept. **Scatter plots may have the axes scaled so that the bottom left of the graph will not be when $x = 0$. When this occurs, the point that looks like the y-intercept is just another point on the graph.**

For example, let's take a look at the same graph from above but the left side of the graph has now been cut off.

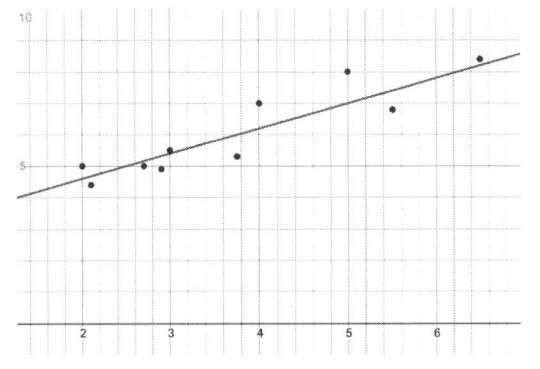

At first glance, it looks like the y-intercept is at $y = 4$, but that would be incorrect. **The graph does not include $x = 0$, so we cannot see the y-intercept.** Make sure that you do not fall for this common trick on test day.

PrepPros

Scatter Plots Practice: Answers on page 333.

For questions 1-6, use the scatterplot below. The height and width of 5 clay sculptures are plotted in the scatterplot below.

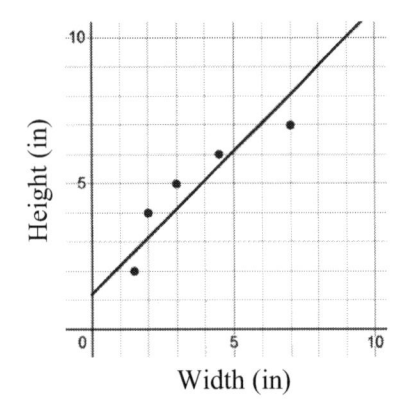

For questions 7-10, use the scatterplot below. On the graph above, the x-axis represents the pounds of steel, in tons, used in a new building and the y-axis represents the price of a new building in thousands of dollars.

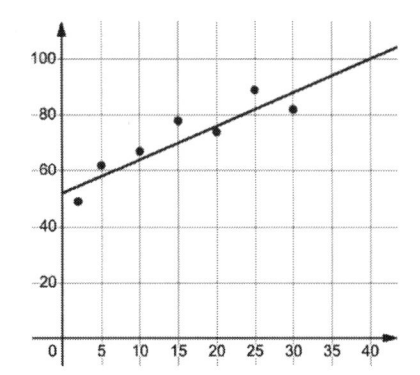

1. For the graph above, for how many data points was the height of the clay sculpture greater than the value predicted by the line of best fit?

    A) 0
    B) 1
    C) 2
    D) 3

2. According to the line of best fit, a clay sculpture with a height of 9 inches is predicted to have a width of how many inches?

3. For the clay sculpture with a height of 5 inches, what was the width of the sculpture, in inches?

4. According to the line of best fit, what is the predicted height of sculpture that has a width of 2 inches?

5. For the clay sculpture with a width of 3 inches, the height predicted by the line of best fit is x inches less than the actual height. What is the value of x?

6. For the clay sculpture that had a height of 7 inches, the actual width is represented by the variable h and the width predicted by the line of best fit is f. What is the value of $f - h$?

7. For the building that had the median price, which of the following is closest to the difference between the actual price and the predicted price of the building in thousands of dollars?

    A) 2
    B) 7
    C) 8
    D) 13

8. For how many data points was the price of the building less than the price predicted by the line of best fit?

9. According to the line of best fit, the building that had a price of $88,000 used approximately how many more tons of steel than predicted by the line of best fit?

    A) 1
    B) 2
    C) 6
    D) 9

10. For the building which was the 3rd most expensive, how many pounds of steel, in tons, were used?

- 250 -

11.

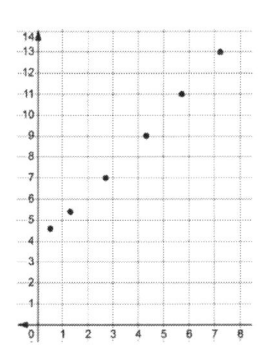

Which of the following equations best models the line of best fit for the scatterplot above?

A) $y = \frac{5}{4}x + 4$
B) $y = x + 3$
C) $y = 2x$
D) $y = 3x + 4$

12.

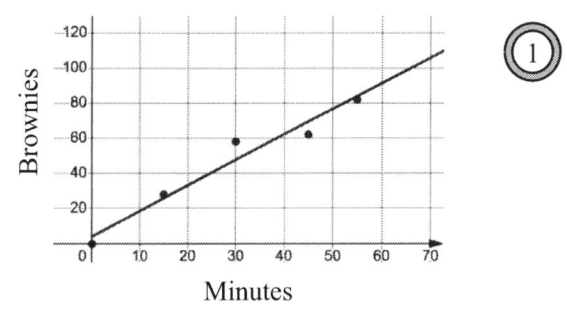

The graph above displays the number of brownies produced at a bakery at different numbers of minutes after opening. Based on the line of best fit, how many minutes after opening is the number of brownies produced expected to be 60?

A) 20
B) 30
C) 38
D) 88

13.

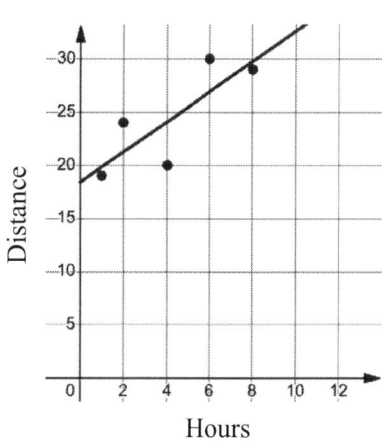

The graph above plots Paula's bike rides last week. What is the number of times that the line of best fit predicted a distance greater than the actual distance?

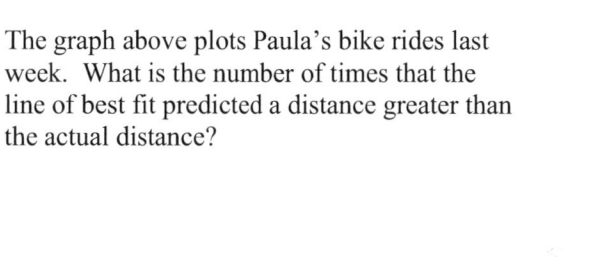

14.

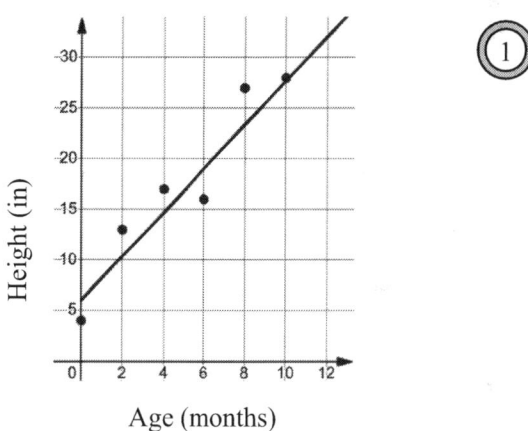

The graph above plots the height, in inches, of a Great Dane on the y-axis and the age, in months, on the x-axis. Which of the following is closest to the difference in centimeters between the actual height of the Great Dane at 8 months and the height of the Great Dane predicted by the line of best fit?

A) 1
B) 5
C) 22
D) 27

15. Which of the following could be the equation for the line of best fit for the data shown in the scatterplot above?

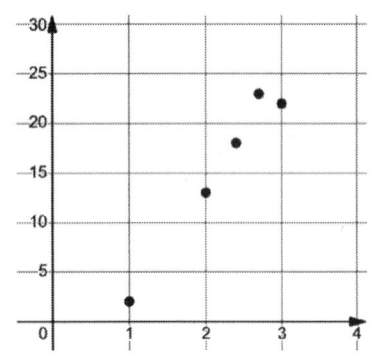

A) $y = 10x - 8$
B) $y = \frac{3}{2}x - 6$
C) $y = 2x$
D) $y = \frac{3}{2}x$

16. Tijuana Daily Border Crossings

Year	Average Number of People Crossing
2007	13,400
2008	14,300
2009	15,500
2010	16,400
2011	17,500

The table above shows the average number of people crossing the Tijuana border per day for the different years listed. If these data points were displayed on a scatter plot with the years after 2007 on the x-axis and the average number of people crossing on the y-axis, which of the following best models the line of best fit?

A) $y = 13,400 + 1,000x$
B) $y = 13,400 + 800x$
C) $y = 13,400(1.1)^x$
D) $y = 13,400(1.1)^{\frac{x}{5}}$

17. The graph above models the relationship between the price, in thousands of dollars, of an airplane since it was purchased in 2020. Let x equal the years since 2020. Which of the following is the equation for the line of best fit?

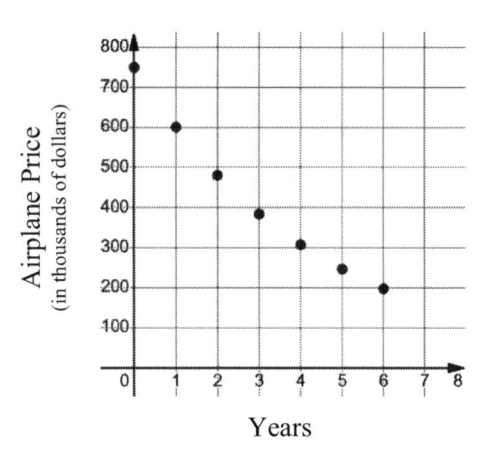

A) $y = 750 - 150x$
B) $y = 750 - 80x$
C) $y = 750(0.2)^x$
D) $y = 750(0.8)^x$

18. The scatterplot above shows the relationship between the years (y) after planting and the number of grapes produced by a vine produced (p) at Frank's vineyard. A line of best fit for the data is shown. Which of the following is the equation of the line of best fit?

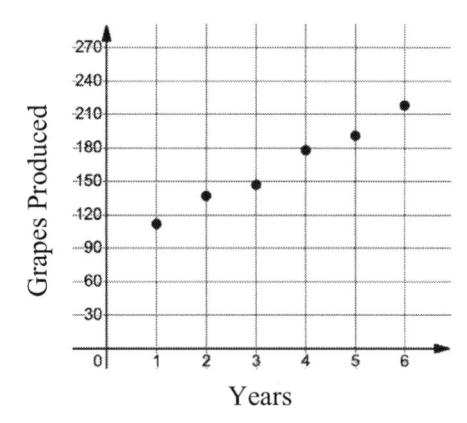

A) $p = 78 + h$
B) $p = 78 + 23h$
C) $p = 23 + 78h$
D) $p = 78h$

Chapter 27: Circles

In order to answer circles questions on the SAT, we need to know the equation for a circle and how to graph a circle.

Equation for a Circle

The equation for a circle with a center at the origin and a radius r is

$$x^2 + y^2 = r^2$$

To make sure you understand this, let's go over this equation with numbers. Let's start with

$$x^2 + y^2 = 16$$

This equation represents a circle with its center at the origin and a radius of 4. Make sure that you remember that the number represents r^2. Many students forget this and mistakenly think the radius here is 16.

The equation for a circle with a center at (h, k) and a radius r is

$$(x - h)^2 + (y - k)^2 = r^2$$

We call this the standard form of a circle. This is the equation that you need to memorize, as questions using this form often appear on test day. Again, let's put some numbers into the equation to make sure we understand how this works.

$$(x - 3)^2 + (y + 5)^2 = 49$$

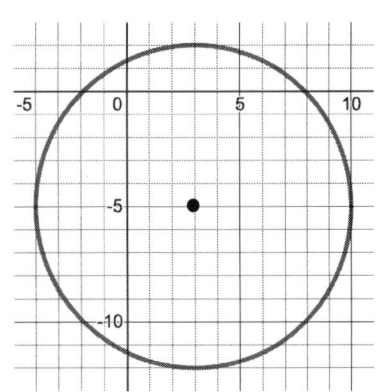

This equation is a circle with a center at $(3, -5)$ and a radius of 7. Make sure that you notice the sign of the h and k values in the equation is the opposite of the actual coordinate of the center (h, k). The term $(x - 3)^2$ shows the x-coordinate is at $x = 3$, not $x = -3$. The term $(y + 5)^2$ shows the y-coordinate is at $y = -5$ not $y = 5$. A common mistake is to think the center of this circle is at $(-3, 5)$.

PrepPros

Example 1: A circle in the xy-plane has a center of $(-9, 4)$ and a radius of 6. Which of the following is the equation of the circle?

A) $(x-9)^2 + (y+4)^2 = 36$
B) $(x+9)^2 + (y-4)^2 = 36$
C) $(x-9)^2 + (y+4)^2 = 6$
D) $(x+9)^2 + (y-4)^2 = 6$

Solution: For this question, we need to properly use the equation of a circle. The radius is 6, so the right side must equal 36. Since the center is at $(-9, 4)$, we need to see the opposite signs of h and k, which here are 9 and -4 respectively, in the circle equation. **The answer is B.**

Other types of circles questions ask you to somehow change the size or location of a circle. For these questions, we again just need to know how the equation of a circle works.

Example 2: $\qquad (x-4)^2 + (y+6)^2 = 25$

The equation for Circle A is shown above. Circle B is drawn by shifting Circle A 3 units left, 8 units up, and increasing the radius by 2. Which of the following is the equation of Circle B?

A) $(x-7)^2 + (y+14)^2 = 49$
B) $(x-1)^2 + (y-2)^2 = 29$
C) $(x-7)^2 + (y-2)^2 = 49$
D) $(x-1)^2 + (y-2)^2 = 49$

Solution: Let's start by finding the radius of Circle B. Circle A has a radius of 5, which we know because 25 is equal to r^2. If we increase that radius by 2, the radius of Circle B is 7, so the right side of the equation must be 49. From this, we know that B is incorrect.

Next, we need to find where the center of Circle B is located. The center of Circle A is at $(4, -6)$. Again, remember that the signs of the numbers in the equation are opposite of the coordinates of the center of the circle. We shift the center of Circle A 3 units left and 8 units up to find the center of Circle B, so the center of Circle B is at $(1, 2)$. **The answer is D.**

TIP – Draw It Out or Use Desmos: If this question is difficult for you, sketch the coordinate plane and draw the circle or use Desmos to graph the circle. The visual can help make sure that you shift the center to the correct point. It is easy to mistakenly shift in the wrong direction if you do not draw it out.

Example 3: $\qquad (x-5)^2 + y^2 = 53$

The equation above represents a circle in the xy-plane. Point $(11, a)$ lies on the circle. If a can be written as $\sqrt{n}$, what is the value of n?

Solution: Since point $(11, a)$ lies on the circle, we can plug the point in for x and y in the circle equation and solve for a.

$$(11-5)^2 + a^2 = 53$$
$$36 + a^2 = 53$$
$$a^2 = 17$$
$$a = \sqrt{17}$$

Since $a = \sqrt{17}$ and we are told that a can be written as $\sqrt{n}$, $n = 17$. **The answer is 17. For any question that gives a point on a circle, we can always plug the point back into the equation to solve for any missing values.**

Example 4: $(x+9)^2 + (y+2)^2 = k$

The equation above represents Circle M in the xy-plane. If point $(-3, 7)$ lies on Circle M, what is the value of k?

Solution: Since point $(-3, 7)$ lies on Circle M, we can plug that point into the equation to solve for k.

$$(-3+9)^2 + (7+2)^2 = k$$
$$6^2 + 9^2 = k$$
$$36 + 81 = k$$
$$117 = k$$

The answer is 117.

General Form and Completing the Square

The SAT also asks questions with the general form of a circle. The general form of a circle is

$$x^2 + y^2 + Ax + By + C = 0$$

This form does not tell us anything helpful about what the circle looks like. In order to find the circle's center and radius, we need to complete the square to get back to standard form.

The steps below show you how to complete the square. For this example, we will use a circle with the equation

$$x^2 + y^2 - 6x + 2y - 15 = 0$$

Step 1: Move any constants to the right side. In this example, we need to move the -15.

$$x^2 + y^2 - 6x + 2y = 15$$

Step 2: Group the x-terms and y-terms together. Leave yourself a space to complete the square.

$$(x^2 - 6x +) + (y^2 + 2y +) = 15$$

Step 3: Complete the square by dividing the coefficient of the middle term by 2 and squaring. For the x-terms, the middle coefficient is -6, so we divide -6 by 2, getting -3, and then square -3, getting 9. We write a 9 in the open space to complete the square. For the y-terms, the middle coefficient is 2, so we divide 2 by 2, getting 1, and then square 1, which is 1. We write a 1 in the open space to complete the square. Be sure to add 9 and 1 to the right side of the equation as well.

$$(x^2 - 6x + 9) + (y^2 + 2y + 1) = 15 + 9 + 1$$

Step 4: Factor both perfect squares. The whole point of completing the square is to create perfect squares. Here we get

$$(x-3)^2 + (y+1)^2 = 25$$

When completing the square, the value in the completed square, here the -3 and $+1$, are always equal to half of the middle terms, -6 and $+2$, that we had before factoring.

Once we have the circle in standard form, **we can see that the center is at $(3, -1)$ and the radius is 5**.

PrepPros

Example 5: Circle P can be written as $x^2 + y^2 + 10x - 4y - 71 = 0$. Which of the following is an equation of Circle P ?

    A) $(x + 5)^2 + (y - 2)^2 = 100$
    B) $(x + 5)^2 + (y + 2)^2 = 71$
    C) $(x + 10)^2 + (y - 4)^2 = 71$
    D) $(x + 5)^2 + (y - 2)^2 = 42$

Solution: Method #1 – Completing The Square: We need to convert Circle P from general form to standard form. To start, we add the 71 to the right side.

$$x^2 + y^2 + 10x - 4y = 71$$

Now, we need to organize the x-terms and y-terms. Remember to leave space to complete the square.

$$(x^2 + 10x +) + (y^2 - 4y +) = 71$$

Next, we complete the square.

$$(x^2 + 10x + 25) + (y^2 - 4y + 4) = 71 + 25 + 4$$

Factoring the perfect squares, we get

$$(x + 5)^2 + (y - 2)^2 = 100$$

The answer is A.

Method #2 – Desmos Equivalent Hack #3 For Equivalent Equations: We can cheat this question and solve it using Desmos! In this question, we are given the general form of Circle P and asked to find the standard form. So, we are asked to find which answer choice, written in standard form, is equivalent to the general form given in the question.

If two expressions are equivalent, the graphs of the expressions are identical. To solve, graph the general form given in the question and then graph the answer choices. If we graph the general form and answer choice A, we only see 1 circle, which tells us that the equations are equivalent. **The answer is A.**

Example 6: For a circle in the xy-plane with the equation $4x^2 + 4y^2 + 24x - 32y = 80$, the radius can be expressed as $3\sqrt{k}$. What is the value of k?

Solution: On more challenging questions, the SAT adds coefficients in front of the x^2 and y^2 terms. **When there are coefficients in front of the x^2 and y^2 terms, we first divide the entire equation by that coefficient.** This removes the coefficients and makes it much easier to complete the square. In Example 6, the coefficient is 4, as we have $4x^2$ and $4y^2$, so our first step is the divide the entire equation by 4 to get

$$x^2 + y^2 + 6x - 8y = 20$$

Now that the x^2 and y^2 terms have no coefficient, we can follow all the steps we learned for completing the square. The constants, 20, are already on the right side, so we can organize the x-terms and y-terms.

$$(x^2 + 6x +) + (y^2 - 8y +) = 20$$

Next, we complete the square.

$$(x^2 + 6x + 9) + (y^2 - 8y + 16) = 20 + 9 + 16$$

Factoring the perfect squares, we get

$$(x + 3)^2 + (y - 4)^2 = 45$$

Since 45 is equal to r^2, the radius is equal to $\sqrt{45}$, which can be simplified to $3\sqrt{5}$. The question says that the radius can be expressed as $3\sqrt{k}$, so $k = 5$. **The answer is 5.**

Advanced Circles Questions

For advanced circles questions, the SAT requires a deeper understanding of two basic circles principles. While these principles may simple, recognizing them is critical to solving advanced circles questions.

Principle #1: The two endpoints of any diameter on a circle have their midpoint at the center of the circle.

Try this on your own. Grab a piece of paper and draw a circle. No matter how you draw the diameter, the center of the circle will be the midpoint of the diameter.

Example 7: Circle P has its center at $(2,7)$. If AB is a diameter of circle P and point A is at $(-3,4)$, which of the following is point B?

A) $(7,10)$ B) $(-8,1)$ C) $(-\frac{1}{2}, \frac{11}{2})$ D) $(6,8)$

Solution: Using principle #1, we know that the center of the circle must be the midpoint of AB. Since we are given point A, we can use the midpoint formula to solve for point B. If you need to review the midpoint formula, go back to chapter 17. To solve for the x-coordinate, we set up

$$\frac{x + (-3)}{2} = 2$$

$$x = 7$$

If we check the answer choices, we already know that **the answer is A**. Be sure to **always check the answer choices once you find either the x-coordinate or y-coordinate of a point.**

To finish solving this question algebraically, we solve for the y-coordinate.

$$\frac{y + (4)}{2} = 7$$

$$y = 10$$

Point B is at $(7,10)$, so **the answer is A.** If you need to review how to use the midpoint formula, go back to chapter 17.

Principle #2: The distance between the center and any endpoint of a diameter of a circle is equal to the radius of the circle.

If this principle seems obvious, it is because it is. It is just the definition of a radius! However, it is helpful to recognize if you are only given two endpoints of a diameter and are asked to find the equation of the circle.

Example 8: In the xy-plane, point $(4,2)$ and $(6,10)$ are the endpoints of a diameter on the circle. Which of the following is the equation of the circle?

A) $(x-1)^2 + (y-4)^2 = 68$
B) $(x-1)^2 + (y-4)^2 = 17$
C) $(x-5)^2 + (y-6)^2 = 68$
D) $(x-5)^2 + (y-6)^2 = 17$

Solution: To find the equation of the circle, we need to find the center and the radius. To find the center, we just need to find the midpoint of the two endpoints of the diameter. The x-coordinate of the center is at

$$\frac{4+6}{2} = x$$

$$x = 5$$

The y-coordinate of the center is at
$$\frac{2+10}{2} = y$$
$$y = 6$$

The center of the circle is at $(5, 6)$. From this, we know that answer choices A and B are incorrect. Now that we know the center, we can find the radius using principle #2. The distance from the center to either of the endpoints is equal to the radius. Here, we will use point $(4, 2)$ to find the radius using the distance formula.
$$r = \sqrt{(5-4)^2 + (6-2)^2}$$
$$r = \sqrt{(1)^2 + (4)^2}$$
$$r = \sqrt{17}$$

If you need to review the distance formula, go back to chapter 17.

Now that we know the radius, we can finish this question. The right side of a circle equation is equal to r^2. Since $(\sqrt{17})^2 = 17$, **the answer is D.**

TIP – Draw It Out: For any questions like this, we recommend making a drawing. Sketching a coordinate plane, the endpoints of the diameter, and drawing the circle can help you identify what steps you need to take to solve the question. Even if you still cannot find the exact answer, you can often at least eliminate some incorrect answers and make a more educated guess after drawing it out.

Finding Points On, Inside, and Outside the Circle

The final type of tricky circles questions asks you to find if a point is on, inside, or outside of the circle. These questions will very likely be written with variables, so we cannot solve them in Desmos. To solve these questions, we need to memorize the rules in the table below.

Point Location	Rule	Summary
On The Circle	$(x-h)^2 + (y-k)^2 = r^2$	If we plug a point into the standard form equation and the left side is equal to r^2, the point is on the circle.
Inside The Circle	$(x-h)^2 + (y-k)^2 < r^2$	If we plug a point into the standard form equation and the left side is less than to r^2, the point is inside the circle.
Outside The Circle	$(x-h)^2 + (y-k)^2 > r^2$	If we plug a point into the standard form equation and the left side is greater than r^2, the point is outside the circle.

If we think about it, these rules make sense. To be on the circle, a point must be at a distance from the center that is equal to the radius, so the left side must equal r^2. To be inside the circle, a point must be at a distance from the center that is less than the radius, so the left side must be less than r^2. And to be outside the circle, a point must be at a distance from the center that is greater than the radius, so the left side must be greater than r^2.

Example 9: In the xy-plane, which of the following points lies outside of a circle with the equation $(x - a)^2 + (y - b)^2 = 50$?

A) $(a + 3, b - 4)$ B) $(a - 7, b + 1)$ C) $(a + 5, b + 5)$ D) $(a - 4, b - 6)$

Solution: To solve, we plug each point in the answer choices into the equation to find which one gives a value on the left side that is greater than 50, as this shows that the point is outside the circle.

Let's start with answer choice A. To plug in answer choice A, we plug in $a + 3$ for x and $b - 4$ for y.

$$(a + 3 - a)^2 + (b - 4 - b)^2$$

Now, we simplify. Notice how the a and b terms cancel, leaving us with

$$(3)^2 + (-4)^2$$

Solving this, we get a value of 25. 25 is less than 50, so we can tell that $(a + 3, b - 4)$ is inside the circle and incorrect.

Next, let's try answer choice B. To plug in answer choice B, we plug in $a - 7$ for x and $b + 1$ for y.

$$(a - 7 - a)^2 + (b + 1 - b)^2$$

Now, we simplify.

$$(-7)^2 + (1)^2$$

Solving this, we get a value of 50, which tells us that $(a - 7, b + 1)$ is on the circle and incorrect.

Now, let's try answer choice C. To plug in answer choice C, we plug in $a + 5$ for x and $b + 5$ for y.

$$(a + 5 - a)^2 + (b + 5 - b)^2$$

Now, we simplify.

$$(5)^2 + (5)^2$$

Solving this, we get a value of 50, which tells us that $(a + 5, b + 5)$ is on the circle and incorrect.

Finally, let's try answer choice D. To plug in answer choice D, we plug in $a - 4$ for x and $b - 6$ for y.

$$(a - 4 - a)^2 + (b - 6 - b)^2$$

Now, we simplify.

$$(-4)^2 + (-6)^2$$

Solving this, we get a value of 52. 52 is greater than 50, so we can tell that $(a - 4, b - 6)$ is outside the circle. **The answer is D.**

Circles Practice: Answers on page 333.

1. In the standard xy-plane, what is the center of the circle $(x-3)^2 + (y+4)^2 = 16$?

   A) $(-3, 4)$
   B) $(3, 4)$
   C) $(3, -4)$
   D) $(4, 4)$

2. In the standard xy-plane, what is the radius of the circle $(x+5)^2 + (y-3)^2 = 36$?

   A) 3
   B) 5
   C) -5
   D) 6

3. What is the diameter of the circle in the xy-plane with the equation $(x-7)^2 + (y+1)^2 = 25$?

4. $$(x+2)^2 + (y-10)^2 = j$$

   The equation above represents Circle B in the xy-plane. If point $(4, 5)$ lies on Circle B, what is the value of j?

5. In the standard (x, y) coordinate plane, what is the area of the following circle?

   $$(x+2)^2 + (y-3)^2 = 144$$

   A) 10π
   B) 12π
   C) 64π
   D) 144π

6. The equation below represents a circle in the xy-plane. If the point $(a, 9)$ lies on the circle and $a > 0$, what is a possible value of a?

   $$(x)^2 + (y-6)^2 = 58$$

7. The equation below represents circle A in the xy-plane. If point, $(2, b)$ lies on circle A, what is the value of b?

   $$(x+4)^2 + (y+3)^2 = 100$$

   A) 2
   B) 5
   C) 6
   D) 8

8. A circle with center $(-a, -b)$ has a radius of $7c$. Which of the following represents the equation of the circle if a and b are positive values?

   A) $(x+a)^2 + (y+b)^2 = 7c^2$
   B) $(x+a)^2 + (y+b)^2 = 49c^2$
   C) $(x-a)^2 + (y-b)^2 = 7c^2$
   D) $(x-a)^2 + (y-b)^2 = 49c^2$

9. Circle A has a center at $(6, -2)$ and a radius of 2. Circle B is formed by moving Circle A down 6 units and to the left by 3 units. Which of the following gives the correct equation for Circle B?

   A) $(x-3)^2 + (y+8)^2 = 4$
   B) $(x-3)^2 + (y-1)^2 = 4$
   C) $(x)^2 + (y+8)^2 = 4$
   D) $(x+3)^2 + (y-4)^2 = 4$

10. In the xy-plane, circle A has an equation of $(x-1)^2 + (y+5)^2 = 16$, and circle B has an equation of $(x-1)^2 + (y+9)^2 = 16$. Which of the following describes the translation of circle B required to obtain circle A?

    A) Shift 4 units down
    B) Shift 4 units up
    C) Shift 4 units left
    D) Shift 4 units right

11. The equation of a circle in the xy-plane is shown below. If the circle is shifted two units left, one unit down, and the radius is increased by two, what is the new equation of the circle?

    $$(x-6)^2 + (y+2)^2 = 9$$

    A) $(x-8)^2 + (y+1)^2 = 25$
    B) $(x-4)^2 + (y+3)^2 = 25$
    C) $(x-8)^2 + (y+3)^2 = 11$
    D) $(x-8)^2 + (y+3)^2 = 25$

12. In the xy-plane, circle A is described by the equation $(x+4)^2 + (y+3)^2 = 16$ and circle B is described by the equation $(x-1)^2 + (y+3)^2 = 64$. What transformations can be applied to circle A to obtain circle B?

   A) Shift the center to the right 5 units and multiply the radius by 2.
   B) Shift the center to the left 5 units and multiply the radius by 2.
   C) Shift the center to the right 5 units and multiply the radius by 4.
   D) Shift the center to the left 5 units and multiply the radius by 4.

13. The equation of a circle in the xy-plane is shown below. What is the radius of the circle?

   $$x^2 + 4x + y^2 - 6y = 12$$

14. The equation of a circle in the xy-plane is shown below. What are the coordinates of the center of the circle?

   $$x^2 + 4x + y^2 - 8y + 5 = 0$$

   A) $(2, -4)$
   B) $(-2, 4)$
   C) $(4, -8)$
   D) $(-4, 8)$

15. In the xy-plane, points $(-4, -2)$ and $(2, 6)$ are endpoints of the diameter of a circle. An equation of this circle is $(x+1)^2 + (y-2)^2 = r^2$. What is the value of r?

16. In the xy-plane, points $(-3, -7)$ and $(11, -7)$ are the endpoints of the diameter of a circle. An equation of the circle is $(x-a)^2 + (y-b)^2 = c^2$. What is the value of $a + b + c$?

17. $$x^2 + y^2 + 4x + 8y - 16 = 0$$

   For the circle above, the center is at point (a, b) and the radius is c. What is the value of $a + b + c$?

   A) 0
   B) 6
   C) 12
   D) 42

18. Which of the following gives the equation of a circle tangent to $y = 6$ with a center of $(6, 3)$?

   A) $(x-3)^2 + (y+6)^2 = 3$
   B) $(x-6)^2 + (y-3)^2 = 3$
   C) $(x-6)^2 + (y-3)^2 = 9$
   D) $(x+6)^2 + (y+3)^2 = 9$

19. In the xy-plane, points $(8, a)$ and $(-2, b)$ are the endpoints of the diameter of a circle. If the center of that circle is (h, k) and $hk = 18$, what is the value of $a + b$?

   A) 6
   B) 12
   C) 18
   D) 24

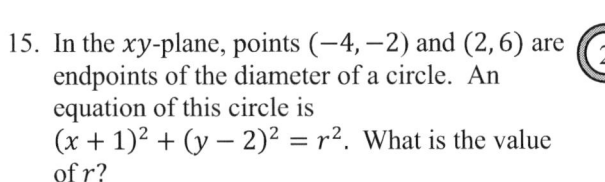

20. The equation below represents a circle in the xy-plane. If the circle is translated so that it is tangent to both the x-axis and y-axis, what is the new equation of the circle?

   $$(x-8)^2 + (y+4)^2 = 25$$

   A) $x^2 + y^2 = 25$
   B) $(x-5)^2 + (y)^2 = 25$
   C) $(x-5)^2 + (y+5)^2 = 25$
   D) $x^2 + (y-5)^2 = 25$

21. The equation of a circle in the xy-plane is shown below. What is the radius of the circle?

   $$x(x-8) + y(y+4) = 5$$

PrepPros

(3) 22. A circle in the xy-plane has its center at $(1, -6)$ and has a radius of 4. An equation of this circle is $x^2 + y^2 + ax + by + c = 0$. What is the value of c?

(3) 27. A circle in the xy-plane has its center at $(-2, 4)$ and has a radius of 9. An equation of this circle is $x^2 + y^2 + ax + by + c = 0$. What is the value of $a + b + c$?

(3) 23. The equation of a circle in the xy-plane is shown below. If the radius of the circle is equal to $2\sqrt{n}$, what is the value of n?

$$x^2 + y^2 - 8x + 10y - 27 = 0$$

(4) 28. In the xy-plane, the graph of the given equation is a circle. Which point lies on the circle?

$$(x + 7)^2 + (y - 6)^2 = 36$$

A) $(-7, 6)$
B) $(7, -6)$
C) $(\sqrt{17} - 7, \sqrt{19} + 6)$
D) $(\sqrt{17} + 7, \sqrt{19} - 6)$

(4) 24. The equation of a circle in the xy-plane is shown below. What is the radius of the circle?

$$2x^2 + 2y^2 + 12x + 16y - 48 = 0$$

(4) 29. In the xy-plane, which of the following points lies on a circle with the equation $(x + a)^2 + (y - b)^2 = 100$?

A) $(a - 3, b + 4)$
B) $(a - 7, b + 7)$
C) $(-a + 5, b + 7)$
D) $(-a - 8, b - 6)$

(4) 25. In the xy-plane, which of the following points lies outside of the circle below?

$$(x - a)^2 + (y - b)^2 = 64$$

A) $(a - 8, b)$
B) $(a + 4, b - 3)$
C) $(a - 4, b + 5)$
D) $(a - 6, b + 7)$

(4) 30. The equation of a circle in the xy-plane is shown below. What are the coordinates of the center of the circle?

$$4x^2 + 20ax + 4y^2 = 3c + 28by$$

A) $(20a, 28b)$
B) $(-5a, -7b)$
C) $(-\frac{5}{2}a, \frac{7}{2}b)$
D) $(-10a, 14b)$

(4) 26. The graph of $\frac{1}{2}x^2 + \frac{1}{2}x + \frac{1}{2}y^2 + \frac{3}{2}y = \frac{157}{4}$ in the xy-plane is a circle. What is the length of the circle's radius?

(4) 31. In the xy-plane, which of the following points lies in the interior of a circle with the equation $(x + h)^2 + (y + k)^2 = 289$?

A) $(-h - 15, -k + 8)$
B) $(-h + 8, -k + 7)$
C) $(-h - 8, -k - 15)$
D) $(-h + 17, -k - 1)$

Chapter 28: Shifting and Transforming Functions

On the SAT, you need to know how lines, parabolas, cubics, and other functions shift and transform in the xy-plane.

Rules for Shifting and Transforming Functions

1. **Numbers inside the parentheses shift a function horizontally.** Adding a number shifts a function that many units to the left and subtracting a number shifts a function that many units to the right.
2. **Numbers outside the parentheses shift a function vertically.** Adding a number shifts a function that many units up and subtracting a number shifts a function that many units down.
3. **A negative sign in front of a function flips the function vertically.**
4. **A coefficient in front of the function causes a vertical transformation.** If the coefficient is greater than 1, it causes a vertical stretch. If the coefficient is less than 1, it causes a vertical compression.

All functions follow the same rules. These rules will be made clearer as we look at some examples for various types of functions. As long as you memorize the rules above, you will be able to solve questions with shifts and transformations of lines, parabolas, and any other type of function.

Lines

Let's start by reviewing the shifts and transformations using the linear function $f(x) = x$.

$f(x) = x$	**Horizontal Shift** $f(x) = (x - 1)$	**Vertical Shift** $f(x) = x + 3$
	Numbers in the parentheses cause a shift right with subtraction (as shown above) and a shift left with addition.	Numbers outside the parentheses cause a shift down with subtraction and a shift up with addition (as shown above).
Vertical Stretch $f(x) = 3x$	**Vertical Compression** $f(x) = \frac{1}{4}x$	**Vertical Flip** $f(x) = -x$
A coefficient that is greater than 1 causes a vertical stretch.	A coefficient that is less than 1 causes a vertical compression.	A negative sign in the front causes the function to reflect over the x-axis.

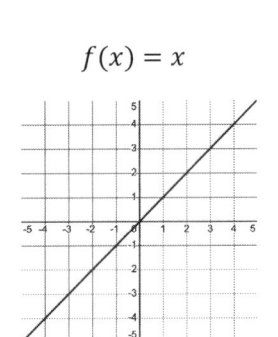

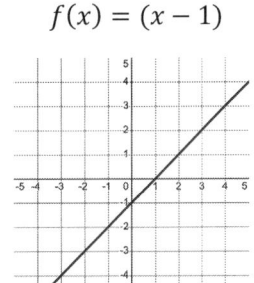

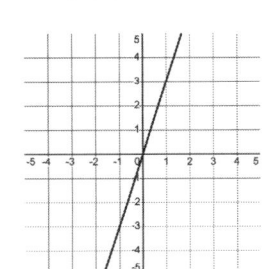

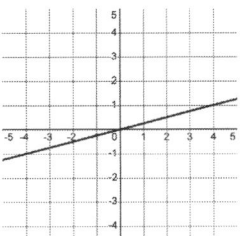

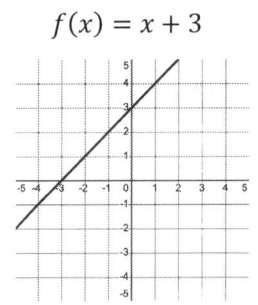

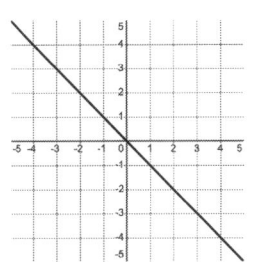

PrepPros

Example 1: The graph of $4x + 2y = 26$ is shifted up 4 units. What is the y-coordinate of the resulting y-intercept?

Solution: Method #1 – Solve Algebraically: First, we need to turn the line from standard form to slope-intercept form. To do this, we isolate y. First, we subtract the $4x$ to get

$$2y = -4x + 25$$

Next, we divide by 2 to get

$$y = -2x + 13$$

The original equation has a y-intercept at $(0, 13)$. If we shift the graph up 4 units, we move the y-intercept up 4 units, so the y-intercept is at $(0, 17)$. **The answer is 17.**

Method #2 – Graph in Desmos: Instead of turning the line from standard form to slope-intercept form, we can simply type in $4x + 2y = 26$ to Desmos to find the y-intercept. The y-intercept of the original equation is at $(0, 13)$. When the graph is shifted up 4 units, the y-intercept shifts up 4 units to $(0, 17)$. **The answer is 17.**

Example 2: The function $h(x)$ is defined as $h(x) = 8(x + 13) - 20$. If $g(x) = h(x - 9)$ and point $(2, k)$ lies on the graph of $g(x)$, what is the value of k?

Solution: The $h(x - 9)$ shifts the original $h(x)$ function 9 units to the right, $g(x)$ is the result of shifting the function $h(x)$ 9 units to the right. To find the equation of $g(x)$, we need to solve for the equation of $h(x - 9)$. To do so, we plug in $x - 9$ for x in the $h(x)$ function.

$$h(x - 9) = 8((x - 9) + 13) - 20$$

Next, we can simplify this equation by distributing the 8 and combining like terms.

$$h(x - 9) = 8(x + 4) - 20$$
$$h(x - 9) = 8x + 32 - 20$$
$$h(x - 9) = 8x + 12$$

Since $h(x - 9) = g(x)$, we know that $g(x) = 8x + 12$. Since point $(2, k)$ lies on the graph of $g(x)$, we plug in $x = 2$ to $g(x)$ find k.

$$g(2) = 8(2) + 12$$
$$g(2) = 16 + 12$$
$$g(2) = 28$$

Since $g(2) = 28$, the point $(2, 28)$ lies on the graph of $g(x)$, so $k = 28$. **The answer is 28.**

For shifting and transforming questions, we expect the SAT to more commonly ask you questions like Example 2, which you cannot easily graph and solve using Desmos. Instead, you will need to understand and apply the shifting and transforming principles to solve these questions correctly on test day.

Parabolas

Next, let's review the shifts and transformations using the parabola function $f(x) = x^2$.

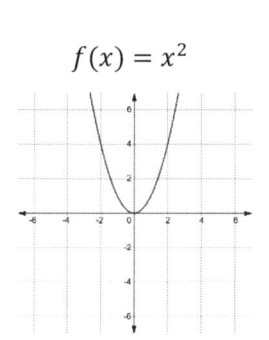

	Horizontal Shift	**Vertical Shift**
$f(x) = x^2$	$f(x) = (x-2)^2$	$f(x) = x^2 - 3$
	Numbers in the parentheses cause a shift right with subtraction (as shown above) and a shift left with addition.	Numbers outside the parentheses cause a shift down with subtraction (as shown above) and a shift up with addition.
Vertical Stretch	**Vertical Compression**	**Vertical Flip**
$f(x) = 4x^2$	$f(x) = \frac{1}{2}x^2$	$f(x) = -x^2$
A coefficient that is greater than 1 causes a vertical stretch.	A coefficient that is less than 1 causes a vertical compression.	A negative sign in the front causes the function to reflect over the x-axis.

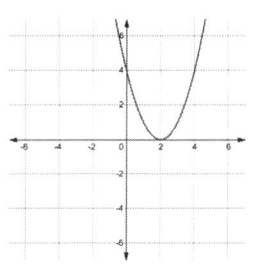

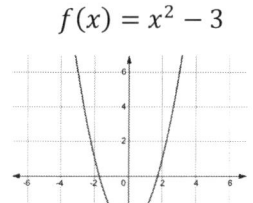

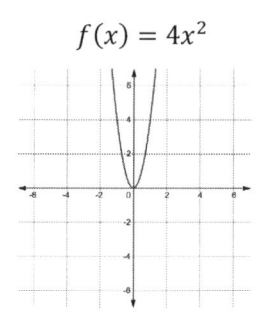

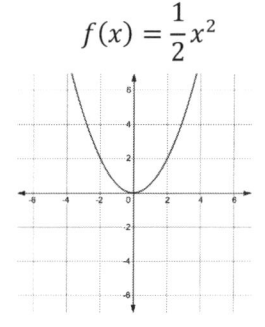

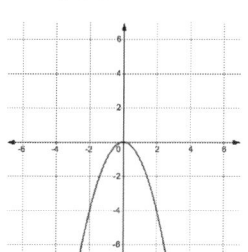

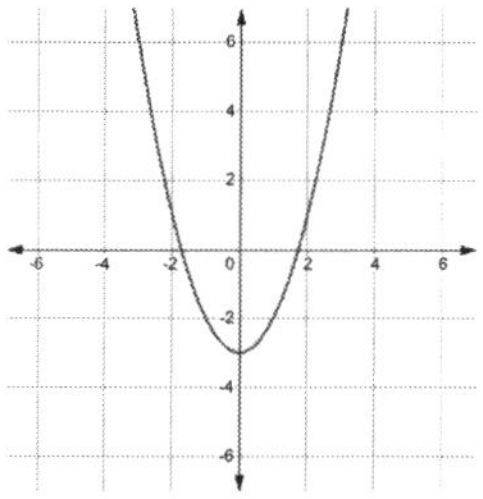

Notice how the shifting and transforming rules for parabolas are the same we saw for lines. Now, let's see how this can be tested on the SAT.

Example 3: The function $f(x)$ is shown in the graph to the right. If $g(x) = f(x+2) + 3$, what is the value of $g(1)$?

A) -1
B) 1
C) 2
D) 3

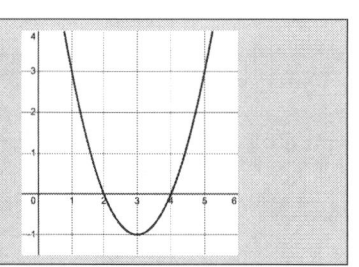

Solution: The function $f(x+2) + 3$ shifts the original $f(x)$ function 2 units left and 3 units up. To find $g(1)$, we have to find the point on $f(x)$ that is shifted 2 units left and 3 unit up to become $g(1)$.

The easiest way to do this is to find the x-value of the point on $f(x)$ that is shifted to $g(1)$. At $g(1)$, the x-value is 1. To find the x-value of the point on $f(x)$, we can reverse the shift and shift 2 unit right from $x = 1$ to $x = 3$. So, we know the point that ends up at $g(1)$ starts at $f(3)$. The point at $f(3)$ is $(3, -1)$.

Now, we can follow the shifts to find $g(1)$. If we shift this point 2 units left and 3 units up, the point $(3, -1)$ is translated to $(1, 2)$. So, $f(1) = 2$ and **the answer is C**.

2-4 All Other Functions

All functions follow the same basic rules for shifting. Lines, parabolas, cubics, exponentials, and any other functions follow the same rules! At times, the SAT asks questions about very weird looking functions. To solve, follow the same rules for shifts and transformations as the lines and parabolas that we just learned.

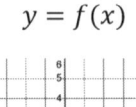

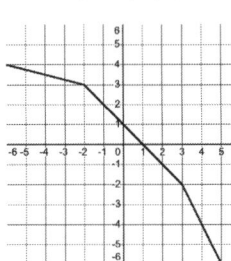

	Horizontal Shift	**Vertical Shift**
$y = f(x)$	$y = f(x + 2)$	$y = f(x) - 3$
	Numbers in the parentheses cause a shift left with addition (as shown above) and a shift right with subtraction.	Numbers outside the parentheses cause a shift down with subtraction (as shown above) and a shift up with addition.
Vertical Stretch	**Vertical Compression**	**Vertical Flip**
$y = 3f(x)$	$y = \frac{1}{3}f(x)$	$y = -f(x)$
A coefficient that is greater than 1 causes a vertical stretch.	A coefficient that is less than 1 causes a vertical compression.	A negative sign in the front causes the function to reflect over the x-axis.

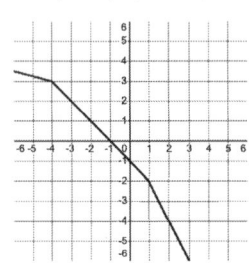

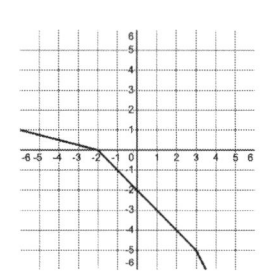

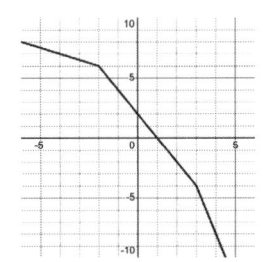

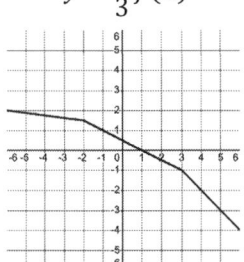

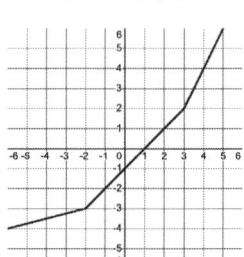

Example 4: The function $p(x + 23) - 18$ is shown to the right. What is $p(24)$ equal to?

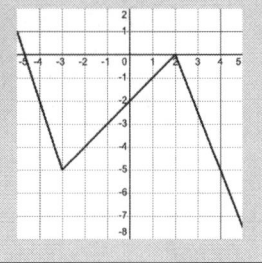

Solution: We are given the graph of the function $p(x + 23) - 18$, which has been shifted left 23 units and down 18 units from the original $p(x)$ function. To find $p(24)$, we have to find the point on the graph of $p(x + 23) - 18$ that $p(24)$ has been shifted to and work backwards.

To start, let's consider the x-values. For $p(24)$, the x-value is 24. When the graph is shifted 23 units left, the x-value becomes 1, so the point $(1, -1)$ on the graph given in the question is where $p(24)$ has been shifted to on $p(x + 23) - 18$. Now that we know the final position of $p(24)$, we can work backwards. Remember, the function $p(x + 23) - 18$ has been shifted 23 units left and 18 units down. To go back to the original $p(x)$ function and find $p(24)$, we shift the point $(1, -1)$ 23 units right and 18 units up to the point $(24, 17)$, which is where $p(24)$ appears on the $p(x)$ function. We find that $p(24) = 17$, so **the answer is 17.**

Chapter 28: Shifting and Transforming Functions

Shifting and Transforming Functions Practice: Answers on page 333.

1. The function $g(x)$ is given below. What is the y-intercept of the graph $g(x) - 7$?

   $$g(x) = 4(16x - 8)$$

2. $$f(x) = x^2$$
   $$g(x) = (x - 7)^2 + 17$$

   Which of the following correctly describes the shift required to transform $f(x)$ into $g(x)$?

   A) Shift $f(x)$ right 7 units and down 17 units.
   B) Shift $f(x)$ right 7 units and up 17 units.
   C) Shift $f(x)$ left 7 units and down 17 units.
   D) Shift $f(x)$ left 7 units and up 17 units.

3. $$h(x) = x^2 - 5$$
   $$g(x) = (x - 2)^2 - 1$$

   Which of the following correctly describes the shift required to transform $h(x)$ into $g(x)$?

   A) Shift $h(x)$ right 2 units and down 4 units.
   B) Shift $h(x)$ right 2 units and up 4 units.
   C) Shift $h(x)$ left 2 units and down 4 units.
   D) Shift $h(x)$ left 2 units and up 4 units.

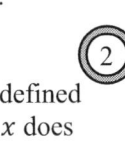

4. The function f is defined by $f(x) = x^2 + 5x + 6$. The function g is defined by $g(x) = f(x) + 3$. For what value of x does $g(x)$ reach its minimum?

5. $$f(x) = (x + 1)^3 + 2$$

   Which of the following functions $g(x)$ shifts $f(x)$ up by 4 units and left by 1 unit?

   A) $g(x) = x^3 + 6$
   B) $g(x) = (x + 5)^3 + 3$
   C) $g(x) = (x + 2)^3 - 2$
   D) $g(x) = (x + 2)^3 + 6$

6. The function $f(x)$ shown below is the result of translating $g(x)$ up 7 units. What is the y-intercept of $g(x)$?

   $$f(x) = (x - 1)(x + 6)(x + 8)$$

7. The graph of $y = f(x) + 17$ is shown below, which of the following defines function f?

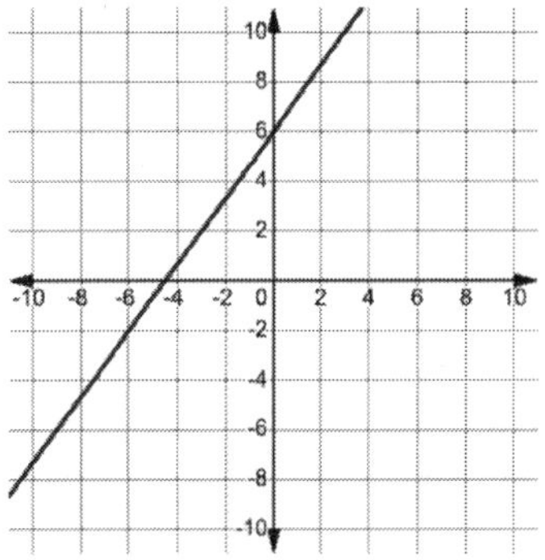

   A) $f(x) = \frac{4}{3}x - 6$
   B) $f(x) = \frac{4}{3}x - 11$
   C) $f(x) = \frac{4}{3}x + 6$
   D) $f(x) = \frac{4}{3}x + 23$

8. The function f is defined by $f(x) = (x - 7)(x - 4)(x + 5)$. In the xy-plane, the graph of $y = g(x)$ is the result of translating the graph of $f(x)$ up 13 units. What is the value of $g(0)$?

9. In the xy-plane, the graph of $y = 7 - (x - 4)^2$ is the image of the graph of $y = 2 - x^2$ after which of the following transformations?

   A) A translation of 5 units up and 4 units to the right.
   B) A translation of 5 units down and 4 units to the right.
   C) A translation of 5 units up and 4 units to the left.
   D) A translation of 5 units down and 4 units to the left.

10. The function below defines $g(x)$. What is the y-coordinate of the y-intercept of the $g(x) + 7$?

    $$g(x) = 17(8x - 15)$$

- 267 -

11. The graph of $f(x)$ is displayed above. Which of the following is the graph of $y = f(x) - 3$?

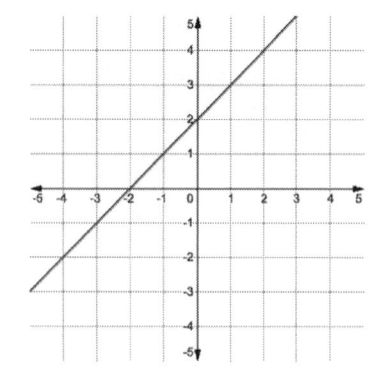

A)

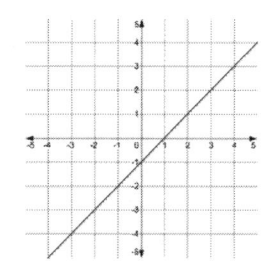

B)

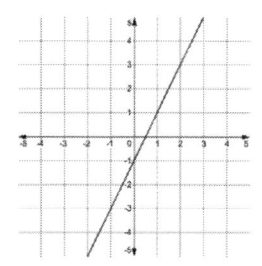

C)

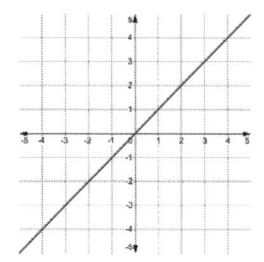

D)

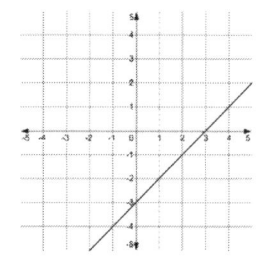

12. The quadratic function f is defined as $f(x) = -3(x + 2)^2 - 1$. In the xy-plane, which of the following could be the graph of $f(x)$ shifted 4 units up?

A)

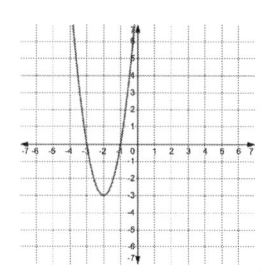

B)

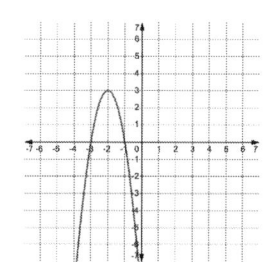

C)

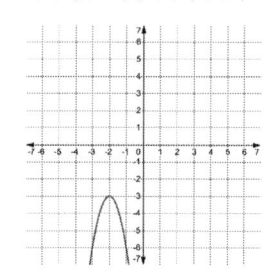

D)

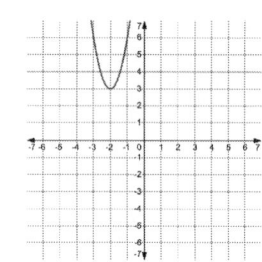

13. $$g(x) = -(x - 2)^2 + 9$$
$$h(x) = -(x + 2)^2 + 11$$

Which of the following transformation are required to turn $h(x)$ into $g(x)$?

A) Shift 2 units left and reflect over the x-axis.
B) Shift 4 units left and 2 units up.
C) Shift 4 units right and reflect over the x-axis.
D) Shift 4 units right and 2 units down.

14.

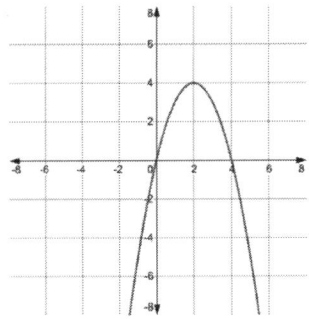

The graph above displays the function for the height of a soccer pass in meters after the referee blew the whistle to restart the game. Which of the graphs below properly model the height of the soccer ball if the player had waited 3 seconds after the referee blew the whistle to make the same pass?

A)

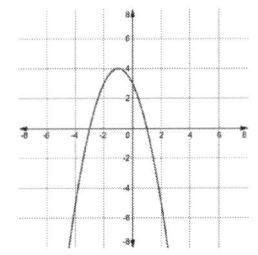

B)

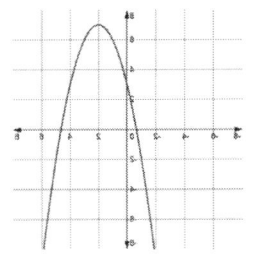

C)

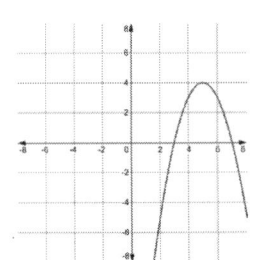

D)

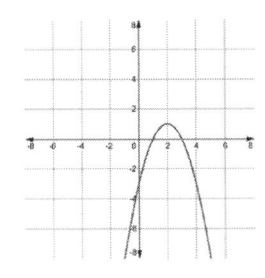

15. The graph of $y = f(x)$ is shown in the xy-plane. The graph of $g(x) = f(x) + 11$. What is the value of $g(0)$?

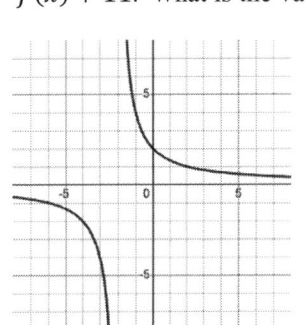

16. The complete graph of the function f is shown in the xy-plane. What is the y-intercept of the graph of $y = f(x-2)$?

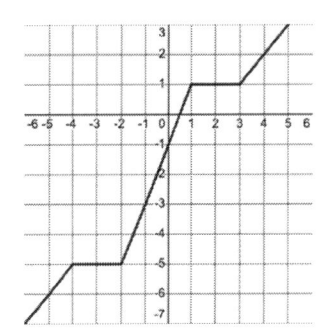

A) -5
B) -3
C) -1
D) 1

17. The graph of $y = f(x) + 2$ is shown below. Which equation defines the function f?

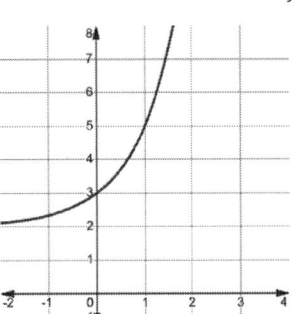

A) $f(x) = 2^x$
B) $f(x) = 3^x$
C) $f(x) = 2^x + 2$
D) $f(x) = 3^x + 2$

18. The function below defines $g(x)$. What is the y-coordinate of the y-intercept of $g(x-3)$?

$$g(x) = 2(25x - 15)$$

19. The graph of $5x + 7y = 12$ is translated down 5 units in the xy-plane. What is the x-coordinate of the x-intercept of the resulting graph?

20.

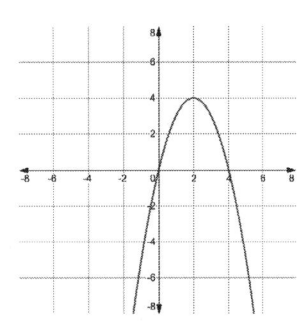

The graph above displays the function $f(x-4) + 1$. Which of the following is the correct equation for $f(x)$?

A) $f(x) = -(x+2)^2 + 3$
B) $f(x) = -(x-2)^2 + 4$
C) $f(x) = -x^2 + 5$
D) $f(x) = -(x-6)^2 + 5$

21. The function f is defined by $f(x) = (-7)(5)^x + 3$. What is the y-intercept of the graph of $y = f(x-2)$ in the xy-plane?

22. The functions f and g are defined as $f(x) = \frac{3}{5}x - 17$ and $g(x) = \frac{1}{3}x + 38$. If $h(x) = f(x) + g(x) - 17$, what is the x-coordinate of the x-intercept of $y = h(x)$ in the xy-plane?

23.

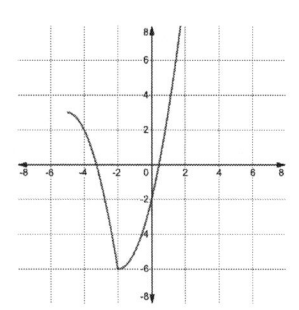

The function $y = f(x+2) + 1$ is show above. What is the y-intercept of $f(x)$?

A) -4
B) -5
C) -6
D) -7

24. Line k contains the points $(14, 166)$ and $(19, 206)$. Line a is the result of translating line k down 7 units in the xy-plane. What is the x-coordinate of the x-intercept of line a?

25. When the quadratic function f is graphed in the xy-plane, where $y = f(x)$, its vertex is $(8.5, -20.25)$, one of the x-intercepts of this graph is $(4, 0)$. If $g(x) = f(x) - 17$, what is the y-intercept of $g(x)$?

26. The function f is defined by the given equation. If $g(x) = f(x+3)$, which of the following equations defines the function g?

$$f(x) = 7(3)^x$$

A) $g(x) = 21(3)^x$
B) $g(x) = 189(3)^x$
C) $g(x) = 21(9)^x$
D) $g(x) = 343(9)^x$

27. The points on the quadratic function $f(x)$ are shown in the table below. If $g(x) = f(x) - 371$. What is $g(0)$?

x	$f(x)$
14	35
16	21
18	35

Chapter 29: Absolute Value

Absolute value is defined as a number's distance from zero. Since a distance can never be negative, the absolute value is always positive.

$$|3| = 3 \quad \text{(3 is three units from zero)}$$
$$|-3| = 3 \quad \text{(−3 is three units from zero)}$$

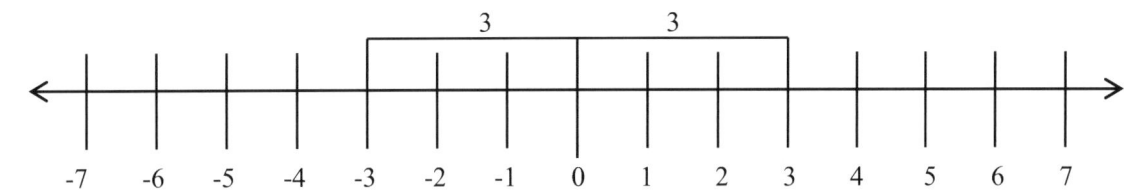

For equations with absolute value bars, **complete any math inside the absolute value bars first**. Then, solve the rest of the equation. For example, to solve

$$|3 - 7| + 2$$

Start by working inside the absolute value bars to get

$$|-4| + 2$$

$|-4| = 4$, so the equation becomes

$$4 + 2 = 6$$

Example 1: $a = |2 + 11| - 2|3 - 5|$

For the equation above, what is the value of a?

Solution: We start by working inside the absolute value bars. The equation becomes

$$a = |13| - 2|-2|$$

$|13| = 13$ and $|-2| = 2$, so we get

$$a = 13 - 2(2)$$
$$a = 9$$

The answer is 9.

Absolute Value and Unknown Variables

What if there is an unknown variable inside the absolute value bars? Let's consider the equation below.

$$|x - 3| = 5$$

For any equation like this, there are two answers. Since $|5| = 5$ and $|-5| = 5$, we need to solve for the values of x when $x - 3 = 5$ and $x - 3 = -5$.

$$x - 3 = 5 \qquad\qquad x - 3 = -5$$
$$x = 8 \qquad\qquad x = -2$$

Both $x = -2$ and $x = 8$ are correct answers.

- 271 -

For any question with an unknown variable inside the absolute value bars, there are multiple solutions. To solve, we must get the absolute value bars on one side of the equation and all other terms on the other side. There are four steps to solve these questions.

1. **Move all terms outside of the absolute value bars to the other side of the equation. First, add or subtracting any constants outside of the absolute value bars.**

2. **Next, divide or multiply any terms directly in front of the absolute value bars.** After this step, we should have the absolute value bar on one side of the equation by itself and all constants on the other side.

3. **Set the term inside the absolute value bars equal to the positive value (1st equation) and negative value (2nd equation) of the term(s) on the other side.**

4. **Solve both equations to get the values of the unknown variable.**

Example 2: For the equation $3|2x + 1| - 6 = 45$, what is a positive value of x that solves the equation?

Solution: Method #1 – Solve Algebraically: To solve, we need to move terms outside of the absolute value bars to the other side of the equation. Here, we have the absolute value bars on the left side of the equation, so we will move all constants outside of the absolute value bars to the right side.

We start with any constants outside of the absolute value bars that can be added or subtracted, which in this case is the -6.

$$3|2x + 1| - 6 = 45$$

To move the -6 to the right side, we add 6 to both sides.

$$3|2x + 1| = 51$$

Next, we must move the 3 to the right side. We can do this by dividing both sides by 3 to get

$$|2x + 1| = 17$$

Now that the absolute value bars are on one side and the constants are on the other, we can solve by setting the term inside the absolute value bar equal to $+17$ and -17 and solving both equations.

$$2x + 1 = 17 \qquad 2x + 1 = -17$$
$$2x = 16 \qquad 2x = -18$$
$$x = 8 \qquad x = -9$$

The question asks for a positive value of x, so **the answer is 8**.

Method #2 – Desmos Hack #1 for Solving Algebra Equations: Write the equations in Desmos as $y = 3|2x + 1| - 6$ and $y = 45$, and look for the points of intersection. The graphs intersect at points $(-9, -45)$ and $(8, 45)$. We are finding the positive x-value in this question, which is $x = 8$, so **the answer is 8**. To review the Desmos Hack #1, go to p. 14.

Using the Desmos Hack for solving algebra equation is easier and faster, so we recommend using this method on test day.

Chapter 29: Absolute Value

Advanced Absolute Value

For advanced absolute value questions, the SAT can include equations that have variables both inside and outside the absolute value bars. We solve these equations using the same steps we have used so far in this chapter, but we have to add one final step at the end: check for extraneous solutions.

Example 3: For the equation $-2|x - 5| = -4x$, what value(s) of x are solutions to the equation?

A) -5 B) $\frac{5}{3}$ C) -5 and $\frac{5}{3}$ D) -5 and 5

Solution – Method #1 – Solve Algebraically: First, we want to isolate the absolute value bars, so we divide both sides by -2 to get

$$|x - 5| = 2x$$

Now that the absolute value bars are isolated, we can solve by setting the term inside the absolute value bar equal to $+2x$ and $-2x$ and solving both equations.

$$x - 5 = 2x \qquad\qquad x - 5 = -2x$$
$$-x = 5 \qquad\qquad 3x = 5$$
$$x = -5 \qquad\qquad x = \frac{5}{3}$$

At first, it looks like answer choice C is correct, but we need to test both of our solutions to make sure that they make the original equation true. Let's first test $x = -5$ by plugging in -5 for x in the original equation.

$$-2|-5 - 5| = -4(-5)$$
$$-2|-10| = 20$$
$$-20 = 20$$

Since $-20 \neq 20$, we find that $x = -5$ does not satisfy the original equation, so $x = -5$ is not a solution. $x = -5$ is an extraneous solution.

Next, let's test $x = \frac{5}{3}$ by plugging in $\frac{5}{3}$ for x in the original equation.

$$-2\left|\frac{5}{3} - 5\right| = -4\left(\frac{5}{3}\right)$$
$$-2\left|\frac{5}{3} - \frac{15}{3}\right| = -\frac{20}{3}$$
$$-2\left|-\frac{10}{3}\right| = -\frac{20}{3}$$
$$-2\left(\frac{10}{3}\right) = -\frac{20}{3}$$
$$-\frac{20}{3} = -\frac{20}{3}$$

We find that $x = \frac{5}{3}$ works and is a solution, so **the answer is B.**

Method #2 – Backsolve: We can also backsolve with the answer choices. If we plug in the answer choices to the original equation, only $x = \frac{5}{3}$ works. **The answer is B.**

Method #3 – Desmos Hack #1 for Solving Algebra Equations: Write the equations in Desmos as $y = -2|x - 5|$ and $y = 4x$. The graphs intersect at the point $(1.667, -6.667)$. The x-coordinate is at 1.667, which is equivalent to $\frac{5}{3}$, so **the answer is $\frac{5}{3}$.** This method is the easiest way to solve Example 3.

- 273 -

Absolute Value with 1 Solution, No Solution, and Infinite Solutions

Advanced absolute value questions ask about equations with 1 solution, no solution, and infinite solutions. To answer these questions correctly, you need to memorize the rules in the table below.

Number of Solutions	Rule	Example
1 Solution	The absolute value equals 0 (or less commonly one of the solutions is extraneous, as we saw in Example 3).	$\|x - 3\| = 0$ The only solution is at $x = 3$
No Solution	The absolute value is equal to a negative number. OR There are absolute value bars on both sides of the equation. The coefficients for the x-terms inside the absolute value bars are identical and the constants are different (this is further explained on p. 283).	$\|x - 3\| = -2$ $\|x - 3\| = \|x + 2\|$ There is no solution.
Infinite Solution	There are absolute value bars on both sides of the equation, and the terms inside the absolute value bars are identical.	$\|x - 3\| = \|x - 3\|$ There are infinite solutions.

*Note: If the term inside the absolute value bars has a squared term and the absolute value is equal to 0, such as $|x^2 - 4| = 0$, there can be 2 solutions. For $|x^2 - 4| = 0$, the solutions are $x = -2$ and $x = 2$.

Example 4: For the equation $|0.8x - 20| + k = 28$, for what value of k does the equation have one solution?

Solution: To have one solution, the absolute value must be equal to 0. If the equation looks like $|0.8x - 20| = 0$, there is one solution. So, we want to isolate the absolute value bars by subtracting k from both sides and then find what value of k makes the right side equal 0.

$$|0.8x - 20| = 28 - k$$

To make right side be equal to 0, k must be equal to 28. **The answer is 28.**

Example 5: Which of the following equations has no solution?

A) $|3 - x^2| + 2 = 1$ B) $5 - 2|4x - 9| = -3$ C) $\left|\frac{1}{2}(x - 22)\right| = \frac{5}{4}$ D) $|2(x - 1)| = |2x - 2|$

Solution: For an absolute value equation to have no solution, the absolute value must be equal to a negative number. To test each answer choice, we need to isolate the absolute value bars on one side of the equation and move the constants to the other side.

Let's start with answer choice A. To isolate the absolute value bars, we subtract 2 from both sides to get

$$|3 - x^2| = -1$$

An absolute value can never be negative, so there is no solution to this equation. **The answer is A.**

Let's solve the other answer choices as well to understand this topic better. For answer choice B, we first subtract 5 from both sides to get

$$-2|4x - 9| = -8$$

Next, we divide by -2 to get

$$|4x - 9| = 4$$

Since the absolute value is equal to a positive number, there are 2 solutions to answer choice B.

Chapter 29: Absolute Value

For answer choice C, we already have the absolute value bars isolated, so we can just look at the equation. Since the absolute value is equal to a positive number, there are 2 solutions to answer choice C.

For answer choice D, we have absolute value bars on both sides. Here, we want to see if the values inside the absolute value bars are identical (infinite solutions) or not identical (no solution). If we distribute the 2 on the left-hand side, we get

$$|2x - 2| = |2x - 2|$$

Since the terms inside the absolute value bars are identical, there are infinite solutions for answer choice D.

Absolute Value Practice: Answers on page 333.

1. $|8 - 5| - |4 - 8| =$

   A) -1
   B) 0
   C) 3
   D) 7

2. $|5(-3) + 4| =$

   A) -11
   B) 4
   C) 11
   D) 19

3. What is the value of $|3x - 4| + 5$ when $x = -7$?

4. If $x = 4$, what is $|3x - 6| + |-4x + 8|$ equal?

5. What is a solution to $|3x + 6| = 24$ where $x > 0$?

6. What is the solution set to $|x + 4| = 8$?

   A) $x = 4$
   B) $x = -4$
   C) $x = -12$
   D) $x = 4, -12$

7. The value of one solution to the equation below is 3. What is the value of the other solution?
   $$|9 - x| = 6$$

8. $$|36 - 3x| + 46 = 64$$
   The value of one solution to the equation above is 6. What is the value of the other solution?

9. What is the sum of solutions to the equation below?
   $$3|1.5x - 4.35| = 294.75$$

10. $$\frac{3}{2}|4a + 4| - 4 = 20$$
    If x and y are the solutions to the equation above, what is $|xy|$?

11. If $|4x - 3| + 2 = 15$ and $|5y + 3| = 17$ what is the smallest possible value of xy?

    A) -20
    B) -16
    C) -11
    D) -4

12. What are all possible solutions to the given equation below?
    $$-4|x - 3| = -16x$$

    A) -1
    B) $\frac{3}{5}$
    C) -1 and $\frac{3}{5}$
    D) 1 and $-\frac{3}{5}$

- 275 -

PrepPros

13. If $|7x - 2| = |3x|$, what is the least possible solution?

14. If $\left|\frac{5}{3}x - 84\right| = \left|\frac{5}{2}x\right|$, what is the greatest possible solution?

15. What is the positive solution to the equation below?
$$6|5 - x| + 3|5 - x| = 63$$

16. The function f is defined by the given equation. For which of the following values of a does $f(a) = 7a$?
$$f(x) = |97 - 5x|$$

A) $-\frac{97}{2}$
B) $\frac{97}{12}$
C) $\frac{97}{2}$
D) 97

17. What is the sum of all possible solutions to the given equation below?
$$-3|4x - 7| = -16x$$

18. What is a negative solution to the equation below?
$$10.75|1.25x + 1.4| - 4.5|1.25x + 1.4| = 22.5$$

19. For the equation below, the solution is equal to a. What is a possible value of a given that $a > 0$?
$$\left|\frac{x + 48}{6x}\right| = \frac{24}{9}$$

20. What is the sum of all possible solutions to the given equation below?
$$|x^2 - 17x + 45| = 4x - 9$$

21. Which of the following equations has no solution?

A) $3 - \left|\frac{9}{4}x + \frac{8}{5}\right| = \frac{20}{3}$
B) $|4x + 182| = |2.75x + 101|$
C) $-3\left|\frac{11}{9}x - \frac{3}{11}\right| = -108$
D) $|x^2 - 6x + 9| = 12$

22. What is the value of $\frac{k}{13}$ if the equation shown below only has one solution?
$$13|x - 7| = k$$

A) -7
B) 7
C) -7 or 7
D) 0

23. Which of the following inequalities gives a value of c where the equation below has no solution?
$$\frac{4}{3}|20 - x^2| = \frac{9}{5} - 12c$$

A) $-\sqrt{20} < c < \sqrt{20}$
B) $c < -\sqrt{20}$ and $c > \sqrt{20}$
C) $c < \frac{3}{20}$
D) $c > \frac{3}{20}$

- 276 -

Chapter 30: Word Problems

One of the challenges of the SAT Math Test is dealing with everyone's least favorite questions: word problems. Word problems are often written in a way that makes it difficult to figure out exactly what is happening in the question. Word problems includes a wide variety of math topics that we have already learned in this book, so we will not cover any particular type of word problem in this chapter. Instead, we will focus on the tips that can help you solve all types of word problems more effectively and efficiently.

Tip #1 – Do Not Be Intimidated

Word problems look scary. Many students see a big paragraph and say, "no way, I can't solve that." They feel intimidated before even trying to solve the question. Do not let this be you! Word problems at their core are no more difficult than any other SAT Math questions. When you see a math question with a big paragraph on test day, take a deep breath and solve it one step at a time.

Tip #2 – Turn Words into Equations

When approaching a word problem, take it one sentence at a time. As you read through the question, identify each key piece of information, and write it down in an equation if necessary. If you can convert the question from a word problem into an equation or equation(s), the question will be much easier to solve.

Often, word problems are actually just systems of equations questions. For questions like these, which we covered in Chapter 12, you will need to write down two equations. Once you have converted the word problem into two equations, you will be able to solve the question with the methods we learned in Chapter 12.

Tip #3 – Backsolve with the Answer Choices

For some word problems, writing your own equation(s) is very difficult. If you cannot write out the equation(s) or are not sure if the equation(s) that you wrote are correct, see if you can use the backsolving method we learned in Chapter 1. Sometimes it is easier to backsolve by taking the answer choices, going through the steps of the word problem, and seeing if the answer choice you selected works. Even if you cannot tell which answer is correct, backsolving can often help you eliminate some answer choices and make a better guess. If you need to review how to backsolve, go back to Chapter 1.

Tip #4 – Guess and Move on (If You Have To)

If you get to a word problem, try using the tips above, and still have no idea how to solve it, mark the question for review, select your best guess, and move on! It is easy to waste a lot of time reading and re-reading long, confusing word problems. Students who do this often end up running out of time. Save those precious minutes to answer more questions that you know how to solve. We know it sounds backwards but giving up quickly on a word problem that you have no idea how to solve may help you actually get a better score.

If you complete the rest of the questions in the section and have time remaining, you can always come back to any questions that you guessed on. Sometimes when re-reading the question, you will realize how to solve it. It is easier to think more clearly when you are no longer worried about finishing the rest of the questions in the section.

Word Problems Practice: Answers on pages 333-334.

1. Last weekend, Jenny made x cookies per hour for 2 hours, and Cara made y cookies per hour for 3 hours. Which of the following represents the total number of cookies made by Jenny and Cara?

   A) $6xy$
   B) $3x + 2y$
   C) $2x + 3y$
   D) $5xy$

2. Jimmy is a lawyer. Every week, Jimmy has new clients who need their Wills drafted. The number of Wills that Jimmy needs to finish each week is estimated by the equation $W = 42 - 7d$, where W represents the number of Wills left and d is the number of days he has worked. What is the meaning of the number 42 in this equation?

   A) Jimmy will finish the Wills in 42 days.
   B) Jimmy finishes 42 Wills per day.
   C) Jimmy finishes 6 Wills per hour.
   D) Jimmy starts each week with an estimated 42 Wills to complete.

3. Chris was skateboarding at 8 feet per second when he came to the top of a hill. After riding down the hill for 3.5 seconds, he was moving at 43 feet per second. Assuming the acceleration was constant, what was his acceleration in feet per second?

   A) 8
   B) 10
   C) 12
   D) 14

4. A company decides to sponsor an employee softball team. The cost to form the team is $75 per member plus a onetime $50 team registration fee. What is the maximum number of team members who can join the team, if the company can spend $780 for the softball team?

5. The equation below relates the number of avocados, x, John buys each week and the number of bananas, y, John buys each week. If each avocado costs $2.25 and each banana costs $0.75, what does the number 35 represent?

   $$2.25x + 0.75y = 35$$

   A) The number of avocados purchased each week.
   B) The amount of money spent purchasing avocados and bananas each week.
   C) The total number of avocados and bananas purchased each week.
   D) The difference between the number of the avocados and the number of bananas purchased each week.

6. Jason bought five burgers for a total of $30.97 including a $0.22 sales tax. What would be the cost without sales tax if Jason bought four burgers?

   A) $18.00
   B) $20.25
   C) $24.60
   D) $28.00

7. The given equation below describes the relationship between the number of trucks, t, and the number of cars, c, that can be serviced at an automobile shop on a given day. If the business services 16 trucks on a given day, how many cars can it service on this day?

   $$34c + 52t = 1{,}070$$

8. John and Matt each ordered food at their favorite restaurant in Italy. The price of John's meal was y dollars and the price of Matt's meal was $6 more than John's meal. Since John is nice, they split the cost of the meal evenly. There was no tip or sales tax. Which of the following expressions represents the amount, in dollars, each of them paid?

   A) y
   B) $y + 6$
   C) $y + 3$
   D) $2y + 6$

9. James, Danny, and John all own stock in an oil company. James owns 40 shares, Danny owns 35 shares, and John owns 28 shares. If the value of one share is $7, what is the value of all of their shares combined?

    A) $441
    B) $476
    C) $721
    D) $796

10. Debbie's Cupcake Company serves an average of 146 people each day in 2020. This is 12 less than half the average number of customers the company served each day last year. How many customers did Debbie's Cupcake Company serve on average every day last year?

11. Jamie makes pies and cookies. It takes her 20 minutes to make a pie and 30 minutes to make a tray of cookies. This weekend Jamie is going to spend 8 hours making pies and cookies. She will make twice as many trays of cookies as pies. How many trays of cookies will she make?

    A) 6
    B) 8
    C) 10
    D) 12

12. A farmer wants to buy horses and cows. The farmer has a budget of $17,000 and wants to buy at least 13 animals. The price of each horse is $1,800 the price of each cow is $1,100. What is the maximum number of horses that can be purchased?

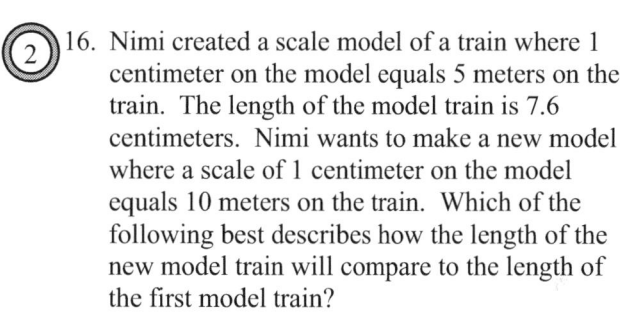

13. The product of 2 positive integers is 84. The smaller integer is one more than one half of the greater integer. What is the smaller integer?

    A) 5
    B) 6
    C) 7
    D) 12

14. Acme Company manufactures sticks of dynamite. This week, Acme Company manufactured 63 more sticks of dynamite on Monday than on Tuesday. If a total of 873 sticks of dynamite were manufactured on Monday and Tuesday, how many sticks did Acme Company manufacture on Tuesday?

    A) 400
    B) 405
    C) 468
    D) 810

15. Danny earns $8.50 per hour for the first 40 hours each week and 1.5 times as much for every additional hour he works. If Danny made $505.75 last week, how many total hours did he work?

16. Nimi created a scale model of a train where 1 centimeter on the model equals 5 meters on the train. The length of the model train is 7.6 centimeters. Nimi wants to make a new model where a scale of 1 centimeter on the model equals 10 meters on the train. Which of the following best describes how the length of the new model train will compare to the length of the first model train?

    A) The length of the new model train will be 10 centimeters longer than the length of the first model train.
    B) The length of the new model train will be 10 centimeters shorter than the length of the first model train.
    C) The length of the new model train will be $\frac{1}{2}$ as long as the length of the first model train.
    D) The length of the new model train will be 2 times as long as the length of the first model train.

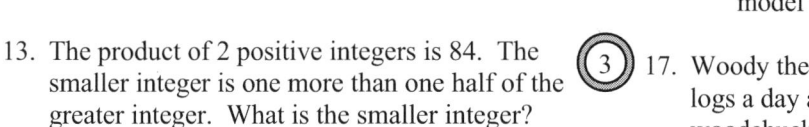

17. Woody the woodchuck can chuck at least 13 logs a day and at most 19 logs a day. Willy the woodchuck can chuck at least 7 logs a day and at most 16 logs a day. Based on this, what is a possible number of days it would take Woody and Willy to chuck 175 logs?

18. A regional train company sells a monthly pass for $275. Tickets for individual trips cost $7.75, $13.50, or $17.50, depending on the length of the trip. What is the minimum number of trips per month for which a monthly pass would cost less than purchasing individual tickets for trips?

19. An industrial printer is loaded with 32,000 sheets of paper. The machine starts a large job and prints at a constant rate. After 12 minutes, the printer has used 5% of the paper. Which of the following equations models the number of sheets of paper, p, remaining in the printer h hours after the printer started printing?

A) $p = 32,000 - 1,600h$
B) $p = 32,000 - 8,000h$
C) $p = 32,000(0.05)^{\frac{h}{5}}$
D) $p = 32,000(0.95)^{\frac{h}{5}}$

20. The area of a rectangular rug is 88 feet. The rug's length x, in feet, is 7 feet shorter than its width. Which equation represents this situation?

A) $x^2 - 7 = 88$
B) $x^2 - 7x = 88$
C) $x^2 + 7 = 88$
D) $x^2 + 7x = 88$

21. Johnny's transport company has a ferry with a weight limit of 35,000 pounds. The ferry is already carrying 13,050 pounds in shipments when it arrives at the dock. If each additional crate weighs 750 pounds, what is the maximum number of new crates that the ferry can transport?

22. A cruise ship has a total of 480 rooms, and on a certain morning, one quarter of the rooms are cleaned. There are 15 housekeepers on duty on the cruise ship that morning, and each housekeeper cleans the same number of rooms, r. Which of the following equations represents the information given in terms of r?

A) $4(15r) = 480$
B) $\frac{1}{4}(15r) = 480$
C) $4(r + 15) = 480$
D) $\frac{1}{4}(r + 15) = 480$

23. The Jones family is throwing a huge surprise party for their grandfather's 80th birthday. The birthday party costs $18,000. All the family members agree to split the cost of the party equally. When 3 members of the family later refused to pay for the event, the remaining members of the family each had to pay an additional $1,000. How many family members were initially going to split the costs for the party?

24. To build a new field, a certain number of companies are going to donate a total of $250,000. Each company will donate the same amount of money. Right at the deadline, 5 more companies decide to donate, and, as a result of the additional companies, each company will pay $2,500 less. How many companies were initially going to donate to pay for the field?

25. A rectangular area consists of 1,372 equal squares where each square has an area of k. If the width of the rectangular area is 1.75 times the length and the length is equal to $x\sqrt{k}$, what is the value of x?

Chapter 31: Solving for Constants

On the SAT, we need to know how to solve for constants that appear in various forms of linear, quadratic, or other polynomial equations. There will be four forms of these questions: solving for constants in equivalent equations and solving for constants in equations with no solution, infinite solutions, and one solution.

Solving for Constants in Equivalent Equations

The SAT asks us to find the value(s) of constant(s) in equivalent forms of the same equation. These questions are easy to spot because you will see an equal sign between the two forms of the equation.

Let's start with an easy example to understand the concept.

> **Example 1:** $\qquad 2ax + 10 = 14x + 10$
>
> For the equation above, a is a constant. What is the value of a?
>
> A) 28 B) 14 C) 7 D) 2

Solution: For the equations to be equal, both sides must be identical. Since both sides already have constants (+10) that are the same, we need to make the x-terms equal.

$$2ax = 14x$$
$$ax = 7x$$

So, we see that
$$a = 7$$

The answer is C.

> **Example 2:** $\qquad (px - 5)(7x + 1) = 14x^2 - 33x - 5$
>
> For the equation above, p is a constant. What is the value of p?
>
> A) 1 B) 2 C) 3 D) 4

Solution: Using our rules for multiplying polynomials (FOIL), we know that we multiply the first 2 terms "px" and "$7x$" in the binomials to get first term $14x^2$, so

$$(px)(7x) = 14x^2$$

We can see that
$$p = 2$$

The answer is B.

> **Example 3:** $\qquad x^4 - 4x(ax^3 + 3) = 13x^4 - 12x$
>
> For the equation above, a is a constant. What is the value of a?
>
> A) −3 B) −2 C) 1 D) 2

Solution: This question is a bit more difficult than the first two we have seen so far. It is important to remember that both sides need to be equal. We can start by distributing the $4x$, so the equation looks like this:

$$x^4 - 4ax^4 - 12x = 13x^4 - 12x$$

The x-terms are already equal on both sides since both sides of the equation have $-12x$, so we just need to make the x^4 terms equal to solve.

$$x^4 - 4ax^4 = 13x^4$$

Combining like terms we get
$$-4ax^4 = 12x^4$$
$$a = -3$$

The answer is A.

Example 4: $\frac{1}{4}(mx + 38) + 2x = \frac{23}{4}x + \frac{19}{2}$

For the equation above, m is a constant. What is the value of m?

A) 21   B) 15   C) 13   D) 9

Solution: As in the last example, we need to make sure both sides are identical. We can start by distributing the $\frac{1}{4}$ to get
$$\frac{1}{4}mx + \frac{19}{2} + 2x = \frac{23}{4}x + \frac{19}{2}$$

The constants, $\frac{19}{2}$, are already equal on both sides, so we just need to make the x-terms equal to solve.
$$\frac{1}{4}mx + 2x = \frac{23}{4}x$$

At this point, we can remove the x's since all terms have an x.
$$\frac{1}{4}m + 2 = \frac{23}{4}$$

To get rid of the fractions, we multiply both sides by 4 to get
$$m + 8 = 23$$
$$m = 15$$

The answer is B.

Solving for Constants in Equivalent Equations with Multiple Unknowns

Solving for constants questions can include multiple unknowns in the same equation. While these questions may look more difficult, we solve them the same way. The key is to identify the terms that each unknown constant value is involved in and make sure these terms are identical on both sides of the equation.

Example 5: $ax - 5(x + 7) = 13x + b + 3$

For the equation above, a and b are constants. What is the value of $a + b$?

A) −56   B) −20   C) 20   D) 56

Solution: To solve this question, we need to first multiply out the left side of the equation.
$$ax - 5x - 35 = 13x + b + 3$$

Now, we can use the fact that the x-terms and constants on each side of the equation must be equal to solve for the values of a and b. a is part of the x-terms, so we only consider the x-terms when solving for a. Similarly, b is part of the constants, so we only consider the constants when solving for b.

Chapter 31: Solving for Constants

To solve for a:
$$ax - 5x = 13x$$
$$ax = 18x$$
$$a = 18$$

To solve for b:
$$-35 = b + 3$$
$$-38 = b$$

So $a + b = 18 + (-38) = -20$. **The answer is B.**

The SAT can also present questions with multiple unknown variables in a question with multiplying polynomials. To solve these questions, we need to identify how the factored binomials multiply to become the expanded equation.

> **Example 6:** $(bx - 6)(3x + 3) = 12x^2 - cx - 18$
>
> For the equation above, what is the value of bc?

Solution: To solve this question, we begin with solving for b. Using our rules for multiplying binomials, we know that
$$(bx)(3x) = 12x^2$$
Here, we find that $b = 4$. Once we know the value of b, our equation looks like
$$(4x - 6)(3x + 3) = 12x^2 - cx - 18$$
Now we have an equation with one unknown. We can multiply out the left side of the equation to solve for c.
$$12x^2 + 12x - 18x - 18 = 12x^2 - cx - 18$$
$$12x^2 - 6x - 18 = 12x^2 - cx - 18$$
For these equations to be equal, $c = 6$. We now know that
$$bc = (4)(6) = 24$$

The answer is 24.

Solving for Constants with No Solution

The SAT also includes questions with constants in equations that have no solution. An algebraic expression with no solution cannot be solved for any value of x. **For this to occur, the expression must have the same coefficients for the variable(s) on both sides and the constants (numbers) must be different.** Some examples of equations with no solution are below:

$$x - 2 = x + 1 \qquad 7x^2 = 7x^2 + 10 \qquad x - 5 = x + 5$$

No matter what value we plug in for x, we can never make any of the equations above true. Notice that the terms with variables (the terms with x or x^2 in the above examples) are equal but the numbers are not. Anytime an equation looks like this, there is no solution.

> **Rule for No Solution**
>
> **The coefficients of the x-terms are the same. The constants (numbers) are different.** Anytime we see these characteristics in an algebraic expression, there is no solution.

> **Example 7:** $a(3x + 6) = 12x - 2$
>
> For the equation above, the value of a is constant. If the equation has no real solution, what is the value of a?

- 283 -

Solution: The trick to solving constants with no solutions questions is to make the x-terms equal. To solve Example 7, we first distribute the 3 on the left side of the equation to get

$$3ax + 6a = 12x - 2$$

Now, we need to make the x-terms equal on both sides to have no solution.

$$3ax = 12x$$
$$3a = 12$$
$$a = 4$$

The answer is 4.

> **Example 8:** $\qquad 4x^2 + 2(ax^2 - b) = 20x^2 - 17$
>
> In the equation above, a and b are constants and $b \neq 8.5$. If the equation has no real solution, what is the value of a?

Solution: To start, we can distribute the 2 to get

$$4x^2 + 2ax^2 - 2b = 20x^2 - 17$$

For no real solution, we need the x^2 terms to be equal on both sides of the equation, so

$$4x^2 + 2ax^2 = 20x^2$$
$$2ax^2 = 16x^2$$
$$2a = 16$$
$$a = 8$$

The answer is 8.

As we see in these examples, if we remember that the x-terms need to be equal for no solution, these questions only require simple algebra to solve.

Solving for Constants with Infinite Solutions

An algebraic expression with infinite solutions must be true for any value of x. **For an equation to have infinite solutions, both sides of the equation must be identical.** Some examples of equations with infinite solutions are below.

$$6x - 12 = 6x - 12 \qquad\qquad 7x^2 = 7x^2 \qquad\qquad x^3 - 4x + 5 = x^3 - 4x + 5$$

For infinite solutions, both the terms with variables (the terms with x, x^2, and x^3 in the examples above) and the constants must be equal. For the expressions above, we can plug any value for x and the expression will be true.

> **Rule for Infinite Solutions**
>
> **Both sides of the equation must be identical. The coefficients of the x-terms and the constants (numbers) must be the same.** Anytime both sides of the expression are identical, any value of x makes the expression true, so there are infinite solutions.

Chapter 31: Solving for Constants

Example 9: $$19x - 5x(a + 3) = -11x$$

For the equation above, a is a constant. What value of a makes the equation have infinite solutions?

A) 3   B) 2   C) 1   D) -1

Solution: **The trick to solving constants with infinite solutions questions is simple: make the values of all terms identical on both sides of the equation.** For this question, we start by distributing the $5x$ to get

$$19x - 5ax - 15x = -11x$$

Then, we combine the x-terms we get

$$4x - 5ax = -11x$$
$$-5ax = -15x$$

To have infinite solutions, we need to solve for the value of a that makes both sides equal. So

$$-5ax = -15x$$
$$-5a = -15$$
$$a = 3$$

The answer is A.

Example 10: $$4(ax + b) - 13x = 15x - 36$$

For the equation above, a and b are constants. If the equation has infinite solutions, what is the value of $b - a$?

A) -16 B) -2 C) 2   D) 16

Solution: To start, let's distribute the 4 to get

$$4ax + 4b - 13x = 15x - 36$$

We need to solve for two unknowns. The a is involved in the x-terms, and the b is involved with the constants. Since we are told this equation has infinite solutions, we need to make sure that the x-terms and constants are identical on both sides of the equation. Let's start by focusing on the x-terms and solving for a.

$$4ax - 13x = 15x$$
$$4ax = 28x$$
$$4a = 28$$
$$a = 7$$

Next, we can solve for b by making the constants equal on both sides.

$$4b = -36$$
$$b = -9$$

Now, we can solve for $b - a$.

$$b - a = (-9) - 7$$
$$b - a = -16$$

The answer is A.

Not too bad, right? The key to solving constants with infinite solutions questions is to remember that both sides need to be identical. If you remember that, you will be able to solve these questions quickly and easily on test day.

2-4 Solving for Constants with One Solution

Any algebraic expression that can be solved for a single value of x will have one solution. For example, if we have the expression.

$$9x - 2 = 5x + 10$$

we can solve for x. Subtract $5x$ from both sides and add 2 to both sides to get:

$$4x = 12$$
$$x = 3$$

We get 1 solution for x. Memorize the rules below to know how to spot this quickly.

> **Rule for 1 Solution**
>
> **The coefficients of the x-terms are different. The constants (numbers) can be the same or different.** Anytime the expression has x-terms with different coefficients and no higher powers of x, such as x^2, there is always 1 solution.

In the example we just solved, the x-terms, $9x$ and $5x$ have different coefficients, so, using the rule for 1 solution, we know there will be 1 solution without having to solve the equation.

> ## Two Solutions for Algebraic Expressions
>
> For a challenge question, the SAT can also include an algebraic expression that has two solutions. For an algebraic expression to have 2 solutions, the equation must either (1) have an x^2-term or (2) have an x-term inside absolute value bars.
>
> ### Two Solutions with an x^2-term
>
> Let's say we are given the algebraic expression $x^2 - 6 = -2$. To solve, we could add 6 to both sides and get
>
> $$x^2 = 4$$
>
> Taking the square root of both sides we get.
>
> $$x = \pm 2$$
>
> **So, we get 2 solutions!** Remember that in Chapter 5 (pg. 23) we learned that when we take the square root of both sides with x^2, we must put a $\pm$ in front of the number.
>
> ### Two Solutions with Absolute Value
>
> Let's say we are given the expression $|x| + 3 = 10$. To solve, we subtract 3 from both sides and get
>
> $$|x| = 7 \rightarrow x = 7 \text{ and } x = -7$$
>
> **When we have a variable inside the absolute value bars, there are 2 solutions.** Remember that in Chapter 28 we learned how to find the 2 solutions to an equation with absolute value bars.

Chapter 31: Solving for Constants

Example 11: Which of the following equations has one solution?
A) $4x - 12 = 4(x - 3)$ B) $3x^2 = 3(x^2 - 5)$ C) $3(2x + 6) = 2x + 3$ D) $-2(3x + 1) = -3(2x - 2)$

Solution: To have one solution, the x-terms must have different coefficients. We can simplify the choices by distributing the value into the terms in parentheses. Once the answer choices are in this form, we can apply our rules and find the number of solutions there are for each answer choice.

A) $4x - 12 = 4x - 12$ (A has infinite solutions, so A is incorrect.)

B) $3x^2 = 3x^2 - 15$ (B has no solution, so B is incorrect.)

C) $6x + 18 = 2x + 3$ (C has one solution, so C is correct.)

D) $-6x - 2 = -6x + 6$ (D has no solution, so D is incorrect.)

For answer choice C, the coefficients for the x-terms ($6x$ and $2x$) are different, so there is one solution. **The answer is C.** Answer choice A is identical on both sides, so it has infinite solutions. Answer choices B and D have the same x-terms and different constants, so both have no solution.

Summary of Rules for One Solution, No Solution, and Infinite Solutions

Type of Solution	x-terms (rule for coefficients)	Constants (numbers)
One Solution	Different	Same or different
No Solution	Same	Different
Infinite Solutions	Same	Same

Solving for Constants Practice: Answers on page 334.

1. In the given equation, k is a constant. The equation has no solution. What is the value of k?

    $$\frac{3}{5}x + 5 = kx - 4$$

2. Which equation has one solution?

    A) $3(x + 7) = x + 7$
    B) $3(x + 7) = 3x + 7$
    C) $3(x + 7) = 3x + 21$
    D) $3x + 7 = 3x + 1$

3. There is no solution to which of the following linear equations?

    I. $3(x - 2) = 3x - 2$
    II. $3(x - 2) = 6x - 6$

    A) I only
    B) II only
    C) I and II
    D) Neither I nor II

4. In the equation below, $a, b,$ and c are constants. If the equation is true for all values of x, what is the value of $a - b + c$?

    $$x(2x - 2) - 2(-x - 4) = ax^2 + bx + c$$

    A) 2
    B) 4
    C) 8
    D) 10

5. In the equation below, a and b are constants. If the equation has infinite solutions, what is the value of $a + b$?

    $$ax + 3(3x - 2) = 5x + b$$

    A) -10
    B) -6
    C) -4
    D) 5

6. $(3x - b)(x + 2) = 3x^2 + 4x - 4$

   For the equation above, b is a constant. If the equation has infinite solutions, what is the value of b?

   A) -2
   B) -1
   C) 1
   D) 2

7. Which linear equation has exactly one solution?

   A) $z = 7 - z$
   B) $z = z - 7$
   C) $z = z + 7$
   D) $z + 7 = z + 7$

8. $6(2x - 17) = a(5x + 1)$

   In the equation above, a and b are constants. If there is no real solution to the equation, what is the value of a?

9. In the equation below, k is a constant. What value of x satisfies the equation?

   $4(x + k) = 3(x + k) + 3 + k + 3$

10. The equation below has no solution, and a is a constant. What is the value of a?

    $8x + 6 = a(-3x + 2) - x$

    A) -3
    B) $-\frac{8}{3}$
    C) 0
    D) 3

11. How many solutions does the equation $3(x + 4) = 9x - 6x + 12$ have?

    A) Zero
    B) Exactly one
    C) Exactly two
    D) Infinitely many

12. Which equation has no solution?

    A) $5(x + 3) = 5x$
    B) $5(x + 3) = 4x$
    C) $5x + 15 = 5(x + 3)$
    D) $2x + 5 = 5x + 2$

13. In the equation below, a is a constant. For which of the following values of a does the equation have no real solution?

    $3x^2 + 12 = 6 + ax^2$

    A) -3
    B) -1
    C) 0
    D) 3

14. In the equation below, a is a constant. If no value of x satisfies the equation, what is the value of a?

    $\frac{1}{3}ax - 12 = 3(x + 4) - 3(1 - 3x)$

    A) 4
    B) 8
    C) 12
    D) 36

15. The equation below, where k is a constant, has exactly one solution. Which of the following could NOT be the value of k?

    $6x - 21 = k(2x - 7)$

    A) 0
    B) 2
    C) 3
    D) 7

16. In the function below, a is a constant. If -5 is a zero of the function, which of the following is a possible value of a?

    $F(x) = x^2 - ax + 15$

    A) -3
    B) -5
    C) 8
    D) -8

Chapter 31: Solving for Constants

17. In the given equation below, a is a constant. If the equation has no solution, which of the following must be true?

$$\frac{1}{7}x + a = \frac{1}{7}x + \frac{9}{2}$$

A) $a > \frac{9}{2}$
B) $a < \frac{9}{2}$
C) $a = \frac{9}{2}$
D) $a \neq \frac{9}{2}$

18. $5x - 3(ax + b) = -31x + 30$

For the equation above, a and b are constants. If the equation has infinite real solutions, what is the value of $b - a$?

A) -22
B) -2
C) 2
D) 22

19. $(ax - 6)(bx + 3) = -2.75x^2 - 14.25x - 18$

For the equation above, a and b are constants. What is the value of ab?

20. $ax^2 + 4(3x^2 + 2b) = 15x^2 + 24$

In the equation above, a and b are constants. If the equation has no real solution, what is the value of a?

A) 2
B) 3
C) 5
D) 12

21. $-7x^4 + 4x(ax^3 + b) = 13x^4 + 24x$

For the equation above, a and b are constants. What is the value of $a + b$?

A) 11
B) 6
C) 5
D) 1

22. In the equation below, k is a constant. The equation has no solution. What is the value of k?

$$-7x + 28kx = 56$$

A) 0
B) 1
C) $\frac{1}{4}$
D) 4

23. In the equation below, a is a constant. If the equation has infinite solutions, what is the value of a?

$$23x - 5x(a + 2) = 4x$$

A) $-\frac{17}{5}$
B) $-\frac{9}{5}$
C) $\frac{9}{5}$
D) $\frac{17}{5}$

24. How many solutions does the equation below have?

$$\frac{3x}{6x - 12} - \frac{x}{2x - 4} = 0$$

A) None
B) One
C) Two
D) Infinitely Many

25. In the equation below, a is a constant. If $x = 5$ is a solution to the equation, what is the value of a?

$$ax^2 + 5x = 115 - 5a$$

26. In the equation below, j and k are constants. If the equation has infinitely many solutions for x, what is the value of k?

$$j(x - k) = \frac{3}{4}x + 15$$

- 289 -

PrepPros

27. How many solutions does the equation below have?

$$\frac{8x}{12x-4} = \frac{2x+1}{3x-1}$$

A) None
B) One
C) Two
D) Infinitely many

28. The equation $7x + 3 = a(x + b)$ where a and b are constants has no solution. Which of the following must be true?

  I. $a = 7$
  II. $b = 3$
  III. $b \neq \frac{3}{7}$

A) None
B) I only
C) I and II only
D) I and III only

29. In the given equation, b is a positive integer constant. Which value could be a solution to the equation?

$$x^2 + bx - 18 = 0$$

A) 3
B) 6
C) 11
D) 17

30. In the given equation a is a positive integer constant less than 30. The equation has exactly one solution. What is the greatest possible value of a?

$$29x - 73 = ax + 30$$

31. If the equation below is true for all values of x, m is a constant and $a < 0$, what is the value of a?

$$m(x^2 - a^2) = (3x - 1)(3x + 1)$$

A) $-\frac{1}{81}$
B) $-\frac{1}{27}$
C) $-\frac{1}{9}$
D) $-\frac{1}{3}$

32. If the equation below is true for all values of x and if a, b, and c are all positive constants, what is the value of $a + b + c$?

$$(3x + 2b)^2 = ax^2 + 8ax + c$$

33. The given expression below is equivalent to $x(ax + 1)(bx + 3)$, where a and b are positive integers. What is a possible value of $a + b$?

$$42x^3 + 27x^2 + 3x$$

34. In the equation below, a and b are constants. If the equation is true for all values of x, what is the value of ab?

$$(x^3 + ax^2 + 5ax - 4) + (2x^3 + bx^2 - bx - 3) = 3x^3 + 8x^2 + 10x - 7$$

A) -2
B) 3
C) 5
D) 15

Chapter 32: Systems of Equations with Infinite Solutions, No Solution, and One Solution

The SAT includes questions asking about systems of equations with infinite solution, no solution, and one solution. While these questions at first seem confusing, once you know the techniques needed to solve, they are easy!

It is important to remember that the equations in most systems of equations questions are lines; they are just in standard form instead of $y = mx + b$. When solving a system of equations (as we learned in Chapter 12), we are finding the point(s) (x, y) where the two functions intersect. But what if the functions do not intersect? Or if the functions are identical? We will outline how to quickly and easily solve these questions below.

It is important to note that **we cannot solve most of these questions with Desmos**, so you need to understand how to solve all questions in this chapter mathematically. We expect these questions to appear more commonly than regular systems of equation on the digital SAT, so this is an important chapter to master.

One Solution (Intersecting Lines)

As we learned in Chapter 12, two lines that intersect at a point (x, y) have one solution at that point. There is one rule we can memorize that tells us how to spot a system of equations with one solution:

A system of equations with 2 lines that have different slopes always has one solution.

As long as 2 lines have different slopes, they must intercept at 1 point. The y-intercepts of the lines can be identical or different. Either way, the lines still intersect at 1 point and have one solution.

Let's consider the lines $2x + y = 20$ and $4x - y = 10$. We can convert these lines to $y = mx + b$ form to find the slopes. If we do that, we get

$$y = -2x + 20 \quad \text{and} \quad y = 4x - 10$$

We can see the slopes of the lines are -2 and 4, so, since the slopes are different, we know there is one solution. If we graph these lines, we see there is 1 point of intersection at $(3, 4)$.

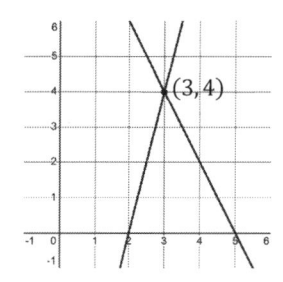

Can we tell the slopes are different without converting the lines into $y = mx + b$ form? Yes! **When written in $ax + by = c$ form, the slope of the line is equal to $-\frac{a}{b}$.** So, we can find the slopes without converting to $y = mx + b$. For the equation $2x + y = 20$, $a = 2$, $b = 1$, so the slope is $-\frac{2}{1} = -2$. For the equation $4x - y = -10$, $a = 4$, $b = -1$, so the slope is $-\frac{4}{-1} = 4$.

Of course, we can also graph the lines in Desmos and look for a point of intersection! We will come back to one solution more in some examples later in this chapter.

No Solution (Parallel Lines)

If two lines are parallel and have different y-intercepts, the lines never intersect. As a result, **there is NO SOLUTION to a system of equations with parallel lines**. This is the first type of unusual systems of equations question that you may see on test day.

Example 1: For the equations below, for what value of k does the system of equations have no solution?

$$3x + 5y = 29$$
$$9x + ky = 12$$

Solution: Ratio Shortcut: To have no solution, the lines must have the same slope and a different y-intercept so that they will never intersect. We could turn both equations to $y = mx + b$ form by isolating y, but that is a lot of work. Instead, we can use our Ratio Shortcut. **For two lines to have the same slope, the ratios of the coefficient for the x-term to the coefficient for the y-term must be identical in both equations.**

A line written in $ax + by = c$ form has a slope of $-\frac{a}{b}$ and a y-intercept of $\frac{c}{b}$. For two lines to have the same slope, we know that $-\frac{a}{b} = -\frac{a}{b}$. We can simplify by removing the negative sign from both sides, so two lines have the same slope if $\frac{a}{b} = \frac{a}{b}$.

Ratio Shortcut: Two lines in $ax + by = c$ form have no solution if $\frac{a}{b} = \frac{a}{b}$ and $\frac{c}{b} \neq \frac{c}{b}$.

For Example 1, we need to make the slopes the same, so we can set up $\frac{a}{b} = \frac{a}{b}$. For $3x + 5y = 29$, $a = 3$ and $b = 5$. For $9x + ky = 12$, $a = 9$ and $b = k$. Plugging in those values, we get

$$\frac{3}{5} = \frac{9}{k}$$
$$3k = 45$$
$$k = 15$$

The answer is 15. This Ratio Shortcut works for any type of no solution systems of equation questions. The constants (numbers) on the right side of the equations correspond with the y-intercepts.

Example 2: For the equations below, what value of k will give the system of equations no solution?

$$y + 2x = -15 - 5y$$
$$6x + 2ky + 3 = 13$$

Solution: Example 2 introduces the SAT's 2 favorite ways to make systems of equations with no solution more difficult: separating like terms and writing the terms out of order. To properly use the Ratio Shortcut, we need to always complete the following 3 steps.

1. **Combine like terms.** If like terms appear on separate sides of the equation, add or subtract to combine the like terms. In the top equation in example 2, we need to combine the y-terms since we have a $+y$ on the left side and a $-5y$ on the right side.

2. **Write the equation in $ax + by = c$ form.** If the equation is not ordered in $ax + by = c$ form, reorder the terms.

3. **Use the Ratio Shortcut.** Write the ratios of two equation as $\frac{a}{b} = \frac{a}{b}$ and solve for the unknown value.

Now, let's follow those 3 steps as we solve Example 2.

Step 1: Combine like terms: For the top equation, we see a y-term on the left (y) and right ($-5y$) sides of the equation, so we must combine the y-terms. We want the y-terms on the left side of the equation, so we add $5y$ to both sides.

For the bottom equation, we see a constant (number) on the left (3) and right (13) sides of the equation, so we must combine the constants. We want the constants on the right side of the equation, so we subtract 3 from both sides.

After completing these steps, we get
$$6y + 2x = -15$$
$$6x + 2ky = 10$$

Chapter 32: Systems of Equations with Infinite Solutions, No Solution, and One Solution

Step 2: Write the equation to $ax + by = c$ form: The top equation is out of order (the y-term is first and the x-term is second), so we must reorder the terms to be in $ax + by = c$ form. The bottom equation is already in the correct form.

$$2x + 6y = -15$$
$$6x + 2ky = 10$$

Step 3: Use the Ratio Shortcut to solve for the unknown value: Since the unknown value k is part of the b-value, we can use

$$\frac{a}{b} = \frac{a}{b}$$

Plugging in the values, we get

$$\frac{2}{6} = \frac{6}{2k}$$

$$4k = 36$$

$$k = 9$$

The answer is 9. For any system of equations question with no solutions, we should always follow the 3 steps that we did in Example 2 and use the Ratio Shortcut to solve.

Infinite Solutions (Identical Lines)

If two lines are identical, they have INFINITE solutions. Two identical lines must have the exact same slope and y-intercept. When a systems of equations question asks for infinite solutions, we need to find a value for the unknown value in the question that makes the two equations identical.

> **Example 3:** For the system of equations below, what value of m gives an infinite number of solutions?
>
> $$8x + 4y = 52$$
> $$4x + 2y = m$$

Solution: To solve this question, we need to find the value of m that makes the equations identical. To accomplish this, there are two methods:

Method #1 – Identical Equations: For two lines to be identical, the ratios of the coefficients for all terms in the equation must be identical, therefore $\frac{a}{a} = \frac{b}{b} = \frac{c}{c}$. In other words, if we can multiply by a coefficient to make the equations identical, there are infinite solutions. For this question, we need to multiply the bottom equation by 2. Once the equations are identical, we can solve for the unknown.

$$8x + 4y = 52$$
$$2[4x + 2y = m]$$

$$8x + 4y = 52$$
$$8x + 4y = 2m$$

Now that the equations are identical, we can see that $2m = 52$. Solving this simple equation, we get $m = 26$, so **the answer is 26.**

Method #2 – Use Ratio Shortcut: The Ratio Shortcut method that we used to solve Examples 1 and 2 also works with one minor tweak: the y-intercepts must be equal.

Ratio Shortcut: Two lines in $ax + by = c$ form have infinite solutions if $\frac{a}{b} = \frac{a}{b}$ and $\frac{c}{b} = \frac{c}{b}$.

For this question, the unknown m is part of the c-value, so we use

$$\frac{c}{b} = \frac{c}{b}$$

PrepPros

Plugging in the values, we get

$$\frac{52}{4} = \frac{m}{2}$$

Once the ratio is setup, we just solve the equation for m.

$$104 = 4m$$
$$m = 26$$

The answer is 26. Since there was no unknown in the a or b values, we do not need to make sure $\frac{a}{b} = \frac{a}{b}$. Just to be thorough, let's plug in the values anyways to confirm the lines are identical. $\frac{8}{4} = \frac{4}{2} \rightarrow 2 = 2$ so we can see that the $\frac{a}{b} = \frac{a}{b}$ condition for infinite solutions is met.

Both methods work for any infinite solutions system of equations question, so you should just memorize whichever one you are more comfortable using.

> **Example 4:** The system of equations below has an infinite number of solutions for what value of k?
>
> $$\frac{1}{4}x - \frac{1}{2}y = \frac{11}{2} - \frac{5}{4}y$$
> $$ky - 22 = -x$$

Solution: As we saw earlier in Example 2, this example is more advanced because the equations are not presented nicely in $ax + by = c$ form. So, we follow the same steps we did in Example 2.

Step 1: Combine Like Terms: For the top equation, we see a y-term on the left $(-\frac{1}{2}y)$ and right $(-\frac{5}{4}y)$ sides of the equation, so we must combine the y-terms. We want the y-terms on the left side of the equation, so we add $\frac{5}{4}y$ to both sides. After completing this step, we get

$$\frac{1}{4}x + \frac{3}{4}y = \frac{11}{2}$$
$$ky - 22 = -x$$

Step 2: Write the equation to $ax + by = c$ form: The bottom equation is out of order. We need to move the x-term to the left side (so add x to both sides) and the constant to the right side (so add 22 to both sides). To reorder the terms to be in $ax + by = c$ form. The top equation is already in the correct form.

$$\frac{1}{4}x + \frac{3}{4}y = \frac{11}{2}$$
$$x + ky = 22$$

Step 3: Solve for the unknown value: To solve for k, we can use the Identical Equations or Ratio Shortcut method. We will start with the Identical Equations method.

Method #1 – Identical Equations: We can multiply by a coefficient to make the equations identical. For this question, we need to multiply the top equation by 4. Once the equations are identical, we can solve for the unknown.

$$4\left(\frac{1}{4}x + \frac{3}{4}y = \frac{11}{2}\right)$$
$$x + ky = 22$$

$$x + 3y = 22$$

Chapter 32: Systems of Equations with Infinite Solutions, No Solution, and One Solution

$$x + ky = 22$$

Now that the equations are identical, we can see that $3y = ky$, so $k = 3$. **The answer is 3.**

Method #2 – Ratio Shortcut: The unknown value is the y-coefficient. We know the values for the x-coefficients and the constants, so we can use either of the conditions in our Ratio Shortcut for infinite solutions. Here, we will use the x-coefficient and y-coefficient to write the ratios as $\frac{a}{b} = \frac{a}{b}$. Plugging in the values, we get

$$\frac{\frac{1}{4}}{\frac{3}{4}} = \frac{1}{k}$$

Once the ratio is setup, we just solve the equation for k.

$$\frac{1}{4}k = \frac{3}{4}$$
$$k = 3$$

The answer is 3. You can use whichever method you prefer to find the unknown value in step 3.

Example 5: The system of equations below has an infinite number of solutions. What is the value of $\frac{k}{m}$?

$$kx + my = 42$$
$$5x + 13y = 14$$

Solution: To make questions appear more difficult, the SAT can include two unknown variables. However, we can solve these questions with the same Ratio Shortcut that we have already learned in this chapter. For infinite solutions, the ratio of the coefficients for the x and y-terms must be the same. As a result, we can solve in one step using $\frac{a}{b} = \frac{a}{b}$.

$$\frac{k}{m} = \frac{5}{13}$$

The answer is $\frac{5}{13}$. This is a great example of an SAT question that appears very difficult until you know the shortcut to solve.

Identifying The Correct System of Equations

The final type of system of equations question gives you one equation in a system and asks you to identify a second equation that creates a system of equations with one solution, no solution, or infinite solutions.

Example 6: One of the equations in a system of two linear equations is $y = 4x + 18$. The system has no solution. Which equation could be the second equation in the system?

A) $-4x + y = 18$ B) $-4x + y = 22$ C) $-8x + y = 36$ D) $-8x + y = 18$

Solution: Method #1: Convert to $y = mx + b$ form: To have no solution, we want to find a second equation that has the same slope but a different y-intercept. Since the first equation ($y = 4x + 18$) is given in $y = mx + b$ form, the easiest way to solve is to convert all the answer choices to $y = mx + b$ form by solving for y. Once the answer choices are in $y = mx + b$ form, we are looking for a line that has the same slope as the first equation but a different y-intercept.

PrepPros

For this question, we have to move the x-term to the right side to convert to $y = mx + b$ form. Below, we have turned all the answer choices into $y = mx + b$ form.

A) $y = 4x + 18$ B) $y = 4x + 22$ C) $y = 8x + 36$ D) $y = 8x + 18$

We can see that answer choice B has the same slope and a different y-intercept, so **the correct answer is B.** A is identical and would have infinite solutions. Answer choices C and D would intersect with the first equation at 1 point and would have one solution.

Method #2: Graph in Desmos: The easiest way to solve this question is graphing in Desmos! All we need to do is graph the original equation ($y = 4x + 18$), graph the answer choices, and see which one never intersects. If 2 lines are parallel and never intersect, there is no solution. You should always solve questions like Example 6 in Desmos if you can. However, you should still understand the math we did with Method #1 in case the SAT gives you a question with variables that you cannot enter into Desmos.

Example 7: One of the two linear equations in a system is $3x - 3y = 6$. The system has exactly one solution. Which equation could be the second equation in this system?

A) $-6x + 6y = -3$ B) $2x - 2y = 4$ C) $-9x + 6y = 7$ D) $x - y = 6$

Solution: Method #1 – Ratio Shortcut: To have one solution, the lines must have a different slope, so when in $ax + by = c$ form $\frac{a}{b} \neq \frac{a}{b}$. Remember, the $\frac{a}{b}$ value corresponds with the slope, so 2 equations with the same $\frac{a}{b}$ value are parallel.

For the equation $3x - 3y = 6$, $\frac{a}{b} = \frac{3}{-3} = -1$. Now, we can check the answer choices to find which one has a different value of $\frac{a}{b}$ and, therefore, a different slope.

A) $\frac{a}{b} = \frac{-6}{6} = -1$ (A has the same slope, so A is incorrect.)

B) $\frac{a}{b} = \frac{2}{-2} = -1$ (B has the same slope, so B is incorrect.)

C) $\frac{a}{b} = \frac{-9}{6} = -\frac{3}{2}$ (C has a different slope, so C is correct.)

D) $\frac{a}{b} = \frac{1}{-1} = -1$ (D has the same slope, so D is incorrect.)

C has a different slope, so **the answer is C.** If the question asked for infinite solutions, the answer would be B since answer choice B is identical to the first equation. $\frac{2}{3}[3x - 3y = 6] \rightarrow 2x - 2y = 4$. Answer choices A and D would have no solution since the $\frac{a}{b}$ value is the same but the $\frac{c}{b}$ value is not the same.

Method #2: Graph in Desmos: The easiest way to solve this question is graphing in Desmos! All we need to do is graph the original equation ($3x - 3y = 6$), graph the answer choices, and see which one intersects.

Summary of Rules for One Solution, No Solution, and Infinite Solutions

Type of Solution	Rules	Ratio Shortcut Rules ($ax + by = c$ form)
One Solution	Slopes are different.	$\frac{a}{b} \neq \frac{a}{b}$
No Solution	Slopes are the same, y-interecepts are different.	$\frac{a}{b} = \frac{a}{b}$ and $\frac{c}{b} \neq \frac{c}{b}$
Infinite Solutions	Slopes and y-interecepts are the same.	$\frac{a}{b} = \frac{a}{b}$ and $\frac{c}{b} = \frac{c}{b}$

Chapter 32: Systems of Equations with Infinite Solutions, No Solution, and One Solution

Systems of Equations with Infinite Solutions or No Solution Practice: Answers on page 334.

1. If the system has no solution, what is the value of b?

   $$5x - 4y = 12$$
   $$bx - 12y = 12$$

   A) -15
   B) -5
   C) 5
   D) 15

2. In the system of equations below, a is a constant. If the system has no solution, what is the value of a?

   $$3x + 4y = 7$$
   $$5x + ay = 14$$

   A) -4
   B) 4
   C) $\frac{20}{3}$
   D) 8

3. In the system of equations below, k is a constant. The system has infinite solutions. What is the value of k?

   $$x + 7y = 5$$
   $$ky - 3x = -15$$

   A) $-\frac{7}{3}$
   B) -7
   C) -14
   D) -21

4. In the system of equations below, a is a constant. If the system of equations has no solution, what is the value of a?

   $$4x + 8y = 15$$
   $$ax + 6y = 14$$

   A) 3
   B) 4
   C) $\frac{16}{3}$
   D) 8

5. In the system of equations below, a and b are constants. If the system has no solution, what is the value of $\frac{a}{b}$?

   $$ax + by = 8$$
   $$6x + 3y = 12$$

6. Which of the following systems of equations has infinitely many solutions?

   A) $2x + 5y = 12$
      $2x - 5y = 12$
   B) $2x - 5y = 12$
      $4x + 10y = -24$
   C) $2x + 5y = 12$
      $-6x + 15y = 36$
   D) $2x + 5y = 12$
      $-4x - 10y = -24$

7. Which of the following systems of linear equations has no solution?

   A) $x = 7$
      $y = 17$
   B) $y = 13x + 8$
      $y = 13x + 9$
   C) $y = 7$
      $y = 3x + 7$
   D) $y = 3x + 9$
      $y = 4x + 4$

8. One of the two equations in a linear system is $3x + 4y = 6$. The system has no solution. Which equation could be the other equation in the system?

   A) $6x - 8y = 12$
   B) $6x + 8y = 12$
   C) $3x - 4y = 6$
   D) $6x + 8y = 6$

9. How many solutions does the given system of equations have?

   $$-5x + 3y = 7$$
   $$-13x + 8y = 7$$

   A) Zero
   B) Exactly one
   C) Exactly two
   D) Infinitely many

10. In the system of equations below, a and b are constants. If the system has infinite solutions, what is the value of $a + b$?

$$3x - 6y = b$$
$$5x - ay = 50$$

A) $\frac{5}{3}$
B) 6
C) 30
D) 40

11. How many solutions does the given system of equation below have?

$$7x - y = 8$$
$$-91x + 13y = -104$$

A) Zero
B) Exactly one
C) Exactly two
D) Infinitely many

12. One of the two equations in a linear system is $7x + 7y = 14$. The system has no solution. Which equation could be the other equation in the system?

A) $8x - 8y = 16$
B) $14x + 14y = 28$
C) $7x - 7y = 14$
D) $7x + 7y = 12$

13. The system of equations below has no solutions. If a and b are constants, what is the value of $\frac{b}{a}$?

$$\frac{2}{3}x = 12 - \frac{1}{4}y$$
$$ax + by = 1$$

14. In the system of equations below, a is a constant. For what value of a does the system have no real solution?

$$12.8x + 1.4y = 9.4 - 0.8y$$
$$15.4y + 11.6 = 2ax$$

15. Which of the following systems of equations has no solution?

A) $4x = 10 - 3y$
   $4x - 3y = 8$
B) $4x + 3y = 10$
   $4x = 8 - 3y$
C) $3y = 10 - 4x$
   $3y - 4x = 8$
D) $3y = 10 - 4x$
   $3y + 8 = 4x$

16. In the given system of equations, J is a constant. If the system has more than one solution, what is the value of J?

$$8x - 12y = 20$$
$$\frac{3}{4}y - \frac{1}{2}x = J$$

17. One of the two equations in a linear system is $5x - y = 7$. The system has exactly one solution. Which equation could be the other equation in the system?

A) $-5x + y = 2$
B) $5x - y = 7$
C) $5x + y = 7$
D) $5x - y = 9$

18. In the system of equations below, a and b are constants. If this system has infinitely many solutions, what is the value of $\frac{a}{b}$?

$$4y = ax + 12$$
$$cy = bx + 6$$

19. In the given system of equations, a and b are constants. The system has infinitely many solutions. What is the value of ab?

$$3x + 8y = 48$$
$$ax + 3y = b$$

Chapter 32: Systems of Equations with Infinite Solutions, No Solution, and One Solution

20. In the given system of equations, k is a constant. If the system has no solution, what is the value of k?

$$9y = 12x - 6y + 14$$
$$4y = -kx + 2$$

21. In the systems of equations below a and b are constants. If the system of equations has infinite solutions, what is the value of $a + b$?

$$4x - ay = 20$$
$$-bx + 3y = 30$$

A) -8
B) -4
C) 4
D) 8

22. In the system of equations below, h is a constant. For what value of h does the system have no real solution?

$$15x + 36y = 28 + 96x$$
$$3hx - 109 = 8y - 200$$

23. In the system of equations below, g and k are constants. If the system has no solution, which statement must be true?

$$y = 4x + 5k$$
$$gx + 5y = 20$$

A) $g = -4, k = 4$
B) $g = -4, k \neq 4$
C) $g = -20, k = \frac{4}{5}$
D) $g = -20, k \neq \frac{4}{5}$

24. In the given system of equations, a is a constant. If the system has infinite solutions, what is the value of a?

$$6y + 5x = -4x + 3$$
$$8y + \frac{45}{2}x = -7y + a$$

25. How many solutions does the given system of equations below have?

$$\frac{5}{2}y - \frac{26}{4}x = \frac{29}{3} + \frac{1}{3}x$$
$$28x + \frac{5}{2}y - \frac{49}{3} = y + 3$$

A) Zero
B) Exactly one
C) Exactly two
D) Infinitely many

26. In the given system of equations, k is a constant. If the system has no solution, what is the value of k?

$$\frac{4}{3}y - \frac{2}{3}x = \frac{5}{4} - \frac{5}{3}y$$
$$\frac{1}{6}x + \frac{4}{5} = ky + \frac{7}{2}$$

27. In the system of equations below, g, k, and z are constants. If the system has infinite solutions, which statement must be true?

$$y = 2x + k$$
$$gx + 9y = z$$

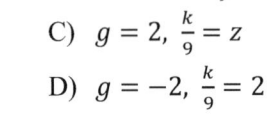

A) $g = 18$, $\frac{z}{9} = k$

B) $g = -18$, $\frac{z}{9} = k$

C) $g = 2$, $\frac{k}{9} = z$

D) $g = -2$, $\frac{k}{9} = 2$

28. Which of the following systems of equations has infinite solutions?

A) $7ax + 2by = 4c$
   $7ax + 2by = -4c$

B) $-8by + 3ax = -12c$
   $24by + 9ax = 36c$

C) $ax + 3by = 4c$
   $18by + 6ax = 24c$

D) $15ax + 30by = 10c$
   $6by - 10x = 3ax$

29. One of the two equations in a linear system is $6ax - by = 10$. The system has no solution. Which equation could be the other equation in the system?

A) $\frac{2}{3}ax = \frac{1}{9}by - \frac{1}{2}$

B) $\frac{12}{5}ax - \frac{2}{5}by = 4$

C) $\frac{1}{2}ax + \frac{1}{12}by = \frac{6}{5}$

D) $-\frac{2}{3}ax - \frac{1}{9}by = \frac{10}{9}$

Chapter 33: Arcs and Sectors

Arcs

The arc of a circle is a portion of the circumference. Arcs can be measured in two ways: the degree measure of the arc or the length of the arc.

Degree Measure of Arc AB

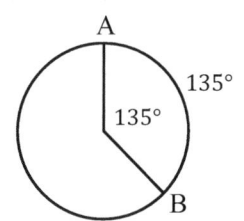

Length of Arc AB

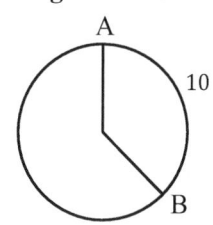

The degree measure of an arc is equal to the measure of the central angle intersecting the arc. The arc length is the actual distance covered moving from point A to point B along the circle.

To solve arc questions, you need to memorize the two equations below. These are different versions of the same equation. Being familiar with both the concept and the actual equation well help you solve different types of arc questions on the SAT.

$$\frac{\text{Arc Length}}{\text{Circumference}} = \frac{\text{Angle Measure}}{360°} \qquad \frac{L}{2\pi r} = \frac{\theta}{360}$$

L = arc length
θ = central angle
r = radius

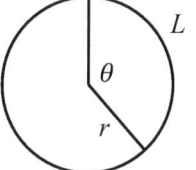

Example 1: In the circle to the right, the length of minor arc BC is 6π and the radius is 8. What is the measure of ∠A in degrees? (Note: Figure not drawn to scale).

A) 270 B) 180 C) 135 D) 100

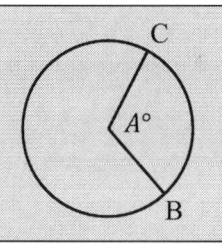

Solution: Using the arc equation, we can setup and solve for the measure of the central angle.

$$\frac{6\pi}{2\pi(8)} = \frac{\theta}{360}$$

$$\frac{6\pi}{16\pi} = \frac{\theta}{360}$$

Now, we can cross multiply and solve for θ.

$$2{,}160\pi = (16\pi)\theta$$

$$\frac{2{,}160\pi}{16\pi} = \theta$$

$$135 = \theta$$

The answer is C.

- 301 -

PrepPros

Example 2: Points X and Y lie on a circle. The length of arc XY is $\frac{1}{5}$ of the circumference of the circle. What is the measure of arc XY in degrees?

Solution: The proportion of the length of an arc to the circumference is equal to the proportion of the measure of an arc to 360°. Here, we know that the proportion of the arc length to the circumference is $\frac{1}{5}$, so we already know the left side of the equation.

$$\frac{1}{5} = \frac{\theta}{360}$$
$$360 = 5\theta$$
$$\theta = 72$$

The answer is 72.

For arc questions that measure the angle in radians, use the equation below. Remember that 2π radians = 360°. When solving for arc length in terms of radians, we replace the 360° with 2π in equations.

$$\frac{\text{Arc Length}}{\text{Circumference}} = \frac{\text{Angle Measure}}{2\pi \text{ radians}} \qquad \frac{L}{2\pi r} = \frac{\theta}{2\pi}$$

Example 3: The length of arc AB is $\frac{5}{2}$ and the circle has a radius of 4. What is the measure of the central angle of arc AB in radians?

Solution: Using the arc equation above, we can setup and solve for the measure of the central angle.

$$\frac{\frac{5}{2}}{2\pi(4)} = \frac{\theta}{2\pi}$$
$$\left(\frac{5}{2}\right)2\pi = \theta(8\pi)$$
$$\frac{5\pi}{8\pi} = \theta$$

The central angle has a measure of $\frac{5}{8}$ radians. **The answer is $\frac{5}{8}$.**

TIP – Inscribed Angle Theorem

An inscribed angle is an angle that has its vertex on the circumference of a circle and whose sides are chords. While that fancy definition may seem confusing, all you need to know for the SAT is the following rule:

For an inscribed angle and central angle that intersect the same portion of the arc, the measure of the inscribed angle is half of the measure of the central angle.

As you can see in the figure, the inscribed angle of 45° is half of the central angle of 90° This rule does not show up often on the SAT, but you should still memorize it just in case.

Sectors

The sector is the measure of the area of a portion of a circle. To solve sector questions, you will need to memorize the equations below.

$$\frac{\text{Sector Area}}{\text{Area of Circle}} = \frac{\text{Angle Measure}}{360°} \qquad \frac{S}{\pi r^2} = \frac{\theta}{360} \qquad \begin{array}{l} S = \text{sector area} \\ \theta = \text{central angle} \\ r = \text{radius} \end{array}$$

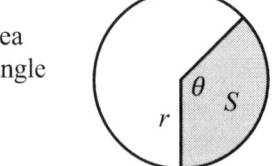

Example 4: For the circle to the right, the radius is 6. If $\angle C = 150°$, what is the area of sector BCD?

A) 8π B) 10π C) 12π D) 15π

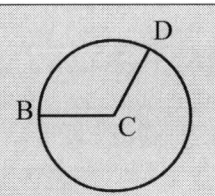

Solution: Using the sector equation above, we can plug in the values from the question and solve to find the area of the sector.

$$\frac{S}{\pi(6)^2} = \frac{150}{360}$$

$$\frac{S}{36\pi} = \frac{150}{360}$$

We can now cross multiply to solve for S.

$$360S = 5{,}400\pi$$

$$S = \frac{5{,}400\pi}{360}$$

$$S = 15\pi$$

The answer is D.

Example 5: Andrew bought a 12-inch diameter pumpkin pie and cut it into 12 equal slices. After eating 2 slices, he calculates that he consumed 480 calories. How many calories are in the entire pie?

Solution: The proportion of calories in two slices to calories in the entire pie is equal to the proportion of the area of the 2 slices of pie to area of the entire pie.

$$\frac{\text{calories in 2 slices}}{\text{calories in the entire pie}} = \frac{2 \text{ slices}}{12 \text{ slices}}$$

$$\frac{480}{x} = \frac{2}{12}$$

$$480(12) = 2x$$

$$x = \frac{480(12)}{2}$$

$$x = 2{,}880$$

The answer is 2,880.

For sector questions that measure the angle in radians, you can use the equation below.

$$\frac{\text{Sector Area}}{\text{Area of Circle}} = \frac{\text{Angle Measure}}{2\pi \text{ radians}} \qquad \frac{S}{\pi r^2} = \frac{\theta}{2\pi}$$

Example 6: Amanda is going to make a pie chart to display how she spends her time each day. She is going to print the pie chart on special circular paper that has a diameter of 12 inches. If Amanda spends 2 hours at volleyball practice each day, what will be the central angle, in radians, of the section of the pie chart that represents the number of hours for volleyball practice?

A) $\frac{\pi}{6}$ B) $\frac{\pi}{4}$ C) $\frac{\pi}{3}$ D) $\frac{\pi}{2}$

Solution: The proportion of hours spent playing volleyball to hours in the day is equal to the proportion of the central angle to the entire radian measure of the circle (2π radians). The diameter of 12 inches is just extra information to confuse you.

$$\frac{2 \text{ hours playing volleyball}}{24 \text{ hours}} = \frac{\text{central angle}}{2\pi \text{ radians}}$$

$$\frac{2}{24} = \frac{x}{2\pi}$$

$$4\pi = 24x$$

$$\frac{4\pi}{24} = x$$

$$x = \frac{\pi}{6}$$

The answer is A.

Arc and Sectors Practice: Answers on page 334.

1. The circle below has a circumference of 30π. What is the length of minor arc AB?

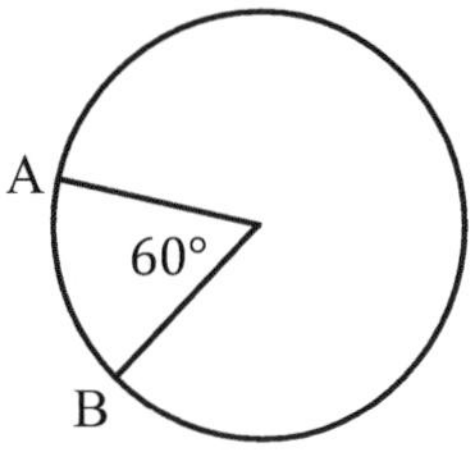

   A) 5π
   B) 6π
   C) 8π
   D) 10π

2. If the circumference of a circle is 18 and the length of arc AB is 6, what is the measure of the central angle that intercepts it?

   A) 30
   B) 60
   C) 120
   D) 240

3. Christine's famous chocolate cake contains 2,700 calories. If the cake is sliced evenly into 9 slices, what is the central angle of each of the slices?

4. The circle below has a radius of 6. What is the area of sector BAC?

   A) π
   B) 2π
   C) 6π
   D) 36π

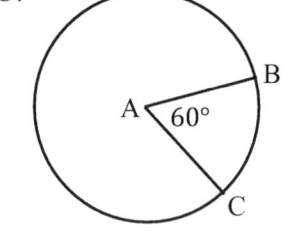

5. Dave is making a pie chart to represent the different fruits he currently has in the house. If he has 8 bananas, 6 apples, 5 oranges, and 6 plums, what is the central angle of the portion of the pie chart that represents the oranges?

   A) 45°
   B) 60°
   C) 72°
   D) 90°

Chapter 33: Arcs and Sectors

6. The length of AB is 10. What is the perimeter of the semicircle below?

    A) 5π
    B) $5\pi + 10$
    C) $10\pi + 10$
    D) 25π

7. The circle below has a radius of 9. The measure of ∠XZY is 120°. The length of the minor arc XY is equal to $a\pi$. What is the value of a?

8. In the circle below, point B is the center of the circle, and the length of arc AC is $\frac{3}{10}$ of the circumference. What is the value of x?

9. The circle below has a radius of 8. If the area of sector CAB is 16π, what is the measure of ∠CAB?

    Note: Figure not drawn to scale.

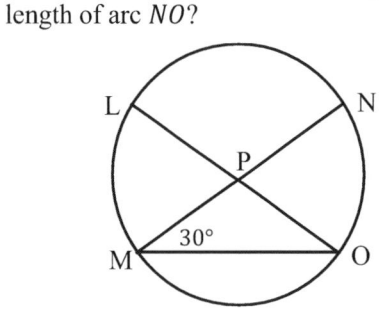

10. If the central angle of an arc is 135°, what proportion of the circumference does the arc intercept?

    A) $\frac{1}{4}$
    B) $\frac{1}{3}$
    C) $\frac{3}{8}$
    D) $\frac{3}{7}$

11. Points C and D lie on a circle with a radius of 2. Arc CD has a length of $\frac{\pi}{2}$. What is the measure of the central angle of arc CD?

    A) 30°
    B) 45°
    C) 60°
    D) 90°

12. Points A and B lie on a circle with a radius of 2, and arc AB has a length of $\frac{\pi}{5}$. What fraction of the circumference of the circle is the length of arc AB?

13. In the circle shown below, chords LO and MN intersect at point P, which is the center of the circle. The circle has a radius of 6, what is the length of arc NO?

    Note: Figure is not drawn to scale.

    A) 2π
    B) 3π
    C) 4π
    D) 6π

- 305 -

14. The length of AD is 6. What is the area of the shape ABCD below?

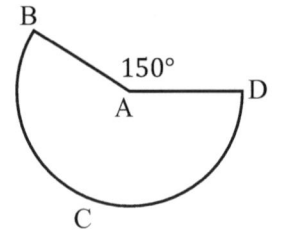

   A) 7π
   B) 14π
   C) 16π
   D) 21π

15. In the circle below, arc AB has a length of 4π. Which of the following is closest to the arc length of ADB?

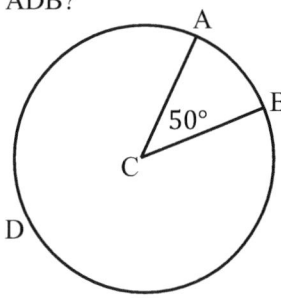

   A) 12π
   B) 18π
   C) 25π
   D) 29π

16. In the figure below, AC is a diameter of the circle and has a length of 12. What is the length of minor arc AB?

   A) 4π
   B) 6π
   C) 8π
   D) 12π

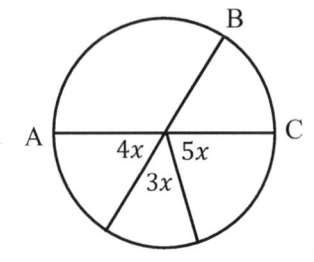

17. In the semicircle below, arc BC has a length of 3.2π, D is the midpoint of AB, and DC = 8. What is the measure of x?

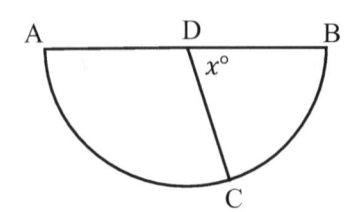

18. In the semicircle below, $\overline{DE}$ and $\overline{DC}$ are radii. The length of arc EC is 20π and $x = 50$. What is the length of $\overline{DE}$?

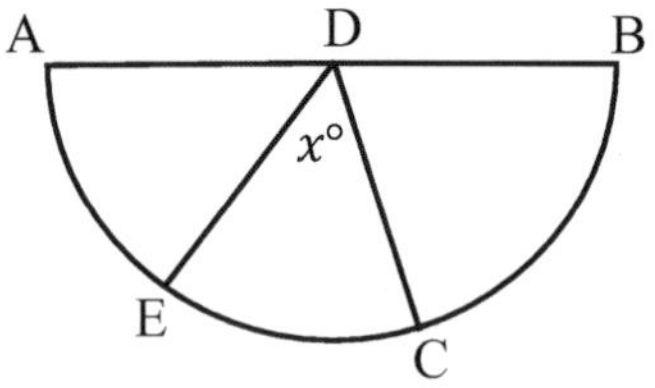

19. An object is traveling around a circle with center O and radius of 6 meters, as shown below. The object travels at a rate of $\frac{1}{8}$ m per second. If the object starts at point B and travels for 18 seconds to reach point A, what is the value of θ in radians?

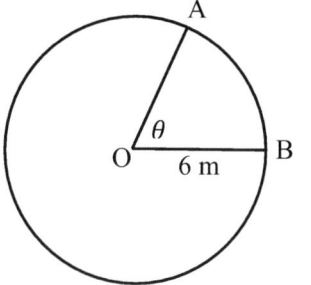

   Note: Figure is not drawn to scale.

   A) $\frac{9}{32}$
   B) $\frac{3}{8}$
   C) $\frac{9}{16}$
   D) $\frac{9}{8}$

20. Point O is the center of the circle with the radius of $\frac{3}{2}$. If the area of sector BOC is written as $k\pi$, what is the value of k?

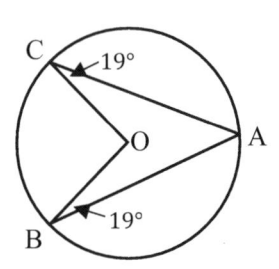

- 306 -

Chapter 34: Extraneous Solutions

The SAT includes algebra questions that have extraneous solutions. Extraneous solutions are "fake" answers that look correct when solving algebraically but do not work when plugged back into the original equation. **Anytime we see variables in the denominator of a fraction or underneath a square root, we need to check for extraneous solutions.** To see how this works, take a look at the example questions below:

Example 1: What value(s) of x satisfy the equation $\sqrt{2x+7} = x + 2$?
A) -3 B) 1 C) $0, 1$ D) $-3, 1$

Solution: Method #1 – Solve Algebraically: To solve this equation, we need to solve for x.

$$\sqrt{2x+7} = x + 2$$
$$(\sqrt{2x+7})^2 = (x+2)^2$$
$$2x + 7 = x^2 + 4x + 4$$
$$0 = x^2 + 2x - 3$$
$$0 = (x-1)(x+3)$$
$$x = 1, -3$$

It looks like the answer here is D, but that is incorrect. We need to plug $x = 1$ and $x = -3$ back into the original equation to test for extraneous solutions.

To test $x = 1$
$$\sqrt{2(1)+7} = 1 + 2$$
$$\sqrt{2+7} = 3$$
$$\sqrt{9} = 3$$
$$3 = 3$$

To test $x = -3$
$$\sqrt{2(-3)+7} = -3 + 2$$
$$\sqrt{-6+7} = -1$$
$$\sqrt{1} = -1$$
$$1 \neq -1$$

We find that $x = 1$ works but $x = -3$ does not. This means that $x = -3$ is an extraneous solution, so the only value of x that works is $x = 1$. **The correct answer is B.**

That is a lot of work to solve, so if you ever see one of these questions on the SAT with answer choices (as we see in Example 1), use the shortcut method below. However, the SAT can ask extraneous solution questions and not provide answer choices, so it is important to understand how to solve algebraically as well.

Method #2 – Backsolve: We can plug the answer choices back into the question and solve. To test answer choice A, we plug in $x = -3$ to the equation:

$$\sqrt{2(-3)+7} = -3 + 2$$
$$\sqrt{-6+7} = -1$$
$$\sqrt{1} = -1$$
$$1 \neq -1$$

Since $x = -3$ does not work, we know that answer choices A and D are both incorrect. To test answer choice B, we plug in $x = 1$ to the equation:

$$\sqrt{2(1)+7} = 1 + 2$$
$$\sqrt{2+7} = 3$$

- 307 -

PrepPros

$$\sqrt{9} = 3$$
$$3 = 3$$

so $x = 1$ works. Now, we need to test $x = 0$ to see if the correct answer is B or C.

To test answer choice C, we plug in $x = 0$ to the equation:

$$\sqrt{2(0) + 7} = 0 + 2$$
$$\sqrt{0 + 7} = 2$$
$$\sqrt{7} \neq 2$$

We find that $x = 0$ does not satisfy the equation. The only value of x that did satisfy the equation was $x = 1$, so **the answer is B.**

Method #3 – Desmos Hack #1 for Solving Algebra Equations: Write the equations in Desmos as $y = \sqrt{2x + 7}$ and $y = x + 2$. The graphs intersect at the point $(1, 3)$. The x-coordinate is at 1, so **the answer is 1.** This method is the easiest way to solve any extraneous solution question and the one that we recommend you always use.

1-4 **Example 2:** What is a possible value of x that satisfies the equation $\frac{x}{x-2} = \frac{1}{2x-4}$?

Solution: Method #1 – "Math Teacher Way": When the question does not include answer choices, we must solve algebraically. Here, we can start by cross multiplying to get

$$x(2x - 4) = 1(x - 2)$$

Distributing the x we get

$$2x^2 - 4x = x - 2$$

Since we have a quadratic, we move all terms to the left side (we subtract x and add 2) and factor.

$$2x^2 - 5x + 2 = 0$$
$$(2x - 1)(x - 2) = 0$$

To solve, we set each factor equal to 0 and solve.

$$2x - 1 = 0 \qquad\qquad x - 2 = 0$$
$$x = \frac{1}{2} \qquad\qquad x = 2$$

It looks like we have two answers: $x = \frac{1}{2}$ and $x = 2$. However, since there are x-terms in the denominator of the fraction in our original equation, we must check for extraneous solutions.

To test $x = \frac{1}{2}$, we plug in $x = \frac{1}{2}$ to the equation:

$$\frac{\frac{1}{2}}{\frac{1}{2}-2} = \frac{1}{2\left(\frac{1}{2}\right)-4}$$

$$\frac{\frac{1}{2}}{-\frac{3}{2}} = \frac{1}{-3}$$

$$-\frac{1}{3} = -\frac{1}{3}$$

so $x = 0.5$ works. To test $x = 2$, we plug in $x = 2$ to the equation:

$$\frac{2}{2-2} = \frac{1}{2(2)-4}$$

- 308 -

Chapter 34: Extraneous Solutions

$$\frac{2}{0} = \frac{1}{0}$$

Since any fraction divided by 0 is undefined, $x = 2$ does not work and is an extraneous solution. Therefore, the only solution to the equation is $x = \frac{1}{2}$ and **the answer is $\frac{1}{2}$ or 0.5.**

Method #2 – Desmos Hack #1 for Solving Algebra Equations: Write the equations in Desmos as $y = \frac{x}{x+2}$ and $y = \frac{1}{2x+4}$. The graphs intersect at the point $(0.5, 0.2)$. The x-coordinate is at 0.5, which is the same as $\frac{1}{2}$, so **the answer is $\frac{1}{2}$ or 0.5.** This method is the easiest way to solve any extraneous solution question.

Extraneous Solutions Practice: Answers on page 334.

1. What value(s) of x are solutions to the equation below?

   $$x - 6 = \sqrt{3x}$$

   A) 3
   B) 12
   C) 6
   D) 3, 6

2. What value(s) of x satisfy the equation below?

   $$-x = \sqrt{6x}$$

   A) 0
   B) 1
   C) 6
   D) 0, 6

3. What value(s) of x are solutions to the equation below?

   $$x - 10 = \sqrt{5x}$$

   I. 5
   II. 20

   A) I only
   B) II only
   C) I and II
   D) Neither I nor II

4. What value(s) of x are solutions to the equation below?

   $$\frac{5}{x+2} = \frac{x-3}{2x+4}$$

   A) 2
   B) 8
   C) 13
   D) 2, 13

5. For the equation $\sqrt{17 - y} - 3 = y$, what value(s) of y are solutions?

   A) -8
   B) 1
   C) 14
   D) $-8, 1$

6. For the equation $x - 4 = \sqrt{3x - 2}$, find a value of x that satisfies the equation.

7. What is a value of x that satisfies the equation below?

   $$\sqrt{2x} = x - 4$$

8. What is a positive value of x that satisfies the equation below?

   $$\frac{3x}{x+4} - \frac{1}{x+3} = \frac{24}{x^2 + 7x + 12}$$

9. Find a value of x that satisfies the equation below.

   $$0 = \sqrt{x + 6} - x$$

- 309 -

PrepPros

10. What is a value of x that makes the equation $(2x + 7)^{\frac{1}{2}} - x = 2$ true?

15. What is the sum of all solutions to the equation below?
$$\frac{5x^2}{12x - 5} + 1 = \frac{1 - x}{5}$$

11. In the equation $\sqrt{x + 14} - 2 = x$, what value of x is an extraneous solution?

16. If $4z + 5$ is an extraneous solution to the equation $x - 8 = \sqrt{30 - 2x} - 5$, what is the value of z?

12. What is a value of x that is an extraneous solution to the equation below?
$$\frac{2x}{x + 1} - 3 = \frac{2}{x^2 + x}$$

17. If z is an extraneous solution to the equation below, what is the value of z?
$$\frac{c}{c + 6} = \frac{72}{c^2 - 36} + 4$$

13. What is a value of x that is an extraneous solution for the equation below?
$$(x + 2)^{\frac{1}{2}} = \frac{1}{3}(3x - 12)$$

18. $a + 3$ is an extraneous solution to the equation below. What is the value of a?
$$\frac{x + 6}{x} - \frac{2}{x + 6} = \frac{12}{x^2 + 6}$$

14. How many solutions are there to the equation below?
$$\frac{1}{x - 2} = \frac{3}{x + 2} - \frac{6x}{x^2 - 4}$$

- 310 -

Chapter 35: Interpreting Constants in Linear, Polynomial, and Exponential Functions

The SAT asks you to interpret constants in linear, polynomial, and exponential functions. To answer these questions correctly, you need to be familiar with various forms of linear, polynomial, and exponential functions and what the constants represent.

Linear Functions

To start, let's look at an easy example with a linear function, which is just a fancy term for a line.

> **Example 1:** The graph of the equation below in the xy-plane is a linear function. Which of the following equivalent forms of the equation includes the y-intercept as a constant or coefficient?
> $$3y = 4x - 6$$
> A) $4x = 3y + 6$
> B) $3y = 2(x - 3)$
> C) $y = \frac{4}{3}x - 2$
> D) $x = \frac{3}{4}y + \frac{3}{2}$

Solution - Method #1 – "Math Teacher Way": We want to convert the line from standard form to slope-intercept form because in slope-intercept form, also known as $y = mx + b$ form, the b-value shows the y-intercept of a line. We divide by 3 to isolate y and turn the equation into $y = mx + b$ form.

$$3y = 4x - 6$$
$$y = \frac{4}{3}x - 2$$

The y-intercept is at -2. The only answer choice that has -2 as a constant is C. **The answer is C.**

Method #2 – Shortcut Method: That works, but there is an easier and faster way! Rather than doing any algebra, we can solve this more quickly by using the answer choices. Once we recognize that we want this line in slope-intercept form (because slope-intercept form shows the y-intercept as a constant), we can look at the answer choices and see that only C is in slope-intercept form. **The answer is C.**

For interpreting constants questions, be sure to **look at the answer choices right away**. These questions almost always have all 4 answer choices that are various equivalent forms of the same equation, so you generally do not need to do any algebra to see if the equations match. You just need to be familiar with what the constant(s) represent in various forms of the same equation.

Make sure you are familiar with various forms of linear equations and what the constants represent.

Linear Equations

Form	Equation	What the Constants Represent
Standard	$ax + by = c$	a, b, and c represent nothing
Slope-Intercept	$y = mx + b$	m is the slope b is the y-intercept
x equals	$x = dy + f$	f is the x-intercept

- 311 -

PrepPros

2-4 Finding the *x*-Intercept and *y*-Intercept

On many questions involving constants, we need to find the *x*-intercept(s) and *y*-intercept(s) of various types of functions. Doing so is easy as long as you remember the 2 rules below:

To solve for the *x*-intercept, set $y = 0$ and solve for *x*.

To solve for the *y*-intercept, set $x = 0$ and solve for *y*.

Be sure to memorize these rules, as they help on a variety of questions throughout the SAT! Now, let's see how these rules can help to solve interpreting constants questions.

Example 2: $\qquad 5x - 3y = 20$

The graph of the equation above in the *xy*-plane is a linear function. Which of the following equivalent forms of the equation includes the *x*-intercept as a constant or coefficient?

A) $3y = 5x - 20$
B) $3y = 5(x - 4)$
C) $y = \frac{5}{3}x - \frac{20}{3}$
D) $x = \frac{3}{5}y + 4$

Solution: To solve for the *x*-intercept, set $y = 0$ and solve for *x*.

$$5x - 3(0) = 20$$
$$5x = 20$$
$$x = 4$$

Now that we know that the *x*-intercept is at $x = 4$, we look at the answer choices to see which ones has 4 as a constant or coefficient. **The answer is D**. The *x*-intercept is positive 4, so the -4 in B is incorrect.

Example 3: $\qquad x^2 - 2y - 10 = 3x$

For the function above, which of the following equivalent forms of the function includes the *y*-intercept as a constant or coefficient?

A) $2y = x^2 - 3x - 10$
B) $y = \frac{x^2}{2} - \frac{3}{2}x - 5$
C) $x(x - 3) = 2y + 10$
D) $y = (x - \frac{5}{2})(x + 2)$

Solution: To solve for the *y*-intercept, set $x = 0$ and solve for *y*.

$$(0)^2 - 2y - 10 = 3(0)$$
$$-2y - 10 = 0$$
$$-2y = 10$$
$$y = -5$$

We find that the *y*-intercept is at $y = -5$, so we need to look at the answer choices to see which one has -5 as a constant or coefficient. **The answer is B.**

Parabolas

Most commonly, interpreting constants questions ask about parabolas. To answer these questions correctly, we need to know how to identify the x-intercepts, the y-intercepts, and the vertices of vertical and horizontal parabolas.

You should memorize the three forms of a vertical parabola below and what the constants represent.

Vertical Parabola

Form	Equation	What the Constants Represent
Standard	$y = ax^2 + bx + c$	c is the y-intercept
Factored	$y = a(x - d)(x - f)$	d and f are the x-intercepts
Vertex	$y = a(x - h)^2 + k$	vertex is at (h, k)

Vertical Parabola

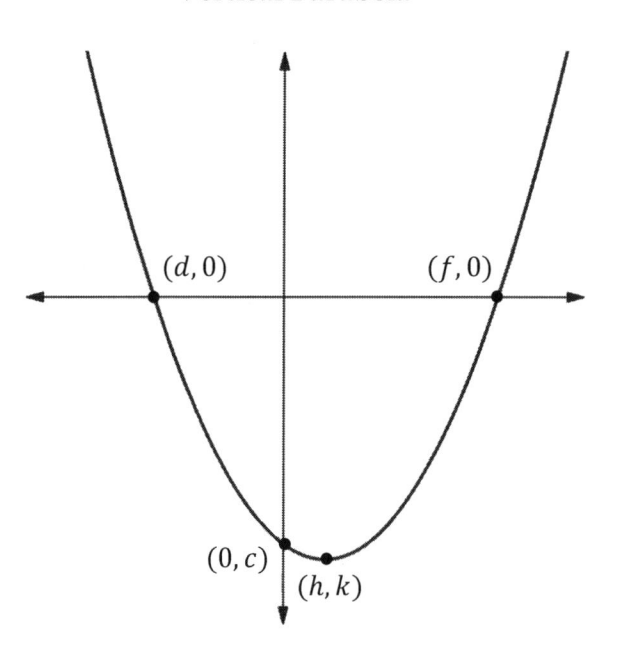

Points labeled: $(d, 0)$, $(f, 0)$, $(0, c)$, (h, k)

Horizontal Parabola

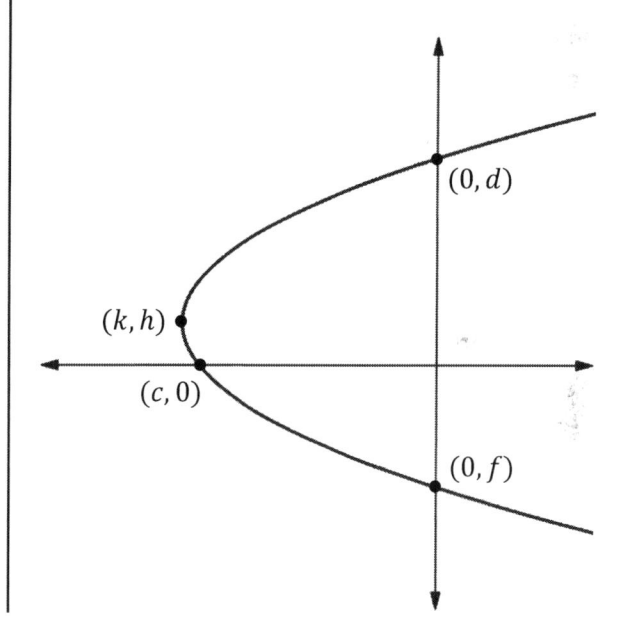

Points labeled: $(0, d)$, (k, h), $(c, 0)$, $(0, f)$

For more difficult questions, you need to know the three forms for horizontal parabolas. These are far less common on the SAT, but you should memorize these in case you see one on test day.

Horizontal Parabola

Form	Equation	What the Constants Represent
Standard	$x = ay^2 + by + c$	c is the x-intercept
Factored	$x = a(y - d)(y - f)$	d and f are the y-intercepts
Vertex	$x = a(y - h)^2 + k$	vertex is at (k, h)

PrepPros

Now that we have learned the rules for parabolas, let's take a look at a few examples of interpreting constants questions with parabolas.

> **Example 4:** $$y = x^2 - 10x + 16$$
>
> The equation for parabola P is written above. Which of the following equivalent forms of the equation shows the coordinates of the vertex of parabola P as constants or coefficients?
>
> A) $y = (x-5)^2 - 9$
> B) $y = (x-8)(x-2)$
> C) $y - 5 = x^2 - 10x + 11$
> D) $16 = y - x(x-10)$

Solution: The question asks us to find the constants for the coordinates of the vertex, so we are looking for a parabola that is written in vertex form. The only equation that is written in vertex form is A, which shows the vertex for this parabola is at the point $(5, -9)$. **The answer is A.**

> **Example 5:** $$x^2 - y + 8x + 12 = 0$$
>
> For the parabola above, which of the following equivalent forms of the equation shows the x-intercept(s) as constants or coefficients?
>
> A) $x(x+8) + 12 = y$
> B) $y = (x+4)^2 - 4$
> C) $y = (x+6)(x+2)$
> D) $x^2 + 8x + 12 = y$

Solution: We need to see the x-intercept(s) as constants, so we are looking for the parabola that is in factored form. The only answer choice that is written in factored form is C, where we can see the x-intercepts of this parabolas are at $x = -2$ and $x = -6$. **The answer is C.**

As you can see from these two examples, these questions are pretty straightforward as long as we know the three forms of vertical parabolas.

Now, let's take a look at 2 questions with horizontal parabolas. Since most students do not use horizontal parabolas nearly as often as vertical parabolas, questions with horizontal parabolas are more difficult and meant to stump you. However, if you memorize the three forms of horizontal parabolas and what the constants in each form represent, you will be prepared to answer these challenging questions correctly on test day.

> **Example 6:** Parabola Q in the coordinate plane has the equation $y^2 - 10y + x - 2 = 14$. Which of the following equivalent forms of the equation shows the x-intercept(s) of the parabola as constants or coefficients?
>
> A) $x = -(y-5)^2 + 41$
> B) $x = 16 + 10y - y^2$
> C) $y = \sqrt{41-x} + 5$
> D) $y(y-10) - 2 = 14 - x$

Solution: Here, we have a horizontal parabola. We can spot horizontal parabolas easily by looking for a y^2-term and an x-term. To find the x-intercept, we set $y = 0$ and solve for x.

$$(0)^2 - 10(0) + x - 2 = 14$$
$$x = 16$$

The x-intercept is at $x = 16$, so we need to look for an answer choice that has 16 as a constant or coefficient. **The answer is B.**

We also could have solved this question by knowing the three forms for horizontal parabolas. The standard form of a horizontal parabola shows the x-intercept. Since B is the only answer choice written in standard form, **the answer is B.**

> **Example 7:** Parabola Z in the coordinate plane has the equation $y^2 - 6y - x - 91 = 0$. Which of the following equivalent forms of the equation shows the y-intercept(s) of the parabola as constants or coefficients?
>
> A) $x = (y + 7)(y - 13)$
> B) $x = y^2 - 6y - 91$
> C) $y(y - 6) = x + 91$
> D) $y = \sqrt{x + 82} + 3$

Solution: We again see a horizontal parabola in this question. The y-intercepts for a horizontal parabola are constants when the equation is written in factored form. The only answer choice in factored form is A, where we can see that the y-intercepts are at $y = -7$ and $y = 13$. **The answer is A.**

We could have also solved this question using our rule to find the y-intercepts: set $x = 0$ and solve for y.

$$y^2 - 6y - (0) - 91 = 0$$
$$y^2 - 6y - 91 = 0$$
$$(y - 13)(y + 7) = 0$$
$$y = -7, 13$$

We find the y-intercepts are at $y = -7$ and $y = 13$. The only answer choice that shows these as constants or coefficients is A. **The answer is A.**

Exponential Functions

We previously covered exponential growth and decay functions in Chapter 19. Let's briefly review the basics of how exponential functions in the form $y = ab^x$ appear when graphed. In this form, **the y-intercept appears at the point $(0, a)$.** When $b > 1$, the function shows exponential growth (as in the graph on the left below). When $0 < b < 1$, the function shows exponential decay (as in the graph on the right below).

Exponential Growth ($b > 1$)
$f(x) = ab^x$
$f(x) = 2(1.25)^x$

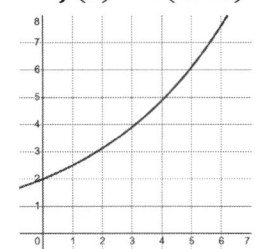

Exponential Decay ($0 < b < 1$)
$f(x) = ab^x$
$f(x) = 6\left(\frac{1}{2}\right)^x$

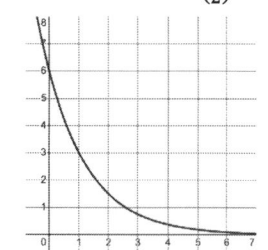

If you need to review exponential graphing and shifting further, go back to Chapter 19.

For interpreting constant questions about exponentials, we need to know three rules:

Rules #1: For an exponential function in the form $f(x) = ab^x$, the y-intercept is at the point $(0, a)$.

To see how this rule works, let's look at the 2 graphs on the previous page. Notice how the y-intercept for $f(x) = 2(1.25)^x$ is at $(0, 2)$ and the y-intercept for $f(x) = 6\left(\frac{1}{2}\right)^x$ is at $(0, 6)$.

Rule #2: For exponential growth ($b > 1$), the y-intercept shows the minimum value on the domain of $x \geq 0$.

Since exponential growth graphs increase as the graph goes to the right, the minimum value on the domain $x \geq 0$ is always at the y-intercept. For the graph of $f(x) = 2(1.25)^x$, the minimum value on the domain $x \geq 0$ is at $(0, 2)$.

Rule #3: For exponential decay ($0 < b < 1$), the y-intercept shows the maximum value on the domain of $x \geq 0$.

Since exponential decay graphs decrease as the graph goes to the right, the maximum value on the domain $x \geq 0$ is always at the y-intercept. For the graph of $f(x) = 6\left(\frac{1}{2}\right)^x$, the maximum value on the domain $x \geq 0$ is at $(0, 6)$.

Now, let's see how we may have to apply these rules on the SAT.

Example 8: Two functions f and g are defined by the equations given below, where $x \geq 0$. Which of the following equations displays, as a base or coefficient, the maximum value of the function it defines, where $x \geq 0$?

I. $f(x) = 85(2.8)^x$
II. $g(x) = 85(0.8)^x$

A) I only   B) II only   C) Both I and II   D) Neither I nor II

Solution: Method #1 – "Math Teacher Way": Let's start by assessing $f(x)$. The function $f(x)$ is an exponential growth function, since the b-value of 2.8 is greater than 1 and has a y-intercept at $(0, 85)$. An exponential growth function increases as the graph goes to the right, so the maximum value of the function is not shown by any base or coefficients. Instead, 85 shows that the minimum value of $f(x)$ is $(0, 85)$ where $x \geq 0$.

The function $g(x)$ is an exponential decay function since the b-value is 0.8. The y-intercept for $g(x)$ is at $(0, 85)$. An exponential decay function decreases as the graph goes to the right, so the maximum value of the function where $x \geq 0$ is at the y-intercept. The 85 shows the maximum value for $g(x)$ is $(0, 85)$ where $x \geq 0$. **The answer is B.**

Method #2 – Graph in Desmos: For students who are not as comfortable with exponential functions, we recommend graphing $f(x)$ and $g(x)$ in Desmos. When we graph $f(x)$, we see an increasing function with no clear maximum value, so the maximum is not shown by any constants or coefficients. On the other hand, when we graph $g(x)$, we see a decreasing function with a maximum value at the y-intercept $(0, 85)$, where $x \geq 0$. Since $g(x)$ has 85 as a coefficient, we can see that **the answer is B.**

Example 9: Which of the following equivalent forms of the function $f(x) = p(3)^{2(x+1)}$ displays, as the base or the coefficient, the y-coordinate of the y-intercept of the graph of $y = f(x)$ in the xy-plane?

A) $9p(3)^{2x}$ B) $3p(3)^{2x-1}$ C) $p(9)^{x+1}$ D) $81p(9)^{2x-1}$

Solution: Method #1 – Find The y-intercept: First, we can find the y-intercept of $f(x)$ by plugging in $x = 0$ and solving.
$$f(0) = p(3)^{2(0+1)} = p(3)^2 = p(9) = 9p$$
The y-intercept of $f(x)$ is at $(0, 9p)$, so we need to see which answer choice includes $9p$ as a base or coefficient. **The answer is A.**

Method #2 – Split The Exponent to Return To Standard Form: To find the y-intercept, we need to turn $f(x)$ into standard $y = ab^x$ form, where $(0, a)$ shows the y-intercept. Right now, $f(x)$ is shifted 1 unit left by the $x + 1$ in the exponent, so the coefficient of p does not show the y-intercept. To find the y-intercept, we need to remove the shift and return to standard form.

To turn $f(x)$ into standard form, we first distribute the 2 in the exponent to get
$$f(x) = p(3)^{2x+2}$$
Next, we split the exponent into two terms, one with $2x$ in the exponent and one with 2.
$$f(x) = p(3)^{2x}(3)^2$$
When exponents with the same base are multiplied, we add the exponents together. In the previous step, we reversed that rule and used it to split the exponents. Next, we can simplify the $(3)^2$ to 9 to get
$$f(x) = p(3)^{2x}(9)$$
We can now combine the p and the 9 to further simplify.
$$f(x) = 9p(3)^{2x}$$
At this point, we only have $2x$ in the exponent, so we have removed the shift. Since the shift is removed, the coefficient now shows the y-intercept. The y-intercept is at $(0, 9p)$. **The answer is A.**

We can even further simplify $f(x)$ by turning 3^{2x} to 9^x. We can write 3^{2x} as $(3^2)^x$, which simplifies to 9^x. So, we could also write $f(x)$ as
$$f(x) = 9p(9)^x$$
Now, this really matches our $y = ab^x$ form. Again, we can see that the y-intercept is at $(0, 9p)$.

For Example 9, splitting the exponent and returning to standard form is a much more advanced and difficult way to solve this question, so we recommend using the y-intercept rule. However, **it is important that advanced math students aiming for top scores understand how to split the exponent to remove a horizontal shift and return to standard form**, as this is a skill that can be tested on difficult exponential interpreting constants questions on test day (and one you will need to use in this chapter's problem set).

Interpreting Constants Practice: Answers on page 334.

1. The graph of the equation below in the xy-plane is a linear function. Which of the following equivalent forms of the equation includes the x-intercept as a constant?

$$y = 2x + 6$$

A) $y - 2x = 6$
B) $\frac{1}{2}y - x = 3$
C) $y = 2(x + 3)$
D) $x = \frac{1}{2}y - 3$

2. The graph of the equation below in the xy-plane is a parabola. Which of the following equivalent forms of the equation includes the x-coordinate of the vertex as a constant?

$$y = x^2 - 8x + 12$$

A) $y = (x - 4)^2 - 4$
B) $y = (x - 6)(x - 2)$
C) $y = x(x - 8) + 12$
D) $y - 12 = x(x - 8)$

3. The graph of the equation below in the xy-plane is a linear function. Which of the following equivalent forms of the equation includes the y-intercept as a constant?

$$2x + 3y = 12$$

A) $x = -\frac{3}{2}y + 6$
B) $3y = -2x + 12$
C) $\frac{2}{3}x - 4 + y = 0$
D) $y = -\frac{2}{3}x + 4$

4. If $f(x) = a(x - b)(x + c)$, where a, b, and c are constants, which of the following lists the x-intercept(s) of $f(x)$?

A) $-ab$ and ac
B) $a, -b,$ and c
C) b and $-c$
D) $-b$ and c

5. The graph of the equation below in the xy-plane is a linear function. Which of the following is a form of the equation that includes the x-intercept as a constant?

$$6x + 4y = 24$$

A) $y = \frac{3}{2}x + 6$
B) $y = -\frac{3}{2}x + 6$
C) $x = -\frac{2}{3}y + 4$
D) $x = -\frac{2}{3}y + 6$

6. If $y = 5x^2 - 16x + 3$ is graphed in the xy-plane, which of the following elements of the graph is displayed as a constant?

A) x-intercept
B) y-intercept
C) x-coordinate of the vertex
D) y-coordinate of the vertex

7. The equation below represents a parabola in the xy-plane. Which of the following equations displays the x-intercepts of the parabola as constants or coefficients?

$$y = x^2 - 13x + 36$$

A) $y = (x - 4)(x - 9)$
B) $y = x(x - 13) + 36$
C) $y = x^2 - 13(x + 3) - 3$
D) $y - 36 = x^2 - 13x$

8. The equation below is quadratic. Which of the following equivalent equations displays the minimum value of y as a constant or coefficient?

$$y + 12x = x^2 + 9$$

A) $y = x^2 - 12x + 9$
B) $y = (x - 6)^2 - 27$
C) $y = x^2 - 2(6x - 4.5)$
D) $y = -x(x + 12) + 9$

9. The equation below represents a parabola in the xy-plane. Which of the following is an equivalent form that displays the y-intercept of the parabola as a constant or coefficient?

$$y = -3(x+2)(x+3)$$

A) $y = -3x^2 - 15x - 18$
B) $y = -3x^2 - 5x - 6$
C) $y = -3x^2 + 15x + 18$
D) $y = -3x - 9x + 6$

10. The equation below represents a parabola in the xy-plane. Which of the following equivalent forms of the equation displays the x-intercepts of the parabola as constants or coefficients?

$$y = x^2 - 6x + 8$$

A) $y - 8 = x^2 - 6x$
B) $y + 1 = (x-3)^2$
C) $y = (x-4)(x-2)$
D) $y = x(x-6) + 8$

11. Parabola X in the xy-plane has the equation of $y = x^2 - z$. Which of the following is equal to the x-intercept(s) of the parabola as constants or coefficients?

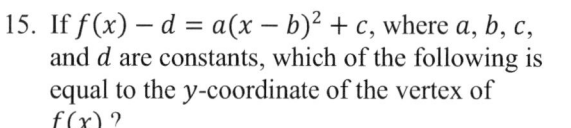

A) $z, -z$
B) $-z$
C) z^2
D) $\sqrt{z}, -\sqrt{z}$

12. The function f is defined as $f(x) = a(1+b)^x$, where a and b are positive constants and $x \geq 0$, which of the following best describes the constant a?

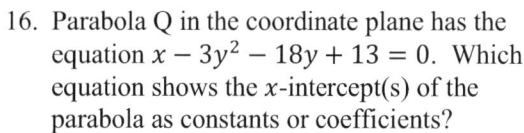

A) The maximum of the function.
B) The x-intercept.
C) The minimum of the function.
D) The rate of increase of the function.

13. The function f is defined by the equation below. In which of the following equivalent forms of the equation does the maximum value of $f(x)$ appear as a constant or coefficient?

$$f(x) = -3x^2 + 24x - 32$$

A) $f(x) = -3x^2 + 18x + 6x - 36$
B) $f(x) = -3x(x-6) + 6(x-6)$
C) $f(x) = -3(x-4)^2 + 16$
D) $f(x) = -3(x-2)(x-6)$

14. Parabola A in the xy-plane has the equation $x - y^2 + 8y + 5 = 2y + 13$. Which of the following is an equivalent form of the equation that shows the y-intercept(s) of the parabola as constants or coefficients?

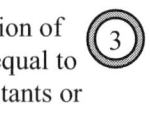

A) $x = y^2 - 6y + 8$
B) $x = y^2 - 6y + 18$
C) $x = (y-4)(y-2)$
D) $x = (y-3)^2 - 1$

15. If $f(x) - d = a(x-b)^2 + c$, where a, b, c, and d are constants, which of the following is equal to the y-coordinate of the vertex of $f(x)$?

A) b
B) $c + d$
C) $-ab$
D) c

16. Parabola Q in the coordinate plane has the equation $x - 3y^2 - 18y + 13 = 0$. Which equation shows the x-intercept(s) of the parabola as constants or coefficients?

A) $x = 3(y-3)^2 - 14$
B) $x = 3y^2 + 18y - 13$
C) $x + 14 = 3(y-3)^2$
D) $y = \sqrt{\frac{x+14}{3}} + 3$

17. If $(y-3)^2 + 8 - 2x = 0$ is graphed in the xy-plane, which of the following elements of the graph is displayed as a constant?

A) x-intercept
B) y-intercept
C) x-coordinate of the vertex
D) y-coordinate of the vertex

18. The functions f and g are defined by the given equations, where $x \geq 0$. Which of the following equations displays, as a constant or coefficient, the minimum value of the function it defines, where $x \geq 0$?

  I. $f(x) = 270(0.7)^x$
  II. $g(x) = 270(1.7)^x$

  A) I only
  B) II only
  C) I and II
  D) Neither I nor II

19. Parabola B in the xy-plane has the equation of $y = x^2 - ax - bx + ab$. Which of the following is equivalent to the x-coordinate for the vertex of the parabola?

  A) $\frac{a+b}{2}$
  B) $\frac{-a-b}{2}$
  C) ab
  D) $\frac{a}{b}$

20. Which of the following equivalent forms of the given function below displays the y-coordinate of the y-intercept of its graph in the xy-plane as a constant?

  $$f(x) = 9^{-(2+x)}$$

  A) $f(x) = \frac{1}{81}\left(\frac{1}{9}\right)^x$
  B) $f(x) = \left(\frac{1}{9}\right)^{(2+x)}$
  C) $f(x) = 3^{-2(2+x)}$
  D) $f(x) = 9^{(-2-x)}$

21. For the exponential function f, the value of $f(1)$ is a, where a is a constant. Which of the following equivalent forms of the function f shows the value of a as the coefficient or the base?

  A) $f(x) = 37(2)^{x+1}$
  B) $f(x) = 70(2)^{x-1}$
  C) $f(x) = 135(2)^{x+2}$
  D) $f(x) = 235(2)^{x-2}$

22. The functions f and g are defined by the given equations, where $x \geq 0$. Which of the following equations displays, as a constant or coefficient, the maximum value of the function it defines, where $x \geq 0$?

  I. $f(x) = 18(0.6)^{x+1}$
  II. $g(x) = 18(0.6)(0.6)^{x-1}$

  A) I only
  B) II only
  C) I and II
  D) Neither I nor II

23. Which of the following equivalent forms of the given function f displays, as the base or the coefficient, the y-coordinate of the y-intercept of the graph of $y = f(x)$ in the xy-plane?

  $$f(x) = 4^{-2(x+1)}$$

  A) $f(x) = \left(\frac{1}{4}\right)^{(2x+2)}$
  B) $f(x) = \left(\frac{1}{16}\right)\left(\frac{1}{4}\right)^{2x}$
  C) $f(x) = \left(\frac{1}{81}\right)^{(-\frac{1}{2}x-\frac{1}{2})}$
  D) $f(x) = 4^{-2x-2}$

24. The functions f and g are defined by the given equations, where $x \geq 0$. Which of the following equations displays, as a constant or coefficient, the minimum value of the function it defines, where $x \geq 0$?

  I. $f(x) = 103\left(\frac{1}{1.1}\right)(1.1)^{x+1}$
  II. $g(x) = 103(1.44)(1.2)^{x-2}$

  A) I only
  B) II only
  C) I and II
  D) Neither I nor II

Chapter 36: Special Quadratics – Perfect Squares and Difference of Squares

Special quadratics questions require you to know the perfect squares and difference of squares formulas. These questions are difficult until you learn how to spot them and the techniques for solving them. To start, let's review the formulas you will need to know.

Equation	Formula	Example
Perfect Square (Addition)	$(x+y)^2 = x^2 + 2xy + y^2$	$(x+2)^2 = x^2 + 4x + 4$
Perfect Square (Subtraction)	$(x-y)^2 = x^2 - 2xy + y^2$	$(x-3)^2 = x^2 - 6x + 9$
Difference of Squares	$(x+y)(x-y) = x^2 - y^2$	$(x+6)(x-6) = x^2 - 36$

Difference of Squares

The SAT most commonly asks you special quadratics questions where you need to use the difference of squares formula. To start, let's take a look at how one of these questions might appear on test day.

Example 1: If $x + y = 3$ and $x^2 - y^2 = -15$, what is the value of $x - y$?
A) -45 B) -15 C) -5 D) 5

Solution: To solve this question, we need to use the difference of squares formula.
$$(x+y)(x-y) = x^2 - y^2$$
The question tells us $(x + y) = 3$ and $x^2 - y^2 = -15$, so we can plug those values in for $x + y$ and $x^2 - y^2$ and solve for $x - y$.
$$(3)(x - y) = -15$$
$$x - y = -\frac{15}{3} = -5$$

The answer is C.

Example 2: If $a - b = 10$ and $a + b = 3$, what is the value of $(a^2 - b^2)(a + b)$?

Solution: We need to spot that this is a difference of squares question. Since $(a^2 - b^2) = (a + b)(a - b)$, we can substitute in $(a + b)(a - b)$ for $(a^2 - b^2)$ and the equation becomes
$$(a + b)(a - b)(a + b)$$
The question tells us $a - b = 10$ and $a + b = 3$, so we can just plug in the values for $(a + b)$ and $(a - b)$ to solve.
$$(3)(10)(3) = 90$$

The answer is 90.

Example 3: If $x^4 - y^4 = 120$ and $x^2 - y^2 = 20$, what is $x^2 + y^2$ equal to?
A) 100 B) 40 C) 12 D) 6

Solution: While this question may look more complicated at first, we can solve it exactly like the previous examples. We need to notice this is still a difference of squares question, only with higher powers now.

PrepPros

$$(x^2 + y^2)(x^2 - y^2) = x^4 - y^4$$

The questions tells us $x^4 - y^4 = 120$ and $x^2 - y^2 = 20$, we just need to plug in the values for $x^4 - y^4$ and $x^2 - y^2$ to solve.

$$(x^2 + y^2)(20) = 120$$
$$x^2 + y^2 = \frac{120}{20} = 6$$

The answer is D.

Example 4: If $x - y = q$ and $\sqrt{x} + \sqrt{y} = 15$, which of the following expressions is equal to $\sqrt{x} - \sqrt{y}$?

A) $\frac{q}{15}$ B) $\frac{15}{q}$ C) $15q$ D) $15 - q$

Solution: To solve, we need to recognize that

$$(\sqrt{x} + \sqrt{y})(\sqrt{x} - \sqrt{y}) = x - y$$

Once we spot this unusual difference of squares, we can substitute in the values of $x - y$ and $\sqrt{x} + \sqrt{y}$ from the question to solve.

$$(15)(\sqrt{x} - \sqrt{y}) = q$$
$$\sqrt{x} - \sqrt{y} = \frac{q}{15}$$

The answer is A.

Questions with unusual difference of squares are difficult to recognize on test day. Just remember that if you ever see a term that looks anything like $x^2 - y^2$, $x^5 - y^5$ or any other variation, you are dealing with a difference of squares question.

TIP – Difference of Squares with Other Powers

The SAT can make difference of squares questions more difficult by using powers other than simple squares as we just saw in examples 3 and 4. **The factors (terms in parentheses) are always half the power of the other terms.** Recognizing this pattern can help you spot advanced difference of squares questions on test day. Below are some examples:

$$(x^3 + y^3)(x^3 - y^3) = x^6 - y^6$$
$$(\sqrt{x} + \sqrt{y})(\sqrt{x} - \sqrt{y}) = x - y$$

Perfect Squares

The SAT also asks questions involving perfect squares. If a question gives you a value for xy and for $(x + y)$, $(x - y)$, or $(x^2 + y^2)$, you are most likely dealing with a perfect squares question.

Let's see how this might appear on the SAT below:

Example 5: If $x^2 + y^2 = 30$ and $xy = 3$, what is the value of $x + y$?

A) 90 B) 15 C) 10 D) 6

Solution: Here, we need to use the perfect square (addition) formula.

$$(x + y)^2 = x^2 + 2xy + y^2$$

We can reorder the terms to make the equation look like this:
$$(x + y)^2 = (x^2 + y^2) + 2xy$$
The question tells us $x^2 + y^2 = 30$ and $xy = 3$, so we can plug in the given values for $x^2 + y^2$ and xy and solve for $x + y$.
$$(x + y)^2 = (30) + 2(3)$$
$$(x + y)^2 = 36$$
$$x + y = 6$$
We see that $x + y = 6$, so **the answer is D**.

> **Example 6:** If $4x^2 - 4xy + y^2 = 9z^2$, which of the following expresses the value of $2x - y$?
>
> A) $9z$ B) $3z$ C) $81z^4$ D) $\frac{9z}{2}$

Solution: This is a more advanced example of a perfect square question. To solve, we need to recognize that
$$(2x - y)^2 = 4x^2 - 4xy + y^2$$
We know that $4x^2 - 4xy + y^2 = 9z^2$, so we can substitute in the $9z^2$.
$$(2x - y)^2 = 9z^2$$
To solve, we now take the square root of both sides and get
$$\sqrt{(2x - y)^2} = \sqrt{9z^2}$$
$$2x - y = 3z$$
The answer is B.

> ### TIP – How to Spot Special Quadratics Questions
>
> All special quadratics questions give you values for terms that include two variables. The five terms you should keep an eye out for are:
>
> $$x^2 - y^2 \qquad x^2 + y^2 \qquad x + y \qquad x - y \qquad xy$$
>
> The SAT can make these questions more difficult by using different variables or using unusual powers (as discussed in the TIP box on the previous page). Below are some examples of how these might appear:
>
> $$m^4 - n^4 \qquad a^2 - b^2 \qquad p + q \qquad \sqrt[3]{c} - \sqrt[3]{d} \qquad ab$$
>
> If you spot anything that looks like these terms, you are most likely dealing with a special quadratics question and will need to use the difference of squares or perfect squares formulas.

Special Quadratics Practice: Answers on page 335.

1. If $a + b = 7$ and $a - b = 3$, what is the value of $a^2 + 2ab + b^2$?

   A) 9
   B) 40
   C) 49
   D) 58

2. If $l + k = 9$ and $l - k = 3$, what is the value of $l^2 - 2lk + k^2$?

   A) 9
   B) 18
   C) 36
   D) 81

3. If $x + y = 11$ and $x - y = 5$, what is the value of $x^2 - y^2$?

   A) 25
   B) 55
   C) 96
   D) 121

4. If $a^2 + 2ab + b^2 = 36$ and $a - b = 9$, what is the value of $a + b$?

   A. 2
   B. 4
   C. 6
   D. 12

5. If $a + b = 12$ and $a - b = 4$, what is the value of $a^2 - b^2$?

   A) 16
   B) 48
   C) 128
   D) 144

6. If $x - y = 5$ and $x^2 - y^2 = 75$, what is the value of $x + y$?

   A) 5
   B) 10
   C) 15
   D) 25

7. If $m + l = 10$ and $m - l = 4$, what is the value of $(m + l)(m^2 - l^2)$?

8. If $a^2 - b^2 = 6$ and $a^2 + b^2 = 12$, what is the value of $a^4 - b^4$?

9. If $x^3 + y^3 = 9$ and if $x^3 - y^3 = 7$, what is the value of $x^6 - y^6$?

10. If $\frac{3^{x^2}}{3^{y^2}} = 3^{12}$ and $x + y = 6$, what is the value of $x - y$?

11. If $(2^{x^2})(2^{-y^2}) = 4^9$ and $x - y = 2$, what is the value of $x + y$?

12. If $a^2 + b^2 = 12$ and $ab = -6$, what is the value of $a - b$?

    A) -2
    B) 0
    C) $2\sqrt{6}$
    D) 6

Chapter 36: Special Quadratics

13. If $\sqrt{x} - \sqrt{y} = 9$ and $x - y = 45$, what is the value of $3\sqrt{x} + 3\sqrt{y}$?

    A) 5
    B) 15
    C) $3\sqrt{5}$
    D) 36

14. What is the value of the expression $x^2 + 2x + 2xy + 2y + y^2$ when $x + y = 12$?

15. If $\dfrac{3^{a^2}}{3^{b^2}} = 9^4$ and $a + b = 2$, what is the value of $a - b$?

16. If $m = a^3 - b^3$, which of the following is equivalent to the expression $x^2 + a^6 - 2a^3b^3 + b^6$?

    A) $x^2 + m^2$
    B) $x^2 + m^3$
    C) $(x + m)^2$
    D) $(x - m)^2$

17. If $x > 1$, $\dfrac{x^{a^2-ab}}{x^{ab-b^2}} = x^{16}$, and $a + b = 8$, what is the value of $a - b$?

18. If $k = c + d$, which of the following is equivalent to the expression $x^2 - c^2 - 2cd - d^2$?

    A) $(x - k)(x + k)$
    B) $(x + k)^2$
    C) $(x - k)^2$
    D) $x^2 - kx - k^2$

19. What is the value of the expression $3x^2 + 10x - 6xy - 10y + 3y^2$ when $x - y = 30$?

Answer Key

Chapter 1 (pp. 3-4)

1. C
2. C
3. B
4. B
5. A
6. A
7. C
8. A
9. C
10. A
11. B
12. D
13. B
14. B
15. A
16. B
17. D

Chapter 2 (pp. 6-8)

1. B
2. C
3. D
4. A
5. B
6. C
7. A
8. D
9. A
10. C
11. B
12. D
13. C
14. A
15. D
16. D
17. C
18. A

Chapter 3 (pp. 12-13):

1. A
2. D
3. D
4. C
5. A
6. A
7. A
8. C
9. B
10. C

11. B
12. A
13. D
14. C
15. C

Chapter 4 (pp.16-17)

1. B
2. A
3. 10.5
4. C
5. -15
6. B
7. C
8. -10
9. 4
10. D
11. B
12. $0.5, \frac{1}{2}$
13. 4
14. 9
15. C

Chapter 5 (pp. 26-29)

1. C
2. A
3. C
4. D
5. B
6. 5
7. D
8. 52
9. 8
10. D
11. $0.125, \frac{1}{8}$
12. 13
13. D
14. 36
15. D
16. A
17. D
18. B
19. D
20. 17
21. C
22. A
23. A
24. 16
25. D

26. C
27. D
28. C
29. A
30. D
31. C
32. B
33. 2
34. -1
35. B
36. 4
37. 6
38. D
39. 6
40. A
41. $1.6, \frac{8}{5}$
42. B
43. B

Chapter 6 (pp. 35-38)

1. $\frac{17}{6}, 2.833$
2. $\frac{7}{20}, 0.35$
3. $\frac{11}{8}, 1.375$
4. $\frac{4a-15}{6}$
5. $\frac{18y-7x}{21}$
6. $\frac{21y+5z}{5y}$
7. $\frac{25}{6x}$
8. $\frac{9}{20}, 0.45$
9. $\frac{3x}{2y}$
10. $\frac{4}{3z}$
11. 4
12. $\frac{49}{2}, 24.5$
13. 2
14. $\frac{43}{30}, 1.433$
15. $\frac{9}{2}, 4.5$
16. B
17. $\frac{1}{4}, 0.25$
18. 15
19. 1
20. A
21. $\frac{6}{5}, 1.2$
22. B

Answer Key

23. $\frac{3}{5}$, 0.6
24. C
25. B
26. C
27. C
28. $\frac{21}{5}$, 4.2
29. A
30. A
31. C
32. A
33. B
34. C
35. D
36. A
37. 5
38. 7
39. B
40. 11
41. D
42. C
43. 35
44. 32
45. 69

Chapter 7 (pp. 40-43)

1. C
2. C
3. C
4. B
5. B
6. D
7. D
8. D
9. B
10. C
11. C
12. C
13. B
14. C
15. A
16. B
17. D
18. C
19. A
20. D
21. C
22. C
23. A
24. C
25. D

Chapter 8 (pp. 48-52)

1. A
2. C
3. A
4. B
5. A
6. B
7. A
8. A
9. C
10. A
11. A
12. A
13. B
14. C
15. C
16. D
17. D
18. C
19. 7
20. B
21. B
22. D
23. 5
24. A
25. B
26. B
27. D
28. 20
29. D
30. A

Chapter 9 (Simple Percentages) (pp. 54-56)

1. B
2. D
3. B
4. B
5. B
6. C
7. A
8. B
9. C
10. D
11. B
12. 150
13. 0.7
14. A
15. C
16. B
17. 18.75
18. D
19. 1300
20. 16
21. A
22. 15
23. A
24. 40

Chapter 9 (Percentage Increase and Decrease) (pp.58-62)

1. B
2. C
3. C
4. D
5. B
6. 1.17
7. 35
8. B
9. B
10. D
11. A
12. D
13. D
14. C
15. 30
16. B
17. D
18. D
19. C
20. A
21. D
22. A
23. B
24. 14.4
25. C
26. C
27. C
28. B
29. 15
30. 500
31. C
32. D
33. 10
34. 800
35. 159.2
36. 35
37. 0.3

Chapter 10
Exponents Exercise (p. 65)

1. x^6y^3
2. $3x^5$
3. $24x^3y^7$
4. $4x^2y^6$
5. $\frac{3y^5}{x^2}$
6. $9x^4$
7. $\frac{9y}{x^3z^2}$
8. $\frac{1}{x}$
9. $\frac{z}{x^4}$
10. $\frac{9x^{10}z^2}{y^4}$
11. $16xy^3$
12. $\frac{25x^{17}}{8y^7}$
13. 1
14. 8
15. 5, −5
16. 1
17. $\frac{11}{6}$
18. 6
19. 6
20. 8

Roots Exercise (p. 69)

1. $2\sqrt{15}$
2. $7\sqrt{6}$
3. $2\sqrt{5}$
4. $7\sqrt{2}$
5. $5\sqrt[3]{6}$
6. $\sqrt{3}$
7. 1
8. $2b^2\sqrt{2a}$
9. $4x\sqrt{y}$
10. $a^3\sqrt{b}$
11. $2x^2y\sqrt[3]{3y}$
12. $4x^5$
13. $\frac{20}{3}$
14. 45
15. 3
16. 90
17. 6
18. $\frac{45}{2}$, 22.5
19. 4
20. 5

Chapter 10 Practice Problem Set (pp. 69-73)

1. C
2. D
3. C
4. D
5. A
6. B
7. $\frac{26}{3}$, 8.666, 8.667
8. A
9. B
10. B
11. B
12. C
13. 1
14. B
15. B
16. A
17. D
18. $\frac{3}{4}$, 0.75
19. D
20. D
21. C
22. D
23. A
24. A
25. B
26. A
27. 9
28. B
29. $\frac{4}{9}$, 0.444
30. 4
31. C
32. 5
33. C
34. D
35. $\frac{1}{18}$, 0.055
36. $\frac{31}{10}$, 3.1
37. B
38. C
39. $\frac{11}{6}$, 1.833
40. $\frac{193}{3}$, 64.333
41. $\frac{5}{9}$, 0.555
42. D
43. D
44. $\frac{8}{3}$, 2.666, 2.667
45. 81
46. D
47. D
48. $\frac{1}{5}$, 0.2
49. $\frac{14}{3}$, 4.666

Chapter 11 (pp. 86-92)

1. D
2. B
3. C
4. D
5. −9, 3
6. 13
7. 14
8. 14
9. A
10. C
11. D
12. 6
13. 1,026
14. A
15. B
16. A
17. A
18. 12
19. D
20. C
21. −8
22. B
23. C
24. −7
25. C
26. D
27. B
28. 3, 4
29. C
30. 180
31. −4
32. C
33. $-\frac{3}{4}$, −0.75
34. C
35. 11
36. A
37. D
38. 12
39. A
40. 784
41. A
42. D
43. 2
44. $\frac{33}{8}$, 4.125
45. 48
46. D

Answer Key

47. A
48. 145
49. B
50. $\frac{7}{2}$, 3.5
51. A
52. 341.3
53. D
54. 8,100
55. C
56. 2
57. $\frac{1}{18}$, 0.055
58. 240
59. C
60. D
61. 237
62. 1,521
63. C
64. 46
65. -4
66. A

Chapter 12 (pp. 97-101)

1. D
2. D
3. B
4. C
5. D
6. 2
7. 3
8. A
9. B
10. A
11. $-9.6, -\frac{48}{5}$
12. D
13. 2.5, $\frac{5}{2}$
14. 75
15. 6
16. 6
17. C
18. B
19. C
20. 100
21. D
22. D
23. $-6, -8$
24. 56
25. 14
26. 16
27. C
28. $\frac{7}{12}$, 0.583

29. C
30. 23.5, $\frac{47}{2}$
31. 360
32. 1
33. $\frac{1}{4}$, 0.25
34. 20
35. $-1,470$
36. D
37. A
38. 175
39. A
40. 32
41. 19
42. 0.55, $\frac{11}{20}$
43. 4

Chapter 13 (pp. 105-109)

1. 25
2. 103
3. 193
4. -22
5. $18x^2 - 7$
6. $-3x + 19$
7. -2
8. -7
9. $5, -5$
10. 7
11. 52
12. $8x^2 - 24x + 11$
13. 91
14. $\frac{1}{3}$
15. $-54x^2 + 31$
16. B
17. C
18. 29
19. 1.5, $\frac{3}{2}$
20. 416
21. 95
22. B
23. 30
24. A
25. C
26. C
27. 4.5, $\frac{9}{2}$
28. C
29. D
30. 4.125, $\frac{33}{8}$
31. 3
32. D

33. B
34. B
35. A
36. -1
37. 36
38. 70
39. D
40. B
41. B
42. 1
43. D
44. A
45. C
46. D
47. 18
48. 36
49. -4
50. A
51. D
52. B
53. 6
54. 0, 10
55. $-\frac{20}{3}, -6.666, -6.667$

Chapter 14 (pp. 113-116)

1. 20
2. C
3. D
4. A
5. B
6. D
7. 67.5
8. C
9. D
10. C
11. 129
12. C
13. B
14. 84
15. C
16. A
17. 135
18. D
19. C
20. D
21. 158
22. B
23. D

Chapter 15 (pp. 125-129)

1. C
2. D
3. 22
4. B
5. A
6. B
7. 12
8. A
9. 64
10. 17
11. C
12. B
13. D
14. 15
15. A
16. C
17. C
18. B
19. A
20. D
21. C
22. 9
23. D
24. $\frac{9}{2}$, 4.5
25. C
26. D
27. D
28. 50
29. 896
30. 40
31. D
32. D
33. 2,700
34. 24
35. C
36. C
37. C
38. B
39. A
40. 48
41. B
42. 400
43. 3
44. C
45. 42

Chapter 16 (pp. 136-140)

1. B
2. B
3. 14
4. 172
5. A
6. C
7. 73
8. B
9. B
10. C
11. 51
12. C
13. A
14. 29.2
15. C
16. B
17. 68
18. C
19. 25
20. $\frac{11}{3}$, 3.666, 3.667
21. D
22. C
23. B
24. 325
25. C
26. C
27. $\frac{19}{4}$, 4.75
28. 9
29. C
30. $\frac{9}{4}$, 2.25
31. 18
32. $\frac{4}{3}$, 1.333

Chapter 17 (pp. 149-154)

1. A
2. C
3. C
4. $\frac{7}{3}$, 2.333
5. D
6. $-\frac{5}{2}$, -2.5
7. D
8. D
9. C
10. C
11. $\frac{5}{3}$, 1.666
12. D
13. C
14. $\frac{12}{5}$, 2.4
15. B
16. A
17. A
18. C
19. 50
20. C
21. $-\frac{4}{9}$, -0.444
22. B
23. -12
24. $\frac{21}{4}$, 5.25
25. C
26. 10
27. $\frac{75}{7}$, 10.71
28. 34
29. A
30. D
31. D
32. A
33. B
34. $\frac{9}{5}$, 1.8
35. $-\frac{102}{5}$, -20.4
36. 3
37. D
38. A
39. B
40. $\frac{50}{3}$, 16.66
41. D
42. C
43. C
44. $\frac{7}{4}$, 1.75
45. A
46. $\frac{2}{3}$, 0.666
47. A
48. B
49. C

Chapter 18 (pp. 158-163)

1. C
2. C
3. A
4. D
5. A
6. A
7. C
8. B
9. A
10. A
11. B
12. B
13. D
14. A
15. D
16. B
17. D

18. C
19. B
20. C
21. D
22. A
23. A
24. B
25. C
26. B
27. C
28. A
29. C
30. A
31. C
32. B

Chapter 19 (pp. 170-176)

1. A
2. D
3. C
4. 1.06
5. D
6. D
7. D
8. 3,136
9. B
10. B
11. C
12. A
13. D
14. C
15. C
16. B
17. A
18. A
19. A
20. 81
21. C
22. D
23. C
24. D
25. B
26. B
27. −2
28. A
29. B
30. B
31. C
32. D
33. D
34. 6
35. B
36. A

37. D
38. C
39. 2.8
40. B
41. D
42. B
43. C
44. C
45. D
46. B
47. $-\frac{1}{2}, -0.5$

Chapter 20
Coterminal Practice Part 1
(p. 188)

1. 135
2. 180
3. 315
4. 240
5. 270
6. 45
7. 315
8. 30
9. 150
10. 150
11. 180
12. 90
13. 225
14. 90
15. 135
16. 180

Coterminal Practice Part 2
(p. 189)

1. $\frac{5\pi}{3}$
2. $\frac{\pi}{2}$
3. $\frac{5\pi}{6}$
4. $\frac{2\pi}{3}$
5. $\frac{\pi}{6}$
6. $\frac{\pi}{4}$
7. $\frac{5\pi}{3}$
8. π
9. $\frac{\pi}{2}$
10. $\frac{2\pi}{3}$
11. $\frac{7\pi}{4}$

12. $\frac{7\pi}{6}$
13. $\frac{4\pi}{3}$
14. $\frac{4\pi}{3}$

Chapter 20 Practice Problem Set (pp. 190-196)

1. C
2. D
3. D
4. D
5. B
6. D
7. B
8. D
9. 405
10. B
11. $\frac{4}{7}, 0.571$
12. C
13. $\frac{3}{5}, 0.6$
14. A
15. $\frac{16}{9}, 1.777, 1.778$
16. A
17. C
18. $\frac{12}{13}, 0.923$
19. A
20. B
21. B
22. A
23. $\frac{5}{17}, 0.294$
24. $\frac{15}{17}, 0.882$
25. $\frac{3}{10}, 0.3$
26. C
27. 24
28. B
29. 18
30. $\frac{21}{29}, 0.724$
31. $\frac{20}{21}, 0.952$
32. A
33. D
34. A
35. C
36. A
37. $\frac{4}{5}, 0.8$
38. 27.5, 55/2
39. $\frac{7}{5}, 1.4$
40. A

41. $\frac{4}{5}$, 0.8
42. B
43. C
44. 11
45. 8
46. C
47. D
48. 10
49. B
50. B
51. B
52. C
53. $\frac{3}{4}$, 0.75
54. A
55. A
56. 0
57. 273.1, 273.2
58. C

Chapter 21 (pp. 202-207)

1. A
2. $\frac{1}{12}$, 0.083
3. C
4. B
5. C
6. B
7. B
8. A
9. C
10. A
11. B
12. D
13. A
14. A
15. D
16. D
17. C
18. D
19. A
20. C
21. D
22. A
23. D
24. B
25. C
26. B
27. B
28. $\frac{17}{25}$, 0.68
29. $\frac{9}{20}$, 0.45
30. $\frac{11}{25}$, 0.44

31. B
32. D
33. 27
34. C
35. $\frac{39}{64}$, 0.609
36. $\frac{3}{11}$, 0.273

Chapter 22 (pp. 216-223)

1. B
2. C
3. B
4. C
5. D
6. A
7. B
8. D
9. A
10. A
11. A
12. D
13. D
14. 62, 63, 64, 65, 66, 67, 68
15. A
16. D
17. C
18. C
19. C
20. A
21. D
22. C
23. C
24. D
25. B
26. A
27. C
28. D
29. B
30. D
31. B
32. B

Chapter 23 (pp. 226-229)

1. A
2. B
3. 7
4. 18
5. D
6. D
7. B
8. D
9. A

10. D
11. 64
12. A
13. C
14. D
15. 75
16. 559
17. A
18. 160
19. D
20. B
21. 48
22. 200
23. C
24. 182
25. B
26. 153
27. $\frac{7}{9}$, 0.778

Chapter 24 (pp. 236-240)

1. B
2. A
3. C
4. 4.5
5. D
6. D
7. A
8. A
9. D
10. B
11. C
12. C
13. C
14. C
15. 23
16. A
17. 3.5, $\frac{7}{2}$
18. B
19. C
20. B
21. B
22. B
23. 32
24. D
25. C
26. C
27. A
28. 0.25, $\frac{1}{4}$
29. 24
30. D
31. 92,900

Answer Key

32. A
33. A
34. 166
35. 70

Chapter 25 (pp. 245-247)

1. C
2. A
3. 132
4. B
5. A
6. 192
7. C
8. D
9. A
10. A
11. D
12. D
13. D
14. 46
15. A
16. 10,560
17. D
18. B
19. D
20. A
21. 34
22. A
23. 1,056
24. 39.83
25. 3.02
26. D
27. 19

Chapter 26 (pp. 250-252)

1. D
2. 8
3. 3
4. Any number from 3.0 to 3.3
5. Any number from 0.7 to 1.0
6. Any number from −0.9 to −1.3
7. A
8. 3
9. C
10. 15
11. A
12. C
13. 3
14. B
15. A
16. A
17. D
18. B

Chapter 27 (pp. 260-262)

1. C
2. D
3. 10
4. 61
5. D
6. 7
7. B
8. B
9. A
10. B
11. B
12. A
13. 5
14. B
15. 5
16. 4
17. A
18. C
19. B
20. C
21. 5
22. 21
23. 17
24. 7
25. D
26. 9
27. −65
28. C
29. D
30. C
31. B

Chapter 28 (pp. 267-270)

1. −39
2. B
3. B
4. $-\frac{5}{2}$, −2.5
5. D
6. −55
7. B
8. 153
9. A
10. −248
11. A
12. B
13. D
14. C
15. 13
16. A
17. B
18. −180
19. $-\frac{23}{5}$, −4.6
20. A
21. 2.72
22. $-\frac{30}{7}$, −4.286
23. D
24. $-\frac{47}{8}$, −5.875
25. 35
26. B
27. 546

Chapter 29 (pp. 275-276)

1. A
2. C
3. 30
4. 14
5. 6
6. D
7. 15
8. 18
9. 5.8
10. 15
11. B
12. B
13. $\frac{1}{5}$, 0.2
14. 20.16
15. 12
16. B
17. $\frac{3}{4}$, 0.75
18. −4
19. $\frac{16}{5}$, 3.2
20. 34
21. A
22. D
23. D

Chapter 30 (pp. 278-280)

1. C
2. D
3. B
4. 9
5. B
6. C
7. 7
8. C

9. C
10. 316
11. D
12. 3
13. C
14. B
15. 53
16. C
17. Any value from 5 to 8.75
18. 16
19. B
20. D
21. 29
22. A
23. 9
24. 20
25. 28

Chapter 31 (pp. 287-290)

1. 0.6, $\frac{3}{5}$
2. A
3. A
4. D
5. A
6. D
7. A
8. 2.4, $\frac{12}{5}$
9. 6
10. A
11. D
12. A
13. D
14. D
15. C
16. D
17. D
18. A
19. -2.75
20. 3
21. A
22. C
23. C
24. D
25. 3
26. -20
27. B
28. D
29. A
30. 28
31. D
32. 159
33. 8, 13, 23, 28

34. D

Chapter 32 (pp. 297-300)

1. D
2. C
3. D
4. A
5. 2
6. D
7. B
8. D
9. B
10. D
11. D
12. D
13. $\frac{3}{8}$, 0.375
14. -44.8
15. B
16. $-\frac{5}{4}$, -1.25
17. C
18. 2
19. 20.25, $\frac{81}{4}$
20. -3.2, $-\frac{16}{5}$
21. A
22. 6
23. D
24. 7.5, $\frac{15}{2}$
25. B
26. 0.75, $\frac{3}{4}$
27. B
28. C
29. A

Chapter 33 (pp. 304-306)

1. A
2. C
3. 40
4. C
5. C
6. B
7. 6
8. 108
9. 90
10. C
11. B
12. $\frac{1}{20}$, 0.05
13. A
14. D
15. C

16. A
17. 72
18. 72
19. B
20. $\frac{19}{40}$, 0.475

Chapter 34 (pp. 309-310)

1. B
2. A
3. B
4. C
5. B
6. 9
7. 8
8. 2
9. 3
10. 1
11. -5
12. -1
13. 2
14. 0
15. $-\frac{43}{37}$ -1.162
16. -2
17. -6
18. -9

Chapter 35 (pp. 318-320)

1. D
2. A
3. D
4. C
5. C
6. B
7. A
8. B
9. A
10. C
11. D
12. C
13. C
14. C
15. B
16. B
17. D
18. B
19. A
20. A
21. B
22. B
23. B
24. C

Chapter 36 (pp. 324-325)

1. C
2. A
3. B
4. C
5. B
6. C
7. 400
8. 72
9. 63
10. 2
11. 9
12. C
13. B
14. 168
15. 4
16. A
17. 4
18. A
19. 3,000

Made in the USA
Middletown, DE
12 August 2024